ALL ▪ IN ▪ ONE

PHR®/SPHR®
Professional in Human Resources Certification

EXAM GUIDE

Second Edition

William H. Truesdell
Christina Nishiyama
Dory Willer

New York   Chicago   San Francisco
Athens   London   Madrid   Mexico City
Milan   New Delhi   Singapore   Sydney   Toronto

Library of Congress Cataloging-in-Publication Data

Names: Truesdell, William H., author. | Nishiyama, Christina, author. |
  Willer, Dory, author.
Title: PHR/SPHR professional in human resources certification : all-in-one
  exam guide / William H. Truesdell, Christina Nishiyama, Dory Willer.
Description: Second edition. | New York : McGraw-Hill Education, [2019] |
  Includes bibliographical references and index.
Identifiers: LCCN 2019000487 | ISBN 9781260453119 (soft cover : alk. paper)
Subjects: LCSH: Personnel management—Examinations—Study guides. | Personnel
  management—Examinations, questions, etc. | Personnel
  departments—Employees—Certification.
Classification: LCC HF5549.15 .P765 2019 | DDC 658.30076—dc23
LC record available at https://lccn.loc.gov/2019000487

McGraw-Hill Education books are available at special quantity discounts to use as premiums and sales promotions, or for use in corporate training programs. To contact a representative, please visit the Contact Us pages at www.mhprofessional.com.

PHR®/SPHR® Professional in Human Resources Certification All-in-One Exam Guide, Second Edition

1 2 3 4 5 6 7 8 9   QVS   23 22 21 20 19

ISBN   978-1-260-45311-9
MHID   1-260-45311-1

Sponsoring Editor Wendy Rinaldi	**Technical Editor** William Kelly	**Production Supervisor** James Kussow
Editorial Supervisor Patty Mon	**Copy Editor** Kim Wimpsett	**Composition** Cenveo Publisher Services
Project Manager Jyoti Shaw, Cenveo® Publisher Services	**Proofreader** Lisa McCoy	**Illustration** Cenveo Publisher Services
Acquisitions Coordinator Claire Yee	**Indexer** Jack Lewis	**Art Director, Cover** Jeff Weeks

To all HR professionals who constantly strive to do better.

—The authors

To all HR professionals who get up each morning
and go to work attempting to do what is right.

—Bill

To Steve, Malea, and Siena for your love and encouragement.
To my father Larry, the best HR mentor.

—Christina

To my husband, Jeff, who is my very own personal cheerleader,
constantly supporting and nudging me to new levels of success.

—Dory

ABOUT THE AUTHORS

William H. Truesdell, SPHR, SHRM-SCP, is president of The Management Advantage, Inc., a human resources management consulting firm he founded in 1987. He spent more than 20 years in management with American Telephone and Telegraph in HR and operations management. Truesdell is an expert on the subjects of employment practices, employee handbooks, equal opportunity, and performance management programs. He is a past president of the Northern California Employment Round Table and for several years was an HR course instructor at the University of California, Berkeley extension program. His classes included Basic HR Management and EEO and Affirmative Action. He is the author of several books, including *Secrets of Affirmative Action Compliance*. He has co-authored four books for McGraw-Hill Education on certification preparation for HR professionals. Truesdell holds the SPHR and SHRM-SCP certifications and a bachelor's degree in business administration from the California State University, Fresno. Bill can be reached at billt@management-advantage.com.

Christina Nishiyama, MBA, SPHR, SHRM-CP, is an executive vice president at Bienati Consulting Group, Inc., a human resources and management consulting firm focused on helping clients in a variety of industries improve organizational and individual effectiveness. Prior to consulting, Christina served as a human resources executive at international hospitality organizations in Las Vegas, and she directed human resources, finance, and information technology operations for a large startup organization. Her expertise lies in establishing people-driven organizational cultures, executive and front-line talent acquisition strategies, employee relations, communication, and competitive total compensation plans that are tightly aligned with financial goals. Christina received her bachelor's degree in economics and psychology from the University of California, San Diego, and her master's in business administration from San Diego State University. Christina is currently pursuing her PhD at University of Nevada, Las Vegas, and also holds her SPHR and SHRM-CP certifications. She previously served on the SHRM National Young Professionals Advisory Council and led the SHRM Southern Nevada Young Professionals for several years. If you would like to contact Christina for consulting inquiries, she can be reached at christina@bienati.com.

Dory Willer, SPHR, SHRM-SCP, PCC, is a certified executive coach with more than 30 years of experience as a senior HR executive, keynote speaker, and strategic planning facilitator. She has broad and diverse experience working for blue-chip and Fortune 100 companies, leaving her last corporate position as a vice president of HR to open Beacon Quest Coaching based in the San Francisco Bay Area. Willer coaches clients and teams in leadership enhancement, performance improvement, and career renewal to unleash their full potential. Additionally, she facilitates strategic planning sessions that stretch paradigms, align activities with behaviors, and hold groups accountable to produce end results. She was among the first graduating classes from Stanford's Executive HR Certification Program (Graduate School of Business, 1994). Willer achieved the designation of SPHR more than 20 years ago, holds a bachelor's degree in behavioral science from the University of San Francisco, and has several advanced certifications in professional coaching. If you would like to contact Dory for speaking engagements or individual and team coaching, you may reach her at Dory@BeaconQuest.com.

About the Contributor and Technical Editor

William (Bill) Kelly, SHRM-SCP, SPHR, PHRca, is the owner of Kelly HR, an HR consulting services practice specializing in providing HR consulting services and support for small businesses, and is, more recently, founder of CalHRSuccess LLP, an HR educational organization dedicated to helping HR professionals successfully take and pass their professional HR certification exams. Bill's experience includes more than 40 years of professional-level HR responsibilities. Bill has been teaching professional PHR/SPHR certification preparation classes for 25 years and California HR certification preparation for 11 years for the Society for Human Resource Management (SHRM) and the Northern California HR Association (NCHRA). Bill was a key player in the introduction and development of California's HR certification credential; he was also the project manager for the team of California HR professionals who developed SHRM's first California Learning System in support of California certification. Bill's professional leadership also includes roles on the board of directors and as national vice president for the Society for Human Resource Management, on the board of directors and as president for the HR Certification Institute, as state director for the California State Council of SHRM, on the board of directors and as president for the Northern California HR Association, and as commissioner and chair for the Marin County Personnel Commission. Bill received his bachelor's degree in political science from Spring Hill College in Mobile, Alabama, and undertook postgraduate studies in organizational management at the College of William and Mary in Williamsburg, Virginia, and the University of Virginia in Richmond, Virginia. Prior to HR, Bill had a military career, achieving the rank of major in the United States Army with tours of duty in the United States, Germany, Thailand, and Vietnam.

CONTENTS AT A GLANCE

CONTENTS

Part II   PHR Body of Knowledge Functional Areas

Part III   SPHR Body of Knowledge Functional Areas

ACKNOWLEDGMENTS

First and foremost, we'd like to thank Wendy Rinaldi and her extremely talented staff at McGraw-Hill Education for making this book happen. She has been a wonderful guide through the development process, showing patience, perseverance, and encouragement.

We'd also like to provide a note of thanks to our literary agent, Carole Jelen. Carole originally identified Dory as the best candidate to author the first edition of this book. Dory reached out to the rest of us with an invitation to contribute to the project.

We'd also like to send a bucket of gratitude to the professionals who contributed to our "In the Trenches" sections: Grant Bassett, Larry Bienati, Susan Chritton, Susan Farwell, Jim Foord, John Fox, Fredi Foye-Helms, Joel Garfinkle, Jane Henderson, Rob Hyde, and our own Christina Nishiyama. These folks have provided insight, expert sage advice, and awesome perspective based on their firsthand experience, which is priceless.

Finally, there is no way this book could have been started, much less completed, without the expert input and guidance of Bill Kelly, our technical editor and contributing author of the compensation and benefits chapter. In addition to Bill's treasure trove of advice about the HRCI exams and his experience as a facilitator/teacher for HRCI exam study groups, it has just been plain delightful and an honor to have his helping hand on this project.

And a special thank-you to co-author Christina Nishiyama. She jumped into the void left by Dory when work schedules would not permit Dory to work on this second edition. Christina is a true HR professional with wonderful communication skills. This second edition could not have been completed without Christina.

INTRODUCTION

Allow us to be the first to congratulate you on making the decision to sit for an HR Certification Institute (HRCI) certification exam and to strive to obtain your Professional in Human Resources (PHR) or Senior Professional in Human Resources (SPHR) certification! Professional certifications are a mark of distinction that sets you apart in the profession, and they speak volumes about your commitment to your craft. More than 140,000 of your colleagues around the globe have obtained the HRCI certifications, including us.

Human resources is most likely part of our DNA makeup; we've lived it and breathed it for many decades. Our purpose is to share with you some strategies and experience that will assist you when you sit for the certification exam(s). It is our intention that this book will provide the knowledge and concepts you are expected to have mastered as a PHR and SPHR candidate. It is our pleasure to share those things with you. You also bring your own professional experience to the process. As you combine your experience with the information included in this book, you will be better able to answer the situational-based and competency-based questions about HR situations that you will find on the exam.

We want you to be successful. It is our belief that the HRCI professional certifications are important because the certifications demonstrate your knowledge and expertise to employers and clients. Having a professional certification has become increasingly important. It may be a requirement of your next job assignment or the promotion you are pining for within your organization. You may decide that these certifications are necessary qualifications for future HR professionals that you hire. In any event, we wish you the best professional regards and success in passing your exam and earning the prestigious designation of PHR and SPHR.

HRCI Certification vs. SHRM Certification

Beginning in 2015 and 2016, the Society for Human Resource Management (SHRM) began rolling out its certification program for HR professionals: the Certified Professional (SHRM-CP) and the Senior Certified Professional (SHRM-SCP).

Initially, SHRM gave "grandfather" status to any individual holding a certification from HRCI. It was only necessary to answer a few questions and prove your active certification status with HRCI to be awarded the status of SHRM's certification program.

That initial transition program has ended. All new SHRM certifications require HR professionals to submit to a written examination and meet designated experience and educational requirements. We have written a study guide for those examinations called *SHRM-CP/SHRM-SCP Certification All-in-One Exam Guide*. It is another fine example of self-study publications from McGraw-Hill Education.

How to Use This Book

This book covers the entire PHR and SPHR Body of Knowledge (BoK). It is organized differently from the first edition, however. This time we have separated the study materials for PHR from SPHR. The greatest volume of material is focused on the PHR level requirements. That is because *both* PHR and SPHR candidates must know everything required at the PHR level. SPHR candidates will be tested more on strategic issues and practical application of all BoK materials in scenarios requiring application of experience as well as knowledge. This time, each functional area has been assigned its own chapter. HRCI has designated specific functions that it will expect certification candidates to have mastered. It even has specified the weight each will have on the exam question selection process. There are separate functional area designations for the SPHR certification requirements. Here they are, as presented by HRCI in 2018.

Functional Areas Designated by HRCI	
PHR	**SPHR**
Functional Area 01: Business Management (20%)	Functional Area 01: Leadership and Strategy (40%)
Functional Area 02: Talent Planning and Acquisition (16%)	Functional Area 02: Talent Planning and Acquisition (16%)
Functional Area 03: Learning and Development (10%)	Functional Area 03: Learning and Development (12%)
Functional Area 04: Total Rewards (15%)	Functional Area 04: Total Rewards (12%)
Functional Area 05: Employee and Labor Relations (39%)	Functional Area 05: Employee Relations and Engagement (20%)

Additionally, within each functional area, we have organized the presentation of topics to follow this same logic. As you progress through the material, we hope you will do so with a feeling of accomplishment at mastering the information presented and thereby increase your drive and motivation to continue.

The following is a brief overview of the organization of this book and how we feel this organization will benefit you.

Chapter 1

In Chapter 1, we explain everything you need to know about PHR and SPHR exams and also discuss the different types of HRCI certifications. Additionally, you'll find information about the process of registering for the exams, the actual exam experience, and what the style and format of questions are on the exams.

Chapter 2

Chapter 2 provides a list of all the U.S. laws and regulations that you will need to know. We placed this information in a chapter rather than an appendix to emphasize the importance of reviewing these laws and regulations prior to diving into the functional areas. Understanding these laws should make it easier for you to grasp the reasoning behind the material that is presented in Chapters 4–13. You will find many questions on the certification exams that are directly related to these laws.

Chapter 3

This chapter lists the 23 additional knowledge items that HRCI has identified as core knowledge items. These items may have applications across more than one functional area. We spell each knowledge item out individually and show you how they link to other knowledge mastery requirements for the certification process.

Chapters 4 Through 13

Chapters 4 through 13 go into the specifics of each functional area and discuss what we believe is essential knowledge for the HRCI exams. These chapters are designed to be concise and yet to effectively communicate the information. Each chapter provides an overview, a list of laws that will be applicable to the topics covered, and court cases that apply to the subject area. At the end of each chapter, there is a review section that briefly summarizes the salient points of the chapter. Chapters 4 through 8 apply to the PHR exam. Chapters 9 through 13 apply to the SPHR exam.

In the Trenches

In the chapters, you will find contributions from experts in the field titled "In the Trenches," which contain valuable insight and sage advice from professionals about a specific topic in that functional area.

Notes

Specially called out *Notes* are part of the chapters, too. These are interesting tidbits of information that are relevant to the topic and point out helpful information.

Questions and Answers

At the end of Chapters 2 through 13, you will find a set of review questions and answers to help you test your knowledge and comprehension. Practice, practice, practice—it will pay off on exam day.

Appendixes

We have also included three appendixes to supplement the information you need to know.

Appendix A　Appendix A is a list of abbreviations. The HR field is notorious for abbreviations creating the jargon in HR language, and these abbreviations have flowed into the everyday business language of employers, employees, and the public at large. It is likely that you will see questions on the exams that include and reference these acronyms, so please familiarize yourself with this list.

Appendix B　In Appendix B, we have listed all of the associated legal cases you should know and review prior to sitting for the exams. The cases are organized by chapter (functional area) and include a brief synopsis of what each case addressed. A URL is provided so that you can review the case in more detail, and we do recommend that you spend time reviewing these cases. You will notice that most of the cases are listed in PHR functional areas. That is because they apply to the foundation of HR professionalism.

Appendix C   Appendix C provides you with additional resources that we feel would be helpful for digging deeper into some of the topics: literature, books, and websites that you can reference for greater insight and expanded information.

Glossary
A glossary of terms has been created for your ease of reference. Using the glossary will help you review the key terms covered in this book.

Index
In the back of the book is an index that will guide you to the appropriate pages where a term is mentioned or discussed.

The Examination
The PHR and SPHR exams are not simple true/false or memory-recall exams. You will be sitting for a four-hour, 175+ question exam that may contain up to five different question types. There will be traditional multiple choice, multiple choice–multiple response, fill in the blank, drag and drop, and scenarios. Knowing how to get the most out of each question is crucial.

Traditional Multiple Choice
These questions ask for you to choose among four possible answers and select the one correct answer. Sometimes, you will be asked to select the one wrong answer. "Correct" answers are determined by a panel of HR subject-matter experts who agree on that selection.

Multiple Choice–Multiple Response
These are also multiple-choice questions, except that there are two or more correct answers rather than only one. You will be told how many answers you should choose for this type of question.

Fill in the Blank
You will be asked to provide a numeral, word, or phrase to complete the sentence.

Drag and Drop
You will be asked to click each option and place it in the proper order or associate it with the proper link option.

Scenarios (Situational Judgment)
Scenario questions present typical HR situations, followed by a series of exam items based on the scenario. These scenarios require you to integrate facts from different subject areas. They depend on both knowledge and experience.

NOTE   The questions included at the end of the chapters and in the practice exams will provide you with good examples of these different question types.

Preparing for the Exam

Preparing for any type of certification exam is not about memorizing information. The PHR and SPHR exams require that established HR professionals with the requisite years of experience be able to demonstrate that they can apply their experience and knowledge in a host of different situations.

 NOTE You have already invested in an education for your career; investing in serious study time and preparation will pay off so that you can pass your exam.

For those with a more limited or the minimal experience qualifications, we suggest you begin preparation and study six months prior to your exam date. For those with significantly more experience and time on the job as an HR professional, three months should be your yardstick. If you want to "shoot from the hip" and not study the material outlined in this book, your chances of passing one of these professional exams will likely be low—even if you have been in an HR exempt position for years. We aren't saying that it can't be done, but your chances of passing the exams are much better if you study the information in this book and the questions in the practice exams we have provided. There is also a separate practice exam book, *PHR/SPHR Professional in Human Resources Certification Practice Exams, Second Edition* (McGraw-Hill Education, 2019), to prepare to sit in front of the computer screen at the testing center for four hours selecting the correct answers. Guessing strategies are not foolproof and not a good substitute for solid study habits in preparation for an exam. The best preparation strategy is one that is focused on committed preparation with study time spent in a productive manner.

Number of certified professionals as of January 31, 2018[1]:

PHR = 76,170
SPHR = 51,393

Pass rates for certification exams as of January 31, 2018:

PHR = 52%
SPHR = 49%

Exam Tips

The following exam tips are exactly what they sound like, tips to assist you in your preparation for the exam:

- Before studying, go for a brief walk to take in some fresh air and clear your mind in preparation for the focused time and new concentration. Put all the other thoughts and projects of the day on a back burner and allow your mind to be a clean slate, setting the intention that this specific amount of time is for the exclusive intention of HRCI studying.

---

[1] https://www.hrci.org/our-programs/what-is-hrci-certification/hrci-exam-statistics

- Make sure your "do not disturb" sign is on your door if you are at home or in the office so others clearly know that nothing is to disturb you during your study time. An hour uninterrupted is plenty of time to devote to studying on a regular set schedule. Most people find that four or five hours a week is sufficient for this type of material.

- Clear your study area. It should be free of anything else that might distract you from studying. Keep your focus on the studying at hand, and to add a little incentive, create a bit of visual incentive for yourself—the desired end result of a letter stating you have successfully passed your exam. Spoof a letter from HRCI, print it, and put it in a nice picture frame and place it in front of you every time you begin your study time. What the mind can conceive, you can achieve!

- Select a time of day that is optimum for you to study. Are you best in the wee hours of the early morning with a cup of coffee prior to work, or perhaps it's the noon hour? Maybe your rhythm is one of a person who kicks in just after dinner. Find that sweet hour and make the appointment on your calendar, listing it as "VIP-HRCI." *You* are the very important person, and this appointment will cause you to think twice before allowing another activity to slip in on your time slot.

- The old adage "practice makes perfect" is not quite right. "Perfect practice makes perfect" is a better way to state the intention. As you make your study time perfect and practice saying "no thank you" to others and other things that would interrupt your study time, you are practicing the perfect combination that will allow you to stay focused and produce the results you are after.

- Beginning two days before the exam, be sure to get a full night's sleep each night, which is typically 7 to 9 hours for most people. Studies prove that a REM state of sleeping is extremely helpful for brain function.

- Hydrate, hydrate, hydrate the day before and the day of the exam. Try to avoid massive amounts of caffeine (it will keep you awake and rob you of precious hydration). Water is good for the body, but even better for the brain, bringing oxygen that helps your brain functions improve.

Here are a couple of other helpful tips about the HRCI exams in particular:

- Nothing that has occurred in the last two years will be covered on your exam. It takes HRCI almost two years to process questions and add them to an exam. So don't worry about current events or a new law that just passed.

- Trust your gut, your first impression. First impressions of the correct answer are many times the best choice. This refers to topics you know that you know. This should not be confused with "guessing along."

- Be careful not to base your answer solely on what your current organization's policy is. Keep focused on generally accepted HR practices.

- There will be no patterns, so don't even try to look for them. The psychometric exam process used for the HRCI exams prevents questions from falling into patterns.

- Only *federal* laws apply—don't mix up federal laws with your state laws.
- The most common weakness of HR test takers is overanalyzing the options. Be thorough but be reasonable in your analysis and selection of the options.
- When stumped, try to eliminate the obvious answers and then just focus on what remains.
- *Do read* all four answer choices—it may be that you need to select the *best* answer choice and yet all answer choices are correct.
- Resist the urge to change your answers—this goes hand in hand with the first tip. If you are absolutely, positively sure that you have an incorrect answer, go ahead. But for the most part, resist the urge to change answers.
- Don't rush. Manage your time. You will have a little over a minute for each question. A clock is visible on your monitor screen counting down what amount of time is left. Keep an eye on it.

Final Thoughts

This book has been designed not only to assist you, the HRCI exam candidate, in studying for the PHR and SPHR exams but also to serve as a reliable reference book to be placed on the shelf in your office as a resource. There is a lot for an HR professional to remember. It is our hope that this book becomes a convenient resource that guides you when something pops up that you need a refresher on. At a minimum, we hope it gives you direction in your effort to improve your HR circumstance.

Finally, thank you for selecting this book. We sincerely hope your PHR or SPHR exam goes well and wish you the absolute best on exam day!

PART I

The Human Resources Profession

Human Resources Certifications

The skills and abilities that a human resources (HR) professional uses to produce desired results requires a mastery of professional skills and techniques. Mastery of any profession will involve a continuous career-long commitment to learning, and that is a foundational truth within the HR profession. HR has been, and continues to be, an evolving component of an organization because its basic focus is on people. The constant changes and outside influences on an organization's workforce increase the demands on HR professionals. HR professionals today walk a tight line and must master the art of staying two steps ahead while having one foot firmly planted in the present.

The HR Certification Institute (HRCI, www.hrci.org) was established in 1976 as an internationally recognized certifying organization for the human resources profession. Its mission has been to develop and deliver the highest-quality certification programs that validate mastery in the field of HR management and contribute to the continued improvement of individual and organizational performance. Nearly 140,000 HR professionals in more than 100 countries have been certified by HRCI.

Professional Certifications

Credentialing as an HR professional demonstrates to your colleagues and your organization that you are committed to a higher standard and ethic and dedicated to the HR profession. When you achieve your HR credential, it signals your mastery of core practices and principles in HR management, raising the confidence of an employer and your peers in your abilities.

A professional certification is not to be confused with a certificate program. Professional certifications are based on work experience and education along with recertification requirements. Certificate programs do not require work experience or an educational component, nor do they require recertification. Figure 1-1 shows the HRCI January 2018 certification data.[1]

Figure 1-1
HRCI certification
Holders as of
January 31, 2018

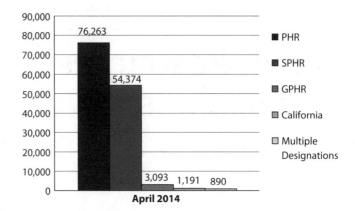

HR Certification Organizations

As of 2018, three certifying organizations offer HR professionals the opportunity to become professionally certified: the HR Certification Institute, which is accredited; the Society for Human Resource Management (SHRM); and the International Public Management Association for Human Resources (IPMA-HR). As of this writing, only HRCI offers a certification for first-level career HR professionals with the aPHR exam. All of the organizations' certifications test knowledge that HR professionals require as their baseline. All three organizations examine individual knowledge and application of that knowledge.

The HR Certification Institute

The HR Certification Institute (www.hrci.org) was established in 1976 as an internationally recognized certifying organization for the human resources profession. Its mission is to develop and deliver the highest-quality certification programs that validate mastery in the field of human resources management and contribute to the continued improvement of individual and organizational performance. Until 2015, HRCI was the only certifying organization for the HR profession and, as of this writing, is the only accredited certifying organization.

HRCI exists to enhance the professionalism of the HR profession with its various certification processes. The HRCI certifications demonstrate relevance, competence, experience, credibility, and dedication to human resources. The institute is a nonprofit (501) (c)(3)[2] separate organization, an IRS designation, from the Society of Human Resource Management, which is a (510)(c)(6)[3] organization. HRCI was accredited by the National Commission for Certifying Agencies (NCCA) in 2008.

HRCI's Body of Knowledge (BoK) is a complete set of knowledge and responsibility statements required to successfully understand and perform generalist HR-related duties associated with each of its credentials, i.e., Associate Professional in Human Resources (aPHR), Professional in Human Resources (PHR), Senior Professional in Human

Resources (SPHR), Global Professional in Human Resources (GPHR), Professional in Human Resources, California (PHRca), Professional in Human Resources, International (PHRi), and Senior Professional in Human Resources, International (SPHRi). The BoK is periodically updated, typically every five to seven years, to ensure it is consistent with and reflects current practices in the HR field. This book, *PHR/SPHR Professional in Human Resources Certification All-in-One Exam Guide,* provides in-depth preparation for the PHR and SPHR exams.

aPHR

HRCI's Associate Professional in Human Resources is the first-ever HR certification designed for professionals who are just beginning their HR career journey. It certifies that a person has knowledge of foundational human resources.

Eligibility Requirements   To sit for the aPHR exam, you must have the following:

- A high school diploma or global equivalent. No experience is required since the aPHR credential is a knowledge-based credential.

PHR

The Professional in Human Resources certification demonstrates that a person has mastery of the technical and operational aspects of HR practices and U.S. laws and regulations. The professionally relevant credential is for the HR professional who focuses on program implementation, has a tactical/logistical orientation, is accountable to another HR professional within the organization, and has responsibilities that focus on the HR department rather than the whole organization.

Eligibility Requirements   To sit for the PHR exam, you must have one of the following:

- A minimum of one year of experience in a professional-level HR position plus a master's degree or higher
- A minimum of two years of experience in a professional-level HR position plus a bachelor's degree
- A minimum of four years of experience in a professional-level HR position plus a high school diploma

SPHR

The Senior Professional in Human Resources certification demonstrates that a person has mastered the strategic and policy-making aspects of HR management as practiced in the United States. The credential is designed for the HR professional who plans (rather than implements) HR policy, focuses on the "big picture," has ultimate accountability in the HR department, has breadth and depth of knowledge in all HR disciplines, understands the business beyond the HR function, and influences the overall organization.

Eligibility Requirements   To sit for the SPHR exam, you must have one of the following:

- A minimum of four years of experience in a professional-level HR position plus a master's degree or higher
- A minimum of five years of experience in a professional-level HR position plus a bachelor's degree
- A minimum of seven years of experience in a professional-level HR position plus a high school diploma

GPHR

The Global Professional in Human Resources is a global, competency-based credential that is designed to validate the skills and knowledge of an HR professional who operates in a global marketplace. The credential demonstrates a mastery of cross-border HR responsibilities that include strategies of globalization; development of HR policies and initiatives that support organizational global growth and employer retention; and the creation of organizational programs, processes, and tools that achieve worldwide business goals.

Eligibility Requirements[4]   To sit for the GPHR exam, you must have one of the following:

- A minimum of two years of experience in a global professional-level HR position plus a master's degree or higher
- A minimum of three years of experience in a professional-level HR position (at least two in global HR) plus a bachelor's degree
- A minimum of four years of experience in a professional-level HR position (at least two in global HR) plus a high school diploma

Global HR experience is defined as having direct cross-border HR responsibilities for two or more countries or regions.

PHRca

The Professional in Human Resources, California demonstrates that an HR professional has mastered the laws, regulations, and HR management practices unique to the state of California. The PHRca is for professionals either who practice in California or who are responsible for human resources management functions in California. You do not have to be located in California or any longer possess a PHR or SPHR certification to earn a PHRca certification.

Eligibility Requirements[5]   To sit for the PHRca exam, you must have one of the following:

- A minimum of one year of experience in a professional-level HR position plus a master's degree or higher
- A minimum of two years of experience in a professional-level HR position plus a bachelor's degree
- A minimum of four years of experience in a professional-level HR position plus a high school diploma

PHRi

The Professional in Human Resources, International is a global, competency-based credential that is designed to validate professional-level core HR knowledge and skills. The credential demonstrates a mastery of generally accepted technical and operational HR principles on a global scale. Independent of geographic region, the credential complements local HR practices. Through demonstrated knowledge, the credential enhances the credibility of HR professionals and the organizations they serve.[6]

Eligibility Requirements   To sit for the PHRi exam, you must have one of the following:

- A minimum of one year of experience in a professional-level HR position plus a master's degree or global equivalent
- A minimum of two years of experience in a professional-level HR position plus a bachelor's degree or global equivalent
- A minimum of four years of experience in a professional-level HR position plus a high school diploma or global equivalent

SPHRi

The Senior Professional in Human Resources, International is a global, competency-based credential that is designed to validate professional-level core HR knowledge and skills. This credential demonstrates a mastery of generally accepted HR principles in strategy, policy development, and service delivery. Independent of geographic region, this credential complements local HR practices. Through demonstrated knowledge, this credential enhances the credibility of HR professionals and the organizations they serve.[7]

Eligibility Requirements   To sit for the SPHRi exam, you must have one of the following:

- A minimum of four years of experience in a professional-level HR position plus a master's degree or global equivalent
- A minimum of five years of experience in a professional-level HR position plus a bachelor's degree or global equivalent
- A minimum of seven years of experience in a professional-level HR position plus a high school diploma or global equivalent

Recertification

Recertification is the process of renewing one's certification. To maintain certification, a certification holder must be prepared to show that they are building their knowledge, growing as a professional, and increasing their experience. HRCI recertification is required every three years through demonstrated professional development (the preferred method) or by retaking the exam. Recertification can be earned in the following categories:

- Continuing education
- Instruction

- On-the-job experience
- Research/publishing
- Leadership
- Professional membership

Recertification requires much more than attending conferences and workshops. Most certified HR professionals earn their recertification credits through the activities they do daily for their organizations.

The Society for Human Resource Management

For more than 65 years, the Society for Human Resource Management (www.shrm .org) has served the human resources profession and HR professionals worldwide. Founded in 1948, SHRM is the world's largest HR membership organization devoted to human resources management. Representing more than 275,000 members in more than 160 countries, SHRM is the leading provider of resources to serve the needs of HR professionals and advance the professional practice of human resources management. SHRM has more than 575 affiliated chapters within the United States and subsidiary offices in China, India, and United Arab Emirates.

SHRM began offering its own certifications in 2015,[8] the SHRM Certified Professional (SHRM-CP) and the SHRM Senior Certified Professional (SHRM-SCP) certifications, which are associated with its defined Body of Competency and Knowledge (BoCK).

SHRM-CP

The SHRM-Certified Professional exam is for HR professionals who implement policies and strategies, serve as a point of contact for staff and stakeholders, deliver HR services, and perform operational HR functions.

Eligibility Requirements The following are the SHRM-CP eligibility requirements to sit for the exam:

Less than a bachelor's degree*	HR-Related Program 3 years in HR role	Non-HR Program 4 years in HR role
Bachelor's degree	HR-Related Degree 1 year in HR role	Non-HR Degree 2 years in HR role
Graduate degree	HR-Related Degree Currently in HR role	Non-HR Degree 1 year in HR role

*Less than a bachelor's degree includes the following: working toward a bachelor's degree, associate's degree, some college, qualifying HR certificate program, high school diploma, or GED.

SHRM-SCP

The SHRM-Senior Certified Professional exam is for HR professionals who develop strategies, lead the HR function, foster influence in the community, analyze performance metrics, and align HR strategies to organizational goals.

Eligibility Requirements The following are the SHRM-SCP eligibility requirements to sit for the exam:

Less than a bachelor's degree*	HR-Related Program 6 years in HR role	Non-HR Program 7 years in HR role
Bachelor's degree	HR-Related Degree 4 years in HR role	Non-HR Degree 5 years in HR role
Graduate degree	HR-Related Degree 3 years in HR role	Non-HR Degree 4 years in HR role

*Less than a bachelor's degree includes the following: working toward a bachelor's degree, associate's degree, some college, qualifying HR certificate program, high school diploma, or GED.

Recertification

Recertification is how you will continue to grow and adapt to the evolving needs of the profession. SHRM-CP or SHRM-SCP credential holders must do one of the following for recertification:

- Earn 60 professional development credits (PDCs) within a three-year recertification period that ends on the last day of the credential holder's birth month
- Retake the certification exam at the end of the three-year recertification period

The International Public Management Association for Human Resources

While HRCI and SHRM offer certifications covering all employment sectors (private, public, international, and federal government), IPMA-HR focuses solely on public-sector human resources professionals. It is international in scope.[9]

IPMA-CP

This designation is for entry to mid-level public-sector HR professionals. It requires that candidates participate in a fee-based Public Sector HR Essentials training course that is currently offered three times a year. Then you may sit for the exam. Once you have passed the exam, you will be certified.

IPMA-SCP

This designation is for public-sector human resources professionals who have reached the manager, director, senior management, or executive level in their profession. Regardless of the educational level achieved, all candidates for this certification must have a minimum of one year of work experience in the public sector. Eight years of HR work experience are required if there is no degree beyond high school. Those with an associate degree must have six years of HR work experience. Bachelor's degree holders must have four years of HR work experience, and graduate degree holders must have a minimum of two years of HR work experience. All must be in jobs that are classified as exempt under the Fair Labor Standards Act (FLSA) at the time an application is submitted for testing.

Benefits of Certification

Earning an HR credential adds a level of recognition as an expert in the HR profession. This certification is a distinction that sets you apart in the profession, indicating you have a high level of knowledge and skills. It adds to your career value and to the organization you work in. Your HR certification could mean the difference between you and your competition. In fact, 96 percent of employers say that an HR-certified candidate applying for a job would have an advantage over a noncertified candidate. In addition, HR professionals who hold certifications tend to make more money than their peers who do not.[10] According to PayScale Human Capital, this pattern is true for all industries and metropolitan areas in the United States. HR certification is becoming an important means for employers to recognize HR expertise and for HR professionals to increase their value and worth.

Earning an HR credential can

- Boost your confidence
- Create recognition for you as an HR professional
- Help you master expert knowledge for the HR profession
- Protect your organization from risk by knowing regulatory compliance
- Help you stand out from other HR candidates in job searches and promotions
- Broaden your perspective in the HR field
- Help you keep up with HR innovations, developments, and legislative/law changes
- Help you demonstrate your commitment to the HR profession

Many organizations, including a number of Fortune 500 organizations, now require or prefer HR certification for their new HR hires or for internal promotions. A May 2014 study from Software Advice, Inc., called "What Employers Are Looking for in HR Positions"[11] revealed that employers will be increasingly demanding certification for their job candidates. The study found the HR certification preferences, broken down by job title, shown in Table 1-1.

Job Title Classification	Certification Required	Certification Preferred	Total
HR business partner	70%	30%	100%
Associate HR director	35%	30%	65%
Senior HR manager	10%+	45%	55%
HR director	10%	45%	55%
HR manager	5%	40%	45%
Senior HR generalist		55%	55%
Senior HR business partner		45%	45%
Employee relations manager		30%	30%
HR generalist		15%	15%
Other		30%	30%

Table 1-1   HR Certification Specifications by Job Title

This survey suggests that certification will be essential for any professional-level HR job candidate. If an individual wants to be considered for a senior-level HR position, then certification is nearly an absolute requirement. Those expectations will be further solidified as time goes on.

The HR Certification Institute's Role

The HR Certification Institute exists to enhance the professionalism of HR professionals with the various certification processes. The institute is a nonprofit separate entity from the Society of Human Resource Professionals. HRCI is responsible for the following:

- Conducting the practice analysis that results in the HR Body of Knowledge
- Developing test questions and maintaining the test bank versions
- Determining a candidate's eligibility to take the exams
- Managing the details of test registration and the testing process
- Approving recertification activities by which certified HR professionals retain their designations

HRCI was accredited by the National Commission for Certifying Agencies in 2008. It partners with PearsonVUE (https://home.pearsonvue.com/hrci) for computerized exam delivery.

The Significance of the Body of Knowledge

HRCI's BoK is the description of the complete set of concepts, tasks, responsibilities, and the knowledge required to successfully understand and perform generalist HR-related duties associated with each of its credentials. The BoK is periodically updated, typically every five years, to ensure it is consistent with and reflects current practices in the HR field. All exam test questions are specifically linked to a BoK item.

The Test Development Process

HRCI follows certification-industry best practices to create and keep their exams updated. The institute's question-writing and review processes are designed to reflect the best practices for exam question writing and review in the certification industry. The institute also ensures that questions are developed by actual HR practitioners for the HR practitioner. The following are the steps used in developing its exams:

- **Step 1** The process begins with a practice analysis study that defines the HR BoK from which exam questions are created. The BoK is a source document that identifies the basic principles, concepts, and knowledge requirements for HR generalists to successfully carry out their duties and responsibilities for each level and type of certification offered by HRCI. A 10-member practice analysis task force is organized that is responsible for conducting critical incident interviews and focus panels to identify and collect current information and practice patterns for HR generalists. This information is sorted into process- and content-based approaches to functional areas of responsibility. The final results are submitted to the HRCI board of directors for approval. The approved result is the HR Body of Knowledge, also called *exam content*. Practice analysis studies are typically conducted every five years. The next PHR/SPHR practice analysis study will occur in 2018.

- **Step 2** Exam item development begins with two U.S. 15-member item writing panels consisting of certified HR professionals who received special training and are tasked to write 35 new test items (questions) each year. Separate 15-member writing panels write test items for the GPHR and California certification exams.

- **Step 3** Questions prepared by the item-writing panels are reviewed by item review panels consisting of veteran writers. These item review panels look to ensure the test questions are reflective of the applicable BoK, are relevant to the HR field, and are adequately supported by the evidence and subject-matter expert literature—literature reviewed by a panel that checks for accuracy and proper coding to the HRCI functional area. Items that pass this review screen are collected into an "item bank" to be selected as appropriate for upcoming exams.

- **Step 4** All questions must pass validity and reliability testing requirements. This happens when a new test item is initially used on an exam. The new test item is part of 25 unscored items randomly distributed on the exam. Their initial appearance is to develop a statistical profile that will determine whether the item meets validity and reliability requirements based on exam results, and is thus usable as a scored item on future exams.

- **Step 5** Exams consist of 175 questions, 25 of which are unscored, and multiple versions of the exam are created and reviewed by another panel.

- **Step 6** A passing score is determined for each of the seven exam versions.

- **Step 7** Each question on the exam version is pre-equated to determine the difficulty level of that version. Item Response Theory (IRT) is used to pre-equate. Because all versions of the exam are pre-equated, the number of questions answered correctly to earn a passing score varies depending on the exam version. The minimum passing score is a scaled score of 500. This is a floating score based on the degree of difficulty of the exam; that is, a more difficult exam will have a lower floating score, while a less difficult exam will have a high floating score.

Figure 1-2 provides a flowchart of the exam test development.

All questions appearing on the PHR and SPHR exams are linked to HRCI's BoK and responsibilities statements, which are located in Chapter 3 and at the front of each functional area in Chapters 4 through 13.

The Exam Experience

All exams are delivered by computer-based testing (CBT). Computer-based testing is the standard for many other test delivery programs. CBT is testing done in person, on a computer, and at an approved testing center. CBT offers a more consistent test delivery,

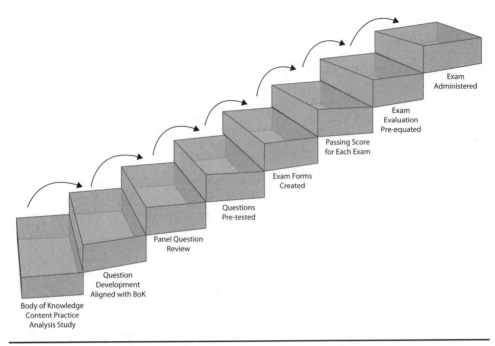

Figure 1-2 HRCI exam development process

faster scoring and reporting, and enhanced test security. Exam takers receive their preliminary pass/fail results before walking out of the testing center. Official pass/fail notices come in the mail a few weeks after the exam.

The PHR, SPHR, and GPHR exams are three hours in length for testing. Both the PHR and SPHR have the same number of multiple-choice questions, 175, of which 150 are scored questions and 25 are pre-test (unscored). The GPHR's makeup of questions is 165 multiple-choice (140 scored questions and 25 pre-test). The SPHRi is lengthier with 170 questions (145 of those are scored, and 25 are pre-test), allowing 3 hours and 25 minutes for the exam. The PHRi allows 2 hours and 30 minutes for the exam consisting of 130 questions (105 scored questions and 25 pre-test questions). The PHRca is allotted 2 hours and 15 minutes and has 125 multiple-choice questions.

Seventy-five percent of the PHR exam and 85 percent of the SPHR exam are heavily experiential—that is, application or situation based. The exams test a knowledge or cognitive comprehension level of 25 percent for the PHR and 15 percent for the SPHR. The PHR and SPHR exams have test questions that require the following:

- Knowledge and comprehension (recall of factual material, translation, or interpretation of a concept)

- Application and problem-solving (solving new, real-life problems through the application of familiar principles or generalizations)

- Synthesis and evaluation (combining distantly related elements into a whole involving critical judgments in terms of accuracy or consistency of logic)[12]

Strict rules are enforced at the testing centers to ensure a secure, consistent, and fair test experience for all exam takers. You will find the testing center information for Pearson VUE at https://home.pearsonvue.com/. Reviewing this is advisable for preparation. Prior to the exam, you may be asked to empty your pockets and turn your pockets inside out, and, if you have one, store your purse in a locker during the test. No cell phones, recording devices, calculators, or other aids will be allowed in the testing room.

New Test Question Formats

Up until 2018, HRCI used one format for its test questions. That was a multiple-choice format with four possible answer selections, with only one correct answer within the four. It has since redesigned its tests to include five types of questions:

- **Traditional multiple-choice**   Four possible answers with only one of them correct.

  Example: The most recognized HR certification organizations are:

  A. Northern California Human Resource Association, Human Resource Certification Institute, and Society for Human Resource Management

  B. Eastern States Professional HR Association, Northern California Human Resource Association, Society for Human Resource Management

  C. International Public Management Association for Human Resources, Human Resource Certification Institute, Society for Human Resource Management

  D. International Human Resource Professionals, Private Sector Human Resource Professionals Association, Society for Human Resource Management

  Answer: C is correct. All three are valid certification organizations.

- **Multiple-choice, multiple-response**   Like the traditional multiple-choice in that there are multiple possible answers, but two or more of them are correct. The question will tell you how many are correct.

  Example: Which of the following are valid HR certifications? (Choose four.)

  A. SPHRca

  B. aPHR

  C. SHRM-CP

  D. IPMA-SCP

  E. Intern-CP

  F. SPHR-SCP

  Answer: B, C, D, and F are correct. Each is a valid certification offered by one of the HR certification organizations.

- **Fill in the blank**   You will need to insert a number, word, or phrase to complete the test question.

  Example: _____ was accredited by the National Commission for Certifying Agencies (NCCA) in 2008.

  Answer: Human Resource Certification Institute (HRCI)

- **Drag and drop**   You will need to match up contents of two columns of information so they are correctly aligned.

  Example: Match the following certification designations to the certifying organization.

  A. SPHRi

  B. aPHR

  C. SHRM-SCP

  D. IPMA-CP

  (1) HRCI

  (2) SHRM

  (3) IPMA-HR

  Answer: A, (1); B, (1); C, (2); D, (3)

- **Scenarios**   Typical HR problems are presented followed by a series of exam questions based on that scenario. You will be required to use both knowledge and experience to blend skill with legality and practicality from various subject areas.

  Example: Amanda has joined the HR department recently. As the newest HR analyst, Amanda has been assigned to provide client departments with monthly reports detailing the HR performance indices. What is the most important factor Amanda should keep in mind while performing this task?

  A. Department managers always have the right to veto any HR initiative.

  B. Any request by the client department should be accepted and provided to them.

  C. Any deliverable she provides will establish her reputation as reliable or unreliable.

  D. Customer reports will eventually be collected and destroyed because of their confidential nature.

  Answer: C is correct. Her reputation will rest on her accuracy, honesty, and ethical behavior.

Practice Questions in This Study Guide

In this study guide we will be providing you with a variety of questions that will give you practice with the formats you can expect to encounter on the real exam. None of the questions you find here will actually appear on the exam. But they are legitimate examples of questions similar to those the exam may contain.

We will offer you practice questions at the end of each chapter. And we offer you two complete practice exams so you can get better acquainted with the type of experience you may have on exam day.

Registering for the Exam   Fitting your certification exam schedule into a testing window is now a thing of the past. HRCI provides year-round testing—an HR industry first. The year-round testing provides you with the most flexibility possible to accommodate your busy schedule. Exam dates for all HRCI certifications are available on a first-come, first-served basis at approved testing centers. HRCI monitors test center usage closely and periodically evaluates test center locations based on customer volume.

You must meet all eligibility requirements to take an exam. The exam approval is valid for 120 calendar days from the application approval date.

The Exam's Design

The PHR and SPHR exams will consist of 175 multiple-choice questions. The PHR exam is more heavily weighted in the functional area of Employee and Labor Relations (39 percent), whereas the SPHR exam is weighted heavily in the functional area of Leadership and Strategy (40 percent). Table 1-2 illustrates the differences in the weightings for each exam and indicates the number of questions you can expect in the specific functional areas.

HRCI produces multiple versions of the exam for each testing level (PHR and SPHR). Prometric operates computerized-based testing centers across the United States, and its system is programmed so that any one of the multiple versions may be used for a testing candidate, which means the person sitting next to you very well may be taking a different exam. Some test versions have a number of questions where knowledge of the related legislation or the name of a court case will be needed (see Chapter 2 and Appendix B); other versions may not dive into that, or only indirectly. The other variable is whether there are any math questions on the exam; some exams have them, some don't. As a result, preparing for the exam should address all of this.

According to HRCI, the January 31, 2018, national pass rates were as follows:

- **aPHR** 85%
- **PHR** 52%
- **PHR**CA 50%
- **PHRi** 62%
- **SPHR** 49%
- **SPHRi** 68%
- **GPHR** 66%

HRCI Functional Area – 2018	PHR		SPHR	
	Weighting	Questions	Weighting	Questions
Business Management	20%	35		
Employee and Labor Relations	39%	68		
Employee Relations and Engagement			20%	35
Leadership and Strategy			40%	70
Learning and Development	10%	18	12%	21
Talent Planning and Acquisition	16%	28	16%	28
Total Rewards	15%	26	12%	21
TOTAL Questions	**100%**	**175**	**100%**	**175**

Table 1-2 PHR/SPHR Exam Weighting

NOTE If you already hold a PHR certification and you do not pass the SPHR exam, you will still retain your PHR certification.

Chapter Review

Professional HR certification serves as an acknowledgment of an HR professional's demonstrated mastery of core HR skills, principles, and knowledge, which are essential to the best practice in human resources. This book provides all the necessary knowledge and principles needed to pass your PHR or SPHR exam. Only your past work experience can provide you with the hands-on experience and critical thinking capabilities that are an additional essential part to earning the PHR and SPHR credentials.

HR certification consists of four key components:

- Eligibility through a combination of past work experience and formal education
- Commitment and demonstration to a high professional ethical standard
- Demonstrated applied knowledge and skills through the exam process
- Ongoing professional development for career lifelong learning through recertification requirements

Having a thorough and complete understanding of the HRCI Body of Knowledge, which is located in Chapter 3 of this book and at the beginnings of Chapters 4–13, is absolutely vital for identifying a correct answer for both the PHR and SPHR exams. You need to know the objective of those laws and regulations inside out.

Remember that the PHR and SPHR exams are based on federal laws and cases and not on local state laws and ordinances (only the PHRca certification has a basis in state law, specifically, California law).

Last, the HRCI website (www.HRCI.org) goes into far greater detail about exam eligibility, registration, recertification, and what the exam questions may look like. Prepare yourself for scenario types of questions, and be sure to take the sample test questions at the end of each chapter in this book. Guessing as a test tactic is not a good substitute for studying in test preparation. Correct answers come from sufficient studying and test practice.

Questions

1. HRCI has been certifying HR professionals since:

   A. 1986

   B. 1976

   C. 2008

   D. 2016

2. In 2008, _____ was accredited by the National Commission for Certifying Agencies (NCAA).

3. HRCI's certification exams have all been _____, meaning they actually measure what they say they measure.

   A. Validated

   B. Expunged

   C. Contested

   D. Proven

4. Simone has just graduated from college and is beginning her first job as an HR analyst with a major employer. She is wondering what certification she should seek to begin her career. You tell her to take the exam for _____.

5. Which of the following are valid HR certifications? (Choose three.)

   A. PHRca

   B. PHRi

   C. NPHR

   D. UPHR

   E. SPHR

6. Someone already certified as a Professional in Human Resources (PHR) must _____ to gain certification as a Senior Professional in Human Resources (SPHR). (Choose two.)

   A. Sit for and pass the SPHR exam

   B. Have a minimum of seven years of experience at a professional HR level

   C. Sit for and pass the SPHRca exam

   D. Have a minimum of four years of experience at a professional HR level

7. HR professionals who operate in a global marketplace are able to demonstrate mastery of cross-border HR responsibilities, including strategies of globalization and development of HR policies and initiatives supporting organizational global growth by achieving a _____ certification.

8. PHRca is a certification that recognizes the unique characteristics of business and employment requirements in _____.

9. Other certification agencies, in addition to the Human Resource Certification Institute, include:

   A. Cross-Border HR Professionals Association and Society for Human Resource Management

   B. Society for Human Resource Management and International Public Management Association for Human Resources

   C. American National Standards Institute and Cross-Border HR Professionals Association

   D. Society for Human Resource Management and Human Resource Standards Acceptance Group

10. Which of the following is *not* a valid HR certification designation?

    A. GPHR

    B. SHRM-SCP

    C. IHRM-CP

    D. IPMA-SCP

11. Studies have shown that _____% of employers are looking for certifications at the HR director level.

12. The HRCI Body of Knowledge (BoK) is:

    A. A list of everything any HR manager should know

    B. A description of the complete set of concepts, tasks, responsibilities, and knowledge required to fulfill the duties of an HR generalist

    C. A list of all the desirable knowledge items any HR manager should understand

    D. A description of the responsibilities undertaken by any HR generalist

Answers

1. **B**. HRCI has been certifying HR professionals since 1976.

2. **HRCI**

3. **A**. All of the HRCI certification exams have been validated.

4. **aPHR**

5. **A, B, E**. NPHR and UPHR are not certification designations.

6. **A, D**. A minimum of four years' experience at the professional HR level and passing the SPHR certification exam are both required.

7. **GPHR**

8. **California**

9. **B**. Both SHRM and IPMA-HR are valid certification agencies.

10. **C**. IHRM-CP is not a valid HR certification designation.

11. **55%**

12. **B**. It encompasses concepts, tasks, responsibilities, and knowledge required of an HR generalist.

Endnotes

1. PayScale Human Capital research report, "The Market Value of PHR and SPHR Certifications," http://resources.payscale.com/rs/payscale/images/report_SPHR_PHR.pdf

2. HRCI Certification Policies and Procedures Handbook, www.hrci.org/certification-handbooks

3. HRCI PHR/SPHR Body of Knowledge Handbook, www.hrci.org/docs/default-source/web-files/phr_sphr-body-of-knowledge=pdf.pdf

4. HRCI GPHR Body of Knowledge Handbook, https://www.hrci.org/our-programs/our-certifications/gphr

5. https://www.hrci.org/our-programs/our-certifications/PHRca

6. https://www.hrci.org/our-programs/our-certifications/PHRi

7. https://www.hrci.org/our-programs/our-certifications/SPHRi

8. https://www.shrm.org/certification

9. https://www.ipma-hr.org

10. "The Value of HR Certification Around the World," exit study 2012, www.hrci.org/docs/default-source/web-files/2014-certification-handbook-pdf.pdf

U.S. Laws and Regulations

In this chapter we introduce the federal laws and legislation that the human resources professional must be knowledgeable of. After studying this chapter and completing the test questions, you should have an understanding of the relevance of these laws to the employment relationship. HR professionals in both small and large companies play an important role in dealing with day-to-day employment issues relating to the recruiting, hiring, managing, and training of employees. Ensuring that an employer's policies and actions follow the law and keeping employers out of legal jeopardy are essential functions valued by employers.

What You Need to Know Concerning Employee Management

We have structured this chapter so that it not only covers the knowledge needed for the HRCI exams but can also be used as a reference tool in your day-to-day work in human resources. The laws are summarized and listed in groupings according to the number of employees an organization has, from 1 to 100+. Included is a reference URL that points to each law's full description. Legal regulation constantly evolves, so when using this guide as a reference book, be sure to reference the URL provided and specific state laws that govern your work locations.

- If you have from 1 to 14 employees, there are 53 federal laws you must abide by. *53*
- If you have from 15 to 19 employees, there are an additional 10 federal laws for *63* your attention.
- If you have from 20 to 49 employees, add another four laws to the list. *67*
- If you have from 50 to 99 employees, add another six laws to the list. *73*
- If you have 100 or more employees, there are a total of 74 federal laws you must *74* know and be in compliance with.
- If you are in a federal agency, you must comply with six laws specifically focused on your employee management issues.

In Part II of this study guide, the Body of Knowledge (BoK) areas within each chapter will direct you to this chapter's specific law for reference. We suggest you thoroughly explore this chapter's information before moving into Part II for greater ease with the HRCI exam's BoK. Then gauge your understanding of the laws by taking the pre-test at the end of this chapter.

1. When You Have One or More Employees

Employers sometimes forget that the moment they hire their first employee they become subject to a host of legal requirements. The following are 53 laws that will impact an employer with one or more employees on the payroll.

1.1 The Clayton Act (1914)

This legislation modified the Sherman Anti-Trust Act by prohibiting mergers and acquisitions that would lessen competition. It also prohibits a single person from being a director of two or more competing corporations. The act also restricts the use of injunctions against labor and legalized peaceful strikes, picketing, and boycotts.

For more information, see 15 U.S.C. Sec.12, www.law.cornell.edu/uscode/text/15/12.

1.2 The Consumer Credit Protection Act (1968)

Congress expressed limits to the amount of wages that can be garnished or withheld in any one week by an employer to satisfy creditors. This law also prohibits employee dismissal because of garnishment for any one indebtedness.

For more information, see www.dol.gov/compliance/laws/comp-ccpa.htm.

1.3 The Copeland "Anti-Kickback" Act (1934)

This act precludes a federal contractor or subcontractor from inducing an employee to give up any part of his or her wages to the employer for the benefit of having a job.

For more information, see www.dol.gov/whd/regs/statutes/copeland.htm.

1.4 The Copyright Act (1976)

The Copyright Act offers protection of "original works" for authors so others may not print, duplicate, distribute, or sell their work. In 1998, the Copyright Term Extension Act further extended copyright protection to the duration of the author's life plus 70 years for general copyrights and to 95 years for works made for hire and works copyrighted before 1978. If anyone in the organization writes technical instructions, policies and procedures, manuals, or even e-mail responses to customer inquiries, it is a good idea to speak with your attorney and arrange some copyright agreements to clarify whether the employer or the employee who authored those documents will be designated the copyright owner. Written agreements can be helpful in clearing up any possible misunderstandings.

For more information, see www.copyright.gov/title17/92appa.pdf.

1.5 The Davis-Bacon Act (1931)

This law requires contractors and subcontractors on certain federally funded or assisted construction projects exceeding $2,000 in the United States to pay wages and fringe benefits at least equal to those prevailing in the local area where the work is performed. This law applies only to laborers and mechanics. It also allows trainees and apprentices to be paid less than the predetermined rates under certain circumstances.

For more information, see www.dol.gov/whd/regs/statutes/dbra.htm.

1.6 The Dodd-Frank Wall Street Reform and Consumer Protection Act (2010)

This law offers a wide range of mandates affecting all federal financial regulatory agencies and almost every part of the nation's financial services industry. It includes a nonbinding vote for shareholders on executive compensation, golden parachutes, and return of executive compensation based on inaccurate financial statements. Also included are requirements to report CEO pay compared to the average employee compensation and provision of financial rewards for whistle-blowers. Congress recently passed legislation signed two days later by the U.S. president that loosens key portions of the act by exempting dozens of banks from strict regulation.

For more information, see www.sec.gov/about/laws/wallstreetreform-cpa.pdf.

1.7 The Economic Growth and Tax Relief Reconciliation Act (EGTRRA) (2001)

Here are modifications to the Internal Revenue Code that adjust pension vesting schedules, increase retirement plan limits, permit pretax catchup contributions by participants older than 50 in certain plans (which are not tested for discrimination when made available to the entire workforce), and modify distribution and rollover rules.

For more information, see www.irs.gov/pub/irs-tege/epchd104.pdf.

1.8 The Electronic Communications Privacy Act (ECPA) (1986)

This is actually and uniquely a law composed of two pieces of legislation: the Wiretap Act and the Stored Communications Act. Combined, they provide rules for access, use, disclosure, interpretation, and privacy protections of electronic communications, and they provide the possibility of both civil and criminal penalties for violations. They prohibit interception of e-mails in transmission and access to e-mails in storage. The implications for HR have to do with recording employee conversations. Warnings such as "This call may be monitored or recorded for quality purposes" are intended to provide the notice required by this legislation. Having cameras in the workplace to record employee or visitor activities is also covered, and notices must be given to anyone subject to observation or recording. Recording without such a notice can be a violation of this act. If employers make observations of employee activities and/or record telephone and other conversations between employees and others and proper notice is given to employees, employees will have no expectation of privacy during the time they are in the workplace.

For more information, see www.justice.gov/jmd/ls/legislative_histories/pl99-508/pl99-508.html.

1.9 The Employee Polygraph Protection Act (1988)

Before 1988, it was common for employers to use "lie detectors" as tools in investigations of inappropriate employee behavior. That changed when this act prohibited the use of lie detector tests for job applicants and employees of companies engaged in interstate commerce. Exceptions are made for certain conditions, including law enforcement and national security. There also is a federal poster requirement.

 NOTE Many state laws also prohibit the use of lie detector tests.

For more information, see www.dol.gov/compliance/laws/comp-eppa.htm.

1.10 The Employee Retirement Income Security Act (ERISA) (1974)

This law doesn't require employers to establish pension plans but governs how those plans are managed once they are established. It establishes uniform minimum standards to ensure that employee benefit plans are established and maintained in a fair and financially sound manner; protects employees covered by a pension plan from losses in benefits due to job changes, plant closings, bankruptcies, or mismanagement; and protects plan beneficiaries. It covers most employers engaged in interstate commerce. Public-sector employees and many churches are not subject to ERISA. Employers that offer retirement plans must also conform with the IRS code to receive tax advantages.

For more information, see www.dol.gov/compliance/laws/comp-erisa.htm.

1.11 The Equal Pay Act (EPA) (Amendment to the FLSA) (1963)

Equal pay requirements apply to all employers. The act is an amendment to the FLSA and is enforced by the EEOC. It prohibits employers from discriminating on the basis of sex by paying wages to employees at a rate less than the rate paid to employees of the opposite sex for equal work on jobs requiring equal skill, effort, and responsibility, and which are performed under similar working conditions. It does not address the concept of comparable worth.

For more information, see www.eeoc.gov/laws/statutes/epa.cfm.

1.12 The FAA Modernization and Reform Act (2012)

Congress took these actions in 2012 to amend the Railway Labor Act to change union certification election processes in the railroad and airline industries and impose greater oversight of the regulatory activities of the National Mediation Board. This law requires the Government Accountability Office (GAO) initially to evaluate the NMB's certification procedures and then audit the NMB's operations every two years.

For more information, see www.faa.gov/regulations_policies/reauthorization/media/PLAW-112publ95[1].pdf.

1.13 The Fair and Accurate Credit Transactions Act (FACT) (2003)

The financial privacy of employees and job applicants was enhanced in 2003 with these amendments to the Fair Credit Reporting Act, providing for certain requirements in third-party investigations of employee misconduct charges. Employers are released from obligations to disclose requirements and obtain employee consent if the investigation involves suspected misconduct, a violation of the law or regulations, or a violation of pre-existing written employer policies. A written plan to prevent identity theft is required.

For more information, see www.gpo.gov/fdsys/pkg/PLAW-108publ159/pdf/PLAW-108publ159.pdf.

1.14 The Fair Credit Reporting Act (FCRA) (1970)

This was the first major legislation to regulate the collection, dissemination, and use of consumer information, including consumer credit information. It requires employers to notify any individual in writing if a credit report may be used in making an employment decision. Employers must also get a written authorization from the subject individual before asking a credit bureau for a credit report. The FCRA also protects the privacy of background investigation information and provides methods for ensuring that information is accurate. Employers who take adverse action against a job applicant or current employee based on information contained in the prospective or current employee's consumer report will have additional disclosures to make to that individual.

For more information, see www.ftc.gov/os/statutes/031224fcra.pdf.

1.15 The Fair Labor Standards Act (FLSA) (1938)

The FLSA is one of a handful of federal laws that establish the foundation for employee treatment. It is a major influence in how people are paid, in employment of young people, and in how records are to be kept on employment issues such as hours of work. The law introduced a maximum 44-hour 7-day workweek, established a national minimum wage, guaranteed "time-and-a-half" for overtime in certain jobs, and prohibited most employment of minors in "oppressive child labor," a term that is defined in the statute. It applies to employees engaged in interstate commerce or employed by an enterprise engaged in commerce or in the production of goods for commerce, unless the employer can claim an exemption from coverage. It is interesting to note that the FLSA, rather than the Civil Rights Act of 1964, is the first federal law to require employers to maintain records on employee race and sex identification.

Provisions and Protections

Employers covered under the "enterprise" provisions of this law include public agencies; private employers whose annual gross sales exceed $500,000 or those operating a hospital or a school for mentally or physically disabled or gifted children; and pre-schools, elementary or secondary schools, or institutions of higher education (profit or nonprofit). Individuals can still be covered, even if they don't fit into one of the enterprises listed. If the employees' work regularly involves them in commerce between the states, they would be covered. These include employees who work in communications

or transportation; regularly use the mail, telephone, or telegraph for interstate communication, or keep records of interstate transactions; handle shipping and receiving goods
moving in interstate commerce; regularly cross state lines in the course of employment;
or work for independent employers who contract to do clerical, custodial, maintenance,
or other work for firms engaged in interstate commerce or in the production of goods
for interstate commerce. The FLSA establishes a federal minimum wage that has been
raised from time to time since the law was originally passed. The FLSA prohibits shipment of goods in interstate commerce that were produced in violation of the minimum
wage, overtime pay, child labor, or special minimum wage provisions of the law.

Recordkeeping

The FLSA proscribes methods for determining whether a job is exempt or nonexempt
from overtime pay requirements of the act. If a job is exempt from those requirements,
incumbents can work as many hours of overtime as the job requires without being paid
for their overtime. Exempt versus nonexempt status attaches to the job, not the incumbent. So someone with an advanced degree who is working in a clerical job may be
nonexempt because of the job requirements, not their personal qualifications. Employers
are permitted to have a policy that calls for paying exempt employees when they work
overtime. That is a voluntary provision of a benefit in excess of federal requirements.
State laws may have additional requirements. People who work in nonexempt jobs must
be paid overtime according to the rate computation methods provided for in the act.
Usually, this is a requirement for overtime after 40 hours of regular time worked during a
single workweek. The act also describes how a workweek is to be determined.

Each employer covered by the FLSA must keep records for each covered, nonexempt
worker. Those records must include the following:

- Employee's full name and Social Security number.
- Address, including ZIP code.
- Birth date, if younger than 19.
- Sex.
- Occupation.
- Time and day of week when an employee's workweek begins.
- Hours worked each day and total hours worked each workweek. (This includes a
  record of the time work began at the start of the day, when the employee left for
  a meal break, the time the employee returned to work from the meal break, and
  the time work ended for the day.)
- Basis on which employee's wages are paid (hourly, weekly, piecework).
- Regular hourly pay rate.
- Total daily or weekly straight-time earnings.

- Total overtime earnings for the workweek.

- All additions or deductions from the employee's wages.

- Total wages paid each pay period.

- Date of payment and the pay period covered by the payment.

There is no limit in the FLSA to the number of hours employees 16 and older may work in any workweek. There is a provision for employers to retain all payroll records, collective bargaining agreements, sales, and purchase records for at least three years. Any time card, piecework record, wage rate tables, and work and time schedules should be retained for at least two years. A workplace poster is required to notify employees of the federal minimum wage.

The federal child labor provisions of the FLSA, also known as the child labor laws, were enacted to ensure that when young people work, the work is safe and does not jeopardize their health, well-being, or educational opportunities. These provisions also provide limited exemptions. Workers younger than 14 are restricted to jobs such as newspaper delivery to local customers; babysitting on a casual basis; acting in movies, TV, radio, or theater; and working as a home worker gathering evergreens and making evergreen wreaths. Under no circumstances, even if the business is family owned, may a person this young work in any of the 17 most hazardous jobs. See Figure 2-1 for a list of the 17 most hazardous jobs.

- Manufacturing or storing of explosives

- Driving a motor vehicle or working as an outside helper on motor vehicles

- Coal mining

- Forest fire fighting and forest fire prevention, timber tract, forestry service, and occupations in logging and sawmilling

- Using power-driven woodworking machines

- Exposure to radioactive substances and ionizing radiation

- Using power-driven hoisting apparatus

- Using power-driven metal-forming, punching, and shearing machines

- Mining, other than coal

- Using power-driven meat-processing machines, slaughtering, meat and poultry packing, processing, or rendering

- Using power-driven bakery machines

- Using balers, compactors, and power-driven paper-products machines

- Manufacturing brick, tile, and related products

- Using power-driven circular saws, band saws, guillotine shears, chain saws, reciprocating saws, wood chippers, and abrasive cutting discs

- Working in wrecking, demolition, and ship-breaking operations

- Roofing and work performed on or about a roof

- Trenching or excavating

Source: "U.S. Department of Labor, eLaws Fair Labor Standards Act Advisor" on July 9, 2013, www.dol.gov/elaws/esa/flsa/docs/haznonag.asp

Figure 2-1   The 17 most dangerous jobs, which may not be performed by workers under 18

For workers aged 14 and 15, all work must be performed outside school hours, and these workers may not work

- More than 3 hours on a school day, including Friday
- More than 18 hours per week when school is in session
- More than 8 hours per day when school is not in session
- More than 40 hours per week when school is not in session
- Before 7 a.m. or after 7 p.m. on any day, except from June 1 through Labor Day, when nighttime work hours are extended to 9 p.m.

Until employees reach the age of 18, it is necessary for them to obtain a work permit from their school district. For workers aged 16 through 17, there is no restriction on the number of hours worked per week. There continues to be a ban on working any job among the 17 most hazardous industries. All of these conditions must be met, or the employer will be subject to penalties from the U.S. Department of Labor.

Overtime Computation

Overtime is required at a rate of 1.5 times the normal pay rate for all hours worked over 40 in a single workweek. An employer may designate that their workweek begins at a given day and hour and continues until that same day and hour seven days later. Once selected, that same workweek definition must be maintained consistently until there is a legitimate business reason for making a change. That change must be clearly communicated in advance to all employees who will be affected by the change. No pay may be forfeited because the employer changes its workweek definition. Compensating time off is permitted for state and local government (public-sector) employees who have a union contract outlining the availability of compensating time off. Under the FLSA it must be given at the same rates required for overtime pay. There are some caps on accrual of compensating hours for police officers and firefighters. State laws sometimes permit compensatory time off for private-sector employees. FLSA does not.

Enforcement

Provisions of the FLSA are enforced by the U.S. Department of Labor's Wage and Hour Division. With offices around the country, this agency is able to interact with employees on complaints and follow up with employers by making an onsite visit if necessary. If violations are found during an investigation, the agency has the authority to make recommendations for changes that would bring the employer into compliance. Retaliation against any employee for filing a complaint under the FLSA or in any other way availing himself or herself of the legal rights it offers is subject to additional penalties. Willful violations may bring criminal prosecution and fines up to $10,000. Employers who are convicted a second time for willfully violating the FLSA can find themselves in prison.

The Wage and Hour Division may, if it finds products produced during violations of the act, prevent an employer from shipping any of those goods. It may also "freeze" shipments of any product manufactured while overtime payment requirements were violated.

A two-year limit applies to recovery of back pay unless there was a willful violation, which triggers a three-year liability.

For more information, see www.dol.gov/whd/regs/statutes/FairLaborStandAct.pdf.

1.16 The Foreign Corrupt Practices Act (FCPA) (1997)

The FCPA prohibits American companies from making bribery payments to foreign officials for the purpose of obtaining or keeping business. Training for employees who are involved with international negotiations should include a warning to avoid anything even looking like bribery payment to a foreign company or its employees.

For more information, see www.justice.gov/criminal/fraud/fcpa/.

1.17 The Health Information Technology for Economic and Clinical Health Act (HITECH) (2009)

The HITECH requires that anyone with custody of personal health records send notification to affected individuals if their personal health records have been disclosed, or the employer believes they have been disclosed, to any unauthorized person. Enacted as part of the American Recovery and Reinvestment Act (ARRA), this law made several changes to HIPAA, including the establishment of a federal standard for security breach notifications that requires covered entities, in the event of a breach of any personal health records (PHI) information, to notify each individual whose PHI has been disclosed without authorization.

For more information, see www.hhs.gov/ocr/privacy/hipaa/administrative/enforce mentrule/hitechenforcementifr.html.

1.18 The Health Insurance Portability and Accountability Act (HIPAA) (1996)

This law ensures that individuals who leave or lose their jobs can obtain health coverage even when they or someone in their family has a serious illness or injury or is pregnant. It also provides privacy requirements related to medical records for individuals as young as 12. It also limits exclusions for pre-existing conditions and guarantees renewability of health coverage to employers and employees, allowing people to change jobs without the worry of loss of coverage. It also restricts the ability of employers to impose actively-at-work requirements as preconditions for health plan eligibility, as well as a number of other benefits.

For more information, see www.hhs.gov/ocr/privacy.

1.19 The Immigration and Nationality Act (INA) (1952)

The INA is the first law that pulled together all of the issues associated with immigration and is considered the foundation on which all following immigration laws have been built. It addresses employment eligibility and employment verification. It defines the conditions for the temporary and permanent employment of aliens in the United States.[1]

The INA defines an "alien" as any person lacking citizenship or status as a national of the United States. The INA differentiates aliens in these ways:

- Resident or nonresident
- Immigrant or nonimmigrant
- Documented and undocumented

The need to curtail illegal immigration led to the enactment of the Immigration Reform and Control Act (IRCA).

For more information, see www.dol.gov/compliance/laws/comp-ina.htm.

1.20 The Immigration Reform and Control Act (IRCA) (1986)

This is the first law to require new employees to prove both their identity and their right to work in this country. Regulations implementing this law created Form I-9, which must be completed by each new employee and the employer. Form I-9 has changed many times since 1986. Please be sure you keep track of the changes as they are issued by the government and make sure that you are using the most current version of the form. There are document retention requirements. The law prohibits discrimination against job applicants on the basis of national origin or citizenship. It establishes penalties for employers that hire illegal aliens.

For more information, see www.eeoc.gov/eeoc/history/35th/thelaw/irca.html.

1.21 The IRS Intermediate Sanctions (2002)

Here you find guidelines for determining reasonable compensation for executives of non-profit organizations. These were enacted by the IRS and applied to nonprofit organizations that engage in the transactions that inure to the benefit of a disqualified person within the organization. These rules allow the IRS to impose penalties when it determines that top officials have received excessive compensation from their organizations. Intermediate sanctions may be imposed either in addition to or instead of revocation of the exempt state of the organization.

For more information, see www.irs.gov/pub/irs-tege/eotopice03.pdf.

1.22 The Labor-Management Relations Act (LMRA) (1947)

Also called the Taft-Hartley Act, this is the first national legislation that placed controls on unions. It prohibits unfair labor practices by unions and outlaws closed shops, where union membership is required to get and keep a job. Employers may not form closed-shop agreements with unions. It requires both parties to bargain in good faith and covers nonmanagement employees in private industry who are not covered by the Railway Labor Act.

For more information, see 29 U.S.C. Sec.141, www.law.cornell.edu/uscode/, and search for *Labor Management Relations Act, 1947*.

1.23 The Labor-Management Reporting and Disclosure Act (1959)

Also called the Landrum-Griffin Act, this law outlines procedures for redressing internal union problems, protects the rights of union members from corrupt or discriminatory labor unions, and applies to all labor organizations. Specific requirements include the following:

- Unions must conduct secret elections, the results of which can be reviewed by the U.S. Department of Labor.
- A Bill of Rights guarantees union members certain rights, including free speech.
- Convicted felons and members of the Communist Party cannot hold office in unions.
- Annual financial reporting from unions to the Department of Labor is required.
- All union officials have a fiduciary responsibility in managing union assets and conducting the business of the union.
- Union power to place subordinate organizations in trusteeship is limited.
- Minimum standards for union disciplinary action against its members is provided.

For more information, see www.dol.gov/compliance/laws/comp-lmrda.htm.

1.24 The Mine Safety and Health Act (1977)

Following a series of deadly mining disasters, the American people demanded that Congress take action to prevent similar events in the future. This law converted the existing Mine Enforcement Safety Administration (MESA) to the Mine Safety and Health Administration (MSHA). For the first time, it brought all coal, metal, and nonmetal mining operations under the same Department of Labor jurisdiction. Regulations and safety procedures for the coal mining industry were not altered, just carried into the new agency for oversight.

For more information, see www.dol.gov/compliance/laws/comp-fmsha.htm.

Provisions and Protections

This law requires the Secretaries of Labor and Health, Education, and Welfare to create regulations governing the country's mines. All mines are covered if they are involved in commerce, which any active mining operation would be. Regulations that implement this law specify that employees must be provided with certain protective equipment while working in a mine. These devices relate to respiration and fire prevention, among other protections. Protecting against "black lung disease" is a key concern, even today, in the coal mining industry.

Recordkeeping Requirements

Employers engaged in mining operations must inspect their worksites and document the results, reflecting hazards and actions taken to reduce or eliminate the hazards. Employees are to be given access to information related to accident prevention, fatal accident statistics for the year, and instructions on specific hazards they will face while working in the mine. Requirements detail the content of written emergency response plans, emergency mapping, and rescue procedures. Individual employee exposure records must be maintained. Each mine operator is required to conduct surveys of mine exposures and hazards, a plan to deal with those problems, and a record of the results. This information must be made available to MSHA inspectors if they request it.

MSHA Standards

This agency enforces mine safety standards that involve ventilation, chemical exposure, noise, forklifts and other mining equipment, mine shoring, and more. Material safety data sheets (MSDS) must be available to employees in mining as they are in other industries overseen by the OSHA agency.

MSHA Enforcement

MSHA has a team of federal inspectors who conduct onsite audits of mining operations. MSHA has the authority to cite mine operators for violations of its regulations, and citations can carry a $1,000 per day penalty in some circumstances.[2]

1.25 The National Industrial Recovery Act (1933)

This was an attempt to help the country move forward from the effects of the Great Depression. It proposed the creation of "Codes of Fair Competition" for each of several different industries. Essentially, every business would have to identify with and belong to a trade association. The association would then be required to create a Code of Fair Competition for the industry. Antitrust laws would be suspended in favor of the code. Of course, the code would have to be approved by the president of the United States, and the administration would issue federal licenses to every business in the country. If a business refused to participate in the code, its license could be suspended, and that would be the signal for that business to end all operations. There were financial penalties as well. This law didn't fare very well. It was declared unconstitutional by the United States Supreme Court in 1935 and was replaced by the National Labor Relations Act later that same year.

For more information, see www.ourdocuments.gov/doc.php?flash=true&doc=66.

1.26 The National Labor Relations Act (NLRA) (1935)

This is the "granddaddy" of all labor relations laws in the United States. It initially provided that employees have a right to form unions and negotiate wage and hour issues with employers on behalf of the union membership. Specifically, the NLRA grants employees the rights to organize, join unions, and engage in collective bargaining and other "concerted activities." It also protects against unfair labor practices by employers. It established the National Labor Relations Board (NLRB), which hears charges of violation and makes rulings as a court would.

Following on the heels of the National Industrial Recovery Act's failures, this law stepped into the void and addressed both union and employer obligations in labor relations issues. It established the NLRB, which would help define fair labor practices in the following decades. The NLRB has the power to accept and investigate complaints of unfair labor practices by either management or labor unions. It plays a judicial role within an administrative setting. This law is sometimes called the Wagner Act. Some key provisions include the following:

- The right of workers to organize into unions for collective bargaining
- The requirement of employers to bargain in good faith when employees have voted in favor of a union to represent them
- The requirement that unions represent all members equally.
- Covers nonmanagement employees in private industry who are not already covered by the Railway Labor Act

For more information, see www.nlrb.gov/national-labor-relations-act.

1.27 The Needlestick Safety and Prevention Act (2000)

This law modifies the Occupational Safety and Health Act by introducing a new group of requirements in the medical community. *Sharps,* as they are called, are needles, puncture devices, knives, scalpels, and other tools that can harm either the person using them or someone else. The law and its regulations provide rules related to handling these devices, disposing of them, and encouraging invention of new devices that will reduce or eliminate the risk associated with injury due to sharps. Sharps injuries are to be recorded on the OSHA 300 log with "privacy case" listed and not the employee's name. Blood-borne pathogens and transmission of human blood-borne illnesses such as AIDS/HIV and hepatitis are key targets of this law. Reducing the amount of injury and subsequent illness because of puncture, stab, or cut wounds is a primary objective. There are communication requirements, including employment poster content requirements.

For more information, see www.gpo.gov/fdsys/pkg/PLAW-106publ430/html/PLAW-106publ430.htm.

1.28 The Norris-LaGuardia Act (1932)

Remember that this was still three years before the NLRA came to pass. When unions tried to use strikes and boycotts, employers would trot into court and ask for an injunction to prevent such activity. More often than not, they were successful, and judges provided the injunctions. Congress had been pressured by organized labor to restore their primary tools that could force employers to bargain issues unions saw as important. Key provisions of this law include the following:

- It prohibited "yellow-dog" contracts. Those were agreements in which employees promised employers that they would not join unions. This new law declared such contracts to be unenforceable in any federal court.
- It prohibited federal courts from issuing injunctions of any kind against peaceful strikes, boycotts, or picketing when used by a union in connection with a labor dispute.
- It defined "labor dispute" to include any disagreement about working conditions.

For more information, see 29 U.S.C., Chapter 6, www.law.cornell.edu/uscode/text/29.

1.29 The Occupational Safety and Health Act (OSHA) (1970)

Signed into law by President Richard M. Nixon on December 29, 1970, the Occupational Safety and Health Act created an administrative agency within the U.S. Department of Labor called the Occupational Safety and Health Administration (OSHA). It also created the National Institute of Occupational Safety and Health (NIOSH), which resides inside the Centers for Disease Control (CDC).

Provisions and Protections

Regulations implementing this legislation have grown over time. They are complex and detailed. It is important that HR professionals understand the basics and how to obtain additional detailed information that applies to their particular employer circumstance. There are many standards that specify what employers must do to comply with their legal obligations. Overall, however, the law holds employers accountable for providing a safe and healthy working environment. The "General Duty Clause" in OSHA's regulations says employers shall furnish each employee with a place of employment free from recognized hazards that are likely to cause death or serious injury. It also holds employees responsible for abiding by all safety rules and regulations in the workplace. Some provisions require notices be posted in the workplace covering some of the OSHA requirements. Posters are available for download from the OSHA website without charge. The law applies to *all* employers regardless of the employee population size.

Recordkeeping Requirements

OSHA regulations require that records be kept for many purposes. It is necessary to conduct and document inspections of the workplace, looking for safety and health hazards. It is necessary to document and make available to employees records about hazardous materials and how they must be properly handled. Employers with 10 or more people on the payroll must summarize all injury and illness instances and post that summary in a conspicuous place within the workplace. That report must remain posted from February 1 to April 30 each year. Certain employers are exempt from some OSHA recordkeeping requirements. They generally are classified by industry Standard Industrial Classification (SIC) code. A list is available on OSHA's website at www.OSHA.gov. Any time there is a serious or fatal accident, a full incident report must be prepared by the employer and maintained in the safety file. These records must be maintained for a minimum of five years from the date of the incident. Known as a log of occupational injury or illness, it must include a record of each incident resulting in medical treatment (other than first aid), loss of consciousness, restriction of work or motion, or transfer or termination of employment. If you are in the medical industry, construction industry, or manufacturing industry, or you use nuclear materials of any kind, there are other requirements you must meet. Key to compliance with OSHA rules is communication with employees. Training is often provided by employers to meet this hazard communication requirement. In summary, then, OSHA recordkeeping involves the following:

- Periodic safety inspections of the workplace
- Injury or illness incident reports
- Annual summary of incidents during the previous calendar year

- Injury and illness prevention program (if required by rules governing your industry)
- Employee training on safety procedures and expectations
- Records of training participation
- Material safety data sheets for each chemical used in the workplace (made available to all employees in a well-marked file or binder that can be accessed at any time during work hours)

Occupational Safety and Health Act Enforcement

OSHA inspections may include the following:

- **Onsite visits that are conducted without advance notice**   Inspectors can just walk into a place of employment and request that you permit an inspection. You don't have to agree unless the inspector has a search warrant. In the absence of the warrant, you can delay the inspection until your attorney is present.
- **Onsite inspections or phone/fax investigations**   Depending on the urgency of the hazard and agreement of the person filing the complaint, inspectors may telephone or fax inquiries to employers. The employer has five working days to respond with a detailed description of inspection findings, corrective action taken, and additional action planned.
- **Highly trained compliance officers**   The OSHA Training Institute provides training for OSHA's compliance officers, state compliance officers, state consultants, other federal agency personnel, and the private sector.

Inspection priorities include the following:

- **Imminent danger**   Situations where death or serious injury are highly likely. Compliance officers will ask employers to correct the conditions immediately or remove employees from danger.
- **Fatalities and catastrophes**   Incidents that involve a death or the hospitalization of three or more employees. Employers must report these incidents to OSHA within eight hours.
- **Worker complaints**   Allegations of workplace hazards or OSHA violations. Employees may request anonymity when they file complaints with OSHA.
- **Referrals**   Other federal, state, or local agencies; individuals; organizations; or the media can make referrals to OSHA so the agency may consider making an inspection.
- **Follow-ups**   Checks for abatement of violations cited during previous inspections are also conducted by OSHA personnel in certain circumstances.
- **Planned or programmed investigations**   Inspections aimed at specific high-hazard industries or individual workplaces that have experienced high rates of injuries and illnesses. These are sometimes called *targeted investigations*.

Two Types of Standards

The law provides for two types of safety and health standards. The agency has therefore developed its regulations and standards in those two categories.

Normal Standards   If OSHA determines that a specific standard is needed, any of several advisory committees may be called upon to develop specific recommendations. There are two standing committees, and ad hoc committees may be appointed to examine special areas of concern to OSHA. All advisory committees, standing or ad hoc, must have members representing management, labor, and state agencies, as well as one or more designees of the Secretary of Health and Human Services (HHS). The occupational safety and health professions and the general public also may be represented.[3]

Emergency Temporary Standards   According to the OSH Act, "Under certain limited conditions, OSHA is authorized to set emergency temporary standards that take effect immediately. First, OSHA must determine that workers are in grave danger due to exposure to toxic substances or agents determined to be toxic or physically harmful or to new hazards and that an emergency standard is needed to protect them. Then, OSHA publishes the emergency temporary standard in the *Federal Register*, where it also serves as a proposed permanent standard. It is then subject to the usual procedure for adopting a permanent standard except that a final ruling must be made within six months. The validity of an emergency temporary standard may be challenged in an appropriate U.S. Court of Appeals."[4]

For more information, see www.dol.gov/compliance/guide/osha.htm.

1.30 The Omnibus Budget Reconciliation Act (OBRA) (1993)

Signed into law by President Bill Clinton on August 10, 1993, this legislation reduces compensation limits in qualified retirement programs and triggers increased activity in nonqualified retirement programs. It also calls for termination of some plans.

For more information, see www.gpo.gov/fdsys/pkg/BILLS-103hr2264enr/pdf/BILLS-103hr2264enr.pdf.

1.31 The Pension Protection Act (PPA) (2006)

Focused solely on pensions, this law requires employers that have underfunded pension plans to pay a higher premium to the Pension Benefit Guarantee Corporation (PBGC). It also requires employers that terminate pension plans to provide additional funding to those plans. This legislation impacted nearly all aspects of retirement planning, including changes to rules about individual retirement accounts (IRAs).

For more information, see www.dol.gov/ebsa/pensionreform.html.

1.32 The Personal Responsibility and Work Opportunity Reconciliation Act (1996)

This law requires all states to establish and maintain a new-hire reporting system designed to enhance enforcement of child support payments. It requires welfare recipients to begin working after two years of receiving benefits. States may exempt parents with children under age 1 from the work requirements. Parents with children under the age of 1 may use this exemption only once; they cannot use it again for subsequent children. These parents also are still subject to the five-year time limit for cash assistance. HR professionals will need to establish and maintain reporting systems to meet these tracking requirements.

For more information, see www.acf.hhs.gov/programs/css/resource/the-personal-responsibility-and-work-opportunity-reconcilliation-act.

1.33 The Portal-to-Portal Act (1947)

By amending the Fair Labor Standards Act (FLSA), this law defines "hours worked" and establishes rules about payment of wages to employees who travel before and/or after their scheduled work shift. The act provides that minimum wages and overtime are not required for "traveling to and from the actual place of performance of the principal activity or activities which such employee is to perform" or for "activities which are preliminary to or postliminary to said principal activity or activities," unless there is a custom or contract to the contrary.

For more information, see 29 U.S.C., Chapter 9, www.law.cornell.edu/uscode/text/29.

1.34 The Railway Labor Act (1926)

Originally, this law was created to allow railway employees to organize into labor unions. Over the years, it has been expanded in coverage to include airline employees. Covered employers are encouraged to use the Board of Mediation, which has since morphed into the National Mediation Board (NMB), a permanent independent agency.

1.35 The Rehabilitation Act (1973)

This replaced the Vocational Rehabilitation Act and created support for states to establish vocational rehabilitation programs. The term originally used in this legislation was *handicapped*. The law was later modified to replace that term with *disabled*.

Table 2-1 notes some of the most important sections of the Rehabilitation Act.

Section	Requirement
Section 501	Requires nondiscrimination and affirmative action in hiring disabled workers by federal agencies within the executive branch
Section 503	Requires nondiscrimination and affirmative action by federal contractors and subcontractors with contracts valued at $10,000 or more
Section 504	Requires employers subject to the law to provide reasonable accommodation for disabled individuals who can perform the major job duties with or without accommodation

Table 2-1   Key Employment Provisions of the Rehabilitation Act of 1973

1.36 The Retirement Equity Act (REA) (1984)

Signed into law by President Ronald Reagan on August 23, 1984, the REA provides certain legal protections for spousal beneficiaries of qualified retirement programs. It prohibits changes to retirement plan elections, spousal beneficiary designations, or in-service withdrawals without the consent of a spouse. Changing withdrawal options does not require spousal consent. It permits plan administrators to presume spousal survivors annuity and reduce primary pension amounts accordingly. Specific written waivers are required to avoid spousal annuity.

For more information, see www.law.cornell.edu/uscode/text/29/1055.

1.37 The Revenue Act (1978)

This law added two important sections to the Internal Revenue Tax Code relevant to employee benefits: Section 125, Cafeteria Benefit Plans, and Section 401(k), originally a pretax savings program for private-sector employees known as individual retirement accounts, subsequently expanded to a second plan opportunity known as "Roth IRA" that permitted funding with after-tax savings.

For more information, see www.irs.gov/pub/irs-utl/irpac-br_530_relief_-_appendix_natrm_paper_09032009.pdf.

1.38 The Sarbanes-Oxley Act (SOX) (2002)

In response to many corrupt practices in the financial industry and the economic disasters they created, Congress passed the Sarbanes-Oxley Act to address the need for oversight and disclosure of information by publicly traded companies.

Provisions and Protections

This law brought some strict oversight to corporate governance and financial reporting for publicly held companies. It holds corporate officers accountable for proper record-keeping and reporting of financial information, including internal control systems to assure those systems are working properly. There are also requirements for reporting any unexpected changes in financial condition, including potential new liabilities such as lawsuits. Those lawsuits can involve things such as employee complaints of illegal employment discrimination.

It requires administrators of defined contribution plans to provide notice of covered blackout periods and provides whistle-blower protection for employees.

This law protects anyone who reports wrongdoing to a supervisor, appointed company officials who handle these matters, a federal regulatory or law enforcement agency, or a member or committee of Congress. It even extends to claims that prove to be false as long as the employee reasonably believed the conduct is a violation of SEC rules or a federal law involving fraud against shareholders.

On March 4, 2014, the United States Supreme Court issued its opinion in the case of *Lawson v. FMR LLC.* (No. 12–3).[5] The 6-3 decision held that all contractors and subcontractors of publicly held companies are subject to the Sarbanes-Oxley Act, even if they are not publicly held. The takeaway from this ruling is that nearly everyone is now subject to the whistle-blower provisions of the Sarbanes-Oxley Act. As Justice Sotomayor suggested in her dissenting opinion:

> For example, public companies often hire "independent contractors," of whom there are more than 10 million, and contract workers, of whom there are more than 11 million. And, they employ outside lawyers, accountants, and auditors as well. While not every person who works for a public company in these nonemployee capacities may be positioned to threaten or harass employees of the public company, many are.

> Under [the majority opinion] a babysitter can bring a … retaliation suit against his employer if his employer is a checkout clerk for the local PetSmart (a public company) but not if she is a checkout clerk for the local Petco (a private company). Likewise the day laborer who works for a construction business can avail himself of [this ruling] if her company has been hired to remodel the local Dick's Sporting Goods store (a public company), but not if it is remodeling a nearby Sports Authority (a private company).

Recordkeeping Requirements

Internal control systems are required to assure that public disclosure of financial information is done as required. The registered accounting firm responsible for reviewing the company's financial reports must attest to the proper implementation of internal control systems and procedures for financial reporting.

SOX Enforcement

Enforcement of the law is done by private-firm audits overseen by the Public Company Accounting Oversight Board (PCAOB). The PCAOB is a nonprofit corporation created by the act to oversee accounting professionals who provide independent audit reports for publicly traded companies. It essentially audits the auditors.

Companies and corporate officers in violation of the act can find themselves subject to fines and/or up to 20 years imprisonment for altering, destroying, mutilating, concealing, or falsifying records, documents, or tangible objects with the intent to obstruct, impede, or influence a legal investigation.

For more information, see http://www.sec.gov/answers/pcaob.htm.

1.39 The Securities and Exchange Act (1934)

When companies "go public" by issuing common stock for trade, it is done on the "primary market." This law provides for governance in the "secondary market," which is all trading after the initial public offering. It also created the Securities and Exchange Commission (SEC), which has oversight authority for the trading of stocks in this country. It extends the "disclosure" doctrine of investor protection to securities listed and registered for public trading on any of the U.S. exchanges.

For more information, see www.law.cornell.edu/wex/securities_exchange_act_of_1934.

1.40 The Service Contract Act (SCA) (1965)

Applying to federal contractors (and subcontractors) offering goods and services to the government, this law calls for payment of prevailing wages and benefit requirements to all employees providing service under the agreement. All contractors and subcontractors, other than construction services, with contract value in excess of $2,500 are covered. Safety and health standards also apply to such contracts.

The compensation requirements of this law are enforced by the Wage and Hour Division in the U.S. Department of Labor (DOL). The SCA safety and health requirements are enforced by the Occupational Safety and Health Administration (OSHA), also an agency within DOL.

For more information, see 41 U.S.C. 351, www.dol.gov/oasam/regs/statutes/351.htm.

1.41 The Sherman Anti-Trust Act (1890)

If you allow yourself to travel back to the latter part of the nineteenth century, you will find that big business dominated the landscape. There was Standard Oil, Morgan Bank, U.S. Steel, and a handful of railroads. They were huge by comparison with other similar enterprises at the time. And people were concerned that they were monopolizing the marketplace and holding prices high just because they could. John Sherman, a Republican Senator from Ohio, was chairman of the Senate Finance Committee. He suggested that the country needed some protections against monopolies and cartels. Thus, the law was created and subsequently used by federal prosecutors to break up the Standard Oil Company into smaller units. Over the years, case law has been developed that concludes that attempting to restrict competition, or fix prices, can be seen as a violation of this law. Restraint of trade is also prohibited.

For more information, see 15 U.S.C. Secs. 1–7, www.law.cornell.edu/uscode/text/15/1.

1.42 The Small Business Job Protection Act (SBJPA) (1996)

This law increased federal minimum wage levels and provided some tax incentives to small business owners to protect jobs and increase take-home pay. It also amended the Portal-to-Portal Act for employees who use employer-owned vehicles. It created the SIMPLE 401(k) retirement plan to make pension plans easier for small businesses. Other tax incentives created by this law include the following:

- Employee education incentive—allowed small business owners to exclude up to $5,250 from an employee's taxable income for educational assistance provided by the employer
- Increased the maximum amount of capital expense allowed for a small business to $7,000 per year
- Replaced the Targeted Jobs Tax Credit with the Work Opportunity Tax Credit
- Provided a tax credit to individuals who adopted a child (up to $5,000 per child) and a tax credit of up to $6,000 for adoption of a child with special needs

For more information, see www.ssa.gov/legislation/legis_bulletin_082096.html.

1.43 The Social Security Act (1935)

The Social Security program began in 1935 in the heart of the Great Depression. It was initially designed to help senior citizens when that group was suffering a poverty rate of 50 percent. It currently includes social welfare and social insurance programs that can help support disabled workers who are no longer able to earn their wages.

The Social Security program is supported through payroll taxes with contributions from both the employee and the employer. Those payroll tax rates are set by the Federal Insurance Contributions Act (FICA) and have been adjusted many times over the years. There are many programs currently under the control of the Social Security Act and its amendments. These include the following:

- Federal old-age benefits (retirement)
- Survivors benefits (spouse benefits, dependent children, and widow/widower benefits)
- Disability insurance for workers no longer able to work
- Temporary Assistance for Needy Families
- Medicare Health Insurance for Aged and Disabled
- Medicaid Grants to States for Medical Assistance Programs
- Supplemental Security Income (SSI)
- State Children's Health Insurance Program (SCHIP)
- Patient Protection and Affordable Care Act

There is currently a separate payroll deduction for Medicare Health Insurance, which is also funded by both the employee and the employer. In addition, the Patient Protection and Affordable Care Act offers the opportunity to provide medical insurance coverage to a greater number of people.

A personal Social Security number is used as a tax identification number for federal income tax, including bank records, and to prove work authorization in this country. Social Security numbers can be used in completing Form I-9, which must be completed for every new employee on the payroll. Also required for Form I-9 is proof of identity.

For more information, see www.ssa.gov/history/35act.html.

1.44 The Tax Reform Act (1986)

This law made extensive changes to the Internal Revenue Service (IRS) tax code, including a reduction in tax brackets and all tax rates for individuals. Payroll withholdings were affected, many passive losses and tax shelters were eliminated, and changes were made to the alternative minimum tax computation. This is the law that required all dependent children to have Social Security numbers. That provision reduced the number of fraudulent dependent children claimed on income tax returns by seven million in its first year. For HR professionals, answers to employee questions about the number of exemptions to claim on their Form W-4 is greatly influenced by this requirement for dependent Social Security numbers.

For more information, see http://archive.org/stream/summaryofhr3838t1486unit/summaryofhr3838t1486unit_djvu.txt.

1.45 The Taxpayer Relief Act (1997)

Congress wanted to give taxpayers a couple of ways to lower their tax payments during retirement, so the Taxpayer Relief Act was passed to create new savings programs called Roth IRAs and Education IRAs. Many individuals were able to achieve a better tax position through these tools.

For more information, see www.gpo.gov/fdsys/pkg/BILLS-105hr2014enr/pdf/BILLS-105hr2014enr.pdf.

1.46 The Trademark Act (1946)

This is the legislation that created federal protections for trademarks and service marks. Officially it was called the Lanham (Trademark) Act, and it set forth the requirements for registering a trademark or service mark to obtain those legal protections. HR people may well have a role to play in training employees in how to properly handle organizational trademarks and the policies that govern those uses.

For more information, see www.uspto.gov/trademarks/law/tmlaw.pdf.

1.47 The Unemployment Compensation Amendments Act (UCA) (1992)

This law established 20 percent as the amount to be withheld from payment of employee savings accounts when leaving an employer and not placing the funds (rolling over) into another tax-approved IRA or 401(k).

For more information, see www.socialsecurity.gov/policy/docs/ssb/v56n1/v56n1p87.pdf.

1.48 The Uniformed Services Employment and Reemployment Rights Act (USERRA) (1994)

USERRA provides instructions for handling employees who are in the reserves and receive orders to report for active duty. The law protects the employment, reemployment, and retention rights of anyone who voluntarily or involuntarily serves or has served in the uniformed services. It requires that employers continue paying for the employee's benefits to the extent they paid for those benefits before the call-up. It also requires that employers continue giving credit for length of service as though the military service was equivalent to company service. There are specific detailed parameters for how long an employee has to engage the employer in return-to-work conversations after being released from active military duty.

This law and its provisions cover all eight U.S. military services and other uniformed services.

- Army
- Navy
- Air Force

- Marines
- Public Health Service Commissioned Corps
- National Oceanic and Atmospheric Administration Commissioned Corps
- Coast Guard
- National Guard groups that have been called into active duty

For more information, see www.dol.gov/compliance/laws/comp-userra.htm.

1.49 The Vietnam Era Veterans Readjustment Assistance Act (VEVRAA) (1974) [as Amended by the Jobs for Veterans Act (JVA) (2008)]

Current covered veterans include the following:

- Disabled veterans
- Veterans who served on active duty in the United States military during a war or campaign or expedition for which a campaign badge was awarded
- Veterans who, while serving on active duty in the Armed Forces, participated in a United States military operation for which an Armed Forces service medal was awarded pursuant to Executive Order 12985
- Recently separated veterans (veterans within 36 months from discharge or release from active duty)

These requirements apply to all federal contractors with a contract valued at $25,000 or more, regardless of the number of total employees.

This veteran support legislation requires all employers subject to the law to post their job openings with their local state employment service. There are three exceptions to that requirement:

- Jobs that will last three days or less
- Jobs that will be filled by an internal candidate
- Jobs that are senior executive positions

Affirmative action outreach and recruiting of veterans is required for federal contractors meeting the contract value threshold. For more information, see www.dol.gov/compliance/laws/comp-vevraa.htm.

1.50 The Wagner-Peyser Act (1933) [as Amended by the Workforce Investment Act of 1998]

The Wagner-Peyser Act created a nationwide system of employment offices known as Employment Service Offices. They were run by the U.S. Department of Labor's Employment and Training Administration (ETA). These offices provided job seekers with assistance in their job search, assistance in searching jobs for unemployment insurance recipients, and recruitment services for employers.

The Workforce Investment Act created the "One Stop" centers within Employment Service Offices. The federal government contracts with states to run the Employment Service Offices and One Stop centers. Funds are allocated to states based on a complicated formula.

For more information, see www.doleta.gov/programs/w-pact_amended98.cfm.

1.51 The Walsh-Healey Act (Public Contracts Act) (1936)

President Franklin Roosevelt signed this into law during the Great Depression. It was designed to assure the government paid a fair wage to manufacturers and suppliers of goods for federal government contracts in excess of $10,000 each. The provisions of the law included the following:

- Overtime pay requirements for work done over 8 hours in a day or 40 hours in a week
- A minimum wage equal to the prevailing wage
- Prohibition on employing anyone under 16 years of age or a current convict

The Defense Authorization Act (1968) later excluded federal contractors from overtime payments in excess of 8 hours in a day.

For more information, see www.dol.gov/compliance/laws/comp-pca.htm.

1.52 The Work Opportunity Tax Credit (WOTC) (1996)

This law provides federal income tax credits to employers that hire from certain targeted groups of job seekers who face employment barriers. The amount of tax credit is adjusted from time to time and currently stands at $9,600 per employee.

Targeted groups include the following:

- Qualified recipients of Temporary Assistance to Needy Families (TANF).
- Qualified veterans receiving Supplemental Nutrition Assistance Program (SNAP) or qualified veterans with a service-connected disability who have one of the following:
  - A hiring date that is not more than one year after having been discharged or released from active duty
  - Aggregate periods of unemployment during the one-year period ending on the hiring date that equals or exceeds six months
- WOTC also includes family members of a veteran who received SNAP for at least a three-month period during the fifteen-month period ending on the hiring date or a disabled veteran entitled to compensation for a service-related disability hired within one year of discharge or unemployed for a period totaling at least six months of the year ending on the hiring date.
- Ex-felons hired no later than one year after conviction or release from prison.

- Designated Community Resident—an individual who is between the ages of 18 and 40 on the hiring date and who resides in an empowerment zone, renewal community, or rural renewal county.

- Vocational rehabilitation referrals, including ticket holders with an individual work plan developed and implemented by an employment network.

- Qualified summer youth ages 16 through 17 who reside in an empowerment zone, renewal community, or rural renewal county.

- Qualified SNAP recipients between the ages of 18 and 40 on the hiring date.

- Qualified recipients of Supplemental Security Income (SSI).

- Long-term family assistance recipients.

These categories change from time to time as well.

In addition to these specific federal laws, there are laws dealing with payroll that HR professionals need to understand. While it is true that accounting people normally handle the payroll function in an employer's organization, occasionally HR professionals get involved and have to work with accounting people to explain deductions and provide input about open enrollment for healthcare benefit programs, among other things. Those things can include garnishments, wage liens, savings programs, benefit premium contributions, and income tax, FICA, and Medicare withholdings.

For more information, see www.gao.gov/new.items/d01329.pdf.

1.53 Whistle-Blowing

Finally, it is important to highlight the issue of whistle-blowing. We do not have a separate section for whistle-blowing because protections against retaliation are embedded in various laws we cover in this chapter. Laws with those provisions and protections include the Civil Rights Acts, OSHA, MSHA, the Sarbanes-Oxley Act, ADA, and more.

Whistle-blower laws usually apply to public-sector employees and employees of organizations contracting with the federal government or state governments. They are designed to protect individuals who publicly disclose information about corrupt practices or illegal activities within their employer's organization. Often, such events occur when someone is mishandling money, contracts, or other assets. Construction projects not being built to specifications can result in whistle-blowing by governmental employees. Employees of financial services companies (banks, credit unions, stock brokerages, and investment firms) have been in the headlines during recent years. They uncovered and disclosed misbehavior among people in their companies and were protected under whistle-blower provisions of various laws. Whistle-blowers are protected from disciplinary action, termination, or other penalty.

For more information, see www.dol.gov/compliance/laws/comp-whistleblower.htm.

2. When You Have 15 or More Employees

Once employers have added 15 or more employees to their payroll, it becomes necessary to comply with an additional 10 major federal laws.

2.1 Americans with Disabilities Act (ADA) (1990)

Prior to this legislation, the only employees who were protected against employment discrimination were the ones working for the federal, state, or local government and federal government contractors. They were captured by the Rehabilitation Act. As a matter of fact, it was the Rehabilitation Act that was used as a model for developing the ADA. Five years after the Rehabilitation Act, the Developmental Disabilities Act of 1978 spoke specifically to people with developmental disabilities. It provided for federally funded state programs to assist people in that category of the population. The ADA had been first proposed in 1988, and it was backed by thousands of individuals around the country who had been fighting for rights of their family members, friends, and co-workers. They thought it was appropriate only for those people to have equal access to community services, jobs, training, and promotions. It was signed into law by President George H. W. Bush on July 26, 1990. It became fully effective for all employers with 15 or more workers on July 26, 1992.

Provisions and Protections

Title I—Employment—applies to employers with 15 or more workers on the payroll. Those employers may not discriminate against a physically or mentally disabled individual in recruitment, hiring, promotions, training, pay, social activities, and other privileges of employment. Qualified individuals with a disability are to be treated as other job applicants and employees are treated. If a job accommodation is required for a qualified individual to perform the assigned job, employers are required to provide that accommodation or recommend an alternative that would be equally effective. The interactive process between employers and employees should result in an accommodation or explanation about why making the accommodation would provide an undue hardship on the employer. Title I is enforced by the Equal Employment Opportunity Commission (EEOC). Part of the interactive discussion about accommodation requests involves the employer investigating other accommodations that may be equally effective yet lower in cost or other resource requirements. Employers are not obligated to accept the employee's request without alteration.

U.S. Supreme Court Interpretation of the ADA

There were several U.S. Supreme Court cases that interpreted the ADA very narrowly. They limited the number of people who could qualify as disabled under the court's interpretation of Congress's initial intent. Reacting to those cases, Congress enacted the ADA Amendments Act in September 2008. It became effective on January 1, 2009.

ADA Amendments Act of 2008

Following the U.S. Supreme Court decisions in *Sutton v. United Airlines,*[6] *Toyota Motor Manufacturing,* and *Kentucky, Inc. v. William,*[7] Congress felt that the Court had been too restrictive in its explanation of who is disabled. It was the intent of Congress to be broader in that definition. Consequently, Congress passed the ADA Amendments Act to capture a wider range of people in the disabled classification. A disability is now defined as "an impairment that substantially limits one or more major life activities, having a record of such an impairment, or being regarded as having such an impairment." Although the words remain the same as the original definition, the Amendments Act went further. It said, when determining whether someone is disabled, *there may be no consideration of mitigating circumstances.* In the past, we used to treat people who had a disability under control as not disabled. An employee with a prosthetic limb did everything a whole-bodied person could do. An employee with migraines that disappeared with medication wasn't considered disabled. Under the old law, epilepsy and diabetes were not considered disabilities if they were controlled with medication. Now, because the law prohibits a consideration of either medication or prosthesis, they are considered disabilities. You can see that a great many more people will be defined as disabled under these more recent changes. The only specifically excluded condition is the one involving eyeglasses and contact lenses. Congress specifically said having a corrected eye problem through the use of glasses is not considered a disability.

An individual can be officially disabled but quite able to do his or her job without an accommodation of any sort. Having more people defined as disabled doesn't necessarily mean there will be more people asking for job accommodations.

For more information, see www.eeoc.gov/laws/statutes/adaaa.cfm.

"Substantially Limits"

Employers are required to consider as disabled anyone with a condition that "substantially limits" but does not "significantly restrict" a major life activity. Even though the limitation might be reduced or eliminated with medication or other alleviation, the treatment may not be considered when determining the limitations. So people who use shoe inserts to correct a back problem or who take prescription sleeping pills may now be classified as disabled. The same might be said of people who are allergic to peanuts or bee stings. Yet there may be no need for any of them to request a job accommodation.

"Major Life Activities"

Caring for oneself, seeing, hearing, touching, eating, sleeping, walking, standing, sitting, reaching, lifting, bending, speaking, breathing, learning, reading, concentrating, thinking, communicating, interacting with others, and working...these all are considered "major life activities." Also included are major bodily functions such as normal cell growth, reproduction, immune system, blood circulation, and the like. Some conditions are specifically designated as disabilities by the EEOC. They include diabetes, cancer, human immunodeficiency virus and acquired immunodeficiency syndrome (HIV/AIDS), multiple sclerosis (MS), cerebral palsy (CP), and cystic fibrosis (CF) because they interfere with one or more of our major life activities.

"Essential Job Function"

An essential job function is defined as "A portion of a job assignment that cannot be removed from the job without significantly changing the nature of the job." An essential function is highly specialized, and the incumbent has been hired because he or she has special qualifications, skills, or abilities to perform that function, among others.

"Job Accommodation"

Someone with a disability doesn't necessarily need a job accommodation. Remember that we select people and place them in jobs if they are qualified for the performance of the essential functions, with or without a job accommodation. Someone with diabetes may have the disease under control with medication and proper diet. No accommodation would be required. However, if it were essential that the employee had food intake at certain times of the day, there could be a legitimate request for accommodation of that need. The employer might be asked to consistently permit the employee to have meal breaks at specific times each day.

Job accommodations are situationally dependent. First, there must be a disability and an ability to do the essential functions of the job. Next, there must be a request for accommodation from the employee. If there is no request for accommodation, no action is required by the employer. It is perfectly acceptable for an employer to request supporting documentation from medical experts identifying the disability. There might even be recommendations for specific accommodations, including those requested by the employee.

Once an accommodation is requested, the employer is obliged to enter into an inter-active discussion with the employee. For example, an employee might ask for something specific, perhaps a new piece of equipment (a special ergonomic chair) that will elimi-nate the impact of disability on their job performance. The employer must consider that specific request. Employers are obligated to search for alternatives that could satisfy the accommodation request only when the specific request cannot be reasonably accommo-dated. This is the point where the Job Accommodation Network (JAN)[8] can become a resource. They can usually provide help for even unusual situations.

Once specific alternatives have been explored, a specific accommodation should be determined. The employer must consider if making that accommodation would be an "undue hardship" considering all it would involve. You should note that most job accom-modations carry a very low cost. Often, they cost nothing. The larger an employer's pay-roll headcount, the more difficult it is to fully justify using "undue hardship" as a reason for not agreeing to provide an accommodation. Very large corporations or governments have vast resources, and the cost of one job accommodation, even if it does cost some large dollar amount, won't likely cause an undue hardship on that employer.

Recordkeeping Requirements

There is nothing in the Americans with Disabilities Act of 1990, or its amendments, that requires employers to create job descriptions. However, smart employers are doing that in order to identify physical and mental requirements of each job. Job descriptions also make it easy to identify essential job functions that any qualified individual would have to perform, with or without job accommodation. It is easier to administer job accom-modation request procedures and to defend against false claims of discrimination when an employer has job descriptions that clearly list all of the job's requirements. It also makes screening job applicants easier because it shows them in writing what the job will entail; then an employer's recruiters may ask, "Is there anything in this list of essential job functions that you can't do with or without a job accommodation?"

If a job requires an incumbent to drive a delivery truck, driving would be an essential function of that job. A disability that prevented the incumbent from driving the delivery truck would likely block that employee from working—unless an accommodation could be found that would permit the incumbent to drive in spite of the disability.

People are sometimes confused about temporary suspension of duty being a permanent job accommodation. If that temporary suspension means the incumbent no longer is responsible for performing an essential job function, the job could not be performed as it was designed by the employer. It is not necessary for an employer to redesign job content to make a job accommodation. It is possible for such voluntary efforts to be made on behalf of an employee the organization wants to retain. Those situations are not job accommodations, however. They are job reassignments.

EEOC procedures prohibit employers from inviting job applicants to identify their disability status prior to receiving a job offer.

Annual review of job description content is required under the EEOC guidelines. It is important to maintain accurate listings of essential job functions and physical and mental job requirements. Annual review will help assure that you always have current information in your job descriptions.

ADA Enforcement

The EEOC enforces Title I of the ADA. The agency will accept complaints of illegal discrimination based on mental or physical disability. Once an employee has established that they are disabled and claim that they have been prohibited some employment benefit because of their disability (hiring, promotion, access to training, or inappropriate termination), there is a *prima facie* case (meaning it is true on its surface). Then the agency notifies the employer of the complaint and asks for the employer's response. This process can work back and forth from employer response to employee response for several cycles. Ultimately, the agency will determine that the case has cause (has a valid claim of discrimination), it has no cause (the claim could not be substantiated), or the case was closed for administrative purposes (the employee asked for the case to be closed). Each of those three outcomes is followed by a "right to sue" letter, allowing the employee to get an attorney and file a lawsuit in federal court seeking remedies under the law.[9]

Once a complaint (called a *charge of illegal discrimination*) is filed with the EEOC, employers are instructed to cease talking about the issue directly with their employee. All conversation about the complaint must be directed through the EEOC. Unfortunately, that complicates the communication process and provides a strong incentive for employers to resolve complaints internally before they reach the formal external complaint stage. Working directly with an employee on the subject of accommodation, or any other personnel issue, is preferable to working through an agency such as the EEOC.

For more information, see www.ada.gov/.

2.2 The Civil Rights Act (Title VII) (1964)

Although this was not the first federal civil rights act in the country,[10] it came to us through a great deal of controversy. It was signed into law by President Lyndon Johnson on July 2, 1964. Following the assassination of President John F. Kennedy the previous November, President Johnson took it upon himself to carry the civil rights banner and urge Congress to pass the law.

For more information, see www.eeoc.gov/laws/statutes/titlevii.cfm.

Employment Protections

Title VII of the act speaks to employment discrimination and cites five protected classes of people. Before the final days when Congress was discussing the issues, there were only four protected classes listed: race, color, religion, and national origin. There was a great deal of opposition in the Senate from Southern states. They decided that they would strategically add another protected category to the list. They thought that if "sex" was added to the list, the bill would surely fail because no one would vote for having women protected in the workplace. Well, it passed…with all five protected categories in place. From that time forward, when making employment decisions, it has been illegal to take into account any employee's membership in any of the protected classifications.

Penalties for Violations

Penalties can be assessed by a federal court. Protocol requires a complaint be filed with the Equal Employment Opportunity Commission (EEOC), the administrative agency tasked with the duty to investigate claims of illegal employment discrimination. Regardless of the outcome of that administrative review, a "right to sue" letter is given to the complaining employee so the case can move forward to federal court if that is what the employee wants to do next.

Penalties that can be assessed if an employer is found to have illegally discriminated against an employee include the following:

- **Actual damages** Costs for medical bills, travel to medical appointments, equipment loss reimbursement, lost wages (back pay), lost promotional increase, and lost future earnings (front pay). The limitation is usually two years into the past and an unlimited number of years into the future.

- **Compensatory damages** Dollars to reimburse the victim for "pain and suffering" caused by this illegal discrimination.

- **Punitive damages** Dollars assessed by the court to "punish" the employer for treatment of the employee that was egregious in its nature. This is usually thought of as "making an example" of one case so as to send a message to other employers that doing such things to an employee or job applicant will be severely punished.

2.3 The Civil Rights Act (1991)

This act modified the 1964 Civil Rights Act in several ways:

- It provided for employees to receive a jury trial if they wanted. Up to this point, judges always heard cases and decided them from the bench.

- It established requirements for any employer defense.

- It placed a limitation on punitive damage awards by using a sliding scale depending on the size of the employer organization (payroll headcount).

- For employers with 15 to 100 employees, damages are capped at $50,000.

- For employers with 100 to 200 employees, damages are capped at $100,000.

- For employers with 201 to 500 employees, damages are capped at $200,000.
- For employers with more than 500 employees, damages are capped at $300,000.

For more information, see www.eeoc.gov/eeoc/history/35th/1990s/civilrights.html.

2.4 The Drug-Free Workplace Act (1988)

This legislation requires some employers to maintain a drug-free workplace. Employee compliance must be assured by subject employers.

Provisions and Protections

This law applies to federal contractors and all organizations receiving grants from the federal government. If you are covered, you are required to assure that all the employees working on the contract or grant are in compliance with its drug-free requirements. Covered employers are required to have a drug-free policy that applies to its employees. To determine that an employer is in compliance with the requirements, drug testing is usually performed on employees and applicants who have received a job offer. Random drug testing is also used in some organizations to assure employees subject to the law or policy are continuing to comply with the requirements. Any federal contractor under the jurisdiction of the Office of Federal Contract Compliance Programs (OFCCP) in the Department of Labor must comply with this legislation.

Employee notification about the policy must include information about the consequences of failing a drug test. Whenever an employee has been convicted of a criminal drug violation in the workplace, the employer must notify the contracting or granting agency within 10 days.

Recordkeeping Requirements

Covered employers are required to publish a written policy statement that clearly covers all employees or just those employees who are associated with the federal contract or grant, depending on the circumstances. Each covered employee must be given a copy of the policy statement, and it is a good idea, although it is not required, to have employees sign for receipt of that policy statement. The statement must contain a list of prohibited substances. At a minimum, it must cite controlled substances.[11]

Some employers choose to include in the policy prohibition of alcohol and prescription drug misuse, although that is not a requirement. Subject employers must also establish a drug-free awareness training program to make employees aware of (a) the dangers of drug abuse in the workplace; (b) the policy of maintaining a drug-free workplace; (c) any available drug counseling, rehabilitation, and employee assistance programs; and (d) the penalties that may be imposed on employees for drug abuse violations. Records should be maintained showing each employee who received the training and the date it occurred.

Drug-Free Workplace Act Enforcement

Federal contractors under the jurisdiction of the OFCCP will find that the agency requires proof of compliance when it conducts a general compliance evaluation of affirmative action plans. Any employee who fails a drug test must be referred to a treatment program or given appropriate disciplinary action. Care should be given to treating similar cases in the same way. It is fairly easy to be challenged under Title VII for unequal treatment based on one of the Title VII protected groups.

Each federal agency responsible for contracting or providing grants is also responsible for enforcing the Drug-Free Workplace Act requirements. These responsibilities are spelled out in the Federal Acquisition Regulation (FAR). Failing to maintain a drug-free workplace can result in the following:[12]

- Suspension of payments for contract or grant activities
- Suspension or cancellation of grant or contract
- Up to five years' prohibition for any further contracts or grants

For more information, see www.dol.gov/elaws/asp/drugfree/require.htm.

2.5 The Equal Employment Opportunity Act (EEOA) (1972)

Amended the Civil Rights Act of 1964 by redefining some terms. It also required a new employment poster for all subject work locations explaining that "EEO is the law."
For more information, see www.eeoc.gov/eeoc/history/35th/thelaw/eeo_1972.html.

2.6 The Genetic Information Nondiscrimination Act (GINA) (2008)

In general terms, GINA prohibits employers from using genetic information to make employment decisions. This legislation was brought about by insurance companies using genetic information to determine who would likely have expensive diseases in the future. That information allowed decisions to exclude them from hiring or enrollment in medical insurance programs. With the implementation of this law, those considerations are no longer legal.
For more information, see www.eeoc.gov/laws/statutes/gina.cfm.

2.7 Guidelines on Discrimination Because of Sex (1980)

The Equal Employment Opportunity Commission (EEOC) published these guidelines to help employers understand what constituted unwanted behavior and harassment. They were issued long before the U.S. Supreme Court considered the leading cases on sexual harassment. This is about the only thing at the time that employers were able to turn to for help in managing the problem of sexual harassment in the workplace.
For more information, see www.ecfr.gov/cgi-bin/text-idx?SID=948f17132a22640b25 9f8e238d0dd410&node=29:4.1.4.1.5.0.21.11&rgn=div8.

2.8 The Lilly Ledbetter Fair Pay Act (2009)

This was the first piece of legislation signed by President Barack Obama after he was inaugurated as the 44th president of the United States. It was passed by Congress in reaction to the U.S. Supreme Court decision in *Ledbetter v. Goodyear Tire & Rubber Co., Inc.*, 550 U.S. 618 (2007).

This law amends the Civil Rights Act of 1964 and states that the clock will begin running anew each time an illegal act of discrimination is experienced by an employee. In Lilly Ledbetter's situation, her pay was less than that for men doing the same job. The old law didn't permit her to succeed in her complaint of discrimination because she failed to file 20 years earlier on the first occasion of her receiving a paycheck for less than her male counterparts. Under the new law, the 180-day statute of limitations for filing an equal-pay lawsuit regarding pay discrimination resets with each new paycheck affected by that discriminatory action.

For more information, see www.eeoc.gov/laws/statutes/epa_ledbetter.cfm.

2.9 The Pregnancy Discrimination Act (1978)

This law modified (amended) the Civil Rights Act of 1964. It defined pregnancy as protected within the definition of "sex" for the purpose of coverage under the Civil Rights Act. It also specifically said that no employer shall illegally discriminate against an employee because of pregnancy. It defines pregnancy as a temporary disability and requires accommodation on the job if it is necessary. It guarantees the employee rights to return to work to the same or similar job with the same pay following her pregnancy disability.

For more information, see www.eeoc.gov/laws/types/pregnancy.cfm.

2.10 Uniform Guidelines on Employee Selection Procedures (1976)

This set of regulations is often overlooked by employers and HR professionals alike. Details can be found in 41 C.F.R. 60-3. For covered employers with 15 or more people on the payroll, this set of requirements is essential in preventing claims of discrimination.

There are two types of illegal employment discrimination: adverse treatment and adverse or disparate impact. The latter almost always results from seemingly neutral policies having a statistically adverse impact on a specific group of people. To avoid illegal discrimination, the guidelines require that all steps in a hiring decision be validated for application to the job being filled. Validity of a selection device can be determined through a validity study or by applying a job analysis to demonstrate the specific relationship between the selection device and the job requirements. Selection devices include things like a written test, an oral test, an interview, a requirement to write something for consideration, and a physical ability test.

Employers can get into trouble when they use selection tools that have not been validated for their specific applications. For example, buying a clerical test battery of written tests and using it to make selection decisions for administrative assistants as well as general office clerks may not be supportable. Only a validity analysis will tell for sure. What specific validation studies have been done for the test battery by the publisher? Any publisher should be able to provide you with a copy of the validation study showing how the test is supposed to be used and the specific skills, knowledge, or abilities that are analyzed when using it. If you can't prove the test measures things required by your job content, don't use the test. According to the Uniform Guidelines, "While publishers of selection procedures have a professional obligation to provide evidence of validity which meets generally accepted professional standards, users are cautioned that they are responsible for compliance with these guidelines."[13] That means the employer, not the test publisher, is liable for the results.

For more information, see www.eeoc.gov/policy/docs/factemployment_procedures .html.

3. When You Have 20 or More Employees

The next threshold for employers occurs when they reach a headcount of 20 employees. At that point, another four major federal laws have influence on the organization.

3.1 The Age Discrimination in Employment Act (ADEA) (1967)

When this law was first passed, it specified the protected age range of 40 to 70. Anyone under 40 or over 70 was not covered for age discrimination in the workplace. Amendments were made a few years later that removed the upper limit. Today, the law bans employment discrimination based on age if the employee is 40 or older. Remedies under this law are the same as under the Civil Rights Act. They include reinstatement, back pay, front pay, and payment for benefits in arrears. Some exceptions to the "unlimited" upper age exist. One example is the rule that airline pilots may not fly commercial airplanes after the age of 65.[14]

For more information, see www.eeoc.gov/laws/statutes/adea.cfm.

3.2 The American Recovery and Reinvestment Act (ARRA) (2009)

The thrust of this legislation was to create government infrastructure projects such as highways, buildings, dams, and such. It was an attempt to find ways to re-employ many of the workers who had become unemployed since the Great Recession began in 2007. There was a provision that provided partial payment of COBRA premiums for people who still had not found permanent job placement. It applied to individuals who experienced involuntary terminations prior to May 31, 2010.

ARRA also modified HIPAA privacy rules. It applies HIPAA's security and privacy requirements to business associates. Business associates are defined under ARRA as individuals or organizations that transmit protected medical data, store that data, process that data, or in any other way have contact with that private medical information. All parties are responsible for proper handling and compliance with the HIPAA rules.

For more information, see www.irs.gov/uac/The-American-Recovery-and-Reinvestment-Act-of-2009:-Information-Center.

3.3 The Consolidated Omnibus Budget Reconciliation Act (COBRA) (1986)

This law requires employers with group health insurance programs to offer terminating employees the opportunity to continue their health plan coverage after they are no longer on the payroll or no longer qualify for benefits coverage because of a change in employment status, i.e., reduction in hours. The cost must be at group rates, and the employer can add a small administrative service charge. It turns out that many employers turn these programs over to vendors that administer the COBRA benefits for former employees. They send out billing statements and provide collection services. Two percent is the maximum administrative overhead fee that can be added. The total cost of COBRA premiums and administrative fees is paid by employees participating in COBRA. The duration of coverage is dependent on some variables, so it may be different from one person to another.

For more information, see www.dol.gov/dol/topic/health-plans/cobra.htm.

3.4 The Older Workers Benefit Protection Act (OWBPA) (1990)

In the 1980s, it was common for employers, particularly large employers, to implement staff reduction programs as a means of addressing expenses. Often those programs were targeted at more senior workers because, generally speaking, their compensation was greater than that of new employees. Reducing one senior worker could save more money than the reduction of a more recently hired worker. Congress took action to prevent such treatment based on age when it passed this law.

The key purposes of the Older Workers Benefit Protection Act (OWBPA) are to prohibit an employer from

- Using an employee's age as the basis for discrimination in benefits
- Targeting older workers during staff reductions or downsizing
- Requiring older workers to waive their rights without the opportunity for review with their legal advisor

For more information, see www.eeoc.gov/eeoc/history/35th/thelaw/owbpa.html.

4. When You Have 50 to 100 Employees

Once the employee head count reaches these higher levels, additional legal obligations become effective for employers. Some of them apply only if the employer is subject to affirmation action requirements as a federal contractor.

4.1 Executive Order 11246—Affirmative Action (1965)

This is the presidential order that created what we now know as employment-based affirmative action. In 1965, President Johnson was past the days when he approved the Civil Rights Act, and he was in the process of examining how it was being implemented around the country by employers. He concluded that the law was pretty much being ignored. He needed something to stimulate implementation of the employment provisions in the Civil Rights Act, Title VII. His staff suggested they require affirmative action programs from federal contractors. A new program was born. President Johnson said that if a company wanted to receive revenue by contracting with the federal government, it would have to implement equal employment opportunity and establish outreach programs for minorities and women. At the time, minorities and women were being excluded from candidate selection pools. If they couldn't get into the selection pools, there was no way for them to be selected.

So, affirmative action programs were created. Outreach and recruiting was the name of the game in these programs. Analysis of the incumbent workforce, the available pool of qualified job candidates, and the training of managers involved in the employment selection process all contributed to a slow movement toward full equality for minorities and women.

The Office of Federal Contract Compliance Programs (OFCCP) is the civil rights enforcement agency that currently has responsibility for enforcing the Executive Order along with other laws. Federal contractors must meet several conditions in return for the contracting privilege. One is the requirement to abide by a set of rules known as the Federal Acquisition Regulations (FAR). And then there is affirmative action for the disabled and veterans. Any business that doesn't want to abide by these requirements can make the business decision to abandon federal revenues and contracts. If you want the contracts, you also have to agree to the affirmative action requirements.[15]

For more information, see www.dol.gov/ofccp/regs/statutes/eo11246.htm.

4.2 The Family and Medical Leave Act (FMLA) (1993)

In general, the Family and Medical Leave Act (FMLA) sets in place new benefits for some employees in the country. If their employer has 50 or more people on the payroll, then they are required to permit FMLA leave of absence for their workers. FMLA provides for leaves lasting up to 12 weeks in a 12-month period, and it is unpaid unless the employer has a policy to pay for the leave time. The 12-month period begins on the first day of leave. A new leave availability will occur 12 months from the date the first leave began. During the leave, it is an obligation of the employer to continue paying any benefit plan premiums that the employer would have paid if the employee had remained on the job. If there is a portion of the premium for health insurance that is normally paid by the employee, that obligation for co-payment continues during the employee's leave time. The 12 weeks of leave may be taken in increments of one day or less.

To qualify, employees must have more than one year of service and must have worked at least 1,250 hours for the employer in the past year. The leave is authorized to cover childbirth or adoption; to care for a seriously ill child, spouse, or parent; or in case of the employee's own serious illness. The employee is guaranteed return to work on the same job, at the same pay, under the same conditions as prior to the leave of absence.

There are provisions for "Military Caregiver Leave" lasting up to 26 weeks of unpaid leave of absence for employees with family members needing care due to a military duty–related injury or illness. The 26-week limit renews every 12 months. The law provides for "National Guard and Military Reserve Family Leave." Employees who are family members of National Guard or Military Reservists who are called to active duty may take FMLA leave to assist with preparing financial and legal arrangements and other family issues associated with rapid deployment or post-deployment activities. An employer may agree to any nonlisted condition as a qualifier for FMLA leave as well.

FMLA provides for "Light Duty Assignments." It clarifies that "light duty" work does not count against an employee's FMLA leave entitlement. It also provides that an employee's right to job restoration is held in abeyance during the light duty period. An employee voluntarily doing light duty work is not on FMLA leave.

There is an employment poster requirement. The notice must be posted at each work location where employees can see it without trouble. A "Medical Certification Process" is part of the new provisions. DOL regulations specify who may contact the employee's medical advisor for information, written or otherwise, and specifically prohibit the employee's supervisor from making contact with the employee's medical advisor.

Specific prohibitions apply against illegal discrimination for an employee taking advantage of the benefits offered under this law. These provisions are enforced by the EEOC.

For more information, see www.dol.gov/whd/fmla/.

4.3 The Mental Health Parity Act (MHPA) (1996)

This legislation requires health insurance issuers and group health plans to adopt the same annual and lifetime dollar limits for mental health benefits as for other medical benefits.

For more information, see www.dol.gov/ebsa/mentalhealthparity/.

4.4 The Mental Health Parity and Addiction Equity Act (MHPAEA) (2008)

This is an amendment of the Mental Health Parity Act of 1996. It requires that plans that offer both medical/surgical benefits and mental health and/or substance abuse treatment benefits provide parity between both types of benefits. All financial requirements (for example, deductibles, co-payments, co-insurance, out-of-pocket expenses, and annual limits) and treatment requirements (for example, frequency of treatment, number of visits, days of coverage) must be the same for treatment of both mental and physical medical problems.

For more information, see www.dol.gov/ebsa/newsroom/fsmhpaea.html.

4.5 The National Defense Authorization Act (2008)

This is the origin of benefit provisions under FMLA for leaves of absence because of military reasons. Qualifying events include notice of deployment, return from deployment, and treatment for an injury sustained while on deployment. The provision is for up to 26 weeks, which can be taken in increments of a day or less if, for example, treatment is required for a service-related injury.

For more information, see www.dol.gov/whd/fmla/NDAA_fmla.htm.

4.6 The Patient Protection and Affordable Care Act (PPACA) (2010)

Signed into law by President Barack Obama on March 23, 2010, this law is commonly referred to as the Affordable Care Act. It has created health insurance trading centers in each state where employees and those who are unemployed can shop for health insurance coverage. These trading centers are the American Health Benefit Exchanges and Small Business Health Options Program (SHOP). Individuals and business owners of organizations with fewer than 100 workers can purchase insurance through these exchanges.

It applies to all employers with 50 or more full-time workers on the payroll. Employers with fewer than 50 full-time workers are exempt from coverage under the law. Effective January 1, 2014, covered employers must either provide minimum health insurance coverage to their full-time employees or face a fine of $2,000 per employee, excluding the first 30 from the assessment. Employers with fewer than 25 employees will receive a tax credit if they provide health insurance to their workers. In 2018, changes in the Affordable Care Act included elimination of the financial penalties for individuals who do not sign up for health insurance. Consequently, the number of people who are uninsured has increased (see https://blog.medicarerights.org/millions-lose-coverage-affordable-care-act-changes-take-effect/). Cost of coverage has been increasing steadily through all of the insurance companies. Congress, however, has failed to pass new legislation that would either replace or repeal the Act.

For more information, see www.dol.gov/ebsa/healthreform/.

5. When You Have 100 or More Employees

The final major threshold for employers is reached when the payroll reaches 100 employees. At that time employers become subject to the WARN Act and are required to submit annual reports to the federal government summarizing their race and sex demographics.

5.1 The Worker Adjustment and Retraining Notification Act (WARN) (1988)

This was the first attempt by Congress to involve local communities early in the private sector's downsizing process. It also prevented employers from just shutting the door and walking away without any worker benefits. It applies to all employers with 100 or more full-time workers at a single facility. The law specifies a qualifying employer to be one that has 100 or more employees who in the aggregate work at least 4,000 hours per week (exclusive of hours of overtime).

Definitions

The term *plant closing* refers to the permanent or temporary shutdown of a single site of employment, or one or more facilities or operating units within a single site of employment, if the shutdown results in an employment loss at the single site of employment during any 30-day period for 50 or more employees, excluding part-time employees.

The term *mass layoff* refers to a reduction in force that is not the result of a plant closing and results in an employment loss at the single site of employment during any 30-day period for (1) at least 500 full-time employees or (2) 33 percent of the total number of full-time employees for employers with 50 to 499 employees.

Required Actions

The law requires 60 days' advance notice to employees of plant closing or mass layoffs. Any employment loss of 50 or more people, excluding part-time workers, is considered a trigger event to activate the requirements. Notification of public officials in the surrounding community in addition to notification of employees is a requirement. The local community leaders must be informed and invited to participate in the process of finding new jobs for laid-off workers. There is a provision that says an employer can be required to pay 60 days' separation allowance if it gives no notice to workers who will be terminated.

Exemptions to Notice Requirement

Notice is not required, regardless of the size of layoff, if the layoff, downsizing, or terminations result from the completion of a contract or project that employees understood would constitute their term of employment. It is not uncommon for workers to be hired in a "term" classification that designates them as employees for the life of a project. When employees are hired with a specified termination date, it will not trigger the WARN Act provisions.

WARN is not triggered in these cases:

- In the event of strikes or lockouts that are not intended to evade the requirements of this law.

- In the event the layoff will be for less than six months.

- If state and local governments are downsizing, they are exempt from the notice requirement.

- In the event that fewer than 50 people will be laid off or terminated from a single site.

- If 50 to 499 workers lose their jobs and that number is less than 33 percent of the active workforce at the single site.

For more information, see www.dol.gov/compliance/laws/comp-warn.htm.

6. For Federal Government Employees

The federal government is subject to some of the same laws as the private-sector employers. Yet there are additional obligations that government employers have. Some of those obligations stem from the U.S. Constitution. Others come from the following laws.

6.1 The Civil Service Reform Act (1978)

This legislation eliminated the U.S. Civil Service Commission and created three new agencies to take its place.

- **The Office of Personnel Management (OPM)**   This is the executive branch's human resources department. It handles all HR issues for agencies reporting to the president.

- **The Merit Systems Protection Board (MSPB)**   This part of the law prohibits consideration of marital status, political activity, or political affiliation in dealing with federal civilian employees. It also created the Office of Special Counsel, which accepts employee complaints and investigates and resolves them.

- **The Federal Labor Relations Authority (FLRA)**   This is the agency that enforces federal civilian employee rights to form unions and bargain with their agencies. It establishes standards of behavior for union officers; these standards are enforced by the Office of Labor-Management Standards in the U.S. Department of Labor.

For more information, see www.eeoc.gov/eeoc/history/35th/thelaw/civil_service_reform-1978.html.

6.2 The Congressional Accountability Act (1995)

Until this law was implemented, the legislative branch of the government was exempt from nearly all employment-related requirements that applied to other federal agencies and private employers. This law requires Congress and its affiliated agencies to abide by 12 specific laws that are already applied to other employers, in and out of government.

- Americans with Disabilities Act of 1990
- Age Discrimination in Employment Act of 1967
- Employee Polygraph Protection Act of 1988
- Federal Service Labor-Management Relations Statute
- Rehabilitation Act of 1973
- Civil Rights Act of 1964 (Title VII)
- Fair Labor Standards Act of 1938
- Family and Medical Leave Act of 1993
- Occupational Safety and Health Act of 1970
- Veterans Employment Opportunities Act of 1998
- Worker Adjustment and Retraining Notification Act of 1989
- Occupational Safety and Health Act of 1970

For more information, see www.compliance.gov/publications/caa-overview/.

6.3 The False Claims Act (1863)

During the Civil War, people were selling defective food and arms to the Union military. This law, sometimes referred to as the Lincoln law, prohibits such dishonest transactions. It prohibits making and using false records to get those claims paid. It also prohibits selling the government goods that are known to be defective. For HR professionals today, it is wise to train all employees about the need to avoid creating records that are inaccurate or, even worse, fictitious. Doing things that are illegal just because the boss says you should will still be illegal. Employees need to understand that concept.

For more information, see www.justice.gov/civil/docs_forms/C-FRAUDS_FCA_Primer.pdf.

6.4 The Homeland Security Act (2002)

This Cabinet-level organization (Department of Homeland Security) was created by Congress and President George W. Bush to consolidate security efforts related to protecting U.S. geography. Immigration and Customs Enforcement (ICE) is a part of this department. The E-Verify system resides here. Used by federal contractors as part of their affirmative action obligations and other private employers on a voluntary basis, the system is intended to assist in the rapid verification of Social Security numbers (SSNs) and confirm that the individual attached to the SSN has a valid right to work in this country.

For more information, see www.dhs.gov/homeland-security-act-2002.

6.5 The Privacy Act (1974)

This law provides that governmental agencies must make known to the public their data collection and storage activities and must provide copies of pertinent records to individual citizens when requested, with some exemptions. These exemptions include law enforcement, congressional investigations, census use for "archival purposes," and other administrative purposes. In all, there are 12 statutory exemptions from disclosure requirements. If employees are concerned about employers using their Social Security numbers in records sent to the government, this act ensures privacy. Although such private information is required by the government, it is prohibited from releasing it to third parties without proper authorization or court order.

For more information, see www.justice.gov/opcl/privacy-act-1974.

6.6 The USA Patriot Act (2001)

The Patriot Act was passed immediately following the September 11, 2001, terrorist attacks in New York City and at the Pentagon in Virginia. It gives the government authority to intercept wire, oral, and electronic communications relating to terrorism, computer fraud, and abuse offenses. It also provides the authorization for collecting agencies to share the information they collect in the interest of law enforcement. This law can have an impact on private-sector employers in the communications industry. It can also have an impact on any employer when the government asks for support to identify and track "lone wolves" suspected of terrorism without being affiliated with known terrorist organizations. HR professionals may find themselves involved in handling the collection and release of personal, confidential information about one or more employees. When legal documents such as subpoenas and court orders are involved, it is always a good idea to have the organization's attorney review them before taking any other action.

For more information, see www.justice.gov/archive/ll/highlights.htm.

Employment Visas for Foreign Nationals

Under some circumstances, it is possible for people from other countries to come work in the United States. There are several classifications of workers that can be used depending on the type of work to be done and the level of responsibilities.

E Nonimmigrant Visas

There are two types of E Nonimmigrant Visas: E-1 Treaty Traders and E-2 Treaty Investors. For more information on E Nonimmigrant Visas, see www.uscis.gov/portal/site/uscis.

E-1 Treaty Traders

The individual must be a citizen of the treaty country; there must be substantial trade; the trade must be principally with the treaty country; the individual must have executive, supervisory, or essential skills; and the individual must intend to depart the United States when the trading is completed.

E-2 Treaty Investors

The individual must be a citizen of the treaty country and be invested personally in the enterprise. The business must be a *bona fide* enterprise and not marginal, and the investment must be substantial. E-2 employees must have executive, supervisory, or essential skills, and E-2 investors must direct and develop the enterprise. The E-2 investor must depart the United States when the investment is concluded.

H Visas

There are five types of H visas that are specific for temporary workers. For more information about H visas, see www.uscis.gov/portal/site/uscis.

H1-B Special Occupations and Fashion Models

These visas require a bachelor's or higher degree or its equivalent. The job must be so complex that it can be performed only by a person with the degree. The employer normally requires a degree or its equivalent for this job. Fashion models also fall into this category.

H1-C Registered Nurse Working in a Health Professional Shortage Area

This requires a full and unrestricted nursing license in the country where your nursing education was obtained. Or you must have received your nursing education and license in the United States. It also requires that you have appropriate authorization from the U.S. Board of Nursing to practice within the United States. H1-C requires that you have passed the examination given by the Commission on Graduates for Foreign Nursing Schools (CGFNS) or have a full and unrestricted license to practice as a registered nurse in the state where you will work.

H-2A Temporary Agricultural Workers

The employer must be able to demonstrate that there are not sufficient U.S. workers who are able, willing, qualified, and available to do the temporary seasonal work. The employer must also show that the employment of H-2A workers will not adversely affect the wages and working conditions of similarly employed U.S. workers.

H-2B Temporary Nonagricultural Workers

The employer must show that there are not enough U.S. workers who are able, willing, qualified, and available to do the temporary work and that the employment of H-2B workers will not adversely affect the wages and working conditions of similarly employed U.S. workers. The employer must also show that the need for the prospective worker's services is temporary, regardless of whether the underlying job can be described as temporary.

H-3 Nonimmigrant Trainee

To qualify, employees must be trainees receiving training in any field of endeavor, other than graduate medical education, that is not available in their home country. Or they must be a Special Education Exchange Visitor who will participate in a special education training program focused on the education of children with physical, mental, or emotional disabilities.

L-1 Intra-Company Transferee

This allows a qualifying organization to move an employee from another qualifying country into the United States for a temporary assignment that is either managerial in nature or requires specialized knowledge.

L1-A Managers and Executives

These are intra-company transferees coming to the United States to work in a managerial or executive capacity. The maximum stay in the United States allowed under this visa is seven years.

Specialized Knowledge

This is someone with specialized knowledge of the employer's product, service, research, equipment, techniques, management, or other interests and its application in international markets, or an advanced level of knowledge or expertise in the organization's processes and procedures. An L1-B visa holder may only stay in the United States for five years.

O-1 Alien of Extraordinary Ability in Arts, Science, Education, Business, or Athletics

These people have a level of expertise indicating that they are among the small percentage who have risen to the top of their field of endeavor. Alternatively, they represent extraordinary achievement in motion picture and television productions, or they have extraordinary ability and distinction in the arts.

P Visa Categories

There are seven variations of athletics-based or art-based occupations visas:

- **P1-A** Individual Athletes or Athletic Teams
- **P1-B** Entertainment Groups
- **P1-S** Essential Support needed for P1-A or P1-B
- **P2** Artist or Entertainer Under a Reciprocal Exchange Program
- **P2-S** Essential Support for P2
- **P3** Artist or Entertainer Under a Culturally Unique Program
- **P3-S** Essential Support for P3

EB Employment-Based Visas

There are five levels of employment-based visas. They are prioritized so that once the first-level immigrant applicants are processed, the next level of priority will be considered. That will continue until the maximum allotment of visas is reached. In recent years, about 140,000 employment-based visas were permitted each year.

EB-1: Alien of Extraordinary Ability

The employer must demonstrate that the alien has extraordinary ability in the sciences, arts, education, business, or athletics, which has been demonstrated by sustained national or international acclaim and whose achievements have been recognized in the field through extensive documentation. It must also be shown that the work to be done in the United States will continue in the individual's area of extraordinary ability. It must also be shown how the alien's entry into this country will benefit the United States; 28.6 percent of the total employment-based visas are allocated to this category.

EB-2: Alien of Extraordinary Ability

This is a classification that applies to any job that requires advanced degrees and people of exceptional ability; 28.6 percent of the employment-based visas are allocated to this category.

EB-3: Skilled Workers

This category requires professionals and even unskilled workers who are sponsored by employers in the United States; 28.6 percent of the employment-based visas are allocated to this category.

EB-4: Certain Special Immigrants

Included here are some broadcasters, ministers of religion, and employees or former employees of the United States government, as well as Iraqi or Afghan interpreters and translators and other similar workers. 7.1 percent of the employment-based visas are allocated to this category.

EB-5: Immigrant Investors

These are people who will create new commercial enterprises in the United States that will provide job creation; 7.1 percent of the employment-based visas are allocated to this category.

Chapter Review

While this chapter is not meant to be a comprehensive statement of each law, studying and learning these laws will help you understand the basics as you perform your human resources management responsibilities. As you read through the chapters in Part II of this book, it's important to remember that one or more of these laws are the underlying basis in the HRCI's Body of Knowledge subject matter. Additionally, while using this list as a reference guide in your day-to-day application as a human resources professional, please also consult the statutes and regulations themselves via the URLs we have provided. A thorough understanding of the various laws and regulations that impact the employment relationship will enhance your ability to protect your organization in matters involving employment and employee relations.

Questions

The following are all questions about U.S. laws and regulations concerning employee management.

1. John, a new employee, has just arrived at the orientation program where everyone completes their payroll forms and signs up for healthcare benefits. He brings his W-4 form to you and says he isn't subject to payroll withholding because he pays his taxes directly each quarter. What is your response?

   A. That's okay. We won't process a W-4 form for you. We will give you a Form 1099.

   B. I'll check with the accounting department to find out whether you can do that.

   C. Unfortunately, all employees are subject to payroll tax withholding.

   D. If you can show me a W-10 form you have submitted to the IRS, we can block your paycheck withholding.

2. The Wagner-Peyser Act protects employees who are:

   A. Unemployed

   B. Injured on the job

   C. Unable to work because of pregnancy

   D. Have two or more jobs

3. Mary has had a bad encounter with her supervisor, Henry. That evening after getting home from work, she pulls out her computer and sends a blistering post to her Facebook page. She names her company and her supervisor. She calls him unfair, pigheaded, and without principles. What can the company do about her posting?

   A. The company can demand that she remove the offensive post. If she doesn't, the company can file legal action against her.

   B. The company can demand that Facebook remove the offensive post. If it doesn't, the company can file legal action against Facebook.

   C. The company is protected against such employee comments by the Fair and Decent Treatment Act and can take disciplinary action against Mary.

   D. The company is prohibited from any action against Mary because she is engaging in protected concerted activity.

4. Pete is sensitive about the security of his personally identifiable information since his credit card has been stolen twice in the past year. He is trying to clear up his credit rating because of the problems with the stolen cards. Now, he has approached the HR manager at his organization and requested that his Social Security number be removed from all company records. He thinks that a mistake could cause him more grief if the Social Security number were to be obtained by thieves. As the HR manager, what should you do?

   A. The company can and should delete the Social Security number from its records to protect Pete.

   B. There is a need for the company to keep the Social Security number for tax reporting.

   C. There is a need for the company to keep the Social Security number for census reporting.

   D. The company has no need for the Social Security number but should keep it regardless.

5. Pat is talking with her colleagues about illegal discrimination at work. Someone mentions that the company is going to be sending out a request for updated race and sex information. Pat says that isn't legal. The company isn't supposed to track any of that information. What would you tell Pat?

   A. Pat has not understood the FLSA requirements that employers keep race and sex data on employees.

   B. The EEOC has issued guidelines that agree with Pat's belief that it is illegal to maintain that information in company records.

   C. Only federal contractors are required to maintain the race and sex identification for employees.

   D. It is only the public-sector employees who are exempt from providing their race and sex identification to employers.

6. The Tractor and Belt Company (TBC) handles conveyor belt installations for many small firms. Each of the customer projects begins on a day that is most convenient for the customer. Sometimes that's Monday; sometimes it's Thursday or some other day. The HR manager says that the company will adjust its workweek to begin when the customer's project starts. That way, each installation team has a separate workweek, and those workweeks can shift several times a month. It's better for the payroll system that way, and the company can usually avoid paying overtime. What would you advise the HR manager to do if you disagree with the policy of changing workweeks?

   A. The HR manager is taking advantage of the FLSA's provisions for flexible workweeks that support small business.

   B. Once the workweek has been designated to begin on a certain day of the week, it should not be changed by the HR manager.

   C. It depends on state laws and regulations whether the workweek begins on any specific day of the week.

   D. The FLSA says a workweek should always begin on Sunday.

7. Sandy is 15 years old and a sophomore at Central High School. She gets a job at the local hamburger drive-in. Her boss says he needs her to work the following schedule during the Spring Break week: 4 hours at lunch time every day, 9 hours on Saturday, and 6 hours on Sunday. Is that schedule acceptable for Sandy given that she has a work permit from the school?

   A. Because it is a school vacation week, there are no restrictions on the hours that Sandy can work.

   B. Only state laws impact what hours Sandy can work because it happens during a vacation week.

   C. Federal law says Sandy cannot work more than 8 hours a day when it is a vacation week.

   D. Because Sandy won't be working more than 40 hours for the week, there is no problem.

8. Gary is a junior at Southpark High School. He is 17 years old. The school needs some help in its warehouse during the summer, and Gary needs a job so he can save money for college. His boss is the manager of facilities. Gary is assigned to work nine hours every day during the week because one of the other employees is on disability leave. And because the other employee was the forklift driver, Gary has been given training in how to drive that equipment around the warehouse and loading dock. He likes that duty because he has been driving a car for only a few months. The forklift is cool. Is there any difficulty with the facilities manager's requirements of Gary?

   A. Everything the facilities manager has required Gary to do is permissible under federal laws.

   B. Since there is no restriction to the number of hours Gary can work, everything should be okay.

   C. Whatever the facilities manager wants Gary to do is okay because it's only a summer job.

   D. Even though Gary can work unlimited hours, he cannot be assigned to drive the forklift because forklifts are classified as a "power-driven hoisting apparatus," which is one of the 17 most dangerous jobs as classified by OSHA that may not be operated by workers under the age of 18.

9. Hank puts in the following hours at his city job: Sunday, 0; Monday, 8; Tuesday, 8; Wednesday, 9; Thursday, 8; Friday, 8; Saturday, 7. His boss says he will give Hank compensating time off for every hour of overtime Hank works. How many compensating hours off should Hank receive for this work time?

    A. One day of compensating time off.

    B. 1.5 days of compensating time off.

    C. 7 hours of compensating time off.

    D. Compensating time off is not permitted under the FLSA.

10. The Tractor and Belt Company (TBC) doesn't have an HR manager. HR is handled by the payroll clerk. When a new employee is assigned to the production department as an assembler, the payroll clerk raises a question. Should the new person be paid the same as all the other employees, all women, in the department, or is it okay to pay her more because she made more at her former job?

    A. There are no restrictions on the amount a new employee can be paid. It is market driven.

    B. The Fair and Decent Treatment Act requires all people doing the same work to be paid the same amount.

    C. There is no restriction on the amount paid because all the incumbents are women.

    D. Once a valid market survey has been done, it can be used to determine starting pay for new people.

11. Finding a life insurance company to provide benefits to her workforce has been difficult for Joan, the HR manager. She decides to recommend that they offer a self-insured plan. What controls might Joan have to consider in her planning?

    A. There are no federal restrictions on a company providing its own life insurance plan to employees.

    B. The Employee Retirement Income Security Act regulates welfare benefit plans, including life insurance.

    C. The Life Insurance Benefit Plans Act has control over what Joan is able to do with her idea.

    D. Only state laws will have an influence on Joan's development of a self-insured benefit plan.

12. Simone has just been hired and is asked to complete a Form I-9. She offers her driver's license as proof of her identity. What else is required for her to complete the document?

    A. She may offer any document authorized on the Form I-9 instructions as proof of her authorization to work in this country.

    B. She must have a Social Security number to submit on the form.

C. Simone has a U.S. passport but is told that she can't use it for her Form I-9.

D. As long as Simone offers to get a Social Security number in the next 30 days, she can submit her Form I-9.

13. Steve is the HR director for a crane operations company. He just got a phone call from one of his field supervisors with tragic news. One of their units has collapsed, and their operator is in the hospital with serious injuries. What should Steve do with that information?

   A. Steve should immediately call the hospital to be sure all the insurance information is on file for their employee.

   B. He should notify the Occupational Safety and Health Administration about the accident and the injuries.

   C. He should notify the Crane Safety Institute of America to be sure they are able to add this accident to their database.

   D. Steve should call the crane operator's spouse to let her know about the tragedy.

14. Every year Donna has to attend training on the use of the company vehicles she drives. She thinks this is a silly waste of time. Donna knows how to drive, and she knows the company vehicles. Why should she attend training every year?

   A. There is no federal requirement for Donna to take yearly training.

   B. OSHA only requires training be done once for vehicle operation.

   C. Only state safety provisions govern how frequently training must be done in Donna's situation.

   D. Safety programs must be developed that provide for refresher training on all equipment operating procedures.

15. Jerry just arrived at work and found a sinkhole in the parking lot. He is early enough that other people have not yet begun arriving for work. Because the hole is about 10 feet across at the moment, what should Jerry be doing about the problem?

   A. If Jerry is a management employee, he should take charge of the situation and begin the process of alerting others to the danger posed by the sinkhole.

   B. If Jerry is a nonmanagement employee, he should give his boss a call and leave a voicemail message, if necessary, about the sinkhole.

   C. If the sink hole poses an immediate danger of death or serious injury, Jerry should call 911 and report it. He should barricade the perimeter of the sinkhole with tape or something else to prevent people from falling in.

   D. Jerry should first test the edges of the sinkhole to see whether it could grow in size. Then he should barricade the perimeter so no one will fall in.

16. Theresa attended a seminar recently that pointed out the need to post a yearly summary of injury and illness cases. Her boss doesn't want to do that, saying he doesn't want to publicize the problems the organization has had. What should Theresa tell him?

A. Posting requirements call for display of the report in a prominent location if there are 10 or more people on the payroll.

B. Posting requirements can be met by putting a report on the back of the closet door in the employee lounge.

C. Posting requirements can be met by making the report available in a binder in the HR manager's office.

D. Posting requirements are optional, but good employers are using the report as a "best practice" in safety programs.

17. An employer routinely works with hazardous chemicals trucking them for delivery to various customer locations. After each load, the truck must be cleaned before being loaded with a different chemical. Cleaning has to be done by someone inside the tanker using special absorbent materials. What else should be considered?

A. Personal protective equipment should be provided by the employer, including breathing apparatus and hazmat suits.

B. Standard coveralls and boot covers should be provided for employees to use if they want.

C. Workers should never be sent into a tanker truck for any reason.

D. Breathing equipment is absolutely a requirement if someone will be in the tanker truck for longer than 30 minutes.

18. Shelly has worked for the same dentist for more than 10 years. In all that time, there has been no mention of any special requirements for handling syringes. She arranges the doctor's equipment trays every day and cleans them up after they have been used. She just tosses the used equipment into the autoclave or into the trash if it won't be used again. If you were advising Shelly about the practices used in her dental office, what would you say?

A. Needles should be broken off before they are thrown into the trash can.

B. Sharps should be triple wrapped in a stiff paper to protect from sticking someone handling the trash.

C. Any possible harm can be prevented if used syringes are placed into an approved sharps container.

D. Putting used syringes into any solid container that is wrapped in red paper is sufficient to meet requirements.

19. The price of gold is climbing, and folks at the Golden Nugget Mine are planning to reopen their operation. They know that safety is an important consideration. But what about federal regulations for gold mines? Are there such things?

    A. There are only OSHA regulations in general. All of those rules still apply.

    B. There are MSHA regulations to be considered, but because they are not in the coal mining business, the Golden Nugget Mine won't have to worry about them.

    C. MSHA rules apply to all mining operations in the United States. The Golden Nugget Mine will have to study those rules and get ready for inspections by the government.

    D. MSHA can tell the mine what to do, but it has no authority to conduct inspections because the Golden Nugget is not a coal mine.

20. Olivia suspects her payroll clerk of embezzlement. She has inspected the records for the past three months, and the pattern is clear. But to be sure it is the payroll clerk and not the accounts payable clerk, Olivia wants to confront her and demand she take a lie detector test.

    A. Good going, Olivia. You caught her. Sure enough, demanding that she take a lie detector test is a good way to confirm your suspicions.

    B. While lie detector tests can be used for some employees, accounting employees are exempt. You can't test her.

    C. Lie detector tests are not permitted for any use by any employer. You can't test her.

    D. Lie detector tests can be required only in limited circumstances, and this isn't one of them. You can't test her.

21. For the past six years, Sam's company has been a federal contractor working on equipment for the Department of Defense. They have additional contract opportunities coming up, and Sam isn't sure if there will be an extra burden related to disabled workers because they are subject to both the Americans with Disabilities Act and the Rehabilitation Act.

    A. Sam should rest easy. The ADA and the Rehabilitation Act are identical in their content and requirements.

    B. Sam's company has already met its recruiting obligations and now only has to worry about meeting ADA requirements.

    C. Handling job accommodation requests is a requirement of the ADA but not the Rehabilitation Act. Things should be easier.

    D. Whatever Sam thinks, the ADA and Rehabilitation Act requirements have applied to his company for six years already. Adding more contracts won't change his current obligations.

22. Arthur has applied for a job with the AB Transit Company. He is told he must take and pass a urine drug test. If he fails the test and any subsequent random drug test after he is hired, he will be dismissed from the company. Arthur reacts loudly and says, "That's an invasion of my privacy! I won't do it." What happens now?

   A. Arthur can call his lawyer and have the drug test waived since he doesn't want to take it.

   B. Arthur can discontinue his participation in the AB Transit Company's employment process.

   C. Arthur can take the test now and still refuse to participate in random tests later.

   D. Arthur can have his friend take the test for him.

23. Cynthia works for a large multistate manufacturing company and approaches her boss one morning and tells him that her husband has just received orders from the Coast Guard to report for deployment to the Middle East. They have a week to get everything ready for his departure. She wants to know whether she can have excused time off during the coming week. If you were her boss, what would you tell her?

   A. She can have the time off, but it will be logged as unpaid and charged as FMLA leave.

   B. She can take the time off, but it will be unexcused because she didn't give more than a week's notice.

   C. If she wants the time off, she will have to use her paid vacation time for the week.

   D. Jennifer has already requested the week off for vacation, and only one person can be off at any one time or the unit won't be able to function. Cynthia's request is denied with regrets.

24. Robert works for a congressional representative and suffers a disabling injury in an automobile accident. Robert cannot work more than three hours per day according to his doctor. Weeks later, when he returns to work, he asks for a job accommodation and is told that it can't be done. When he presses the point, his supervisor says the reason is:

   A. Congressional staff people aren't covered by the ADA so they don't have to even discuss his request.

   B. The request he has made would exempt him from several of his job's key responsibilities.

   C. The request he has made would set a precedent that other representatives' offices would have to follow.

   D. Because congressional staff members have to meet the public every day, they can't have people seeing disabled workers in the office. It doesn't look good.

25. Jimmy has heard that he will be getting healthcare coverage from his company because of the new Obamacare law. His company employs only 10 people, but Jimmy is excited that he will finally get some insurance. He hasn't been feeling very well lately.

   A. Jimmy might have to wait until he can arrange for insurance through one of the exchanges.

   B. Jimmy should get an enrollment form from his boss because all employees will be covered by the new requirements that employers must provide health insurance for workers.

   C. Jimmy is out of luck. The new law only covers employers with 50 or more people, and there is no way Jimmy will be getting health insurance under the new law.

   D. Jimmy's boss just ran out of forms, but he will get some more from HR and then have Jimmy sign up for his coverage.

Is Safety the Most Important Policy?—A Case Study

A company manufactured batteries for automobiles. The battery manufacturing process used lead as a main ingredient. It is generally known that exposure to lead can cause serious health problems. Even though the company provided personal protective equipment (PPE) to its workers, there was still a chance that some exposure could happen to the folks out on the manufacturing line. One of the dangers was related to harm that could be done during pregnancy to both the mother and the baby.

Because of the sensitivity the company had to the safety and health of its employees, its policy was to prohibit any pregnant worker from being on the production line. It didn't want to be responsible for harming any of its employees or their children.

One pregnant employee objected to that policy, and her union sued the company. The company stood by its policy claiming safety trumps all other concerns.

Did the company have a valid policy? Why?

Answers

   1. **C.** If the new worker is classified as an employee and is on the payroll, the IRS demands that income tax, Social Security tax, and Medicare tax be withheld. The law does not allow employees to opt out because they want to file their own tax payments each quarter.

   2. **A.** The Wagner-Peyser Act of 1933 provides for federal unemployment insurance and sets guidelines for state unemployment insurance programs.

   3. **D.** Mary is protected by the National Labor Relations Act (NLRA) of 1935. The National Labor Relations Board has taken the position that almost all postings on the Internet, whether complaining about supervisors or employers or making charges that employees are treated unfairly, are protected concerted activities under the act.

4. B. Both the FLSA and the IRS regulations require employers to obtain and report Social Security numbers from all employees. A Social Security number is required for completion of the Form I-9 to prove authorization to work in this country. The company may not remove it from its records, regardless of how concerned Pete may be.

5. A. Race and sex data is specifically required by the FLSA. For employers with 15 or more people on the payroll, who are engaged in interstate commerce, EEOC regulations also require maintenance of those data records.

6. B. The FLSA requires employers to designate a day as the beginning of the workweek. To change that designation, there should be a significant business reason. Moving the workweek to begin based on projects is not acceptable. The FLSA requires consistency because of the need to pay overtime for hours in excess of 40 in a workweek. Constantly moving a workweek could deprive employees of earned overtime.

7. C. The FLSA prohibits people aged 14 and 15 from working more than 8 hours in a day even when school is not in session.

8. D. Driving a "power-driven hoisting apparatus" is one of the 17 most dangerous jobs that may not be performed by workers younger than 18. At Gary's age, the FLSA has no restriction on the hours he may work in a week.

9. B. The FLSA requires all hours of work in excess of 40 in a week be paid overtime for city workers at the rate of 1.5 times the normal hourly pay rate. Compensating time off in lieu of overtime pay must be given at the rate of 1.5 hours for every overtime hour. So a day of overtime (8 hours) should be compensated for with 1.5 days of compensating time off.

10. C. The Equal Pay Act requires men and women doing the same work to be paid the same rate. If there are no men in the job, only women, there is no Equal Pay Act issue. If all the incumbents are women, there is no employment discrimination based on sex because there is only one gender represented. So with those conditions, there is no barrier to paying the new employee more based on her previous job's compensation. However, considering previous compensation in hiring decisions is now illegal in some states, so be careful.

11. B. ERISA specifically regulates welfare benefit plans such as health insurance and life insurance. That is in addition to the regulation of pension and retirement plans offered by employers. It makes no difference who underwrites the life insurance—the employer or a vendor. ERISA will still provide requirements.

12. A. The deadline for completing a Form I-9 is three days after hire. Any documents listed on the form are acceptable. The employer may not designate certain documents as requirements. A Social Security number is one way to demonstrate authorization to work in this country. A valid U.S. passport is also a way to demonstrate both identity and work authorization.

13. **B.** The company has eight hours after the accident to file its report of serious injury with OSHA. We don't know how long ago the accident happened, but it was long enough that the operator is now in the hospital. Steve should gather all the information needed for the report and get it called in to the OSHA office.

14. **D.** Injury and illness prevention programs are required by OSHA. Part of the identification and remediation of workplace hazards is employee training. Even if employees have been trained on equipment operation, periodic refresher programs can help overcome bad habits that might have developed. Refresher programs conducted on a yearly basis represent a reasonable interval for Donna's situation.

15. **C.** It doesn't matter if Jerry is a manager. All employees should be trained to react to imminent dangers by taking immediate action to prevent anyone from serious injury. And walking up to the edge to see whether it is going to collapse is just nuts.

16. **A.** If she must, Theresa should show her boss the requirement in OSHA regulations. A prominent display location excludes places such as the back of a closet door or inside a binder somewhere in the manager's office.

17. **A.** Working inside an enclosed space with dangerous fumes calls for hazmat equipment and adequate breathing equipment. OSHA regulations specify the personal protective equipment (PPE) necessary in this and other working conditions.

18. **C.** The Needlestick Safety and Prevention Act requires all sharps be disposed of in approved sharps containers. It also requires posting of warnings and information about blood-borne pathogens.

19. **C.** The Mine Safety and Health Administration has jurisdiction over all mining operations, not just coal mines. It handles safety complaints and conducts inspections of both above-ground and underground mining operations. All mine operators are required to conduct their internal safety inspections and maintain records of those inspections.

20. **D.** Except for law enforcement, security officers, and people who handle controlled substances, lie detectors are no longer permitted in the workplace. They were commonly used prior to 1988's Employee Polygraph Protection Act.

21. **D.** Sam's company will not incur any additional obligations for disabled workers if they seek additional government contracts. They have been obligated under both laws for six years.

22. **B.** Arthur has to decide whether he wants to continue seeking employment with the AB Transit Company. If so, he must participate in their drug testing program. If he wants to avoid testing, he must drop out of the job application process and seek employment elsewhere.

23. **A.** Under the FMLA, Cynthia is entitled to an unpaid leave of absence as a spouse of a covered military service worker. It will be logged as unpaid time off, unless she wants to use some of her accrued paid time off. It will also be logged in her record as excused FMLA leave.

24. **B.** Even the congressional offices are subject to the ADA's requirement to consider and discuss requests for job accommodation. Job accommodations must be made to make it easier for an employee to perform one of the job's essential functions. If he can't do that, even with an accommodation, he is not eligible for assignment to that job. If there is no other job available, the employer can't return him to work until his status changes.

25. **A.** Employers are required to provide health insurance coverage or pay a penalty in lieu of that insurance only if they have 50 or more full-time workers. With only 10 employees, Jimmy's employer is not obligated to provide health insurance coverage. Jimmy may purchase it for himself through one of the exchanges set up for that purpose.

Case Study Outcome

The case was *Automobile Workers v. Johnson Controls, Inc.* 499 U.S. 197 (1991). The decision of the Court was that the company policy on fetal protection was a violation of Title VII of the Civil Rights Act of 1964 as amended by the Pregnancy Discrimination Act (PDA). It impacted only women and, as such, was illegally discriminating against women based on sex.

Justice Harry A. Blackmun wrote, "Danger to a woman herself does not justify discrimination." The Court concluded that it is the woman's decision to make about her safety and that of her fetus. Blackmun then said, these decisions "must be left to the parents…rather than the employers. It is no more appropriate for the courts than it is for individual employers to decide whether a woman's reproductive role is more important to herself and her family than her economic role." Thus, in this instance, Title VII trumps safety concerns for the employer. (For a copy of the complete Supreme Court opinion, go to http://supreme.justia.com/cases/federal/us/499/187/case.html.)

Endnotes

1. "Instructions for Employment Eligibility Verification," U.S. Department of Homeland Security, U.S. Citizenship and Immigration Services, accessed July 9, 2013, www.uscis.gov/files/form/i-9.pdf.

2. "Federal Mine Safety & Health Act of 1977, Public Law 91-173, as amended by Public Law 95-164," U.S. Department of Labor, Mine Safety and Health Administration, accessed July 9, 2013, www.msha.gov/regs/act/acttc.htm.

3. "OSH Act, OSHA Standards, Inspections, Citations and Penalties," U.S. Department of Labor, Occupational Safety and Health Administration, accessed July 9, 2013, www.osha.gov.

4. Ibid.

5. *Lawson v. FMR LLC*, U.S. No. 12-3, retrieved from www.supremecourt.gov/opinions/13pdf/12-3_4f57.pdf on March 7, 2014.

6. *Sutton v. United Air Lines, Inc.*, 527 U.S. 471 (1999).

7. *Toyota Motor Manufacturing, Kentucky, Inc. v. Williams*, 534 U.S. 184 (2002).

8. The Job Accommodation Network (http://askjan.org or 800-526-7234) is a free resource for employers. It is a service provided by the U.S. Department of Labor's Office of Disability Employment Policy (ODEP). JAN has been providing services for more than 25 years.

9. "Disability Discrimination," U.S. Equal Employment Opportunity Commission, accessed July 10, 2013, http://eeoc.gov/laws/types/disability.cfm.

10. The first was the Civil Rights Act of 1866, which protected the right to enter into contracts regardless of race.

11. A list of controlled substances can be found in Schedules I through V of Section 202 of the Controlled Substances Act (21 U.S.C. 812) and as further defined in Regulation 21 CFR 1308.11–1308.15.

12. "eLaws—Drug-Free Workplace Advisor," U.S. Department of Labor, accessed July 10, 2013, www.dol.gov/elaws/asp/drugfree/screenr.htm.

13. 41 C.F.R. 60-3.7.

14. Fair Treatment of Experienced Pilots Act (December 13, 2007) Public Law 110–135.

15. 41 CFR 60.

HRCI Core Knowledge

The HR Certification Institute (HRCI) has reabsorbed the "core knowledge" components that it used to cluster together. Now, each knowledge area is listed within the functional area to which it belongs. Nonetheless, each of these pieces of information is critical to both levels of HRCI certification, Professional in Human Resources (PHR) and Senior Professional in Human Resources (SPHR). Without a firm grasp of each of these knowledge areas, it would be difficult for a human resources (HR) professional to achieve certification and, more importantly, succeed on the job.

In this chapter, we discuss each of the knowledge items individually and show how they link to the other knowledge mastery requirements in the certification process. Be sure you understand each of them, and carefully study the details in each of the individual functional areas so you have a firm grasp of the subjects.

Core Knowledge Requirements

Nearly all of these core knowledge requirements apply to more than one functional area. That's why they are considered core requirements. In this analysis, we are identifying major applications and linkages. One risk of scattering these knowledge areas into each of the functional areas is that some people may interpret that to mean they apply to only one area of the HR professional functions. They are truly interdependent rather than independent. The related functional areas are listed in the boxes under each core knowledge requirement. Look there for more details.

Employee Communications

- PHR functional area 1—Business Management
  - Employee communications
- SPHR functional area 3—Learning and Development
  - Effective communication skills and strategies (for example, presentation, collaboration, sensitivity)

Presentation skills are applicable in all functional areas for HR professionals. Having the ability to make presentations to small groups as well as large gatherings is critical when addressing policy makers in the boardroom and employee assemblies to present or discuss policy or program changes. Understanding how to select the proper communication tool contributes to strategic plans for policy implementation.

HR professionals will find themselves presenting a variety of timely messages to a vast array of audiences. The skills needed for effective communications include written and verbal skills that involve persuasion, collaboration, influencing, sensitivity, tact, and diplomacy.

Generally, communication falls into two categories: oral and written. Skills in each category are critical for HR professional success. From the mid-1950s to the mid-1980s, the Bell System's Management Progress Study tracked college hires placed in management positions. They were observed and assessed on 25 variables thought to contribute to management success.[1] Two of the variables that lasted throughout the study were communication skills.

- **Oral communication skill** How effective would this person be in presenting an oral report to a small conference group on a subject the person knew well?
- **Written communication skill** How effective would this person be in composing a communicative and formally correct memorandum on a subject this person knows well?

The key assessment measurement always boils down to this: does the message come across as intended? If it does, the communication was successful.

There are an unlimited number of sources that want to tell you how to effectively communicate with others. Use your judgment to determine which resources will be of greatest value to you and then study them carefully. In the end, practice is what will hone your skills as a communicator.

Ethical and Professional Standards

- PHR functional area 1—Business Management
  - Ethical and professional standards
- SPHR functional area 5—Employee Relations and Engagement
  - Ethical and professional standards

Ethics is a field of intense interest among many organizations these days. For HR professionals, ethics is tied to the proper and fair methods used to manage employees in an employment environment. It also involves HR professionals participating with senior management to define ethical standards for their organizational behavior and employee expectations. SHRM and HRCI have formally published standards for professional behavior for the HR profession. The SHRM Code of Ethical and Professional Standards in Human Resource Management can be viewed in its entirety at www.shrm.org/about/pages/code-of-ethics.aspx. Ethical standards follow these six core principles:

- Professional responsibility
- Professional development
- Ethical leadership
- Fairness and justice
- Conflicts of interest
- Use of information

HRCI's Model of Professional Excellence sets standards for honesty, reliability, fairness, and cooperation.

Reporting Tools for Supporting Both HR and the Greater Organization

> - PHR functional area 1—Business Management
>   - ○ Existing HRIS, reporting tools, and other systems for effective data reporting and analysis
> - SPHR functional area 3—Learning and Development
>   - ○ Techniques to assess training program effectiveness, including the use of applicable metrics

Technology can accomplish many things. It can reduce the number of employees necessary in performing repetitive and menial duties. It can assist employees with records management, updating information as it changes through time. Technology can assist when training employees, processing job applicants, and handling employee information. Exactly which technology to use in any given situation is a decision to be made by HR professionals and their colleagues. There are four mainstays of technology in human resources:

- **Human resource information system (HRIS)**   A repository of information for storing employment files and individual employee records
- **Applicant tracking and hiring system**   An automated method for keeping track of applicants and the hiring process
- **Employee self-service system**   Gives employees access to their own employment and benefit records on the company intranet 24/7
- **Learning management system**   Tracks, enrolls, and organizes employee training requirements, needs, and progression

Change Management Theory, Methods, and Application

- PHR functional area 1—Business Management
  - Change management theory, methods, and application
- SPHR functional area 1—Leadership and Strategy
  - Change management processes and techniques

In 1962, Everett Rogers wrote a book called *Diffusion of Innovations*[2] that described how people adapt to new ideas and technologies. Many scientists have followed with their own versions of studies examining how organizations can identify an end result and then plan to manage the change process to achieve that result. Particularly in large businesses, change management has become an identifiable function on the organization chart. In others, it is a function that is either part-time or hired in through consulting firms. The notion that large organizational changes can be properly managed is important in the fast-paced world of mergers, acquisitions, and other upheavals such as restructuring and downsizing. Only 10 percent of the population is known as a *change agent*—people simply resist change.[3] HR professionals must be masters of understanding, orchestrating, and getting others to accept change. As the saying goes, "Change is good—you go first!"

Risk Management Techniques

- PHR functional area 1—Business Management
  - Risk management
- SPHR functional area 1—Leadership and Strategy
  - Risk management

Nearly every aspect of HR management impacts the function of risk management in one way or another. Employee satisfaction can be captured through monitoring complaints. Safety can be expressed in terms of workers' compensation experience. The cost of employee health benefits is impacted by employer programs that support smoking cessation, exercise, and a good diet. Computer security programs can block unauthorized access to confidential employee and business records. Privacy of records can be expressed in financial terms. All of these issues have a potential impact on the profit or loss of an employer's organization. Even nonprofits and governmental agencies have budgets they are expected to live within. Huge, unexpected expenses related to undue risk exposure can cause instant budget failure. HR professionals can have a great impact on the organizational finances by preventing large losses through effective risk management programs.

Qualitative and Quantitative Methods and Tools for Analysis

- PHR functional area 1—Business Management
  - Qualitative and quantitative methods and tools for analytics
- SPHR functional area 1—Leadership and Strategy
  - Qualitative and quantitative methods and tools used for analysis, interpretation, and decision-making purposes

As HR professionals gain access to the executive suites of senior management, knowledge of business strategies and measurements is critical. It is not just a question of how many employees it takes to produce a given product or the cost of healthcare plans per employee. Now it is a question of the dollar benefits produced by a diversity program or the increased production per employee realized by providing an in-house childcare center. All of these are fair game for measurements (metrics) that demonstrate they add value to the employer's organization and its ultimate mission. Knowing which method to utilize for research, data collection, and analysis is essential for the information presented.

Quantitative methods involve measuring numbers. How many employees were hired in the past 90 days? What percentage of employees were registered for healthcare coverage in this cycle? How many employees are being paid outside the compensation band for their job title?

Qualitative methods involve measuring things that aren't subject to hard numbers. To make measurement possible, we ordinarily create rating scales to demonstrate where the result has landed along the scale. For example, what is the amount of communication skill improvement as a result of a training program? What is the change in employee attitudes about the employer over a six-month period? How has the employee population attitude toward dental benefits changed over the last year? Scales are created that have "high" and "low" results and descriptions of the amount of result seen between each of them. This approach is particularly valuable when HR professionals are trying to measure the amount of behavior they see among a selection of employee candidates for promotion. Scales can be helpful in describing all of the soft people skills such as leadership, tolerance of uncertainty, and decision-making.

Human Relations Concepts and Applications

For example: Emotional Intelligence, Organizational Behavior

- PHR functional area 5—Employee and Labor Relations
  - Human relations, culture and values concepts, and applications to employees and organizations
- SPHR functional area 5—Employee Relations and Engagement
  - Human relations concepts and applications

Human relations focuses on the relationship between supervisors and subordinates in an employment organization. Organizational behavior is what results from the impact individuals, systems, and groups have on the overall organizational effectiveness. Emotional intelligence refers to the ability to perceive, control, and evaluate emotions. Emotionally intelligent individuals are able to motivate themselves, have awareness of others' emotions, are able to manage relationships, and can control their reactions to emotions. Applying these concepts can provide a valuable benefit to any employment organization. The more supervisors understand these concepts, the better they will be able to influence subordinate behavior and organizational results.

Methods for Assessing Employee Attitudes, Opinions, and Satisfaction

For Example: Surveys, Focus Groups/Panels

> - PHR functional area 5—Employee and Labor Relations
>   - Review and analysis process for assessing employee attitudes, opinions, and satisfaction
> - SPHR functional area 5—Employee Relations and Engagement
>   - Methods for assessing employee attitudes, opinions, and satisfaction

It is wise for any organization large enough to have one or more HR professionals on staff to engage in activities to gather feedback from employees about their experience on the job. Even smaller organizations can avail themselves of consulting support to do the same thing. Providing employees with an opportunity to be heard and express their opinions assists management and HR in many areas, including building good employee relationships and avoiding third-party interventions. Structured investigations through the use of focus groups, surveys, or panel discussions can yield a wealth of information about employee reactions, attitudes, and expectations. This information is important as a component of strategic planning and in the design of HR systems and programs. The process of gathering employee input should be repeated periodically because attitudes, expectations, and reactions change over time as the environment changes.

Diversity Concepts and Applications

For Example: Generational, Cultural Competency, Learning Styles

> - PHR functional area 5—Employee and Labor Relations
>   - Diversity and inclusion
> - SPHR functional area 5—Employee Relations and Engagement
>   - Diversity and inclusion concepts and applications

Diversity issues impact every aspect of employment these days. Types of diversity include employee representation (demographics), educational background, and cultural experience. Taking advantage of viewpoints molded by those differing experiences can result in more effective decisions.

It can also take longer to resolve questions simply because you need to discuss differing viewpoints. A key consideration involves people from different generations having different values, beliefs, and expectations that can lead to difficulties and conflict.

Making decisions in a group of people with similar backgrounds and experiences can be faster but may not include considerations of cultural issues outside that experience. So, even though groups with a multitude of backgrounds and experiences will discuss issues for a longer period, the decisions they make will typically be more workable and apply to a broader target population.

This same variety of perspectives from a diverse workforce can also create a cultural competence to add strength to an organization. Military veterans have had different experiences and thus have developed the ability to problem-solve in different ways than those without a military background. Disabled people are able to bring viewpoints that those without disabilities cannot readily see. The amalgam of all these differences can bring together organizational policies and outcomes. The results can be much stronger and more effective than are seen in organizations without such diversity.

Employee Records Management

For Example: Electronic/Paper, Retention, Disposal

- PHR functional area 5—Employee and Labor Relations
  - Recordkeeping requirements
- SPHR functional area 5—Employee Relations and Engagement
  - Data security and privacy

Knowing what records to keep is critical. So is knowing what records to destroy. Records management is an area of responsibility that can be a part-time assignment in a small organization or a full staff responsibility in a large organization. Employee records include an employee's personnel file, medical records, investigation records, training records, and security clearances. Depending on the organization, there can be other categories of records retained for employees—for example, safety records. Some records are required for government compliance, such as W-4 forms, I-9 forms, W-2 forms, work time records, hazardous exposure records, workers' compensation reports, and more. Other records are maintained for the convenience and use of the employer—for example, commendation and disciplinary records, training records, and performance appraisals. Some records are required by law and must be retained for designated periods of time. Other records have no retention requirements. Generally speaking, any record other than one made by an attorney can be discovered through the legal process and is often sought in lawsuits against employers, including informal electronic communications. Retaining records beyond their required period can be detrimental to employers, so employers should create and follow a purging schedule, especially of electronic records.

Job Descriptions and Job Analysis

- PHR functional area 4—Total Rewards
  - Job analysis and evaluation concepts and methods
- SPHR functional area 4—Total Rewards
  - Job analysis and evaluation methods

Job analysis is usually the first step in developing a job description. Several things usually happen at this stage of the process:

- **Observation** A job analyst prepares lists of all activities and behaviors performed by an incumbent or group of incumbents and then consolidates those lists of duties and responsibilities. Observation can involve time and motion studies. For accuracy of results, job analysts should be properly trained in the process rather than using untrained observers.

- **Questionnaire** A written questionnaire can be used to gather input from incumbents, supervisors, and managers about job content and incumbent requirements.

- **Interview** A job analyst interviews incumbents to determine the job content qualifications for successful incumbents and the physical and mental requirements of the job.

Some people are under the impression that federal law requires employers to have written job descriptions. That is not true. Even the Americans with Disabilities Act (ADA) does not require employers to have job descriptions. But job descriptions make it much easier for employers to entertain requests for job accommodation. Job descriptions contain key descriptions of the job, including the following:

- List of duties and responsibilities
- Identification of the amount of time spent (by percentage) on each duty and/or responsibility
- List of knowledge categories required to perform the job
- List of skill categories required to perform the job
- List of ability categories required to perform the job
- List of physical requirements of the job
- List of mental requirements of the job
- Identification of qualifications not mentioned elsewhere in the job description (such as educational requirements or amount of specific experience required to be successful on the job)

So, while job descriptions are not a legal requirement, they are a practical necessity. They make it easy to hand a job candidate the job description and ask, "Can you perform all of these requirements, with or without accommodation?" It may also be that a job candidate objects to one or more of the duties or responsibilities. With a job description in hand, that can become readily apparent.

Organizational Documentation Requirements

- PHR functional area 5—Employee and Labor Relations
  - Recordkeeping requirements
- SPHR functional area 5—Employee Relations and Engagement
  - Performance management strategies

Documentation is the lifeblood of human resource managers. Attorneys are careful to point out, "If it isn't documented, it didn't happen." When legal challenges pit employees against their employers, jury sympathy tends to swing to the "little guy" (the employee) rather than to the employer organization. Employers are expected to expend the energy necessary to make a record of events that take place during employee management. Supervisors must be trained in effective documentation techniques for employment actions and performance issues, and it is the responsibility of HR professionals to be sure supervisors are fulfilling that duty.

Third-Party or Vendor Selection, Contract Negotiation, and Management, Including Development of RFPs

- PHR functional area 5—Employee and Labor Relations
  - Using third-party experts for complaint investigations, generating reports, or report analysis
- SPHR functional area 1—Leadership and Strategy
  - Third-party or vendor selection, contract negotiation, and management, including development of requests for proposals (RFPs)

Requests for proposals are a common tool used in selecting vendors to fulfill projects that usually carry a significant cost or require specialty skills that are unavailable in the organization. They are a structured method for outlining the desired organizational outcome while allowing competing vendors to demonstrate how they will reach that outcome and how much the project will cost. RFPs allow organizations to compare "bid" responses from multiple vendors using the same format. Negotiation of final details can be facilitated through the RFP content.

With an increasing number of HR functions being outsourced, the need for HR professionals to effectively manage third-party contractors becomes vitally important. For a successful contractor relationship, it is critical that a clear understanding of the deliverable be established in the RFP and final contract.

Generally, an RFP will follow a format such as this:

1. Brief overview

2. Qualifications of vendor

3. How the service/product will be supplied by the vendor

4. Project team from both vendor and client organization—with responsibilities and accountabilities described

5. Delivery timeline

6. Billing and pricing schedule

7. Deadline for final submission of RFPs

Once the RFPs have been submitted, an evaluation of the proposals occur. There are various factors to consider that will be specific to the needs request, including the reputation of the vendor. Once a vendor is selected and the contract drafted, negotiated, and entered into, it is important to have an ongoing evaluation of the project/service to ensure the deliverable is meeting the expectations as outlined in the contract.

Project Management Concepts and Applications

> - PHR functional area 1—Business Management
>   - Dealing with situations that are uncertain, unclear, or chaotic
> - SPHR functional area 1—Leadership and Strategy
>   - Project management (for example, goals, timetables, deliverables, and procedures)

The area of project management represents skills involving planning, executing, controlling, accountability, and lessons learned. Project management involves working with project evaluation and review technique (PERT) charts, critical path method (CPM) planning processes, and other similar techniques to guide a project through to completion while controlling resources, manpower, and deliverables. For HR professionals, managing projects is a necessary skill and factor for success. Projects can occur in just about every area of the HRCI functional areas.

Business management requirements present only one type of project management opportunity. Other functional areas are also filled with opportunities for project management. Employee and labor relations offers a chance to apply project management techniques to contract negotiations. Learning and development offers the opportunity to apply project management skills to new course development requirements.

Budgeting, Accounting, and Financial Concepts

- PHR functional area 2—Talent Planning and Acquisition
  - Planning concepts and terms (for example, succession planning, forecasting)
- PHR functional area 4—Total Rewards
  - Budgeting, payroll, and accounting practices related to compensation and benefits
- SPHR functional area 1—Leadership and Strategy
  - Budgeting, accounting, and financial concepts (for example, evaluating financial statements, budgets, accounting terms, and cost management)

Business competence is a requirement of HR professionals just as it is of any other member of senior management. It is necessary for HR professionals to be able to create and manage within a financial budget, understand accounting reports, and be able to discuss financing issues. Chief executive officers (CEOs) expect HR professionals to have a grasp of business concerns and be able to express in financial terms how HR programs are contributing to the "bottom line." HR programs often must be justified in business terms so senior executives can understand the impact they will have on organizational financial results. There are several types of budget development processes. The most used are zero-based budgeting and historical information budgeting.

Types of Organizational Structures

For Example: Matrix, Hierarchy

- PHR functional area 1—Business Management
  - Business elements of an organization (for example, other functions and departments, products, competition, customers, technology, demographics, culture, processes, safety, security)
- SPHR functional area 1—Leadership and Strategy
  - Business elements of an organization (for example, products, competition, customers, technology, demographics, culture, processes, safety, security)

HR professionals can make a significant contribution to the organization when designing its structure. There are three key types of structures employers usually implement: functional, divisional, and matrix. Other structures less used are product-based and geographic. Functional structures are those that group organizational segments according to their purpose—for example, production, accounting, and shipping. Divisional structures group organizational segments according to product type or market segments—for example, large-screen TV division, computer monitor division, audio equipment division, Pacific states division, and Midwest division. Matrix organizations rely on relationships to determine the structure. For example, a reorganization task force can pull members from traditional accounting, HR, manufacturing, marketing, and other functional areas. Matrix organizations can often create situations where individuals report to more than one supervisor.

Environmental Scanning Concepts and Applications

For Example: Strengths, Weaknesses, Opportunities, and Threats (SWOT) and Political, Economic, Social, and Technological (PEST)

- PHR functional area 3—Learning and Development
  - Organizational development (OD) methods, motivation methods, and problem-solving techniques
- SPHR functional area 1—Leadership and Strategy
  - Methods of gathering data for strategic planning purposes (for example, strengths, weaknesses, opportunities, and threats [SWOT], and political, economic, social, and technological [PEST])

Environmental scanning is the process of monitoring and detecting events or conditions that will have an impact on the employer's organization. Over time, the process has been structured by some scientists to produce methods that can be applied by laypeople in HR management and other functional areas. SWOT and PEST are two examples of methods for environmental scanning. The degree to which the internal environment of an organization matches its external environment is expressed as its *strategic fit*. Strengths and weaknesses are considered by the method as internal elements, while opportunities and threats are considered external elements. PEST analysis has been expanded since its inception as a strategic management tool and can be represented by the acronym STEEPLED: social, technological, environmental, economic, political, legal, ethics, demographics. Through quantification and anecdotal examples, this method allows for unmasking issues to be considered in strategically preparing for the organization's future.

Needs Assessment and Analysis

- PHR functional area 3—Learning and Development
  - Instructional design principles and processes (for example, needs analysis, process flow mapping)
- SPHR functional area 3—Learning and Development
  - Instructional design principles and processes (for example, needs analysis, content chunking, process flow mapping)

Needs assessment is a structured process of measuring the difference between current status and the desired level or quantity of any given organizational condition. A needs assessment can become input to strategic planning or training program development. It can also be done in support of individual developmental planning for career enhancement.

The following are the most common steps in needs assessment analysis:

1. Describe the objective.

2. Define the current condition.

3. Conduct a gap analysis.

4. Prioritize a list of what must occur.

5. Determine options.

6. Evaluate best options with cost-budget associations.

7. Recommend a solution and action plan.

Adult Learning Processes

- PHR functional area 3—Learning and Development
  - Adult learning processes
- SPHR functional area 3—Learning and Development
  - Adult learning processes

Recent decades have brought us a continuing flow of behavioral science about how adult learning is different from children's learning. While the working of brain synapses may be similar, there are huge differences in what it takes to motivate students to learn. Adults must be shown "what's in it for them." What benefit will they derive from their efforts to learn new materials? HR professionals are often thrust into the role of instructor and must understand the adult learning process so they are able to properly facilitate the training experience for their employees.

Malcolm Knowles identified the following characteristics of adult learning:

- **Self-concept**   Moving from dependency on others to autonomy and self-directed learning

- **Experiential learning**   Drawing on past experience for future learning

- **Readiness to learn**   Needs specific to the current condition

- **Orientation to learning**   Applying information in current situations to solve immediate issues

- **Motivation**   Coming from a source of personal inspiration and desire versus outside conditions

Knowles also identified three types of learners:

- **Auditory learners** A process of learning that suits those who have a preference to "hear" information
- **Visual learners** A process of learning that suits those who have a preference to see information to commit it to memory
- **Tactile/kinesthetic learners** A process that suits those who have a preference to be physical, involving a sense of touch and hands-on learning

Training Techniques

- PHR functional area 3—Learning and Development
  - Training program facilitation, techniques, and delivery
- SPHR functional area 3—Learning and Development
  - Training and facilitation techniques

There are many training delivery techniques. Some of them are as follows:

- Classroom lecture
- Online computer-based training (CBT)
- On-the-job training
- Facilitation
- Small work group assignments
- Self-study

Chapter Review

This chapter has provided you with an overview and basic understanding of the concepts and applications that are common to PHR and SPHR knowledge requirements. As you read the specific topic information in Parts II and III, notice how these core knowledge statements have implications in several functional areas. There are volumes of books, courses of study, and journals that address the many subject topics presented here. An understanding of the concepts is what will be required for the HRCI exams.

Questions

1. There are some areas of HR knowledge that are known as _____ _____ because they apply to all HR professionals at all levels.

2. Needs assessment and analysis is an area of required knowledge that applies to this functional area:

  A. Employee communications

  B. Ethical and professional standards

  C. Instructional design principles and processes

  D. Environmental scanning concepts and applications

3. Needs assessment can be applied to which of the following processes? (Choose three.)

  A. Benefits planning, vacation assessments, attendance programs, and employee training needs

  B. Strategic planning, public relations, and emergency awareness

  C. Published industrial results

  D. Staffing forecasts, training planning, and budgeting

4. Vendor selection can involve which of the following list of activities?

  A. Reference checking, financial assessment, comparison with similar projects

  B. Interviewing, background checking, financial stability assessment

  C. Appointment of contract manager, review of financial statements, review of similar projects

  D. Development of RFPs, evaluation of match to project requirements for each vendor, background checking, financial stability

5. Organizational documentation requirements can impact these functional areas of professional HR management:

  A. Parking policy, payroll compliance, orientation

  B. EEO/AA, employee records management, performance management

  C. Magazine subscriptions, amusement park discount programs, forms management

  D. Vacation selection system, cafeteria menu planning, parking lot space assignments

6. HR professionals must be concerned about adult learning processes because they impact these areas of the organization:

  A. Human resource development, training and development, compensation and benefits

  B. Payroll, employee orientation programs, training and development

  C. Job description development, vacation planning, government compliance

  D. Safety compliance, compensation and benefits, employee training

7. Which of the following is not considered a business management competence requirement for HR professionals?

   A. Performing a standard deviation analysis of employee movement

   B. Creating and managing within a financial budget

   C. Understanding financial reports

   D. Discussing financial issues

8. Employee training is a function that falls within human resources development. The following are generally accepted training techniques:

   A. Texting, lecturing, small group discussions

   B. Reading, group discussions, e-mail

   C. Lecturing, self-paced online, subgroup exercises

   D. On-the-job, classroom, recess

9. Yvette has told her supervisor that she feels her co-workers are harassing her because she is Hispanic. They point to her and laugh, exclude her from their table in the break room, and have damaged her work so it has had to be redone. She believes they have also punctured her car tire on more than one occasion. Is this really illegal harassment?

   A. Who can say if it is illegal or not? It sure sounds like it is inappropriate behavior.

   B. Harassment can only be sexual harassment. You can't be harassed because of your Hispanic heritage.

   C. Even though Hispanic is an ethnicity, it is treated like a race when harassment is concerned. She may have a case against her co-workers because of their behavior.

   D. Since Hispanic is an ethnicity, it is excluded from racial comparisons and therefore cannot be the reason cited for the harassment complaint.

10. Jolene has come to the HR department to file a complaint of race discrimination against her boss, who is Asian. She says he won't allow her to go to a key training program simply because she is White and he wants to train the Asians first. He says to her, "You can't complain because you're White." What would you tell Jolene?

   A. Jolene's boss is right. She can't file a race complaint because she is White.

   B. You should really speak with the company attorney before even talking with Jolene about this complaint. She needs to find out whether it would be alright to accept the complaint before doing anything else.

   C. The only comparison with White is Black. Asians can't be the cause of an illegal race complaint when Jolene is White.

   D. Everyone has a race, and White is a government-designated race. Treating someone differently because of their race is not legal. You should accept Jolene's complaint.

11. Wilmington is a newly appointed first-level supervisor. Riley knows him fairly well because she was involved in the discussions about his promotion. He now wants to talk with her about a problem he is having with two of his workers. One is Black, and one is Native American. The Black employee is saying he was not given a bonus check because of his race. He wants to have his money. The Native American employee received a bonus check. What would be a legitimate reason for withholding the bonus payment to the Black employee? (Choose two.)

   A. 15 days of absence from work beyond using all of the paid time off available

   B. Missing three project deadlines

   C. Bringing cakes and cupcakes to share every Friday

   D. Passed latest training program with highest score in the class

   E. Announced she would quit if she didn't get her bonus

12. You are asked to prepare a presentation for the senior management and executive team on the subject of the updated insurance benefit packages available for the coming year. What should you consider the highest priority for your presentation?

   A. Finding the most dazzling PowerPoint slide templates

   B. Getting some scientific research references to support your information

   C. Being sure all the information you present is up-to-date and accurate

   D. Getting some slides from the insurance companies to help with formatting

13. Your boss asks you to prepare a memo that will be distributed to all employees explaining the new company policy on sick leave. You hate writing, especially something that will be as widely seen as this. What should you do?

   A. Plead with your boss to give the assignment to one of your colleagues.

   B. Hunker down and start learning what facts you need to convey and design the best way for that to happen.

   C. Delegate the assignment to your support clerk. She writes well.

   D. Go to a friend who works at a different company and ask if they have anything like this that you can use as a model.

14. Charlene has come in to ask you to give her a set of labels with employee home addresses on them. She wants to send some new marketing materials to everyone in hopes of selling her beauty aid products. What will you tell Charlene?

   A. Sure. No problem. We can get them to you in a couple of days.

   B. It will never happen. We can't spend the money on labels for such projects.

   C. It would be unethical for us to provide home address labels for employees to anyone, even Charlene. It is a violation of privacy standards.

   D. Without approval from the organization's CEO there is no way HR is going to be able to agree to issue Charlene the address labels.

15. One of the organization's HR supervisors has told a line manager that it is OK to use the company copy machine to make flyers for their new business. The company doesn't mind, and it won't amount to much money. What is your response to this advice?

   A. I will have a serious conversation with the HR supervisor. It is not acceptable to suggest the company will permit use of the copy machine for personal business. If the company did approve of such use, it would need to extend that same offer to every employee.

   B. I will have a talk with the HR supervisor and tell that person to keep such things really quiet. We don't want a general announcement about people who are doing such things.

   C. I will ignore the issue. It isn't such a big deal anyway.

   D. I will terminate the HR supervisor on the spot.

16. Everyone seems to be talking about leadership these days. Why is it so important? What is leadership anyway?

   A. Leadership is someone giving orders and charging off to whatever the goal is.

   B. Leadership is briefing everyone about the goal and then sending them off to get there.

   C. Leadership is getting people to understand the goal and willingly (voluntarily) following the leader to that goal.

   D. Leadership is always taking credit for the achievements of the group.

17. HR reporting tools can include:

   A. Applicant tracking, learning management, U.S. Census Bureau requests

   B. HRIS, learning management, U.S. Postal Service master mailing list

   C. Employee self-service systems, learning management systems, HRIS

   D. HRIM, applicant tracking, production schedules

18. Employer risks can result in:

   A. Industry reports on collective results

   B. National averages for financial results

   C. Quarterly injury results

   D. Monthly sales results

19. Today, giving employees electronic access to their personal information is more common. When doing so, employers should:

   A. Make sure the records are no more than six to eight months old

   B. Provide a secure access system that will permit employees to see only their own records

    C. Give access to union representatives so they will be able to reconcile their union dues payments

    D. Permit employees to make any changes they want on their records

20. Quantitative measurements can include all but:

    A. Number of days a job requisition is open before being filled

    B. Accidents by department

    C. Job performance decision-making ratings

    D. Number of people attending new employee orientation in their first week

21. Qualitative measurements can include all but:

    A. Ratings of employee promotability

    B. Workers' compensation insurance claims per quarter

    C. Employee survey ratings of working conditions

    D. Opinion ratings of employee cafeteria offerings

22. The ability to perceive, control, and evaluate emotions is known as _____ _____.

23. Job descriptions:

    A. Are required by law

    B. Have no real practical value

    C. Can be helpful in defending against union claims of work hours violations

    D. Can be helpful in processing requests for job accommodation

24. Is it permissible to create outreach and recruiting programs specifically targeted at females and minorities?

    A. Yes. Anything to bring the number of women and minorities up in the organization.

    B. No. All focus on race or sex (gender) when recruiting is illegal.

    C. Yes. Targeting by race and sex (gender) is acceptable when creating candidate pools.

    D. No. Even if the quantity of females and minorities is really low, any openly targeted system would be illegal.

25. Employee personnel file records should include:

    A. Medical information about disabilities

    B. Investigation file information about complaints

    C. Personal training history

    D. Detailed security clearance information

26. Match the following recordkeeping requirements with the laws requiring them.

    A. Employee race and sex

    B. Right to work in the United States

    C. Social Security number

    D. Serious injury and death

    (1) Occupational Safety and Health Act

    (2) Immigration Reform and Control Act

    (3) Internal Revenue Service Regulations

    (4) Fair Labor Standards Act

27. Form I-9 is used to prove employees' _____ and _____ in this country.

28. Three key types of structures employers usually implement are _____, _____, and _____.

29. Two methods of environmental scanning are

    A. PERT, CPM

    B. SWOT, PEST

    C. CCRG, USGS

    D. USDA, FICA

30. Which of the following is not a type of adult learner?

    A. Tactile/kinesthetic learner

    B. Psychic absorption learner

    C. Auditory learner

    D. Visual learner

Answers

1. **Core knowledge**

2. **C.** Needs assessment and analysis apply to instructional design.

3. **A, B, D.** Published industrial results are not subject to needs assessment.

4. **D.** RFPs should be the foundation of vendor-assigned projects. Vendor selection should be based on the match of vendor capabilities to RFP requirements, background investigation, and financial stability.

5. **B.** In fact, all of these things are going to require documentation. The most correct answer is B because it has the widest impact across the employer's organization.

6. **A.** Like the previous question, this is the correct answer because it has the widest impact on an employer's organization.

7. A. Standard deviation analysis is important for disparity analysis but does not involve business management competencies.

8. C. Texting, e-mail, and recess are not commonly accepted training techniques.

9. C. Race is a protected category when harassment is alleged.

10. D. All races are protected against illegal discrimination.

11. A, B. Specific job-related or performance results are legitimate reasons for withholding a bonus payment as long as others who are similarly situated are treated in the same way.

12. C. HR credibility rests on the accuracy, honesty, and truthfulness of its information.

13. B. If your boss recognizes that you need to practice your writing skills, this assignment may be designed for that purpose. Delegating to someone else or trying to get out of it some other way would not be appropriate.

14. C. Employee home addresses are considered private and confidential information. Giving them out to someone, even an employee, for use in a private venture is unethical.

15. A. It is important to talk with the supervisor about the precedent being set when such permission is given to one employee. That permission may also violate company policy.

16. C. Getting people to willingly follow toward the accomplishment of a specific goal is an ideal leadership skill.

17. C. Employee self-service systems, learning management systems, and the HR information system are all examples of HR reporting tools.

18. C. Quarterly injury results are an example of employer risk tracking.

19. B. Employee access should be limited to their own personal records.

20. C. Ratings for decision-making are a qualitative measurement, not a quantitative one.

21. B. Claims per quarter is a quantitative measurement.

22. Emotional intelligence

23. D. Statements in a job description related to physical and mental job requirements can be helpful in determining what job accommodation can be made when requested by the applicant or employee.

24. C. Targeting by race and gender is acceptable when identifying people to include in a candidate pool. Selecting someone from that candidate pool must be done using nondiscriminatory processes that do not include consideration of race or gender.

25. C. Personal training records should be part of an employee personnel file.

26. A4; B2; C3; D1

27. Identity and **right to work**

28. Functional, divisional, matrix

29. B. SWOT and PEST are the correct response.

30. B. Psychic absorption is not a valid type of adult learner.

Endnotes

1. Bray, Douglas W., Richard J. Campbell, Donald L. Grant, Formative Years in Business: A Long-Term AT&T Study of Managerial Lives, John Wiley & Sons, New York, 1974

2. Rogers, Everett, *Diffusion of Innovations (5th Edition),* Free Press, 2003

3. Barker, Brenda, "Energizing Organizational Readiness," Queen's University (2007). http://irc.queensu.ca/articles/energizing-organizational-readiness

PART II

PHR Body of Knowledge Functional Areas

Business Management

Business Management is the foundation of the overall HR function and an important part of the PHR exam. Twenty percent of the PHR exam will focus on this area of knowledge. A wealth of information is available in case law to guide HR professionals in their compliance with federal legislation and regulations in this topic. Common sense can help as well.

This area of knowledge is where you will find all the information about vision, mission, values, corporate governance, ethics, database tools, change management, and risk management.

The official HRCI Business Management functional area responsibilities and knowledge statements are as follows:

Responsibilities

- Interpret and apply information related to general business environment and industry best practices
- Reinforce the organization's core values and ethical and behavioral expectations through modeling, communication, and coaching
- Understand the role of cross-functional stakeholders in the organization and establish relationships to influence decision-making
- Recommend and implement best practices to mitigate risk (for example, lawsuits, internal/external threats)
- Determine the significance of data for recommending organizational strategies (for example, attrition rates, diversity in hiring, time to hire, time to fill, return on investment [ROI], success of training)

Knowledge Of

- Vision, mission, values, and structure of the organization
- Legislative and regulatory knowledge and procedures
- Corporate governance procedures and compliance
- Employee communications

- Ethical and professional standards
- Business elements of an organization (for example, other functions and departments, products, competition, customers, technology, demographics, culture, processes, safety and security)
- Existing HRIS, reporting tools, and other systems for effective data reporting and analysis
- Change management theory, methods, and application
- Risk management
- Qualitative and quantitative methods and tools for analytics
- Dealing with situations that are uncertain, unclear, or chaotic

Key Legislation Governing Business Management

Now that you've reviewed the Business Management functional area responsibilities and knowledge statements, we recommend you review the federal laws that apply to business management (see Figure 4-1). It would benefit you to refer to Chapter 2 on these specific laws prior to reading any further in this chapter.

While legislation is important, of equal value is the case law that comes from court interpretations. There are no case laws that directly impact the Business Management functional areas of responsibility for HR professionals.

Vision, Mission, Values, and Structure of the Organization

While a great deal of involvement with these organizational components involves senior HR professionals, every HR professional must have a grasp on how these factors interact. Further, it is imperative that each HR expert know how to contribute to and support them.

Vision

An organizational vision statement outlines what the organization wants to be in the future. Normally, this is created by the board of directors, the senior executives, or a combination of the two. It is becoming more common for other employees or managers to have an opportunity to contribute to the creation of the vision statement.

• The Fair Labor Standards Act of 1938	• The Immigration Reform and Control Act of 1986
• Drug-Free Workplace Act of 1988	• The Lilly Ledbetter Fair Pay Act of 2009

Figure 4-1 Key legislation governing business management

A plumbing service could say its vision is to grow into a regional service company that offers the installation, repair, and removal of water and sewer systems to residential and business customers. An aircraft manufacturer could say its vision is to become the foremost private-sector space transportation vehicle provider to U.S. customers.

Mission

An organizational mission statement describes what will be achieved by organizational success. For example, a newspaper may say its mission is to inform readers about local and national events that impact daily living. An auto repair shop could say its mission is to restore damaged or worn vehicles to safe operating condition so they can be safely used on the road.

Values

Every organization has values, whether they are formalized and documented or not. Unstated values will always exist even in the absence of documentation. How are people expected to act within the organization? Does the organization claim "employees are our most valued asset" yet make every decision based on where the next big customer is located rather than the location of its workforce? Following is a list of positive and negative core values (see Table 4-1).

Business Structures and Functions

There are six types of organizational structures:

- Departmental
- Chain of command
- Span of control
- Work specialization
- Centralized or decentralized
- Matrix

Positive Core Values	Negative Core Values
Treating everyone, regardless of position, with respect.	Managers expected to answer text messages or phone calls during vacations.
Innovation, thinking outside paradigms.	Creative tension, challenging everything.
Acting in an environmentally friendly way.	Management personnel arrive prior to non-exempt employees in the morning.
The customer is always right.	Providing preference to parent employees over non-parent employees for vacation requests during school holidays.
Quality and safety first.	Eating and working at desk during lunch break.

Table 4-1   Driving Core Organizational Values

Departmental

For this structure, tasks are divided into separate duties, grouping people and jobs together. The purpose is so that work can be coordinated. It can be functional in nature, divisional, or matrix.

Chain of Command

This is a structure where an employee typically reports to one manager in an up-down format, with a clear line of decisions and authority. Chain of command is becoming less recognized in organizations today because, more and more often, organizations are pushing decision-making down matrix lines, which causes the line of authority to look more lateral.

Span of Control

This organizational structure refers to the number of individuals who report to a single supervisor. It's hierarchical in nature through a chain of command, with executives at the top, managers, then supervisors, and then direct reports—much like a pyramid. In organizations where many workers are skilled and require little supervision, employees may report to one supervisor. This would be considered a "flat organization."

Work Specialization

Work specialization was first associated with the assembly line. It is where tasks are divided into specific jobs and workers are considered skilled labor. It may offer a more efficient manner of productivity, but it can lead to worker boredom. Organizations using this organizational structure today will typically rotate job functions on a regular basis, training the workers in skills that add variety to their tasks.

Centralized or Decentralized

To centralize or decentralize, that seems to be the question and the cycle of several long-standing organizations. Centralizing pulls decision-making authority to a central level of management, such as a headquarters. Decentralizing is pushing the authority level and decisions out to units, such as regional divisions.

The centralizing and decentralizing continuum is also applicable to HR departments. With decentralized structures, corporate headquarters will create policy and develop programs; rollout and applications are then carried out by the HR staff in their regional divisions. When it is centralized, HR headquarters makes the policy and coordinates the rollout activities or administrative functions.

Matrix

Matrix structures create a dual, rather than a single, chain of command. A function such as HR reports to the local division executive at a facility, along with a direct reporting function to the head of HR in the headquarters office, which is typically located in another geographical area. As a result, the HR manager at the division location has two managers, with neither manager having a superior role over the other in this reporting relationship. A huge disadvantage for this type of reporting relationship is the potential for conflicting priorities between the division and the headquarters. The employee with two direct superiors is attempting to follow the direction of one, and the other is competing for their priority. It can be a bit of a tug-of-war.

Legislative and Regulatory Knowledge and Procedures

Legislation affecting employers can come from any level of government. Federal legislation comes from Congress. It includes laws shown in Chapter 2 for which employers must maintain compliance. States also pass laws affecting employers. Consider how many states have stricter overtime rules than the Fair Labor Standards Act. Some states have laws governing unemployment insurance benefits and workers' compensation. Some cities and counties offer another layer of legislation that places yet more controls on employers. San Francisco, for example, requires a significantly higher hourly rate for minimum wage than either the federal or state laws require.

Legislation

Employment-based legislation always seems to be a "work in progress" at both the state and federal levels. Some laws, such as the Equal Pay Act, require equal pay for men and women doing the same work in essentially the same working conditions. Other laws are meant to modify or amend existing provisions for some employment condition. An example is the Americans with Disabilities Act Amendments Act. Originally, Congress passed the Americans with Disabilities Act (ADA) in 1990 with a definition of *disabled* that courts later found to be quite limiting. The U.S. Supreme Court ruled in several cases that *disabled* was a more restrictive term than was being applied in practice. Under the case rulings by the high court, employees would not be able to receive protections under the law. So, Congress went back to work and passed the ADA Amendments Act in 2008. It said when determining whether someone is disabled, there may be no consideration of mitigating circumstances. (Mitigating circumstances include medication, physical prosthetics, and other similar devices or methods to permit the disabled person to function with some normalcy.) The only specific exclusion from the definition of disability according to Congress involves eyeglasses and contact lenses as mitigations for vision difficulties.

HR professionals are key players in monitoring these legislative processes. Determining what new proposals are being introduced and when they get passed, signed into law, and become effective is often the job of an HR professional. Your company attorney can help with this process, but there are many sources available to help HR professionals in this task. Some of the most readily available are provided by the Society for Human Resource Management (SHRM). Members are given periodic updates about newly introduced congressional bills. SHRM even provides HR professionals to testify before congressional committees during the approval process. Some provisions are supported, while others that are onerous to employers and/or employees are not supported. If you are not now a member of SHRM, give it some serious consideration. It is a wonderful resource for all HR professionals. But you must be a member to access those resources.

Monitoring Legislative and Regulatory Issues

Some industry associations have legislative monitors or lobbyists to keep track of state and federal legislatures. It is only the larger employers who find it beneficial to employ their own representatives to the legislative process. Collective funding for common interests is often quite effective, and it is done by most industries, including the pharmaceutical, automobile, high-technology, and the lumber and paper industries. Many more can be added to that list.

When legislation is proposed that will have an impact on the employers within an industry, these representatives work with legislators and their staffs to understand the impact proposals will have on the work done by people in those groups. It is common for these discussions to take place and for lobbyists to try to convince legislative representatives that their industry's interests should be considered when considering legislative action.

Individual employers may find it advantageous to perform their own monitoring of state and federal legislatures, so they participate by testifying at hearings or submitting comments regarding their suggestions for new laws.

Federal regulations are published in the *Federal Register* and thus are available for review by the general public. When new regulations are developed, opportunities are available for employers to offer comments on the impact those regulations will have on them. It is frequently in the best interest of employers to participate in that process, yet few actually do. All employers should be alert to what is going on in Washington, D.C., and in state capitals.

The Legislative Process

While each state legislature follows much the same process, for federal law when a legislative proposal is passed by both the House and the Senate and approved by the president, it becomes law. The following are the steps that are followed (see Figure 4-2):

1. Bills introduced in the House are designated HR, while bills introduced in the Senate are designated SB. Any member can introduce a piece of legislation.

2. One of either the House or Senate committees, depending on which is the originating chamber, is assigned to consider the bill.

3. Either a subcommittee or the full committee considers the bill, marks it up, and votes on whether to pass it along to the full House or Senate. Subcommittees must report out on the bill to the full committee by a majority vote. The committee must report out on the bill to the full House or Senate. The "report out" includes a recommendation for passage.

4. The bill goes to the full House or Senate for a vote by all members. Amendments can be made by representatives or senators. If an amendment passes, it becomes part of the bill. A vote of the entire body will result in passage by simple majority or defeat if a majority is not achieved.

5. The bill is then sent to the other body for consideration. The same process is followed. Committees and subcommittees are involved and may hold hearings to listen to experts talk about the proposed law. Once passed by the committee, the bill goes to the full body for consideration.

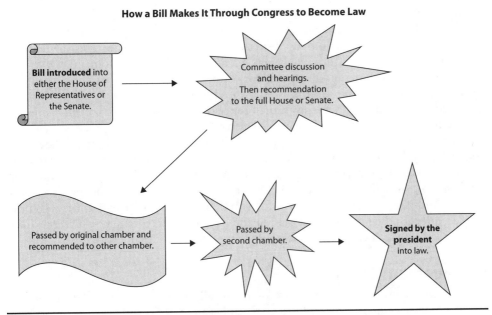

How a Bill Makes It Through Congress to Become Law

Bill **introduced** into either the House of Representatives or the Senate.

Committee discussion and hearings. Then recommendation to the full House or Senate.

Passed by original chamber and recommended to other chamber.

Passed by second chamber.

Signed by the president into law.

Figure 4-2   How a bill makes it through Congress to become a law

6. If the Senate version and the House version of the bill are different, the bill goes to a joint committee of both bodies to resolve those differences. It is now called a *conference bill*. When a final joint agreement is reached, the bill goes back to each body for another vote.

7. Once passed by both congressional bodies, the bill goes to the president for signature. If the president signs the bill, it becomes law in the time specified in the law. If the president opposes the bill, the president can veto it. It then goes back to Congress for a veto override consideration. If the president takes no action after Congress has adjourned its second session, it is a pocket veto, and the legislation dies.

8. Congress can override the president's veto by a two-thirds roll call vote of the members who are present (meeting sufficient numbers for a quorum) in each house.

Regulatory Knowledge and Procedures

Regulations are rules that are established by governmental agencies or departments. The rules tell how the laws passed by Congress will be implemented. The Civil Rights Act of 1964 outlined what was permitted and what was prohibited employer behavior in Title VII. (A *title* in a law is like a chapter in a book.) Title VII applies to equal employment opportunity. Title III applies to desegregation of public facilities. Title IV speaks to desegregation of public education. All in all, there are 11 titles in that law. Also created by that law was the Equal Employment Opportunity Commission (EEOC). The EEOC was designed as the enforcement agency with authority to investigate and remedy complaints of illegal discrimination based on any of the protected categories in the Civil Rights Act of 1964. Out of the Civil Rights Act and the EEOC have come rules that govern nondiscrimination requirements, nonharassment requirements, and employee testing validation requirements. You must know everything about these regulations so you can be sure your employees are given the proper protections but also so you can assure your employer that you have a reasonable grasp of the risks to the corporation.

HR professionals are expected to know and, more importantly, understand the regulations promulgated by the government's executive branch. It is your responsibility to track developments as they happen and react with compliance efforts that will permit your employer to maintain its legal position. There is no excuse for not knowing. It's part of the job. And you are accountable for it. If you don't have a company attorney who can provide you periodic updates to legislation and regulation developments, subscribe to an information source such as Bloomberg's Bureau of National Affairs (BNA).[1]

Management Skills

Management skills were first measured scientifically in the American Telephone and Telegraph Management Progress Study,[2] which began in 1956 and lasted for more than 30 years. It followed the careers of managers within the Bell System, first in Michigan Bell and then nationally. That study led to the first industrial assessment centers, measuring the amount of management skills exhibited by participants in the assessment process.

The program measured the following skills:

- Oral and written communication skill
- Human relations skill (later called *leadership skill*)
- Personal impact (forcefulness and likeability)
- Perception (environmental and perception of people)
- Creativity
- Self-objectivity
- Social objectivity
- Behavior flexibility
- Goal flexibility
- Organization and planning
- Decision-making (willingness to make decisions and the effectiveness of decisions)

In addition, nonskills were observed and measured. These included things such as the following:

- Tolerance of uncertainty
- Resistance to stress
- Energy

- Range of interests
- Primacy of work
- Inner work standards
- Need for approval of supervisors
- Need for approval of peers
- Need for advancement

There are other functions involved in managing. These typically involve four identified management functions that the early management theorist Henri Fayol identified and are the basis of most of today's management theories.

Planning

Forecasting, setting goals and objects, determining actions and courses of direction—these activities are key to keeping HR activities in a proactive position rather than a reactive one. The HR department needs to perform strategic planning for its function to ensure that its programs and activities are aligned with the organization's needs. Having a big-picture view of how HR activities intertwine with the organization's objectives is necessary.

Organizing

Organizing is the process of creating order out of chaos. It involves collecting process steps and information about the desired goal and then structuring the methods to achieve the goal. Ordering and sequencing are done while organizing.

HR professionals have huge organizational responsibilities. There are employee data systems to construct, benefit programs to identify, open enrollment to conduct, the interview selection process to design, and payroll processing to handle. HR professionals must create structures that effectively align the people of an organization with the organization's goals and administration.

Directing

These days, directing work in an organization is thought of as leadership. It involves getting people to willingly do what is wanted or needed. Even in military organizations, it is rare for managers/officers to issue blunt orders. In most situations, it is appropriate to lead a group of people to the desired end without dictating. (That doesn't necessarily apply to combat.)

Once a goal has been determined and a path chosen, the task of directing requires a manager to encourage people to willingly do what is necessary by engaging people in activities that contribute to the desired business outcomes.

Controlling

The function of controlling involves a monitoring activity to ensure that everything is carried out according to a plan. Managers monitor their organizations' activities and results, determine the difference between what was planned and what actually happened, and then take corrective action to redirect the organization to the goals.

Corporate Governance Procedures and Compliance

There are some differences for compliance if the organization has only a few people or if it is a multinational enterprise. There are considerations to be made for financial and fiduciary compliance, human resource compliance, and sales and marketing compliance.

Financial Compliance

The Sarbanes-Oxley Act of 2002 attempted to plug the holes on many corrupt practices in the financial industry. Publicly traded companies are captured within the provisions of this law, and certain reporting requirements are imposed. Corporate officers are personally liable for the accuracy of the reporting. Financial control systems are required, and their effectiveness must be verified.

The Internal Revenue Service imposes additional regulatory requirements in the form of payroll taxes and employer income taxes. Noncompliance can be a criminal offense. Your chief financial officer is the person responsible for these financial oversights.

Human Resource Compliance

The Fair Labor Standards Act (FLSA) requires employers to maintain employment records for hours worked, race and sex identification, and work permits for minors. The Civil Rights Act of 1964 requires employers to validate all employment screening processes, including written tests and interviews. The Equal Pay Act requires employers to confirm that men and women are being paid the same if they are doing the same work under the same or similar conditions. The Americans with Disabilities Act requires employers to provide job accommodations when requested and when it would not impose an undue hardship on the employer. The Occupational Safety and Health Act (OSHA) requires employers to monitor work locations to assure they are safe, correcting any safety problems before an injury can happen. It also requires posting results of the employer's safety results in most cases. The Immigration Reform and Control Act of 1986 requires each new employee to complete Form I-9 proving they have the right to work in this country and that they are who they say they are. Employers are responsible for confirming the documentation presented meets the requirements as specified on the form.

These are only some of the laws requiring human resource involvement in compliance. HR professionals are responsible for many other such requirements. See the list of laws in Chapter 2 for more about compliance requirements as they relate to human resource management.

Sales and Marketing Compliance

You might not think that people who are outselling the employer's products or services would have any worries about compliance. Yet they do. The Foreign Corrupt Practices Act of 1997 prohibits American companies from making bribery payments to foreign officials for the purpose of obtaining or keeping business. What used to be a common sales technique is now illegal. The False Claims Act of 1863 makes it illegal for organizations to sell defective food and arms to the military using fictitious records to create the sale.

Ethical and Professional Standards

Ethical standards apply to both the employer organization and the individuals within it. HR professionals are expected to set an example for other employees when it comes to ethical behavior. If HR professionals behave unethically, there is little hope that the general employee population will feel compelled to do any differently.

Corporate Ethics

Corporate ethics define the moral principles and values that establish an organization's expectations of conduct from its leadership and employees. Where corporate values define desired behaviors, corporate ethics are the code for attitude and norms. Identifying an organization's ethics and establishing them go hand in hand with creating its vision, mission, and values, helping clearly identify what an ethical workplace is for new hires and existing employees.

Organizations have a responsibility and even a legal requirement thanks to the Sarbanes-Oxley Act (SOX, see Chapter 2) to interact with its employees, stakeholders, and communities in an ethical and trustworthy manner. Responsibilities are wide and vary, ranging from decisions involving local community environmental hazard notifications to the treatment of customers or employees with truth and integrity. HR's role in organizational ethics is an important one because ethical issues raised are generally about honesty, truthfulness, fairness, social responsibility, and legal governance, typically coming from within the workforce.

SOX made many of the practices of organizations come under added scrutiny, providing penalties and even jail time for executives for violations. The following are scrutinized under SOX:

- *Insider trading,* which is illegal and monitored by the Securities and Exchange Commission, occurs when investors receive information that could be known only by internal organizational sources and this information impacts buy-sell shares of that company. For example, your benefits manager in HR discloses a planned merger (which has not been made public yet and would likely increase the value of shares) to your third-party employee benefit firm's account executive. If that account executive were to increase his or her own shares and/or share that information with friends who invested, this would be considered insider trading.

- *Conflicts of interest* happen when either an individual or the organization is involved in a situation of multiple interests, one of which could possibly influence or corrupt motivation. For example, an executive in an organization has a spouse with a separate business that provides products or services to the organization, and that executive has a say in awarding the contract.

- *Kickbacks, bribes,* and *payoffs* are common terms used for payoffs of some nature for doing something such as awarding a contract. For example, buyers in the procurement department of an organization can get caught in this unethical behavior if they accept tickets to the Super Bowl from a vendor in exchange for awarding the procurement contract to that vendor. Acceptance of gifts by an employee and the amount of the gift need to be clearly defined in a policy.

PART II

NOTE   Not all unethical behavior may be illegal.

Personal Ethics

Unethical behavior is something most employers abhor. Given the U.S. laws that prohibit kickbacks to government representatives or bribes to foreign institutions, ethics is a high-level expectation in the employment relationship. It is compliance with not only the letter of the law but the intent of the law that counts.

Here are some examples of employer expectations that might be included in a code of conduct. Each of these would be a violation of that code of conduct.

- Misusing company time (not focusing on work production for the entire workday)
- Bullying or other abusive behavior
- Theft of any kind (from supplies to misusing a company car)
- Lying to anyone in the workplace about anything
- Taking credit for work done by someone else
- Undermining or sabotaging someone else's work
- Following your boss' instructions even though you know it to be wrong
- Deliberate deception of a customer, vendor, media representative, boss, or co-worker

SHRM Code of Ethics

The Society for Human Resource Management (SHRM) has created a Code of Ethics[3] that all SHRM members are obliged to follow. Other HR professionals, not members of SHRM, would be well advised to keep these guidelines in mind also. Here are some of the guideline highlights:

- Adhere to the highest standards of ethical and professional behavior
- Measure the effectiveness of HR in contributing to or achieving organizational goals
- Comply with the law
- Work consistent with the values of the profession
- Strive to achieve the highest levels of service, performance, and social responsibility
- Advocate for the appropriate use and appreciation of human beings as employees
- Advocate openly and within the established forums for debate to influence decision-making and results
- Measure the effectiveness of HR in contributing to or achieving organizational goals

- Be ethical; act ethically in every professional interaction
- Question pending individual and group actions when necessary to ensure that decisions are ethical and are implemented in an ethical manner
- Seek expert guidance if ever in doubt about the ethical propriety of a situation
- Through teaching and mentoring, champion the development of others as ethical leaders in the profession and in organizations

Ethics Investigations

SHRM's *Business Literacy Glossary of Terms* defines *business ethics* as "A philosophy principle concerned with opinions about appropriate and inappropriate business conduct or behavior by individuals or groups of individuals." Some organizations are subject to legal expectations about ethical behavior. (See Chapter 2 and the Sarbanes-Oxley Act of 2002.)

It is fairly common these days for employers to have telephone hotlines for employees to report instances of unethical behavior. Once an issue is reported, the employer can investigate and resolve any problems that may exist.

Behavior is influenced by rewards, so it is critical that HR professionals be sure to think through how behavior is rewarded. For example, are sales representatives told that they should reach their sales quotas "at all costs"? If that is the case, there may be some incentive for people to cut corners and do things that aren't exactly proper. Some people may find it reasonable to do things that aren't even legal to reach their quotas. That disconnect between rewards and behavioral expectations is something to guard against.

Business Elements of an Organization

There are typically common elements that make up each enterprise regardless of what type of business or organization is involved. It can be a nonprofit community service organization, a for-profit entrepreneurial organization, a multinational corporation, or a governmental agency.

Here are some of those elements.

Products

In the broadest sense every organization has some output, be it a physical product or a service. Some organizations produce giant flat-screen TVs. Other organizations provide shelter for the homeless. Still others offer legal or accounting consulting. Whatever the output is, that suggests a primary reason for the organization's existence.

Competition

It is a rare organization that lacks competition. Most companies and community service organizations have some form of competition. Think of the local hospice organization, the hospital volunteers, and the local church charity. Each of them is likely to have a retail outlet for the donations of clothing and household goods they receive. Sales at their store support their charitable operations. And they are in competition with one another.

They need to consider how to survive in the face of that competition. For-profit organizations face the same problem. Even the government in some instances has competitors. Consider organizations that see a need to deliver training on coping with government enforcement procedures. Law firms often fill that need. In recent times, the government has responded with new educational programs it offers for free to its target enforcement population.

Customers

Customers can be people or other business entities. When General Motors sells trucks to the military, the government is its customer. It can sell the same trucks to state and local governments, school districts, and large corporations. Each of those entities becomes a customer when the truck transaction happens. An accounting firm sells its services to its clients. Each of them is a customer. When a local church serves lunch to the homeless, each of those individuals is a customer.

Technology

One pervasive element of employer organizations these days is technology. From computers on each desk to storage of data in "the cloud," it is impossible to conduct business without technology. People are paying their bills at Starbucks each morning by waving their cell phone at a terminal on the counter next to the Danish. There are experiments being done with self-serve grocery markets that know who you are by the phone signature you carry. You select your products and walk out. You are automatically billed for the selections you have added to your shopping cart. Uber and Lyft respond to your cell phone call for rides. Your account is billed automatically when you get out of the car at your destination. All of this technology is relatively new to the world. And it will be joined by new developments as time passes.

Demographics

Look at the demographics of U.S. employer organizations 40 years ago. You will find few, if any, disabled workers. The number of working women was considerably lower than it is today. Shifting demographics are driving diversity management programs, so employers can take advantage of these rich people resources.

Culture

Sum up the idea of culture and it can be said it is "the way we do things around here." If your employer places great emphasis on safety, it will be a primary focus in every staff meeting and tailgate get-together. If employees are included in developing plans for future expansion, that is something that will impact morale. What does the boss emphasize? More importantly, what does the boss reward? If a bank rewards its loan officers for opening accounts, people can get the wrong idea and begin cheating by opening accounts for people who didn't request them. Culture and rewards go hand in hand.

Processes

Processes are the "how" of goal achievement. They represent the way in which we get to where we are going.

- **Manufacturing** Production process, quality assurance process
- **Finance** Billing process, expense reimbursement process
- **Employment** Application process, drug testing process
- **Banking** Audit trail process, security of accounts process
- **HR** Employee data tracking process, policy development process
- **Compliance** Form I-9 audit process, IRS reporting process

Safety and Security

Here you will find risk analysis, identification of safety threats, workplace violence prevention programs, injury and illness prevention programs (IIPPs), and domestic violence issues. These days, every employer should have a crisis management plan in place for dealing with a workplace shooting event. Once the event begins, it will be too late. All employees need to know how to react, protecting themselves and their co-workers. Executives need to know who will act as a company spokesperson. Planning is critical for personal and employer survival.[4]

Other Functions and Departments

Sometimes functions are not large enough to warrant staff support. So, having someone on the payroll for a full year to work on something for only a few weeks is not cost effective. An example is creating and updating an annual set of affirmative action plans. This is a specialty that every employer doesn't need to have on staff. There are plenty of consultants available for hire that can do the project for a lot less than it would cost to have an employee on the payroll.

Likewise, having a department dedicated to compliance with government regulations may not be a viable notion either. It is easy to hire a law firm to conduct a SOX compliance review or use a certified public accountant (CPA) to assess compliance with IRS rules. Such decisions about organizational elements must be made based on the business case that can support them.

Existing HRIS, Reporting Tools, and Other Systems for Effective Data Reporting and Analysis

Performing data tracking and reporting manually is not only impractical, but it may be impossible if you have any quantity of employees on your payroll. If you have more than 10 workers, data tracking becomes complicated. Therefore, it is always recommended that you have some type of mechanized system to help with your employee information and report preparation. It used to be that we could successfully use Excel to track various fields of employee information. After all, it has virtually unlimited capacity for data fields (columns), and employee entries (lines) can capture whatever data you want to put into them. The problem comes with the need to extract reports about that data. It can be more satisfying, less frustrating, and more cost effective (staff time versus software cost) to purchase or rent software designed for that specific purpose. Output is really the reason to have a database. It isn't so much what you put in, although that input must be accurate; it is more what you can get out of it that will help you manage your HR operations.

If you have existing software, learn how to use it. Learn what reports are standard. Then learn how you can create your own reports for the data output and analysis you want to have. When the HRIS doesn't embrace payroll, you may have to seek some reports from the payroll system. There can be differences between the two, so you need to be aware. Your HRIS compensation information for each employee represents the "planned" compensation for the year. The payroll system tracks "actual" pay as you go through the year. They may not necessarily be the same. What if you wanted to guide someone through selecting the amount of money to set aside in their health savings account (HSA)? Using actual payroll to date may not be entirely accurate. Nor would it always be accurate to use last year's payroll total. The plan for this year's compensation may include a bonus amount and a promotional increase. Knowing where to look for the information you want is as important as having the information available for retrieval.

Change Management Theory, Methods, and Applications

Many theories are available to explain how to manage change. We have chosen a few of the most popular for discussion here.

Lewin's Change Management Model[5]

Kurt Lewin is sometimes called the founder of social psychology. He was one of the first to study social dynamics and organizational development. In the early part of the twentieth century, Lewin concluded that there are three stages of change management that are good for use with deep dives into organizational changes.

- **Unfreeze the organization** Once recognized that change is needed, it is necessary to break down the existing organization before it is possible to create a new one.

- **Change the organization** Resolve uncertainties and actually implement the changes needed.

- **Refreeze the organization** Return to the stability of the organizational structure with job assignments that can be maintained for a period into the future.

McKinsey 7-S Model[6]

This model calls for analyzing seven aspects of an employer organization and determining how they interact with each other. Here they are:

- **Strategy**   Formal enough to permit successful competition and flexible enough to adapt to changes without breaking the organization.
- **Structure**   What is your actual structure? Not the structure you think you have. How do people actually interact and report to one another?
- **Systems**   Official processes, unofficial shortcuts, rules, and tracking processes.
- **Shared values**   Linking culture and values to the change process will permit employees to move easily through known territory to the desired change result.
- **Style**   Assessing management and leadership styles used in your organization.
- **Staff**   Are all required positions actually filled?
- **Skills**   Assess what you know your staff skills are and then assess the perception your customers have of what your staff skills are.

Kotter's Theory[7]

This approach relies on the senior executives driving a sense of urgency about the changes required, all based on the premise that current conditions demand that they be made. John P. Kotter suggests there are eight steps in a successful change management process:

- *Create a sense of urgency.* Explain to your team what is happening in the world that impacts your group or employer organization. Outline why it is so important to react to those threats.
- *Build a guiding coalition.* Convince your key leaders and stakeholders of the need to change.
- *Form a strategic vision.* Define your vision and the changes that will get you there.
- *Enlist a volunteer army.* Spread your ideas for change to the remainder of your organization.
- *Remove barriers and reduce friction.* If training is needed to help bring skills up to speed, make those arrangements. Clear the path for your people to do what they need to do in contributing to the change.
- *Generate short-term wins.* Spotlight the small successes achieved by your people in their effort to implement the change. Reinforce their efforts and praise their accomplishments.
- *Sustain acceleration.* This is about creating new habits, including new work patterns, new skill applications, and new methods.
- *Make the changes institutional.* The culmination of the process is to be sure it is all properly documented and that the organization's culture reflects the new changes. You have a new set of "how we do things around here."

Risk Management

Risk management covers many functional areas in the employment world. Some of them are complying with federal employment laws, identifying workplace hazards and developing safety plans to protect employees and the public, and preparing job descriptions to be used both as a communication tool and also as a means to address the physical and mental requirements of each job. Risk management explores how technology can help manage the liability that comes with operating an employment organization. Finally, risk management addresses the rapidly evolving field of social media, Internet, technology, and e-mail use.

Risk management addresses issues related to employees, customers, clients, the public, and vendors/suppliers. Risk management is the process of managing liabilities related to these populations in ways that will protect the employer organization and not be so heavy handed that the organization can't function well in performing its mission. HR professionals are the key to striking a balance in that delicate effort—developing; implementing/administering; and evaluating programs, procedures, and policies to provide a safe, secure working environment and to protect the organization from potential liability. There are lots of exciting things to think about.

Hazard (Risk) Identification and Communication

The process of protecting an organization from financial harm by identifying, analyzing, financing, and controlling risk is a shared responsibility among several areas in an organization. Risk is the threat of an event or action that will adversely affect an organization. Risk arises from missed opportunities as well as possible threats. HR is relied upon to be the keeper of accountability and the developer of policies and procedures in risk management.[8] Effective risk management is a progression of actions that are taken with the purpose of minimizing losses or injuries within the organization. HR's responsibilities fall within the following areas:

- Occupational safety and health
- Legal compliance
- Privacy
- Security
- Disaster recovery for business continuity

The identification of current and potential risks is an essential role for the human resource professional. Weighing in on the probability and acceptability of the risk is valuable to integrate with business decisions that are made with other business units. It is a goal for the HR professional to be consulted as a business partner within the organization. The focus should be on *proactive* and *management*.

Risk Management Techniques

There are four techniques for managing risk:

- **Risk avoidance** Eliminate the risk at any cost. For example, terminate an employee who had a car accident in a company vehicle to avoid claims of negligent retention. Or do not permit public tours of the facilities because of the possibility for liability if a visitor gets hurt.

- **Loss control** Reduce the number of occasions that loss occurs. For example, at least once a month, an employee gets injured by slipping and falling when the bathroom floors are being washed. Control could be obtained by washing the floors at a time when employees would not be using the facilities.

- **Risk retention** For larger employers, this is common when they self-insure such things as workers' compensation or other loss risks. This approach requires that a reserve fund be established to pay for any loss since the employer is self-insured under this model.

- **Risk transfer** Insuring against a particular loss will move the liability from the employer to an insurance carrier. For a fee, nearly everything is insurable. Employers are more frequently turning to insurance to prevent large financial losses because of things such as sexual harassment or supervisor misbehavior. Those types of policies carry large deductibles (paid by the employer) before the insurance begins paying for additional loss.

Occupational Injury and Illness Prevention Programs

On January 26, 1989, OSHA published in the *Federal Register*[9] a notice with general guidelines for voluntary adoption by employers. That set of guidelines was identified as standards 1910, 1910.1200, 1915, 1917, 1918, and 1926.

OSHA refers to these injury and illness prevention programs as *voluntary protection programs* (VPPs) because employers are not required to adopt them but encouraged instead. A VPP is broken down into four sections, as noted in the following outline, and although not a requirement, it would benefit organizations to create and maintain policies and programs that correlate with the VPP outline.

Injury and Illness Prevention Programs

- Section 1: Management Leadership and Employee Involvement
  - Written safety and health management system
  - Management commitment and leadership
  - Planning
  - Authority and line accountability
  - Contract employees
  - Employee involvement
  - Safety and health management system evaluation

- Section 2: Work Site Analysis
  - Baseline hazard analysis
  - Hazard analysis and significant changes
  - Hazard analysis and routine activities
  - Routine inspections
  - Hazard reporting
  - Hazard tracking
  - Accident/incident investigations
  - Trend analysis
- Section 3: Hazard Prevention and Control
  - Disciplinary system
  - Emergency procedures
  - Preventative/predictive maintenance
  - Personal protective equipment (PPE)
  - Process safety management
  - Occupational healthcare program
  - Recordkeeping
- Section 4: Safety and Health Training
  - Requirements for managers and employees
  - Delivery systems
  - Results measurement

A key component of any safety program, as listed in Section 3, is the provision of PPE. This can be as simple as safety glasses and earplugs or can include hard hats, breathing apparatus, and hazmat suits. PPE is provided by the employer based on the job conditions and hazards faced in doing that work. Employers that are cavalier about these protection requirements are liable to find themselves in jail or paying a big fine if one of their workers is injured because of a bad decision on their part.

What are some of the consequences of failure to keep workers safe and free of injury?

- Employees get injured or die.
- Workers' compensation costs increase because of experience modifications.
- Executives and management risk criminal prosecution for negligence or intentional acts.
- Companies are assessed financial penalties for workplace injuries.
- The company's existence is threatened because of marketplace reactions to accidents.

Safety programs should be part of a business's strategic plan. Because of that level of importance, this topic is considered critical for SPHR certification.

General Health Practices

Policies will vary from employer to employer primarily because the health risks associated with employers vary widely. An accounting firm employee will face health risks that are quite different from those faced by Level 4 Containment Lab workers at the Centers for Disease Control, or even people in a local physician's office. And, in all work locations, the objective is the same: to protect workers from health risks whenever possible.

Personal Protective Equipment   In high-risk environments, PPE plays a key role in health protection. In some environments, full hazmat suits are a requirement. In other environments, a gauze mask may be appropriate because of the number of people coughing and sneezing. In a normal office environment, there may be no PPE requirements. These are other examples of PPE:

- Rubber/latex/nitrile gloves
- Protective aprons or overcoats
- Goggles or safety glasses

Workplace Environment Management   Developing a checklist for auditing the environment is something every HR professional should be able to do. There should be an identification of health hazards caused by the workplace and those brought into the workplace by employees and visitors. On that list should be considerations such as those in an environmental hazard checklist of considerations and inspections. Here are some items you may find on such a checklist:

- **Dust, debris, hazards (construction environment)**   Are these in the primary work site, or are they intruding from outside the site? What mitigation options exist?
- **Electrical and gas hazards**   Are there exposed electrical terminals? Are there devices used in the workplace that pose an electrical hazard? Is natural gas, propane gas, gasoline, or other fuel used in the workplace posing a hazard? What potential for leaking gas exists in the workplace? What mitigation options exist?
- **Respiratory hazards**   Is there a risk of exhaust from gasoline engines entering the workplace? Is there a risk of carbon monoxide poisoning from gas heaters or other appliances? Could other substances such as refrigerant gases like ammonia or Freon escape into the workplace? Is it possible for chlorine gas to find a way into the workplace and cause problems for workers? What mitigation options exist?
- **Noise**   Are there machine noises in the workplace? Are other sources of noise generating potentially damaging noise? What mitigation options exist?
- **Moisture**   Are there sources of water that could potentially cause flooding in the workplace? Are there misting sources in the workplace that could cause respiratory issues for workers? Might they cause slip-and-fall hazards? Could moisture cause skin reactions for workers? What mitigation options exist?

- **Temperature** Does the workplace experience extreme high or low temperatures? Is work done outside in direct sun without shade? Is work done in a refrigerated environment? What mitigation options exist?

- **Ergonomic** Does the work require constant movement in repetitive motion? Are there physical response requirements that demand fast reaction or extreme extensions of limbs? Are long periods of sitting, standing, or walking required? What mitigation options exist?

ISO 14001 is known as a generic environmental management system standard, meaning that it is relevant to any organization seeking to improve and manage its environment more effectively.[10] The International Standards Organization (ISO) develops and publishes organizational and product standards for the world stage. This includes the following:

- Single sites to large multinational companies

- High-risk companies to low-risk service organizations

- Manufacturing and the service industries, including local governments

- All industry sectors including public and private sectors

- Original equipment manufacturers and their suppliers

 NOTE The key for any employer is to perform an analysis of the workplace to determine what type of health hazards exist and then develop plans for dealing with those hazards.

General Safety Practices

Because all employers are accountable under federal law for maintaining a safe and healthy work environment (General Duty Clause) and, in many industries, are required to have written safety programs called injury and illness prevention programs, it is necessary to understand what key components exist within those programs.[11]

Evacuation Plans A basic component of every safety plan is evacuation. Fire is a threat in nearly every workplace. And although fire is likely the primary reason, it is not the only reason for having an evacuation plan for your workspace.

Employer workspaces vary from single office facilities to multiple floors in high-rise buildings to entire campus installations composed of many buildings. In each case, employees should be provided with instructions about how to evacuate their work site and what to do following evacuation. Re-assembly areas should be designated in the evacuation plan, and someone should be designated as the authority to verify that everyone successfully got out of the quarters. Figure 4-3 provides a sample evaluation plan.

Once the plan has been properly drawn up, employees should be trained in how it should be implemented and the signals that will alert them to the need to evacuate.

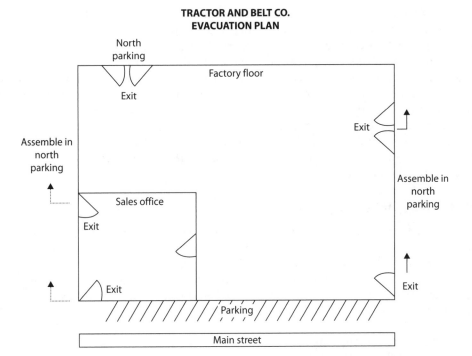

**TRACTOR AND BELT CO.
EVACUATION PLAN**

North parking

Factory floor

Exit

Exit

Assemble in north parking

Assemble in north parking

Sales office

Exit

Exit

Exit

Exit

Parking

Main street

Figure 4-3   Sample evacuation plan

Ergonomic Evaluations

These days, finding employees who have no need for ergonomic work stations is only a dream. Fortunately, these days, more and more resources are available to assist employers in preventing injury due to ergonomic problems. These are some of the areas for concern:

- Repetitive-motion injuries (wrists, hands, arms, legs, backs)
- Sitting (accommodations are desk chairs, table-height "standing" desks)
- Keyboard use, including use of the mouse (carpal tunnel syndrome, arm and shoulder ailments; accommodations are split keyboards, separate portions for each hand, wrist support pads for mouse and keyboard)
- Lifting, bending (cranes, exoskeletons, robot substitute)
- Telephone use (neck pain, shoulder pain; accommodations are headsets with microphones to avoid having to hold handsets between the ear and neck)

Safety Audit and Communication Plans

A good safety program will always have periodic inspections built into the program. As a function, "safety" can often be included in the human resource department. In some organizations, it is found in a department all its own (the safety department). Or, it can be located in another part of the organization such as operations or facilities management.

It is a good idea to have each manager and supervisor perform monthly inspections of their individual and crew work areas. If there is a safety officer for the organization, that person should inspect every part of the physical facility at least once per quarter. Each inspection should be documented and notations made about the need for follow-up and problem correction. Part of every supervisor's personal safety responsibility is to inspect the audit reports made by subordinates. If nobody checks to be sure safety inspections were actually done, they will sometimes get "missed" because of other important things that demand a supervisor's attention.

See Figure 4-4 for a sample safety inspection report. It is necessary to create one inspection form for every type of work area and hazard present. Figure 4-5 illustrates a sample safety action report.

Return-to-Work Policies

When choosing a policy, employers have a wide range of choices. On the one hand is a policy that says no one may return to work until they are 100 percent recovered and able to perform the full range of work duties their job requires. On the other hand is a policy that says just as soon as an employee is able to perform some of the job functions, he or she should return to work, and the balance of their duties can be handled by others until they regain full recovery.

Modified Duty Assignments

Somewhere in the middle of that spectrum is a policy that says that once an employee is able to return to work, we will modify her job responsibilities on a temporary basis so we can get her back to work as early as possible. Some medical people suggest that returning to work early can aid in recovery. Because what we do in our job is so often integral to the person we see ourselves as being, assurances that the job will still be available to the employee can be psychologically beneficial.

In a modified duty assignment, some tasks or duties will be forgiven or handed off to other employees for a period of time. If the employee has just returned from back surgery, waiving the need to lift objects that would be normal work tasks could be an example of modified duty.

Reasonable Accommodation

Reasonable accommodations can present an opportunity to get the employee back on the job with some alterations to the job that don't relieve the employee of any duties or responsibilities. The same employee who had back surgery may find it necessary to alternate standing and sitting. Providing the opportunity for that to take place is an example of job accommodation. If frequent rest breaks are needed to help someone return to work, the employer could agree to allow the employee to take several additional breaks throughout the day. In many cases, these accommodations are temporary and will go away in time. In other cases, the job accommodation may be a permanent thing. When an employee returns to work after having been diagnosed with diabetes, it may be that you are faced with an accommodation request to provide a firm schedule of meal and rest breaks so there are opportunities to take insulin injections and eat food at precise intervals throughout the day.

SAFETY INSPECTION REPORT		
Date:	**Evaluations:** S = Satisfactory	
Inspector Name:	U = Unsatisfactory	
	NA = Not Applicable to Area	
Inspector Signature:		
	If an unsatisfactory rating is provided for a particular item, company Form 4 must be completed for that item.	
Area Inspected: Desks, Work Stations, Chairs		
	Rating	**Additional Comments**
Pencils stored, points away		
No overhanging objects on desks		
Cords not a trip hazard		
Storage: Knives, letter openers		
Storage: Scissors		
Ashtrays: Not near flammables		
Plants/water not near electric outlets		
Chair castors function properly		
Chair armrests function properly		
Chair adjustments function properly		
Broken furniture is not being used		
This sheet is Page _____ of _____ pages		

Figure 4-4 Safety inspection report

Independent Medical Exam

Of course, any injury or illness that requires medical attention will be followed closely by the employee's own medical team. But when the employee calls and says he or she is ready to return to work, what do you do?

First, if the absence has required medical attention, you should ask for a return-to-work release from the employee's physician.

Inspector/Manager Name:		Telephone Extension:		
Inspector/Manager Signature:		Date Report Completed:		
Description and Location of Unsafe Condition and Date			Completion Date	
Discovered by Management	Action to be Taken		Planned	Actual
Concrete cracked and chipped at front entrance.	Work with facilities management to repair.			
Carpet at the entrance to the warehouse is frayed and a trip hazard.	Ask facilities management to repair the damage.			
Binders are stacked on top of filing cabinets creating a hazard if they should fall on someone.	Relocate binders to proper storage site.			
File drawers left open and unattended.	Train staff to close file drawers when not in use.			
IMPORTANT: Hazards which pose a risk of serious or substantial injury to employees must be corrected immediately. Other hazards should be corrected as soon as reasonably possible but in no case later than __ days from the date of discovery by management. Any deviation from these time requirements must be reported to the Program Administrator immediately.				
This is page _____ of _____ pages				

Figure 4-5   Safety action report

Second, you should make an appointment for the employee to visit a physician who is hired by the employer to evaluate the individual's abilities to perform the specific job requirements, meaning a physician who is an expert in occupational medicine. You should provide to that physician a copy of the employee's job description, including a listing of the physical and mental requirements of the job.

If there is a difference of opinion between the two physicians, you can send the employee for a third evaluation, or you can simply elect to use the guidance from your employer's medical expert. HR professionals should be cautioned that it is unwise to make conclusions of a medical nature if you are not a qualified physician yourself. Allow protocol and procedure to obtain the required expert input and then rely on it for your decision-making about the situation.

Plans to Protect Employees and Minimize Organization Liability

HR professionals are responsible for the workforce in many ways, including recruiting and counseling on employee management issues, record management, and the management of organizational liabilities related to employees. There are many disasters that can befall an employer. Airlines experience airplane crashes. Investment institutions experience embezzlement. Manufacturers experience product contamination or other defects. There may just be an accident that causes fire in the building. Who knows what will happen when we get up in the morning?

Emergency Response Plans

A primary safety axiom is that proper planning can save lives and property. It is a good idea to have a written plan specifying what actions will be taken in any of many various scenarios. There are some basic alternatives for dealing with a disaster, large or small.

This consideration goes beyond the emergency evacuation plans discussed earlier in this chapter and relates to the entire universe of emergency planning. Evacuation is just one type of response to an emergency.

The first step toward having an emergency response plan is to conduct a risk assessment for your work location. Look at the physical facilities, emergency exits, fire suppression systems, electrical and gas shut-off access, hazardous materials used in the workplace, protective equipment needed for operations, employee training for special equipment, use of proper lock-out tag-out procedures when working on electrical equipment, and proper handling of carcinogenic substances such as copy machine toner. Answer hypothetical questions such as "What would we do if someone with a gun walked through our front door?"

Engage key personnel in the development process. Ask people on the production line and in the office what they would do in some circumstances. Get input from experts and nonexperts alike. Then list the responses that should happen for each emergency you listed.

Finally, once the plan is developed, be sure everyone in the workplace knows about it and what to do if an emergency happens.

Business Continuation

If there is a flood or fire and your workplace is destroyed, the computers, hard drives, on-site backup systems, and filing cabinets may no longer be available. How will you open your business tomorrow morning?

Employers must have a plan for how they will continue operating their organization. What about customer records, accounting records, client data, and payroll information?

This is an area of responsibility where HR professionals should work with others in the organization such as professionals in information technology (IT) and accounting. It should be common practice for backups to be made of all technology systems, especially an HRIS system. And those backups, or at least duplicates of them, should be stored off-site at some secure location. It is necessary for the survival of your organization that it be able to continue operations as quickly as possible with all the records it requires for that to happen.

What will your plan dictate regarding where employees should report to work after such a disaster? Do you plan to use e-mail, text messages, or a telephone tree to contact everyone and pass along instructions? How will you keep supervisors and managers informed? Who will handle media inquiries about the disaster and your plans for the future?

Password Usage

Some common mistakes are made by employees in handling passwords for computer program access. If you look around your workplace, you will likely find examples of the following.

Password Problems   Here are some common problems found when analyzing password usage:

- **Sticky notes passwords**   Some people write passwords on sticky notes, especially employees who can't seem to remember their passwords. No effort is made to conceal the password. Sometimes this note is pressed to the computer monitor to make it even more available.

- **Desk drawer passwords**   You will find some employees who make a list of their passwords and stick that list into their top desk drawer or workbench drawer. Again, this is for convenience, but it is easily discoverable by anyone with dishonorable intentions.

- **Personal information passwords**   Employees will often create passwords by using their birthday, their home street address, their child's name, or their wedding anniversary. Any of these can be fairly easily discovered by looking elsewhere in the workstation. A family photo with a special date stamp, a diary with the password notations in the front or back, or some other personal notations will be available to anyone who wants to access the employee's work information.

- **Password binders**   What could be handier for a thief than to have sitting in plain sight a binder labeled "Passwords"? With all the access points we must have in the HR world these days, it is common for people to keep binders and address books filled with passwords for each of those programs. But keeping the binder in plain sight shows a low level of concern for security. Perhaps it could be locked up in a cabinet or desk drawer?

Password Examples   Passwords should be made of random or nonsensical characters. They should not be recognizable words.

Bad passwords might look something like this: Easter2015, Hellen1234, 1776July4th, InkPen, RadioKQRT, Mary7789, and Phone593.

Strong passwords might look something like this: HyRtP73N, 84XcMH59, and Ak9BrzE45. Some software today requires the use of symbols in passwords to add further complexity (for example, * & % $ # @ + = !). Use both uppercase and lowercase letters interspersed with numerical characters.

Why Passwords Matter   HR professionals have many pieces of information entrusted to them. You know from Chapter 2 that you have a legal obligation to protect the privacy of employee data and medical information. If you take that responsibility seriously, you will treat passwords with the respect they deserve. The last thing you want to have to tell someone is "I'm afraid someone has accessed your data file and taken a copy."

Social Engineering

Social engineering refers to using electronic communications and the Internet to manipulate someone into compromising their organization's cybersecurity by revealing critical information. With the role of human resources, personally identifiable information (PII) is the target. It is a term that describes a kind of intrusion that often involves tricking other people to break normal security procedures.

A social engineer runs what used to be called a "con game." Social engineers often rely on the natural helpfulness of people as well as on their weaknesses. Virus writers use social engineering tactics to persuade people to run malware-laden e-mail attachments, phishers use social engineering to convince people to divulge sensitive information, and scareware vendors use social engineering to frighten people into running software that is useless at best and dangerous at worst. They might, for example, call the authorized employee with some kind of urgent problem that requires immediate network access. Appeals to vanity, appeals to authority, appeals to greed, and old-fashioned eavesdropping are other typical social engineering techniques. Social engineering attacks may even be internal within an organization, such as searching wastebaskets for valuable information or gaining access codes by looking over someone's shoulder (shoulder surfing).

Security experts propose that as our culture becomes more dependent on information, social engineering will remain the greatest threat to any records and data system. Organizations need to raise the level of awareness of all their people about the dangers of social engineering and keep it at a high level at all times. Con and scamming games are as old as civilization itself. The methods never really change because human nature never changes. Only the technology does.

Disaster Recovery

There are many resources for disaster recovery on the Internet. Here are some of those you may find useful:

- **Federal Small Business Administration**
  www.sba.gov/content/disaster-recovery-plan

- **Federal Emergency Management Agency**
  www.fema.gov/disaster-recovery-centers

- **Federal Disaster Assistance web service**
  www.disasterassistance.gov

Needless to say, every employer organization should have a disaster recovery plan. It should identify the types of disasters that might hit the organization (for example, earthquake, fire, flood, workplace violence), how each of those situations would be handled, who would be assigned to speak for the organization (to the employees and to the press), what employees should do following a disaster, how the organization could regain an ability to resume operations, and how employee injuries or fatalities should be handled. What alternative work site has been chosen to accommodate the resumption of operations? Who will manage the business if the existing leaders are not available for some reason?

If you want a model of crisis management planning, look to the airline industry. They have worked through almost every possible scenario that could impact their business and have developed plans for how each would be handled. They know it is possible for a disaster to happen in their business, and they have prepared themselves for managing those possibilities.

If you would like to have a desk reference on the subject of disaster recovery, we suggest *Manager's Guide to Crisis Management* (McGraw-Hill Education, 2011).

Workplace Violence

Like the other areas of risk management, the area of workplace violence demands planning. HR professionals will be required to have written workplace violence prevention programs in some states. Under the General Duty Clause of OSHA requirements, employers are responsible for providing a safe work environment. Preventing workplace violence would fall within that requirement.

Preventing workplace violence begins with identifying the types of violence that might occur in your workplace. Sources can come from inside or outside the organization. Retail establishments might consider robbery as a possible risk. The same could be said for banks or credit unions. Disgruntled customers or former employees can pose a risk.

Once identified, each risk should be addressed with an action plan detailing how the organization will respond if the violence actually happens. What will the business leaders do? What will the HR manager do? What are employees expected to do? Where should employees go in a violent event? How should they protect themselves if violence happens? Who will address the media? Who will coordinate with law enforcement?

Perhaps the most important consideration is employee communication. Keeping people informed as events unfold is a big part of keeping them safe and reassured. But making sure employees know where to go and what to do in advance depends on careful planning and training. HR professionals must allocate resources to those things, or a disaster can result.

Budgeting, Accounting, and Financial

There is always a risk of employee theft. Embezzlement can happen in the smartest of organizations. If someone wants to game the system, it is only a matter of time before that happens. It is an area for more planning. The senior financial executive in the organization (the chief financial officer) should be involved with that planning effort.

There are commonsense things to consider when planning for the financial security of the organization. For example, never allow a single person to have access to money or other resources without a second person involved in the transaction. When two or more people are required to access accounts, the likelihood of theft is reduced. Have a record of each financial transaction and who it served as an audit trail so it will be possible to identify who is accessing funds for any purpose.

But oversight is going to remain a primary requirement. Frequent review by managers is important. When employees know they will be observed and their work reviewed, there is less chance they will try to take what they shouldn't.

These types of financial risks can be significant depending on the employer. Planning should include identifying the type of risk that could occur, what action plans will be activated in each instance, and how the organization will recover from the problem after the fact.

In some situations, it will be necessary to inform federal agencies of the problem. This is often required when the employer is a publicly held entity. The Securities and Exchange Commission (SEC) and other federal agencies may have requirements that specifically address your type of organization. You should plan accordingly.

Substance Abuse

Substance abuse is a risk not only because it can harm employee health and personal life but also because it can lead to problems such as embezzlement, workplace violence, and workplace injuries.

In some organizations, it is necessary to assure that you are maintaining a drug-free workplace. (See information about the Drug-Free Workplace Act in Chapter 2.) That can involve drug testing on either a regular or random basis. It can also require drug testing following accidents when an employee has been operating equipment or motor vehicles. Federal laws require drug testing for some truck drivers, train engineers, and airline pilots if they are involved in an accident.

If employees must be able to drive on their job, they must do so without impairment by drugs or alcohol, whether the drugs are prescription or illegal. It is up to the HR professional to establish systems necessary to assure that happens and can be verified.

Employers risk the torts of negligent hiring and negligent retention if they knowingly hire or keep on the payroll someone who is a drug or alcohol abuser who does harm to someone else while on the job. If the employee is involved in an automobile accident while under the influence on the job, the employer can be held accountable in some situations.

Policies must be developed that specify what will happen to employees if they fail to pass one or more drug tests. Sometimes policies will provide for employees to use a leave of absence to address drug or alcohol dependence. Will the employer sponsor employee participation in a rehabilitation program? Is there a state or local program that will help pay for the type of program? What will happen if the employee has another incident of involvement with drugs? How will someone who appears to be under the influence of drugs or alcohol be handled if they report to work while impaired?

Don't forget to develop action plans for how you will handle the situation when one of your employees does become involved in an on-the-job incident because of drugs or alcohol.

Theft

There are lots of ways theft can happen in the workplace. Here are some examples:

- Embezzlement of funds

- Taking company equipment (for example, computers, printers, scanners, calculators)

- Taking company supplies (for example, paper, toner/ink, staplers, tape, batteries)

PART II

- Taking time (for example, long breaks for coffee and meals, wandering through the workplace chatting with other workers, playing games on the computer, texting and social media)
- Falsifying records (for example, time cards/payroll input, untrue overtime claim, extended time off for union activities, untrue sickness reports)
- Unauthorized credit card charges (claiming personal expense as company expense)
- Copying employer software for personal use in violation of copyright law

HR professionals need to work with the accounting professionals to develop appropriate policies that explain how these things are unacceptable under the organization's code of conduct. A policy should be clear about what will happen if an employee is discovered to have participated in these types of activities. And management should follow through with discipline according to that policy. Consistency in treatment is critical. Inconsistency can bring charges of illegal discrimination based on any number of classifications.

Sabotage

The term *sabotage* is believed to have originated in the fifteenth century.

Today, workplace sabotage includes the following:

- Throwing items into machinery to destroy or disrupt production
- Removing parts of equipment to cause a shutdown
- Tampering with software or passwords for access to programs
- Attacking computer systems by hacking
- Destroying computer records
- Creating a false workload by filing inaccurate or false claims

Without a doubt, sabotage is a difficult problem to handle. HR professionals should approach such issues with basic investigative techniques. Conduct a proper investigation, and it is possible that some witnesses will surface or the code of silence will be broken, and the truth will come out. When sabotage reaches the criminal vandalism level, always involve law enforcement with proper reports so they can conduct their own inquiries.

Social Media, Internet, and E-mail Use Policies

Social media is here to stay. There is no going back. According to one source, in February 2014 the membership and usage of some principal social media websites was impressive.[12]

- **Facebook**   2.23 billion users
- **Instagram**   1 billion users
- **LinkedIn**   546 million users
- **Pinterest**   200 million users

- **Twitter**   330 million users
- **YouTube**   1.8 billion users

This is just a sampling of websites involved in e-commerce and personal communication. Needless to say, with these membership and usage numbers growing each month, how employees use social media and e-commerce sites is an issue that employers must address in their policies and workplace practices. (Please note that these usage figures change daily. If you need exact usage figures, please conduct a current investigation to be sure you have the accurate data you need.)

Social Media

Social media embraces Internet sites that permit person-to-person communications or posting of general comments on almost any subject. Messages can be directed to a single individual or to the world at large. Also included are services such as YouTube.com that permit people to upload video files that can then be accessed by anyone with an interest. Consider a policy that explains to employees that they should have no expectation of privacy while in the workplace. Of course, careful review of all policies should involve your attorney before any announcements are made to employees.

Internet Access

When it is necessary for employees to have access to the Internet to conduct their business, there should be a written policy describing how that access is to be accomplished and what websites are unacceptable. The policy should also provide for disciplinary activity for someone who engages in accessing Internet sites that are unacceptable. Unacceptable websites can include personal use of pornographic sites, political sites, gaming sites, shopping sites, or others. Use of company equipment and company time to access such sites could be cause for discipline as a misuse of work time and employer equipment.

E-mail Use

E-mail has grown to include texting as a means of written communication from one person to another. It is so common now that we've seen distracted people get into car accidents, walk into automobile traffic, and stumble into water fountains while concentrating on text messaging. Here, once again, employers should consider policy content that controls the use of organizational equipment and the limitation of personal use. But also consider the issue of employees using personal smart phones for texting and e-mail. If this happens during work time, it can be as big a problem as other nonwork diversions. Policies should explain that work equipment is intended only for work applications.

Needs Analysis (Audits)

Conducting a comprehensive risk management needs analysis is an important activity. A comprehensive risk management assessment is a useful tool to uncover and identify risks. When you conduct a risk management needs assessment, you must start with identifying a number of areas and goals and use an appropriate method for audit.

Qualitative and quantitative methods and tools for analysis, interpretation, and decision-making purposes—such as metrics and measurements, costs-benefit analysis, and financial statement analysis—are frequently used in risk management.

PART II

In the Trenches

Social Media's Impact on the Workplace Community

Jane E. Henderson, EdD, timner@comcast.net

Potluck dinners and ice cream socials have long been traditions across America. These events brought communities together to share stories and pictures, make new friends, welcome new neighbors, and build bonds that often lasted a lifetime, all while enjoying delicious food and sweet treats. Originally, foods such as ice cream were considered delicacies that were enjoyed only by royalty, but eventually American presidents served it to their guests who attended gatherings. However, these community gatherings quickly became universally adopted as centerpieces of social life in the early communities. Today, social networks, such as Facebook, Flickr, Twitter, LinkedIn, live chat, blogs, and MySpace, offer a virtual environment in which people replicate these types of community activities but with an added benefit. Now, more than 400 social media and social networking sites allow millions of people to connect both in general socializing and more specifically for the purpose of sharing common interests, such as education, cooking, music, and movies.

Traditional "networking" in the workplace and through professional organizations required physical appearances on company grounds or travel to conference sites. The technologically savvy employee today will have an advantage by being comfortable in the new world of online networking and community building. This advantage will not only enhance the employee's potential within the organization but will also contribute to career development goals. Also, as companies expand globally, online social media provide employees opportunities to build relationships and to nurture them over time without sharing the same physical space.

It is in the connection to such virtual social networks that the concepts of the "potluck dinner or ice cream social" can be applied to provide an environment in which employees have the opportunity to build stronger team bonds, especially if they are working on projects with peers in remote locations. It further supports the notion that the skills and behaviors practiced in the online environment enhance workplace skills and career development.

Despite concerns, social media will expand its influence in the workplace if in no other way than through use by tech-savvy employees who are accustomed to multitasking and integrating such tools throughout their workday.

There are numerous risks possible in the modern workplace. For HR, the focus is usually on things related to the employee's body and its day-to-day exposures. These are some HR risks:

- Employee complaints of illegal discrimination (EEO issues)
- Employee complaints of illegal financial processes (Sarbanes-Oxley and SEC issues)

- Employee injuries on the job (workers' compensation issues)
- Safety practices and procedures (OSHA/MSHA issues)
- Emergency plans for use in the event of fire, earthquake, tornado, flood, hurricane (OSHA/MSHA issues)
- Imbalance of compensation programs (equal pay issues)
- Loss of federal contract revenues by noncompliance with affirmative action requirements
- Responses to crisis conditions (embezzlement, production interruption, natural disaster, key person disappearance)

Recordkeeping Requirements

There is a saying among HR professionals: "If it isn't documented, it didn't happen." Actually, many management attorneys agree with that sentiment. When employer meets employee in a courtroom, juries tend to root for the little guy (the employee) and have little sympathy for the big guy (the employer). That means the employer must be ready to "prove" everything they claim during the course of defending themselves against claims such as wrongful termination, illegal discrimination, and so on.

Documentation is so important that almost every management attorney will offer instructions to their clients about how to prepare documentation of actions involving employee treatment. The problem is that people are inherently lazy. It takes time and effort to prepare documentation. If there is a choice between spending a half-hour writing up the conversation a supervisor just had about an employee performance problem or getting out of work early, the documentation will slide. Eventually, it will be forgotten. And there will be nothing in the file to prove a supervisor had that conversation with that employee about that performance problem. Whatever the supervisor claims to recall will be suspect without the written document to demonstrate that the recollection is accurate.

 NOTE   One of the highest-impact activities an HR professional can have on any organization is to teach managers and supervisors the proper way to prepare documentation.

Once prepared, it is usually dependent upon state laws and company policy whether the employee is given a copy. In some states, that is a requirement, while it is not in other states. Federal law doesn't specify one way or the other. It is not necessary for an employee to sign documentation about a disciplinary conversation with the supervisor, but if you get an employee signature, it is a good practice to provide a copy of the document to that employee. Why isn't it necessary to get an employee signature? Supervisor notes are made by the employer and don't require employee agreement. Unless it is a contract with the employee, the supervisor is merely writing what happened from his or her perspective.

Generally speaking, documentation should include the following:

- The date of the event and when the documentation was prepared. (They should be the same in most situations. Supervisors should always prepare their notes for file soon after the event took place.)

- A description of what was said. It is not necessary to quote verbatim. It is important to capture the key thoughts, who agreed to what, and the details about any deficiencies or issues the supervisor pointed out. The level of detail depends on the topic and how important details were to the conversation.

- How the conversation ended. What action plan was agreed to by both people?

- Will there be a follow-up meeting?

These same guidelines should apply to HR professionals in their documentation of conversations they have with employees, supervisors, and managers. It may be necessary at a future date to show someone your notes about what was said on a particular occasion.

The thing about documentation is that you don't know if it will be important until you reach the future when someone requests it. By the time you discover it is important, it's too late to create it.

Here is a quick word about creating documentation after the fact. While it is always best to be able to say that your notes were made right after the event or conversation, it is also possible to create your notes in the days following that event. When you write notes after the fact, always put the date on them representing when you wrote them. If you had a conversation on January 2 with an employee but didn't get around to writing your notes until three days later, mark your notes with the January 5 date. That way, there will be no question about the fact that you prepared them after the event. It could be beneficial if you stuck in a note saying what caused the delay in preparing the documentation.

In the Trenches

Investigating a Sexual Harassment Complaint

It was a Friday morning when the phone rang and a young man on the other end of the line said he wanted to file a complaint about his supervisor. He said he was calling from an airport 2,500 miles away from his work location and some of his co-workers helped him escape from his boss. He claimed that his life was at risk because his boss threatened him when he was confronted.

That began a complaint investigation that lasted for six months, involved travel halfway across the country for the investigators, consumed six investigators for the entire six months, and cost an enormous amount of money…just for the investigation. This young man claimed his supervisor (another male) had physically assaulted him and made sexual advances in the process.

Because he was a new hire and would be relocating from another state, the boss invited him to live at his house temporarily. The boss said it would save money and give them time out of work hours to get to know one another. The boss was single, having divorced several years before.

(continued)

The assault, as it was told, took place in the boss's home while the two men were working out together. When the sexual advances were rebuffed by the young man, he said his boss got angry and started to punch him. The boss threatened to kill the new employee if he ever told anyone about the incident.

Over the next three weeks, while still living at the boss's home, the young man identified two people in his workgroup that he felt he could trust. He enlisted them in a plan so he could escape the constant oversight of the boss. The boss wanted to know where the young man was at every moment of the day. He wasn't permitted to leave the work site, nor was he permitted to make any trips without supervision away from the home. It was claimed that everything the boss did was intended to isolate this employee from the rest of the workgroup. Still, he managed to get two co-workers to help him get away.

There was no way the employee could take his clothing or personal effects from the house, so he abandoned them. The co-workers arranged an off-site meeting as an excuse for being away from the office. The employee claimed he was going to use the restroom, but instead, he left the building and climbed into the trunk of his co-worker's car. The co-worker drove directly to the airport where the employee got out of the trunk and bought a ticket with borrowed money. The plane was headed 2,500 miles away. That's where he made the call to the company HR manager.

That investigation yielded a "he said/he said" situation. Interviews with the accused manager and with the employee produced credible stories from each one. Sometime after the investigation began, documentation revealed that the boss had been found to have done something similar in years past. That history of behavior tipped the balance. Deeper digging revealed some of the young man's co-workers had also experienced some form of sexual advance from the accused manager.

The case was closed after the manager was fired. Criminal assault charges were never brought.

Investigating Complaints

There are several ways in which HR professionals can manage the employee complaint process, and there are several reasons why you could be faced with the need for an investigation. It may become necessary because of a discrimination complaint, employee bad behavior (code of conduct violation, embezzlement), safety issue (serious employee injury or death), disagreement with the employee's supervisor, and so on.

When you recognize the need for an investigation, you can take one of several approaches to getting that done:

- *Investigate the complaint yourself.* As an HR professional, investigations are often just another of the many responsibilities that come with the job.

- *Hire an outside expert to conduct the complaint investigation.* This might be a consultant specializing in the investigation of complaints of the type you face.

It might also be an attorney who specializes in investigating complaints for clients. It is generally possible to protect files created by an outside legal counsel as attorney work product. The files are part of the legal advice provided to the client organization. You should be aware of any state or local requirements that investigators be licensed before performing such work. Using unlicensed investigators when a license is required could expose the organization to additional risks.

- *Have your internal legal expert conduct the complaint investigation.* It may or may not be possible to protect investigation materials from disclosure under attorney-client privilege when you use your internal attorney. An argument is sometimes made that a lawyer who provides legal advice and is also a participant (investigator) in the same situation invalidates the claim to attorney-client privilege. You'll have to talk with your own legal counsel to determine the best course of action for your organization.

The following steps should be taken in an investigation:

- *Plan the investigation.* Identify the key people involved (complainant, supervisor, witnesses, experts). Identify what is needed from each of them. What questions should be asked based about the complaint? Who saw what? Who did what? Is there any documentation available? Are there any videos or photos available?

- *Interview the employee who filed the complaint.* Determine the details. Be sure the complaint is in writing, naming names and being specific about what happened. Document the encounter.

- *Interview the witnesses.* Determine whether they can corroborate the claims of the complaining employee. Find out whether they have any documentation or other evidence to support their observations. That might include videos or photographs. Document each interview.

- *Interview the accused.* Explain the charges. Explain the documentation and witness testimony about what happened. Ask for comments from the accused in reaction to each of those pieces of input. Document the responses.

- *Follow up on any questions remaining.* Re-interview individuals if necessary.

- *Make a determination and provide feedback to both the accused and the complaining employee.*

Documentation of each step in the process is important. Note that it will be difficult to protect the documents you create from disclosure requests in the event of a lawsuit at some point in the future. That means you should "write for the jury" by explaining everything in detail, especially the reasons you had for making the decisions you did as you progressed through the investigation. Make sure your written documentation can stand on its own if you are not available to testify about what you did in that investigation.

Employee Communications

Communication skills are critical in all walks of life, but communicating effectively in the workplace is critical to professional success. Whether interacting with colleagues, subordinates, managers, customers, or vendors, the ability to communicate effectively using a variety of tools is essential (Figure 4-6).

When someone sends a message, it is generally received by the other person. However, the sender doesn't really know that what was said has been understood unless there is some sort of feedback to indicate understanding.

Think about driving a car. When you step on the brakes, your brake light turns on to alert the driver behind you. When that message is received, the car behind begins to slow, giving you feedback that the message was received. If the car doesn't slow, well... bad things happen.

Similar disasters can happen when communication between people goes awry. If your boss tells you not to send the announcement until later but you understand the message to be, "Send the announcement, it will get there later," then the outcome won't be what the boss wants, and he may send you another message. When your doctor tells you take three pills twice a day and you hear, "Take three pills every two days," things won't go as planned in your recovery. Communication clarity matters.

One of the claims that invariably emerges from every complaint of sexual harassment is "That isn't what I meant at all." Confusion in communication is reduced substantially when people insist upon getting feedback about what they have just said.

One tactic for making sure that the communication cycle is working as you want is to ask for feedback after you have given an important set of instructions. "Tell me what you are going to do..." is an example. Another is "What do you understand I just said?" Any number of other tests will solicit the feedback you want so that there is assurance your message got across as you wanted.

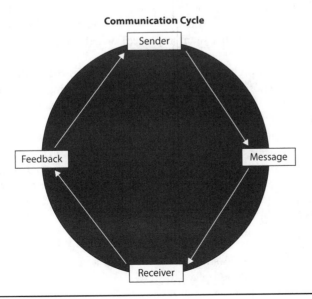

Figure 4-6 The communication cycle

A second important part of communication is the realization that the sender controls intent, but the received controls the impact. Remember what accused parties usually say when confronted with a complaint that they sexually harassed someone? "That isn't what I meant at all." Well, it is often true. That isn't what they intended the message to be. The receiver in our example heard something other than what the sender of the message intended. Incomplete or inaccurate communication can create large liabilities for both individuals and organizations.

In the employment world, communication is critical to properly and successfully running the organization. Supervisors must successfully communicate to subordinates their task assignments, deadlines, expectations, methods, guidelines, and more.

As a message receiver (perhaps in a staff meeting), it can be helpful to repeat your understanding of the expectations or instructions that were just passed along to you: "So, I will be…" or "As I understand it, you want…."

Be clear that the sender controls the intent, but the receiver controls the impact of any message. Tell someone something they don't want to hear (about job performance or policy violation) and you will likely see them react with upset. That emotion can run the gamut from mildly irritated to physically violent. Cavalier approaches to employee communication sessions can hurt feelings and permanently damage relationships. Terminating someone for cause without being careful to protect their self-esteem can lead to bad things such as active shooters coming back to seek retribution against supervisors and even HR people.

Workplace communication is the process of exchanging information, both verbal and nonverbal, within an organization. An organization may consist of employees from different parts of the society. These may have different cultures and backgrounds and can be used to different norms. To unite activities of all employees and restrain from any missed deadline or activity that could affect the company negatively, communication is crucial. Effective workplace communication ensures that all the organizational objectives are achieved. Workplace communication is tremendously important to organizations because it increases productivity and efficiency. Ineffective workplace communication leads to communication gaps between employees, which causes confusion, wastes time, and reduces productivity.

Effective communication with clients plays a vital role in the development of an organization and the success of any business. When communicating, nonverbal communication must also be taken into consideration. How a person delivers a message has a lot of influence on the meaning of this one.

The two types of communication are verbal/oral and written. So much of our interaction with employees, peers, and even our bosses is done by e-mail or text these days that written communication has taken a leap in its importance. Verbal communication has taken a beating as a result. People can be sitting across the table from one another and elect to text message back and forth rather than just talk to one another.

With that increase in importance of e-mail and texting, here are some tips for etiquette when using those methods of communication:

- *Start on a personal note.* A simple thank-you for a previous conversation or chance to meet in person is a good place to start.

- *Tame the emotions.* Particularly if you are upset and want to "unload" all that negative emotion in your message, keep it under control.

- *Keep it short and sweet.* Be accurate. Be brief.

- *Read it twice.* Give yourself a chance to catch any typos or misspellings. Those things make you look less professional.

- *If it's a critical e-mail, do not under any circumstances send it right away.* Allow some time (an hour or two, or a day or two) before you hit Send. Let yourself review the message after you have "cooled off" for a little while. If it is still accurate and honest, go ahead and send it. Just prepare for the consequences.

- *Master the subject line.* The first thing that the receiver will see is your subject line. Capture them at that point, or your message may never be read.

Communication Skills and Strategies

Not much happens properly within a modern workplace unless adequate communication systems are in place to help workers understand what work needs to be done, how safety enters into the process, when to stop a given procedure, and hundreds of other applications you can think of that happen each day.

Communication Methods

With today's technology and real-time accessibility, a conscientious approach and clarity of message are vital. HR becomes a bridge communicating to various sectors within the organization and also outside the organization. Determining the most effective method to communicate can be just as important as what is communicated. Figure 4-7 illustrates the various communication methods for HR.

Strategy involves selecting the best tool for the job. In terms of communication strategy, how a message is to be communicated is often as important as what the message contains. The timing of a message can also be critical. Getting an e-mail message saying all performance appraisals were due last Thursday isn't much help if you don't get it on time to meet the deadline. When you are asked to provide some content to a bid proposal, delay can mean you lose business and the revenues associated with it. Picking the proper communication channel or media is often quite important.

Strategic Communication Planning

You can control the message in many different ways. What strategy you elect to use in conveying your message is dependent upon your answers to the key questions of who, what, when, where, and why. It's not silly. And it's not inane. These are important questions for anyone who doesn't want to go through their professional career "winging it." That cavalier approach won't work for long in the role of an HR professional.

Ask yourself who should receive the message. What is the purpose of the message? When should your message arrive? Where will it be going? Finally, why should the message be sent? If you can answer those questions, you can select the best strategic communication process/media for your message.

Written Communication

- Personal letter or note
- E-mail message
- Website message
- Webinar
- Newsletter article
- Form filled with information
- PowerPoint presentation
- Texting

Oral Communication

- Personal visit/talk
- Group meeting
- Conference call
- Personal telephone call
- Voicemail message
- Speech or lecture
- Artistic performance

Strategic Communication Planning

Answering these questions will help you determine what strategy to use in your communication.

1. What message do you want to send?
2. What do you want the receiver to do with the message (action, planning, etc.)?
3. How fast must the message arrive (no rush or emergency/life dependent)?
4. Should the message go to a group or only an individual (one worker or whole staff)?
5. Do you want to be known as the sender (author or agent for author/boss)?
6. Is the message confidential or public information (medical condition or congressional testimony)?
7. Must the message meet some legal requirements for content (Securities and Exchange Commission filing or vendor contract)?
8. Is a form required to convey the message (performance appraisal or job application)?
9. What professional conventions must be met (patient treatment record, investigation interview documentation, training learning points)?
10. Who should convey the message (you or someone else)?

Figure 4-7 Communication methods

Obviously, this analytical approach isn't necessary for all messages. We send many messages every day as a matter of routine. Some, however, will require more thought. If you are involved in a merger or acquisition, a corporate downsizing, or the introduction of a new vendor for your healthcare programs, some amount of thought should be put into what your message will be and how you will communicate it properly. Your employees will depend on your message being clear and easy to understand. Your executive team will be depending on you to accomplish the objective you have targeted. Success of your communication will depend a great deal on the strategy you select for its delivery.

Human Relation Concepts and Applications

Helping structure an organization's policies and culture to make people feel welcome is a critical HR responsibility. If done properly, morale will remain high, and risks can be controlled.

Job Analysis and Job Description Methods

As noted in Part I under Laws Affecting HR Management, the Americans with Disabilities Act (ADA) does not require employers to prepare job descriptions, but it does require that those who do should review them for accuracy at least once each year. Federal contractors, subject to affirmative action obligations, must review their job descriptions every year. Therefore, most federal contractors are required to prepare and maintain proper job descriptions. If that requirement doesn't apply to you, your organization may choose to have them or not have them.

Preparing and Reviewing Job Descriptions

So why should you write job descriptions for your organization? Job descriptions can do the following:

- Identify key duties and responsibilities
- Communicate to incumbents their job content
- Communicate to job applicants the job content
- Communicate to job supervisors/managers what an incumbent should be doing
- Aid in organizational structuring to identify which jobs will perform which duties
- Provide input for the evaluation of job value in a compensation system
- Assist in determining how much incumbents should be paid
- Provide an objective reference for the preparation of work performance reviews or evaluations
- Assist in succession planning
- Provide a reference for disability accommodation requests

Usually, job descriptions contain some typical subjects. They might be described as follows:

- List of duties and responsibilities
- Identification of the amount of time spent (by percentage) on each duty and/or responsibility
- List of knowledge categories required to perform the job
- List of skill categories required to perform the job
- List of ability categories required to perform the job
- List of physical requirements of the job
- List of mental requirements of the job
- Identification of qualifications not mentioned elsewhere in the job description (such as educational requirements or amount of specific experience required to be successful on the job)

Figure 4-8 is an example of a standard job description.

Organizational Name
Job Description*

Job Title: Administrative Support Specialist
Department: Marketing
Reports to: J. C. Jones, Marketing Manager
FLSA Status: Nonexempt
Prepared by: J. C. Jones, Marketing Manager
Prepared Date: 3/5/2019
Approved by: T. L. Smith, Vice President
Approved Date: 3/10/2019

<u>Summary</u>: Schedules appointments, gives information to callers, processes inventory orders, and otherwise relieves marketing manager of clerical work and minor administrative and business detail by performing the following duties.

<u>Essential Duties and Responsibilities:</u>
Include the following. Other duties may be assigned.

20%	Writes, types, or enters information into computer to prepare correspondence, bills, statements, receipts, checks, or other documents, copying information from one record to another.
5%	Proofreads records or forms. Counts, weighs, or measures material. Sorts and files records.
15%	Processes orders for catalog merchandise from customers. Shrink-wraps products as orders and inventory demand. Receives money from customers and deposits money in bank. Processes credit card payments using credit card processing agent to secure authorization on each purchase.
5%	Composes and types routine correspondence.
5%	Organizes and maintains file system and files correspondence and other records.
5%	Answers and screens telephone calls, conveys messages, and runs errands. Answers basic questions on products or product order processing.
5%	Arranges and coordinates travel schedules and reservations.
10%	Conducts research and compiles and types statistical reports.
5%	Coordinates and arranges meetings, prepares agendas, reserves and prepares facilities.
10%	Makes copies of correspondence and other printed materials.
10%	Prepares outgoing mail and correspondence, including e-mail and faxes. Processes outgoing bulk mailings as required.
5%	Orders and maintains supplies and arranges for equipment maintenance.
100%	Total Time Allocation

<u>Supervisory Responsibilities</u>: This job has no supervisory responsibilities.

<u>Qualifications</u>: To perform this job successfully, an individual must be able to meet each of the essential duties satisfactorily. The requirements listed below are representative of the knowledge, skill, and/or ability required. Reasonable accommodations may be made to enable individuals with disabilities to perform the essential functions.

Figure 4-8 Job description example *(continued)*

Education and/or Experience: High school diploma or general education degree (GED); or one to three months related experience and/or training; or equivalent combination of education and experience.

Language Skills: Ability to read and interpret documents such as safety rules, operating and maintenance instructions, and procedure manuals prepared in the English language. Spanish language skills would be an advantage, but are not a requirement.

Mathematical Skills: Requires an ability to add, subtract, multiply, and divide in all units of measure, using whole numbers, common fractions, and decimals. Also requires an ability to compare rate, ratio, and percent and to draw and interpret bar graphs.

Reasoning Ability: The job requires ability to apply commonsense understanding to carry out instructions furnished in written, oral, or diagram form. This job requires an ability to deal with problems involving several concrete variables in standardized situations.

Certificates, Licenses or Registrations Required: None

Physical Demands: While performing the duties of this job, the employee is regularly required to sit. The employee frequently is required to use hands to finger, handle, or feel; reach with hands and arms; and talk or hear. The employee is occasionally required to stand and walk. Stooping and bending are required when accessing filing cabinet contents and supplies in the storage room. The employee must occasionally lift and/or move up to 50 pounds. Specific vision abilities required by this job include close vision. Keyboard typing skills are required and used up to 50 percent of any work day. Hands and fingers are involved with repetitive movements on standard keyboard.

Work Environment: While performing the duties of this job, the employee is occasionally exposed to moving mechanical parts (computer printers), toxic or caustic chemicals (copy machine toner, correction fluid, etc.), risk of electrical shock (computers and related equipment), and risk of radiation (computer monitors). The noise level in the work environment is usually quiet.

[* Prepared with the help of *DescriptionsNow* software, Insperity, Kingwood, Texas]

Figure 4-8 Job description example

NOTE   Reviewing your job descriptions at least once each year is essential if you are to keep them representative of the actual job content and incumbent requirements. If you are a federal contractor, you must be prepared to attest that you have periodically reviewed your job descriptions to be sure they are accurate.

Job Analysis

When trying to determine the content of a job so a job description can be written, there are several approaches to the task:

- **Observation**   A job analyst prepares lists of all activities and behaviors performed by an incumbent or group of incumbents and then consolidates those lists of duties and responsibilities. Observation can involve time and motion studies. For accuracy of results, job analysts should be properly trained in the process rather than using untrained observers.

- **Questionnaire** A written questionnaire can be used to gather input from incumbents, supervisors, and managers about job content and incumbent requirements.

- **Interview** A job analyst interviews incumbents to determine the job content, qualifications for successful incumbents, and the physical and mental requirements required of the job.

After a draft of the job description has been prepared, it should be shared with the incumbents, supervisors, and managers so they can have an opportunity to comment on the content. After considering the feedback received from the subject-matter experts, a final description should be prepared and submitted for approval.

Each year, or at some more frequent schedule if the job is undergoing rapid changes, the incumbent and supervisor should be asked to submit their comments about changes needed in the written job description. Those changes should be worked into the description and resubmitted for approval.

There is more information about job descriptions and essential functions in Chapters 5 and 7.

Review of Job Descriptions

While job descriptions are not required, affirmative action compliance requires employers to review physical and mental job qualification standards annually. This review must be in writing and made available to compliance officers from the Office of Federal Contract Compliance Programs if requested during an audit of affirmative action plans for the disabled.[13]

Communication to Employees

Organizations live and die by communication. It is when people stop talking with one another that their organizations get into trouble and flounder. To prevent such a disastrous result, HR professionals should be alert to healthy communications within the organization and do all they can to foster those conversations.

Keys to Healthy Organizational Communication

Each of the following types of communication should be encouraged within any employment organization. It is incumbent upon the HR professional to be sure each type thrives and is reinforced and encouraged.

- *Keep employees up-to-date on what is happening in the organization.* Senior executives (and HR professionals) sometimes overlook how important it is to the average worker to understand what's going on with the organization. If employees can be made to feel that they are given information about situations as developments occur, it will be easier for them to believe they really are contributing to the organizational success.

- *Reinforce with employees why their jobs are important.* When employees understand the "big picture" about where the organization is headed (and why), they will be more willing to keep their performance levels high. If they think they are being excluded from the "big picture," their enthusiasm for the job will diminish.

- *Deal effectively and immediately with rumors.* Organizational effectiveness can be severely impacted by rumors working their way through the workforce. Rumors often start when people "suspect" something will happen but don't have confirmation that it is really true. Sometimes rumors are intentionally started in an effort to derail what is thought to be something bad for workers. It could be something to do with the organization or something to do with individuals in the workgroup. Whenever untrue rumors take hold, managers should react quickly to address them openly and correct misunderstandings where they exist. If rumors deal with confidential issues, they should still be dealt with quickly and with as much openness as possible. You can always say, "We don't have information about that yet, but as soon as we do, we'll let you know." Or, "These things are personal and hurtful to those involved. Consider how you would feel hearing something like this about yourself. Even though we can't discuss them because of their personal nature, we hope you will not discuss things like this that can't be confirmed as accurate."

- *Ask for feedback.* Many employees would be willing to contribute ideas or suggestions if they thought there was a chance someone would actually listen. If we believe no one will listen or, worse, have actually been told to keep our ideas to ourselves, we are not likely to be open with ideas in the future. HR managers should protect upward communication by requesting input from employees when it is appropriate. That may mean training managers and supervisors in how to request and accept employee feedback. You might have to prepare organizational leaders in how to behave when employee suggestions surface. Some of those ideas will be good ones. It is not necessary to have formal "employee suggestion programs" for there to be requests for employee feedback. Feedback can be handled formally or informally, but if it is not handled at all, workers will become discouraged at not being able to contribute. Frustration will lead to dissatisfaction and lower production. Give folks the chance to contribute their ideas.

- *Give feedback.* Let your workers know how they are doing. If they are meeting your expectations, give them that acknowledgment. You don't need a formal job performance appraisal system to provide that input to your employees. When something happens that you like or there is a remarkable achievement, let employees know that you appreciate what they did. Likewise, when things go wrong that could have been handled differently, make suggestions for doing it differently next time. People have a need to understand where they fit into an organization and what their supervisors think of the contributions they are making.

HR Technology Activities

Besides the government, the HR function was notorious for being an intensive paper user. It was one of the first organizational functions to jump into the paperless movement via the development of technology, specifically human resource information systems and, soon after, applicant tracking systems. The cost savings of going digital and paperless were astounding. HR technology continues to develop and basically serves two purposes: as a repository of necessary information and as an aid to good decision-making. Let's review the various technology that exists today for HR.

Employee Records Management

These days, records management invokes thinking about not only the method of record-keeping but the safety of those records. For employers larger than 10 to 20 employees, keeping records manually is difficult. That is particularly true with the reporting requirements that exist for federal contractors and subcontractors. A great deal of attention is given to record security, yet there are not many pieces of legislation that speak to employer obligations in that regard. Most of them on the books deal with medical information. (See Chapter 2 for more information about the Fair Credit Reporting Act, the Health Insurance Portability and Accountability Act, and the Americans with Disabilities Act.) Today, hardly a week goes by that there isn't news of another illegitimate access and release of private information from some database somewhere. From a risk management perspective, there are many commonsense protections that can be put in place to prevent the embarrassment of such disclosures and the expense of following up with people whose records have been jeopardized. It can be costly to notify hundreds or thousands of employees that their records have been subject to theft. It erodes employee relations along with HR trust and credibility.

HR Information Systems

Employee records involve fields of data, including those shown in Figure 4-9. This is not an exhaustive list. Many other records are maintained by some employers.

Birth date	Department	Home phone	Original job title
Building code	Educational degree	Home state	Original pay rate
Cell phone	Employee ID number	Home ZIP	Past job title
Certifications	Exempt/nonexempt	Job group/EEO code	Race/ethnicity
Current job title	Healthcare plan	Last employer	Sex
Current pay rate	Home address	Licenses	Social Security number
Dental plan	Home city	Name	Vision plan

Figure 4-9   Types of data included in employee records

HR information system (HRIS) programs range from those serving employee groups up to 100 people to systems that can handle unlimited data fields and unlimited numbers of employees. Obviously, the prices of such software systems vary according to the capabilities they offer. PII is a crucial concern with HRIS and other systems in protecting employee data.

Employee Self-Service

There are many ways to offer employee self-service related to personal employee records. Some large employers use kiosks in central locations equipped with computer terminals that offer individual employees the opportunity to make changes to their employee records. Those changes might include marital status, health plan selections during open enrollment, addition of licenses or certifications, and more.

Employers often offer employee self-service through remote access and internal intranets so they can connect from the convenience of home during off-duty hours. It is obvious that such systems require security to assure that only authorized employees can gain access and that employees can only access their own personal record and not others. It's not a good thing to have one employee searching through other employee records. In some cases, employers have even offered telephone access to employee data with the ability to make updates from the touchtone keypad. The latest hardware, offering touch-screen technology, makes reviewing and updating employee records quick and easy.

It used to be that employers would default to using Social Security numbers as employee numbers in their HRIS or even in file folders. That is no longer such a good idea with identity theft on the rise. In some states, it is no longer permissible to print the entire Social Security number on paychecks for that same reason. Instead, consider using sequential numbers, with 1 representing the first employee hired, and so on. Or you could use compound numbers such as 2013-1 to reflect the year and the hiring priority within the year. Another approach is to use the employee's phone number as the employee number. Because Social Security numbers are used for so many sensitive purposes, such as bank account reporting to the Internal Revenue Service income tax filings and payroll withholding reports, protecting them by not using them as employee ID numbers is a reasonable protection to take.

E-learning

Only a few years ago, e-learning was not an option in the workplace. Learning was accomplished by attending a classroom session lasting from a few hours to several days, weeks, or months. Today, employees are able to log on to a computer access point and participate in training programs at their own pace, on their own schedule. These e-learning systems provide materials, review, and testing to assure the employee has accomplished specific learning objectives before moving to the next training step. They also offer an audit trail to report on who has participated in each program. That is handy when you have to be sure everyone has gone through specific training programs. There is no need for an instructor. Each individual works with the materials presented, and perhaps some reference materials, to meet the training objectives.

One of the more popular e-learning systems involves classroom-type groups with an instructor and a group of students, all participating remotely from anywhere in the world. There is no longer a need when using these systems for the group to collect into one physical setting. The savings on travel time alone have been significant for organizations using these types of learning programs. This approach is used by almost all major universities and colleges around the country.

Applicant Tracking Systems

For most small employers, an applicant tracking system consists of a file folder filled with job application forms. Larger employers are not able to operate with manual records any longer. During the Great Recession, with unemployment running up to double digits, an employer could count on receiving hundreds or thousands of job applications for every job opening announcement. Processing them manually was not feasible.

More and more, applicant tracking is accomplished on employer websites. People interested in a given job opening can submit their application information online and in some cases can even submit résumé files and cover letters for consideration. These mechanized programs allow employers to sort through the massive amounts of data to find the few candidates who might be a good fit for the job opening.

Federal contractors with 50 or more employees and $50,000 or more in contracts are required to maintain applicant flow logs so they can perform analysis compared to new-hire data. The objective, of course, is to determine whether there are significant disparities among various groups for race and gender. Don't forget that "race" includes all races. All people have a race, and all races are protected, not just minorities.

See more about applicant tracking systems in Chapter 5.

Techniques for Forecasting, Planning, and Predicting Impact of HR Activities

One of the largest challenges facing HR professionals is having the right people resources available for the organizational needs precisely when they will be needed. Forecasting can be accomplished in many ways but often relies on the professional experience of people with institutional knowledge about organizational history.

Mathematically Based Forecasting Techniques

In some situations, it is possible to bring objective analysis to the forecasting effort. Using mathematical techniques can help create confidence in the forecast.

- **Staffing ratios** Compare the number of support personnel needed for every 10 production workers. This method can be used to estimate any support group requirements from accounting to HR to legal.

- **Sales ratios** Compare the number of employees required to support each different level of sales activity.

- **Regression analysis**   This type of analysis can be used much like the other ratio approaches to use various pieces of information to determine the likely workload and employee requirements based on sales, production levels, economic indicators, and so on. This method can get complicated quickly but is aided somewhat by the availability of software aids within programs such as Microsoft Excel.

Judgment-Based Forecasting Techniques

Judgment requires experience and knowledge to be effective in forecasting. The following are some manners of judgment-based forecasting techniques:

- **Simple estimates**   Based on what input may be available to the HR manager, this is simply an approximate valuation for the number of people required based on what is known subjectively and objectively about the future.

- **The Delphi technique**   This uses input from a group of individuals who are experts in the area of HR forecasting. Input is gathered through the use of questionnaires; it is compiled/aggregated, and then the anonymous responses are recirculated to the experts for another set of opinions. It is a type of orchestrated survey system that seeks to reach a "correct" response through consensus.

- **Focus group or panel estimates**   Using people gathered into a conference room setting, the group is asked to voice their opinions based on a set of facts given to them.

- **Historically based estimates**   Using historical records, best judgments are made extrapolating history into the future.

In the Trenches

Historical Telephone Company Operator Scheduling

In the 1920s through the 1970s, the telephone company scheduled its operators based on 15-minute increments of workload projection. Many years of data were retained and used by the "Force Manager" to determine how work schedules would be allocated. Notes were kept on such things as special events for the day (Super Bowl, Mother's Day, political inaugurations, or elections) and local events or celebrations (parades, sports contests with local rival organizations, special TV programming). People used the telephone at TV commercial time, just like they used the bathroom at those program breaks. Of course, there are times when historical events cannot reliably project into the future for workforce planning. Examples include the assassination of President Kennedy, explosion of the Space Shuttle Challenger, 9/11, the 2013 Boston Marathon bombing, and other disasters. Success in using this approach to forecasting relies a great deal on personal experience and professional judgment. Today, the retail industry lives and dies by these kinds of staffing forecasts.

Diversity Concepts and Applications

Diversity and inclusion practices embrace internal and external groups. Social media can be effectively used to reach out to groups you have found are underrepresented in your workforce, your vendor and supplier groups, or your customer and client groups. One example is found in how popular LinkedIn has become in the recruiting arena. It has been said that more than half of white-collar workers are being placed through that website each year. Why not use those avenues of communication to increase the diversity of the employee population?

Of course, the risk of liability for failing to treat people equally is that complaints about disparate treatment will be filed. When cases go directly to external enforcement agencies, the employer loses the ability to provide an early remedy or explain to employees why the actions were not discriminatory.

Ethical and Professional Standards

As mentioned earlier in the chapter, the Society of Human Resource Management has compiled and published a Code of Ethics.[2] It calls for HR professionals to set an example for others in their organization: "HR professionals are expected to exhibit individual leadership as a role model for maintaining the highest standards of ethical conduct."

Privacy Issues

The U.S. Supreme Court has weighed in on the question of employee privacy when using employer-owned equipment intended for use as a business tool and not a private communication device. The court has said, regarding public employees, they should have no expectation of privacy when the equipment is owned by the employer and they are directed to use it for work-related business only.[14]

Social media has become such a powerful influence in the lives of American citizens that private employers in some locations began asking job applicants for their Facebook usernames so a review of their Facebook content could be included in the background check. In 2012 Congress failed to pass the Password Protection Act, but that didn't stop six states from passing their own legislation preventing employers from demanding such information.[15]

Another privacy issue for employers is embedded in the National Labor Relations Board ruling on employee freedom to engage in "concerted activities." Late in 2012, the board ruled that employees have a right to discuss employer policies and their personal treatment in a forum such as Facebook.[16]

Internal Privacy Issues

Privacy issues within an organization surround employee expectations and the type of business the organization conducts. Here are some reasons why you might want to explain to employees that they should have no expectation of privacy while at work:

- Security cameras monitor work areas as well as the grounds outside.
- Telephone calls are monitored and recorded for training and quality purposes.

- Computer use is monitored and reviewed for quality purposes.

- E-mails are subject to review at any time.

- Lockers and desks are employer property and subject to search at any time without notice.

- Personal bags and briefcases are subject to search when entering or leaving the building.

External Privacy Issues

When communicating with people and locations outside the employer's organization, it is necessary to consider the possibility that those communications could be intercepted and read by unauthorized people. Today, there is a growing problem of "bad guys" stealing e-mail messages to mine personal data such as credit cards and Social Security numbers. One way to contain the problem is to use encryption for e-mail messages. That scrambles the message so it is not readable by anyone other than someone with the encryption tool needed to decode the message.

Electronic access to bank accounts, tax records, credit card merchant accounts, or other sensitive data is at risk. Such data transfer processes should be done only with a secure link on the Internet. Credit card information should be transmitted only across secure connections. It is time to recognize that there are people sitting and watching electronic traffic. If they have an opportunity to steal such information for personal gain, they will do so. It is incumbent upon the HR professional to assist the organization in constructing systems to prevent that from happening.

Protection of Data

Risks abound in the subject of data protection. Consider these types of data employers generally handle:

- Personal and private employee information (name, Social Security number, bank account number for payroll deposit, driver's license number, passport number, medical records, disability identification)

- Financial records belonging to customers (credit card number, credit card expiration date, credit card security code, bank account number for wire transfers)

- Financial records belonging to the employer's organization (tax records, bank account numbers, accounting records including customer contact information)

The question becomes one of how to protect such information from unauthorized disclosure. Here are some considerations:

- Provide an audit trail in software so financial records can be checked.

- Require two people for authorization of transactions above a given dollar amount.

- Secure employee records with physical locks and a sufficient password policy.

- Restrict access to customer records through a sufficient password policy.
- If it is warranted, require a supervisor to input authorization on each occasion before an employee can gain access to sensitive record systems.

Ensuring that such policies and procedures are not only implemented but properly maintained by all people in the organization is something HR professionals can help with. The alternative is the unauthorized disclosure of employee personal information or customer financial information and the expense it will require to "clean up" after the fact. And that doesn't include the loss of trust people will have in the organization having once experienced exposure that should not have happened. Typically, organizations that have had a breach of security and loss of personal or financial data will offer six to twelve months of credit report monitoring through one of the three major credit bureaus. Even with the expense that represents for thousands of people whose records may have been disclosed, often the basic security for the data systems doesn't get changed and the same risk carries forward. Through proper attention to such matters, HR professionals can help their organizations avoid such catastrophes.

Password Protections, Monitoring Software, and Biometrics

Passwords are problematic because people generally treat them in a cavalier manner. They are posted on notes under plastic desktop protectors or taped to the computer monitor in plain sight. Sometimes, a modicum of effort is made to hide them by putting the note inside the desk drawer or under a blotter.

Employers and HR professionals should have well-considered policies about passwords. The best systems have passwords controlled by a single coordinator who changes passwords on a regular basis or require users to create new passwords on a regular basis. Storing passwords is an issue that should be discussed with all departments. Proper handling can easily be the subject of a brief employee training program.

Monitoring software is available that will permit employers to track the type of usage on company PCs. These are some of the types of tracking that can be done:

- Websites visited
- Searches conducted
- Keystroke logging
- E-mail sent and received
- Document tracking
- Website blocking
- Application blocking
- Keyword blocking

All of these types of tracking can be performed remotely by supervisors or other authorized surveillance personnel. There are many such programs available for less than $100.

NOTE It is necessary to inform employees that such monitoring systems are being used and that they have no privacy when working on company equipment.

Biometrics is the collective use of personal biological characteristics to identify authorized personnel for system access. Biometrics can include retina scans, fingerprint scans, or palm-print scans. The level of sophistication in this technology is increasing rapidly. A quick Internet search will unveil hundreds of websites that offer information or products related to biometric security systems. The federal government even has a website dedicated to the subject at www.biometrics.gov/.

Identity Theft

This is the result we want to avoid. Identity theft is the generic term used to describe the situation when someone co-opts personal information such as credit card numbers and Social Security numbers to steal money from the person those things belong to. Often that happens without anyone being aware of it until the arrival of the next credit card statement. It should be noted, however, that banks and other credit card issuing organizations are becoming much more sophisticated about their monitoring of credit card purchases. They look for purchases that don't belong in the individual's buying pattern or for charges made outside the country.

When someone has had their identity stolen and their credit rating demolished, they will need to invest a significant amount of effort to set things right again. That can take months or years and some amount of money in correspondence and notary fees.

If employee information is jeopardized, a policy should be in place that specifies how the organization will respond to the problem. It should lay out the communication that will take place and any support that will be provided to employees who experience identity theft–type events as a result of the data loss.

Workplace Monitoring

Aside from the computer monitoring we have already discussed, there are some organizations that find it beneficial to monitor their workplace by using video equipment. Examples include gas stations, convenience stores, check cashing businesses, and banks. Monitoring is done for the benefit of employees as much as for the organization's protection.

Of course, retail establishments are concerned about theft of products as well as robbery. "Shrinkage," as product theft is called, cost retailers $119 billion in 2011 according to the *RFID Journal*. Radio frequency identification (RFID) is being used more and more to protect expensive products from pilferage. Fast-forward to 2016 and the technology has improved considerably.[17] As the cost of those small devices decreases, they are finding their way into less expensive products. A transponder chip inserted into the packaging will trigger an alarm when exiting the store if it is not disarmed at the cash register first. As technological changes continue to expand, you will be accountable for monitoring what most recent updates mean to your HR management applications.

PART II

Policies should be in writing and clearly communicated to employees so they understand any monitoring that is conducted in the workplace.

Methods for Assessing Employee Attitudes, Opinions, and Satisfaction

Some risks can be reduced if employers are aware of them in advance. If employee attitudes are sliding from positive to negative, the employer would want to know that and have a chance to correct whatever problems exist before they become irreversible.

Small employer organizations can make use of PC-based software products that can perform surveys and survey reporting with some limitations. Larger organizations will likely want to use more sophisticated software or the help of external survey experts. Often these are members of the American Psychological Association (APA).

Most organizational success experts stress the importance of monitoring employee attitudes and opinions on a regular basis. Almost every large organization spends a great deal of energy and resources on monitoring customer satisfaction. But that's only half of the equation. It also takes satisfied employees as the other part of the equation. HR professionals can help their organizations understand the benefits and importance of budgeting for this important effort.

Use of Third Parties or Vendors

There will come a time in the professional life of every HR manager when there won't be sufficient internal resources available to do the tasks required. It could be the need to do open benefits enrollment, affirmative action plan development, employee attitude surveys, or HRIS implementation. It could be any number of other things.

When vendors are needed to perform a function or task, selecting them should be a serious undertaking. It is a multistep process.

Developing Requests for Proposals

A request for proposal (RFP) is different from requests for information (RFIs) or requests for quotation (RFQs).

An RFI is a formal request for information about products or services available on the market that might fit the buyer's needs. Think of them as "off the shelf" or "ready to wear." There is little or no customization involved with an RFI. Examples are software packages that will track job applicants or an HRIS database for employee information.

An RFQ seeks pricing for a product or service that the buyer already understands. There is no need for the buyer to engage a vendor in discussions about how the request will be fulfilled. The basic information needed is a price for the deliverable. This can be useful when shopping for salary survey reports or safety kits to be posted throughout the workplace.

The RFP is generally used for more complex products and services. When you need to have a vendor provide healthcare benefits programs or payroll services, you will want to publish an RFP and distribute it to vendors you believe would be able to respond adequately.

Contents of an RFP should include the following:

- **Organization and project background**   This is a statement about the organizational history that brought about the need for this program or project. What generated the need?

- **Work to be done**   This is a statement about what the project will entail. This is where a description of the product or service will be found. It can be brief or extensive depending on the complexity of the deliverable involved.

- **Timelines and deadlines**   Write clear expectations for the milestones to be met during the project. Attach dates to each step or review point. Vendor responses should be based on these deadlines and expectations. If payments are to be made to the vendor at interim points along the way, that should be explained here.

- **Vendor bid**   This is the statement of expense the vendor will provide. If necessary, the buyer may request more than a "bottom-line number" for the cost statement. It might be that there are identifiable subdivisions of work that can be priced for budgeting purposes.

- **Payment conditions**   Explain the number of days it will take to generate a check after a vendor invoice is received. Of course, this is something that should involve the accounting department and any policy on the subject. Will there be monthly invoice requirements, one invoice at the end of the project, or only one invoice for delivery of the product being purchased?

- **RFP evaluation criteria**   This is the statement about how the buyer will evaluate the RFP responses. Will there be interviews? Will there be follow-up questions requiring vendor response? Will a committee be making the decision or is that to be done by an individual? What will be considered for evaluating the RFPs? Cost will be one, but other factors could include the ability to meet the milestone dates, background and experience of the vendor and its staff, responses from references provided by the vendor, and location of the vendor's work site in relation to the buyer's facilities. Almost any business criteria could be applied to evaluating vendor responses; whatever they are should be included in the RFP document.

Contract Negotiation

If you are going to select a vendor or supplier without going through the RFP process, it will be necessary to reach agreement on the details of delivery and payment. These things are usually covered in an RFP.

When negotiating, first identify the legal requirements for the situation. Are there local or state laws that govern building permits or zoning that will impact your project? Are there sales tax requirements that will be involved with the purchase? Your organization's legal advisor or financial officer can be helpful in identifying these requirements.

Next, prepare for your negotiating sessions.

- *Prepare a list of topics you want to address.* Identify the facts and figures associated with each topic. Know the details before you go into the meeting.

- *Identify the facts that you think both parties might be able to agree on.* List those that you think will be controversial.

- *Highlight the items you believe are absolute requirements and those you would be willing to compromise on.* Attach some cost estimates to each of the items so you will be ready to discuss the expenses if you do compromise.

- *Meet the other side with respect.* Treat the vendor, or others, as you want to be treated.

Contract Management

Once a contract has been negotiated and approved, someone should be designated as the contract manager. This should be a single person who will be responsible for following up to assure the contract requirements are met. These include verifying that the timeline is working as planned and that all deadlines or milestones are met. If contract changes are needed, work with the attorney to prepare an amendment and then implement the changes. Your organizational attorney will be of help in identifying how to oversee the contract's implementation.

Qualitative and Quantitative Methods and Tools for Analysis

Often, managers will have a need to assess their workforce and what things are influencing it. Questions arise such as "Why is turnover so high?" and "Why are new hires only lasting for six months before leaving?" Some of the following analysis techniques can help determine the answers:

- **Supply analysis techniques**   Do a strategic evaluation of supply chain options such as sourcing alternatives, plant locations, and warehouse locations.

- **Trend and ratio analysis**   Ratio analysis compares current results or historic results but always at a point in time. Trend analysis compares historical results with current results and identifies what may happen in the future based on the trend of data in the past.

- **Turnover analysis**   There are many possible reasons for employees leaving the payroll, including resignation, dismissal, death, long-term disability, and transfer to another subordinate company within the same parent company. Identifying the reasons that employees are leaving provides the data needed to analyze trends and identify potential problems within the organization. If supervisors are causing high resignation rates, it may be appropriate to train the supervisors or take some other action to reduce the rate at which their subordinates are leaving.

- **Flow analysis**   This can involve analysis of data, analysis of production line movement, or analysis of order processing, among other possibilities. How processes operate and how flows of products, data, or other items go through those processes is the objective of this type of monitoring.

- **Demand analysis techniques**   It is interesting to look forward to determine what customers, clients, or patrons will want in the future.

- **Judgmental forecasts**   These are projections based on subjective inputs. This method is often used when there is a short time for drawing a conclusion or data is outdated or unavailable.

- **Managerial estimates**   An individual or a group of management people uses their experience and knowledge to identify the most likely future characteristics without any additional data analysis.

- **Delphi technique**   This is a method of determining the future outcome and then manipulating a group to reach that conclusion or goal statement. A group of people is forced into polarized positions; then the facilitator suggests a resolution and guides people to support that idea. Ultimately, the group will endorse the facilitator's suggestion because the group has accepted the facilitator as one of its own. It is unethical and used more frequently than might be suspected.

- **Nominal group technique**   A variation on the brainstorming process for group creativity, the nominal group technique alters that process a bit. As a forecasting process, the facilitator can ask a question such as, "What will be our best-selling product next year?" The large group is then divided into small groups of five or six members. Each person spends several minutes silently brainstorming on their own, seeking all the possible ideas they can come up with. Next, each group collects its members' ideas by sharing them around the table, and each is written on a flipchart. No criticism is allowed, but clarification in response to questions is encouraged. Each person then evaluates the ideas and individually and anonymously votes for the best ones using some form of grading system (for example, a score of 5 for the best idea, 4 for the next best, and so on). The group then collects and tabulates the points awarded to each idea, and the one with the highest score is the winner.

- **Statistical forecasts**   These approaches to analysis use mathematical formulas to identify patterns and trends. Once identified, the trends are analyzed again for mathematical reasonableness.

- **Regression analysis**   Linear regression is a tool often used in forecasting and financial analysis. It compares relationships among several variables. A variable is something for which the value changes over time. In hiring, one variable is the number of job openings to be filled. Another variable is the number of job applicants received for each job opening. How these things can be related and used in predicting the number of people who will meet the job requirements can be determined through linear regression analysis.

  Multiple regression analysis allows us to ask the question, "What is the best predictor of…?" If we want new employees to remain on the job successfully for at least one year after hiring them, we can use multiple regression analysis to determine how factors such as educational degree, educational institution, general experience, specific job experience, multiple language skills, or community involvement can contribute to that longevity requirement.

PART II

- **Simulations** We can simulate a process or condition to predict an outcome. For example, we can build a simulation of a management problem in order to measure how nonmanagement people handle the problem. That allows us in turn to predict whether each participant would be successful if promoted to a management position. This is commonly done in industrial assessment centers.

- **Gap analysis techniques** Measuring the distance (or difference) between where you are and where you want to be is known as *gap analysis*. If you have to train all employees in certain safety procedures, you can use gap analysis to determine what portion of the population has yet to receive the training or any portion of the training.

- **Solution analysis techniques** Another approach is to define the problem, identify a variety of solutions, and then assess each solution through use of statistical comparisons. It involves asking the question, "What is the likelihood of success for this solution?" It can employ the mathematical process of regression analysis to assess the variables influencing each solution's implementation. For example, it might be possible to solve the problem of turnover by creating a management skills training program. It also might be possible to solve the turnover problem by providing different employee benefits more appealing to the workers. It could also be that offering continuing education to employees would have an impact on turnover. Each of those solutions could work. You can determine how well each works by using regression analysis to calculate the contribution each could make to the problem of turnover control. This analysis considers that there is some value to be contributed by each different solution. If you can't choose all of them, where will you get the greatest impact for your investment of time and money?

Dealing with Situations that Are Uncertain, Unclear, or Chaotic

According to Glenn Llopis,[18] "To successfully manage change and uncertainty, you must engage your employees by empowering them to be part of the solution, rather than giving them reason to perceive they are part of the problem. Oftentimes you'll find leaders that keep a low profile and that say as little as possible during times of change and uncertainty. It's as if they are trying to protect themselves and their careers, instead of leading those that demand and expect great leadership from them. Uncertainty in an organization has the tendency to create hearsay, amplify political rumblings, and cause break room conversations amongst employees; this further fuels uncertainty and makes it difficult for employees to trust the workplace culture and its leadership, which impacts their ability to perform at their highest levels.

"Great leaders know that managing uncertainty is a matter of putting themselves in the shoes of their employees and delivering the compassionate leadership they expect. People don't want good intentions from their leaders during times of uncertainty; they want their leaders to be not only strong, confident and decisive, but transparent and vulnerable enough in their leadership role to express a sense of genuine care and concern."

It is possible for uncertainty to become confidence and predictability. Lack of clarity can become brightness and precision. Chaos can become order and calmness. It all depends on how you, the HR professional, lead the organization through its time of trouble. Perhaps facilitating a planning session will be helpful. Perhaps a new management and/or employee training program could help folks understand how policies will be changing in the future. And helping people understand how to cope with uncertainty can bridge the gap they believe exists between their personal status quo and an unknown future.

The most important way you can deal with these problems is to actively engage employees. That prevents the water cooler talk and rumor mill from causing upset among your workers. That upset can create serious production problems at every level. Do something to bring truth to the conversation. Tell it like it is, at least as much as you legally can. There may be constraints preventing you from sharing some information, and you can explain that to your people. Tell them why you can't say more at the moment. Promise to get back to them as soon as those constraints have been lifted. Information is your most powerful tool. Use it wisely.

Seven Steps to Successfully Dealing with Chaos and Uncertainty[19]

Gordon Tredgold published in *Inc.* his list of seven steps to overcoming chaos and uncertainty:

1. *Communicate. Communicate. Communicate.* As soon as you are able within legal constraints (such as in a merger or acquisition), tell people what you know about the changes that are coming and the impact they will have on each of the employees. Be sure you also tell them the things you don't yet know about the changes they can expect. Explain the timing of those changes so they know when to expect things that will impact them. (For example, a reorganization of departmental structures may cause two departments to be consolidated. Who will be the surviving manager? What will be done about work shift assignments? Will there be any jobs eliminated due to the consolidation? How will this impact annual bonuses? Will there be a change in work locations?) Write a list of all the questions you can anticipate your staff will be asking. Add to it the questions you can expect employees in the two departments will be asking. Then go to work to do a Q&A that can be published for all employees addressing all the questions you are able to answer at the moment. Tell them, too, when you expect you will be able to pass along answers that aren't available right now.

2. *Explain your plan.* Employees will expect you to have a plan that deals with all the things that you actually may not be able to deal with right now. So, plan. Use the information you have currently, identify the information you don't expect to have for a while, and assemble answers to the questions you know people will want answered. Why are you making the decisions you are making? Your objective is to build trust with your workforce as you guide them through this journey for which you can't clearly see the path right now. If you are confident about the process and communicate that confidence, you will have people trust your relationship with them. Make it genuine. Don't try to fool anyone with guesses or misinformation.

3. *Ask for input.* Leaders aren't expected to have all the answers to all the questions at the start of the change process. They are expected, however, to seek input from employees as that input can be used in decision-making along the way. Accepting employee input can raise the sense of involvement among workers and increase the level of satisfaction with their involvement in the process. Cutting people out of the data gathering and decision-making process results in a sense of powerlessness. That, in any amount, is bad for morale and can kill trust.

4. *Be flexible and adaptive.* When new problems arise or better solutions present themselves, we must be willing to adapt to those changes. Often, given the chance, employee suggestions about alternative approaches can result in improved solutions. Acknowledge the employees who made the suggestions and point out in your communication that those suggestions were accepted and resulted in these specific changes in the plan. Then outline the changes.

5. *Be positive.* Nobody enjoys being around a pessimist, especially if that pessimist is the leader in a chaotic situation. Leaders must be positive and optimistic. They must show confidence in the plan and its outcome. HR professionals are particularly expected to be positive about the plan and its implementation. Don't create a false story just to appear positive. But be positive about the real story. When there are uncertainties, explain them. You can still be positive about how you will get past those uncertainties.

6. *Create small wins.* If you have a detailed plan, you can identify early achievements as the plan is implemented. Spotlight accomplishments and the people who were involved. Publicize those accomplishments and help everyone know that progress is being made successfully.

7. *Be visible and stay engaged.* HR professionals have a leadership role to play in organizational redesign. They actually have to wear many different specialty hats. As the leader, the HR professional must be engaged with the workforce during times of uncertainty and doubt. Avoiding negative feelings or even panic among the workers is going to be possible only if the leader is visible and interacting with people who are going through the changes. Strong leaders who are active participants with the workers can have a powerful impact on people's stress reduction.

In the Trenches

Supervisor Meltdown

The manager's organization of 152 employees was undergoing some major changes in its operating procedures, and thus there was a headcount reduction planned. Seven supervisors reported directly to the manager. Each supervisor handled a different component of the department. The manager was keeping everyone as fully appraised of the plan and its progress as possible. There were weekly meetings with the supervisors and biweekly meetings with the entire department. Rumors were addressed, and expectations were aligned with the plan.

One morning the manager came in early as was the custom. He immediately found one of the supervisors huddled under her desk, curled up into a tight ball, whimpering and rocking back and forth. An ambulance took the supervisor to get medical attention.

Later, it was determined that the supervisor's decision to retire at the conclusion of the reorganization put too much stress on her. She really didn't want to retire even though she had 32 years of service. She just went along with it to please everyone else. That conflict caused her tragic reaction. It took a year for her to recover. Ultimately, she realized that she didn't want to continue as a supervisor, and she could find happiness volunteering in the community, using her talents to help others without all the hassle of the work world.

The manager continued to see the reorganization completed. As sad as it was, that was the only tragic negative reaction to the reorganization. All the workers were placed in jobs that assured them continued employment with the company. The department eventually shrunk to 110 employees. That represented a massive 28 percent reduction in the department headcount. Could the manager have prevented the serious mental trauma the supervisor experienced? Possibly. More one-on-one attention with each of the supervisors might have helped.

Even when you think you are doing all the right things, things can go wrong. Address each of the problems as they arise. Empathy and understanding are great allies.

Chapter Review

This chapter reviewed business management issues and how HR professionals can contribute to the organization's business success. We determined that every decision must fit into the strategic business plan for both the HR organization and the total enterprise. HR's role has expanded considerably beyond the processing of benefit and payroll information. It is now a problem-solving role within the enterprise. It serves two masters: employees and the employer. There is a great need for HR professionals to understand and speak in terms of business management.

Questions

1. One of the primary HR responsibilities in business management is:

  A. Deciding which goal to choose when only one can be achieved

  B. Selecting the CPA who will audit the payroll records

  C. Identifying competitive organizations and the size of market they hold

  D. Interpreting and applying information related to general business environment and industry best practices

2. It is not necessary for HR professionals to be concerned with:

  A. Organizational and HR visions

  B. Building and record security

  C. Employee ethics

  D. Getting everyone flu shots in the fall each year

3. Which of the following are parts of a SMART goal? (Choose three.)

  A. Relevant

  B. Strength

  C. Time bound

  D. Measurable

4. Mikhael is the shipping and receiving manager at your Sri Lanka parts plant. He has experienced problems with getting shipments through Customs for timely delivery to the United States. His contact at Sri Lanka Customs informs him that he can expedite the shipments if Mikhael would pay him a gratuity for his service in cash. Your organization's ethics clearly state that bribes are considered unethical behavior; however, this "gratuity" seems to be in the best interest of the organization. What is your best course of action?

  A. Authorize Mikhael to make the payments out of petty cash.

  B. Report the bribe incident to the local Sri Lankan Customs head officer.

  C. Ask executive management for "special outside-of-policy" authorization.

  D. Adhere to the organization's no-bribe ethics policy and seek other solutions for the shipment delay issue.

5. Taylor is the quality assurance director at her organization and reports to both the division VP at her facility and the VP of quality assurance located at the headquarters office. This is an example of what type of organizational structure?

  A. Span of control

  B. Formalized

  C. Matrix

  D. Chain of command

6. Elton has hired a consultancy firm to perform an environmental scanning on his organization. The report indicates that a global competitor is moving into a state where Elton's company has existed for decades. Elton should present this information to executive management as a(n):

   A. Opportunity

   B. Weakness

   C. Strength

   D. Threat

7. Which of the following HR functions is not appropriate for outsourcing?

   A. Benefit administration

   B. Development of HR goals aligned with the organization's strategic plan

   C. New employee orientation/onboarding

   D. Open enrollment

8. _____ is the most important foundational issue of organizational effectiveness.

9. Which of the following actions taken by HR Manager Chris is the most ethical?

   A. Working exclusively with a technical contracting agency for the IT group to qualify for a random prize drawing for customers

   B. Not standing up and voicing displeasure about a discriminatory decision made by a superior

   C. Referring a qualified friend for a vacant position at the company

   D. Deleting low-paying companies from salary survey results of HR positions

10. The matrix type of organizational structure is uniquely suited to managing a group of activities that are:

   A. Narrow and interrelated

   B. Narrow in focus and unrelated

   C. Diverse and unrelated

   D. Diverse and interrelated

11. The process of analyzing and identifying the need for availability of human resources so that the organization can meet its objectives is known as:

   A. Strategic planning

   B. PEST analysis

   C. Human resource planning

   D. Organization planning

12. In an organizational structure, what is centralized?

    A. The degree to which decision-making authority is restricted to senior management

    B. The degree to which decision-making authority is given to lower levels in an organization's hierarchy

    C. The hierarchical division of labor that distributes formal authority and establishes how critical decisions will be made

    D. The degree to which decisions are made by committees

13. Government regulations are published in the _____ _____.

14. Colin is the HR manager at a tax preparation firm. During the tax season, Colin contracts with a temporary agency for seasonal help. The seasonal workers receive payroll checks from the temporary agency and not Colin's organization. What type of contract will Colin sign with the temporary agency for the seasonal workers?

    A. Temporary contract

    B. Seasonal contract

    C. Third-party contract

    D. Direct contract

15. Yoko's organization is acquiring another smaller company. What is the first step for her HR department to be involved with?

    A. Survey the existing workforce of both companies.

    B. Eliminate the redundant positions.

    C. Review the collective bargaining agreements that exist.

    D. Assure OSHA compliance.

16. Which of the following is a legal consequence of the Sarbanes-Oxley Act?

    A. Organizations are allowed to conduct their own stock appraisal.

    B. Shareholders are prevented from suing the company.

    C. CEOs may be punished, including jail time, for fraudulent financial reports.

    D. Audit firms must alternate every two years.

17. Which of the following is not a knowledge requirement of HR professionals in the area of business management?

    A. Corporate governance procedures

    B. Payroll management theory

    C. Change management theory

    D. Dealing with situations that are uncertain, unclear, or chaotic

18. The role of human resource management has changed over the last few decades because more focus is now placed on:

    A. Finding people with qualifications in high technology that can meet today's challenges

    B. Strategic management of the organization with less focus on labor relations

    C. Recruiting and less focus on paperwork

    D. Supporting the executive suite and the programs that the officers want implemented

19. Financial contributions from the HR department are important because:

    A. Training and staffing are the easiest areas to cut and gain back budget.

    B. Executives expect the HR department to be the most flexible in budget terms.

    C. There is little impact from reducing the HR department's budget.

    D. Every strategic decision must contribute to the financial performance of the organization.

20. Management skills have been identified over a long period of time through the work of:

    A. Various universities around the country and their studies of manufacturing plants

    B. Various consulting firms across the country and their studies of university environments

    C. Studies such as the Management Progress Study conducted by American Telephone and Telegraph beginning in 1956 and continuing over the next 30 years

    D. IBM's study of management individuals that lasted for 35 years

21. Complex project management is made easier through the use of:

    A. PARK/ITEM planning charts

    B. Gaunt PERK planning charts

    C. PACK/CWA planning charts

    D. PERT/CPM planning charts

22. The AB Trucking Co. is expanding its routes and hiring more people. Those changes will mean that employees will have to take on different work assignments. How should the HR manager handle those changes with the workforce?

    A. Explain the coming changes to all employees and solicit their help in deciding how to assign the new routes. Prepare a project plan and make sure everyone has a chance to see it before the implementation date.

    B. Explain the coming changes and tell the truckers that assignments will be made based on seniority. The new people will be assigned last.

C. Explain the coming changes and let the senior executives handle the questions about how new job assignments will be made.

D. Explain the coming changes and let the employees discuss among themselves how they want to assign routes to the workforce.

23. When the AB Trucking Co. makes its organizational changes, it plans to alter its reporting relationships. If it elects to have each supervisor report to an operations manager and also to a financial manager, what type of organizational structure will AB Trucking Co. be using?

A. Formalized. This is a firm structure that can be charted, regardless of how many reporting lines exist from one job to another.

B. Matrix. This is a perfect example of when multiple reporting relationships exist for certain jobs.

C. Span of control. The span of control will be exceedingly easier to manage with multiple reporting relationships.

D. Work specialization. Because there are multiple reporting relationships, the specialization of each will increase.

24. Mergers and acquisitions (M&A) provide HR managers with special problems of cultural differences. To make sure that the cultures don't clash after the merger, the HR manager should:

A. Assign a subordinate to monitor the complaint levels and report on problems that are being addressed.

B. Conduct meetings with key players from each organization to outline the cultural values of each organization and determine how best to protect them in the blended employer unit.

C. Send memos to department heads that specify the new cultural characteristics and express the expectation that the department heads will "make it happen."

D. Provide written complaint forms to all employees and express a willingness to listen to any comments the employees have to make about the merger.

25. The AB Trucking Co. is considering outsourcing its HR, accounting, and safety functions to vendors. What considerations should be given to issues impacting that decision?

A. How the decision will fit into the organization's strategic plan and whether it will be cost effective

B. How the employees will react

C. How much money can be saved and what workload can be eliminated from the company executives

D. How all the compliance work can be done by someone else

Answers

1. **D.** General business environmental knowledge and industry best practices awareness are responsibilities of HR professionals. All other answer choices are not primary HR responsibilities.

2. **D.** Flu shots are not an HR responsibility. All other answer choices are.

3. **A, C, D.** SMART goals and objectives are specific, measurable, attainable, relevant/realistic, and time bound. Strength is not included in the list.

4. **D.** A bribery demand is not only a violation of the company's policy but also a violation of the Foreign Corrupt Practices Act of 1997 (see Chapter 2). Paying such a bribe could be a criminal act under federal law.

5. **C.** When the organization calls for reporting to two or more supervisors, the organization is known as a matrix organization.

6. **D.** Competition constitutes a threat to the company. During strategic planning and SWOT analysis, all perceived threats should be considered seriously.

7. **B.** The employer should always retain control of its goal determination function so it can be assured the goals will support the organization's strategic plan.

8. **Ethics** determine how we behave with employees, vendors, customers, clients, and other stakeholders. They govern "how we do things around here." They are constant references for employee decision-making and behavior.

9. **C.** Suggesting a friend apply for a job opening at the employer's organization is perfectly ethical. It even demonstrates a willingness to support the employer as a good place to work.

10. **D.** Matrix organizations allow for great flexibility and quick reaction to outside changes.

11. **C.** Human resource planning involves all facets of people management issues. Forecasting the need for more or fewer people, budget considerations, and recruiting sources comes into play. How HR can be used to support the organization's strategic plans is critical.

12. **A.** The greater grasp senior management retains on decision-making, the more centralized the organization.

13. **Federal Register**

14. **C.** Because Colin doesn't contract directly with the employees, he instead contracts with a third party for the services of the employees.

15. **A.** Part of the due diligence is surveying the workforce to determine not only how many employees are in the organization but what they are doing and their certifications/licenses/skills.

16. **C.** SOX brought criminal liability to the most senior manager in the organization. There is some personal incentive for the CEO to insist that employees behave and follow the rules.

17. **B.** Payroll management theory is not part of business management. It falls within the compensation category. All other answers are listed in the business management knowledge requirements.

18. **B.** Designing strategic support programs for human resource management is critical in today's fast-paced employment world. Competition is more stringent, and legal requirements are constantly expanding. While supporting executive wishes has always been part of the HR job, the design of strategic programs is relatively new.

19. **D.** It is not just a matter of budget dollars, but the contribution they make toward the organizational "bottom line."

20. **C.** It was the psychologists at AT&T who gathered data about management skills over more than 30 years. They identified characteristics of successful managers in the process.

21. **D.** Program Evaluation and Review Technique charts handle multiple project requirements and can be enhanced by the critical path method in visual charts.

22. **A.** Whenever possible, involving employees in designing the plan for accommodating organizational changes will be the best for employee morale.

23. **B.** Matrix structures involve multiple reporting relationships.

24. **B.** Involving key managers from each organization can provide a foundation for whatever cultural values the new organization could like to build.

25. **A.** Key factors are the organizational strategic plan and the budget. If outsourcing will fit nicely into those two considerations, it may be a good alternative. But there are also other factors to be considered such as employee morale, responsiveness of the vendor, and more.

Endnotes

1. https://www.bna.com/

2. Bray, Douglas W., Richard J. Campbell, Donald L. Grant, *Formative Years in Business: A Long-Term AT&T Study of Managerial Lives*, John Wiley & Sons, NY

3. https://www.shrm.org/about-shrm/pages/code-of-ethics.aspx

4. Beighley, Jay C., WAR in the Workplace: A Practical Guide to a Safer Workplace, The Management Advantage, Inc., 2016

5. https://www.sciencedirect.com/science/article/pii/S2444569X16300087

6. https://www.mindtools.com/pages/article/newSTR_91.htm

7. https://www.kotterinc.com/research-and-perspectives/

8. 29 CFR 1910.1200

9. 54:3904–3916

10. https://www.epa.gov/ems/frequent-questions-about-environmental-managment-systems

11. https://www.osha.gov/laws-regs/oshact/section5-duties

12. "How Many People Use the Top Social Media, Apps & Services," July 25, 2018, Craig Smith, Digital Marketing Ramblings blog. http://expandedramblings.com/index.php/resource-how-many-people-use-the-top-social-media/

13. https://www.dol.gov/odep/

14. States with laws barring employers from demanding social media account passwords from employees or job applicants as of 2017 include: Arkansas, California, Connecticut, Delaware, Illinois, Maine, Maryland, Michigan, Montana, Nebraska, New Hampshire, New Jersey, Oregon, Vermont, Virginia, and West Virginia. http://www.ncsl.org/research/telecommunications-and-information-technology/employer-access-to-social-media-passwords-2013.aspx

15. NLRB Case Ruling, *Hispanics United of Buffalo, Inc. and Carlos Ortiz.* Case 03-CA-027872

16. https://www.employmentmattersblog.com/Board%20Decision%20282%29.pdf

17. http://www.rfidjournal.com/articles/view?14284/2

18. https://www.forbes.com/sites/glennllopis/2015/02/16/5-certain-ways-to-engage-employees-during-uncertain-times/#1e88bd0527a3

19. https://www.inc.com/gordon-tredgold/7-ways-successful-leaders-deal-with-chaos-and-uncertainty.html

PART II

Talent Planning and Acquisition

Talent planning and acquisition is the foundation of the overall HR function and an important part of the PHR exam. Sixteen percent of the PHR exam will focus on this area of knowledge. A wealth of information is available in case law to guide HR professionals in their compliance with federal legislation and regulations in this topic. Common sense can help as well.

This area of knowledge is where you will find all the information about workforce planning, sourcing methods and techniques, recruiting, interviewing, equal employment opportunity, affirmative action, job offers, new employee orientation, metrics for staffing effectiveness, and retention. Master these and you will have a strong foundation for HR performance in your employment group.

The official HRCI Talent Planning and Acquisition functional area responsibilities and knowledge statements are as follows:

Responsibilities

- Understand federal laws and organizational policies to adhere to legal and ethical requirements in hiring (for example, Title VII, nepotism, disparate impact, Fair Labor Standards Act [FLSA], independent contractors)
- Develop and implement sourcing methods and techniques (for example, employee referrals, diversity groups, social media)
- Execute the talent acquisition life cycle (for example, interviews, extending offers, background checks, negotiation)

Knowledge Of

- Applicable federal laws and regulations related to talent planning and acquisition activities
- Planning concepts and terms (for example, succession planning, forecasting)
- Current market situation and talent pool availability
- Staffing alternatives (for example, outsourcing, temporary employment)

175

- Interviewing and selection techniques, concepts, and terms
- Applicant tracking systems and/or methods
- Impact of total rewards on recruitment and retention
- Verbal and written offers/contract techniques
- New-hire employee orientation processes and procedures
- Internal workforce assessments (for example, skills testing, workforce demographics, analysis)
- Transition techniques for corporate restructuring, mergers and acquisitions, due diligence processes, off-shoring, and divestitures
- Metrics to assess past and future staffing effectiveness (for example, cost per hire, selection ratios, adverse impact)

Key Legislation Governing Talent Planning and Acquisition

Now that you've reviewed the Talent Planning and Acquisition responsibilities and knowledge statements, we recommend you review the federal laws that apply to this area (see Figure 5-1). It would benefit you to refer to Chapter 2 on these specific laws prior to reading any further in this chapter.

While legislation is important, of equal value is the case law that comes from court interpretations. Over the decades since the civil rights laws began to impact the country in earnest, the U.S. Supreme Court has heard and provided its clarification to many questions. See Figure 5-2 for the vitally important cases dealing with talent planning and acquisition.

For more information on each of these cases, see Appendix B.

• The Civil Rights Act of 1964	• Federal Contractors & Subcontractors: Executive Order 11246 (41 CFR 60-1, 60-2 & 60-4)
• The Civil Rights Act of 1991	• Federal Contractors & Subcontractors: Rehabilitation Act of 1973
• Pregnancy Discrimination Act of 1978	• Federal Contractors & Subcontractors: Vietnam Era Veterans' Readjustment Assistance Act of 1974
• Age Discrimination in Employment Act of 1967	• Federal Contractors & Subcontractors: Jobs for Veterans Act of 1974
• Americans with Disabilities Act of 1990	• The Uniformed Services Employment and Reemployment Rights Act of 1994

Figure 5-1 Key legislation governing talent planning and acquisition *(continued)*

- Americans with Disabilities Act Amendments Act of 2012

- Genetic Information Nondiscrimination Act of 2008

- The Fair Credit Reporting Act of 1970

- The Immigration and Nationality Act of 1952

- The Portal to Portal Act of 1947

- Drug-Free Workplace Act of 1988

- The Employee Polygraph Protection Act of 1988

- The Equal Pay Act of 1963

- The Fair Labor Standards Act of 1938

- The Immigration Reform and Control Act of 1986

- The Work Opportunity Tax Credit of 1996

- The Lilly Ledbetter Fair Pay Act of 2009

Figure 5-1   Key legislation governing talent planning and acquisition

Case Citations

- *Griggs v. Duke Power Co.* (401 U.S. 424)

- *Phillips v. Martin Marietta Corp.* (400 U.S. 542)

- *McDonnell Douglas Corp. v. Green* (411 U.S. 792)

- *Espinoza v. Farah Manufacturing Co.* (414 U.S. 86)

- *Corning Glass Works v. Brennan* (417 U.S. 188)

- *Albermarle Paper v. Moody* (422 U.S. 405)

- *Washington v. Davis* (426 U.S. 229)

- *McDonald v. Santa Fe Transportation Co.* (427 U.S. 273)

- *Hazelwood School District v. U.S.* (433 U.S. 299)

- *Trans World Airlines, Inc. v. Hardison* (432 U.S. 63)

- *Regents of University of California v. Bakke* (438 U.S. 265)

- *St. Mary's Honor Center v. Hicks* (509 U.S. 502)

- *Taxman v. Board of Education of Piscataway* (91 F.3d 1547, 3rd Circuit)

- *McKennon v. Nashville Banner Publishing Co.* (513 U.S. 352)

- *Robinson v. Shell Oil* (519 U.S. 337)

- *Faragher v. City of Boca Raton* (524 U.S. 775)

- *Oncale v. Sundowner Offshore Service, Inc.* (523 U.S. 75)

- *Bragdon v. Abbott* (524 U.S. 624)

- *Kolstad v. American Dental Association* (527 U.S. 526)

- *Gibson v. West* (527 U.S. 212)

- *Grutter v. Bollinger* (539 U.S. 306)

- *Gratz v. Bollinger* (539 U.S. 244)

Figure 5-2   Case law that applies to talent planning and acquisition *(continued)*

Case Citations

- *United Steelworkers v. Weber*
  (443 U.S. 193)

- *Connecticut v. Teal*
  (457 U.S. 440)

- *EEOC v. Shell Oil Co.*
  (466 U.S. 54)

- Meritor Savings Bank v. Vinson
  (477 U.S. 57)

- *Johnson v. Santa Clara County
  Transportation Agency* (480 U.S. 616)

- *School Board of Nassau v. Arline*
  (480 U.S. 273)

- *Watson v. Fort Worth Bank & Trust*
  (487 U.S. 977)

- *City of Richmond v. J. A. Croson Company*
  (488 U.S. 469)

- *Price Waterhouse v. Hopkins*
  (490 U.S. 288)

- *Wards Cove Packing Co. v. Antonio*
  (490 U.S. 642)

- *Harris v. Forklift Systems Inc.*
  (510 U.S. 17)

- *O'Connor v. Consolidated Coin Caterers Corp.*
  (517 U.S. 308)

- *General Dynamics Land Systems, Inc. v. Cline*
  (540 U.S. 581)

- *Pennsylvania State Police v. Suders*
  (542 U.S. 129)

- *Smith v. Jackson, Mississippi*
  (544 U.S. 228)

- *Leonel v. American Airlines*
  (400 F.3d 702, 9th Circuit)

- *Ledbetter v. Goodyear Tire & Rubber Co.*
  (550 U.S. 618)

- *Ricci v. DeStefano*
  (No. 07-1428)

- *Vance v. Ball State Univ.*
  (No. 11-556)

- *University of Texas Sw. Med. Ctr. v. Nassar*
  (No 12-484)

- *St. Mary's Honor Center v. Hicks*
  (509 U.S. 502)

- *Taxman v. Board of Education of Piscataway*
  (91 F.3d 1547, 3rd Circuit)

- *O'Connor v. Consolidated Coin Caterers Corp.*
  (517 U.S. 308)

- *Ellerth v. Burlington Northern Industries*
  (524 U.S. 742)

Figure 5-2   Case law that applies to talent planning and acquisition

Equal Employment Opportunity and Affirmative Action

While it is true that the Civil Rights Act of 1964 was the first civil rights law in the United States that embraced employment issues, it was not the first civil rights law in the country. That would have been the Civil Rights Act of 1866, which said that anyone born in the United States is a citizen and any citizen, regardless of race, has the right to enter into contracts, sue, and be sued.

Before the assassination of President John Kennedy in November 1963, Congress had argued for many months about extending protections from discrimination based on race, religion, national origin, and color. The Senate just couldn't make any progress.

Then some senators from Southern states devised a strategy to end the arguments and defeat the bill once and for all. They proposed an amendment that would add "sex" as a protected category. They reasoned that nobody would vote in favor of protecting women against discrimination in the workplace. Well, the idea didn't work out so well for them. It backfired, and the bill passed with five protected categories, including sex. President Johnson signed the bill into law in 1964.

In 1965, President Johnson looked around the country and noticed that the Civil Rights Act he had signed the previous year was pretty much being ignored by employers of all sizes. He asked his staff to evaluate the problem and come up with some recommendations about how he should address it. They devised a program called *affirmative action* that would force certain federal contractors to implement the Civil Rights Act. President Johnson issued Executive Order 11246 requiring contractors to take affirmative action for minorities and women in their hiring and promotion programs. That didn't have much impact, however. It wasn't until President Nixon's administration implemented some regulations and created an oversight agency that employers began to pay attention.

Equal Employment Opportunity Commission

In 1964, President Johnson signed the Civil Rights Act, which had been working its way through Congress since the time of Presidents Eisenhower and Kennedy. Title VII of that law deals with employment-related equal opportunity provisions. Sometimes these terms are used interchangeably, although they should not be. The Civil Rights Act of 1964 has other titles dealing with public housing, education, and more. (A title in a law is like a chapter in a book.)

The Civil Rights Act of 1964 created a five-member commission that stands alone with allegiance to no government department. Its commissioners are appointed to five-year staggered terms. A council general, the commission's head lawyer, is also appointed by the U.S. president. All appointments must be confirmed by the U.S. Senate. There is a chair, vice chair, and three commissioners. By design, three of the positions are appointed from the sitting U.S. president's political party, and the other two are selected from the political party not in power. Even though the U.S. president appoints the commissioners, the Equal Employment Opportunity Commission (EEOC) does not report to the White House. It is independent.

Commissioners can file charges against employers, but more often the EEOC staff receives complaints of employment discrimination from employees and job applicants. Because the Civil Rights Act of 1964 applies only to employers with 15 or more employees, whose business is engaged in interstate commerce, smaller employers are not subject to its oversight. The EEOC also has jurisdiction over federal government agencies that are considered part of the executive branch, reporting to the U.S. president, and state and local governmental units as well. Size of payroll does not matter for governmental employers. That limitation applies to private employers only. The EEOC has divided its staff into two specialty groups, one handling the public sector and the other handling the private sector.

The EEOC has enforcement authority for the following:

- Civil Rights Act of 1964 (CRA)
- Age Discrimination in Employment Act of 1967 (ADEA)
- Pregnancy Discrimination Act of 1978 (PDA)
- Americans with Disabilities Act of 1990 (ADA)
- Equal Pay Act of 1963 (EPA)
- Genetic Information Nondiscrimination Act of 2008 (GINA)

When the EEOC investigates a complaint and determines that there is justification for that complaint, it says the case has "cause." When a case has cause, the EEOC will attempt to find a "make-whole" remedy that can include any of the following reimbursements:

- Back pay (for up to two years)
- Reimbursement for out-of-pocket expenses (for example, job search, doctor visits)
- Front pay—unlimited (based on how long it might take to get another job)
- Compensatory damages (for example, pain and suffering, emotional distress)
- Punitive damages (for example, punishment of the employer with dollar limits based on payroll head count as specified by the Civil Rights Act of 1991, shown in Table 5-1)

Table 5-1 notes the limits on punitive damages relative to the number of employees within an organization.

Table 5-2 notes the number and nature of EEOC charges filed in fiscal year (FY) 2017.

EEOC Complaint Investigation Procedures

Complaints must be filed with the EEOC within 180 days from the date on which the action was taken that caused the charge of illegal discrimination. In states that have a reciprocity agreement between the state's Fair Employment Practices agency and the EEOC, the filing period is 300 days.

Table 5-1 Cap on Punitive Damages for Title VII Cases[1]	Employer Head Count	Limit on Punitive Damages
	15 to 100 employees	$50,000
	101 to 200 employees	$100,000
	201 to 500 employees	$200,000
	Over 500 employees	$300,000

Basis for Charge	FY 2017 Count	FY 2017 Percentage
Total	84,254	100.0
Race	28,528	33.9
Sex	25,605	30.4
National origin	8,299	9.8
Religion	3,436	4.1
Color	3,240	3.8
Retaliation—all statutes	41,097	48.8
Retaliation—Title VII only	32,023	38.0
Age	18,376	21.8
Disability	26,838	31.9
Equal pay	996	1.2
GINA	206	.2

Table 5-2
Quantity of EEOC
Charges in Fiscal
Year 2017[2]

The charge must be made in writing. It must contain the following:

- The employee's name, address, and telephone number
- The name, address, and telephone number of the employer (or employment agency or union) the employee wants to file this charge against
- The number of employees employed there (if known)
- A short description of the events the employee believes were discriminatory (for example, the employee was fired, demoted, harassed)
- When the events took place
- Why the employee believes he or she was discriminated against (for example, because of race, color, religion, sex [including pregnancy], national origin, age [40 or older], disability or genetic information)
- The employee's signature

It is common for the compliance officer to ask the employee what remedy he or she would like in the situation. That can become important during a conciliation conference if the charge is found to have merit.

Once the complaint has been received by the commission, a letter will be sent to the employer within 10 days explaining the charge and asking for the employer's response.

As a first step, the employer should conduct an internal investigation if that has not already been done. Unfortunately, once a charge has been filed with either the EEOC or a state enforcement agency, the employer is banned from speaking about it with the employee. There may be no direct contact between the employee and employer on that issue. Of course, normal day-to-day interactions are permitted, but nothing related to the charge of illegal discrimination. If an internal investigation has not been conducted before the EEOC's notice of filing, it will be handicapped by the ban on interaction with the employee.

At the completion of the internal investigation, the employer will prepare a written response to the commission explaining what it has found in its investigation. This is the employer's opportunity to explain its side of the story. Based on that input, the EEOC's compliance officer (CO) will either suggest mediation or open an investigation so it can gather more information. There may be requests for more written information from the employer. There may be an onsite visit so interviews can be conducted with people involved in the issue, and there may be witnesses to what happened. How long that will take is an open question. It could be a relatively short period of time (two to three months), or it could go on for a couple of years. Typically, cases are resolved within 12 to 18 months. The EEOC's case backlog continues to hover around 60,000.[3]

At the conclusion of the EEOC's investigation, it will always issue a Right to Sue or a Notice of Rights letter, which explains to the employee their right to file a lawsuit in federal court. Each investigation concludes with one of the following types of findings:

- **No reasonable cause**   The charge of illegal discrimination could not be substantiated.

- **Reasonable cause**   The charge of illegal discrimination is substantiated by the evidence, and a letter of determination is sent to the employer and employee inviting the parties to join the agency in seeking to resolve the charge through conciliation. If conciliation fails, the EEOC will issue a Right to Sue letter to the employee, who is then free to locate an attorney and proceed to federal court. The commission may also decide to pursue legal action itself. It can sue the employer on behalf of the employee.

- **Administrative closure**   If the employee requests the case be closed without an investigation or during an investigation, the commission will cease its activities on the case and issue the employee a notice that he or she has the right to proceed to federal court.

Remedies for cases found to have merit can range from back pay (up to two years), retroactive promotion, retroactive benefits, reimbursement of medical expenses, and other out-of-pocket costs along with other "make-whole" compensation. Those are called *actual damages*. If the employee wants to pursue reimbursement for compensatory damages (emotional and psychological damages) and punitive damages (punishment to the employer), it is necessary to pursue the complaint in federal court.

EEOC Guidelines

Since 1979, the EEOC has issued more than 40 policy statements, policy guidance, enforcement guidance, and revised guidelines. Some of them have been rescinded. These are the most important ones:

- National Origin Discrimination (November 2016)
- Retaliation and Related Issues (August 2016)
- Pregnancy Discrimination and Related Issues (June 2015)

- Consideration of Arrest and Conviction Records in Employment Decisions under Title VII (April 2012)
- Employment Tests and Selection Procedures (December 2007)
- Unlawful Disparate Treatment of Workers with Caregiving Responsibilities (May 2007)
- Reasonable Accommodation and Undue Hardship Under the Americans with Disabilities Act (October 2002)
- Disability-Related Inquiries and Medical Examinations of Employees Under the Americans with Disabilities Act (July 2000)
- Application of EEO Laws to Contingent Workers Placed by Temporary Employment Agencies and Other Staffing Firms (December 1997)
- Americans with Disabilities Act and Psychiatric Disabilities (March 1997)
- Workers' Compensation and the ADA (September 1996)
- Current Issues of Sexual Harassment (March 1990)
- Veterans' Preference Under Title VII (August 1990)
- Indian Preference Under Title VII (May 1988)
- Guidelines on Sexual Harassment (1980)

NOTE   You can find a complete listing on the EOCC website at www.eeoc.gov.

One particular highlight in the EOCC publications are the Guidelines on Sexual Harassment from 1980. These were issued to aid employers in traversing the legal minefield of evolving employment requirements *before* the U.S. Supreme Court began issuing its opinions on the subject in the 1990s. They are still relevant today.

Uniform Guidelines on Employee Selection Procedures (1978)

The Uniform Guidelines, as they are generally known, are among the least understood regulations in equal employment law. They are actually ensconced in the Code of Federal Regulations at 41 CFR 60-3.

NOTE   To find a copy of the regulations, you can search the Internet for *41 CFR 60-3*. Any professionally certified human resource manager should possess a copy of this regulation.

Any employer with 15 or more workers on the payroll is subject to the Uniform Guidelines. (Any employer subject to the Civil Rights Act of 1964 is also subject to the Uniform Guidelines.) They require validation of all employment selection steps and tools. As an example, let's assume that our employment selection process involves the following steps. We are required to determine that each step is free from illegal discrimination (disparate impact) and that it has validity for selecting someone to fill the specific job in question.

Our employment selection steps are as follows:

- Job application form completed (or résumé submitted)
- Written test (specific skills such as typing or accounting and specific knowledge such as building codes or engineering practices)
- Interview with job's supervisor
- Interview with co-workers
- Background check

One of the greatest liabilities employers accept comes through purchasing an "off-the-shelf" employment test. If said test has not been validated as a nondiscriminatory selection tool for your specific job content, you probably shouldn't use it. You can find tests through online searches, in some stationery stores, and in large office supply warehouses. They often have no validation information that would indicate what type of job knowledge or skills they are designed to test. Employers should avoid these products if they don't plan to conduct validation studies themselves.

The Uniform Guidelines requirements exist so that disparate impact can be controlled. Disparate impact, also known as *adverse impact,* means one or more groups suffer a numerical disadvantage compared to other groups. This usually occurs when a seemingly neutral policy or employment selection device (or process) results in discrimination against a Title VII protected class. Numerical and statistical analysis are tools used to detect disparate impact. HR professionals should be acquainted with the "80 percent test," which is sometimes called the "4/5ths rule." Simply said, if any protected group is selected at a rate (percentage) that is less than 80 percent the selection rate of the most favorably treated group, there is possibly a problem. Courts have acknowledged that it is necessary to use statistical analysis techniques to eliminate the possibility of chance in the selection results. So, often we see statistical significance testing methods such as standard deviations and probability analysis being used. Ultimately, the only method available to "prove" disparate impact is multiple regression analysis. Statisticians love that because they are usually the only ones who understand it. Regulations say, "Users are cautioned that they are responsible for compliance with these guidelines." It is not the publishers of the test that are liable; it is the employer who uses the test that carries the liability.

 NOTE HR professionals should be cautious about what employment selection tools are used in their organizations. While it may be difficult to corral managers and executives who feel it is okay to use any technique or tool they want, it is necessary to have them understand that they can single-handedly cost the organization a lot of money if they are cavalier about these requirements.

Validation of Each Selection Step Is Required by the Uniform Guidelines

The Uniform Guidelines say, "If the information [required] shows that the total selection process for a job has an adverse impact, the individual components of the selection process should be evaluated for adverse impact." For our purposes, the terms *adverse impact* and *disparate impact* will have the same meaning. So, test the overall results, and if a problem pops up in that test, drill down to the individual steps in the selection process and test each of them. You may find the following information about validation on the exam.

Jumping back into the selection process, recall that we have discussed the Uniform Guidelines on Employee Selection Procedures (in Chapter 2 and earlier in this chapter). If you have 15 or more employees and are involved in interstate commerce or are a government entity at the state or local level, you must comply with these requirements for validation of your employment selection steps.

Content Validity

If you use testing that is specifically related to what is done on the job and how it is done on the job, then you will have met the Uniform Guidelines requirements. This is called *content validity*. Don't fudge. You must test for the knowledge, skills, and abilities that are specifically required on the job. And you must test them in the same way they are used on the job.

For example, a township fire department asked each firefighter candidate to take a physical test that was conducted behind the firehouse. There was a starting line, a ladder, and a hose connected to a water source. The candidate was required to pick up the ladder and run it over to the firehouse, lift it into position against the firehouse, return for the hose, carry it up the ladder, and squirt the roof of the building. Some people objected to that test, and the judge hearing the case asked if that was exactly what was done on the job. The fire chief said, "Yes, it is, except for one thing." The judge asked what that one thing was. The chief replied, "The job requires all of those things to be done, but we normally assign people to work in pairs." So, the department was testing for what was done on the job, but not the *way* it was done on the job.

Criterion-Related Validity

Demonstrating this type of validity involves empirical studies producing data that shows the selection procedures are predictive or significantly related to important elements of job performance. This is a scientific study of the test used with a sufficient number of successful incumbents to determine there is a statistically significant correlation with the job content. These studies are, by their nature, long and expensive. They should be performed by the test publisher. Or by the test user, which is the employer. Remember that the guidelines state that it is the test user (employer) who is responsible for any disparate impact caused by use of the test. It isn't the publisher who is liable.

You can use your own written test without a criterion-related validity study *if* you make the test specifically related to the work done on the job. Otherwise, if you purchase a test "off the shelf," for example, you must be able to demonstrate that it is predictive of success on the job for which you will use it.

One employer purchased a general clerical test that tested basic arithmetic skills, typing skills, and spelling skills. That test was administered to *all* job applicants in the organization. So, anyone applying for a clerical job would have to take the tests, but so would anyone applying for a laboratory cleaning job, a delivery driver job, or a food service job. Clearly, the test didn't apply to many of the jobs for which it was being used. The employer was wrong in how it applied the tests.

Construct Validity

Construct validity is another data-based way of determining that an employment test has validity for the job in question. It should show that the "procedure measures the degree to which candidates have identifiable characteristics which have been determined to be important in successful performance in the job...."[4] Those measurements are done through detailed study of the test results and success of incumbents on the job. Such validation can be extremely expensive to demonstrate.

Federal Contracting and Affirmative Action Requirements

In 1965, President Johnson recognized that employers were not implementing equal employment opportunity provided for in the Civil Rights Act of 1964, so his administration created affirmative action requirements to force the portion of the employer community engaged in federal contracting to implement the new law. Affirmative action requirements demand the inclusion of all qualified individuals in consideration for job openings.

It was common practice in 1965 to fill jobs without any announcement. Decisions were made in private (secret), and, in particular, minorities and women had no knowledge that a job opening even existed. Affirmative action rules changed that for federal contractors. They said contractors had to assess their workforce and determine where there was a need for more minorities and women. Then the regulations required contractors to implement "outreach and recruiting programs" to invite qualified minority and female candidates to participate in the selection process.

Federal Regulations

Congress passes laws that direct the executive branch of the government to do certain things. It is up to the administration to write the regulations that will cause those congressional mandates to happen. Regulations have the force and effect of law. Regulations are sometimes referred to as *rules*. On the other hand, *guidelines* issued by agencies such as the EEOC do not have the same weight as regulations. Employers may not be forced to abide by guidelines, while they are compelled to abide by regulations.

When an employer decides it wants to get revenue from the federal government, it subjects itself to these rules governing that process. Just as it is necessary for any organization earning money in this country to pay income taxes according to Internal Revenue Service (IRS) regulations, it is necessary to abide by U.S. federal government contracting rules if you want to have the revenue from selling goods or services to the government.

 NOTE Construction contractors who want to get revenues from building roads, dams, or office buildings for the government are also subject to affirmative action requirements, although rules for construction contractors are different from those for goods and service contractors.

Goods and Services Contractors

If the employer has 50 or more employees on the payroll *and* it has contracts valued at $50,000 or more, there are affirmative action obligations that must be met. There are also other obligations under the Federal Acquisition Regulation (FAR). FAR obligations are usually managed by the accounting department, and affirmative action obligations are usually managed by the human resource department.

Under the employment affirmative action obligations, there are three types of affirmative action plans required. One covers minorities and women. Another covers disabled people. The third covers certain veterans of the U.S. uniformed services. Written plans are required for each type of affirmative action effort. As mentioned, affirmative action requirements are the government's way of ensuring that equal employment opportunity laws were properly implemented. They got a bad reputation because people used them in ways that they should not have. Today, the U.S. Supreme Court has clarified that affirmative action programs are not quota systems. Nor are they set-aside or preferential treatment systems.

Executive Order 11246 sets the basic requirements upon which these regulations were established. 41 CFR 60-1 and 60-2 set out what is required for minorities and women. Affirmative action for disabled people is regulated by 41 CFR 60-741. Finally, affirmative action programs for covered veterans is governed by 41 CFR 60-250 and 60-300.

Construction Contractors

Unlike the obligations for goods and service contractors, those who engage in construction projects have a different set of requirements. Known as the *16-point program,* the regulations are found at 41 CFR 60-4 and apply to any contractor or subcontractor with a federal or federally assisted construction contract in excess of $10,000. The construction affirmative action plan requirements focus on craft and laborer jobs with specific numerical targets for total minorities based on the job location. A table of locations and goals for minorities can be found in 46 F.R. 7533. If you haven't looked at this table recently, don't worry; the table has not been changed since 1980. There is one uniform goal for representation of women in construction jobs, and that is 6.9 percent. No management or professional jobs are included in these requirements.

Affirmative Action Plans

Affirmative action plans (AAPs) are documents containing information and commitments to take action that will improve the representation of minorities, women, disabled people, and veterans in the workforce. Specifically, there are affirmative action plans required for minorities, women, disabled people, and veterans. There are narrative requirements, action plan requirements, and data analysis requirements. All together these are referred to as *affirmative action*. Employment affirmative action has nothing to do with affirmative action for educational admissions or affirmative action for minority- or female-owned supplier enterprise programs.

Sometimes, *affirmative action program* is used to describe the affirmative action plan. *Affirmative action requirements* is a term referring to the federal regulation requirements. Plans and programs are the synonymous documents and action plans need to meet those regulations. An *action plan* is a step-by-step list of actions to be taken to accomplish a specific goal. AAP documents must contain action plans for reaching the AAP goals in each AAP establishment. An *AAP establishment* can be either a street address (or campus) where 50 or more of the contractor's employees work or a functional segment of the workforce such as marketing or engineering at all work locations in the country. AAP regulations apply only to U.S.-based employee locations.[5]

Affirmative action programs involve outreach and recruiting. Equal employment opportunity means equal access. So, if you are building a pool of candidates for a given job opening, anyone who is qualified for the position should have access to the pool (equal opportunity), and you should reach out to qualified groups of minorities and women to invite them to participate in the selection process (affirmative action). Once the pool has been established with qualified candidates, the nondiscriminatory selection process should be applied to ultimately make a job offer to the best qualified person. The notion of affirmative action is that if people aren't in the candidate pool, they can't possibly be selected. So, we must be sure that minorities and women are represented in the candidate pools.

 NOTE An employer that must meet the construction contractor requirements may not need to meet the requirements of goods and services contractors. An exception to that rule might be a design-and-build engineering and construction company that has both a service contract for engineering and a construction contract for building the project.

A separate set of AAP documents must be created for each work location (or campus facility) where 50 or more people are assigned to work. Work locations with fewer than 50 people should have those jobs and incumbents "rolled up" into the plan where their boss works. If there are no remote work locations with 50 or more people, all company employees should be reported in the corporate headquarters plan.

Compliance Evaluations by OFCCP

Enforcement of affirmative action regulations is accomplished by an agency in the United States Department of Labor called the Office of Federal Contract Compliance Programs (OFCCP). The chances of a federal contractor or subcontractor being audited by the OFCCP is around 2 percent.[6] There are three primary types of compliance evaluation that the OFCCP conducts:

- **Normal compliance evaluation** This is an audit of the physical establishment identified by a street address or campus location. This can be for either a goods and services contractor or a construction contractor. The requirements are different, but the offsite and onsite activities are much the same.

  - **Opening conference** The compliance officer will visit the contractor and interview the senior executive, discussing the employer's EEO/AA policy and its implementation.

  - **Desk audit** A Scheduling letter is sent by the OFCCP to the contractor requesting a response with specific documentation in the employer's response. These documents will be examined by the OFCCP compliance officer in the OFCCP office. There may be additional documentation demands, and they will be examined in the OFCCP office as well. If all compliance requirements have been met, the evaluation can be closed with a No Violation letter.

  - **Onsite visit** The compliance officer may find it necessary to visit the contractor's work location to interview management or nonmanagement personnel. The CO also may find a need to inspect the physical facilities to determine that there are proper and equal restrooms or changing rooms for both men and women. Poster inspection is another task undertaken during the onsite visit. The OFCCP has said it will make an onsite visit in every 50th audit even if there is no "indication" of a problem at the desk audit stage.

  - **Closing conference** A meeting when the CO provides feedback to the contractor about violations found and expectations for corrective action.

  - **Closure of the evaluation** The OFCCP will close the audit once it has finished its evaluation of all regulatory requirements.

    - **Notice of No Violation** This is given to contractors that meet all the requirements.

    - **Notice of Violation** This is given to contractors that have one or more deficiencies in meeting the requirements. This usually results in a Conciliation Agreement, which can permit the OFCCP to monitor the contractor for up to two years going forward. A Conciliation Agreement is a formal contract with the government that specifies corrective actions the contractor must take. It can also specify a remedy for a discriminatory practice with back-pay awards and other such financial settlements.

- **Functional AAP Compliance Evaluation** When a contractor has gained approval of the OFCCP for its functional establishment, it becomes subject to selection of a compliance evaluation of that functional establishment. A functional establishment is composed of everyone in the contractor's enterprise working in a functional area such as sales and marketing or administrative support.

- **Corporate Management Compliance Evaluation** Sometimes called a *glass ceiling audit,* this audit looks at the corporate headquarters organization and analyzes issues surrounding executive compensation, succession planning, mentoring programs, and developmental programs. This type of compliance evaluation was created by the OFCCP to identify illegal discrimination at senior corporate levels. *Glass ceiling* is the term that refers to an invisible barrier beyond which women may not progress in the organization. Since the term was first used, its meaning has expanded to encompass minorities as well as women.

It is the current policy of the OFCCP to avoid another compliance evaluation in the same AAP establishment for a period of two years following the successful closure of an audit.

Affirmative Action Reporting Requirements

In addition to the affirmation action requirements for contracting, there are annual reporting requirements for federal contractors. EEOC rules require all employers with 100 or more employees to submit a report showing sex and race/ethnicity head count by job category, and that report is also required of federal contractors that are subject to affirmative action requirements. That means federal contractors with 50 or more workers must submit the required reports even before they have grown to a 100-person payroll.

One report set is known as Standard Form 100. Today, it includes the EEO-1, EEO-3, EEO-4, and EEO-5. Reports labeled EEO-2, EEO-2E, and EEO-6 have all been discontinued.

- EEO-1 applies to private-sector employers and is required annually by March 31.

- EEO-3 applies to local unions with 100 or more members. Filing is required biannually in even-numbered years.

- EEO-4 applies to state and local governments with 100 or more employees. Filing is required biannually in odd-numbered years.

- EEO-5 is formerly known as the Elementary-Secondary Staff Information Report and is a joint requirement of the EEOC and the Office for Civil Rights (OCR) and the National Center for Education Statistics (NCES) of the U.S. Department of Education. It is conducted biennially in the even-numbered years and covers all public elementary and secondary school districts with 100 or more employees in the United States.

Another report that is required of all federal contractors by September 30 each year is the VETS-4212, previously the VETS 100A. Any federal contract dated after December 2003 requires submission of the VETS-4212 report.

The Vietnam Era Veterans' Readjustment Act (VEVRA) requires federal contractors and subcontractors with contracts worth $25,000 or more to annually collect and report certain data on the covered veterans in their workforce on the Federal Contractor Veterans' Employment Report VETS-100 report form. The Jobs for Veterans Act of 2002 (JVA) amended VEVRA's reporting requirements and tasked the DOL with the responsibility for these amendments. In 2008, the DOL issued regulations that created new requirements for the VETS-4212 report form starting September 30, 2009, for all contracts entered into or modified after December 1, 2003, of $100,000 or more.

The following are the covered veteran categories for the VETS-4212 form:

- Disabled veterans
- Active duty or wartime campaign badge veterans
- Recently separated veterans (within the past three years)
- Armed Forces Service Medal veterans

NOTE Completion of each report, the Standard Form 100 and the VETS-4212, requires an employer identification number that can be obtained online. Once the employer identification number has been issued for each report, it will be reused in each subsequent filing period.

Contrary to what some people believe, it is not necessary to "file" your affirmative action plans with the government each year. Only when you get a notice of audit called a Scheduling Letter is it necessary to send copies of your AAP documents to the Office of Federal Contract Compliance Programs. That is the U.S. Department of Labor agency that has been given authority and responsibility to enforce the federal regulations requiring affirmative action on the part of federal contractors. AAP documents are created by the contractor for use by the contractor in the implementation of action plans contained in the AAPs.

In 2007, the EEOC changed the race/ethnic and job categories in the EEO-1 report. Those changes were not made in the EEO-4 or any other Standard Form 100. Tables 5-3 and 5-4 show how race/ethnicity and occupational categories are now defined.

Placement-Rate Goals and Good Faith Efforts

As part of affirmative action, each year qualifying federal contractors also have to re-compute the gap between their incumbency race and sex mix and the availability of qualified workforce within a reasonable recruiting area. This must be done for every job group separately. A job group is a collection of similar job titles with similar responsibilities and compensation with similar developmental or promotional opportunities. The gap can be large enough to require a placement-rate goal. That means for the coming year, special outreach and recruiting efforts will be made for the job group to ensure representation of each candidate pool created for that job group will contain at least the percentage of minorities and women that availability analysis tells us exists.

Race	Definition
Hispanic or Latino (can be combined with any race but is reported as Hispanic)	A person of Cuban, Mexican, Puerto Rican, South or Central American, or other Spanish culture or origin regardless of race
White (not Hispanic or Latino) race	A person having origins in any of the original peoples of Europe, the Middle East, or North Africa
Black or African American (not Hispanic or Latino) race	A person having origins in any of the black racial groups of Africa
Native Hawaiian or other Pacific Islander (not Hispanic or Latino) race	A person having origins in any of the peoples of Hawaii, Guam, Samoa, or other Pacific Islands
Asian (not Hispanic or Latino) race	A person having origins in any of the original peoples of the Far East, Southeast Asia, or the Indian subcontinent, including, for example, Cambodia, China, India, Japan, Korea, Malaysia, Pakistan, the Philippine Islands, Thailand, and Vietnam
American Indian or Alaska Native (not Hispanic or Latino) race	A person having origins in any of the original peoples of North and South America (including Central America) and who maintain tribal affiliation or community attachment
Two or more races (not Hispanic or Latino)	All people who identify with more than one of the earlier six races

Table 5-3   EEO-1 Report Race/Ethnicity Categories

Occupational Category	Definition
Executive/Senior Level Officials and Managers Category 1.1	Individuals who plan, direct, and formulate policies; set strategy; and provide the overall direction of enterprises/organizations for the development and delivery of products or services within the parameters approved by boards of directors or other governing bodies. Examples are chief executive officers, chief operating officers, chief financial officers, line of business heads, presidents or executive vice presidents of functional areas or operating groups, chief information officers, chief human resources officers, chief marketing officers, chief legal officers, management directors, and managing partners.
First/Mid-Level Officials and Managers Category 1.2	Individuals who serve as managers, other than those who are in the more senior Category 1.1 jobs, including those who oversee and direct the delivery of products, services, or functions at group, regional, or divisional levels of organizations. These managers receive direction from more senior managers. They implement policies, programs, and directives of senior executives through subordinate managers and within the parameters set by senior executives. Examples of these jobs are vice presidents and directors; group, regional, or divisional controllers; treasurers; human resources, information systems, marketing, and operations managers. Also included are first-line managers and supervisors, team managers, unit managers, and branch managers.

Table 5-4   EEO-1 Occupational Categories *(continued)*

Occupational Category	Definition
Professionals Category 2	Most jobs in this category require bachelor and graduate degrees and/or professional licensing or certification. Examples of these jobs are accountants, auditors, airplane pilots and flight engineers, architects, artists, chemists, computer programmers, designers, dieticians, editors, engineers, lawyers, librarians, scientists, physicians and surgeons, teachers, and surveyors.
Technicians Category 3	Jobs in this category include activities requiring applied scientific skills, usually obtained by post-secondary education of varying lengths. Examples of these jobs are drafters, emergency medical technicians, chemical technicians, and broadcast and sound engineering technicians.
Sales Workers Category 4	These jobs include nonmanagerial activities that wholly and primarily involve direct sales. Examples of these jobs are advertising sales agents, insurance sales agents, real estate brokers and sales agents, wholesale sales representatives, securities or other financial services sales agents, telemarketers, demonstrators, retail salespersons, counter and rental clerks, and cashiers.
Administrative Support Workers Category 5	These jobs involve nonmanagerial tasks providing administrative and support assistance, primarily in office settings. Examples of these jobs are bookkeeping, accounting and auditing clerks, cargo and freight agents, dispatchers, couriers, data entry operators, administrative assistants, typists, proofreaders, and general office clerks.
Craft Workers Category 6	Most jobs in this category include higher skilled occupations in construction and natural resource extraction. Examples of these jobs are boilermakers, brick and stone masons, carpenters, electricians, painters, glaziers, pipe layers, plumbers, pipe and steam fitters, plasterers, roofers, elevator installers, and derrick operators.
Operatives Category 7	Most jobs in this category include intermediate skilled occupations and include workers who operate machines or factory-related processing equipment. Jobs in this category include textile machine workers, laundry and dry-cleaning workers, photographic process workers, weaving machine operators, electrical and electronic equipment assemblers, semiconductor processors, and testers, graders, and sorters.
Laborers and Helpers Category 8	Jobs in this category require only brief training to perform tasks that require little or no independent judgment. Examples include production and construction worker helpers, vehicle and equipment cleaners, laborers, freight or material movers, service station attendants, septic tank servicers, and refuse materials collectors.
Service Workers Category 9	Jobs in this category include food service, cleaning service, and protective service activities. In this category are medical assistance, hairdressers, janitors, porters, transit and railroad police, and fire fighters, guards, private detectives, and investigators.

Table 5-4 EEO-1 Occupational Categories

In the Trenches

Control Your Applicant Flow—Beware the Law of Big Numbers

John C. Fox, Partner, Fox, Wang & Morgan P.C., San Jose, California jfox@ foxwangmorgan.com

This is *the* most important lesson of the FedEx settlement (OFCCP conciliation agreement with FedEx Ground Package System, Inc., and FedEx SmartPost, Inc., March 2012). This was not a case of unlawful discrimination. This was a series of what I call "the law of big numbers" cases defense lawyers see weekly. FedEx's greatest crime was that it allowed its applicant flow to swell to too large a size. *Any* employer that allows an applicant flow greater than approximately 1,000 to occur for even a large number of jobs will trip a statistical violation meter known as 2 standard deviations, unless the employer hires literally "by the numbers," meaning that the employer hires very close to the exact percentage of protected groups represented in their applicant flow. And the more applicants the establishment in question has, the larger the statistical confidence level (the more standard deviations) will be. This is because the "law of big numbers" will cause a *prima facie* finding of unlawful discrimination *almost always* when you have thousands of applicants. The U.S. Supreme Court was not thinking about this complex law of statistics when it sanctioned the pattern and practice (P&P) disparate treatment class-type theory of unlawful discrimination in the *Hazelwood* and *Teamsters* case decisions on May 31, 1977. Had an attack on the statistics been in one of those cases, I doubt we would today have the P&P theory. It is time for the courts to revisit the P&P theory with the advance in statistical education that the last 30 years of class litigation has brought us.

NOTE   Even the government recognizes that it is difficult to hire less than one whole person. Therefore, goals need be set only when the gap exceeds one whole person.

Federal regulations require the contractor to make "good faith efforts" to address the placement-rate goal. These efforts will likely involve special outreach and recruiting actions, such as contacting associations of minority or women professionals and asking for qualified candidates for job openings or reaching out to universities and technical clubs specifically for minorities and women. Remember that it is necessary to document all of the good faith efforts so they can be discussed during any possible audit from the OFCCP.

Office of Federal Contract Compliance Programs

When affirmative action programs were first created, there were several enforcement agencies, nearly one in each federal department. It wasn't until 1978 that President Jimmy Carter consolidated all of the enforcement groups into one agency that would eventually be called the Office of Federal Contract Compliance Programs (OFCCP). Organizationally, it came to rest in the U.S. Department of Labor (DOL).

The OFCCP has responsibility for enforcing the following:

- Executive Order 11246 (affirmative action plan requirements for minorities and women)
- Section 503 of the Rehabilitation Act (affirmative action requirements for disabled)
- Vietnam Era Veterans' Readjustment Assistance Act (affirmative action requirements for veterans)
- Americans with Disabilities Act (job accommodation requirements for disabled)
- Americans with Disabilities Act Amendments Act

The OFCCP has developed regulations for contractors to follow during their implementation of these laws and executive orders. Those regulations have the weight of law and specify what federal contractors are expected to do and how they will be audited by the OFCCP when they are randomly selected from the contractor pool. In that regard, the OFCCP is a law enforcement agency. The EEOC is also a law enforcement agency. They are just enforcing administrative laws rather than criminal laws. These regulations are in the Code of Federal Regulations at 41 CFR 60. Chapter 60 has many different components that give the OFCCP its administrative power over contractor affirmative action programs.

Affirmative action plans for minorities and women must contain the following:

- Commitment to Equal Employment Opportunity
- Responsibility for implementation
- Internal review and reporting systems
- Problem identification
- Development and execution of action-oriented programs
- Statistical analysis reports (including Workforce Analysis [or Organizational Structure Report], Job Group Analysis, Availability Analysis, Analysis of Incumbents Compared to Availability, Placement Rate Goals, and Goals Progress Report)

In 2014, regulations for affirmative action plans for disabled people and veterans were amended. Prior to 2014, statistical analysis requirements were not outlined for these categories; only narrative requirements were. As a result of new amendments, a 7 percent target[7] was established for disabled persons, and an 8 percent target[8] was established for veterans. Expanded requirements for data collection, an invitation to self-identify, new equal employment opportunity language, and records access procedures are some of the major changes in both categories. For veterans specifically, changes were also made to the requirement for listing job openings with the local state employment service so veterans have a better chance at referral for openings.

Outreach and Recruiting Requirements for Affirmative Action

The purpose of affirmative action programs is the establishment of outreach and recruiting efforts. To better understand this, it is helpful to look at a comparison of EEO and affirmative action.

Equal employment opportunity (EEO) is the foundation of affirmative action. EEO means anyone who is qualified for a job opening should have access to that job opening. Before the Civil Rights Act of 1964, it was common practice for employers to fill some job openings with "hand-selected" incumbents. Sometimes the position was never even announced until it had been filled. The Civil Rights Act of 1964 said that type of employment practice was not acceptable. Today, openings should be announced and candidate pools established. Anyone who is qualified for a job should be given access to the candidate pool. Then, sorting and selection should be done based on nondiscriminatory procedures. (Remember the discussion of the Uniform Guidelines on Employee Selection Procedures earlier in this chapter?) The objective of EEO selection procedures should be to include everyone who is qualified and then select the best qualified from among all candidates.

As EEO is supposed to provide equal access, affirmative action is supposed to provide outreach and recruiting efforts where there are gaps between incumbent representation and computed availability. If you compute the availability of women among professional civil engineers to be 40 percent in your recruiting geography and your incumbents have a 20 percent representation of women, you will likely be required to establish a placement rate goal of 40 percent for your professional civil engineer job group. That means you should have at least 40 percent women in your candidate pool for that job group. Each time you have a job opening in that job group, at least 40 percent of the candidates will be women. And because there are more trained and experienced women in that type of work these days, you will undoubtedly be finding some to be best qualified in your selection process. Gradually, your female representation will grow. It may take a few years of effort, but you will see the demographics shift so that your incumbency more closely mirrors availability. The same type of comparisons need to be done for each of the minority race and ethnic categories.

In summary, employers must abide by many administrative laws. EEO and affirmative action requirements are only two of them. EEO is equal employment opportunity. It requires all individuals to be given access to job opportunities for which they are qualified. Affirmative action is a program requiring employers that are federal contractors to engage in outreach and recruiting to entice qualified minorities, women, disabled individuals, and veterans into the job applicant process.

Recordkeeping Requirements

One regulation the OFCCP has put in place is a definition for *Internet applicant* that governs much of how federal contractors collect and retain data on job applicants. This definition applies to applications submitted through the Internet, by fax, or by any other electronic process. It does not apply to applications taken in person or through the U.S. mail unless the contractor wants to apply the same definition to those sources.

An Internet applicant is someone who

- Submits an application, résumé, or other expression of interest in employment
- Has been considered for a specific job opening
- Possesses all the basic job qualifications for the open job
- Did not self-eliminate from considerations by taking another job elsewhere, stating he or she is no longer interested, or failing to respond to employer communications

In addition to the job applicant records, contractors are required (under 41 CFR 60-1.12) to keep and maintain the following:

- Any record created by the employer pertaining to hiring, assignment, promotion, demotion, transfer, layoff or termination, rates of pay or other terms of compensation and selection for training or apprenticeship
- Other records having to do with request for reasonable accommodation and results of any physical examination
- Job advertisements or postings
- Applications
- Résumés
- Any and all expressions of interest through the Internet or related electronic data technologies, such as online résumés or internal résumé databases
- Records identifying job seekers contacted regarding their interest in a particular position
- A record of each résumé added to its internal resume databases and a record of the date each résumé was added to the database
- A record of each position for which a search of an internal database was made and, corresponding to each search, the substantive search criteria used and the date of the search
- A record of the position for which each search of an external database was made, and corresponding to each search, the substantive search criteria used, the date of the search, and the résumés of job seekers who met the basic qualifications for the particular position who are considered by the contractor
- Tests for employment screening or selection
- Interview notes

Gender Discrimination and Harassment in the Workplace

As recent media at the time of this book has made us aware, discrimination against employees based on sex or gender has not been eradicated from the workplace. There is still a thriving complaint-handling business in both the private and public sectors. To help combat that problem, the federal government has provided general guidelines.

Gender-Neutral Job Advertisements

Returning to the discussion of EEOC guidelines, the EEOC has issued guidance on how employment ads should be constructed. In 1964, most employment advertisements were seen in local newspaper classified sections. Prior to the Civil Rights Act, it was common practice for newspapers to have separate categories for "Jobs for Men" and "Jobs for Women."

The EEOC guidelines say such designations are illegal under the law. There are some exceptions where jobs require either men or women, but those are few and they must be justified based on a bona fide occupational qualification (BFOQ). Examples of jobs that might be gender or sex-specific would include restroom attendant, wet nurse, actor, or actress. Today most gender-specific job titles have been changed to gender-neutral titles. For example, *mailman* has been changed to *mail carrier*, *waitress* and *waiter* have been changed to *server*, and *stewardess* has been changed to *flight attendant*.

The EEOC guidelines also require a "tag line" in all job advertisements. At minimum, employers should show "EEO Employer" or "Equal Opportunity Employer" at the bottom of each job advertisement. Additional wording may be added if the employer wants. Some have used sentences such as, "Minorities, women, disabled, and veterans encouraged to apply."

Types of Harassment

In addition to providing protection for gender discrimination, the Civil Rights Act has provided for protection against harassment. Before the Civil Rights Act and the case law that has come out of its application, harassment on the job was a fact of life for some individuals, and these folks were faced with the option of putting up with the harassment or quitting their job and going to work somewhere else, hoping that harassment wouldn't be a problem at the new location.

Sexual Harassment

Sexual harassment has been defined by the courts over the last several decades (see Figure 5-2: *Meritor Savings Bank v. Vinson, Harris v. Forklift Systems Inc., Faragher v. City of Boca Raton, Ellerth v. Burlington Northern Industries, Oncale v. Sundowner Offshore Service, Inc.*). If you go back to the Civil Rights Act of 1964, you will not find the term *sexual harassment* in the law. It has been created from these court cases. As it turns out, there are two types of sexual harassment: quid pro quo and hostile work environment.

Quid pro quo means "this for that." It is usually an issue when a supervisor makes sexual demands of a subordinate. It represents abuse of power. It can literally mean, "If you give me sexual favors, I'll let you keep your job."

Hostile work environment harassment can happen to employees by other employees (peers) or even people who are not employees—for example, by vendor representatives just visiting the employee's workplace to deliver drinking water or office supplies. Hostile environment sexual harassment exists when behavior is repeatedly unwelcome and of a sexual nature. It can be verbal, physical, or visual, involving any of these types of behavior:

- Verbal conduct such as epithets, derogatory jokes or comments, slurs or unwanted sexual advances, invitations, or comments
- Visual conduct such as derogatory and/or sexually oriented posters, photography, cartoons, drawings, or gestures
- Physical conduct such as assault, unwanted touching, blocking normal movement, or interfering with work because of sex, race, or any other protected basis
- Threats and demands to submit to sexual requests as a condition of continued employment, or to avoid some other loss, and offers of employment benefits in return for sexual favors
- Retaliation for having reported or threatened to report harassment

It should be noted that an employee is not required to give notice to the employer that the behavior is unwelcome. Sometimes fear for one's job or simple social discomfort will prevent people from speaking up to say they don't like what is going on. It might come out only in a complaint to the EEOC at some later time. "She laughed along with the rest of us" is not a valid defense to charges of sexual harassment if the behavior was something that should have not been permitted in the workplace to begin with. The only acceptable form of touching in the American workplace these days is the handshake.

What is the standard for employers who learn of a problem with sexual harassment in their organization? The federal requirement is that employers address the problem rapidly and thoroughly. Some state laws require employers to go as far as to guarantee that the problem does not occur again and require sexual harassment training on a regular basis, which is beyond federal requirements.

Harassment of Other Types

It isn't only sexual harassment that is illegal in the American workplace. Harassment based on race, age, religion, national origin, color, disability, pregnancy, or genetic information is also illegal. In fact, harassment on the basis of any protected class is illegal.

 NOTE Remember that jokes at the expense of others are usually not a good idea. And if you are a supervisor or manager engaging in such behavior, you can plan on some serious consequences if you end up in court.

Employment liability for workplace injuries is usually handled with liability insurance. These days, insurance is available to address employment decisions, but it is expensive and it comes with a high deductible. That insurance is called *employment practices liability insurance* (EPLI). It does offer employers some amount of coverage to protect against judgments against the employer and the punitive compensation awards that might accompany those judgments. EPLI covers employers for harassment or other illegal discrimination complaint charges and violation of laws about working conditions, among similar alleged bad acts. They usually have a large deductible requirement and carry expensive premiums.

These injuries are not workers' compensation injuries. They are psychological and financial impacts felt by employees subjected to illegal employment discrimination. Peace of mind and the financial security of employment can be taken away in these situations. Courts assign dollar damage awards to compensate for such injuries.

For individual supervisors and managers who engage in employee harassment, no insurance protection is available, and the employer is not obligated to defend the supervisor against legal challenges. Ordinarily a supervisor would be indemnified by the employer because although the supervisor was making individual decisions, it was done within the scope of their job as an agent of the employer. It is when the supervisor steps outside the boundaries of the normal job requirements that things get sticky. Employers depend on managers and supervisors to make decisions every day. However, harassment is not a duty assigned by the employer to any manager or supervisor. It is behavior that is illegal and in most cases runs counter to employer policy. No insurance policy will pay for such illegal behavior unless it is a specific covered hazard in the policy. Additionally, supervisors who engage in harassing behavior with their employees will find that their homeowner's liability coverage won't protect them either. It will decline coverage saying that it was an intentional act, not an accident. Think of someone who gets behind the wheel of their car and intentionally runs over the neighbor's garden. Their automobile policy won't cover them because it was an intentional act. Thus, any court assessments or fines will have to come from the supervisor's personal financial resources. Some have lost their houses because of that insurance provision.

Employer Prevention Obligations

Under federal provisions, employers subject to the Civil Rights Act of 1964 are responsible for having a policy that clearly states what behaviors are considered unacceptable in the workplace. Additionally, they are responsible for enforcing that policy with disciplinary actions when necessary. That may include dismissal in some instances.

As with any other discipline, it should be consistently applied. Similar situations should produce similar outcomes. Treating people differently because of their race, sex, or other basis could generate its own set of discrimination complaints. Regular training with managers and employees on appropriate workplace conduct is recommended to prevent such conduct from happening in the first place. Prompt investigation of complaints can also help to resolve issues before they become an even larger problem.

Nepotism

One potential area of risk for employers that is not as extensively covered by law is nepotism. *Nepotism* is when someone with a high-level position or a high level of influence at an organization hires friends or relatives over other, potentially more qualified candidates. The only law that prohibits nepotism specifically applies to public officials in government: U.S. Code 3110. Although nepotism is technically not illegal for employers outside of government, hiring someone less qualified because of a personal relationship violates a slew of other laws and regulations. Favoritism can be founded upon discrimination, harassment, or retaliation.

One way that employers take steps to avoid nepotism and the potential negative outcomes it can cause is through internal policies and procedures. A policy governing employment of relatives can be a helpful way for HR and management to objectively review hiring decisions that involve relatives of employees. This policy may include some workplace relationships that are prohibited. A common one is a supervisor being related to a direct report. Job applications often include a question such as "Do you have any relatives working for this organization?" While some reporting relationships may be prohibited by a policy, it is well documented that employee referrals are generally successful hires. So, like all HR activities, it is a fine balance determining whether a hiring decision is appropriate.

Fair Labor Standards Act

The last of the key laws governing employment that we will cover in this chapter is the Fair Labor Standards Act. For a refresher on the law, please review Chapter 2. You might remember that the FLSA influences how people are paid, the employment of young people, and how records are kept on employment issues such as hours of work. The Wage and Hour Division (WHD) of the Department of Labor oversees compliance with the FLSA and the federal minimum wage. Although the federal minimum wage has not changed recently, many states have established their own minimum wage laws. Whenever an employee lives in a state where he or she is subject to both federal and state minimum wage laws, the employee is entitled to whatever minimum wage is higher.

Employees of an organization are considered either exempt or nonexempt from the provisions of the FLSA. A job that is exempt means that an employee is not entitled to overtime pay regulations defined in the FLSA. A job that is nonexempt means that an employee is eligible to receive overtime pay, as defined by federal regulations such as the FLSA or, often, state regulations. Most states outline specific requirements for when a nonexempt employee is eligible to receive overtime, frequently for time worked over 40 hours in a week, 8 hours in a day, or the sixth or seventh consecutive day of work in a workweek. While state laws will not be covered on the PHR or SPHR exams, it is important to pay attention to what state laws may apply to your organization. Violating the FLSA may result in criminal prosecution, fines, and back pay.

Determining whether an employee is exempt or nonexempt from the FLSA depends on how much an employee is paid, how they are paid, and what kind of work the employee does. First, to be exempt from overtime, an employee must be paid at least $23,660 per year. This equates to $455 per week. In 2016, President Obama attempted to nearly double this salary threshold since it has not been updated in more than 20 years. That change was not approved. While the amount of pay is part of the determination of FLSA exemption status, how the employee is paid is also important. To be FLSA-exempt, an employee must be paid on a salary basis. This means that an employee receives a predetermined amount of compensation and it cannot be reduced because of variations in the quantity or quality of an employee's work. So, an exempt employee will be paid the same amount whether working 28 hours in a week or 48 hours in a week.

Lastly, even if an employee meets the salary tests required for FLSA exemption, equally as important is the duties test. FLSA exemptions are limited to employees who generally perform high-level work. Table 5-5 outlines the major types of FLSA exemptions defined by the U.S. Department of Labor and the requirements necessary to qualify for them.

Executive Exemption
To qualify for the executive employee exemption, all of the following tests must be met:

- The employee must be compensated on a salary basis (as defined in the regulations) at a rate not less than $455 per week.

- The employee's primary duty must be managing the enterprise or managing a customarily recognized department or subdivision of the enterprise.

- The employee must customarily and regularly direct the work of at least two or more other full-time employees or their equivalent.

- The employee must have the authority to hire or fire other employees, or the employee's suggestions and recommendations as to the hiring, firing, advancement, promotion, or any other change of status of other employees must be given particular weight.

Administrative Exemption
To qualify for the administrative employee exemption, all of the following tests must be met:

- The employee must be compensated on a salary or fee basis (as defined in the regulations) at a rate not less than $455 per week.

- The employee's primary duty must be the performance of office or nonmanual work directly related to the management or general business operations of the employer or the employer's customers.

- The employee's primary duty includes the exercise of discretion and independent judgment with respect to matters of significance.

Professional Exemption
To qualify for the learned professional employee exemption, all of the following tests must be met:

- The employee must be compensated on a salary or fee basis (as defined in the regulations) at a rate not less than $455 per week.

- The employee's primary duty must be the performance of work requiring advanced knowledge, defined as work which is predominantly intellectual in character and which includes work requiring the consistent exercise of discretion and judgment.

- The advanced knowledge must be in a field of science or learning; and

- The advanced knowledge must be customarily acquired by a prolonged course of specialized intellectual instruction.

To qualify for the creative professional employee exemption, all of the following tests must be met:

- The employee must be compensated on a salary or fee basis (as defined in the regulations) at a rate not less than $455 per week.

- The employee's primary duty must be the performance of work requiring invention, imagination, originality, or talent in a recognized field of artistic or creative endeavor.

Table 5-5 FLSA Exemption Categories[9] *(continued)*

Computer Employee Exemption

To qualify for the computer employee exemption, the following tests must be met:

- The employee must be compensated either on a salary or fee basis (as defined in the regulations) at a rate not less than $455 per week or, if compensated on an hourly basis, at a rate not less than $27.63 an hour.

- The employee must be employed as a computer systems analyst, computer programmer, software engineer, or other similarly skilled worker in the computer field performing the duties described next.

- The employee's primary duty must consist of the following:

  - The application of systems analysis techniques and procedures, including consulting with users, to determine hardware, software, or system functional specifications.

  - The design, development, documentation, analysis, creation, testing, or modification of computer systems or programs, including prototypes, based on and related to user or system design specifications.

  - The design, documentation, testing, creation, or modification of computer programs related to machine operating systems.

  - A combination of the aforementioned duties, the performance of which requires the same level of skills.

Outside Sales Exemption

To qualify for the outside sales employee exemption, all of the following tests must be met:

- The employee's primary duty must be making sales (as defined in the FLSA) or obtaining orders or contracts for services or for the use of facilities for which a consideration will be paid by the client or customer.

- The employee must be customarily and regularly engaged away from the employer's place or places of business.

Highly Compensated Employees

Highly compensated employees performing office or nonmanual work and paid a total annual compensation of $100,000 or more (which must include at least $455 per week paid on a salary or fee basis) are exempt from the FLSA if they customarily and regularly perform at least one of the duties of an exempt executive, administrative, or professional employee identified in the standard tests for exemption.

Table 5-5   FLSA Exemption Categories[9]

Independent Contractors

To be covered by the FLSA, an individual must be an employee of an organization. An area of particular concern to both the IRS and DOL over the years is the misclassification of employees as independent contractors. An *independent contractor* is someone who is self-employed and provides goods or services to another organization under verbal or written agreement.

Several U.S. Supreme Court cases have ruled on the classification of employees versus independent contractors. From these cases, key factors in determining whether someone is an independent contractor are noted in the following list.[10] We will start with the legal definition from the case rulings and provide some examples.

- The extent to which the services rendered by the independent contractor are an integral part of the business the independent contractor performs work for.

For example, if an independent contractor supervises employees in an organization and performs a major function associated with business operations, the independent contractor might be misclassified.

- The permanency of the relationship between the company and independent contractor. An independent contractor generally performs an assignment or assignments for a specified length of time outlined by a contract with the company.

- The amount of the independent contractor's use of company facilities and equipment. For example, independent contractors generally bring their own equipment and materials to perform their work.

- The degree of independent business operation and control of the independent contractor. Independent contractors should control what, when, and how they do their work. They are not subject to the same policies that an employee might be. For example, independent contractors should not be required to wear a specific uniform on the job.

- The independent contractor's opportunities for profit and loss. Independent contractors generally carry their insurance for the services they perform. Independent contractors also control their own billing and taxes. Rather than being on a company's payroll, an independent contractor customarily invoices a company for his or her services.

- The amount of initiative, judgment, or foresight in open market competition with others required for the success of the independent contractor. Independent contractors do their own advertising. For example, an independent contractor will generally have his or her own website for marketing purposes. The company he or she performs services for might be listed as a client on the website.

Organizational Staffing Requirements

Staffing is the lifeblood of an organization. People are required to make any organization run. Getting the right people into the right jobs is the function known as *staffing*. Staffing is an extensive process and covers an array of activities, starting with forecasting and planning staffing needs.

Forecasting Staffing Needs

Identifying job openings before they exist is the activity known as *forecasting*. It is best performed with the aid of operations managers who will be supervising the new positions. Given what is anticipated for growth (or force reduction), a manager is able to convert workload into staff requirements. Determining the portion of jobs that will be part-time versus those that will be full-time is another contribution of the forecasting process. Forecasting staffing needs is usually done in terms of the number of full-time equivalent people. That unit value is also favored for budgeting activities. Here's the equation:

Full-Time Equivalent People (FTE) Required = Total Functional Work Load / Work Load Handled by One Person

Forecasting results can be converted into employee head count and budget impact, and the consequences can demand other staffing needs. Adding production workers can cause an increase in payroll support work levels, for example. Forecasting may be needed for temporary changes in business needs. An example is when a toy manufacturer has more demand for product over the holidays and needs more staff members during that time. In this example, forecasting the expected business demand during the holidays (total work load) will help the organization determine the right number of staff members needed to get the work completed. Sometimes, staffing forecasts are needed for long-term business changes as well. We'll talk about this more in the next section.

Corporate Restructuring

A corporate restructure is when an organization changes its business structure in some fashion. This can happen for many reasons. It can be a result of two or more organizations joining together, known as a *merger*. Or it can be when one organization buys another organization, known as an *acquisition*. If an organization is in financial distress, it may need to reorganize or reduce internal staff to meet financial obligations. This can happen in the form of a *divestiture*, which is when an organization sells all or part of its business. Or an organization may decide to move operations to a different country, known as *off-shoring*.

The list of reasons for why a corporate restructure might occur are endless. But one thing that is consistent across the board is the importance of HR's involvement in the corporate restructure process. Whether an organization is growing, downsizing, or moving, each HR functional area that we talk about in this book will need to be reviewed and potentially revamped. Talent planning and acquisition is especially affected. An organization may need to hire a large number of new employees, reduce or reorganize its current staff, or simply find the best way to retain its staff during a time of change and uncertainty.

Mergers and Acquisitions

The unfortunate reality is that an estimated 70 percent to 90 percent of all mergers and acquisitions (M&As) fail to achieve their anticipated strategic and financial objectives.[11] Oftentimes, this is a result of HR-related factors. Combining workplaces, overhauling policies and benefits programs, re-training, and adding or reducing staff members are difficult and sensitive processes. But most notably, change is difficult for people. During an M&A, employees experience mixed emotions. Excitement, fear, anger, and uncertainty are only a few. That is why there is an entire HR function called *change management* dedicated to it. We will talk more about change management in Chapter 10.

One of the first steps in the M&A process is *due diligence*. Due diligence is when the two organizations considering an M&A analyze whether it is a good decision from a strategic, legal, technological, financial, and operational standpoint. Undertaking an M&A is a hefty investment of time and resources, so due diligence is naturally an intensive process that lasts months. HR involvement is critical to understanding key information like organizational structure, employment contracts, polices, benefits, and compensation plans. Many of these activities are completed at the senior HR level, but an HR professional may be tasked to help create organization charts, gather information about benefits and policies, and help with assessments in these areas to determine whether it is worth it for an organization to begin an M&A.

Off-Shoring

Over the years, it has become increasingly popular to move business to another location, often to obtain a cost savings. When business is moved to another country, it is called off-shoring. This decision is commonly made when the cost of operations or the cost to employ staff members in another location is cheaper. There are often tax benefits for organizations that decide to off-shore as well. Car manufacturing is a common example. Because of the cost of production, many of the cars that we drive in the United States are manufactured in another country.

When off-shoring, talent planning and acquisition can more complicated. Labor laws can be entirely different in another country, and there will be cultural and societal differences to navigate as well. HR tasks such as relocating current employees or hiring new employees will require attention to all the laws, regulations, and cultural differences in the new country.

Divestitures

Rather than growing, some organizations make the decision to downsize to meet strategic or financial goals. A divestiture can happen through a sale of part or all of a company's business. Sometimes the decision to undertake a divestiture may come after an M&A. When two businesses merge and become fully operational, a certain business unit or location may be redundant or not perform as well financially as others.

During a divestiture, HR will generally be tasked with reducing staff, also known as a *layoff* or *reduction in workforce*. Once the decision is made to reduce employees, there is a lot of planning and communication that needs to occur, such as the following:

- Forecasting the right number of staff needed to operate the business and the number of staff to reduce.

- Determining a method for staff reduction that does not violate any law or regulation, especially discrimination. How will the organization determine who stays and who does not? How will this change be executed in a fair and unbiased way?

- Checking for other laws the organization may be subject to as a result of this change. A common one is the Worker Adjustment and Retraining Notification Act (WARN Act). We will review this in the next section.

- Creating a separation package for employees to assist with their transition out of the workplace.

- Determining how to communicate this change to staff members being separated from the organization and staff members who are staying. Organizational changes can be extremely difficult for the employees who stay with the organization.

Many of these steps are handled at the senior HR level. However, a divestiture or any corporate restructure involves tremendous HR support. You may find yourself assisting with this process by gathering data about employee performance, hire dates, or demographics to help select a method of staff reduction. Or, you might help develop new organization charts or assist in the preparation of separation packages for employees.

NOTE   Organizations often opt to reduce their workforce based on seniority, or date of hire. This means that the employees with the most recent hire date (least seniority with the organization) are selected for layoff first. This is a popular option because date of hire is the only criterion used for determining who stays with the organization and who does not. There is a low risk for discrimination or bias when using this selection method.

Compliance with WARN Act

When you have 100 or more employees and undergo a large downsizing of your staff, as you read in Chapter 2, you may be subject to the Worker Adjustment and Retraining Notification (WARN) Act.

Should it be necessary to reduce your employee head count by 50 or more full-time workers, you must comply with the WARN Act requirements. At least 60 days before the layoff is to occur or the plant is to be closed, notice should be sent to the State Rapid Response Dislocated Worker Unit as well as the chief elected official of the local government where the layoff or closure will occur. Notice must also be given to each union or other employee representative at the facility that will experience the force reduction. In companies without union representation, each affected worker must receive this notice. Specific content is required of these notices, including the following:

- The name and address where the mass layoff or plant closing is to occur, along with the name and telephone number of a company contact person who can provide additional information
- A statement as to whether the planned action is expected to be permanent or temporary and, if the entire plant is to be closed, a statement to that effect
- The expected date of the first separation and the anticipated schedule for making separations
- The job titles of positions to be affected and the name of affected employees in each job classification

The WARN Act Employers Guide states, "An employer who violates WARN is liable to each affected employee for an amount equal to back pay and benefits for the period of violation, up to 60 days. This liability may be reduced by any wages the employer pays over the notice period. WARN liability may also be reduced by any voluntary and unconditional payment not required by a legal obligation."[12]

Sourcing Methods and Techniques

Sourcing methods and techniques are different ways to find people to fill the jobs that need to be filled. There are many different options available to source applicants. Before a job can be effectively sourced, an accurate job description, including compliance with all legal requirements such as EEO and ADA, should be in place.

Current Market for Talent

At the time of writing this book, unemployment is low. Unemployment is a monthly calculation done by the Bureau of Labor Statistics (BLS) of the Department of Labor. The goal of calculating unemployment is to determine the amount of people in the United States who do not have jobs, are looking for a job, or are looking for more work.

The goal is always to keep unemployment at a low level. Low unemployment is a good thing for workers. It means that a higher percentage of people who are looking for work have jobs. On the other hand, it can put hiring managers in a tough position. When more workers already have jobs, it means there is less available talent looking for positions. At the time of this book, there is also a shift in generations in the workforce. In the years following World War II, between approximately the 1940s through the 1960s, there was a noticeable increase in the birth rate. The generation born during this time is called the Baby Boomers. Many Baby Boomers are now making the decision to retire, leaving more open jobs.

With more open jobs and less available talent, sourcing techniques become even more important. To find the right person for the job, employers have to use creative techniques to attract talent to their organization. There are many different options for sourcing talent, and different approaches may be best suited for different positions. With all sourcing, it is important that HR professionals take the time to develop their recruitment plan and determine the best solution to meet organizational needs and legal requirements.

Internal and External Recruitment Sources

Often, employers search both inside and outside their organizations for someone who can fill a job opening.

Internal Sources

Some organizations overlook their own workforce as a legitimate source of qualified candidates when job openings occur. Internal recruiting can be handled either formally or informally. In union-represented organizations, a procedure for internal job postings is usually specified in the memorandum of understanding (MOU) or union contract (collective bargaining agreement [CBA]). Details within union contracts (CBAs) might specify what information should be included in job postings and how long job openings will remain posted. Sometimes internal recruiting must happen for a specified number of days prior to any external recruiting efforts being made. In the absence of unions, the employer will have the opportunity to develop its own policies and procedures in this staffing area.

Often there are internal resources that might fill the needs of the job opening in question. Current employees are constantly changing, through education or temporary job assignments. They may be working on certifications that would better qualify them for a different job. It is important to consider these resources because they represent less expensive candidate pools than those built with external candidates. And it begs the question of whether it is necessary to have a database that tracks current employee skills and certifications. Training accomplishments, new educational achievements, and demonstrated skill performance should all be identified periodically (annually or more often) and the data entered into these types of databases.

Succession planning is a process of organizing the internal staffing process. It depends on identifying when job openings may occur, who is currently qualified to perform that job, and, alternatively, who could be qualified through more training and/or development. Properly done, succession planning will enable you to identify two or three key candidates for each senior executive position in the organization. It will also enable you to identify the developmental process that will be implemented to prepare each of those candidates for the ultimate placement in the higher position. Developmental activities can include temporary task force assignments, temporary job assignments, rotational job assignments, or job swapping where two people change positions for mutual benefit. Succession plans are usually closely guarded because they contain very special and sensitive information. Sometimes HR professionals below the senior executive level in HR are not even privy to succession plan content. Early in your HR career, initial involvement in the succession planning process will include tasks such as preparing assessments under the guidance of senior HR professionals and helping to develop training programs to fill noted skill gaps. Implementing a quality succession plan can take a year or more.

One tool that can assist the internal recruiting process is an employee skills database. Information tracked in this database will be confidential to a large extent. Yet it can help you identify qualified candidates for internal placement when the need arises. Your list of data content will likely be different from that created by other HR professionals in different types of organizations. Some of the basics could include the following:

- Typing (rate and accuracy)
- Specific software application skills (Microsoft Office, accounting programs)
- Driving (automobiles, trucks, forklifts)
- Licenses (attorney, physician, pharmacist, private investigation, nursing)
- Certifications (CPA, PHR, SPHR, surveyor, architect)
- Computer programming (languages)
- CPR/first aid
- Credentials (teaching specialty)
- Craft specialty (welding, plumbing, electrician, carpentry)
- Advanced degree (master's, functional specialty)

- Executive training
- Task force leadership
- Languages (specific language fluency)

Internal recruiting can contribute substantially to your overall placement needs. Generally speaking, internal candidates are less expensive to obtain than external candidates. When people are already on the payroll, transferring them to a new job assignment reduces the costs associated with recruiting, hiring, and even sometimes Social Security and Medicare tax.

Here are some internal sources that can be considered before publishing a job opening in external sources:

- **Promotions and transfers** Internal sources include promotions and transfers. People can transfer within the same department, to other departments, or to other associated subsidiary companies. A promotion can be defined as an increase in job level, an increase in compensation, or an increase in responsibilities. Usually, morale is positively affected when workers see the employer making opportunities available to the existing workforce before searching outside for job candidates. Upgrades and, strangely, downgrades or demotions can also be considered internal sources for job placements.

- **Diversity groups** Diversity groups are sometimes called *employee affinity groups*. They typically are organized along race, gender, disability, or veteran status (for example, African American Employees Association, Women Engineers Club, or AB Trucking Veterans Association). Sometimes they are sponsored by employers; sometimes they are not. Often, employers provide meeting space and refreshments in exchange for conversations with the groups on topics of diversity management, employee relations, employee development, and so on. Such groups can be a valuable resource for employer human resource management. Diversity groups should be included in external recruiting efforts, encouraging further referrals of job candidates from minority, women, disabled, and veteran populations.

- **Retired employees** A resource who is already trained, has organizational knowledge, and is experienced in job requirements should not be overlooked. It may be cheaper in the short run to bring back a retired worker to "fill in" temporarily than to hire another type of temporary worker.

- **Employee referrals** Because internal employees are already well versed in organizational policies and procedures and the work environment, when an internal employee refers a new hire, statistics have shown that the new hire will be more successful. The old saying, "It takes one to know one" can apply to this scenario. Employee referrals are also generally a cheaper method of sourcing. Rather than spending the staffing budget on external job postings and other sourcing methods, hiring an employee referral can avoid these expenses altogether.

Many employers create programs to incentivize employee referrals because of the success of new hires found through this method and the cost savings associated with it. Such programs often provide an employee referral bonus to the internal employee who referred the new hire. Bonuses are often paid once the new hire has completed an introductory period of employment, or at least 90 calendar days on the job. Referral bonuses may also continue when the referred new hire completes certain milestones, such as one or five years of employment.

External Sources

In contrast to internal recruiting is external recruiting, which is just as it sounds. External recruiting sources include the following:

- **State employment services**   These are free postings for job openings of all kinds.

- **Industrial associations**   If the employer is a member of an industrial association, there are frequently job posting services offered by such associations, and they are usually free.

- **Local educational institutions**   High schools, community colleges, and universities will usually be glad to post job opening information so their graduating students can find employment in their chosen field of work.

- **Veterans organizations**   Sometimes state employment agencies have linkages to veterans organizations and often have veterans coordinators on their staff to maintain those relationships. Get to know these people and how they can help with your recruiting efforts.

- **Organizations for disabled**   Many qualified job seekers are classified as "disabled" for one reason or another. In many cases, the disability will have no impact on that person's ability to perform the essential job functions. Don't overlook a valuable resource.

- **Advertising or posting on web services**   In this day and age, most recruiting is done online. Popular websites for recruiting include Indeed.com, Monster.com, ZipRecruiter.com, and others. Some websites require fees for postings, and others do not. Some websites will offer a base job posting service for free, for a short length of time, or at a reduced level of advertising exposure to applicants. To get more exposure for your job posting, you can pay a fee. On some sites like Indeed .com, you can set a maximum daily amount you want to spend for your job posting, which helps manage your recruitment budget.

- **Advertising or posting on social media**   It has been said that, today, more than half of all white-collar jobs are being filled through LinkedIn. LinkedIn is a free social media site where anyone who has signed up for the service can create a profile, which is essentially a résumé. Employers can pay to post a job on LinkedIn and source candidates through the website. It is also a great way for people who are looking for jobs to display their credentials and experience to employers.

With the vast array of social media options available, you will also find employers maximizing free resources for job posting on platforms such as Facebook, Twitter, and Instagram.

- **Traditional advertising**   Newspaper and magazine print advertising can take the form of classified ads or display ads. These days, magazines and newspapers have companion editions online. Buying advertising in one format can also provide the same advertising in the other format. There are also free job search newspapers that can be found in dispensing racks at local supermarkets, on street corners, and at newsstands. These list job openings only within a given geography. They are sustained by paid advertising related to job opportunities and placement, like those related to training institutions and universities, for example.

In the Trenches

Req-less Recruiting

Grant D. Bassett, VP of Talent, Workday, Inc.

As the advantages of creating connections through social media grow, online professional networks continue to make finding talent easier and easier. I believe we're at the cusp of a hard left turn in the recruiting profession where the real value of a recruiting function will clearly be talent engagement and conversion.

Imagine a company with 10,000 employees, all of whom actively manage their social networks as well as cultivate their professional networks. It is reasonable to believe that through the connections of those 10,000 employees, every person that company might want to hire is known to someone within that network. So, finding them isn't the issue any more. It's curating and distributing content in a way that attracts, engages, and ultimately converts those individuals into people who will be interested in talking about a career move.

All of this points away from a job requisition being the order that is placed to kick off recruiting efforts and toward a model where key talent profiles are built and communicated across a company, communities are created that will feed those profiles, and compelling, engaging content is developed that can be used by all employees to share with their networks.

Every employee becomes a recruiter, and the ultimate goal is 100 percent employee referral, or, stated another way, 100 percent of hires come from our networks. The requisition goes away, the success profile becomes key, and the role of the talent acquisition function becomes a true center of excellence (COE) focused on successful profile creation, talent community creation, content creation and distribution, and other key programs aimed at enabling all employees to engage and convert talent that feeds the needs of the company.

State Employment Services

Each state maintains an agency that has a resource for job placement assistance. Usually it is the same agency that manages the unemployment insurance distribution system. Federal contractors are required to post their job openings with the state employment service for the state in which the job will be located. Other employers are encouraged to post their job openings at these agencies, but they are not required to do so. There is no fee for employer use of these agencies. Anyone using the sites should retain a copy of the filings they post so there is no confusion in the future about what job content was described.

Flexible Staffing

Traditionally, full-time employment was thought of as one of the three eight-hour periods in a workday: 8 AM to 5 PM, 4 PM to 1 AM, or 12 AM to 9 AM. (Each is nine hours long because of a planned meal period of one hour.) These days, we don't have quite the lock-step approach to staffing that used to exist, and there are many alternatives to full-time employees.

Temporary Employees

One change to full-time employment is the use of temporary employees. It is not necessary to hire people by putting them on the payroll. Employers can expand their workforce quickly and easily by contracting with temporary talent agencies to satisfy their need for additional people. Temporary workers can be used on production lines, in accounting departments, or in any other portion of an organization experiencing a workload that cannot be handled by the permanent staff. Agencies pay their employees, take care of payroll withholding and tax reporting, add a profit margin, and then pass the final rate to the employer contracting for that help.

Job Sharing

Job sharing is an employment technique that you hear about more and more these days. It offers two or more workers the opportunity to collectively constitute one full-time equivalent employee. One person works the job in the morning, and another works the same job in the afternoon. Considerations involve briefing the "job sharing partner" on the current issues to be dealt with during the next portion of work time. There are some financial considerations, too. Each employee will require the employer's full contribution toward Social Security and Medicare. That may cost the employee more than if one person were to occupy the position.

 NOTE Job sharing can increase morale and provide staffing in situations that otherwise might be difficult.

In the Trenches

Mother Nature, the Sherpa of Job Sharing/Telecommuting

In 1989 a catastrophic earthquake, Loma Prieta, hit the San Francisco Bay Area, causing freeways to collapse, modes of public transportation to hiccup, and buildings to be red-tagged as uninhabitable. With all of that disruption, the launch of the era of telecommuting was officially born. Companies were scrambling to figure out how to get business done when key employees were unable to physically make it into the workplace due to lengthy road and bridge closures. The terms *telecommuting* and *job sharing* were tossed into the ring as viable options for keeping business moving. It was helpful that San Francisco was in close proximity to the technology capital of the world, Silicon Valley, whose professional and technical types of employees had already been successfully working within the parameters of telecommuting.

Yet this was a time when most other industry organizations were still struggling to get their executive and senior management staff to learn how to dial into bridge/conference lines, let alone use a PC. Many HR professionals turned to the California Telecommuting Pilot Project, which was initially planned in 1985 and began with its pilot in mid-1987 as a resource for help. Though this pilot program had a controlled group of mostly supervisory personnel and individual contributors such as technical staff, nevertheless it was helpful to review the "how to" on implementing telecommuting. Organizations didn't have the luxury of time to create a well-thought-out project plan, and most were just plain shell-shocked by the events, so the local media was brought into the loop to help spread the option. IT staff were taking laptops to key employees' homes, setting them up with modems, and dialing in to intranet e-mail systems, providing personal one-on-one instructions on the use of keyboard function keys (those were the days prior to a "mouse").

And the story expands from there, because folks were having issues with their own personal matters from the earthquake's aftermath and having to juggle family/home issues while still attending to their careers. That's when the concept of job sharing expanded. In that era, job sharing was mostly for new parents in the workplace whose job capacity was identical to others, such as accounting. With Mother Nature as a catalyst, it caused many more occupations and employees to design the job share both to help overcome the needs of the business and take care of the personal crisis. Eventually, there was no turning back once business as usual resumed and the transportation infrastructure was fixed. Telecommuting and new roles for job sharing were here to stay as the effectiveness and productivity became widespread. HR was quickly developing aligned policies, and IT groups geared up for the technology training and hookups.

(continued)

Today, telecommuting and job sharing have affected almost every aspect of contemporary life, from fundamental job patterns such as having to reserve office space (i.e., hoteling) when going into the office to the physical structure of communities such as solo home offices and the additions of cable/fiber optics to the suburbs. Interesting how a kick from Mother Nature can cause an idea to explode into reality and the everyday way of now doing work.

Part-Time vs. Full-Time

In addition to contributions toward Social Security and Medicare, there are many financial considerations related to full-time versus part-time workers. Where local employment taxes are based on head count, part-time workers can cost more than a full-time staff.

Under the Affordable Care Act, employers can escape paying for benefit coverage of some workers if they maintain a part-time status. By policy, other benefit programs may or may not be available to part-time workers. It is not uncommon to have access to an individual retirement account (IRA) or other retirement programs based on the number of hours worked each week. The amount of supervision available can also impact the ratio of full-time to part-time workers.

Project Hires/Contract Labor

Using project hires and contract labor is another alternative to full-time employment. Project hires are people who are recruited and placed on the payroll with the understanding that their employment will be terminated once the project is completed. It is common in organizations that seek out projects from client organizations. A staff is hired for the project and then let go when the project comes to an end.

Contract labor refers to people who are hired for a specific period of time. An organization may believe that the workload will last until this time next year. So, it contracts with people to handle that workload for the year. At the end of the contract, those folks will come off the payroll, whether or not the project has concluded. They could be "extended" (payroll status maintained) for a designated period of time if the workload has not diminished.

Phased Retirement

As opposed to instant full-time retirement, phased retirement is another alternative to full-time employment, which allows an individual to take partial retirement while continuing to work a reduced schedule. It can take the form of job sharing, part-time, seasonal, temporary, or project work.

 NOTE A major advantage of phased retirement is that it allows employees to get used to working less and having more time to themselves. It prevents the sudden shock of not having a work routine that comes with traditional retirement.

Retiree Annuitants

Retiree annuitants are folks who have retired from the organization but are called back to work because of emergencies, unexpected workload, or other unforeseen need. They are defined by the IRS[13] as people who are entitled to be drawing benefits from their retirement program while earning compensation from their employer for continuing employment whether or not they are continuing to pay into the retirement program.

Payrolling

When a job needs to be done and the organization does not want to hire someone onto its own payroll to do that job, an alternative is to contract with a vendor who will hire someone to do the job at the client organization. Contractor payrolling is used when you need to adjust to seasonal fluctuations, fill a vacancy while searching for a permanent replacement, bridge the gap in personnel when there is unexpected growth, or use interns for a set period of time. It has many applications, and the greatest benefit is in protecting against charges that the person hired is not an independent contractor but an employee, a problem that cost the company Microsoft just under a $100 million in payroll taxes, penalties, fines, and legal fees. This is usually a process used for less than an entire workforce. When single employees or small groups of employees are needed, payrolling services can solve the need.

Employee Leasing and Professional Employer Organizations (PEOs)

Similar to payrolling, employee leasing is a process of moving employees to another company's payroll as a service for a client organization. Typically, professional employer organizations (PEOs) will take over the entire workforce in a client company. PEOs provide payroll services, tax tracking and depositing, retirement program management, healthcare benefit program management, and even employee counseling and support services. In essence, employee leasing is the outsourcing of the human resource department and the payroll function together. Employees usually become employees of both organizations, the client where they perform their work and the vendor (PEO) that handles the payroll and HR functions for the client. It means both employers are liable for legal compliance.

Outsourcing and Managed Service Providers

Another alternative is outsourcing. Outsourcing is shifting a workload out of the organization through a contract with another employer organization, either here in this country or somewhere else in the world. Managed service providers (MSPs) offer to manage functions as part of a strategic decision to move operations or support functions out of an employment organization to a vendor that can perform them less expensively. Such a decision is designed to allow the client company to focus on key activities within its core business while a vendor handles support activities for the client.

Temp-to-Lease Programs

When a need exists for employees on a seasonal basis or for jobs that will last longer than a few days or weeks, it is possible for employers to lease their workers from a vendor organization. The vendor provides the underlying employment relationship with the worker. When temporary needs stretch into longer-term needs, it still may not be wise to increase payroll in the client organization. That's when contracting for temporary agency workers can be converted into long-term employee leases. These workers often have no benefits provided to them. The client organization pays an employment agency a fee in addition to the pay received by the worker assigned to the client. All payroll operations are maintained by the temporary service agency.

Rehires and Transfers

When workloads rise unexpectedly, it is sometimes difficult to bring in new hires quickly enough to respond to that increased demand. Rehiring laid-off workers and bringing in transfers from other portions of the organization can sometimes be good solutions. Rehired workers are already trained and can be productive immediately. Transfers from other portions of the organization have the advantage of already knowing the culture, and if coming from similar or identical types of work, they can also be productive rather quickly.

Relocation

Moving workers from one location to another outside the normal commute radius requires finding them new living quarters. This can be done on a temporary or permanent basis. If relocation is used to respond to union strikes or increased workload, it will likely be a temporary condition. Employers sometimes rent blocks of rooms in long-term hotel facilities so workers can have cooking and laundry facilities along with living quarters.

Permanent relocation can involve workers selling and buying homes and packing household belongings and shipping them long distances, sometimes across the country or internationally. There are many variables in such action on the part of the employer. Enticing employees to accept relocation can be a high hurdle to overcome. Forcing the change for a spouse's employment, moving children from one school to another, and accepting a higher cost of living at the new location can require employers to provide financial incentives. Those incentives can include such things as the following:

- **Home purchase/lease escape fees**   Guaranteed purchase of the employee's old home following an appraisal of value. The employee can accept or reject the company's offer if it might be possible to achieve a higher selling price some other way. When there is a fee involved for canceling property leases, employers can pay that fee for employees.

- **Real estate processing fees**   Escrow fees for selling and buying real property can amount to many dollars. Paying these expenses for a relocating employee can lift that burden and remove another objection to relocating.

- **Mortgage subsidy**   In an inflationary economy, mortgage rates rise. It can sometimes be necessary for employers to pay a portion or all of the increased mortgage rate to get an employee to accept relocation.
- **Packing/shipping/unpacking**   Paying the bill for a moving company to pack, ship, and unpack at the destination is another way to relieve employees of financial burden.
- **Funds for taxes on increased taxable income**   When there are income tax consequences for employees as a result of a relocation, employers sometimes compute a "tax obligation roll-up" and pay that to the employee in a lump sum as withholdings.

Applicant Tracking

Once there is a sourcing method in place, it is a matter of good management that some form of applicant tracking be used in any organization hiring employees. In federal contractor organizations and employers with 100 or more workers, there are additional obligations that require maintaining records of job applicants. Table 5-6 provides basic information that an applicant tracking records system should track.

Résumés vs. Job Applications

So far, no state or federal law or regulation requires employers to use job applications or résumé forms in their employment process. That means employers are left to their own devices about how to process job applicants. Evaluating differences among job applicants is the primary task. Carefully crafted job application forms can help HR professionals in that evaluation process.

What is required by state and federal law is that employers meet the requirements of equal employment opportunity laws and be able to demonstrate that they made their employment decisions without regard to any of the protected categories. Some organizations prefer to use résumés rather than job applications, and in some companies neither is a requirement.

If a job application is used, it can be designed by the employer to contain requests for information the employer deems to be necessary in making the employment decision. Obviously, information categories should not include things such as birth date, race, sex, marital status, or other reference to protected categories.

Race and gender/sex are required data points for employees. Employers must either capture that information through employee self-identification or by observation best guess. Affirmative action employers (federal goods and service contractors) must invite job applicants to self-identify their race and gender/sex when they submit their application. That information is supposed to be diverted from view of the hiring manager or recruiter. Normally, it is routed to the HR professional responsible for accumulating and analyzing the database it will be entered into.

There are countless ways to write a résumé, and not all of them will contain the same data elements. Further, résumés almost never provide written authorization for

Information Element	Element Content
Applicant name	Applicant name.
Address	Applicant's current mailing address.
Telephone number	Applicant's current telephone number (home, cell, work).
E-mail or other method of contact	Applicant's e-mail address.
Self-identification of race and sex	This information should not be passed on to the selecting manager(s).
Self-identification of protected veteran and disabled status	This information should not be passed on to the selecting manager(s).
Source	How did this person get information about your job opening?
Position applied for	Always insist on applicants identifying the specific job opening they are interested in. This might be a job requisition number or a job title.
Job location	If more than one location is available, ask for a preference.
Qualifications for the job	This could be satisfied by a resume or CV. Or you can require every applicant to complete your specific job application form.
Availability	How soon will the candidate be available to start work?
Compensation desired	While many people won't answer this question, it is good to ask it anyway. If someone replies with a number significantly above your budget range, you do not need to waste any more time on their candidacy. Some states have recently passed state laws forbidding questions on a job application about salary history. Be sure to pay attention to state laws that may affect your organization in this area.
References	Be sure to track references provided by the job applicant, including educational institutions (and degrees), former employers (with job titles and compensation amounts), and personal references.

Table 5-6   Applicant Tracking Data

employers to gather information from previous employers. Job application forms can be designed with those authorizations and liability release statements to facilitate background checking.

Online vs. Hard Copy

There are many folks today who prefer to dispense with paper copies of documents, and there are legitimate environmental reasons for moving to electronic copies. There are advantages to each approach.

Hard-Copy Records   Job applications and résumés can provide an insight into the candidate's organization and language skills. Sloppiness and misspellings can be readily detected on paper records, particularly on résumés. Asking applicants to fill out a form can offer some insights into their reading skill, penmanship, written articulation, and inner work standards. When such records are converted to electronic format, the same types of information may not be as obvious.

Online Records   The most obvious advantage of electronic records is that they can be shared by multiple people at the same time. In the case of group interviews, this can be particularly nice. Many years ago, there were problems with the legality of electronic signatures on e-documents. The Uniform Electronic Transactions Act of 1999[14] remedied that problem for the most part.

Advantages of Job Application Forms

While there is no requirement for employers to use job application forms, they can be enormously helpful. As an employer, you might expect to gain some or all of these benefits:

- Consistently gather the same data in the same format from each prospective employee. With an employment application, employers gain standardization of information requested.

- Gather information about the applicant's credentials that candidates would not usually include in a résumé or cover letter. Examples include reasons why the applicant left the employ of a prior employer, felony or misdemeanor crime convictions, and names and contact information for immediate supervisors.

- Obtain the applicant's signature attesting that all statements on the employment application are true.

- Obtain the applicant's signature enabling a potential employer to check the veracity of all data provided on the employment application, including employment history, education history, degrees earned, and so forth. Fraudulent claims and information on application materials, including fake degrees, exaggerated claims about former job responsibilities or compensation, fake dates of employment, and other falsehoods are a significant problem.

- Get the applicant's signature to attest that he or she has read and understands certain employer policies and procedures that are spelled out on the employment application. These typically include the fact that the employer is an at-will employer; that the employer is an equal opportunity, nondiscriminating employer; and any other facts that the employer wants the applicant to read and understand on the employment application. When applicable, this may include the requirement that the applicant must pass a drug test prior to hire.

> - Obtain the applicant's signature agreeing to a background check, including criminal history, driving record (for certain jobs), and anything else required by the job.
> - Obtain voluntary self-identification data about race, sex, disability, and veteran status to enable proper reporting to government organizations as required and analysis of employment data by the employer.
>
> These days, it is more a function of employer policy and organizational preference as to which type of record format will be used.

Invitations to Self-Identify as Part of the Application Process

We know from the Fair Labor Standards Act (see Chapter 2) and the EEOC requirement for annual filing of the EEO-1 report that many employers are required to establish and maintain records of employee demographics. This information should be treated as confidential just as all other HR data is considered confidential.

Race and Gender/Sex

All employers with 100 or more employees and all federal contractors with 50 or more employees and contracts of $50,000 or more (or a construction contract valued at $10,000 or more) must maintain sex and ethnic identification of each employee.

There are seven race/ethnic categories on the EEO-1 form. So, an invitation to self-identify given to employees and job applicants should contain all seven categories.

- White (not Hispanic)
- Black or African American (not Hispanic)
- Hispanic
- Asian (not Hispanic)
- Native Hawaiian or Other Pacific Islander (not Hispanic)
- American Indian, Native American, Alaska Native (not Hispanic)
- Two or more races (not Hispanic)

In the public sector, the EEO-4 report has not expanded its list of five race/ethnic categories. They remain as follows:

- White (not Hispanic)
- Black or African American (not Hispanic)
- Hispanic
- Asian (not Hispanic, Including Hawaiian and Other Pacific Islander)
- American Indian, Native American, Alaska Native (not Hispanic)

NOTE Any form requesting job applicants or employees to identify their race should conform to the choices to the type of EEO report you will have to file.

When an employee fails to self-identify, the employer is responsible for making an observation and best guess as to the race category in which the employee should be reported. If the employee later decides to report their race/ethnicity, that information should be accepted and recorded by the employer.

The government has decided that for tracking and reporting purposes, the Hispanic ethnicity trumps all race categories. That is to say, someone who says they are Hispanic and some other race in addition should be recorded as Hispanic. Race categories are used only for non-Hispanic individuals.

The invitation to self-identify should also ask for identification of gender/sex, either male or female. Again, if the individual refuses to self-identify, the employer is obligated to make a selection based on observation.

Veteran and Disabled Status

Federal contractors with $25,000 or more in contract value must abide by regulations related to affirmative action requirements for disabled and veterans. As of 2014, all federal contractors are required to invite self-identification as disabled and veteran from both applicants and employees. When talking about veterans, we mean U.S. veterans. Someone who has served in the armed forces of a foreign country is not included in the government's definition.

The EEOC has determined that it is acceptable to request identification of disability prior to an employment offer being extended as long as the invitation form is the one specified by the Office of Federal Contract Compliance Programs (OFCCP) and it is in an effort to comply with affirmative action obligations. Of course, any request for accommodation during the application process should be handled as required by the Americans with Disabilities Act.

Each of the four categories of veteran should be clearly identified on the self-ID request form. The applicant or employee should be able to choose from that list. A brief explanation of each category should be given so the form user can understand what they mean.

The disability identification should be available as a selection, along with an opportunity to request any job accommodation or applicant accommodation that might be desired.

Selection

"Pick me. Pick me!" Employment selection is a competition of talent identification. It is rare for someone to walk into a business and ask for a job and then to be hired on the spot. Although it might still happen in small employer organizations, more typically selection is a multiple-step process. It can involve an initial application and/or résumé, telephone interview, written testing, in-person interview (perhaps several), a team interview (panel interview), background check, job offer, and post-offer physical exam. Then, there is usually a probationary period that is now more often called a *training period* or *introductory period*.

Selection Systems

There are many possible selection systems. Pick every sixth person on the list, presuming all on the list meet the basic qualifications of the job. Pick the tenth person, without any further consideration or screening. Pick the first person to respond. These are all valid selection processes, and they are nondiscriminatory. They don't, however, offer much in the way of screening or filtering for nuances of skills and abilities.

Quantitative Selection Systems

How often have you heard operations managers say, "I want to pick my own people"? Usually, what they are saying is, "I want to be sure the chemistry is right and that I can work with the person who is selected."

Quantitative selection systems are those that use numerical performance levels and allow for specific numerical cutoffs as qualification thresholds. Written paper and pencil tests are the easiest example. Giving a test involving true-false or multiple-choice answers permits scoring the test by the number of correct responses. The raw number of right answers can be used, or it can be converted into a rate or percentage. The percentage of 76 correct out of 134 questions is 57 percent. If the "pass" level was initially set at 66 percent, this person would not have passed the written test.

 NOTE The PHR/SPHR exam is another example of a quantitative selection system. Only those with a passing score will be awarded the certification.

Subjective Selection Systems

How often have you heard someone say, "I'll know it when I see it, but it can't be measured…it's too subjective." Of course, that's nonsense. Anything can be measured. Things such as behaviors and accomplishments can be measured in relation to other things, similar or not. Behaviors are what we say and do. Behaviors can be measured along a scale that is created just to measure those behaviors or their characteristics. Think of measuring the amount of leadership someone demonstrates or measuring the amount of communication skill they can display. Behaviors can be measured against a standard or norm, and a person can be determined to have less or more of that behavior than the norm. Consider a measurement of inner work standards. A furniture painter with exceptionally high inner work standards compared to a typical furniture painter is a person who paints the top of the top shelf and the bottom of the bottom shelf, even if no one will ever see those surfaces.

Rating Scale

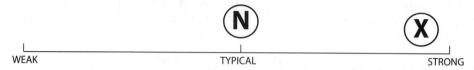

Shows all possible amounts of leadership skills from weak to strong. The N is the norm. It represents the amount of leadership skills observed in the person or group of successful individuals who are at the same job level as the incumbent being rated. X represents the incumbent's amount of leadership skills observed.

Figure 5-3   The amount of leadership observed

Teachers and instructors are perfect examples of people who perform jobs that some folks think would be difficult to measure. It's not so. Giving it a little thought, you will discover that the behaviors of good teachers can be thought of as the norm or standard you would like all teachers to "measure up to." Then it is only necessary to identify the specific behaviors you would like to measure in teachers. Here are some examples:[15]

- **Skills**   Verbal, interpersonal, leadership, reading, organizing and planning, platform skills, decision making, analytical, problem solving, feedback, questioning, writing, management of diverse groups
- **Knowledge**   Subject matter, organization, adult learning needs, trainee group
- **Qualifications**   Educational degree, license, certification, train-the-trainer course
- **Experience**   Technical, training, supervisory, management, operations or staff
- **Characteristics**   Energy, enthusiasm, commitment, integrity, self-objectivity

Pick any of those on the list, and you will be able to create a measurement for it. For example, let's choose "leadership." First, we must define what the term means related to the job at hand. So, we will say, "Leadership is the ability to get other people to willingly follow suggestions." Now, we can create a scale on which we can measure the amount of "leadership" each instructor demonstrates. It might look like Figure 5-3.

"N" is the amount of leadership seen in the person being referenced as the norm. "X" is the amount of leadership being seen in the person being evaluated against the norm.

Measuring performance in HR functions can be done in the same way. Consider the "norm" for each behavior, characteristic, skill, or knowledge to be "What you would expect to see in someone performing the job successfully." Not the best ever. Not what just gets by. But what you expect to see in a successful performer.

Criteria for Selection

Before beginning the actual selection process, criteria for selection should be determined. These criteria should measure the degree to which a candidate possesses the job qualifications listed in the job description. Lack of a college degree may be a problem, or it may be compensated for by demonstration of specific experience on identified duties and responsibilities. Criteria might specify the degree of physical involvement required by citing how heavy the materials are that must be lifted and carried a specified number of times during a work shift. Mental criteria could include certain mathematical abilities, literacy achievements, or speaking ability. Demonstrated leadership skills could also constitute a job selection criterion.

Whatever is listed as a basic requirement must be demonstrated by any person selected for the position. Selecting someone who does not have a required qualification invalidates the job requirements and could entirely invalidate the employer's selection process. Care should be taken to be sure the basic qualifications are actually required and that no one is selected who does not have all of them.

Employment Testing

Proper testing is conducted by using validated selection tools. That was explained earlier in this chapter. Be sure to understand the various types of validation studies that can be used under the Uniform Guidelines on Employee Selection Procedures.

Interviewing Candidates

In addition to testing, interviewing is an important part of the selection process. A large portion of the workforce is hired only after one or more interviews with the prospective employer. There are several primary types of interviews employers can select from.

Structured

An interviewer asks every applicant the same questions along with follow-up probes that may be different depending on the initial response. Structured interviews make it possible to gather similar information from all candidates.

Patterned

In the patterned interview, sometimes called a *targeted interview,* an interviewer asks each applicant questions that are from the same knowledge, skill, or ability (KSA) area; however, the questions are not necessarily the same. They differ depending on the candidate's background. For example, questions asked of a recent college graduate may differ from those asked of a candidate with years of related experience.

Stress

In this type of interview, an interviewer creates an aggressive posture—in other words, deliberately creating some type of stress to see how the candidate reacts to stressful situations. For example, using a room where the candidate has to face an open window with the sun in his or her eyes can put the candidate under stress. This type of interview is used more often in law enforcement, air traffic control, and similar high-stress occupations. The stress interview was more common in the 1970s and 1980s. Today, it is not recommended because of the likelihood that it will be interpreted as personal bias.

Directive

In this type of interview, an interviewer poses specific questions to the candidate, maintaining tight control; it is a highly structured interview. Every candidate is asked exactly the same questions.

Nondirective

In this type of interview, the interviewer asks open-ended questions and provides only general direction; the interviewer allows the candidate to guide the process. A response to one question dictates what the next question will be.

Behavioral

In a behavioral interview, an interviewer focuses on how the applicant previously handled actual situations (real, not hypothetical). The interviewer probes very specific situations looking for past behaviors and how the applicant handled those experiences. The questions probe the knowledge, skills, abilities, and other personal characteristics identified as essential to success on the job. The interviewer looks for three things: a description of an actual situation or task, the action taken, and the result or outcome. The principle behind behavioral interviewing is that past performance is the best predictor of future performance.

Situational

In a situational interview, the interviewer elicits stories and examples that illustrate the applicant's skills and qualifications for the job. Situational interviewing is similar to behavioral interviewing; the only difference is that in a behavioral interview, the interviewer is probing for actual past experiences, whereas in a situational interview, the interviewer develops hypothetical situations and asks the applicant how he or she would handle them.

Group

Group interviews happen when multiple job candidates are interviewed by one or more interviewers at the same time. Group interviews are used in specific situations where a number of candidates are being considered for the same job in which the duties are limited and clearly defined, such as a merry-go-round operator. A *fishbowl interview* brings multiple candidates together to work with each other in an actual group activity or exercise. It is similar to an in-basket exercise except it involves a group of candidates. A *team interview* typically involves a group of interviewers with a perspective of the actual interactions associated with the job. This might include supervisors, subordinates, peers, customers, and so on. It is like a 360° exercise. Finally, in a *panel interview,* questions are distributed among a group of interviewers, typically, those most qualified in a particular area. At the conclusion of the panel interview, the panel caucuses with the purpose of coming to a group consensus regarding the result.

 NOTE   Panels can be structured or unstructured. In the public sector, consistency is often a key factor in selection decisions, so structured interviews are conducted by panels.

Panel members will sometimes ask the same question of each candidate, and sometimes the panel members will alternate their selection of questions to be asked. Panel size also varies from two to something more. It is common to see panels composed of three to four individuals. Because this is an expensive approach to interviewing (it requires multiple people to spend their time), it is usually reserved for professional and managerial job selections.

Documentation of Selection Decisions

Once you've gone through testing and interviewing, you have a decision to make. All employment decisions should be documented, none more so than those that involve hiring and termination. All notes made about the reasons for selecting one candidate over another are subject to the retention requirements for holding documentation up to two years beyond the decision.

Documentation about interviews and hiring decisions should

- Be factual
- Contain job-related information only
- Not contain opinions or personal biases

Marginal notes on résumés should not contain comments about age, disability, race, or other protected category. As surprising as it seems, there are still interviewing supervisors who write things such as "This one is too fat!" or "She's way too old for the job," or "Customers will never accept an Asian." It is okay for marginal comments to contain notes about how résumé content relates to job requirements.

The Selection Approval Process

Each organization has its own structure of approving authorities. That is usually controlled by the accounting department. Those structures tell what management level is authorized to approve expenditures of given amounts, approve the hiring of people at given job levels, and so forth. Policies are established based on those structures. Authority to hire is closely related to authority to spend money. Sometimes there are multiple steps in the authorization process. First, the budget must contain authorization for the full-time equivalent (FTE) position. Then, there must be authorization to fill the position. Finally, there must be authorization to hire a specific individual to fill that job. Small organizations have fewer steps, and larger organizations can have more steps in the process. Before making a job offer, be sure you have the approval of your "hiring authority" to do so.

Employment Policies, Practices, and Procedures

Employment policies, practices, and procedures all impact selection efforts. An employer with a policy requiring all hiring decisions to be approved by executives at a certain authority level in the organization wants definite budget control over the hiring process. A staffing practice that says a job opening may not be advertised outside the organization until internal postings have lasted for at least three days gives existing employees "first chance" at any new opportunities. A procedure requiring at least two in-person interviews will have an impact on budget because it involves two or more interviewers and it may cost money to bring a candidate in from out of town. All of these organizational preferences have consequences. Those consequences can be financial, production impacts, government compliance issues, or morale-related. It is up to the HR professionals to analyze them all and make senior management aware of those consequences so they may consider them before approving any changes.

The Impact of Total Rewards on Recruitment and Retention

When someone agrees to work for an employer, they are also agreeing to a total rewards package. Total rewards encompass an employee's annual salary or hourly pay rate, performance-based pay such as commissions or bonuses, health benefits, financial benefits such as a 401(k) plan, vacation benefits, holiday pay, and much more. The items noted in the last sentence are, among other things, tools for recruiting and retaining quality employees. An employer can't hope to recruit top talent unless it is willing to pay a wage or salary that is competitive in the marketplace. Benefits take on a similar role and help with recruiting and retention.

Recall that there are no legal requirements that demand employers provide paid vacation time to employees. Vacation is an invention that comes either through union agreements/contracts or from the need to be competitive in the employment market. Imagine a company trying to hire people today if it did not offer some competitive number of paid vacation days. Not many people would like to work at that place if vacation weren't part of the employment package. So, by policy, employers offer paid time off to their workers. Other benefit programs that add to the employment enticement package include retirement programs, savings plans, medical benefits, employee cafeterias, employee spas, rest and recovery centers, and pizza Fridays.

All of the benefits can be quantified, and their contribution to employment and retention efforts can be computed. There is no doubt that total rewards are a major factor in every employer's efforts to attract and retain talent on its payroll. HR professionals should be prepared to include this information in employment offer conversations. We discuss this topic in more detail in Chapter 7.

Negotiation Skills and Techniques

When you are ready to make an offer, first identify the outcomes you want to achieve from the process. It might be as simple as "hiring the best candidate for an amount of money that doesn't break the budget." Before a written offer is made, then, the amount of compensation should be discussed and agreed on by both you and the candidate. Oftentimes, this is done during a phone call or face-to-face meeting with a candidate before a written offer is developed. You explain what amount is offered, and the candidate accepts or explains that more is wanted. If you have more to give without violating some equal pay circumstance, then make the enhanced offer. Other points of negotiation can include hours of work, frequency of shift changes, work location assignment(s), travel requirements, bonus provisions, criteria for performance, and stock awards.

NOTE   The best negotiators are those who make it seem like a common conversation rather than a championship boxing match.

Employment Offers

Once the candidate has accepted all the job conditions that you have explained, it is time to put the offer in writing. The offer letter will detail the compensation, start date, job title, organization, and immediate supervisor. As we discussed earlier in this chapter, it is wise to also include specifics on the compensation for the position such as whether the employee will be paid on a salary or hourly basis and whether the job is or is not eligible for overtime pay. Components of the total rewards package such as health benefits, bonus potential, and vacation time are also typically included in an offer letter. You should have a signature block at the bottom of the letter for the candidate to sign as acceptance of the terms. One copy should be returned to you with the signature.

NOTE   It is wise to attach a copy of the job description to the offer letter.

Employment Reference Checks, Background Checks, and Credit Reports

Job offers are often conditioned upon successful completion of background checks, reference checks, and sometimes even credit checks. In some instances, a job offer could be conditioned on passing a medical evaluation or a drug screen.

Before conducting background checks or credit checks, review the current legal limitations on their use. The EEOC has issued guidelines on consideration of conviction records due to potential disparate impact on certain racial groups. While you will not be tested on state laws in the PHR exam, some states have also created laws to remove questions about criminal history on job applications. Removing such questions ensures that candidates are not denied a job offer based on criminal history.

Often what organizations do is make a job offer "contingent," or dependent, on a candidate successfully passing a background check. If criminal infractions are found, rescinding or revoking an offer of employment must be based on criminal history that is directly tied to the job and presents a potential risk to the employer. For example, a finance employee with a felony for theft is a good example of a risk to the employer. It is best to consult with an employment attorney before you take any employment action as a result of a background or credit check.

New Employee Orientation

It is a common belief that the first 90 days of a worker's experience on a new job will determine how the relationship goes for the balance of her/his employment. One way to get off on the right foot is to provide a quality orientation program (also referred to as *onboarding*) to every new employee.

A strong orientation program will include such things as these:

- **Welcome by the CEO/senior executive**   Providing evidence that senior management cares about employees can begin during orientation. Senior executives who believe it isn't worth their time convey a strong message also.

- **Discussion about culture**   This is an opportunity to discuss "the way we do things around here." What does the employer value? What gets rewarded in the organization? What type of image does the employer want to project to the world? What are expectations of ethics?

- **Enrollment in benefit programs**   This is an opportunity to complete payroll tax forms, benefit enrollment forms, and self-identification forms for race, sex, disability, and veteran status.

- **Tour of employee common areas**   This can include the cafeteria or break room, the location for labor law compliance posters, and restrooms.

- **Safety equipment and emergency exits**   This is often overlooked when it should be on the orientation agenda. If there are emergency breathing apparatus, eye wash stations, emergency shutdown switches, first aid stations, or other important safety points of interest, this is the time to show each new worker where they are. Safety training in how to use emergency equipment will come later.

- **Introduction to co-workers and supervisors**   Guide the employees to their new work locations and introduce them to their new co-workers and supervisors, even if they may have met some of them during the interviewing process. Have someone designated to explain where to get office supplies, how to access computer terminals, and whom to ask when questions come up. These things are just common employment courtesy.

Human Resources Analysis and Metrics

There are many reasons why an organization may need to assess or analyze its workforce. Some examples include tracking employee skills, training and certifications to help with internal promotion decisions, tracking demographic data needed for EEO reporting, or determining metrics like the average time it takes to recruit for a position. As such, it is helpful to track employee information in a database. There are many options available to HR folks that are full-service options to assist with employee recordkeeping, payroll, and finance needs.

As part of the employee skill database, fields of data are often gathered through assessment of individual employees. At the same time, a different database of records can be maintained containing organizational assessment information. There are different reasons for performing an assessment of an organization and its employees. First, the organization may need to be assessed for effectiveness. Second, employees may need assessment as a way of determining developmental needs as well as current strengths.

PART II

Organizational Assessment

If you believe that you need more information about the health of your organization, these assessment tools can be of help.

- **360-degree evaluations**   Designed to assist individual managers and management teams in knowing where developmental effort should be focused
- **Workforce involvement**   Identification of the degree of engagement felt by the people on your payroll

Individual Assessment

Once you are sure about the health of your organization, it may be helpful to add more information about individual employees. These techniques can do that.

- **Job assessment**   Identifies the best fit for individual interests and skill sets
- **Talent profile**   Identifies specific current skills
- **Readiness for promotion**   Likelihood of success if promoted now

Many of these assessments are done by professional psychologists or through the use of tests developed by psychologists. Any HR professional considering such programs would be best served by consulting with someone qualified in the field to determine the best approach for the current need.

Workforce Analysis Techniques

Often, managers will have a need to assess their workforce and what things are influencing it. Questions arise such as "Why is turnover so high?" and "Why are new hires only lasting for six months before leaving?" Some of the following analysis techniques can help determine the answers:

- **Supply analysis techniques**   These include a strategic evaluation of supply chain options such as sourcing alternatives, plant locations, and warehouse locations.
- **Trend and ratio analysis**   Ratio analysis compares current results or historic results but always at a point in time. Trend analysis compares historical results with current results and identifies what may happen in the future based on the trend of data in the past.
- **Turnover analysis**   There are many possible reasons for employees leaving the payroll, including resignation, dismissal, death, long-term disability, and transfer to another subordinate company within the same parent company. Identifying the reasons that employees are leaving provides the data needed to analyze trends and identify potential problems within the organization. If supervisors are causing high resignation rates, it may be appropriate to train the supervisors or take some other action to reduce the rate at which their subordinates are leaving.

- **Flow analysis**   This can involve analysis of data, analysis of production line movement, or analysis of order processing, among other possibilities. How processes operate and how flows of products, data, or other items go through those processes is the objective of this type of monitoring.

- **Demand analysis techniques**   It is interesting to look forward to determine what customers, clients, or patrons will want in the future.

- **Judgmental forecasts**   These are projections based on subjective inputs. This method is often used when there is a very short time for drawing a conclusion or data is outdated or unavailable.

- **Managerial estimates**   An individual or a group of management people use their experience and knowledge to identify the most likely future characteristics without any additional data analysis.

- **Delphi technique**   This is a method of determining the future outcome and then manipulating a group to reach that conclusion or goal statement. A group of people is forced into polarized positions; then the facilitator suggests a resolution and guides people to support that idea. Ultimately, the group will endorse the facilitator's suggestion because the group has accepted the facilitator as one of its own. It is unethical and used more frequently than might be suspected.

- **Nominal group technique**   A variation on the brainstorming process for group creativity, the nominal group technique alters that process a bit. As a forecasting process, the facilitator can ask a question such as, "What will be our best-selling product next year?" The large group is then divided into small groups of five or six members. Then each person spends several minutes silently brainstorming on their own, seeking all the possible ideas they can come up with. Next, each group collects its members' ideas by sharing them around the table, and each is written on a flipchart. No criticism is allowed, but clarification in response to questions is encouraged. Each person then evaluates the ideas individually and anonymously votes for the best ones using some form of grading system (for example, a score of 5 for the best idea, 4 for the next best, and so on). The group then collects and tabulates the points awarded to each idea and the one with the highest score is the winner.

- **Statistical forecasts**   These approaches to analysis use mathematical formulas to identify patterns and trends. Once identified, the trends are analyzed again for mathematical reasonableness.

- **Regression analysis**   Linear regression is a tool often used in forecasting and financial analysis. It compares relationships among several variables. A variable is something for which the value changes over time. In hiring, one variable is the number of job openings to be filled. Another variable is the number of job applicants received for each job opening. How these things can be related and used in predicting the number of people who will meet the job requirements can be determined through linear regression analysis.

Multiple regression analysis allows us to ask the question, "What is the best predictor of…?" If we want new employees to remain on the job successfully for at least one year after hiring them, we can use multiple regression analysis to determine how factors such as educational degree, educational institution, general experience, specific job experience, multiple language skills, or community involvement can contribute to that longevity requirement.

- **Simulations**   We can simulate a process or condition to predict an outcome. For example, you can build a simulation of a management problem to measure how nonmanagement people handle the problem. That allows us in turn to predict whether each participant would be successful if promoted to a management position. This is commonly done in industrial assessment centers.

- **Gap analysis techniques**   Measuring the distance (or difference) between where you are and where you want to be is known as *gap analysis*. If you have to train all employees in certain safety procedures, you can use gap analysis to determine what portion of the population has yet to receive the training, or any portion of the training.

- **Solution analysis techniques**   Another approach is to define the problem, identify a variety of solutions, and then assess each solution through use of statistical comparisons. It involves asking the question, "What is the likelihood of success for this solution?" It can employ the mathematical process of regression analysis to assess the variables influencing each solution's implementation. For example, it might be possible to solve the problem of turnover by creating a management skills training program. It also might be possible to solve the turnover problem by providing different employee benefits more appealing to the workers. It could also be that offering continuing education to employees would have an impact on turnover. Each of those solutions could work. You can determine how well each works by using regression analysis to calculate the contribution each could make to the problem of turnover control. This analysis considers that there is some value to be contributed by each different solution. If you can't choose all of them, where will you get the greatest impact for your investment of time and money?

Measurements and Metrics of Staffing

Overall there are many measurements that can be applied to human resource management. In fact, many books have been written about the subject. One of particular value is *How to Measure Human Resources Management* by Jac Fitz-enz and Barbara Davison.[16] Measuring staffing is valuable because it can tell you the cost of each step in the process as well as the overall cost of a new hire, and knowing costs associated with recruiting can help with budgeting for future staffing requirements.

Some Ways to Measure Hiring

Other valuable recruitment measurements that can be undertaken include the following:

- **Response time to obtain a new hire**   How long it takes from the authorization to hire until someone is actually on the payroll. This can be monitored separately for various candidate sources (newspapers, social media, employer website, or other source).

- **Recruiting efficiency**   The amount of time it takes to collect a viable number of qualified candidates, process candidates through interviews, and get people on the payroll. Each can be measured individually, and the total can be measured.

- **Quality of hire**   Includes the job performance rating of new hires, the percentage of new hires promoted within a year, the percentage of new hires retained after a year, and any number of other possibilities.

- **Employee retention**   Grasps the percentage of new hires that are retained for a year (or any other designated period of time). Retention can be computed in budget terms because the cost per hire can be computed and allow identification of retention costs.

- **Turnover cost**   The opposite of retention; measures the rate of employee loss. It can include unemployment insurance expense, workers' compensation expense, the cost of training a replacement, the cost of recruiting and hiring a new employee, and other factors.

There are a host of possible measurements associated with compensation programs as well (payroll taxes, revenue per employee, employee cost including benefits, net income per employee, average pay per grade, percentage of employees paid over grade maximum, and so forth). There are also measurements for employee training, production tooling, engineering expense, percentage of project cost associated with permits, inspections, and reworking. Almost anything you can observe in a workplace can be measured. Chapter 9 offers an expansion on this topic.

American National Standards Institute Standards for Hiring Metrics

The Society for Human Resource Management (SHRM) has partnered with American National Standards Institute (ANSI) to develop and publish many types of measurements for HR management. One set of those standards relating to hiring has been published. It offers methods for measuring cost per hire and a recruiting cost ratio.[17]

Cost per Hire   This measurement uses external costs and internal costs to determine overall cost per person hired during any given time period. This formula looks at the number of hires and the costs to obtain them. It enables you to derive expenses for each new hire stated as an average.

$$\text{Cost Per Hire} = \frac{(S(\text{External Costs}) + S(\text{Internal Costs}))}{(\text{Total Number of Hires in a Time Period})}$$

External costs are those expenses such as external agency fees, advertising costs, job fair costs, travel costs, and other similar expenses for the time period being analyzed.

Internal costs are expenses that can include fully loaded salary and benefits of the recruiting team and fixed costs such as physical infrastructure.

$$\text{Cost Per Hire} = \frac{(\text{External Costs} = \$100{,}000 + \text{Internal Costs} = \$100{,}000)}{(\text{Total Number of Hires in a Time Period} = 50)}$$

$$\text{Cost Per Hire} = \$4{,}000$$

Recruiting Cost Ratio   This measurement looks at the cost per hire based on compensation rather than head count.

$$\text{Recruiting Cost Ratio} = \frac{(\text{S(External Costs)} + \text{S(Internal Costs)} \times 100)}{(\text{Total First-Year Compensation of Hires in a Time Period})}$$

The RCR tells us how much we spent recruiting for every dollar of first-year compensation paid to the new hires.

$$\text{Recruiting Cost Ratio} = \frac{((\text{External Costs} = \$100{,}000 + \text{Internal Costs} = \$100{,}000) \times 100)}{(\text{Total First-Year Compensation of Hires in a Time Period} = \$2{,}000{,}000)}$$

$$\text{RCR} = 10\%$$

Obviously, the lower the percentage, the better (more efficient).

Recruitment Yield Ratio   Another measure of recruiting efficiency and effectiveness is the recruitment yield ratio. It can be calculated at each step of the recruiting and hiring process to determine how successful you are at each stage of the process.

- How many people were minimally qualified compared to total responses?
- How many people were sent to the hiring manager compared to minimally qualified?
- How many people were interviewed compared to those sent to the hiring manager?
- How many people were hired compared to those interviewed?

At each stage, you can compute a ratio or percentage. The greater the percentage, the better.

$$\text{RYR} = \frac{\text{Number of Hires}}{\text{Number of Interviews}}$$

$$\text{RYR} = 3 \,/\, 15 = 20\%$$

Achieving a higher ratio (percentage) means your yield is greater for whatever comparative group you are using.

Here is an example:

> We have hired 25 new computer programmers. It took an average of four interviews for each new hire. So, our recruitment yield ratio (RYR) is 25 / 4 = 6.25. If we only required an average of three interviews per new hire, the RYR would be 25 / 3 = 8.33. The higher our RYR, the better. It allows us to recognize that many interviews in the hiring process add to the cost of hiring. Lowering the average number of interviews per new hire will raise our ratio.

Chapter Review

As we have reviewed in this chapter, talent planning and acquisition covers a wide range of human resource functions that are critical to understand both on the PHR exam and in your professional career. There is a reason why talent planning and acquisition is one of the first functional areas in HRCI's Body of Knowledge. An organization cannot operate without employees. Hiring the right employees and complying with all federal laws during the employment process is the foundation of the human resource function. To best prepare for the exam, familiarize yourself with federal laws and key organizational policies that set the basis for the employment function. Ethics and common sense play an important role, too. While most decisions in the talent planning and acquisition function are guided by law, many require critical thinking and evaluation of the most ethical resolution for the organization and its employees.

Questions

1. Stewart was working late when his boss approached him and asked if he would like to go get a drink. His boss then put his hand on Stewart's backside and gave it a little squeeze. What is going on here?

   A. Nothing. It is simply his boss showing a little affection for Stewart. No problem.

   B. Whether or not it is a problem depends on Stewart's reaction. If it is unwelcome, there might be a problem.

   C. If Stewart agrees, they can have a drink without anyone being the wiser.

   D. It is a problem only if one of Stewart's co-workers saw what happened.

2. A _____ selection system uses numerical performance levels and allows for specific numerical cutoffs as qualification thresholds.

3. Alonzo is the HR manager for Top Notch Trucking. One of the biggest issues facing Top Notch Trucking is high turnover in the first 90 days of employment. Employees frequently comment during exit interviews that they do not feel connected to the organization and communication is poor. Given exit interview results, what is the best course of action to help reduce high turnover in the first 90 days?

    A. Ask supervisors to communicate more frequently with new employees.

    B. Create a task force to schedule more employee events.

    C. Add a question to the job application about applicant communication styles.

    D. Create a new employee onboarding program to introduce employees to the organization and include regular check-ins between supervisors and new hires during the first 90 days of employment.

4. Lebron serves his employer as the HR director. It is a startup company, and his bosses want him to hire people fast so they have given him some tests to use in the screening process. He was told to hire the applicants with the best scores. Are these tests something Lebron should use?

    A. It is okay to use tests if they are job-specific in their measurement.

    B. No way. He should not use any tests that he hasn't bought from a legitimate test publisher.

    C. Tests are just fine. He should be sure the passing scores are set so they can get the best people.

    D. If the boss says to use the tests, he has little choice. He just has to be sure to score them properly.

5. The two types of sexual harassment are _____ and _____.

6. Pat has just discovered that her organization has signed a contract with the federal government to provide computer products and installation services. The contract value is $600,000. The organization just hired its 61st employee. Does Pat's organization now need to prepare an affirmative action plan?

    A. No. When they get to 100 employees, they will need to develop an AAP.

    B. Because the contract value is less than $1,000,000, they are exempt from the AAP requirement.

    C. Yes. An AAP is needed for minorities, women, disabled people, and veterans.

    D. Yes. Only an AAP for minorities and women is necessary.

7. Elton heads a company that contracts to build office buildings for the federal government. He isn't sure if he has any affirmative action obligations because of his work. What would you tell him if you were his HR advisor?

    A. Don't worry. Construction firms are not classified as providers of goods and services. There is no affirmative action plan obligation for Elton's company.

    B. Elton may have to prepare a 16-point affirmative action plan that is required of all federal construction contractors if the contract value exceeds $10,000.

    C. Elton has to meet the same requirements as all other federal contractors that sell anything to the government.

    D. Elton should revisit the question once his contracts exceed $1,000,000.

8. Julia has been asked to identify her race and sex for her employer. She is uncomfortable doing that, thinking that she might be the target of some discrimination if she tells them. If you were Julia's HR manager, what would you tell her?

   A. It's okay. We can put down whatever we want to identify your race and sex.

   B. Don't be concerned, Julia. Discrimination is something we don't tolerate, and it is also illegal. We are required by the government to keep the race and sex data.

   C. If you don't tell us what you want recorded, we will just have to leave your information blank in the database.

   D. Julia should be sent to the HR department so they can tell her she has no choice. She must identify her race and sex for the company records.

9. Marina is new to the compensation department and has to make her first job offer to a new employee. Which is the best tactic to use?

   A. Conduct the entire process in writing over e-mail for documentation purposes.

   B. Call the candidate to offer the job verbally first, share the total rewards package, negotiate compensation, and provide a written offer for the candidate's signature.

   C. Call all the candidates who are not going to be offered a job first to get that out of the way and then send a written offer to the candidate being offered the job.

   D. Call the candidate to offer the job verbally, share the total rewards package, and let management know via e-mail that the candidate accepted the job.

10. Which of the following are types of exemption from the Fair Labor Standards Act? (Choose three.)

    A. Executive exemption

    B. Technical exemption

    C. Administrative exemption

    D. Professional exemption

    E. Sales executive exemption

11. Solomon is from an island off the coast of India and has always been told he is classified as Asian. Now Andrew, his HR manager, is telling him something else. How should Solomon be classified?

    A. Always default to White when there is a question.

    B. Solomon should identify himself as being Two or More Races.

    C. Because he comes from an island off the coast of India, he really should be classified as a Pacific Islander.

    D. People who originate in the Indian subcontinent should be classified as Asian.

PART II

12. Affirmative action plans have a great deal to do with altering the demographics of an employer's organization. They do this by:

    A. Creating "set-asides" for job openings that are underrepresented in certain race categories

    B. Providing preferential selection for the underrepresented race category

    C. Creating placement rate goals and letting a nondiscriminatory selection process select the best qualified people

    D. Moving applicants with a certain race up to the top of the selection list

13. Gerardo manages the HR function along with the accounting department. He is involved in an OFCCP audit of his affirmative action plans. The agency wants him to sign a conciliation agreement saying he will hire a certain number of women into one job title and give back pay to a group of Hispanics who weren't hired. What would you advise Gerardo to do with the conciliation agreement?

    A. Review it with his legal counsel and senior executives. Determine whether the OFCCP claims are accurate and negotiate something else as a consequence if they are not.

    B. Go ahead and sign the conciliation agreement. It's just a promise and doesn't really matter.

    C. Whenever there is a document like this coming from the federal government, there should be a set of instructions that comes along with it telling the contractor what to do. Gerardo should look for that list.

    D. Gerardo should read it and make sure there isn't anything that talks about illegal discrimination. He should scratch out any references to discrimination and send it back to the OFCCP with his signature.

14. Guillermo supervises a group of six women in the accounting department. They are responsible for all payments and receipts. On Friday, Eleanor invites Guillermo to her apartment for a home-cooked dinner. He accepts. Under the various U.S. Supreme Court opinions on the subject, is this classified as sexual harassment?

    A. Very likely. Anytime a supervisor has a relationship with a subordinate, it is classified as sexual harassment.

    B. Probably not. The subordinate initiated the relationship, if indeed there actually is one. It is hard for a subordinate to harass a supervisor because in the end the supervisor is the one with the organizational power.

    C. It all depends on what happens after dinner. Guillermo is the one with the supervisory power. If he initiates anything, he can be in trouble.

    D. If they are having an affair, there is likely sexual harassment involved.

15. Which two fields in applicant tracking systems should *not* be shared with hiring managers?

    A. Applicant's age

    B. Applicant's self-identification of race and sex

    C. Applicant's desired compensation

    D. Applicant's self-identification of disabled and veteran status

16. Every month, Ali has to provide a report to the executives that details what employee complaints have been received. This month's report shows complaints of harassment from two people. One was based on race, and the other was based on religion. The executives are challenging those classifications, saying harassment can be based only on sexual conditions. What would you tell the executives if you were Ali?

    A. It shouldn't have been classified as harassment, rather just plain discrimination. There really can't be any harassment other than sexual harassment.

    B. We should really get our attorney to set the classifications for us. We're not sure if there can be harassment based on anything other than sex.

    C. Of course, there can be harassment based on race, religion, age, national origin, or a number of other categories.

    D. Executives should be encouraged to avoid getting into such details. It isn't really important. In the end, we just have two complaints of discrimination.

17. Times are still hard for the AB Trucking Company. They are going to have to close one of their work locations. That will take 146 full-time people off the payroll who will have to look for other work with other employers. What should the company consider in their layoff planning?

    A. WARN kicks in, and they must notify the local government as well as employees who will be affected at least 60 days before the layoff date.

    B. WARN kicks in, but they don't have to notify anybody until a week before the layoff date.

    C. Because they are in the transportation industry, the WARN Act doesn't apply. They have *carte blanche* in how they handle the layoff.

    D. WARN kicks in, and they have to notify employees 60 days in advance, but notifying the local government is a voluntary decision.

18. Lawana has just been given the job of preparing an EEO-1 for her employer group. She finds some gaps in the employee race and gender data she will need to use in reporting. How should she handle that problem?

    A. Ignore the missing data and just report what data she has. She should not guess about any of the race or gender identifications.

    B. Talk with each employee and ask if the person has been invited to self-identify. If the employee chooses not to self-identify, speak with the supervisor and get a determination based on observation.

C. Take the best guess possible and fill in the blanks.

D. Where data is missing, it is usually a good idea to default to White as a race and male as a gender. Statistically, those are the most common entries.

19. Match the type of staffing to the appropriate description.

A. Retiree annuitant

B. Contract labor

C. Project hires

D. Phased retirement

(1) Temporary employee hired for a specific period of time.

(2) Temporary employee hired to complete a specific project.

(3) Retired employee called back to work for a previous employer.

(4) Employee who works a reduced schedule leading up to retirement.

20. Denny's Drywall hired 10 employees in August. Advertising the job openings cost $1,000, and the recruiting specialist, Debbie, spent 100 percent of her work time in August hiring these employees. Debbie's monthly salary is $5,000. Denny's Drywall also had to house the new employees in a satellite office location for the month that cost $4,000. What is the cost per hire?

Answers

1. **B.** If the behavior of his boss is unwelcome, this could be an incident of *quid pro quo* sexual harassment. We need more information to know for sure. If Stewart's co-workers saw what happened, they might also object should Stewart go along with the boss's sexual advance. Co-workers could be negatively affected because of favoritism or perceived favoritism toward Stewart on the part of his boss, and there could be other problems as well.

2. **Quantitative.** A good example of this type of selection system is a written test that requires a certain threshold as a passing score.

3. **D.** Onboarding programs are the best way to communicate company expectations at the outset of employment. It can be a stressful time for a new employee, and a structured program that is managed by human resources helps ensure that supervisors are meeting expectations required of them as well.

4. **A.** Remember that it is the user of a test who holds the liability, not the publisher of the test. If a test has been validated to properly predict success in specific jobs with specific knowledge and skill requirements, it can be used for those jobs. Using it for *all* jobs is not a good idea. If the boss insists, he needs to be told what the consequences can be.

5. **Hostile work environment** and *quid pro quo*. A hostile work environment by definition is pervasive, severe conduct that discriminates against a protected classification. *Quid pro quo* means "this for that" in Latin. Often, it involves a manager or other authority figure offering or merely hinting that he or she will give the employee something (a raise or a promotion) in return for that employee's satisfaction of a sexual demand.

6. **C.** The contract exceeds $50,000, and there are more than 50 employees, so an AAP is required for minorities and women. A plan for disabled people and another for veterans are required as well because the contract is over $10,000 for disabled AAP requirements and $100,000 for veteran AAP requirements.

7. **B.** If his contract exceeds $10,000, Elton will need an affirmative action plan that satisfies regulatory requirements for construction contractors. The 16-point plan they must develop is not the same as the plans required of goods and services contractors.

8. **B.** Identifying race and sex is voluntary. The employer is required to keep records of every employee's race and sex identification, however. When someone doesn't volunteer the information, the employer must make a determination by observation and keep a record of the race and sex of the individual.

9. **B.** Job offers are best done verbally at first, allowing both the candidate and employer to negotiate the terms of the job. Then, offers should be documented in writing once both parties have agreed. While it may seem like the nice thing to do to call candidates who are not being selected first, there is no guarantee your top choice for the position will agree to take the position.

10. **A, C, D.** Although technical exemption can easily be confused with computer employee exemption and sales executive exemption might sound similar to outside sales exemption, these are not correct.

11. **D.** According to the EEO-1 instructions, the category of Asian includes all people from the Indian subcontinent. The fact that he lived on an island off the coast is irrelevant.

12. **C.** Preferences and set-asides are illegal under case law. Outreach and recruiting so a candidate pool reflects a mix of race and sex can allow a nondiscriminatory selection system to pick the best qualified person. In some cases, that will be a woman or racial minority.

13. **A.** A conciliation agreement is a legal contract. When it comes from OFCCP, it means they will come back every six months or so to be sure you are doing what it promises you will do. If not, they can take you through the enforcement process to force you to comply. Always get your management attorney involved before signing such a contract.

14. **B.** It's probably not *quid pro quo* harassment because the invitation came from a subordinate. It's likely not hostile environment harassment because the person being harassed has to suffer unwanted advances of a sexual nature. She is actually the one initiating the invitation.

15. **B, D.** Although age is a protected classification and compensation provided to employees must be in alignment with laws like the Equal Pay Act, hiring managers may need to know this information. For example, some jobs require an employee to be at least 21 years of age (e.g., a bartender), and knowing what an applicant's desired wage is helps with the budgeting and negotiation process. At the time of this book, some states prohibit collecting or using salary history information from applicants, but there is no federal law that prohibits asking about desired compensation.

16. **C.** Harassment has been recognized by the courts when it is based on sex but also when it is based on race, ethnicity, religion, and other protected categories. Executives need to understand that these are all liabilities for the organization.

17. **A.** WARN applies because the layoff will involve more than 100 full-time people at a single location. It requires 60 days advance notification to both the employees and the local government officials.

18. **B.** Employees should always be invited to self-identify. If they refuse and since employers are obligated to maintain the data, the next best way to get it is to ask the supervisor to make a personal observation and record it in the data fields.

19. **A3; B1; C2; D4.** A retiree annuitant is a retired employee called back to work for a previous employer. Contract labor is a temporary employee hired for a specific period of time. A project hire is a temporary employee hired to complete a specific project. Lastly, phased retirement is when an employee works a reduced schedule leading up to retirement.

20. **Cost per hire = $1,000. Cost per hire = ((External costs of $1,000) + (Internal costs of $5,000 and $4,000)) / 10 total hires.**

Endnotes

1. EEOC.gov (June 14, 2018) https://www.eeoc.gov/employers/remedies.cfm

2. EEOC.gov (June 14, 2018) https://www.eeoc.gov/eeoc/statistics/enforcement/charges.cfm

3. EEOC.gov https://www.eeoc.gov/eeoc/newsroom/release/11-9-17.cfm

4. 41 CFR 60-3.5B

5. Truesdell, William H. SPHR, *Secrets of Affirmative Action Compliance,* The Management Advantage, Inc., Walnut Creek, CA 2014.

6. U.S. Government Accountability Office: https://www.gao.gov/products/GAO-16-750 (June 22, 2018)

7. OFCCP: https://www.dol.gov/ofccp/regs/compliance/section503.htm

8. OFCCP: https://www.dol.gov/ofccp/regs/compliance/vevraa.htm

9. U.S. Department of Labor, Wage and Hour Division (June 17, 2018) https://www.dol.gov/whd/overtime/fs17a_overview.pdf

10. U.S. Department of Labor, Wage and Hour Division (June 17, 2018) https://www.dol.gov/whd/regs/compliance/whdfs13.htm

11. Christensen, C.M., Alton, R., Rising, C., & Waldeck, A. (2011, March). The Big Idea: The New M&A Playbook. *Harvard Business Review.*

12. U.S. Department of Labor, WARN Act Employer Guide (June 15, 2018) www.doleta.gov/layoff/pdf/EmployerWARN09_2003.pdf

13. Internal Revenue Service (June 19, 2018) https://www.irs.gov/government-entities/federal-state-local-governments/rehired-annuitants

14. "The Uniform Electronic Transaction Act," retrieved from the Uniform Law Commission on 6/18/18 from www.uniformlaws.org/ActSummary .aspx?title=Electronic%20Transactions%20Act.

15. Powers, Bob, and William J. Rothwell, *Instructor Excellence: Mastering the Delivery of Training*, 2nd edition, Pfeiffer (John Wiley and Sons), San Francisco, CA 2007.

16. Fitz-enz, Jac, and Barbara Davison, *How to Measure Human Resources Management*, 3rd edition, McGraw-Hill Education, 2002.

17. Cost per hire standard developed by SHRM, referenced on June 22, 2018, https://www.shrm.org/ResourcesAndTools/business-solutions/Documents/shrm_ansi_cph_standard.pdf.

Learning and Development

Learning and development focus on the talent, knowledge, and performance of the workforce in an organization in an effort to meet the current and future needs of the organization. Developing, implementing, and evaluating activities and programs that address employee training and development, performance appraisal, and performance management is at the core of HR responsibility. The PHR exam carries a 10 percent weight on the exam.

Responsibilities

- Provide consultation to managers and employees on professional growth and development opportunities
- Implement and evaluate career development and training programs (for example, career pathing, management training, mentorship)
- Contribute to succession planning discussions with management by providing relevant data

Knowledge Of

- Applicable federal laws and regulations related to learning and development activities
- Learning and development theories and applications
- Training program facilitation, techniques, and delivery
- Adult learning processes
- Instructional design principles and processes (for example, needs analysis, process flow mapping)
- Techniques to assess training program effectiveness including the use of applicable metrics
- Organizational development (OD) methods, motivational methods, and problem-solving techniques
- Task/process analysis
- Coaching and mentoring techniques

- Employee retention concepts and applications
- Techniques to encourage creativity and innovation

Federal Laws That Apply to This Body of Knowledge

Now that you've reviewed the Learning and Development responsibilities and knowledge statements, we recommend you review the federal laws that apply to learning and development (see Figure 6-1). The federal laws fall into these two categories:

- Laws that regulate content and intellectual property
- Laws that protect the rights of employees

It would benefit you to refer to Chapter 2 on these specific laws prior to reading any further in this chapter.

Training and Development

Training and development (T&D) are core value functions of the HR department. The process of training provides skills and abilities, plus knowledge that is focused on a specific outcome. The intent is a short-term focus for the immediate application for on-the-job use by trainees.

On the other hand, with development activities, there is a longer-term focus that prepares intended trainees for future job skill or knowledge needs to increase their effectiveness for the organization.

In all T&D activities, it is imperative that the learning objectives and programs developed be aligned with the strategic goals and objectives of the organization, along with a strong level of support from line management.

A systematic process is used to determine the needs for training, develop the training, and evaluate the outcomes. One of the most widely used standard processes is known as the ADDIE model.

- The Copyright Act (1976)
- The Trademark Act (1946)
- Uniform Guidelines on Employee Selection Procedures (1978)
- Age Discrimination in Employment Act (1967)

- The U.S. Patent Act
- Title VII of the Civil Rights Act (1964)
- The Americans with Disabilities Act (1990)
- Uniformed Services Employment and Reemployment Rights Act (1994)

Figure 6-1   Federal laws that apply to human resource development

ADDIE represents the following:

- **Assessment**   In this first phase, data is received and collected to identify where there may be lack of productivity or gaps in desired performance. Individually or within groups, this assessment will point the way to what specific knowledge, skills, and abilities are lacking and the need to be addressed for training and development objectives.

- **Design**   The initial information from the assessment phase is decided upon for course content, delivery methods, and tactics for delivery. The result is an outline of what the training design will be and the order of presentation.

- **Development**   The pencil meets the paper in this phase, and the actual training materials and coursework are created. Courses and training materials may already be available off the shelf, or a customized or modified creation may occur. For training that is highly specific and customized to the organization, a course may be developed from scratch to fit the specific objectives to reach the desired outcome, such as in a new product launch for a product that has never before existed. An example might be the new Apple Watch.

- **Implementation**   In this phase, the training program is delivered to the trainees. A pilot training program might first occur to work out any kinks and revise certain material if needed. Participant selection and scheduling occur during this phase and the where, when, and whom to deliver occur in this phase, too.

- **Evaluation**   Just as the label indicates, the end results and outcomes of the training require an evaluation—both from the participants trained and from the learning objectives measured. The evaluation phase will typically last some months after the training to measure the changes and performance indicators for sustained results.

Training Needs Assessment and Analysis

As the ADDIE approach suggests, the first phase in training is to conduct a needs assessment and analysis. The needs assessment is a process in which HR identifies the training needs and identifies the specific training designed to help the intended trainees meet the organization's objectives. A thorough needs assessment will dive into the possible training needs on three levels: organizational, task, and individual.

When conducting a needs assessment, processes used in strategic planning are utilized. Processes such as environmental scanning and a SWOT analysis (strengths, weaknesses, opportunities, threats) are helpful. A needs assessment model that follows a problem-solving structure is helpful for HR's role in strategic management. For some organizations, an outside vendor is utilized for the needs assessment phase.

Here are some steps to take when you are going to assess your training needs.[1]

1. Identify a clear business goal that the training supports.

2. Determine the tasks workers need to perform so the company can reach that goal.

PART II

3. Determine the training activities that will help workers learn to perform the tasks.

4. Determine the learning characteristics of the workers that will make the training more effective.

Content Chunking

Content chunking is the technique of breaking up content into shorter, bite-size pieces that are more manageable and easier to remember.[2]

In 1956, Harvard professor George A. Miller said that short-term memory could hold only five to nine chunks of information at a time. Since then, scientists have argued about the exact number of knowledge chunks people can hold, but the concept of breaking training into chunks remains a concept created by Dr. Miller.

Chunking as a technique has been applied quite successfully to online training programs. Actually, any self-paced training program can benefit from the chunking design technique. Teaching materials in small chunks has been demonstrated to offer greater success with participants than a constant flow of information in one large stream.

Process Flow Mapping

Process flow mapping is a visual way to understand how things work. You start at the beginning and then determine what must be done next. Then, you determine what action comes after that and so forth. Eventually, you will have a chartable list of action steps that will result in a fully functional training program (see Figure 6-2).

This same process can be used to chart the action steps for any project, not just training. Consider using it for new employee orientation, benefits program open enrollment,

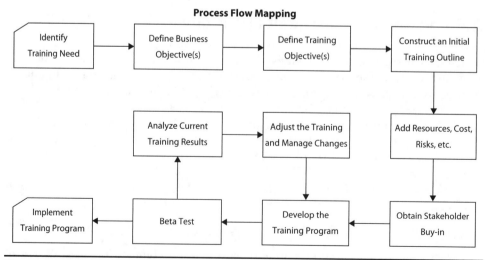

Figure 6-2 Process flow mapping

or an employee complaint investigation. Mapping a process can make clear all of the steps that are necessary parts for project completion.

Establishing Training Objectives

Determine what training objectives are necessary for measuring the outcome of the training. Objectives relate to the results that the participants will be able to do in the training or perform at the end of the program. They focus on design. Objectives provide a guide for training participants on what they are intended to know by the end of the training. The objectives assist in ensuring that there is the intended knowledge/skill transfer. Objectives provide a means to measure what was learned. When designing training objectives, much like the design of an individual's performance goal objectives, employing the use of the SMART outline is helpful. (SMART stands for specific, measurable, action-oriented and achievable, realistic/relevant, and timed.) Composing objectives with the SMART outline and the use of action verbs such as *identify, describe,* and *define* will guide the objective of the learning. An example of an objective might be something like this: "With the knowledge and techniques taught in this three-day training course on operating the new widget processor, the participant will be able to operate the widget processor at a 100 percent production capacity."

When writing training objectives, keep in mind that action is needed. Saying that an objective is for participants in a training program "to understand . . ." is not an action statement. How will you know if they understand? It is better to say something like, "demonstrate," "explain," "answer 80 percent of the test questions correctly," or "teach someone else to successfully...."

Instructional and Delivery Methods

There is no one perfect teaching method for every situation. As a matter of fact, the method that should be used will depend upon the training circumstances and the material being covered. There are teacher-centered instructional methods and learner-centered instructional methods.[3] Instructional methods are the manner in which materials are presented to students.

Adult Learning Processes and Principles

Adult learning principles have a single-track focus, trainability.[4] *Trainability* is concerned with the readiness to learn and its associated motivation. *Andragogy* is the study of how adults learn, and it is based on five assumptions about learning in adults as compared to children. As people mature, they shift to the following:

- **Self-concept**   Their concept of self moves toward self-direction and self-sufficiency.
- **Experience**   They accumulate more experience that can be tucked away and accessed in learning situations.
- **Readiness to learn**   They adjust to a readiness state for learning because of the developmental requirements associated with developmental needs that correlate to the stage of life and the social roles they live (for example, parent, homeowner).

- **Orientation to learning**   They shift from subject-focused to problem-focused learning that has immediate applicability.
- **Motivation to learn**   Motivation for learning comes from an internal source within rather than external.

As training programs are being designed and delivered, these needs of adult learners should be incorporated. Real-world examples and an emphasis on how the training is going to be immediately applied are helpful.

Learning Styles

All adults have a particular learning style that best suits their ability to learn. Understanding these learning styles will assist you in the creation of a learning environment within your organization, allowing you to accommodate each style with the delivery of training.

Additionally, as a presenter or trainer, knowing your own learning style will enhance your ability to adjust your preference of delivery methods so you won't fall into the comfort of just your style and can better shift your delivery to meet the needs of all participants. Also, knowing your own learning style will assist you in your career with problem-solving, managing conflict, negotiations, teamwork, and career planning.

There are three learning styles: auditory, visual, and kinesthetic.

- *Auditory learners* tend to benefit most from a lecture style. Present information by talking so they can listen. Auditory learners succeed when directions are read aloud or information is presented and requested verbally because they interpret the underlying meanings of speech through listening to tone of voice, pitch, speed, and other nuances.
- *Visual learners* rely upon a "seeing" presentation style: "Show me and I'll understand." These learners do best when seeing facial expressions and body language. It helps them understand the content of what is being taught because they think in pictures, diagrams, charts, videos, computer training, and written directions. These students will value to-do lists, flip charts, and written notes. They need and want to take detailed notes to absorb the information.
- *Kinesthetic learners* are also called tactile learners. They learn via a hands-on approach and prefer to explore the physical aspects of learning. Sitting for long periods of time is difficult for these learners, for they need activity to learn. Kinesthetic learners are most successful when totally engaged with the learning activity such as in role playing, practicing, and with topics that can use the sense of feeling and imagining.

Learning Curves   Besides having different learning preference styles, adults also learn at different rates. This is referred to as *learning curves*. A learning curve is a graphical representation of the increase of learning (vertical axis) with experience (horizontal axis). The following are the factors that determine how quickly an adult will learn:

- The person's motivation for learning
- The person's prior knowledge or experience

- The specific knowledge or task that is to be learned
- The person's aptitude and attitude about the knowledge or skill to learn

The following are the four most common learning curves:

- **Increasing returns**   This is the pattern that comes into play when a person is learning something new. The start of the curve is slow while the basics are being learned. The learning increases and takes off as knowledge or skills are acquired. This curve assumes that the individual will continue to learn as time progresses. An example would be when an IT programmer needs to learn a new coding language. Learning will be slow at first until they grasp the new coding protocol, and after mastering the basics, the learning becomes easier and/or quicker as they learn more about the particular language.

- **Decreasing returns**   This pattern is when the amount of learning increases rapidly in the beginning and then the rate of learning slows down. The assumption with this learning curve is that once the learning is achieved, the learning then stops. This occurs with routine tasks learning and is the most common type of learning curve. An example is when a data entry clerk learns how to enter a sales order—the learning is complete.

- **S-shaped**   This learning curve is a blend of the increasing and decreasing returns curves. The assumption with this learning curve is that the person is learning something difficult, such as problem-solving or critical thinking. Learning may be slow at the beginning until the person learning becomes familiar with the learning material, and at that point, learning takes off. The cycle continues with a slow to faster progression as new material is presented. An example of this is when a production lead is trained on new equipment, yet this equipment has not been utilized in the production of the product before. There might be a trial and error for adjustments until the new production equipment is working as expected and is adjusted to the new product. Then when another product is introduced, the equipment and process needs adjusting again until everything works smoothly.

- **Plateau curve**   Just as the name suggests, learning on this curve is quick in the beginning and then flattens or plateaus. The assumption is that the plateau is not permanent and that with additional coaching, training, and support the person learning can ramp up again. With this curve, it can be frustrating for the learner if they are not getting the support and additional training needed to master the task. An example of the plateau curve is a salesperson who has met quotas in the past, and when a new line of equipment is introduced into the product line, the salesperson is provided a minimal level of training/knowledge about it but not enough training to answer all the questions of the prospective customers. The anticipation of additional sales with the new product is not being achieved because the salesperson requires more training in order to pitch the new product and convince the customer to purchase it.

Figure 6-3 illustrates the four most common learning curves.

Figure 6-3
Learning curves

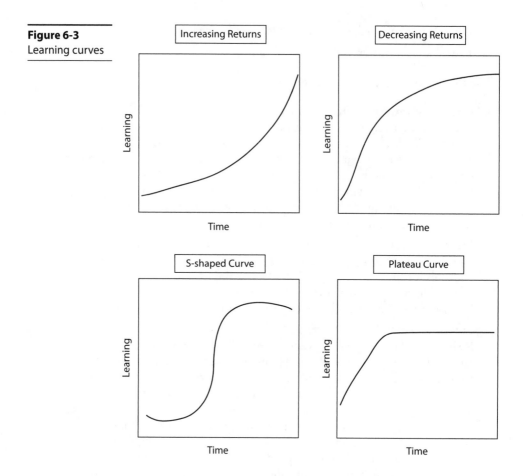

Learning Levels Knowing the styles of learning and learning curves is essential, yet understanding the levels of adult learning is critical to being able to meet adult learning objectives. According to the principles of classification known as Bloom's taxonomy, training objectives are divided into three domains: cognitive, affective, and psychomotor (which is loosely described as "knowing/head," "feeling/heart," and "doing/hands"). Within the domains, there are six levels of cognitive learning.[5]

- **Knowledge** This level of cognitive learning is where the learner recalls specific facts and instruction.

- **Comprehension** This level of learning allows the learner to interpret information.

- **Application** This is the ability to use the learned information in new experiences and situations.

- **Analysis** This cognitive learning is the understanding of information and being able to apply it and see how it connects and fits together with other information.

- **Synthesis**   This level is where the learner is able to respond to new experiences and dissect problems, considering appropriate tactics for solutions.
- **Evaluation**   This is the highest level of cognitive learning wherein the learner will make judgments.

Motivation Concepts

Three underlying principles of human behavior are directly linked to motivation.

- All human behavior is caused. This means people have a reason for doing what they do.
- All behavior is focused on achieving an end result, or goal. People do things to attain something, tangible or intangible. Their behavior is not random, though it could be unconscious.
- Every person has a unique fingerprint and is unique in that no one has the exact experience, heredity, or environmental/relationship influences.

Understanding these principles of human behavior will assist you as an HR professional with motivational pursuits, not just in the learning process, but in all matters related to the work and employment relationship, especially engagement.

There are several other long-standing motivational theories that we will briefly review to refresh your memory about what you most likely learned in your secondary educational endeavors.

Maslow's Hierarchy Needs   In Maslow's theory, there are five basic human needs arranged in a pyramid, necessitating that the first level (bottom of the pyramid) must be met first before moving up the pyramid. Figure 6-4 shows Maslow's hierarchy of needs. Lower-level needs on the pyramid will always have some influence on behavior.[6]

You can fulfill these needs in the workplace through the following:

- **Safety and security**   Employment security such as an employment contract, pay and benefits, working conditions
- **Belonging and love**   Teams, good leadership, participation in groups, employee associations, customer base assignments
- **Esteem**   Training, recognition, awards, special assignments
- **Self-actualization**   Job growth opportunities, project team participation, becoming a mentor

---

   NOTE   It's important to recognize that not all motivational models of Western culture, like Maslow's hierarchy of needs, are going to apply in many of the global and diverse organizations of today.

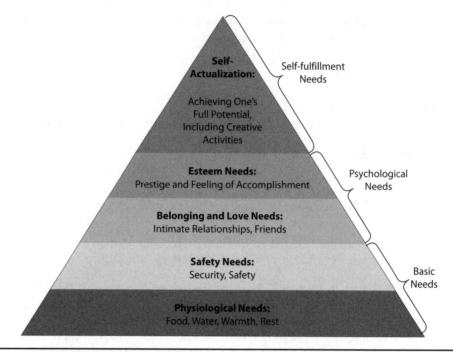

Figure 6-4   Maslow's hierarchy of needs

Herzberg's Motivation-Hygiene Theory   This theory asserts that employees have two different categories of needs and that they are essentially independent of each other, but they affect behavior in differing ways: hygiene factors, which are considered extrinsic, and motivational factors, which are considered intrinsic (see Table 6-1). The latter is associated with recognition, achievement, and personal growth–related events in the job,

Hygiene Factors	Motivation Factors
Company policy and administration	Personal achievement
Supervision	Recognition
Interpersonal relations	Growth possibilities
Compensation (wage/salary)	Career advancement
Status	Level of responsibility
Job security	The job itself (work challenges/satisfaction)
Personal life	
Working conditions	

Table 6-1   Herzberg's Motivation-Hygiene Factors

whereas hygiene factors are associated with job security, pay, working conditions, supervision, and co-worker relations that can quickly lead to job dissatisfaction.

Hygiene factors are motivators for short periods of time, but their impact fades rather quickly. Motivation from the second group of factors lasts longer and often has a greater initial impact as well.

Much of Herzberg's research was done in automobile manufacturing plants. He would observe workers doing their job and then ask them questions about what they liked and didn't like about the work they did. He would explore what kept them motivated to continue doing their job. It has been said that one assembly line worker was tightening a single bolt on a car chassis as they passed his work station. Herzberg saw him using his right hand to twist the bolt each time. When Herzberg asked the worker what he would like to do differently, he said, "I'd like to use my left hand once in a while."

It was Herzberg who suggested employers could use three methods to increase the motivational factors for their employees.

- **Job enlargement**   More of the same type of work. Eliminate the boredom of slack times. Fill up the day so time will pass more quickly.

- **Job rotation**   Give people a chance to learn more than one job. A repair technician might be cross-trained on repair of washing machines as well as dishwashers.

- **Job enrichment**   Providing greater levels of responsibility for the job. Rather than just assemble parts, expand the job so quality control is included in the work.

McGregor's Theory X and Theory Y   McGregor's theory offers two approaches to motivating employees: Theory X, which suggests an authoritative management style because it assumes that employees inherently do not like to work and must be controlled and closely monitored; and Theory Y, which suggests a participative style of management, under the belief that employees dislike controls and inherently want to do their best (see Table 6-2). Arguments have abounded for decades about the value of these theories in modern management. Both suggest that motivation comes from the supervisor, external to the employee. McGregor said that how the supervisor deals with employees will determine how they respond to the motivating techniques. In actuality, each theory is represented by its own scale, rather than as commonly thought, being two ends of the same scale. The scale can explain the amount of the behavior exhibited by the supervisor.

McGregor suggests that these two management approaches to employees will result in quite different organizational behaviors. Each of these approaches has advantages and limitations.[7] As part of the history of industrial psychology, McGregor's theories offer some insights to the early studies conducted in workplaces. Theory X managers are thought to have more concern for tasks than for people. If managers focus on tasks, the people will take care of themselves because they need strong direction. Theory Y managers are thought to have more concern for relationships than for tasks. If you focus on people and relationships, the task accomplishments will take care of themselves because people really do care about their jobs and the work they produce.

Theory X Managers Believe	Theory Y Managers Believe
Employees have little ambition.	Employees are internally motivated.
Employees want to avoid responsibility.	Employees enjoy their jobs.
Employees are self-centered and goal-oriented.	Employees take responsibility for their work.
Employees work solely for sustainable income.	Employees do not need close supervision.
Employees are inherently lazy.	Employees want to create quality.

Table 6-2 McGregor's Theory X and Theory Y

Teacher-Centered Approaches

Elements of a teacher-centered approach include the following:

- **Demonstration**   Showing participants how something is done.
- **Direct instruction**   Conveying concepts and skills.
- **Lecture**   Passive participants, reception of instruction.
- **Lecture-discussions**   Questions added to lecture.

Learner-Centered Approaches

The following are elements of a learner-centered approach:

- **Case studies**   Require application of knowledge to respond to a "real" problem.
- **Cooperative learning**   Small group working on solving a problem or completing a task.
- **Discussion**   Classroom or online interaction among participants and with the teacher.
- **Discovery**   Using prior knowledge and experience to discover new things.
- **Graphic organizers**   Diagrams, maps, and webs as illustrations of material.
- **Journals/blogs**   Recordings of reflections and ideas.
- **K-W-L**   Structured table showing columns with what participants know (K), what they want to know (W), and what they learned in the end (L).
- **Learning centers**   Independent or small group work aimed at completing a task.
- **Role-play**   Solving problems through action or performance.
- **Scaffolding**   Teacher modeling skills and thinking for participants, allowing participants to take over those expressions based on the initial structure provided by the teacher.
- **Problem-based learning (inquiry learning)**   The teacher provides a problem where inquiry must be utilized to reach a solution.

- **Simulations**   Situations designed to be as realistic as possible without the risk of a real-life circumstance.

- **Storytelling**   Use of multimedia technology (for example, PowerPoint) to present interactive opportunities involving any subject.

HR's Role in Organizational Development

First, let's define what organizational development (OD) is. The following is a long-standing definition created by Richard Beckhard in his 1969 book *Organization Development: Strategies and Models*:[8]

> Organization Development is an effort (1) planned, (2) organization-wide, and (3) managed from the top, to (4) increase organization effectiveness and health through (5) planned interventions in the organization's "processes," using behavioral-science knowledge.

The best way to describe HR's role in organizational development is as a masterful change agent because planning and managing change are the cornerstones in OD. Helping the workforce adapt to change, embrace the changes, and see the potential possibilities for the organization's benefit is the responsibility of HR professionals.

Of all the many competencies required for the HR professional, being a masterful change agent is probably the most important because HR professionals not only serve as the catalyst in communicating the change but will also be charged with the evaluation of the change and with design or implementation interventions for the change. They will have their hands in diagnosing the environment to determine the readiness of the workgroup that is impacted and needing to accept the change. Then HR professionals move into developing an action plan that determines the strategies to be used to implement the plan. Lastly, they are responsible for evaluating the change to measure the planned effectiveness and behavioral results against what was intended.

Learning Organization

A learning organization is a place "where people continually expand their capacity to create the results they truly desire, where new and expansive patterns of thinking are nurtured, where collective aspiration is set free, and where people are continually learning how to learn together." It is a systems-level concept in which the organization is characterized by its capacity to adapt to changes in its environment. The organization responds quickly to situations by altering the organizational behavior. A good example is when social media became more than just staying in touch with friends and family. Businesses quickly learned how much power they had to influence customers, and thus businesses began creating their own customer fan pages to communicate with customers and provide time-sensitive offers.

The importance of aligning HR initiatives and activities with the overall strategic plan of the organization will require the application of concepts of both a learning organization and organizational learning.

In a learning organization a systems-thinking approach is used, change is embraced, risk is tolerated, and failures are lessons learned. Peter Senge's *The Fifth Discipline* outlines the five disciplines that interface and support one another with this systems-thinking concept.

- **Personal mastery**   Connects personal and organizational learning, merging an individual's personal vision with their current reality. Commitments happen between the organization and the individual.

- **Mental models**   Ingrained assumptions that influence how individuals understand their reality and what actions they take.

- **Building shared vision**   Develops a projection of the future that is shared and creates a genuine commitment on all individuals involved.

- **Team learning**   Aligns the shared vision of a group and develops their capacities to produce the results the team desires.

- **Systems thinking**   A framework for seeing patterns and how things interrelate and how to change things.

When the five disciplines are in use in an organization, learning is matched to employees' learning preferences, leaders become stewards and teachers, people take responsibility for their own development and learning, and there is an understanding on how to learn, not a sole focus on what needs to be learned. The learning is easily tied to business objectives, and it creates a performance-based culture where solving problems and learning new ways not previously used are rewarded. Basically, a learning organization focuses on employees who want to learn to develop new capabilities and reacts to adapt to its environment.[9]

Organizational Learning

Organizational learning describes the particular activities or processes that occur in an organization with both individuals and teams. An example would be a new payroll cloud-based processing software that all payroll clerks are required to learn to use. In organizational learning, individual learning takes place through self-study, instruction, and observation. Group learning occurs through increasing knowledge, skills, and group instruction.

The following are the characteristics of a culture that supports organizational learning:

- Recognition of continuous learning in the work environment being as important as the day-to-day work itself

- Quality improvements driving organizational initiatives

- Well-defined core competencies in job descriptions

- Performance rewards based on individual and group learning achievements

- Employees having access to important information such as strategic plans

- A focus on creativity exists

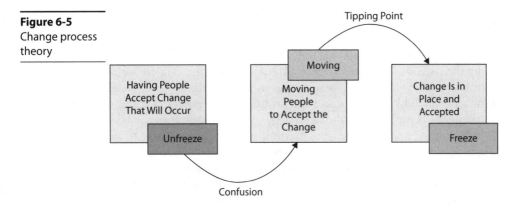

Figure 6-5
Change process theory

The distinction between organizational learning and a learning organization is that organizational learning exists in every organization.

Change Process Theory

OD and change process theory go hand in hand. Just as there is a predictable series of emotions that occurs with significant emotional events in organizational change, social psychologist Kurt Lewin[10] identified three stages of the change process in organizations, as depicted in Figure 6-5. The first stage is called *unfreezing* and involves shifting and dismantling the existing mind-set or paradigms. The second stage, labeled *moving*, is the moment change occurs. It is generally a phase of confusion marked by not knowing what's next and difficulty in letting go of old ways. The final and third stage is called *freezing*. This is when the new paradigm is taking shape and a tipping point of comfort with the new change is taking hold.

Like all good planning methods, with organizational changes, communication must be crystal clear on the long-term goals for the change, along with actions steps on how the change will take place.

In the Trenches

The Five Misconceptions of What OD Really Is

Larry Bienati, Ph.D., SPHR, CCP

I am grateful to my HR-OD mentor Fred Jackson, who always conveyed the importance of an organizational development mind-set in how I led the HR vision of the organization. Over the last 35 years Fred's good counsel still rings true, and it has led me to lament the five misconceptions of what OD really is.

(continued)

PART II

The first misconception is thinking that it is all about "training" or anything "done to an organization." Those seeking the valued HR business partner role by their senior leadership team realize that OD is the catalyst for delivering the transformational leadership outcome in an organization. Its purest definition was captured by Wendell and French when they referred to OD as "a response to change, a complex educational strategy intended to change the beliefs, attitude, values, and structure of an organization so it can better adapt to new technologies, markets and the business strategy." I have always viewed OD as a process to engage the hearts and minds of your human resources by providing a vision of the future, involving employees in that vision, and enlisting their ideas, commitment, and ownership of the process to bring about a desired result.

The second misconception is to focus strictly on the process and fail to engage the people in that process of understanding. I recall many failures of process improvement strategies like Total Quality Management (TQM), reengineering, and other management fads of the month. Kotter got it right in his legacy work on the eight steps of *Leading Change*—a must-read and model for any successful OD practitioner! He captured the eight deadly sins and reminded us of the importance of creating that sense of urgency, ensuring top-level commitment, sharing the vision, exhaustive communication, board-based action, removing barriers, aligning systems, and celebrating success.

The third misconception is failing to clearly align the HR-OD strategy to the organizational business plan. Each year I would meet with the key functional leaders in the organization and ask how HR could support their business imperatives. This resulted in various service level agreements with each "customer" and ensuring our HR-OD program aligned in some measure to their key performance objectives. We focused on two objectives per customer. We established appropriate success measures and communicated with the customer on a regular basis to show impact.

The fourth misconception is failing to demonstrate the "ROI effect in the OD process." Sadly, OD is viewed as another touchy-feely HR program by many. The prescription: Can you show in soft and hard dollars what the economic value and what the cost-benefit of the OD effort will be? Will it increase revenue, decrease costs, improve productivity, or achieve some critical aspect of the business plan? Whenever possible, I always demonstrated the financial impact of our OD process—what got measured got done.

The fifth misconception is thinking the change management process is a 90-day process of immediate success. Sure, we might see immediate returns initially if we scope the project correctly, pursue realistic objectives, and pursue small victories through deeds—actions and not words. Be prepared to stay the course, and achieve success through incremental wins realizing it may take a 36-month time frame for the full outcome effect. Good luck on your OD journey!

Talent Management

Talent management involves all the HR strategies and processes that are involved in attracting, developing, engaging, and retaining the skills/knowledge/abilities of the workforce to meet the organization's needs. Talent management goals are simple: manage the human resources initiatives that directly result in employee productivity and that address current and future business needs.

Employee Development Programs

Employee development programs are an important aspect of talent management, providing employees with opportunities to learn new knowledge and skills, preparing them for future responsibilities and job changes, and increasing their capacity to perform in their current jobs. Job rotation, enlargement, and enrichment form one avenue for employee development. Another could be an apprenticeship program that relates to skills training.

NOTE   The U.S. apprenticeship system is regulated by the Bureau of Apprenticeship and Training (BAT).[11]

Higher education tuition reimbursement programs are also offered by many organizations as part of their employee development program. The pursuit of education is normally restricted to an employee's current occupation or an occupation that exists within the organization.

Other employee development programs that are increasingly on the rise within organizations are those associated with wellness training, stress management, and work-life balance.

Skills Training

Skills training generally encompasses specific skill sets associated with jobs as identified in job descriptions. Skill development is a constantly moving target because of the nature of changing workplace requirements. With the added complexity of technology and rules/regulations, most jobs will have changing skill set requirements throughout their existence in the organization. Categories of skills training will normally include the following:

- Sales training
- Technology training
- Technical skills
- Quality training
- Communication skills training
- Emotional intelligence
- Basic on-the-job training

Other skills training may be specifically targeted to supervisory-level positions such as leadership/supervisory skills training, discrimination/harassment prevention training, or diversity and ethics training.

Instructor Evaluation

Instructor jobs are among those that some people say can't be evaluated. They depend entirely on soft skills that can't be measured but can be recognized when seen. Besides being incorrect, that position is a slap in the face to really effective instructors and a "free pass" for incompetent instructors.

According to Bob Powers in the book *Instructor Excellence,*[12] there are 17 critical instructor skills that can be measured and should be used in screening candidates for instructor jobs.

- **Verbal skills**   The ability to speak effectively
- **Interpersonal skills**   The ability to work effectively with others
- **Leadership skills**   The ability to get others to accomplish objectives without creating hostility
- **Reading skills**   The ability to read and comprehend course materials
- **Organizing and planning**   The ability to establish priorities and structures and develop and carry out plans, designs, and so on
- **Platform skills**   The ability to establish and hold eye contact, speak with a variety of inflections, move naturally, and gesture with ease
- **Decision-making skills**   The ability to make sound decisions, given the information available
- **Flexibility**   The ability to change plans to meet objectives
- **Analytical skills**   The ability to comprehend and interpret information
- **Problem-solving skills**   The ability to constructively handle unexpected problems
- **Acceptance of feedback**   The ability to provide and receive motivational and developmental feedback
- **Questioning skills**   The ability to ask questions in a way that produces a response
- **Participation**   The ability to get people to participate
- **Initiative**   The ability to initiate action
- **Managing diverse groups**   The ability to successfully manage a mix or variety of people
- **Risk taking**   The willingness to take unplanned action to accomplish objectives
- **Writing skills**   The ability to write clearly and concisely to accomplish an objective

A rating scale can be created for each of these skills. Measurements can be made based on comparison with successful instructors in the type of training programs this job will

Figure 6-6 Platform skill rating

be part of. The "standard" comes from answering the question, "What do I see a completely successful instructor doing in this type of program?" Then the job candidate or incumbent can be rated in relation to that mark along each scale. Figure 6-6 shows an example of how to rate the amount of behavior seen in one of these skills.

Using this approach, each of these instructor skills can be measured/evaluated. It is helpful to work with the incumbents to develop the amount of behavior that can be observed in a successful instructor. That way, their comparison along the evaluation scale will be better understood and accepted.

How do you observe behavior in a job interview? You ask the candidate to demonstrate the skill given a specific training outline and audience. Making it job specific can be easy if you extract a segment of the program the instructor will be teaching after being hired. Observing incumbents can be done by sitting in on a class as an observer, rating each of the skills, and making notes to identify what behaviors were being demonstrated. Immediate feedback is appropriate at the end of the class. The accumulation of these observations over a quarter or a year can constitute a performance evaluation. They should be frequent, and any improvement needs should be revisited at the following observation to note improvements.

Training Platforms

There are multiple methods for delivering training, known as *training platforms*. Some newer approaches are overtaking traditional approaches in popularity. Here are a few to consider:

- **Classroom**   Involves an instructor and a group of students/participants gathered together in a single room. Delivery methods can include lecture, interactive discussion, individual exercises, small group exercises, or large group exercises.

- **Online group**   Involves an instructor-led group that uses Internet-based audio/visual tools to help move the group through the class material outline. Participants can be located anywhere on the globe (or above it as in the International Space Station).

- **Online self-paced individual package**   Participant is an individual without any other people for interaction. There is no instructor. Materials move the participant along at the individual's pace, so materials can be absorbed at a rate acceptable to the participant.

- **Self-study book**   Participant reads and absorbs knowledge from a book designed to provide the information necessary to accomplish the training objectives. The pace of progress is controlled by the individual participant.

Training Program Evaluation

Evaluating training programs can be done in several ways. Here are some of the possible metrics you can use:

- **End of program participant survey**   Request feedback from program participants about the program content, the instructor, and the value of the content to their job performance
- **Specific job transfer measurement**   Periodic measurement of the impact the training program had on participant's job performance.
- **Instructor evaluation of the program and its participants**   A thoughtful analysis by the instructor of the class group and its reaction to the program contents
- **Participant demonstration of skills or knowledge**   In-class demonstration of mastery over skills and knowledge that can be transferred to on-the-job application
- **Cost per person**   How much expense is involved in having one person participate in the training?
- **Instructor preparation cost**   What time is required for instructors to "get up to speed" and able to teach the program?
- **Training development cost**   What expense is involved in researching, designing, writing, and publishing the training program?

Teams

Bringing together a group of people who can address a given set of issues or problems is the process of team creation. How effective the group will be depends on many things, such as the team leadership and the experience of each member. Teams permit the focus of talent on specific organizational goals.

Employee development strategies could include team participation, involvement on committees, and work teams to expose a group to decision-making and collaborative processes. Team assignments can enrich an employee's experience and perspective, assisting with an employee's career planning initiatives.

For a team to be effective, all participants need to be clear on the goals they are working toward and what expectations they are to meet and fulfill.

Project Teams

Project teams are formed when specific projects must be completed. People with a specific talent or experience are recruited into the group to contribute their knowledge and skills to resolving the problem or accomplishing some other goal. There is often a team leader who can be an organizational superior or peer of other team members.

Self-Directed Teams

Self-directed teams are groups of people who are given general direction by assignment to resolve an issue or solve a problem. The group selects its own leadership, identifies its own direction, and holds itself accountable for accomplishments.

Task Forces

A cousin of teams, task forces are groups of people assembled to research and address major organizational issues. They are composed of individuals with specific experience or knowledge and are expected to "fix" problems that could have significant impact on the organization. Task forces are sometimes used to address system failures (for example, computer or software) or to handle crises (for example, natural disaster or sudden inability to transport goods through a region due to a new local ordinance). Once the solution is found or issue resolved, the task force disbands.

Work Teams

When formed to facilitate production or performance, the group is sometimes referred to as a *work team*. These are people from the same type of work, usually of the same or similar job class, who are working together to generate the production for their segment of the organization. Types of work teams include the following:

- **Functional work teams**   These are groups of people from the same function working together to generate production. On an assembly line or in the accounts receivable department, groups handle the work load as a unit rather than as individuals.

- **Cross-functional work teams**   These are groups of people from different functions working together to generate production. On the assembly line or in the engineering department, individuals with different talents work together to create a unified output. (For example, an engineer works with drafters and technicians to create work drawings for a project. The group may include electricians, construction supervisors, and other interior designers. All functions work together to create one unified result.)

- **Virtual work teams**   With virtual work teams, members are not located in the same facility and, in fact, may work in different parts of the globe. They come together via technology such as Internet FaceTime meetings to accomplish team assignments that could fall within the scope of work teams.

Career Development

Career development is the lifelong individual process that involves planning, managing, learning, and transitions at all ages and stages in work life. In organizations, it is an organized approach used to match employee goals with the business's current and future needs. An individual's work-related preferences and needs continuously evolve throughout life's phases. At the same time, organizations are also continuously adapting to economic, political, and societal changes.

Career Development Processes

There are two processes in career development: career planning and career management. With career planning, the focus is on the individual. Career management has a focus on the organization.

In career planning, assessing an individual's skills, talents, experiences, and potential abilities occurs to give direction to a person's career. HR professionals typically assist with these activities, but many self-assessment instruments are available online for individuals to use.

With career management, this involves implementing and monitoring employee career paths at an organizational level. The individual employee is actively involved; however, the organization is typically providing the development programs and opportunities associated with internal career progression opportunities and succession planning. The intention with career management from the organizational perspective is to assist with aligning existing workforce talent with new business objectives, create an atmosphere of positive morale, and for employee retention of needed talent.

Roles in Managing Career Development

It is not just the individual employee and HR involved in career development. The direct line of management and the organization's leaders have a role to play, too.

Individuals bear the primary responsibility for their own career. Today, individuals are required to be proactive in planning their career progression and not rely on an organization to direct their career path. Being keenly aware of current assessed traits and skills, along with needs for increased knowledge, skill, and experience associated with the individual's career ambitions, is largely the responsibility of an individual employee. Figure 6-7 illustrates the stages of an individual's career development.

The direct line of management normally serves as support in helping an individual assess his or her current effectiveness and potential and provides a broader view of the organization's career paths. The direct supervisory management will wear many hats, including coach, appraiser, guidance counselor, and resource referral in the employee's career development planning.

The HR professionals are involved in the development of career pathing, personal development programs, and skill development training to enable employees to achieve their career aspirations and goals. Creating a skill inventory database along with work and educational experience of the current workforce is needed in helping the organization assess its current workforce talent. Additionally, HR professionals monitor training and development needs and create programs to meet those needs, along with the communication of job progression opportunities.

The organizational leader's role in career development includes the communication of the organization's mission and vision to the workforce to link the organization's initiatives and changes with the anticipated talent needs. Fostering a culture of support and internal opportunity for career development is another important function of the organizational leader's role.

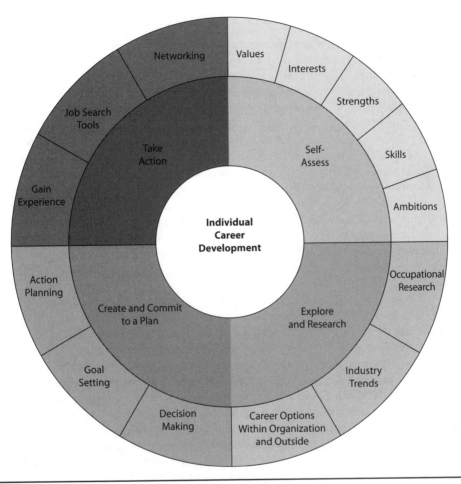

Figure 6-7 Individual career development

In the Trenches

Personal Branding and You

Susan Chritton, author of Personal Branding for Dummies,
http://susanchritton.com

What do people think of when they think about you? Are you thought of as intelligent, honest, and creative, or do people associate you with poor-quality work and someone who doesn't finish what they start? You have a personal brand whether you know it or not.

(continued)

So, what exactly is a *personal brand?* Very simply it is your reputation. Your personal brand is the way others remember you through your actions, your knowledge, and the emotional connections you make. Your personal brand becomes the promise you make about who you are and what you do that is strengthened every time people connect with you.

Personal branding is the strategic process of building a positive set of experiences for the people who need to know about you. Personal branding is about expressing your authentic self by allowing you to be the person you are meant to be. Personal branding helps you connect with your unique promise of value and employ it in the world to act as a filter that helps you make decisions that are congruent with who you are and what you stand for. It identifies what makes you unique and clearly communicates your individuality to the people who need to know about you.

Having a personal brand sounds like a great idea, but how do you get one? If you're serious about developing your personal brand, you will need a clear plan to get you there.

To begin the process, you need to spend time up front studying yourself and figuring out what you really want. Only with a strong sense of yourself can you undertake the steps to build a personal brand. You will need to define who you are and understand both your target audience and who your competitors are.

After you know your brand, your next challenge is to communicate it clearly, concisely, and consistently to the people who need to know about you. Finally, you'll want to examine your *brand ecosystem*, which are those things that encompass every element of your life—from your clothes to your professional colleagues—and influence how your target audience perceives you.

Personal branding supports and enhances your work. Your best success comes when you recognize your own gifts and are able to represent your personal brand in all that you do. Your personal brand helps you make the most of what you have to offer by understanding who you are and what sets you apart from every other person. It helps you navigate the direction of your life. Your personal brand is your own success story waiting to be written.

Career Development Programs

Many large organizations create full-fledged career development programs. Some will be self-paced and opt-in by individual employees, and some are created with particular objectives in mind, such as management development programs, where high-potential employees are invited to participate. A typical model for a career development program will include stages of the following:

- **Occupational preparation** This stage is where occupations are assessed, an occupation is decided upon, and necessary education and skill levels are pursued.

- **Organizational entry**   This is the stage where a person obtains and decides on job offers from organizations they want to work for, or they learn of internal changes within the company they work in and they decide on whether they want to go for that.

- **Early career establishment**   In this phase, an employee learns a new job, along with organizational norms and rules for fitting into the job, company, or industry. An employee gains work experience and career skills.

- **Mid-career**   In this phase, an employee evaluates his or her career objectives, with an understanding of his or her current life situation, and may choose to shift career direction.

- **Late career**   In this last phase, employees focus on retirement planning and, again, choices associated with life considerations as to the hours they want to work and the extra effort that may cause additional mental stress. Climbing career progression ladders is not normally in their career plans at this phase, yet mentoring of employees in early career phases would be.

 NOTE   By understanding the focus of each stage, HR professionals are better equipped to prepare and manage the transitions the employees in their organization will experience.

Dual-Ladder Program

Dual-ladder career development programs allow mobility for employees without requiring that they be placed into the managerial enclave. Mostly associated with technical, medical, engineering, and scientific occupations, this type of program is a way to advance employees who are not interested in pursuing a management track. These individuals exhibit one or more of the following characteristics:

- Have substantial technical or professional expertise beyond the basic levels

- Have licensure or required credentials

- Are known for innovation

- May or may not be well suited for management or leadership roles

An objective within a dual-ladder development program is to increase complexity and value to the organization, enabling the organization to increase employee salaries to improve employee retention and satisfaction. Lateral movement may occur within a dual-ladder program such as team membership, internal consultative roles, mentorships, or larger facility rotation. Figure 6-8 shows an example of a dual-ladder career path.

Coaching and Mentoring

More organizations are realizing the advantages of having coaching and mentoring programs as part of their overall career management strategy. These programs are advantageous

PART II

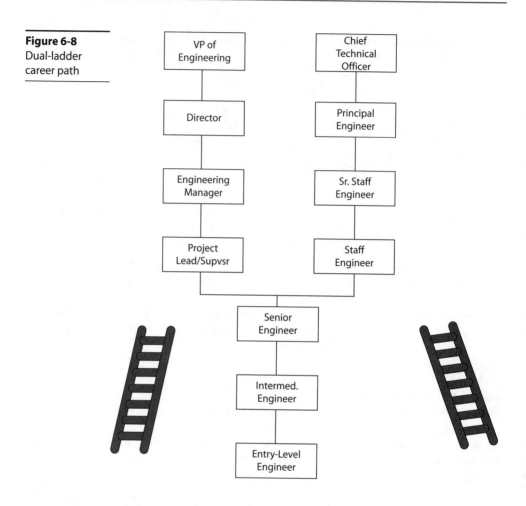

Figure 6-8 Dual-ladder career path

for HR because of their effectiveness in working one-on-one with individuals, allowing HR the ability to maintain an unbiased position.

Coaching involves one-on-one discussions between the employee and a "coach." The coach can be internal or external. An internal coach could be a member of the HR team or a line manager. Coaching can involve ongoing activities with a direct supervisor or HR professional that provide discussions focused on the career objectives of an employee, including perspective assessments such as poor job fit or potential growth tracks. External coaches are professionals hired at the organization's expense who typically work on the development of an employee in a particular area—for example, presentation or communication—or to hone and shift leadership skills. This type of coaching is focused solely on the employee and is confidential and private. At the level of executive coaching, which is more prevalent in organizations of all sizes, a third-party vendor-certified executive coach is utilized to allow executives the freedom to discuss aspects of career-life balance with a high level of trust and nondisclosure.

Mentoring is an action-oriented relationship between two people within the organization, usually a senior and junior colleague. It involves advising, providing opinion and perspective, role modeling, and sharing contacts and networks, along with support. The mentee receives career support and learns the ropes in the organization, and the mentor has the opportunity to share his or her knowledge and perhaps pass the baton of the job responsibilities on to afford the mentee a chance to move out of a current role. Mentorships can occur at all levels in an organization. They can be formally designed by HR, such as part of the onboarding orientation process, or they can be part of a succession planning program.

Employee Retention

According to the SHRM's Future of the U.S. Labor Pool Survey Report,[13] three out of ten employees in the workforce are retiring each year for the next 12 years. That creates a large knowledge gap and an emphasis on passing institutional knowledge on to employees via replacement/succession planning. Yet a plan is only going to work as designed if the identified candidates remain employed with the organization. Retention is the ability to keep talented employees. The importance of retention has moved to the top of the priority list in today's global competitive marketplace because of the following factors:

- An improved economy rebounding from the recession causing the job market to improve
- Retirement of the Baby Boomers and a likely shortage in skills/knowledge-based labor
- The increase of global competition
- Economic factors resulting in cost of living substantially increasing
- Technological advancements
- Generational motivation differences

How can you improve your employee retention results? Here are some key elements of a good retention program:

- **On-boarding and employee orientation programs** From the beginning of day one, make the new employee feel comfortable and welcome. There should be smiles in the workplace.
- **Mentorship programs** These provide linkages between experienced, more senior people who are willing to give advice and council to a new employee. They fill the "big brother" or "big sister" role in a long-term relationship.
- **Employee compensation** There should be competitive pay rates at all levels. Money may not be a long-term motivator, but it can help reduce turnover.
- **Recognition and rewards systems** Operate with the belief that everyone likes to be recognized for their contributions. Build systems that can encourage supervisors and managers to say "Thank you" when things go well, and offer

extra incentives for going the extra mile. It could involve gift cards, a day off with pay, acknowledgment in the company newsletter, or some other form of spotlight on the accomplishments.

- **Training and development**   If people have an opportunity to attend training programs that will expand or enhance their skills, that alone can sometimes offer incentive for remaining with the employer.

Retention means you have made your organization a highly desirable place to work. It can be thought of as a destination for job candidates. When "everybody wants to work here," you will be able to say you have a low employee turnover.

Employee Suggestion Systems

Having an employee suggestion system is an employee engagement and involvement strategy that goes hand in hand with employee retention. When employees feel their opinion counts or their perspective is "heard," they are more likely to turn away from third-party representation.

Employee suggestion systems, anonymous or not, can provide management with a way to "hear" the workforce for both positive ideas and negative issues or perceptions. Many improvements are discovered through employee suggestion systems that are considered at upper management levels in an organization. Often, HR is the gatekeeper responsible for screening or compiling the employee suggestions. It's important that employee suggestions are acknowledged and given serious consideration and that responses are provided in a timely manner.

Employee Focus Groups

When a large cross-section of employee opinions or perspectives is needed, an employee focus group from various units, functions, and facilities in an organization is used. Surveys can solicit the input from the entire employee population, and there are survey instruments that can compile this input for HR, but a focus group offers the opportunity to have two-way dialogue for clarity and probing purposes. The employees, however, must feel safe providing candid and honest feedback, which is a reason why either HR or an outside consultant will conduct employee focus groups.

When an organization is bleeding from key and high performers exiting, a focus group of existing employees might be in order to learn what the root cause of the exodus is.

Challenges in Talent Management

Organizations may not always realize why they are losing talent. There exist special challenges in talent management, even though the organization may have a plethora of training and development programs in place. Not all careers will take an upward or positive direction for every employee. In fact, some long-term employees may hit a wall and go nowhere.

Plateaued Careers

How do you maintain the productivity, loyalty, and commitment of an employee who is not considered promotable? They have been good performers in the past, and they may be years away from retirement, though suddenly their performance growth hits a mile-long plateau. The challenge is in seeking ways to expand skills, create new levels of motivation and interest, keep the employee engaged in the organization's vision, and work them into a process where their knowledge and talents due to lengthy experience can benefit the organization. Some employees see this as a pigeon-hole, and yet their high salary expense can become an issue as their cost of employment becomes inequitable to their productivity.

Glass Ceilings

Glass ceiling is another talent management issue as well as a federal legal issue. The federal government found it to be such a big issue that the Federal Glass Ceiling Commission was created in 1991, and its mandate was to identify the glass ceiling barriers that have blocked the advancement of minorities and women. The commission also studies the successful practices and policies of organizations that have led to breaking glass ceilings and advancing minorities and women into decision-making power positions. Organizations are recognizing that glass ceilings are not healthy for business because of shifts in labor force demographics, changes in their marketplace, and, of course, the globalization of their industries.

Boards of directors and senior management are creating glass-ceiling initiatives to help all employees, regardless of gender and ethnicity, reach their full employment potential. There is bottom-line value and economic advantages to the business, and then there is the practicality of keeping the EEOC from issuing an audit notice.

Creativity and Innovation

Business Insider tells us, "The main difference between creativity and innovation is the focus. *Creativity is about unleashing the potential of the mind to conceive new ideas.* Those concepts could manifest themselves in any number of ways, but most often, they become something we can see, hear, smell, touch, or taste.

"Innovation, on the other hand, is completely measurable. *Innovation is about introducing change into relatively stable systems.* It's also concerned with the work required to make an idea viable. By identifying an unrecognized and unmet need, an organization can use innovation to apply its creative resources to design an appropriate solution and reap a return on its investment."

Organizations often chase creativity, but what they really need to pursue is innovation. Theodore Levitt puts it best: "What is often lacking is not creativity in the idea-creating sense but innovation in the action-producing sense, i.e., putting ideas to work."[14]

HR professionals have responsibility for helping leaders in the enterprise understand and act on the resources available for creative and innovative contributions to the strategic plan.

Performance Management

Performance management is a systematic process that helps improve organizational effectiveness by providing feedback to employees on their performance results and improvement needs. It is employee accomplishments and contributions that drive the business results of an organization, so a regular feedback system discussing individual performance is at the core of a good performance management system. It ensures that employees are on course for the completion of tasks and goals that are aligned with the organization's goals and that the resources and support are provided for the employee to perform such functions.

Employee performance management systems include the following:

- Delegating and planning work
- Setting expectations for performance results
- Continually monitoring performance
- Developing a capacity to perform to new levels for personal and professional growth
- Periodically rating performance in a summary fashion
- Providing recognition and rewarding good performance

As discussed in Chapter 4, creating and communicating the organization's vision, mission, strategies, specific goals, and values form the foundation that is needed for the performance management system. Then performance standards are agreed upon by both the line management and the employee on what the job requires and what will be measured. At this stage, it is essential that employees clearly understand the standards, including expected behavior standards set forth for their jobs. Feedback is the next stage and can be both informal and formal. Formal feedback would entail a written performance appraisal.

Performance Standards

Employees need to know and understand what specific performance is expected of them in performing their jobs and the acceptable behavior. This communication begins with the first discussion in a job interview and certainly with the job offer and new hire onboarding orientation. The discussion continues on a consistent basis both with the reinforcement of organizational standards that are outlined in employee handbooks and other written material and with performance appraisal review sessions. The clearer the expectations set for employees, the greater the success in having expectations met.

 NOTE For employees to meet job expectations, there needs to be a direct relationship between the job description's competency requirements and the performance objectives.

Performance Appraisal Methods

Performance appraisals satisfy three purposes:

- Providing feedback and coaching
- Justifying the allocation of rewards and career opportunities
- Helping with employee career planning and development plans

For the organization, performance appraisals can foster commitment and align people to contribute to initiatives with their upcoming performance contributions. The most common performance appraisal method involves just two people: the employee and his or her direct supervisor. In some companies, others are asked to be involved in the appraisals such as peers, another level of management, and sometimes colleagues in the organization whose job function interacts with the employee. These are known as *360-degree appraisals.*

Methods for rating the performance can be completely narrative, management by objectives (MBO) discussed in Chapter 11, behaviorally anchored ratings (BARS), category rating, and comparative ratings with others in like functions.

The least complex of the methods is the category rating where the reviewer simply checks a level of rating on a form. Three types of rating formulas are typically used in category ratings:

- **Graphic scale**   The most common type, where the appraiser checks a place on the scale for the categories of tasks and behaviors that are listed. A typical scale is 5 points, where 1 means not meeting expectations or low and 5 means exceeding expectations or high. These types of performance appraisals normally have a comments section that the appraiser completes that provides justification for the rating.

- **Checklist**   Another common appraisal rating in which the appraiser is provided with a set list of statements/words to describe performance. The appraiser selects the one word or statement that best describes the performance—for example, "Employee consistently meets all deadlines" or "Employee consistently misses deadlines."

- **Forced choice**   A variation of the checklist approach, but in the checklist method, the appraiser is required to check two of four statements. One check is for the statement that is most like the employee's performance, and the other check is for the statement that is least like the employee's performance—a combination of positive and negative statements. This method can be difficult to convey to employees and understand from an employee's perspective.

With comparative methods, employee performance is compared directly with others in the same job. The appraiser will rank the employees in a group from highest to lowest in performance. This causes a forced distribution known as a *bell curve.* Ten percent will fall in the highest and lowest of the rating scale, another 20 percent will fall on either

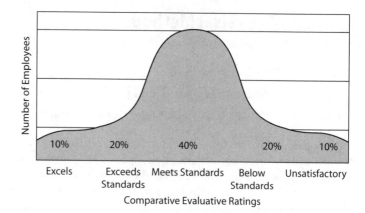

Figure 6-9
Bell curve distribution

side, and then 40 percent will meet job standards and expectations. An obvious fault with this type of system is suggesting that a percentage of employees will fall below expectations. Figure 6-9 displays a bell curve distribution.

Narrative evaluations are time consuming for an appraiser to complete, yet they can be the most meaningful to the employee being evaluated. There are three methods that are the most common for the narrative appraisal:

- **Essay format**   The appraiser writes an essay type of narrative describing each category of performance.

- **Critical incident**   The appraiser is logging dates and details of both good and not-so-good performance incidents. This method requires the appraiser to be keeping good, detailed notes on a routine basis during the appraisal period and not relying solely on an employee's most recent performance.

- **Behaviorally anchored rating methods**   Referred to as BARS, this appraisal method describes desirable behavior and undesirable behavior. Examples are then compared with a scale of performance level for the rating. BARS works well in circumstances in which several employees perform the same function. A BARS appraisal system requires extensive time to develop and maintain to keep the performance dimensions up-to-date as the job functions change. However, the BARS methods offer a more accurate gauge of performance measurement, provide clearer standards to employees, and have more consistency in rating.

Self-Assessment

Coupled with the direct supervisory management evaluation, many employees are asked to self-assess their performance. This approach assists with creating a truly two-way dialogue in the evaluation interview and offers an opportunity for the employee to provide his own perception of his performance. Additionally, it engages employees in a proactive means of creating goals and objectives, along with triggering a discussion about career development. Figure 6-10 provides an example of a self-assessment—both a category rating and open-ended questions to elicit a narrative commentary.

Self-Assessment Performance Appraisal
For the appraisal period of January 1, 2022 – December 31, 2022

Employee Name: _____ EE # _____

Department: _____
Position Title: _____
Supervisor: _____
Facility: _____

Instructions:
Please complete your self-assessment evaluation and return it to your supervisor by (date)_____.
Your participation in the annual performance appraisal process helps to facilitate a comprehensive evaluation of your performance and accomplishments against set standards, goals, and objectives.

1. Describe your accomplishments and contributions since last review period.
2. Describe the activities you have participated in that have produced favorable outcomes.
3. Since your last appraisal, what new skills have you acquired?
4. Describe skills that you have increased and provide an example of their effective application on the job.
5. List new training and/or development programs you have completed.
6. Describe areas you wish to improve to enhance your job performance and capabilities.
7. State three or more job objectives for this next year and how you plan to achieve them.

Please provide your self-assessment rating in the following categories using the rating scale below.

Rating Scale:

4 - Outstanding **3** - Very Competent or High Level **2** - Satisfactory **1** - Inexperienced or Improvement Needed

Category	Self-Rating
a. Technical Skills (job specific)	_____
b. Job Knowledge (up-to-date on industry, articles, and best practices)	_____
c. Quality of Work Product (comprehensive, accurate, timely)	_____
d. Productivity	_____
e. Professionalism (punctuality, attendance; conduct; responsiveness and follow through)	_____
f. Collaboration & Teamwork	_____
g. Computer Skill Applications	_____
h. Time Management & Organizational Skills	_____
i. Interpersonal Skills	_____
j. Communication Skills - Verbal/Written	_____
k. Innovation or Creativity	_____

Date: _____   Employee Signature: _____

Figure 6-10   Self-assessment performance appraisal

Shortcomings of Performance Appraisals

As with any subjective system, performance appraisals are subjective because they are based on people's perceptions and opinions, so there can be shortcomings. Here are the most common errors made on the part of appraisers:

- **Halo**   This occurs when the employee is doing well in one area and is therefore rated high in all areas.

- **Horn**   This occurs when an employee is demonstrating a strong weakness and is thus rated low in all other areas.

- **Bias**   This happens when the evaluator's bias (consciously or unconsciously) influences and distorts his or her perspective.

- **Recency**   A recency error occurs when more emphasis is placed on a recent occurrence and all earlier performances during the review period are discounted.

- **Primacy**   The opposite of recency. The evaluator gives more weight and emphasis to earlier performances, discounting more recent performance.

- **Strictness**   An evaluator is reluctant to give high ratings, and his or her standards are higher than other evaluators.

- **Leniency**   The evaluator does not provide low scores and instead gives all employees a high rating on their appraisals.

- **Central**   An evaluator rates all of his or her employees in the same range and does not consider differences of actual performance among the group rated.

- **Contrast**   The evaluator is providing an employee rating based solely on a comparison to that of another employee and not to objective standards.

 NOTE   These common errors can be avoided with narrative format methods.

Chapter Review

Learning and development are the integrated use of training, organizational development, and career development efforts to improve individual, group, and organizational effectiveness. This HRCI functional area focuses on the behavior, skills, and competencies for employees to further the organization's goals. Learning and development activities need to align and support the organization's strategic goals and objectives, and it is the HR professional's responsibility to develop, evaluate, and measure the direct effectiveness to ensure that they are in alignment. By providing input in the development and fully understanding the organization's strategic plan, the HR professional can then develop, select, and implement learning and development programs and activities that provide the organization's workforce with the necessary skills and competencies to meet the current and future organizational job demands.

Learning and development play a strong role in helping employees acquire skills and knowledge and in assisting with the changes and outside influences through the development of training and development programs, change management, performance management, employee career planning, and job enhancement.

Questions

1. When conducting a needs assessment, which processes are used in strategic planning? (Choose two.)

   A. Environmental scanning

   B. Healthcare scanning

   C. Opinions from local supervisors and managers

   D. SWOT analysis

2. A good training objective should begin with "The participant will be able to:"

   A. Understand

   B. Perform

   C. Expect

   D. Absorb

3. According to Maslow's hierarchy, which needs must be met first?

   A. Social needs

   B. Security/safety needs

   C. Self-actualization needs

   D. Belonging/loving needs

4. Leslie has moved into a new supervisory position in the creative services department. She intends to set a good example for her subordinates. She recognizes that there are already strong creative partnerships within the department, so she tries to foster even more cooperation. What style of leadership is Leslie practicing?

   A. Authoritarian leadership

   B. Team style

   C. Democratic leadership

   D. Collaborative leadership

5. ADDIE is an instructional design tool. What is not part of ADDIE?

   A. Delivery

   B. Implementation

   C. Design

   D. Development

6. Trainability is concerned with the _____ ____ _____ and its associated motivation.

7. The Tasty Good corporation downsized because of intense global competition and modified its strategic business plan for the year. The most important task that the HR department's training and development function needs to do to support the change is to:

    A. Cost-justify training

    B. Work with employees on accepting the change

    C. Evaluate the effectiveness of all training programs

    D. Link training and development to the new strategic plan

8. Adult learners in comparison to child learners have which of the following characteristics?

    A. Resistance to change

    B. Inflexibility

    C. Focus on real-world issues

    D. Directed by others

9. One of the most important competencies of an HR professional is:

    A. Skilled project manager

    B. Skilled masterful change agent

    C. Excellent time management skills modeler

    D. Listening modeler

10. When an HR intervention has a focus on emotional intelligence (EQ), the goal is to:

    A. Heighten emotions

    B. Always improve co-worker relationships

    C. Cause EQ rating to align with IQ rating

    D. Improve or increase an individual's interactions and behaviors

11. Training and development manager Joey received a request from the operations director to develop a team-building program that would focus on blending the values of Gen X with the Baby Boomers. Joey does not possess the knowledge of generational issues for team building. Which of the following is a justification Joey can use to sell his boss on purchasing an already existing team-building training program from a third-party consultant?

    A. Outside expertise will generate higher credibility from the Gen X participants because Joey is from the Baby Boomer generation.

    B. The time required to develop a training program in-house by Joey would take too long.

C. There are many vendors that offer this kind of specific training.

D. A Gen X training facilitator would be better to deliver this type of training program.

12. What performance evaluation method increases employee engagement and dialogue the most?

   A. Self-assessment evaluation

   B. Behaviorally anchored rating scale method (BARS)

   C. A forced-choice method

   D. Paired comparison method

13. Providing motivation by increasing job responsibility is known as:

   A. Job enlargement

   B. Job rotation

   C. Job enrichment

   D. Job training

14. In managing career development, it is which of the following who has primary responsibility?

   A. Supervising managers

   B. Individuals

   C. HR managers

   D. Training managers

15. A large technology company has identified a group of key managers in various departments who were hired with employment contracts that included large equity options. The company went public two years ago and continues to see a steady increase in stock value. There is a realization that many of these managers may retire when they are eligible to exercise their stock options in three more years. What OD activity should HR be focused on related to this circumstance?

   A. Review the organization's retirement plan and begin counseling discussions

   B. Expand the vacation policy for this group of managers

   C. Design a succession plan and identify high-potential employees

   D. Hire executive coaches to help this group of management with work-life balance

16. Herzberg's Motivation-Hygiene Theory is based on which two categories of needs?

   A. Psychological and basic needs

   B. Motivational and security needs

   C. Extrinsic and intrinsic needs

   D. Safety and self-esteem needs

17. What type of team involves a group that is given general direction to resolve an issue or solve a problem?

    A. Self-directed team

    B. Task force

    C. Project team

    D. Work team

18. Kiara has been working at her company for close to 18 years out of her 25 years as a programmer. What stage would probably best describe Kiara's career development?

    A. Late-career

    B. Mid-career crisis

    C. Occupational preparation

    D. Mid-career

19. Mark and Gwen are co-workers whose cubicles are located in a 12-by-10 enclosed room. Their manager is unable to resolve a conflict that they are having related to the temperature in the room, and the matter has escalated to HR. Which would be the best tactic to use in resolving their conflict?

    A. Use the seniority system; the person with the most seniority gets to decide on the temperature.

    B. Provide a portable fan for the cubicle and desk of the person who is too warm.

    C. Facilitate a conversation with the two of them in the same room to try to find common agreements.

    D. Create a schedule of telecommuting so that they are not in the same office at the same time.

20. Which is *not* one of the leadership practices that Kouzes and Posner identify for effective leadership?

    A. Enable

    B. Persuade

    C. Model

    D. Encourage

21. In a low-context culture, which is true?

    A. Tasks must be spelled out explicitly.

    B. Behaviors must be spelled out explicitly.

    C. People know how to behave.

    D. People have connections over long periods of time.

22. _____ is an action-oriented relationship between two people within the organization, usually a senior and junior colleague.

23. You have observed that your employee Matthew consistently has a notebook in hand and is taking notes in the training sessions. Which learning style is Matthew exhibiting?

  A. Visual

  B. Auditory

  C. Kinesthetic

  D. Tactile

24. Which learning curve is the most common?

  A. Increasing returns

  B. S-shaped curve

  C. Decreasing returns

  D. Plateau curve

25. When a large cross-section of employee opinions or perspectives is needed, what is the method that should be used?

  A. An employee suggestion system

  B. A general employee meeting with the CEO

  C. A call for written recommendations from employees for specific problems

  D. An employee focus group(s)

26. Performance standards are a good tool to use because:

  A. They offer specific descriptions of the minimum job performance requirements

  B. They offer a best-case, hoped-for expectation of job performance

  C. They offer management a reason for having job descriptions

  D. They offer employees stretch-objectives for their job growth program

Answers

  1. A, D. Environmental scanning and SWOT analysis are valuable components of needs assessment and strategic planning.

  2. B. Performing includes demonstrating, showing, selecting, listing, citing, and any number of other activities that can prove the participant actually learned from the training experience.

  3. B. Safety and security needs must be met first before moving up the pyramid of hierarchal needs according to Maslow's theory.

  4. B. The team style of leadership encourages teamwork and commitment among employees.

5. **A.** ADDIE is an instructional design model that follows phases of assessment, design, development, implementation, and evaluation.

6. **Readiness to learn**

7. **D.** Linking training and development activities to the new strategic plan is the first step to ensure that activities and resources are aligned with the organization's new initiatives.

8. **C.** As people mature, they shift in their motivation for learning. Real-world examples and emphasis on how the training is going to be immediately applied is most helpful.

9. **B.** Although all those skills listed are important to the profession, being a masterful change agent is most important because change agents serve as a catalyst in helping others work through and accept change, along with implementing processes and programs that align with the change.

10. **D.** Emotional intelligence (EQ) interventions involve skill and coaching or mentoring to cause a person's interactions to improve by changing an ineffective behavior.

11. **B.** Sometimes it is more cost and time effective to utilize an already developed training program that is available from a third-party vendor.

12. **A.** More organizations are having their employees complete a self-assessment on their performance and submit it prior to their evaluation interview meeting. This affords an opportunity for the employee to be more engaged with setting their job goals for the next review period and focuses discussions on their career development in the organization.

13. **C.** Job enrichment expands the amount of responsibility the job is given.

14. **B.** Individuals bear the primary responsibility for their own career, including development if that is what the individual wants.

15. **C.** A succession plan is a key component for business success and should be part of every organization's learning and development program to be sure that there is no gap in knowledge that cripples an organization because of the departure of key human capital.

16. **C.** Hygiene factors are considered extrinsic and associated with job security, pay, working conditions, and relationships, whereas motivational factors are considered intrinsic, associated with recognition, achievement, and personal growth–related events in the job.

17. **A.** Self-directed teams as a group select their own leadership and identify their own direction, holding themselves accountable for the intended accomplishments.

18. **D.** Mid-career is a phase when evaluation of career objectives occurs. It is too soon for retirement but a time of life when work-life family issues are more of a factor and can shift a person's motivations about work.

19. **C.** Any and all small agreements assist with the stages of conflict resolution. Agreeing on the problem and on some small changes gives a feeling of compromise to both parties so you can begin the process of looking at all possible acceptable solutions.

20. **B.** The five leadership practices Kouzes and Posner identify in *The Leadership Challenge* are challenge, inspire, enable, model, and encourage.

21. **B.** Behaviors must be clearly identified.

22. **Mentoring**

23. **A.** Matthew is a visual learner. Writing things down gives him that visual reference.

24. **C.** Most often, decreasing returns is the type of learning curve adults experience.

25. **D.** A focus group offers the opportunity to have two-way dialogue for clarity and probing purposes.

26. **A.** Performance standards offer employees clear descriptions of the minimum requirements expected of them.

Endnotes

1. https://www.convergencetraining.com/blog/how-to-create-an-effective-training-program-8-steps-to-success

2. https://elearningindustry.com/4-tips-for-content-chunking-in-e-learning

3. https://education.cu-portland.edu/blog/classroom-resources/which-is-best-teacher-centered-or-student-centered-education/

4. https://www.ncbi.nlm.nih.gov/pmc/articles/PMC4005174/

5. Benjamin Bloom, Engelhart, M. D. Furst, E. J. Hill, W. H. Krathwohl, D. R. Taxonomy of Educational Objectives: The Classification of Educational Goals. Handbook I: Cognitive Domain (New York: David McKay Company, 1956)

6. Abraham Maslow, "A Theory of Human Motivation," Psychological Review, 50, 370–96, 1943

7. https://www.managementstudyguide.com/theory-x-y-motivation.htm

8. Richard Beckhard, Organization Development: Strategies and Models (Addison-Wesley, 1969)

9. Peter Senge, The Fifth Discipline, Revised and Updated edition (New York: Doubleday, 2006)

10. Kurt Lewin, "Frontiers in Group Dynamics: Concept, Method and Reality in Social Science; Social Equilibria and Social Change," Human Relations Journal (June 1947), http://hum.sagepub.com/content/1/1/5

11. https://www.dol.gov/apprenticeship/

12. Powers, Bob and William J. Rothwell, Instructor Excellence: Mastering the Delivery of Training, 2nd Edition, Pfeiffer, John Wiley and Sons, 2007

13. SHRM, Talent Management Future of the U.S. Labor Pool Survey Report, 2013, www.shrm.org/india/hr-topics-and-strategy/strategic-hrm/talent-development-strategy

14. https://www.businessinsider.com/difference-between-creativity-and-innovation-2013-4

Total Rewards

The function of total rewards is composed of all employer programs that are used to attract, motivate, and retain employees. You have probably heard the terms *compensation* and *benefits* before. These are the two primary programs that make up total rewards, in addition to many other programs that will be reviewed in this chapter. In many ways, the total rewards function is the lifeblood of the employment relationship between the worker and the employer. Rewards have a significant effect on the quality and quantity of work produced by employees. Fifteen percent of the PHR exam will focus on this area of knowledge.

The official HRCI Total Rewards functional area responsibilities and knowledge statements are as follows:

Responsibilities

- Manage compensation-related information and support payroll issue resolution
- Implement and promote awareness of noncash rewards (for example, paid volunteer time, tuition assistance, workplace amenities, and employee recognition programs)
- Implement benefits programs (for example, health plan, retirement plan, employee assistance plan, other insurance)
- Administer federally compliant compensation and benefit programs

Knowledge Of

- Applicable federal laws and regulations related to total rewards
- Compensation policies, processes, and analysis
- Budgeting, payroll, and accounting practices related to compensation and benefits
- Job analysis and evaluation concepts and methods
- Job pricing and pay structures
- Noncash compensation
- Methods to align and benchmark compensation and benefits
- Benefits programs policies, processes, and analysis

A Total Rewards Philosophy and Strategy

People are willing to work in exchange for rewards they receive from the work they do. The objective is to provide a balance between what work is performed and the reward received for doing the work. *Total rewards* includes the financial incentives and rewards (such as direct pay, cash-based incentives, and benefits) as well as nonfinancial incentives and rewards (such as the value of a desirable job as well as a good working environment). Employers strive to offer an attractive compensation package, including a fair base pay, incentives, and benefits, in addition to a good job match and working environment to attract employees and retain them.

Total rewards includes compensation that is both direct and indirect. Direct compensation (e.g., cash) applies to a variety of pay programs that are, in one way or another, cash-based, whereas indirect compensation (e.g., benefits) applies to programs primarily designed to provide recognition and benefits and, therefore, are indirectly cash-based. Common examples of these two types of compensation are listed in Table 7-1.

Some of the direct compensation programs are discretionary, i.e., cash awards, differential pay, and certain bonuses, while others are mandatory and governed by federal, state, and, in some cases, local law and regulation (base pay and incentives). Some of the indirect compensation programs are also discretionary—that is, they are employed at the option of the employer. They include paid vacation, sick leave, paid time off, 401(k) and similar retirement plans, and pensions. Finally, some benefits are mandatory and governed by federal law and regulation. Social Security, workers' compensation, and unemployment insurance are examples. Even discretionary programs are subject to regulation when they are employed.

 NOTE The single difference between direct and indirect compensation is that direct compensation results in some form of a cash reward, while indirect compensation results in some form of a desired benefit for the employee.

Direct Compensation (Cash)	Indirect Compensation (Benefits)
Base pay (wages and salary)	Social Security
Commissions	Unemployment insurance
Bonuses	Disability insurance
Merit pay	Pensions
Piece rate	401(k) and other similar programs
Differential pay	Health care
Cash award	Vacations
Profit sharing	Sick leave
Gainsharing	Paid time off

Table 7-1   Direct and Indirect Compensation

While Table 7-1 lists many common total rewards programs, this is an area of constant innovation in the human resource field. Attracting, retaining, and motivating employees is equally as important as it is challenging. As such, it continues to be an area where new and innovative programs are top of mind for employers. From workplace gyms, wellness coaches, childcare facilities, tuition assistance, and recreation rooms to countless different types of recognition programs, there are many ways to add value to an employee's total rewards package.

Total Rewards and the Budget

Arguably more than any other human resource function, total rewards programs require a close partnership with the organization's finance function. Most compensation and benefits programs have a direct tie to an organization's overall budget because they are expensive. If you take a bird's-eye view of any organizational budget, the compensation and benefits categories probably make up a hefty portion of an organization's overall expenses.

While executives or the human resource department may have a certain total rewards program in mind, all total rewards decisions are ultimately tied to the bottom line. For example, an organization may want to give a $2,000 bonus to each employee in a tight labor market to keep employees from taking a job with another company. However, the cost, or expense, of this bonus must be weighed against current and future revenue for the organization to be sure the organization can afford this program. Smart total rewards decisions are those that align well with the current and future budget for the organization and do their part to attract, motivate, and retain employees.

Federal Laws That Impact Compensation

Federal, state, and local governments play a significant role in the management of employee compensation. The federal government sets minimum standards relative to how much and how employees are paid through the following legislation. Key federal laws that impact compensation are listed in Figure 7-1.

- Davis-Bacon Act (1931)
- Walsh Healey Act (1936)
- Portal-to-Portal Act (1947)
- Service Contract Act (1965)
- Work Opportunity Tax Credit (WOTC)
- Dodd-Frank Wall Street Reform and Consumer Protection Act (2010)

- Copeland "Anti-Kickback" Act (1934)
- Fair Labor Standards Act (FLSA) (1938)
- Equal Pay Act (EPA) (1963)
- Age Discrimination Act (ADA) (1967)
- Lilly Ledbetter Fair Pay Act (2009)
- IRS Intermediate Sanctions (1996)

Figure 7-1 Key federal laws impacting compensation

PART II

NOTE Detailed descriptions of these federal laws and regulations can be found in Chapter 2 of this book.

Federal Agency Nondiscrimination Enforcement

The following federal agencies have a significant legal oversight role in the rules and regulations applicable to total rewards.

United States Department of Labor

The mission of the United States Department of Labor (DOL) is to foster, promote, and develop the welfare of the wage earners, job seekers, and retirees of the United States; improve working conditions; advance opportunities for profitable employment; and assure work-related benefits and rights. The Department of Labor enforces the Fair Labor Standards Act (FLSA), which sets basic minimum wage and overtime pay standards and has created restrictions on the engagement of child labor in the workplace. These standards are enforced by the department's Wage and Hour Division. The Department of Labor's Unemployment Insurance (UI) programs provide unemployment benefits to eligible workers who become unemployed through no fault of their own and meet certain other eligibility requirements.

Fair Labor Standards Act

The employer's responsibilities administering its compensation practices are, for the most part, governed by the Fair Labor Standards Act, commonly referred to as the Wage and Hour Law. The DOL has issued a number of guidelines that explain how the FLSA should be interpreted and administered. This information is available on the Internet at https://www.dol.gov/whd/regs/compliance/hrg.htm as well as in the following bulletins:

- Regulations, Part 541: Defining the Terms "Executive," "Administrative," "Professional," and "Outside Sales"
- Regulations, Part 778: Interpretive Bulletin on Overtime Compensation
- Interpretive Bulletin, Part 785: Hours Worked Under the Fair Labor Standards Act of 1938
- Child Labor Requirements in Nonagricultural Occupations Under the Fair Labor Standards Act[1]
- Recordkeeping Requirements under the Fair Labor Standards Act[2]

HR practitioners should make it a point to carefully read and study these publications. Only the major topics will be summarized in this book.

Exempt and Nonexempt Status

As a human resource professional, you frequently hear the terms *exempt* and *nonexempt*. Determining whether an employee is exempt or nonexempt from the FLSA will have important implications in an employee's total compensation, as well the organization's compensation program. Under the FLSA, most employees must be paid at least the federal minimum wage for all hours worked and overtime at time and a half the employee's regular rate of pay for all hours worked over 40 in a single workweek. Section 13(a) exempts bona fide executive, administrative, professional, outside sales employees, and computer professionals from FLSA's minimum wages and overtime payment requirements, but to do this, employees in exempt positions generally must meet certain salary and job duties tests. Nonexempt jobs generally are those that are covered by FLSA's minimum wage and overtime requirements. Please refer to Table 5-5 in Chapter 5 to review the key salary and job duty tests to determine FLSA exemption.

Incumbents in nonexempt jobs are paid on the basis of time—that is, on an hourly basis. They include most manual workers such as technicians, blue-collar workers, maintenance and construction workers, technicians, laborers, and other semiskilled workers. Job titles do not count. Job content, also called *job duties,* are the sole criteria for determining the applicability of the FLSA's minimum wage and overtime requirements.

There are some limited exceptions to these general rules. As an example, certain types of farm workers, babysitters, and persons hired as companions for the sick or elderly are treated as exceptions to the general minimum wage and overtime requirements.[3]

Equal Employment Opportunity Commission

As we have reviewed in previous chapters, the U.S. Equal Employment Opportunity Commission (EEOC) is responsible for enforcing federal laws that make it illegal to discriminate against a job applicant or an employee because of the person's race, color, religion, sex (including pregnancy), national origin, age (40 or older), disability, or genetic information. It is also illegal to discriminate against a person because the person complained about discrimination, filed a charge of discrimination, or participated in an employment discrimination investigation or lawsuit.

Most employers with at least 15 employees are covered by EEOC laws (20 employees in age discrimination cases). Most labor unions and employment agencies are also covered.

The laws apply to all types of work situations, including hiring, firing, promotions, harassment, training, wages, and benefits.

Office of Federal Contract Compliance Programs

The purpose of the Office of Federal Contract Compliance Programs (OFCCP) is to enforce, for the benefit of job seekers and wage earners, the contractual promise of affirmative action and equal employment opportunity required of those who do business with the federal government.

In carrying out its responsibilities, the OFCCP uses the following enforcement procedures:

- Offers technical assistance to federal contractors and subcontractors to help them understand the regulatory requirements and review process
- Conducts compliance evaluations and complaint investigations of federal contractors and subcontractors' personnel policies and procedures

- Obtains conciliation agreements from contractors and subcontractors who are in violation of regulatory requirements

- Monitors, through periodic compliance reports, contractors' and subcontractors' progress in fulfilling the terms of their agreements

- Forms linkage agreements between contractors and Labor Department job training programs to help employers identify and recruit qualified workers

- Recommends enforcement actions to the Solicitor of Labor

The ultimate sanction for violations is debarment—the loss of a company's federal contracts. Other forms of relief to victims of discrimination may also be available, including back pay for lost wages.

The OFCCP has close working relationships with other departmental agencies, such as the Department of Justice, the Equal Employment Opportunity Commission, and the DOL's Office of the Solicitor, which advises on ethical, legal, and enforcement issues; the Women's Bureau, which emphasizes the needs of working women; the Bureau of Apprenticeship and Training, which establishes policies to promote equal opportunities in the recruitment and selection of apprentices; and the Employment and Training Administration, which administers Labor Department job training programs for current workforce needs.

The OFCCP has a national network of six regional offices, each with district and area offices in major metropolitan centers. It is important to note that many district offices will be shuttered in 2019 because of budget restrictions. The OFCCP focuses its resources on finding and resolving systemic discrimination. The agency has adopted this strategy to

- Prioritize enforcement resources by focusing on the worst offenders

- Encourage employers to engage in self-audits of their employment practices

- Achieve maximum leverage of resources to protect the greatest number of workers from discrimination

The OFCCP enforces Executive Order 11246, including the ban on compensation discrimination, consistent with Title VII's flexible, fact-specific approach to proof. This involves factual investigation and data and legal analyses that allow OFCCP to identify and remedy all forms of compensation discrimination. Compliance officers tailor the compensation investigation and analytical procedures to the facts of the case as appropriate under Title VII. This case-by-case approach to compensation discrimination includes the use of a range of investigative and analytical tools. Statistical analyses, such as multiple regression, and nonstatistical analyses, such as the use of comparators or cohort analysis, are applied as feasible and appropriate given the factual questions and the available data and evidence. Compliance officers seek anecdotal evidence but will investigate and remedy compensation discrimination regardless of whether individual workers believe they are being underpaid or whether the OFCCP has any anecdotal evidence.

This case-by-case approach is designed to eliminate unnecessary barriers to OFC-CP's ability to protect workers from discrimination. It ensures OFCCP fully takes into account explanations or responses from contractors and that OFCCP conducts an analysis tailored to a contractor's compensation systems and practices.

Job Evaluation

The systematic determination of the relative worth of jobs in an organization is known as *job evaluation*. Job evaluation is a critically important pay equity concept applied through a formalized process. It is designed to prevent internal pay inequities as employers create structure within the organization's budget while responding to its workforce expectations. Conducting a job evaluation is an essential first step in creating an appropriate wage structure that accommodates different jobs within an organization while it preserves internal pay equity. Market compensation surveys are frequently used in this process. They are a tool that enables organizations to understand and recognize comparative compensation for positions with an objective of external equity.

Job Evaluation Methods

Job evaluation methods can be nonquantitative or quantitative. The primary objective of a nonquantitative method is to establish a relative hierarchy of jobs based on the jobs' relative worth. Nonquantitative methods often are referred to as *whole-job* methods because they rank jobs as a whole based on their perceived worth without placing a numerical value on each job. An example of a nonquantitative method would be to rank a clerical job below a supervisory job on the basis of their relative, nonquantitative worth.

Quantitative job evaluation methods include *point-factor* and *factor comparison* methods. Quantitative methods evaluate factors on a defined measurable scale and provide a score as the result that is a measurable comparison of one job to another (see Table 7-2). Some examples of job factors that are evaluated in quantitative methods are knowledge required for a job or the level of education needed to perform the job.

Job Ranking

The job ranking method is often called a *whole-job* comparison because it is a comparison of the whole job compared to another whole job rather than a comparison based on each job's measurable factors. Job ranking using the "whole job" method is quick and easy but not precise. It is easy to explain, which is why it is popular, but it leaves unanswered why one job is worth more than another as well as how much of a "gap" exists between jobs.

	Nonquantitative Methods	Quantitative Methods
Job-to job comparison	Job ranking	Factor comparison
Job-to-predetermined-standard comparison	Job classification	Point-factor

Table 7-2 Job Evaluation Methods

When there are a large number of jobs to evaluate, a paired-comparison method of ranking can be used. This method enables each job to be compared with every other job. Jobs are methodically compared to the next job and, depending on the perceived worth, moved up or below the next job. Ultimately, the job with the highest number of upward movements is the highest ranked. Other jobs are ranked accordingly.

Job Classification

Jobs can be compared to an outside scale. This also can be done on a whole-job basis called a *job classification* method. Job classification is the result of grouping jobs into a predetermined number of grades or classifications. Each classification has a class description. The federal government has a classification system known as the General Schedule. The General Schedule (GS) is the predominant pay scale for federal employees, especially employees in professional, technical, administrative, or clerical positions. The system consists of 15 grades, from GS-1, the lowest level, to GS-15, the highest level. There are also 10 steps within each grade. The grade level assigned to a position determines the pay level for that job.

Classes can be further identified by using benchmark jobs that fall into each class. Benchmark jobs have the following characteristics:

- The essential functions and knowledge, skills, and abilities (KSAs) are established and stable.
- They represent the entire range of jobs in each class.
- A significant percentage of workers is employed in these jobs.
- External market rates for these jobs are an acceptable basis for setting wages.

The job classification method is a nonquantitative job evaluation method. In the job classification method, a job may be compared to a similar job or to other jobs in the General Schedule to determine its relative ranking. This is considered a nonquantitative method called a *job-to-predetermined-standard comparison*. Job classification comparisons are a good method when evaluating a large number of jobs and are understandable by employees but may not be effective when jobs overlap, as they only look at whole jobs.

Point-Factor Method

The most commonly used job evaluation method is the *point-factor method*, which uses specific compensable factors as its reference points to measure relative job worth. Compensable factors are significant job characteristics that contribute to the value of the work and organization as a whole. Two well-known systems used to identify compensable factors are

- **The Hay Plan** Uses a standard criteria comprising three compensable factors: know-how, problem-solving, and accountability.
- **The Factor Evaluation System (FES)** Determines levels of duties and responsibilities using a point rating system to evaluate selected positions. Uses weighted factors to address the major position characteristics of responsibility, education/experience, job conditions, physical requirements, supervision, training, and so on.

There are five steps involved in the point-factor method of job evaluation.

1. *Identify key jobs.* These are benchmark jobs, not necessarily the most important jobs in the organization but jobs that are equitably paid, stable, and well defined.

2. *Identify the compensable factors.* These are the factors that will be used to distinguish one job from another. Six to eight factors are generally sufficient. Experience, responsibility, and education are most often used. Other factors that can be considered, depending on their general applicability, include physical demands, mental requirements, skill, working conditions, and supervisory responsibilities.

3. *Weight the factors according to their overall worth.* Usually, the most heavily weighted factors are knowledge, responsibility, experience, education, degree of difficulty, and supervisory responsibilities.

4. *Divide each job factor into degrees that range from high to low.* Assign points to each degree. The number of points assigned to each degree should correspond with the weighting of the factors. As an example, if the factor for skill is weighted 40 percent, the factor of working conditions is weighted 10 percent, and both factors have five degrees, then degree two for skill should have four times as many points as degree two for working conditions.

5. *The final result will be a table (see Table 7-3) that gives a complete range of points from 50 (the least number, column 1) to 200 (the most, column 5).* Based on the assigned point values, the job in this example is 126 on a scale of 50 to 200 points. Points usually determine the pay grade to which the job will be assigned.

Point-Factor Job Evaluation Method						
Compensable Factor	**Weighted Percentage**	**Degrees/Points**				
		1	2	3	4	5
Skill	(40%)	20	32	48	72	100
Responsibility	(30%)	15	24	36	54	75
Effort	(20%)	10	16	24	36	50
Working conditions	(10%)	5	8	12	18	25

Example: Machine Operator	**Compensable Factor**	**Degree**	**Points**
	Skill	3	48
	Responsibility	2	24
	Effort	4	36
	Working Conditions	4	18
	Total points		*126*

Table 7-3 Point-Factor Job Evaluation Method

Factor Comparison Method

The *factor comparison method* is more complex than the ranking, classification, and point-factor methods and is rarely used. It involves ranking each job by each compensable factor and then, as an additional step, identifying dollar values for each level of each factor to develop an actual pay rate for the evaluated job.

The factor comparison method is most often used in union negotiations as part of a labor contract and in limited cases where wages are steady over a period of time and the organization uses a flat rate for each job.

Market-Based Evaluation

A market-rate system is not a true job evaluation system, but in some cases, market value can be used to price jobs—particularly when the organization is sensitive to competition. These prevailing rates are used to represent the relative worth of the jobs. In this approach, key jobs are measured and valued against the market, and the remaining jobs are inserted into a hierarchy based on their whole-job comparison to the benchmark jobs.

 NOTE When matching a job with the competition, it is important to compare duties, scope, and reporting relationships, but not titles, because they are often misleading.

Market-based evaluation can be particularly beneficial when an organization has similar jobs in various locations throughout the United States. The disadvantage of a market-based evaluation is that the data will be reliable only when gathered for a significant number of jobs in the organization. Market-based evaluation results are more vulnerable to legal challenge than job-content approaches. Another disadvantage is that market-based evaluations do not recognize internal job value and, as a result, are more likely to lead to discontent from within the organization.

Pay Surveys

Many organizations rely on pay surveys as a systematic way to collect, evaluate, and classify their jobs, adjust pay structures, and provide market information to top management. Pay surveys collect data on prevailing market rates and provide information such as starting wage rates, base pay, pay ranges, overtime pay, shift differentials, and incentive pay plans.

Options to collecting pay survey data include whether the survey should be conducted internally or gathered externally. Organizations that want to maintain maximum control over their pay information often choose to sponsor a custom survey. The advantage of this approach is that the organization has the ability to design the survey, manage its administration, do its own data analysis, and customize its report specifically for its own use. Another advantage is that the organization is able to maximize its control over the transfer of data, thereby reducing the risk of an inappropriate disclosure of highly sensitive confidential information.

While choosing to conduct its own internal survey, an organization should contract with an outside consulting group or independent consultant to design the survey and process the data received in a confidential manner. Using an outside person or group relieves pressure on the organization and ensures compliance with Department of Justice antitrust guidelines.

External surveys have different options. National surveys are widely available through the U.S. Department of Labor and the Bureau of Labor Statistics. Many professional groups such as the Society of Human Resource Management (SHRM) and consulting firms conduct surveys of wage and job data for a wide range of professions and organizations.

Data Analysis

Organizations have an interest in survey data based on their market exposure, competition, their product or service, and employees. To be accurate, survey data must be verified and often aged, leveled, and factored for geography.

In the Trenches

Compensation Surveys: The Good, the Bad, and Really?

Compensation surveys are essential tools for establishing the pay level of positions and staying competitive in the marketplace. In the "golden gilded age" of comp management (1990s to early 2000s), HR was delighted with the increased availability and access to market data, thanks to technology. Compensation information was enabling companies to balance their internal equity pay structures with what the local market was providing for high-demand talent. The data was imperfect, but it was credible when HR would wave a ream of data to support their conclusions for talent bleeding (the loss of key and high-potential employees). That was the *good*: ease of accessing data timely and directly. The cost savings were great as well because high-powered consultancy firms were no longer needed to gather information.

In more recent decades, the focus of compensation surveys has shifted to calibrating pay levels primarily with the external market and that in turn has created enormous pressure to obtain and ensure the data is accurate, timely, and an "apple-to-apple" comparison in terms of usefulness. Today there are thousands of published surveys that an HR professional can obtain for various job families, industries, geographical areas, and just about everything else you can sort data on. So, there is a wealth of information at your fingertips, yet beware: *just because you read it on the Internet, doesn't mean it's true.* And here comes *the bad*: only a fraction of companies participate in surveys. There are millions of organizations, large and small, in the United States, yet a low percentage of them participate in compensation surveys. A survey that has 2,500 participants might sound great, yet 2,500 participants represent less than 1 percent of all companies that have

(continued)

more than 500 employees. What is most disturbing is that more companies use compensation survey data than contribute to the surveys as participants. Additionally, those companies participating are normally participating in multiple surveys, causing data to be two-dimensional.

Participation is the key to obtaining quality data, and all HR professionals have a responsibility for feeding the data that calibrates our economies. Data needs to be accurate, reliable, and timely for the critical needs of attracting or retaining human capital. Just think what a mere 10 percent increase in participation would create—a more robust data source for decision-makers to rely on in organizations. So, participate, participate, participate!

Measurement Terms   The following are terms that are used to refine the accuracy of survey data:

- **Aging**   This is a technique used to make outdated data current, a phenomenon that regularly occurs with printed data as a result of the time lapse between when the data is collected, organized, printed, and published. An example of aging occurs when pay movement or increases average 1.5 percent a year. If you use a pay survey that is one year old, to be reasonably accurate, you would increase the survey data by 1.5 percent.

- **Leveling**   Pay surveys provide summary descriptions of each job surveyed. In many cases, this description is close but not an exact match with the organization's job. To accommodate this separation between the two jobs, a leveling technique is used. Leveling consists of adjusting the survey number by an appropriate percentage needed to achieve a match. As an example, an organization's Engineering I job description indicates an approximate 10 percent less scope of responsibility than described in the same job in a pay survey. Reducing the pay survey job data with a 10 percent reduction would be an appropriate technique to provide an accurate match.

- **Geography**   While many surveys are developed with a specifically described geographical location identified, in cases where this is not done, it would be appropriate to determine the percent difference in job value for a given location and factor that into the comparison.

Frequency Distribution and Tables   The following are techniques used to organize data in a logical manner for ease and accuracy of interpretation:

- **Frequency distribution**   This is a listing of grouped pay data from lowest to highest.

- **Frequency tables**   This is the number of workers in a particular job classification and their pay data.

	Survey	Mean Pay	Number of Participants
Table 7-4	A	$40,000	5
Weighted and	B	$25,000	2
Unweighted	C	$35,000	4
Mean Calculation	D	$50,000	1
	Total	$150,000	12

Measures of Central Tendency   Another way to measure pay data involves the four standard measures of central tendency: mean (average), weighted average, median, and mode.

- **Mean (average)**   The arithmetic average or mean is the average value arrived at by giving equal weight to every participant's actual pay. This method is appropriate when the data to be determined is the average pay for a given job as opposed to actual pay levels applicable to that job. This figure is also known as the *unweighted average*.

- **Weighted average**   This number provides an average result considering the number of participants and each participant's pay. This figure is also known as the *weighted average*.

  Based on the data shown in Table 7-4:

  - The unweighted mean (average) pay is $37,500 ($150,000 ÷ 4 organizational participants A, B, C, and D).
  - The weighted mean (weighted average) is $36,666.66 ($440,000 total pay of all individual participants ÷ 12 participants).

- **Median**   This number is sometimes referred to in pay surveys as the *50th percentile*. This is the middle number in a range. The median is calculated by averaging the two middle numbers in a range when the range data is sorted from lowest to highest.

- **Mode**   This is the most frequently appearing number ("wage" in a pay survey) in a range.

Pay Structure

After an organization has determined its relative internal job values—i.e., job evaluation—and collected appropriate market survey data through pay surveys, work begins on developing the organization's pay structure, including creating pay grades and establishing pay ranges. An organization's pay structure helps set the baseline for the appropriate range of pay for each job at an organization and often includes guidelines on how compensation decisions or changes are made.

Pay Grades

Pay grades, or job groups, are the way an organization organizes jobs of similar values. The valuation is a result of the job evaluation process. Jobs, even though dissimilar in function, of the same or comparatively the same value, are paid within the same pay grade.

No fixed rules apply to creating pay grades; rather, the number of pay grades and their structure are more of a reflection of organizational structure and philosophy. Issues that should be considered include the following:

- The size and structure of the organization
- The "distance" between the lowest and the highest job in the organization
- The organization's pay increase and promotion policy
- The grouping of nonexempt and exempt jobs as well as job families (i.e., clerical, technical, professional, supervisory, and management jobs)
- Creating sufficient grades to permit distinguishing difficulty levels but not so many that the difference between adjoining grades is insignificant

Well-structured pay grades enable management to develop a well-coordinated pay system rather than having to create a separate pay range for each job.

Pay Ranges

Pay ranges establish the upper and lower boundaries of each pay grade. Market data for a benchmark job (ideally, a "key" job that will link to market value) in each pay range helps to determine the range midpoint. The range spread reflects the equal dispersion of pay on either side of the midpoint to the lower and upper range boundaries.

Quartiles and Percentiles

Quartiles and percentiles show dispersion of data throughout a range. These are commonly recognized reference points an organization uses to measure its position against the market as well as for internal compensation management purposes.

Range Spread Calculation

Range spread is calculated by subtracting the range minimum from the range maximum and dividing that figure by the range minimum. Range spread is expressed as a percentage.

$$\frac{Maximum - Minimum}{Minimum}$$

Example: The range spread for a pay range with a $30,000 minimum and a $45,000 maximum would be as follows:

$$\frac{\$45,000 - \$30,000}{\$30,000}$$

$$= 50\%$$

Range Spreads

The range spread is the dispersion of pay from the lowest boundary to the highest boundary of a pay range.

Typical range spreads in organizations are:

- **Nonexempt jobs**   40%
- **Exempt jobs**   50%
- **Executive jobs**   60%

Generally, lower-level jobs have a narrow range between minimum and maximum pay ranges. Jobs at a lower level tend to be more skill-based, which provides for more movement opportunity than higher levels where jobs are more knowledge-based and progression is slower.

Ranges should overlap so that progression is steady within a pay grade; as a worker's pay increases with movement to a higher range quartile, the opportunity for managed movement is possible in a measured way.

There also should be a large enough distance between range midpoints so that pay compression between a lower pay grade and a high pay grade does not occur.

Broadbanding

Broadbanding combines several pay grades or job classifications with narrow range spreads with a single band with a wider spread. Organizations usually adopt broadbanding as a way to simplify their pay levels and reduce management oversight requirements. As a result, broadbanding typically is more popular in large organizations than smaller ones.

While broadbanding has some advantages, it also has some disadvantages. In some cases, broadbanding does not work well with the organization's compensation philosophy. This is particularly true in organizations that focus on promotional opportunities. The reduction of pay grades as a result of broadbanding correspondingly reduces the number of opportunities for promotion. Another disadvantage of broadbanding is the exposure employers receive under the Equal Pay Act. Because broadbanding creates large compensation spreads within a pay band, it is easy to have men and women paid quite differently for the same work.

Compa-ratios

Compa-ratios are indicators of how wages match, lead, or lag the midpoint, normally an indicator of market value. Compa-ratios are computed by dividing the worker's pay rate by the midpoint of the pay range.

The compa-ratio formula is: $\text{Compa-ratio} = \dfrac{\text{Pay rate}}{\text{Midpoint}}$

Compa-ratios less than 100 percent (usually expressed as a compa-ratio less than 1.00) mean the worker is paid less than the midpoint of the range. Compa-ratios above 100 percent (1.00) mean that wages exceed the midpoint.

Base Pay Systems

After an organization has analyzed, evaluated, and priced its jobs, as well as designed its pay structure, the next step is to determine a type of base pay system that will help attract, motivate, and retain employees. In most cases, employees receive some type of base pay, either as an hourly wage (paid to hourly employees) or as a salary (a fixed wage that doesn't change regardless of the hours worked). Base pay system choices include single or flat-rate systems, time-based step rate systems, performance-based merit pay systems, productivity-based systems, and person-based systems. Each of these systems is designed to best achieve the objectives of attracting, motivating, and retaining employees, each under a different set of circumstances.

Single or Flat-Rate System

In the single, or flat-rate, system, each worker in the same job has the same rate of pay regardless of seniority or job performance. This pay system is most commonly found in elected public-sector jobs or in a union setting. The single pay rate (or flat pay rate) usually is directly linked to an applicable market survey. This system is also used as a training rate under circumstances when the worker is being trained for a job.

Time-Based Step Rate System

The time-based step rate system bases the employee's pay rate on the length of time in the job. Pay increases are published in advance on the basis of time. Increases occur on a predetermined schedule. This system has three variations, as described in the sections that follow.

Automatic Step Rate

In the automatic step rate system, the pay range is divided into several steps, each a predetermined range apart. At the prescribed time interval, each employee with the required seniority receives a one-step pay increase. This system is common in public-sector jobs and in a union environment.

Step Rate with Performance Considerations

The step rate with performance considerations system is similar to the automatic system except that performance can influence the size or timing of the pay increase.

Combination Step Rate and Performance

In the combination step rate and performance system, employees receive step rate increases up to the established job rate. Above this level, increases are granted only for superior job performance. To work, this system requires a supporting performance

Performance Rating	1st Quartile	2nd Quartile	3rd Quartile	4th Quartile
Exceeds Performance Objectives	6–7%	5–6%	4–5%	3–4%
Meets Performance Objectives	4–5%	3–4%	2–3%	1–2%
Needs Improvement	2–3%	1–2%	0–1%	0%

Table 7-5   Merit Guidelines Example

appraisal program as well as good communication and understanding by the workers paid under this system.

Performance-Based Merit Pay System

The performance-based merit pay system is based on an employee's individual job performance. A performance-based pay system is often referred to as *merit pay* or *pay for performance*. In this system, employees are typically hired at or near the minimum for their applicable pay range. Pay increases are normally awarded on an annual basis (or annualized if awarded on other than an annual basis) and influenced by the individual's overall job performance. A document identifying the percent pay increase linked to levels of performance and the individual's position in the applicable pay range is communicated to employees as an incentive to increase their performance, thereby earning a higher percentage increase. This document is known as *merit guidelines*. A merit guidelines example is illustrated in Table 7-5.

To be effective, the merit pay system must be understood by employees affected by the system. In addition to the merit pay system, a clearly stated performance appraisal program is required to support the merit pay system. Key points that should be addressed in designing and implementing an effective merit pay system include those depicted in Table 7-6.

Merit Pay System	Performance Appraisal Program
Merit pay figures within quartiles can be either a range or a single number depending on the experience of the raters.	Performance ratings should clearly link to documented pre-agreed performance objectives.
Use a range for experienced raters, a single number for inexperienced raters.	Performance ratings are for overall performance.
Use one standard (range) or the other (single number) for the entire program.	Not more than three performance levels should be used (as shown).
Gap between one performance level and the next should be at least 2 percent to be a significant incentive.	"Needs Improvement" ratings should be placed into a Performance Improvement Program with a defined period (usually not more than 90 days) to improve overall performance.

Table 7-6   Merit Pay and Performance Appraisal Key Points

Productivity-Based System

In the productivity-based system, pay is determined by the employee's output. This system is mostly used on an assembly line in a manufacturing environment. The following sections describe two types of productivity-based systems.

Straight Piece Rate System

With the straight piece rate system, the employee receives a base rate of pay and is awarded additional compensation for the amount of output produced.

Differential Piece Rate System

In the differential piece rate system, the employee receives one rate of pay up to the production standard and a higher rate of pay when the standard is exceeded.

 NOTE Both the straight piece system and the differential piece rate system focus on quantity rather than quality. As a result, other quality control programs may be required to ensure the required quality standard is met. It is important to consider whether your program is incentivizing the kind of results you want.

Person-Based System

In the person-based system, employee capabilities, rather than how the job is performed, determine the employee's pay. For example, two employees do the same work, but one employee with a higher level of skill and experience receives more pay. There are three types of person-based systems, as described in the sections that follow.

Knowledge-Based Systems

In the knowledge-based system, a person's pay is based on the level of knowledge he or she has in a particular field. This system is often used in the learned professions such as lawyers and doctors.

Skill-Based Systems

Employees paid in the skill-based system are paid for the number and depth of skills that they have that are applicable to their job. Heavy equipment operators are typically paid in this system.

Competency-Based Systems

In the competency-based system, pay is linked to the level at which an employee can perform in a recognized competency. In HR, a professional with specialty skills in organizational development or labor relations will typically be paid for his or her competency—for example, organizational development or labor relations, in the HR field.

Variations in Pay

Pay ranges must be periodically evaluated and adjusted to reflect organizational and market changes. Red circle rates, green circle rates, and cost of living adjustments are some of the techniques used to adjust to these changes.

Red Circle Rates

Organizations use red circle rates as a method to increase an employee's pay to a new rate higher than the maximum for the assigned pay range. This situation occurs more often in smaller organizations where promotional opportunities may be limited. When this happens, an employee's next pay raise indicated by the organization's merit guidelines might place the new pay level above the maximum for the applicable pay range.

An example of this is the accounting manager who is paid $95,000 per year and is currently 5 percent from the top of the range. Based on job performance, the manager would be entitled to a 7 percent increase. The next promotion step is the CFO job. In this case, the company may decide to process the 7 percent increase as a red circle rate 2 percent above the range maximum for an accounting manager. Typically, when this is done, the new pay level is frozen until the maximum of the pay range moves upward to exceed the accounting manager's pay level. This would usually happen when the comparative market numbers increase, thereby allowing a change to the pay range.

Green Circle Rates

Green circle rates occur when a new employee is hired at a pay rate lower than the minimum rate for the applicable grade. It can also happen when a "fast-track" employee is promoted to a new job in a high pay grade under circumstances where the percentage pay increase needed to reach the new grade is excessive and might create an unwanted precedent. In this case, the pay increase may result in a pay level below the minimum level of the new pay grade, thus creating a "green circle rate."

Situations such as this should be avoided whenever possible and should be allowed only as a last resort because they can create serious morale issues and, even worse, may create an arguable case of pay discrimination. In any case, such actions should be carefully considered and justified in writing after all of the possible consequences are considered.

Cost-of-Living Adjustments

A cost-of-living adjustment is a pay increase given to all employees on the basis of market pressure, usually measured against the consumer price index (CPI), which is a measure of the price of goods and services in a given area over a period of time.

COLAs can be paid as a lump sum or over a period of time and usually are a negotiated practice in a unionized environment argued on the basis that they simply reflect the increased cost of living. This argument might be more persuasive during periods of high inflation.

Nonunion employers typically resist the pressure to provide COLAs because, once started, they are difficult to stop, thereby diminishing the organization's ability to control its labor costs.

Types of Pay Increases

Pay increases differ depending on the circumstances and the purpose for which they are given. The following are typical pay increases.

General Pay Increases

In some limited circumstances, nonunion employers may want to provide a general pay increase to their employees without the precedent-setting basis of a COLA. A general pay increase is a pay increase given to all employees regardless of their job performance and not linked to market pressures. Usually, the only criteria is the desire to provide all employees with a pay increase subject only to the ability to fund the increase.

Seniority Pay Increases

Whenever a pay increase is given based solely on length of service, it is considered a seniority pay increase. As with a general pay increase, it is simply a basis on which to award a pay increase. Seniority pay increases are common in a unionized setting. In a nonunion setting, pay increases usually combine seniority with performance.

Lump-Sum Increases

A lump-sum increase can be either a stand-alone performance bonus or part of an annual pay increase. Because a lump-sum increase is a single lump-sum payment, it has some advantages that other pay increases don't have. Most other pay increases impact a series of wage and benefits actions such as base wage, overtime, shift differentials, sick leave, vacation pay, and holiday pay in that each increases in proportion to the size of the increase. This is because most pay increases are added to base pay and paid over a number of pay periods in a year, in other words, creating a proportional increase in all of these wage and benefits categories.

A lump-sum increase is a single lump-sum payment subject to applicable tax and withholding that is not added to the employee's base rate of pay because of its character as a single lump-sum payment. This provides the full cash payment to the employee in a single lump-sum payment.

 NOTE In a red circle rate situation, the lump-sum increase can be used for the amount that would otherwise exceed the range maximum without increasing the employee's base rate of pay beyond the range maximum.

Market-Based Increases

When employee retention is threatened because employee pay is not competitive with the market, employers can create market-based increases to adjust an employee's pay by better matching market levels.

> **NOTE** Market-based pay increases are sometimes called *equity increases*.

Pay Differentials

A pay differential is additional compensation paid to an employee as an incentive to accept what would normally be considered adverse working conditions, usually based on time, location, or situational conditions. The same pay differential is paid to all employees under the same circumstances or conditions. Pay differentials benefit the employer by incentivizing employees to accept work they might not otherwise accept; they benefit the employee as additional compensation for accepting the work.

Premium Pay

Some employers pay premium pay, i.e., overtime, at a higher rate than required by law for working paid holidays or vacation days, for the sixth or seventh day of work in a single workweek, or after eight hours in a day. Premium pay for these working conditions may be company policy, required by a union contract, or required by state law, as it is in California.

> **NOTE** As a matter of principle, the Fair Labor Standards Act recognizes that when state and federal law conflict, the entitlement that is most beneficial or protective for the employee prevails.

Hazard Pay

The hazard pay type of differential pay occurs when employees are called to work under adverse conditions either caused by the environment or because of the circumstances. Work generally considered putting an employee at risk for safety or health purposes would typically qualify for hazard pay differential.

Travel Pay

Hourly (nonexempt) employees typically receive travel pay for time traveling between one location and another under other than routine conditions. Under the Portal-to-Portal Act, normal commute time to and from work is not compensable time, but time traveling from one work location to another normally qualifies for travel pay unless the time spent traveling is *de minimis*.

Labor Cost Differentials

Employers differentially structure their local compensation plans to match their competition. In areas where labor rates are high, without a locally differentiating compensation program, employers will be unable to compete for the best available talent, thereby sacrificing productivity. In the opposite situation where local labor rates are low, without a locally deferential program, employers increase their labor costs over the local market, thereby losing a competitive advantage.

Geographic-Based Differential Pay

Geographic-based differential pay is a type of differential pay that responds to geographic issues associated with where the employee works. Companies with locations in multiple regions of the United States have the challenge of customizing their compensation programs to be locally competitive. The result is a differentially structured pay program designed to respond to the local market in a way that is consistent with the company's strategic objectives.

Location-Based Differentials

Sometimes locations are undesirable because of their remoteness, a lack of amenities, climatic conditions, and other adverse conditions. To attract workers, in extreme cases employers will add a location-based differential to the employee's pay package.

Time-Based Differential Pay

Sometimes called *shift pay,* generally time-based differential pay rewards the employee who works hours normally considered undesirable such as a night shift or hours that are in addition to the employee's regular work schedule, i.e., overtime. Time-based differential pay may be a specified amount per hour or a percentage of the employee's regular rate of pay. Except for overtime, federal law does not legally require employers to pay a differential rate of pay, although state requirements may differ.

Overtime Pay

The Fair Labor Standards Act requires employers to pay nonexempt employees one and a half times their regular rate of pay when they work more than 40 hours in a single workweek.

Some employers pay more than the legally required time-and-a-half rate for overtime. The FLSA allows employers, at their discretion, to pay more than the FLSA requires; they may not pay less.

 NOTE   A workweek is a fixed and regularly recurring period of 168 hours, or seven consecutive 24-hour periods.

Regular Rate of Pay

The FLSA requires employers to pay overtime based on an employee's regular rate of pay. Where an employee in a single workweek works at two or more different types of work for which different straight-time rates have been established, the regular rate for that week is the weighted average of such rates. That is, the earnings from all such rates are added together, and this total is then divided by the total number of hours worked at all jobs. In addition, section 7(g)(2) of the FLSA allows, under specified conditions, the computation of overtime pay based on one and a half times the hourly rate in effect when the overtime work is performed. The requirements for computing overtime pay pursuant to section 7(g)(2) are prescribed in 29 CFR 778.415 through 778.421.

Where noncash payments are made to employees in the form of goods or facilities, the reasonable cost to the employer or fair value of such goods or facilities must be included in the regular rate.

Payroll

Payroll is a function that directly impacts compensation and thereby traditionally affects every employee in the organization. It has traditionally been treated as an administrative function responsible for issuing paychecks and maintaining payroll records. Today's payroll function is responsible for the following:

- Legal compliance (federal, state, and local)
- Ongoing periodic reporting
- Record generation and maintenance
- Control and security

Payroll integration, the cost of legally compliant payroll services, and the quality of services are all issues that influence the organization's approach to its payroll function. Payroll may be an in-house function, an outsourced function, or some combination of these approaches. In some cases, payroll responsibility may be an HR responsibility, although, in most cases, payroll is part of the organization's finance and accounting function. In any case, payroll extensively interacts with HR, and vice versa.

Most organizations rely on a combination of technology and automation in an effort to reduce direct payroll costs and the amount of transactional work involved. Employees expect their paychecks to be issued in the correct amount and on time. Their expectations are reinforced by a multitude of legal requirements associated with payroll.

Payroll Administration

Administering the payroll function is complex given the multitude of requirements that must be met, compliance with federal, state, and local legal requirements being chief among the requirements that must be met. Coupled with issuing paychecks, this administrative burden is significant.

Employers are required to keep a master file of employment records for the federal government in addition to an accurate master file to track their labor costs and maintain an organized pay process. This master file contains information that includes the following:

- Personal data on each employee (including name, gender, birth date, and Social Security number)

- Employment data (including date of hire, hours worked per day and per week, and employee's regular rate of pay)

- Tax and payroll data on each employee (including Form W-4 data, allowances claimed, marital status, time records, and Form W-2 for individual income tax purposes)

- Form 1099 for independent contractors who earn $600 or more for services they provide

- Payroll data for the organization, including Form 941, the employer's quarterly federal tax form with local wages subject to federal, state, and local income taxes; total income; Social Security and Medicare tax withheld; payroll ledgers, worksheets, and reconciliation; copies of payroll tax deposit information; and Form W-3 (Transmittal of Wage and Tax Statements sent to the Social Security Administration)

Under the Fair Labor Standards Act (FLSA) and the Age Discrimination in Employment Act (ADEA), employers must retain payroll records for three years. States may have longer retention requirements. Employers may want to retain payroll records at least as long as the applicable state statute of limitations for contracts claims.

After an employee's termination of employment, payroll records should include a copy of the termination record as well as all wages, salaries, commissions, and any other compensation paid to the employee.

Payroll Systems

Most organizations use a computerized payroll system either outsourced or linked to an in-house server as part of an online or networked system. A customized system often includes integrated human resource information system (HRIS) and payroll capabilities. This minimizes the chance for data processing errors, eliminates redundancies, and ensures the HRIS and payroll systems are current and synchronized.

Other issues that should be considered include the following:

- The system's capability to service the organization's needs. Employees depend on the payroll system to receive timely and accurate paychecks; the organization needs a cost-efficient system that can reliably and dependably meet all of its payroll requirements.

- A good payroll system includes a series of checks and balances designed to accurately produce results with the capabilities to detect error, fraud, or any misuse of data.

- The HRIS and the payroll systems must be compatible. They must be able to share data and make changes to data so that records in one system are accurately and timely reflected in the other system.

- Outsourced payroll services are designed to provide the advantage of overall cost savings, better payroll expertise, accuracy, reliability, and accountability. Choosing a payroll vendor is an important decision that must be carefully made given the significance of the payroll function and, by extension, its link to the HRIS, both critically important to the organization.

Payroll Issue Resolution

With an employee's compensation being the primary motivator to come to work each day, it goes without saying how important it is for paychecks to be correct. When a payroll or HRIS system is implemented, the HR or payroll administrator is often heavily involved in the system setup to ensure that the system provider or in-house team processing payroll is well versed on all state and legal requirements and has accurately input key information like Social Security numbers or bank account information for direct deposit of paychecks. Even one small error or mistake that delays an employee's pay can understandably be a stressful situation. It is good practice to check and recheck any payroll information that you, the reader, might handle in your position and work with senior human resource professionals at your organization to develop a policy for quickly rectifying payroll mistakes or concerns.

Objectives of Benefits

Benefit programs, as we discussed at the beginning of the chapter, also called *indirect compensation,* are designed to promote organizational loyalty, reward continued employment, enable employees to live healthy lives, help them care for their families, and help provide for retirement benefits.

In addition to helping employees, benefits programs help employers to

- Attract and retain talent
- Increase the employee's loyalty and commitment to the organization
- Provide tax-advantaged health and welfare benefits

Federal Legislation Impacting Benefits

Federal, state, and local government play a significant role in the management of compensation, including benefits programs. It is important to know and understand the impact that applicable laws, rules, and regulations have on employer benefits (see Figure 7-2). Laws that affect the tax treatment of benefits are listed in Figure 7-3.

- Employee Retirement Income Security Act (ERISA) (1974)

- Consolidated Omnibus Budget Reconciliation Act (COBRA) (1986)

- Older Worker's Benefit Protection Act (OWBPA) (1990)

- Family and Medical Leave Act (FMLA) (1993)

- Mental Health Parity Act (MHPA) (1996)

- Pension Protection Act (PPA) (2006)

- Retirement Equity Act (REI) (1984)

- Health Insurance Portability and Accountability Act (HIPAA) (1996)

- Unemployment Compensation Amendments (UCA) (1992)

- Uniformed Services Employment and Reemployment Rights Act (USERRA) (1994)

- Genetic Information Nondiscrimination Act (GINA) (2008)

- Patient Protection and Affordable Care Act (PPACA) (2010)

Figure 7-2   Key federal laws impacting benefits

Chapter 2 of this book addresses the provisions of all of the laws identified in Figures 7-2 and 7-3 and discusses their impact on employer benefits programs.

Other related federal legislation includes the following:

- Securities and Exchange Act
- Sarbanes-Oxley Act

Tax and Accounting Organizations with Benefits Oversight

Private and public tax and accounting organizations play a significant role in affecting employee benefits programs. These organizations include those discussed in the sections that follow.

- Revenue Act (1978)

- Omnibus Budget Reconciliation Act (OBRA) (1993)

- Tax Relief Act (TRA) (1997)

- Tax Reform Act (1986)

- Small Business Job Protection Act (SBJPA) (1996)

- Economic Growth and Tax Relief Reconciliation Act (EGTRRA) (2001)

Figure 7-3   Key federal laws that affect the tax treatment of benefits

U.S. Internal Revenue Service

The Internal Revenue Service (IRS) is the revenue service of the United States federal government. It is a bureau under the Department of the Treasury and is responsible for collecting taxes and for interpreting and enforcing the Internal Revenue Code. Its regulations effectively influence the types of benefits plans that employers can provide to their employees and the manner in which they fund and operate these plans.

Pension Benefit Guaranty Corporation

The Pension Benefit Guaranty Corporation (PBGC) is an independent agency of the U.S. government that was created by the Employee Retirement Income Security Act (ERISA) of 1974. Its purpose is to encourage the continuation and maintenance of voluntary defined benefit pension plans, ensure the timely and uninterrupted payment of pension benefits to retirees, and keep pension insurance premiums at the lowest level necessary to carry out its operations. The PBGC is not funded by general tax revenues. Rather, its funds come from insurance premiums paid by sponsors of defined benefit plans—in some cases, assets held by pension plans it takes over, recoveries of unfunded pension liabilities, and investment income.

Financial Accounting Standards Board

The Financial Accounting Standards Board (FASB) is a private, not-for-profit organization whose primary purpose is to develop generally accepted accounting principles (GAAP) in the public's interest within the United States. The Securities and Exchange Commission (SEC) designated the FASB as the organization responsible for setting accounting standards for public companies in the United States. In this role, the FASB-established standards impact the accounting practices of public companies and how they report their financial information to their shareholders.

Government-Mandated Benefits

Some benefits are mandated by law. They must be provided and cannot be altered by the employer even when the employer may feel they are not necessary. Currently, federal law mandates Social Security/Medicare, healthcare under the Patient Protection and Affordable Care Act (PPACA), unemployment insurance, workers' compensation, COBRA, and FMLA. The PPACA, COBRA, and FMLA are described in detail in Chapter 2.

Social Security

Social Security originally was intended to provide retirement income for older workers. It has since expanded to include retirement, disability, death, and survivors' benefits. For tax purposes, the system is split into two programs, Social Security and Medicare. To qualify for Social Security, a person must earn a number of "quarters," usually 40 quarters, which takes at least ten years.

There is no age limit for Social Security. Employees who continue to work while receiving Social Security payments must also pay into it. The employer matches the employee's contributions; independent contractors and self-employed individuals pay both the employer's and employee's shares of the tax. The amount of monthly retirement income depends on the individual's average earnings on jobs covered by Social Security. Workers can begin to receive reduced benefits at age 62 but are entitled to full benefits if they wait until their retirement age, which is determined on a graduated scale.

Disability Benefits

Disability benefits are paid to workers if they have a medically determined physical or mental impairment that keeps them from working for at least five months and is expected to continue to at least one year or result in death. There is a five-month waiting period before monthly benefits start.

Survivor Benefits

Survivor benefits are paid monthly to eligible dependents who are the following:

- A surviving spouse age 60 or older (50 if disabled)
- A surviving spouse at any age caring for a child under the age of 16 or disabled
- Unmarried children under age 18
- Disabled children of any age if disabled before age 22
- Dependent parents age 62 or older

Medicare

Medicare covers hospital insurance (Part A) and voluntary supplemental medical insurance (Part B) for people who reach age 65. If an employer provides health insurance coverage, the employer's health plan must be the primary healthcare plan for active employees. If the individual is retired, Medicare is the primary carrier, and the employer's insurance is secondary. If the employer has fewer than 20 employees, Medicare can be primary for employees age 65 and older.

Medicare provides voluntary Part C (Medicare Advantage Plans). These plans allow an individual to participate in several optional healthcare delivery systems such as HMOs and PPOs, which offer extra coverage beyond Parts A and B and usually include prescription drug coverage.

Part D (prescription benefits) coverage is also optionally provided by private companies, but all Medicare plans must provide a minimum standard level of coverage. Benefits vary depending on the drug plan selected.

EEOC Ruling on Medicare

Effective December 26, 2007, an EEOC ruling allows employers to reduce health benefits for Medicare-eligible retirees to avoid paying premiums that are higher than those paid for retirees not covered by Medicare. If an employer provides retiree health benefits, the health insurance benefits received by Medicare-eligible retirees can be the same, or cost the same, as health insurance benefits received by younger retirees.

Unemployment Insurance

Unemployment insurance (UI) is a federally mandated program administered by the states that provides unemployment benefits to eligible workers who are unemployed through no fault of their own and who meet other eligibility requirements of applicable state law. UI benefits are designed to provide temporary financial assistance to unemployed workers. Each state administers its own unemployment insurance program within guidelines established by federal law. Eligibility for unemployment insurance, benefit amounts, and the length of time benefits are available are determined by state law. In the majority of states, benefit funding is based solely on a tax imposed on employers. The amount a person receives is based on the person's salary up to a monthly maximum amount.

Eligibility

To qualify for UI, individuals must meet requirements for wages earned or time worked during an established period of time referred to as the *base period*. In most cases, the individual must be unemployed through no fault of his or her own, must be available and actively seeking work, cannot be terminated for misconduct, and must not be unemployed because of a labor dispute.

Individuals must file weekly or biweekly claims and respond to questions concerning their continuing unemployment. Any job offers or refusal of work must be reported for the period claimed.

Duration

Most states grant UI benefits for up to 26 weeks, but this is often extended during periods of high unemployment by Congress with the approval of the U.S. president.

Workers' Compensation

Workers' compensation is a type of insurance paid for by the employer that provides wage replacement income and medical care benefits to employees who suffer work-related injuries or illnesses in return for giving up the employee's right to sue his or her employer for negligence. Benefits are regulated by the states, not the federal government. Individual states prescribe the rules governing coverage, eligibility, types of benefits, and the funding of benefits.

Work-Related Disability

Workers' compensation defines a work-related disability as a physical condition that can result in an accident or illness and is caused, aggravated, precipitated, or accelerated by a work activity or environment. Workers' compensation covers only worker health problems that are identified as work-related disabilities, injuries, or illnesses.

Workers' compensation benefits include the following:

- Paid medical expenses and wage replacement benefits under certain circumstances
- Four types of workers' wage replacement benefits, listed here:
  - **Income benefits** These benefits replace income that might be lost because of a work-related injury or illness. Income benefits can include temporary income benefits, impairment income benefits, supplemental income benefits, and lifetime income benefits.
  - **Medical benefits** These benefits pay for necessary medical care to treat a work-related injury or illness.
  - **Death benefits** These benefits replace a portion of lost family income for eligible family members of employees who are killed on the job.
  - **Burial benefits** These benefits pay for some of the deceased employee's funeral expenses to the person who paid the expenses.
- Vocational rehabilitation or, in some cases, supplemental job displacement benefits
- Permanent and temporary partial or total disability benefits
- Survivor's benefits in cases of fatal work injuries or illnesses

Healthcare Benefits

Health insurance is a major benefit to the average American worker. Although considered an essential part of a worker's benefits package, it was not a legally mandatory benefits program until the 2010 enactment of the Patient Protection and Affordable Care Act, also referred to as the Affordable Care Act (ACA) or Obamacare. The goal of this law is to increase the quality and affordability of health coverage by expanding public and private insurance coverage and reducing the costs of healthcare for individuals and the government. The original law included mandates and subsidies and created new insurance exchanges to accomplish its goals. In the first few years after ACA implementation, health insurance coverage was mandatory for individuals either through their employers or through newly created state health insurance exchanges.

As a result of President Trump's Tax Reform Plan signed into law at the end of 2017, the insurance coverage mandate of the ACA was affected. Fines associated with not having health coverage are no longer enforceable beginning in 2019. At the time of this book, the law and its implementation continue to face challenges in Congress and the federal courts as well as some state governments, certain advocacy groups, and private business associations. With the expiration of government insurance subsidies, the cost of coverage has been ballooning. Many individuals without coverage through their employers have been dropping their health insurance as a result.

Regardless of the current legal and political landscape associated with offering medical insurance to employees, most employers offer one or more types of medical plans. It remains one of the key aspects of an employee total rewards package.

Fee-for-Service Plans

In the past, this was the traditional health plan sponsored by employers. In recent years, the fee-for-service plan has been largely replaced with various types of managed-care plans. In a fee-for-service health plan, subscribers can go to any qualified physician, healthcare provider, hospital, or medical clinic and submit claims to the insurance company. Fees are generated on the basis of the service provided, thereby creating an incentive for the medical provider to provide more services.

Managed-Care Plans

The concept behind the managed care plan is that this plan is structured to provide managed care to its subscribers. The core objective of a managed care plan is that the medical care a subscriber receives is medically necessary and provided in a cost-effective manner. All of the managed care plans typically offer basic medical coverage including hospitalization, outpatient services, doctor visits, and some forms of extended care.

Health Maintenance Organization

The most common type of managed care plan is the health maintenance organization (HMO) plan. The HMO plan is a capitated healthcare plan in which the healthcare provider is paid on a capitated basis, that is, on a "per-person" basis rather than on the basis of the services provided. Members enroll by paying a monthly or annual fee. Members must use HMO healthcare providers and facilities for their expenses to be covered under their plan. HMO plans are relatively low-cost and often do away with claims and reimbursements when services are provided under their plan. Two types of HMOs include the individual practice association (IPA), where groups of healthcare providers in private practice also provide services through the HMO, and staff model HMOs in which the healthcare providers are directly employed by the HMO. Kaiser Permanente is an HMO organized under the staff model concept.

Some other types of HMOs include those described in the material that follows.

Preferred Provider Organization   A preferred provider organization (PPO) plan includes an in-network and an out-of-network option. PPO plans are one of the most popular types of plans in the health insurance market. PPO plans allow you to visit whatever in-network physician or healthcare provider you want without first requiring a referral from a primary care physician. In-network services receive discounted co-payments or deductibles. The out-of-network option provides access to the physicians and healthcare providers who are "out of network" but with higher co-payments and deductibles. PPOs simply provide a wider range of medical choices and costs.

Point of Service   A point-of-service (POS) plan has some of the qualities of HMO and PPO plans with benefit levels varying depending on whether your care is received in or out of the health insurance company's network of providers. Like an HMO plan, the subscriber may be required to designate a primary care physician (PCP) who will then make referrals to network specialists when needed. Depending upon the plan, services rendered by the PCP are typically not subject to a deductible. Under the ACA, preventive care benefits are included at no cost. Like a PPO plan, the subscriber may receive care from out-of-network providers but with greater out-of-pocket costs. Subscribers may also be responsible for co-payments, coinsurance, and an annual deductible.

Prescription Drug Plans

Most non-Medicare prescription drug plans require a minimum co-payment for prescriptions or a percentage of the cost subject to a minimum and ceiling. In some cases, plans may also require the use of generic-brand drugs or the use of formulary drugs. A drug formulary may include generic or brand-name prescription drugs that are covered by the health plan. Some plans require subscribers to fill their prescriptions at specified pharmacies at a predetermined cost.

Dental Plans

Dental plan coverage is generally subject to a high adverse selection rate; that is, subscribers with dental issues are more likely to enroll in a dental plan than those who do not have dental issues. This affects the cost of coverage. To avoid the resulting cost issues, underwriting an employer-sponsored dental plan may require high enrollments, often with a cap on the benefits. Other approaches include a managed care form of coverage with coverage restricted only to network providers. Another approach is the indemnity plan style coverage in the form of reimbursements based on reasonable and customary charges regardless of the provider.

Vision Care Plans

Vision plans generally limit the frequency of coverage along with a monetary cap on coverage. The majority of plans limit new lenses, frames, or contact lenses. In addition, most plans place a monetary cap on allowances for a standard set of lenses, frames, or contact lenses. Some plans provide discounts for laser vision correction surgery.

Healthcare Funding

Employers have some flexibility in how they fund their healthcare coverage, ranging from fully funded plans to self-funded plans.

Fully Funded Plans

In a fully funded plan, the employer pays the insurance carrier premiums that cover all of the costs associated with the level and type of coverage. This includes the insurance carrier's cost of coverage for medical charges, administrative costs, sales commissions, fringe costs, taxes, and profits. On an annual basis, the carrier adjusts their premiums to coordinate with the employer's claims experience. In the fully funded plan, the carrier bears all of the risk; the carrier experiences either profits or losses based on its underwriting acumen. State insurance laws govern the terms and conditions within their state and vary from state to state.

Minimum Premium Plan

A minimum premium plan is a variation of a fully insured plan. This approach shifts some of the risk to the employer. When there are fewer claims, and therefore lower costs, in the previous year, the minimum premium plan passes a percentage of the savings to the employer. Conversely, when there are more claims, and therefore more costs, the employer potentially pays more.

Self-Funded Plans

When the employer has a self-funded health plan, the employer takes on the role of the insurance carrier and assumes all or most of the risk. Self-funded arrangements are subject to annual nondiscrimination testing requirements to ensure the plan does not discriminate in favor of highly compensated employees either in eligibility for coverage or benefits. There are two different approaches to self-funded plans:

- **Administrative services-only (ASO) plan**   In the ASO plan, all of the risk is assumed by the employer. The employer hires only the claims department of the insurance company for its claims services.

- **Third-party administrator (TPA) plan**   In the TPA plan, as in the ASO plan, the employer assumes all of the risk. The employer hires an independent (not an insurance company's) claims department.

Because there is no insurance involved in an employer's self-funded benefits plan, state insurance laws cannot dictate the content and coverage of such plans because ERISA preempts state rights to regulate employee benefit plans except for the regulation of insurance.

Partially Self-Funded Plans

With partially self-funded plans, the employer purchases one or two types of stop-loss insurance coverage, either specific and/or aggregate stop-loss coverage.

- **Specific stop-loss coverage**   Under this type of stop-loss coverage, the plan is protected against the risk of a major illness for one participant, or one family unit, covered by the plan.

- **Aggregate stop-loss coverage**   Under this type of stop-loss coverage, the plan is protected against the risk of large total claims from all participants during the plan year.

Typically, partially self-funded plans utilize the administrative services of either an ASO or TPA as described previously.

Health Insurance Purchasing Cooperatives (HIPCs)

Health Insurance Purchasing Cooperatives (HIPCs) act as purchasing agents for a large group of employers. They use the size of the cooperative over the size of the individual organizations to negotiate and purchase health insurance plans for their members. Their goal is to provide small organizations with the advantage of their size in negotiating health plan contracts.

Healthcare Costs

All organizations are concerned with their ability to manage or control their healthcare costs. The following are some actions that can help with this effort:

- *Change the delivery system.* The type of healthcare delivery system has a major effect on costs. Managed-care systems include HMOs and PPOs. HIPCs can help by negotiating better terms than might otherwise be possible with direct negotiations between the carrier and the organization.

- *Let employees choose.* Provide a benefits program with choices such as an HMO and a PPO or an indemnity plan. This is a way to avoid offering healthcare services that are not wanted or needed.

- *Redesign the programs.* Examine the balance between the employer share and the employee share of the premium. Changing the balance can also include the following:

  - Increasing deductibles and out-or-pocket requirements. Employers can mitigate shifting the burden to employees by allowing employees to pay these costs through pretax Section 125 healthcare spending accounts.

  - Requiring generic substitutions and/or mail-order drugs.

- *Promote prevention and wellness.* A number of programs can help.

  - Incentives for quitting smoking

  - Onsite fitness facilities and/or discount memberships to offsite facilities

  - Health wellness programs

  - Encouraging healthy and safe behaviors—for example, promoting bicycling, and so on

High-Deductible Health Plans

The objective of consumer-directed healthcare accounts is to allow employees to make more decisions about their healthcare while helping employers better control their costs. Health reimbursement accounts (HRAs) and health savings accounts (HSAs) are two types of consumer-directed healthcare programs. These programs help employers lower their costs and allow employees with set-aside money to pay for out-of-pocket medical and medical-related expenses. These plans are particularly attractive to younger healthy employees who don't want the financial burden of a health plan that does not match their needs but still want healthcare coverage for major injuries and illnesses.

Chapter 7: Total Rewards

Health Reimbursement Accounts

The HRA is a tax-advantaged benefit that allows both employees and employers to save on the cost of healthcare. HRA plans are employer-funded medical reimbursement plans. The employer sets aside a specific amount of pretax dollars for employees to pay for healthcare expenses on an annual basis. Based on the plan design, HRAs can generate significant savings in overall health benefits. The primary requirements for an HRA are that the plan must be funded solely by the employer and cannot be funded by salary reduction, and the plan may provide benefits for substantiated medical expenses only. HRAs may be designed in many fashions to suit the specific needs of employer and employees alike. It is one of the most flexible types of employee benefits plans, making it attractive to most employers.

Health Savings Accounts

The HSA is a tax-advantaged medical savings account available to taxpayers in the United States who are enrolled in a high-deductible health plan. The funds contributed to an account are not subject to federal income tax at the time of deposit. Unlike a flexible spending account (FSA), funds roll over and accumulate year to year if not spent. HSAs are owned by the individual, which differentiates them from company-owned health reimbursement accounts that are an alternate tax-deductible source of funds paired with either high-deductible or standard health plans. HSA funds may currently be used to pay for qualified medical expenses at any time without federal tax liability or penalty. However, over-the-counter medications cannot be paid with HSA dollars without a doctor's prescription. Withdrawals for nonmedical expenses are treated similarly to those in an individual retirement account (IRA) in that they may provide tax advantages if taken after retirement age and they incur penalties if taken earlier.

Section 125 Cafeteria (Flexible Benefit) Plans

A cafeteria plan (includes premium-only plans and flexible spending accounts) is an employee benefits program designed to take advantage of Section 125 of the Internal Revenue Code. A cafeteria plan allows employees to pay certain qualified expenses (such as health insurance premiums) on a pretax basis, thereby reducing their total taxable income and increasing their spendable/take-home income. Funds set aside in FSAs are not subject to federal, state, or Social Security taxes.

Premium-Only Plan

In a premium-only plan, employers may deduct the employee's portion of the company-sponsored insurance premium directly from said employee's paycheck before taxes are deducted.

Flexible Spending Account

In an FSA, employees may set aside a pre-established amount of money on a pretax basis per plan year. The employee can use the funds in the FSA to pay for eligible medical, dependent care, or transportation expenses.

Employers may add an FSA plan as a key element in their overall benefit package. Because an FSA plan offers a tax advantage, employers experience tax savings from reduced FICA, FUTA, SUTA, and workers' compensation taxes on participating employees. These tax savings reduce or eliminate altogether the various costs associated with offering the plan. Meanwhile, employee satisfaction is heightened because participating employees experience a "raise" at no additional cost to the employer.

An employee who participates in the FSA must place a certain dollar amount into the FSA each year. This "election" amount is automatically deducted from the employee's check (for that amount divided by the number of payroll periods). For example, an employee is paid 24 times a year and elects to put $480 in the FSA. Thus, $20 is deducted pretax from each paycheck and is held in an account (by the plan administrator) to be reimbursed upon request.

Plan Year and Grace Period

The plan year for the Section 125 plan is one full year (365 days) and generally begins on the first of a month. Many employers design their flexible spending plan to run on the same plan year as their insurance program. Short plan years are allowed in certain instances.

The grace period is a time frame up to 75 days after the end of the official plan year during which employees may use up any funds remaining at the end of the plan year. For example, if the plan year runs from July 1 through June 30, the grace period for that plan may continue up to September 15. If an employee incurs an expense after June 30 but before September 15, she can utilize the remaining funds from the previous plan year and submit requests for reimbursement. In addition to the 75-day grace period, plan participants have a 90-day run-out period in which they can submit requests for reimbursement for expenses incurred during the dates of service within the plan year and grace period.

Uniform Coverage

Uniform coverage is an aspect of Section 125 that allows an employee to be reimbursed for qualified medical expenses that exceed their contributions to date. While this is a great benefit for the employee, it poses a potential risk to the employer. A case in point is when an employee terminates with a negative balance in her medical FSA. This risk should be offset because some other employees do not spend all of their FSA funds, so the risk is minimal.

This rule states that for the medical expense account, a participant may claim the full amount of her annual election even if she has contributed only a portion of the total. For example, Sue Summers decides to contribute $480 for the year to her FSA account. To accomplish this, $20 is deducted pretax from each of her 24 payrolls for the year. Her plan starts in January. In March, Sue experiences a medical expense that costs $400. To date, she has contributed only $20 on six payrolls, meaning she has only $120 actual dollars in her FSA account. However, because of the uniform coverage rule she can claim and be reimbursed for the full $400 because of the assumption that her biweekly contributions will continue and she will eventually contribute the $480 total.

This honor system is a huge advantage for participants and allows them to experience medical expenses at any time of the year with no worry about having the funds available at the time the expense is incurred.

Uniform coverage applies to the medical FSA only; it does not apply to a dependent care FSA.

NOTE With a dependent care FSA account, a participant's reimbursement may not exceed the balance in the FSA account at the time the claim was made.

The Use-It-or-Lose-It Rule

This rule states that any funds remaining in the participating employee's FSA account at the end of the plan year will be forfeited to the employer. Although the rule is clear, many users of an FSA largely misunderstand the result of the rule. Loss of funds can be easily avoided.

Let's look at an example: Joe Smith chooses to participate in the FSA and elects to fund $500 for the year. After the plan year and grace period are complete, Joe finds that he spent only $400 of the original $500 he put away. He fears he has lost $100, but because of the taxes he saved on the $500 he has not. Let's say Joe is in the 28 percent tax bracket. By putting $500 away in his FSA, he saved $140 in taxes (money that was not taken out of his paycheck and given to the IRS). In sum, even if Joe leaves $100 in his FSA account, he has still saved $40! This vital key issue must be explained completely to potential FSA participants.

The maximum amount of salary reduction contributions that the participant is permitted to make under §125(i) of the code is $2,650 for 2018.[4] This number often increases slightly on an annual basis.

Cafeteria plans are qualified, nondiscriminatory benefit plans, meaning a discrimination test must be met based on the elections of the participants combined with any contribution by the employer.

Nondiscrimination Testing

Section 125 of the Internal Revenue Code requires that cafeteria plans be offered on a nondiscriminatory basis. To ensure compliance, the Internal Revenue Code sets forth testing requirements that must be satisfied. These testing requirements are in place to make certain that cafeteria plan benefits are available to all eligible employees under the same terms and that the plan does not favor highly compensated employees, officers, and owners.

Full Cafeteria Plans

A full cafeteria benefits plan allows employees to choose from a menu of eligible qualified benefits prior to the start of the plan year or coverage period. In these types of plans, employees typically are given credits that they can spend on a variety of qualified benefit items choosing not only between different benefits but also between items within a given benefit. As an example, an employee may choose to use credits for additional disability coverage while purchasing a more conservative health option. In some cases, employees may cash out unused credits or buy additional benefits through pretax salary.

Common Benefits Provided to Employees

A number of benefits help employers to attract and retain employees. The following list provides a brief overview of tangible benefits that many employers provide:

- Disability benefits
- Life insurance
- Long-term care insurance
- Employee assistance programs (EAPs)
- Retirement plans
- Supplemental unemployment benefits (SUBs)
- Paid time off (PTO)
- Paid leaves

Disability Benefits

Employer disability plans normally cover three phases:

- **Employer sick leave**   Sick leave provided by employer policies typically pays 100 percent of pay for a specified number of accrued days. Accrual is usually based on length of employment and subject to a maximum cap. Absences due to employee illness or injury and, in many cases, that of a family member are covered. Absences that exceed the average accrual rate may be covered by short-term disability. While there is no federal law requiring paid sick leave benefits for employees, some states laws address this.

- **Short-term disability (STD)**   This coverage usually begins where sick leave ends. STD typically covers only a portion of lost income and may require a waiting period. In some cases, organizations may self-fund their STD. Typically, STD provides up to 50 to 70 percent of coverage of the employee's base salary up to six months. Five states have mandated short-term disability plans. They include California, Hawaii, New Jersey, New York, and Rhode Island. In addition, Puerto Rico has mandatory insurance requirements.

- **Long-term disability (LTD)**   LTD coverage usually begins after short-term disability coverage ends. LTD is always underwritten by a commercial insurance company because of the risk associated with the coverage. When a disabled employee is also eligible for Social Security disability benefits, the LTD is often integrated with the Social Security coverage to avoid duplication of coverage.

When employees go on LTD, their employment ends with their organization even though they are collecting LTD benefits. During their first two years of LTD coverage, individuals must be unable to perform their own occupation. After two years, a person must be unable to engage in any occupation or do any work to continue on LTD (unless their plan indicates otherwise). Benefits cease when a person returns to work or dies prior to normal retirement age. There are no income levels applicable to LTD coverage.

Life Insurance

Employees are concerned about care for their families if they were to die prematurely, leaving their families without adequate resources. Group term life insurance provides benefits that address this issue.

Group term life insurance provides a lump-sum benefit to beneficiaries. The benefit may be in the form of a flat amount or a multiple of salary. Also, the amount may vary by length of service or position.

NOTE   Many employers keep the value of the group term life insurance to $50,000 because plans kept at that level or less are not taxable when nondiscriminatory. When plans exceed $50,000, the amount over $50,000 is referred to as *excess group-term life insurance* and treated by the IRS as imputed income subject to tax. Imputed income is added to other income and appears on the employee's W-2 Form.

Long-Term Care Insurance

Long-term care (LTC) insurance covers the cost of long-term care in a number of settings including care at home, in an assisted living facility, in a nursing home, or as an inpatient in a hospice. If LTC is offered, it must provide care for people who are chronically ill for at least 90 days. The premium payments are not counted as employee income, and employers can deduct their part of the insurance premiums from their annual income tax liability.

Employee Assistance Programs

Employee assistance programs (EAPs) are employer-sponsored benefits that provide a number of services that help promote the physical, mental, and emotional wellness of individual employees who otherwise would be negatively impacted by health-related crises. EAPs help employees find professional resources to deal with their problems. Services are provided by licensed counselors typically through third-party organizations with a high degree of confidentiality for employees. Depending on the specific program, services can help employees meet personal goals, reduce stress and anxiety, and improve overall emotional and physical health.

Retirement Plans

Retirement plans can take many forms. 401(k), 403(b), or pension plans are commonly offered by employers. Whatever plan is selected, the goal of the benefit is ultimately to help employees save money for retirement and invest in their financial security. Employees make contributions through payroll deductions. Employee-contributed dollars may also be matched up to a certain percentage by employers to provide an added benefit to participating in the plan, essentially "free money." As interest compounds over time, small contributions can grow into significant retirement savings. Since the plans are intended to provide a retirement benefit, there are taxes and penalties associated with removing funds from a plan before retirement age. There are many other types of retirement plans often used in total rewards programs at the executive level that will be covered in Chapter 12.

Supplemental Unemployment Benefits

Supplemental unemployment benefits are unemployment benefits in addition to government benefits offered by some employers. SUBs are common in union environments. Under the Internal Revenue Code, SUBs may be exempt from federal income taxes for employers but not for employees.

Paid Time Off

Many employers combine vacation and sick leave into a single program called paid time off or PTO. PTO is a concept that allows employees to earn, typically by accrual over time, credits that the employee can then use whenever circumstances require that they be absent from work. PTO does not require justification for an absence, simply an approval in the event of a planned absence or the accrued balance to be used in an unplanned absence.

 NOTE In some states where PTO is offered, PTO accrual is treated in the same manner as vacation; that is, PTO is subject to the same rules that are applicable to vacation.

Paid Leaves

Many employers have found that paid time off as a reward for service provides the employee with relief from the ongoing demands of work as well as benefits the employer with increased morale and commitment. Types of paid leaves are described in the sections that follow.

Paid Holidays

While paid holidays are not legally required, employers find that both employers and employees benefit from them. The number of paid holidays vary from 6 to 12 a year, generally including New Year's Day, Memorial Day, Independence Day, Labor Day, Thanksgiving Day, and Christmas Day. Paid holidays are generally paid on the basis of the employer's schedule for a regular workday.

Paid Vacation

The standard vacation policy is based on an accrual system measured on an employee's length of service. State laws vary on the management of vacation accrual. Some states do not allow a "use-it-or-lose-it" policy, while others are silent on the subject. In some cases, vacation can be carried over from year to year with a provision for a reasonable cap. Many employers have a cash-out policy that allows an employee in states in which there is no rollover who hasn't taken his or her accrued vacation by the end of the year to receive cash back for their unused accrued vacation. Generally, employees must receive advance approval to use their vacation so as not to disrupt the employer's workflow.

Sick Leave

Organizations that otherwise have paid vacation policies usually also have paid sick leave policies to provide for time off due to illness or injury. These sick leave programs are primarily intended for the benefit of the employee, although in recent years, sick leave programs have often been expanded to cover an employee's time off to care for a family member. Some states mandate that a portion of the employee's sick leave accrual must be allowed for family care.

Sabbatical

Some professions or industries allow long-term employees to take a paid leave of absence as a way to complete a course of study, do research, or engage in other learned pursuits. This practice is particularly evident in the teaching profession, although it is not restricted only to that profession. Some organizations allow its long-term employees with high-balance sick leave accounts to take extended unpaid time off with the opportunity to use a portion of their sick leave for paid time off during this absence.

Bereavement Leave

Most organizations have policies that provide for paid time off to attend a funeral of a family member. In some cases, this benefit is available to extended family members as well as close friends.

Personal (Floating) Days

Many organizations allow a limited number of paid days off for employees' personal needs. These are often referred to as *floating holidays* because when they are taken is determined by the employee. Typically, approval is required in advance. Because these paid days off are determined by the employee, some states apply the same rules to these days as they do to vacation or PTO.

Severance Packages

While not legally required, some organizations give employees who are terminated for a reason other than cause a severance package, which may include the following:

- Salary continuation for a specified period of time (for example, one week of pay for each year of service)

- Outplacement services such as résumé assistance, interview preparation and placement counseling, testing, and job search assistance
- Retraining in some cases
- Paid benefits premium assistance for a limited period of time

Severance packages may have legal implications. As such, legal assistance should be sought whenever circumstances arise that include a potential severance package.

Noncash Rewards

While traditional compensation and benefits are generally directly tied to a bottom-line cost in an organization's budget, the function of total rewards continues to grow beyond its traditional definition. While some rewards noted in this section can easily be assigned a cash value, others cannot. The key with all programs is the added value perceived by employees and the program's ability to help attract, retain, and motivate employees.

Tuition Reimbursement

Many employers support employee education development by providing financial support to employees who undertake local educational courses related to their work or for general professional development purposes at recognized educational institutions. In some cases, employer tuition reimbursement programs also provide financial support for books and other ancillary supplies. In most cases, employers require a passing grade to qualify for tuition reimbursement support. There is an annual dollar limit on the amount of reimbursement eligible for income inclusion for tax purposes.

Paid Volunteer Time

A growing trend that aligns well with social responsibility programs in organizations is paid volunteer time. Employees are paid their normal wages while volunteering for a nonprofit or underserved community organization. Paid volunteer time is often offered in increments of one day within a certain time period. Not only can this be a great team-building activity to get employees out of the office and establish a sense of pride for supporting a good cause, but it provides a great benefit to the organization being served.

Workplace Amenities

With the advent of technology and demands for 24/7 services in some industries like hospitality and lodging, workplace amenities offer employees an opportunity to make the workplace "a home away from home." Workplace eateries and cafeterias, recreation and game rooms, onsite gyms and fitness classes, and even nap pods are some of the amenities being offered at various organizations. Employers opt for this type of benefit because it is especially attractive to younger generations in the workplace who thrive for collaborative work environments that stray from the traditional office environment and make "work" a more exciting place to spend 40 or more hours per week.

Employee Recognition Programs

While we have spent a great deal of this chapter focused on rewards tools that motivate employees, recognition programs are one of the more common ways to motivate high performance. Many organizations offer recognition programs such as an employee of the month program or team rewards to meeting certain performance goals. On-the-spot recognition programs are also a popular way to surprise an employee for exhibiting an organization's core values or providing great customer service. Recognition programs may also be tied to an employee's length of service with an organization, and awards may be provided for meeting certain service milestones such as five, ten, or twenty years of service. Some organizations also provide recognition for personal milestones such as an employee's birthday or birth or adoption of a child. There are many options for recognition programs, and it is important to not select programs at random. Recognition programs are the best catalyst for motivation when they are truly valued by employees. Conducting an employee opinion survey to determine which programs are most valued by employees is a good way to figure this out.

Other Benefits Provided to Employees

Although less commonly provided, employers have other benefits options to consider adding to a total rewards package. Such benefits should be formally published in an employee handbook as a way to ensure consistent and fair treatment of employees as well as for legal liability protection.

Childcare Services

Employers can provide a variety of childcare services to help working parents deal with the ongoing needs of preschool or school-aged children.

- Supportive time-off policies
- Resource and referral services to identify available community services and childcare providers
- Direct financial assistance through a flexible benefit program (Section 125 program)
- A flex-time program for working hours
- Work options such as job sharing and part-time work

Elder Care

Demographic changes often place family support pressures on employees and their elders as well as their children. Organization support services include the following:

- Supportive time-off policies
- Employer-sponsored group long-term care insurance
- Counseling assistance through an EAP

- Resource and referral services
- A flex-time program for working hours

Commuter Assistance

Most organizations have a significant number of employees who commute to work in their own car because the cost of public transit is either too expensive or not easily accessible to satisfy the employee's work requirements. Some organizational support services that can help include the following:

- Resource and referral services
- A flex-time program for working hours
- Mass transit cost assistance (tokens, transit passes, and so on)
- Van pooling or carpooling assistance
- Dedicated parking for employees at or near the employee's place of employment

Prepaid Legal Insurance

Although not as popular as it was several years ago, some employers continue to provide prepaid legal insurance that covers the cost of routine legal services such as developing a will and assistance with real estate matters, divorces, and other basic legal assistance. This often is a relatively high-cost benefit that is utilized by a relative few employees, which may explain why this benefit is not widespread.

In the Trenches

The Total Rewards Proposition: When $15 per Hour Really Equals $30 per Hour

Larry Bienati, Ph.D., SPHR, CCP, Vice President, Organizational Development, The Cooper Companies, Inc.

When an employee joins the organization, it is so important to clearly articulate the total rewards/compensation equation (salary + variable compensation + short-term benefits + long-term benefits + the delta factor). Too often, we focus on base pay, the next pay increase, or top-end base compensation, if all performance expectations hold true, in an effort to attract, retain, and motivate that key employee. It is therefore important to promote the value proposition of compensation beyond the base salary. Whether a private, public, or not-for-profit sector organization, you are likely spending 30 percent to 60 percent of the total compensation dollar on direct and indirect compensation. Direct compensation includes salary, bonuses, and other short-term incentives. Indirect compensation

(continued)

includes short-term and long-term incentives such as medical, dental, life, disability, sick leave, vacations, educational support, and other variable benefits like 401(k) offering/matching, profit sharing, pension plans, stock, and other perks. We have a fifth bucket called the *delta factor*, or what I call the key differentiator of being a truly great workplace. This includes culture and quality of work-life opportunities that cannot always be measured in hard dollars but that have a profound impact in the retention and job satisfaction proposition. It is the extrinsic and intrinsic value proposition of being a great workplace with high levels of trust, pride, camaraderie, fairness, and sense of place, not to mention the delicate balance of work-family-career and "give back" to the community you serve.

Enlightened HR/OD professionals who are viewed by their boards and senior management as trusted advisors, are true business partners, and have a respected seat at the C-suite table believe that your most important organizational human assets come and go each day. Most important, these assets may constitute 70 percent of an organization's expense structure. Here is where the ROI and value proposition of enlightened total rewards practices can clearly impact the organization fiscal imperatives.

So, tell the story! Do the math! Set up the formula for your company on a simple Excel spreadsheet; see whether your enterprise resource planning (ERP) system can offer this calculation. Consider reminding your employees of their complete total rewards package on an annual basis. I would regularly produce, at the end of the fiscal year, a summary of all elements of total rewards equation, even including the protections offered by Social Security and other mandated state and federal benefits. When you celebrate another great year, you could present the total rewards package for that year (usually around the holidays in most companies) so employees could truly appreciate the company's commitment to provide a fair, responsive, and protective compensation offering.

Benefits: Taxable and Nontaxable

Employee benefits fall into two categories: taxable and nontaxable benefits. Both categories include direct compensation and indirect compensation (employer-paid coverage or reimbursements). Table 7-7 identifies some of the benefits we've discussed in this chapter in each category (the list is only generally indicative; it is not all-inclusive).

Communicating Total Rewards Programs

For employees to perceive a value add from total rewards programs, it is important that they are clearly communicated and understood. Implementing a costly benefit program that employees fail to participate in because they are not aware of it or understand it can be a big human resource and financial problem. There are also some communications that are required by law.

	Taxable Benefits	**Nontaxable Benefits**
Direct Compensation	• Base pay • Differential pay • Severance pay • Paid time off	• Wages paid after death in a new year
Indirect Compensation	Employer paid or reimbursed: • Disability benefits when employer pays the premium • Life insurance when employee pays with pretax dollars • Gifts, prizes, and awards over certain dollar amounts • Personal use of a company vehicle • Sick pay	Employer paid or reimbursed: • Work-related expense reimbursements • Childcare (subject to limitations) • Company vehicle use (only work-related) • De minimis ($25 or less) • Group life insurance plans, $50,000 or less coverage • Educational expenses (subject to annual limits) • Medical, dental, health plans (employer contributions) • Employee-paid disability benefits when purchased with after-tax dollars

Table 7-7 Taxable and Nontaxable Benefits

Legally Required Communications

ERISA-required reporting and communicating requirements that must automatically be distributed to every employee include the following:

- **Summary plan description (SPD)** Contains information on what the plan provides in lay terms. Distribution is required within 120 days after the plan's establishment or 90 days after eligibility. The SPD must be updated no less frequently than every five years.
- **Summary annual report (SAR)** Contains financial information about the plan. Distribution is required within seven months after the end of the plan year.
- **Summary of material modifications (SMM)** Required whenever any of the plan's features have been significantly changed or within 201 days after the end of the plan year.

Other Required Communications

Other required communications include the following:

- (Employers with 50+ employees) An FMLA policy statement in all employee handbooks
- (Employers with 20+ employees) General notification of federal (and state if applicable) COBRA rights
- Notice of special HIPAA enrollment rights and privacy rights

The preceding list is not all-inclusive. Due diligence is required so that all organizations understand the requirements of applicable laws, regulations, and instructions for any official forms or other official guidance. There are also many state laws that govern required communications.

Communicating Through Employee Self-Service Technologies

The communication requirements described in this section are influenced by the introduction of self-service technologies that are rapidly improving the communications abilities of organizations. Self-service technologies will continue to improve the ability of the organization to effectively implement its communications responsibilities. Employee self-service (ESS) applications will play a more active role in payroll and benefits by providing quick and easy access to information, which benefits the organization in the following ways:

- Increasing the accuracy of employee data
- Improving the timeliness of employee transactions
- Reducing HR costs associated with handling of traditional delivery channels

With increased benefits, ESS brings responsibilities:

- The application must be protected from hackers.
- Unauthorized internal and external access must be monitored.
- Access to payroll data and benefits information must be protected.

HR can help promote the success of ESS technology by ensuring that employees do the following:

- Understand the purpose of this technology, what functions are available, and how to apply the functions to meet their needs
- Recognize the benefits of ESS technology when compared to traditional methods
- Make the effort to use the technology to their advantage

Chapter Review

This chapter examined how to implement, promote, and manage an organization's total rewards system. In this chapter, you examined direct compensation (that is, pay systems) and indirect compensation (that is, benefit and recognition programs). You began the chapter by examining the laws that affect compensation programs. Next, you looked at compensation and benefits as an intrinsic part of the organization's strategic direction as well as how HR can leverage compensation and benefits as a competitive advantage. This chapter also examined methods to determine internal and external job value followed by a review of the payroll function and its role in the management and administration of compensation and benefits. Finally, this chapter reviewed the evaluation of the organization's compensation and benefits system and its associated communication requirements.

Questions

1. According to COBRA, a company with 20 or more employees must offer:

   A. Health insurance to its employees

   B. Continued medical insurance coverage to employees terminated for gross misconduct

   C. COBRA benefits to workers if the company terminates its health plan

   D. COBRA benefits up to 36 months to spouses of covered deceased workers

2. An employee elects a $500 annual deferment in his Section 125 flexible benefits plan. His employer pays an FSA claim for $500 in March. In April, the employee terminates his employment after deferring only $290 to his plan. What happens in this situation?

   A. The employee must pay the company $290 for the amount in excess of his actual deferral.

   B. The employer may withhold $290 from the employee's final paycheck.

   C. The employee is entitled to the full reimbursement for $500.

   D. The employee becomes ineligible for the full FSA reimbursement.

3. A window manufacturer guarantees its installers a base wage plus an extra $25 for each job completed to specifications. The employer is using a:

   A. Merit pay system

   B. Productivity-based pay system

   C. Competency-based system

   D. Flat-rate system

4. Under the factor comparison method, jobs are evaluated through the use of:

   A. Predetermined wage classes

   B. A wage/salary conversion table

   C. A scale based on compensable factors

   D. A comparison with market pricing

5. To which of the following job evaluation methods does the paired comparison method belong?

   A. Ranking

   B. Job classification

   C. Point-factor

   D. Factor comparison

6. Which of the following is not a pay differential?

   A. Hazard pay

   B. Shift pay

   C. Base pay

   D. Overtime

7. Which of the following terms refers to collapsing multiple pay ranges into a single wide pay range?

   A. Wide banding

   B. Pay compression

   C. Green circle rates

   D. Broadbanding

8. The following two programs are common noncash rewards programs:

   A. Tuition assistance

   B. Legal assistance

   C. Medical benefits

   D. Paid volunteer time

9. A _____ is an employer-sponsored benefit that provides a number of services to help promote the physical, mental, and emotional wellness of employees.

10. This law requires an administrator of an employee benefit plan to furnish participants with a summary plan description (SPD) describing their rights, benefits, and responsibilities under the plan.

   A. Health Insurance Portability and Accountability Act (HIPAA)

   B. Employee Retirement Income Security Act (ERISA)

   C. Family and Medical Leave Act (FMLA)

   D. Consolidated Omnibus Budget Reconciliation Act (COBRA)

11. Which of the following laws do not directly relate to a company's compensation or benefits programs?

   A. Equal Pay Act

   B. Fair Labor Standards Act

   C. Americans with Disabilities Act

   D. Uniform Guidelines on Employee Selection Procedures

12. Social Security, COBRA, and Medicare are examples of:

   A. Medical benefits

   B. Social benefits

   C. Government-sponsored benefits

   D. Legally mandated benefits

13. Employee benefits are indirect compensation given to employees for:

   A. Loyalty

   B. Organizational membership

   C. Performance

   D. Organizational incentives

14. A _____ includes a statement of the qualifications necessary to perform a job.

15. Which job evaluation method is most difficult to use?

   A. Factor comparison method

   B. Ranking method

   C. Classification method

   D. Point-factor method

16. The simplest method of job evaluation is the:

   A. Job ranking method

   B. Point-factor method

   C. Classification method

   D. Factor comparison method

17. A(n) _____ system is a productivity-based system in which an employee is paid for each unit of production.

   A. Incentive

   B. Merit

   C. Results-oriented

   D. Piece rate

18. The Equal Pay Act prohibits wage discrimination on the basis of:

   A. Race

   B. Sex

   C. Seniority

   D. Merit

19. A _____ job is one that is found in many organizations and performed by several individuals who have similar duties that are relatively stable and that require similar KSAs.

   A. Key

   B. Comparable

   C. Benchmark

   D. Red-circled

20. Which of the following two benefits are taxable?

   A. Disability benefits when employer pays the premium

   B. Employee-paid disability benefits when purchased with after-tax dollars

   C. Base pay

   D. Work-related company vehicle use

Answers

1. D. COBRA provides up to 36 months' continuation of group health benefits in the event of a divorce or death of the employed spouse. None of the other choices is a valid COBRA provision.

2. C. Flexible spending accounts are authorized under Section 125 (cafeteria) plans. FSAs offer employees a pretax method to defer pay toward their group health plan costs as well as their out-of-pocket medical costs. FSA health care claims below the annual elected deferral must be paid by the employer when they are incurred even though the employee's FSA payroll deductions have not created a sufficient balance to cover the expense.

3. B. The employer is using an incentive program based on performance results, which is considered a productivity-based system. A merit-pay system does not address incentive pay. A competency-based system addresses capabilities, whereas a flat-rate system establishes a fixed rate of pay.

4. C. The factor comparison job evaluation method involves a set of compensable factors identified as determining the worth of jobs. Typically, the number of compensable factors is small. Next, benchmark jobs are identified. Benchmark jobs should be selected as having certain characteristics such as equitable pay and be distributed along a range. The jobs are then priced, and the total pay for each job is divided into pay for each factor. This process establishes the rate of pay for each factor for each benchmark job. The other jobs in the organization are then compared with the benchmark jobs, and rates of pay for each factor are summed to determine the rates of pay for each of the other jobs.

5. A. This is an example of ranking jobs. The paired comparison method involves plotting all of the jobs into a matrix. You then compare each job with every other job.

6. C. Hazard pay, shift pay, and overtime are all differentials. Base pay is the foundation of an employer's compensation program.

7. D. Broadbanding is a term that refers to pay ranges with a wide spread. This is often done to facilitate the management of pay levels within the pay range. A side effect of broadbanding is to reduce the opportunity for promotions due to a smaller number of ranges. That can adversely affect morale.

8. A, D. Legal assistance is a less commonly offered noncash reward program, and medical benefits are not considered a noncash reward.

9. Employee Assistance Program

10. B. Among other things, ERISA requires plan administrators to furnish an SPD when a participant first becomes covered by a plan and then at regular intervals thereafter.

11. C, D. In 1978, the Civil Service Commission, the Department of Labor, the Department of Justice, and the Equal Opportunity Commission jointly adopted the Uniform Guidelines on Employee Selection Procedures to establish uniform standards for employers for the use of selection procedures and to address adverse impact, validation, and recordkeeping requirements. The Americans with Disabilities Act prohibits discrimination against individuals with disabilities. The other choices are laws that directly relate to employers' compensation programs.

12. C. Social Security, COBRA, and Medicare are all government-sponsored benefits.

13. B. Employee benefits are indirect compensation given to employees for organizational membership. The other choices are incorrect.

14. Job description

15. A. The factor comparison method is a systematic and scientific method of job evaluation. It is the most complex method of the four recognized methods. Under this method, instead of ranking complete jobs, each job is ranked according to a series of factors. These factors include mental effort, physical effort, skill needed, responsibility, supervisory responsibility, working conditions, and other such factors. Pay will be assigned in this method by comparing the weights of the factors required for each job and divided among the factors weighted by importance. Wages are assigned to the job in comparison to its ranking on each job factor.

16. A. The simplest method of job evaluation is the ranking method. According to this method, jobs are arranged from highest to lowest, in order of their value or merit to the organization. Jobs can also be arranged according to the relative difficulty in performing them. The jobs are examined as a whole rather than on the basis of important factors in the job; the job at the top of the list has the highest value, and obviously the job at the bottom of the list will have the lowest value. The ranking method is simple to understand and practice; it is best suited for a small organization. This kind of ranking is highly subjective in nature and may offend many employees.

17. D. The piece rate pay method compensates employees a set amount for each unit of work completed. For example, in a manufacturing setting, an employee receives a set amount for each item he produces, regardless of how fast or slow he works.

18. B. The Equal Pay Act requires that men and women be given equal pay for equal work in the same establishment. The jobs need not be identical, but they must be substantially equal. It is job content, not job titles, that determines whether jobs are substantially equal.

19. **C.** Benchmark jobs are positions that remain consistent across the industry in terms of salary, responsibilities, and seniority and can therefore be compared from organization to organization. Data is widely available on the key metrics of these jobs, including salary and career route.

20. **A, C.** Employee-paid disability benefits when purchased with after-tax dollars are not taxable because they have already been taxed. Work-related company vehicle use is also not taxable.

Endnotes

1. "Child Labor Requirements in Nonagricultural Occupations Under the Fair Labor Standards Act (FLSA)", US Department of Labor. https://www.dol.gov/whd/regs/compliance/childlabor101.htm.

2. "Fact Sheet #21: Recordkeeping Requirements under the Fair Labor Standards Act (FLSA)", US Department of Labor. https://www.dol.gov/whd/regs/compliance/whdfs21.htm.

3. "Executive Administrative, Professional, Computer, and Outside Sales Exemptions - FLSA," U.S. Department of Labor Field Operations Manual,§13(a)(1)(29 U.S.C. §213(a)(1))

4. "2018 FSA Contribution Cap Rises to $2,650", Society for Human Resource Management. https://www.shrm.org/resourcesandtools/hr-topics/benefits/pages/2018-fsa-contribution-limits.aspx

Employee and Labor Relations

Early in the existence of employee-employer relationships, there was little a worker could do but say "yes" to every employer instruction or demand. There was no recourse for employees. If the employee didn't like the employer or the way he or she was being treated, the only option in many cases was to resign the position and look for another. Unfortunately, good references were often required by new, would-be employers so they would know the worker was responsive and responsible. Without those written references, obtaining work elsewhere was difficult at best.

In the nineteenth century, a fledgling union movement from the previous century began to gain traction, and employee recruitment to union organizations swelled. It seems employees don't like being powerless in the employment relationship. Who can blame them?

In this chapter, we examine the nuances of employee and labor relations. You will learn how the early union protections regarding work rules, terminations, and other actions have been recently migrating into law. Today, even nonunion-represented employees have many protections that once were afforded only to union members.

This topic will be heavily tested on the PHR exam. Thirty-nine percent of PHR test questions will focus on this body of knowledge. The official HRCI Employee and Labor Relations functional area responsibilities and knowledge statements are as follows:

Responsibilities

- Analyze functional effectiveness at each stage of the employee life cycle (for example, hiring, onboarding, development, retention, exit process, alumni program) and identify alternative approaches as needed

- Collect, analyze, summarize, and communicate employee engagement data

- Understand organizational culture, theories, and practices; identify opportunities and make recommendations

- Understand and apply knowledge of programs, federal laws, and regulations to promote outreach, diversity, and inclusion (for example, affirmative action, employee resource groups, community outreach, corporate responsibility)

- Implement and support workplace programs relative to health, safety, security, and privacy following federal laws and regulations (for example, OSHA, workers' compensation, emergency response, workplace violence, substance abuse, legal postings)

- Promote organizational policies and procedures (for example, employee handbook, SOPs, time and attendance, expenses)

- Manage complaints or concerns involving employment practices, behavior, or working conditions, and escalate by providing information to appropriate stakeholders

- Promote techniques and tools for facilitating positive employee and labor relations with knowledge of applicable federal laws affecting union and nonunion workplaces (for example, dispute/conflict resolution, antidiscrimination policies, sexual harassment)

- Support and consult with management in performance management processes (for example, employee reviews, promotions, recognition programs)

- Support performance activities (for example, coaching, performance improvement plans, involuntary separations) and employment activities (for example, job eliminations, reductions in force) by managing corresponding legal risks

Knowledge Of

- General employee relations activities and analysis (for example, conducting investigations, researching grievances, working conditions, reports, etc.)

- Applicable federal laws and procedures affecting employment, labor relations, safety, and security

- Human relations, culture and values concepts, and applications to employees and organizations

- Review and analysis process for assessing employee attitudes, opinions, and satisfaction

- Diversity and inclusion

- Recordkeeping requirements

- Occupational injury and illness prevention techniques

- Workplace safety and security risks

- Emergency response, business continuity, and disaster recovery process

- Internal investigation, monitoring, and surveillance techniques

- Data security and privacy

- The collective bargaining process, terms, and concepts (for example, contract negotiation, costing, administration)

- Performance management process, procedures, and analysis

- Termination approaches, concepts, and terms

Federal Laws That Apply to This Body of Knowledge

Now that you've reviewed the Employee and Labor Relations functional area responsibilities and knowledge statements, we recommend you review the federal laws that apply to employee and labor relations, as listed in Figure 8-1. It would benefit you, the reader, to refer to Chapter 2 on these specific laws prior to reading any further in this chapter.

While legislation is important, of equal value is the case law that comes from court interpretations. Over the past five decades, the U.S. Supreme Court has heard and provided its clarification to many challenges involving employment and labor laws. Figure 8-2 lists the vitally important cases applying to employee and labor relations.

For more information on each of these cases, see Appendix B.

- Davis-Bacon Act of 1931

- Employee Polygraph Protection Act of 1988

- Fair and Accurate Credit Transactions Act of 2003

- Fair Labor Standards Act of 1938

- Immigration Reform and Control Act of 1986

- Labor-Management Reporting and Disclosure Act of 1959 (Landrum-Griffin Act)

- Norris-LaGuardia Act of 1932

- Railway Labor Act of 1926

- Federal Insurance Contributions Act of 1935 (Social Security Act)

- Vietnam Era Veterans Readjustment Assistance Act of 1974

- Walsh-Healey Act of 1936 (Public Contracts Act)

- Civil Rights Act of 1991

- Genetic Information Nondiscrimination Act of 2008

- Pregnancy Discrimination Act of 1978

- Age Discrimination in Employment Act of 1967

- Occupational Safety and Health Act

- Electronic Communications Privacy Act of 1986

- Equal Pay Act of 1963

- Fair Credit Reporting Act of 1970

- Immigration and Nationality Act of 1952

- Labor-Management Relations Act of 1947 (Taft-Hartley Act)

- National Labor Relations Act of 1935

- Portal-to-Portal Act of 1947

- Service Contract Act of 1965

- Uniformed Services Employment and Reemployment Rights Act of 1994

- Wagner-Peyser Act of 1933 (Amended by Workforce Investment Act of 1998)

- Civil Rights Act of 1964 (Title VII)

- Drug-Free Workplace Act of 1988

- Lilly Ledbetter Fair Pay Act of 2009

- Uniform Guidelines on Employee Selection Procedures of 1976

- Worker Adjustment and Retraining Notification Act of 1988

- Needlestick Safety and Prevention Act

Figure 8-1 Key federal laws impacting employee and labor relations

Case Citations

- *DeBartolo Corp. v. Gulf Coast Trades Council* (485 U.S. 568)

- *E. I. DuPont & Company v. NLRB* (311 NLRB 893)

- *PepsiCo. Inc. v. Redmond* (No. 94-3942 7th Cir)

- *NLRB v. Weingarten, Inc.* (420 U.S. 251, 254)

- *Ronald Lesh v. Crown Cork and Seal Company* (334 NLRB 699)

- *Phoenix Transit System v. NLRB* (337 NLRB 510)

- *Oil Capitol Sheet Metal, Inc., v. NLRB* (349 NLRB 1348)

- *Syracuse University v. NLRB* (350 NLRB 755)

- *Staub v. Proctor* (131 U.S. 1186)

- *Kepas v. Ebay* (131 S.Ct. 2160)

- *UGL-UNICCO Service Company v. NLRB* (01-RC-022447)

- *Harris v. Quinn* (S. Ct. No. 11-681)

- *Janus v. American Federation of State, County, and Municipal Employees* (S.Ct.No. 16-1466)

- *Electromation, Inc., v. NLRB* (Nos. 92-4129, 93-1169 7th Cir)

- *NLRB v. Town & Country Electric* (516 U.S. 85)

- *Circuit City Stores v. Adams* (532 U.S. 105)

- *IBM Corp. v. NLRB* (341 NLRB 148)

- *EEOC v. Waffle House* (534 U.S. 279)

- *Toering Electric Company v. NLRB* (351 NLRB 225)

- *Dana Corporation/Metaldyne Corporation v. NLRB* (351 NLRB 434)

- *KenMor Electric Co., Inc. v. NLRB* (355 NLRB 173)

- *AT&T Mobility v. Concepcion* (S.Ct. No. 09-893)

- *Specialty Healthcare and Rehabilitation Center of Mobile v. NLRB* (15-RC-008773)

- *D. R. Horton, Inc. v. NLRB* (12-CA-25764)

- *Wright v. Universal Maritime Service Corp.* (525 U.S. 70)

Figure 8-2   Case law that applies to employee and labor relations

Common Law and the Napoleonic Code

There are two separate legal heritages we draw from in the United States. One is from England, and the other is from France. They are quite different.

Napoleonic Code

This type of law comes from old Roman law, which predominated in Europe. Germanic law influenced how the Napoleonic Code developed, and it all came together in France. Napoleon I between 1800 and 1804 established a written set of laws called the Napoleonic Code. It drew upon the private laws of France that governed transactions and relationships between individuals. It was intended that these laws could be available to all citizens. The Napoleonic Code specifically forbade judges from altering laws through the establishment of precedence in their rulings. Our modern civil codes come from this type of legal system. The province of Quebec and the state of Louisiana use a legal system based on the Napoleonic Code.

Common Law

The system called *common law* comes to us from medieval English law. Judges were expected to create precedence through their interpretations of the king's laws. Other judges were then bound by those precedent decisions, and the result was known as *common law*. In the United States, it is the state courts that are primarily responsible for creating and using common law.

Labor Laws Currently

Over the years, many things have changed in the area of labor law. There are differences between public-sector and private-sector provisions for labor laws, as well as similarities. All in all, many legal protections exist for employees and are the same in each of the two major employment sectors, for instance, equal employment opportunity protections against employment discrimination and wage and hour requirements requiring payroll actions. Benefit and pension programs, on the other hand, are governed by different laws but generally offer similar protections to employees. It is in the area of privacy expectations that the two sectors diverge.

- **Private sector** Generally, private employers are able to apply an employment-at-will relationship with their employees as long as they don't violate public policy when terminating someone. Warrants are not required for employers to access lockers, desks, computer files, or e-mail accounts. Even social media is subject to content review if the employer wants to do so.

- **Public sector** Constitutional protections against unreasonable search and seizure in the Fourth Amendment protect employees of the federal government and, in some cases, those in state and local governments. These conditions have an impact on an employee's right to privacy in the workplace. Government employers can find themselves in a position where they need either the employee's permission or a court-approved warrant to access lockers, desks, computer files, e-mail accounts, and the like.

Employment Types

Employment types are usually defined under applicable employment laws. They have evolved over the years from early European legal foundations.

Employment at Will

"During the late 19th and early 20th centuries a new set of legal rules emerged in the United States governing the relationship between employer and employee.

These rules were called 'employment-at-will' and provided that, absent express agreement to the contrary, employment was for an indefinite time and could be terminated by either party, for any reason, or for no reason at all. This doctrine is a unique product of American common law, created by state and federal judges, and continues, substantially unchanged, until today."[1]

Currently, employment at will exists in most states, and it is state law that usually governs these employee relationships. In other countries using different legal systems, employment may be terminated only for cause. That means employers must justify their decisions to end the employment relationship with someone. Behavior of the individual is usually the justification.

Employment at will exists only in the absence of a contract that details the employment agreement between employer and employee. Those contracts can be related to a group, as union memorandums of understanding, or to individuals, such as chief executive officers. Since roughly the 1930s, American courts have been instrumental in identifying conditions under which employers may not arbitrarily discharge people, even though they are at-will employees. Some of those restrictions include the following:

- Civil service rules
- Constitutional protections
- Protections against employment discrimination (based on race, color, national origin, religion, sex, age, genetic information, physical disability, mental disability, pregnancy, veteran status, use of family and medical leave)
- Whistleblowing protections

Written Employment Agreements and Oral Contracts

When it is in the best interest of both parties, an employment agreement can be developed. For senior executives (usually CEOs and other positions particularly sensitive to the employer organization, such as a chief information technology officer in a high-tech company), employment contracts are particularly desirable. They protect the individual in compensation issues and in the terms of the agreement. They also protect the employer by citing the performance requirements that must be met for compensation thresholds. They also protect the company by requiring the individual to remain in the position for a specified period of time, saving the organization the recruiting expense of an early departure, or limiting the ability to immediately work with a competitor.

Written Employment Contracts

Written employment contracts will typically contain several sections:

- **Job description** Lists duties and responsibilities.
- **Statement of authority** Details expenditure limits, hiring authority, and what conditions require approval of the board of directors or other authority.
- **Agreement length** Identifies the beginning and ending dates of the contract.

- **Performance requirements**   Documents performance requirements for compensation increases or bonuses. These can include revenue targets, sales targets, or other measurable performance standards.

- **Compensation and benefits**   Details the base rate of pay, pay calculation (hourly, salaried, commissioned), how increases will be achieved, how bonuses will be achieved, how compensation will be paid (cash, stock, bonds, future payments), pension program (company and employee contribution scheme), healthcare benefits programs (medical, dental, vision, individual or family), perquisites (company car, airplane, driver, concierge, entertainment tickets for concerts and sporting events), and any other compensation condition upon which the relationship will be based.

- **Other important issues**   Can include agreements about who owns copyright and patent rights to things produced by the employee during the contract period, nondisclosure agreements for employer intellectual property protection, and noncompete provisions.

- **Termination provisions**   Can include personal behavior and ethics requirements and other reasons or "causes" for separating the employee from the organization. In many contracts these reasons are specified in great detail. If there is to be a "buy out" for time remaining on the agreement, that should be specified here. "Golden parachutes" are often large sums representing the "buy out" for early separation such as in a merger.

Oral Employment Contracts

Oral employment contracts can be expressly made or made by mistake and still be valid and enforceable, much to the dismay of employers that fall into those traps.

Oral contracts can be created in some unusual circumstances. Supervisors and managers can inadvertently enter into oral contracts and should receive training to help them avoid such pitfalls.

Some examples of oral contracts include the following:

- An in-house recruiter tells a job applicant that this is a great organization and anyone who keeps their record clean "can expect to have a lifelong career here." Within a year, the new employee's division was closed, and all employees were laid off.

- A manager tells a subordinate that "nothing short of stealing from the company" will be cause for termination. Within a year the employee was terminated for inadequate performance.

- A manager tells a new employee, "Sure, you can bet that you'll be here at least five years, so go ahead and sell your house in another state and move your family here." The employee was part of downsizing six months later.

- A supervisor says to an employee, "Don't worry about your performance rating. Nobody pays any attention to them here anyway." Within a few months the employee was terminated because of poor performance.

Collective Bargaining Agreements

When workers have chosen to be represented by a union, the employer and the union discuss and agree on a written contract through the process of collective bargaining. The *collective bargaining agreement* (CBA) specifies the working conditions in their workplace and the duties of each of the parties. Normally, a CBA will contain specifications for these and other topics:

- Shift assignments and scheduling (for example, hours of work, overtime)
- Seniority provisions
- Time off (for example, vacation, sick time, leave of absence, holidays)
- Termination procedures
- Other benefits (for example, health insurance, disability insurance)
- Rights of management
- Rights of the union
- Grievance procedure (complaint procedure)
- Compensation schedule (for example, by title, by location, by level, by seniority)
- Labor-management committee
- Health and safety
- Length of contract agreement (start date, end date)

Union contracts are sometimes referred to as *memoranda of agreement* (MOU). Contracts are negotiated following an election brought about by a qualifying event such as a show of interest among employees that is sufficient to generate the National Labor Relations Board (NLRB) sanctioning the election. There is usually a period between qualifying and the election that allows both union and management to present their positions to employees. Once the vote is taken and it authorizes the union to represent workers, the process of negotiating begins.

When the negotiations are completed and the contract has been submitted to the general employee body for approval, implementation begins. Periodically, union contracts must be renegotiated. They usually last from two to five years. Some are shorter. Some are longer.

Some unions are national in scope. Others are local. It is not uncommon for a local branch of a national union to be the point of contact for a particular employer. One example is the local union office of the International Brotherhood of Teamsters. Other examples are the Communication Workers of America, the Service Employees International, United Food and Commercial Workers International Union, American Federation of Teachers, National Association of Letter Carriers, Longshore and Warehouse Union, and the International Brotherhood of Electrical Workers. There are dozens of others. When an employer works with one of these large union organizations, it is almost always through a local branch that has its own cadre of officers and workplace stewards. The stewards are the first point of contact between the union and employees. It is often the stewards who are appointed to represent employees in a grievance handling process, in an attempt to settle any workplace disagreements.

Right-to-Work States

There are 28 states[2] that have passed right-to-work laws. A right-to-work law guarantees that no person can be compelled as a condition of employment to join a labor union. They also prohibit unions from collecting mandatory dues from every employee. That means a *closed shop* (employers may hire only dues-paying union members) is not a legal form of unionization in those states. A *union shop* is one in which employers agree to hire only union members or those nonmembers it hires must join the union within a designated time. Union dues are required. An *agency shop* does not require employees to join the representing union, but they are required to pay a fee to the union for its representation if they don't join as members. *Open shops* are workplaces where the employees do not have to pay dues to or join the representing union.

Limitations to Agency Shop

Over the years, a few Supreme Court cases have limited agency shops, especially in regard to fees from members who do not want to join a union. On June 30, 2014, the U.S. Supreme Court issued its ruling in the case of *Harris v. Quinn* (S.Ct. No. 11-681). The court said, "The First Amendment prohibits the collection of an agency fee from [employees] who do not want to join or support the union."[3] On June 27, 2018, the U.S. Supreme Court overturned a major public union precedent in *Janus v. AFSCME* (S.Ct. No. 16-1466). The court said, "States and public-sector unions may no longer extract agency fees from nonconsenting employees. The First Amendment is violated when money is taken from nonconsenting employees for a public-sector union; employees must choose to support the union before anything is taken from them."[4]

Exceptions to Employment at Will

The idea that employers can hire and fire at will, with or without a valid reason, left open the possibility that there would be improper treatment of employees through management by whim of the boss.

Public Policy

Over the years, legislative bodies have created laws limiting employers' at-will rights, and courts have reached conclusions that public policy takes precedence over individual employer interests, thus also limiting employment at will. An example is the body of non-discrimination law that exists at both state and federal levels. Public policy says we may not dismiss employees based on race, color, national origin, religion, sex, genetic information, and other characteristics (depending on jurisdiction). So, employers are not free to take employment action against any employee if that action would violate public policy.

Implied Contract

Employers can sometimes create an implied contract for employment by doing things that seem to be okay on the surface but actually make promises that the employer must then keep. For example, a supervisor makes a job offer to a job applicant and says, "You're going to love it here. Nobody gets laid off here." That is a promise that can be interpreted as an implied contract. The employer implies a contract for lifetime employment. That invalidates the claim of employment at will.

Covenant of Good Faith and Fair Dealing

There is a general assumption in the law of contracts that says people will treat each other with respect and honesty and that they will fulfill their promises to one another. It is known as the *covenant of good faith and fair dealing*. In employment terms, it means the employer must not do things in an underhanded way when dealing with employees. Employment may not be ended based on a trumped-up charge without any basis in fact. If a new worker was promised access to certain benefits and left their former job based on that promise, the employer is obligated to fulfill the promise. To do otherwise would break the covenant of good faith and fair dealing.

Invasion of Privacy

The electronic age has brought with it faster communication, and this communication can sometimes contain information that is illegal or inappropriate in the workplace. Sexual and racial jokes are two examples. Employers want to prevent these things from happening in their workplaces. To do that, they often resort to monitoring telephone and e-mail message content. There are legal limitations to that monitoring, however. Wire-tapping laws require that participants in the telephone communication be notified that the conversation is being recorded or monitored; that's why you are probably familiar with the announcement at the beginning of every call to a help desk that says something like, "Your call may be monitored or recorded for training and security purposes." That puts you, the caller, on notice that you will be monitored and the practice is acceptable. If you continue the call, you are presumed to have agreed with the condition.

Claims of invasion of privacy are hard to support when the parties have been placed on notice that they will be subject to inspection of one sort or another. That is the reason employee policy manuals and handbooks have privacy policies that state something like, "While at work, you should have no expectation of privacy. Anything placed in your company-owned desk or conversations held over company-owned equipment are subject to review by the employer if conditions should indicate that it is necessary. Lockers assigned to employees, company vehicles assigned to employees, desks assigned to employees, and computers and computer systems owned by the company are all examples of tools that the company has the right to inspect if it chooses to do so." It is usually a good idea to place employees on notice that they should have no expectation of privacy and all company equipment, systems, and facilities are subject to search at any time without notice.

Privacy issues are wrapped up in other topics such as personal financial information, criminal background checks, polygraph tests, and credit reports. You will find more information about those topics elsewhere in this book.

Public-sector employees have different rights of privacy because public-sector employers are constrained by the Constitution's Fourth Amendment. The Fourth Amendment prohibits unreasonable search and seizure by government entities. Federal and sometimes state employers are prohibited from inspecting personal workspaces in some instances without getting either the employee's permission or a search warrant from a judge.

Common Law Tort Claims

A *tort* is harm done to someone in legal terms. Negligent hiring and negligent retention are examples of legal torts. A claim for negligent hiring is based on the concept that an employer is liable for harm resulting from an employee's negligent acts. This may happen when an organization knowingly hires an unqualified employee and does not train the person. Negligent retention is similar. It involves placing an employee in a position that the employer knew or should have known would potentially commit harm in a position and where the employee actually does commit harm. This is why pre-employment background checks can be helpful. You will find more about both of these tort conditions in the "Employment Legal Issues" section in this chapter.

Defamation (Slander/Libel)

Defamation is the act of damaging someone's reputation. *Slander* is verbal defamation, and *libel* is written defamation. If someone says or writes something about another person and it is true, there is no defamation. The truth is an absolute defense against a claim of defamation. However, if someone says or writes something about another person that is false, made up, or unfounded, it can be defamation if it harms that person's reputation. Employees can cause themselves problems on the Internet by posting comments about others (including supervisors) that are not true. Employers (including supervisors) who respond with untrue comments can also find themselves in hot water.

Fraudulent Misrepresentation

When someone represents something to be true knowing it is false, or represents something as fact recklessly without knowing it is true, there can be the possibility of fraudulent misrepresentation. Some other things have to come into the equation before you can say for sure. Such misrepresentations must be made with the intention that another person rely on them. Finally, the other person must have suffered damages as a result. For example, an employer makes a statement such as, "If you join our company, you can plan on getting at least a 20 percent bonus payment every year." Should a job applicant leave an existing job and come to work for the employer promising a bonus, the harm comes when the bonus isn't paid and overall compensation falls below what would have been earned at the previous job.

Other Factors Involved in the Employment Relationship

The employment relationship depends on other factors beyond employment at will and the covenant of good faith and fair dealing.

Employer Expectation of Employee Loyalty

From common law comes this concept of the duty owed to employers by employees. Some states have added it to their laws. In California, it is part of the Labor Code. Section 2860 says, "Everything which an employee acquires by virtue of his employment, except the compensation which is due to him from his employer, belongs to the employer, whether acquired lawfully or unlawfully, or during or after the expiration of the term of his employment." The duty of loyalty requires that employees will not compete with the employer by running a similar business or take from the employer private and confidential information such as customer lists.

Unfair Competition and Noncompete Clauses

Employers depend on their workers to keep confidential all the information that might benefit competitive organizations. Disclosure of proprietary and confidential information can harm the employer whose information is lost in the process. Employees have an obligation to avoid helping anyone outside their employer's organization if that could bring harm to their employer. Giving aid to a competitor can foster unfair advantage to the other company. That is described as *unfair competition*.

Employers have sometimes tried to protect themselves by having employees sign noncompete agreements. In some cases, when challenged, state courts have determined that the noncompete agreement was overly broad and could not be justified. Trying to prevent an employee from ever working for some competitive company can deprive that person of the ability to make a living. If the noncompete agreement simply prevented activity that directly harmed the employer, it could be acceptable to court scrutiny. Insisting employees agree not to take a job with a direct competitor's organization for six months might be supportable.

Concept of Inevitable Disclosure

This legal concept holds that an employer may prohibit a former employee from working in certain jobs for competitors of the employer. It is based on the belief that if the former employee were to do so, it would inevitably result in the disclosure of the former employer's trade secrets to the competing employer.

Workplace Policies and Procedures

Organizations need a set of guidelines that explain how the workplace will be managed, what will happen when there are disagreements, and what expectations employees should have for employment conditions and benefits.

Frequently, employers prepare written employee handbooks that contain their policies for employment issues. Having them written can be beneficial if they are thought out carefully. And, of course, any employee policies should be reviewed with an employment attorney before implementation.

Developing and Communicating Policies

Many states have rather strict laws about employment policies and their communication to workers. Case law helps clarify what expectations employees should have about policies and their implementation. Generally, it is not acceptable to make policies effective retroactively. Plan to circulate any policy changes or additions to your employees with sufficient time for them to digest and adjust to the requirements before the implementation date.

NOTE Some attorneys recommend having employees sign a document acknowledging receipt of the policy changes. It doesn't mean they agree but that they have received a personal copy. This is particularly important when there are changes having to do with privacy and other similarly sensitive issues.

Policy development is a process that can take a short time or considerable time. Some organizations use teams of people in policy development; other organizations have one person generate policies. In all cases, it is a good idea to have the proposed policy circulated among executives and select employees to get feedback about their content and the changes that they will bring. If the organization has unions, it may be necessary to negotiate policy changes through the collective bargaining process.

Employee Handbooks

Employee handbooks are the documents that represent the employer's policies concerning employee management. They outline the following types of topics:

- Equal employment opportunity
- Sexual and other types of harassment
- Selection and placement of employees
- Employment-at-will employment relationship
- Personnel records and personal employee information
- Employer recordkeeping requirements
- Employee conduct
  - Weapons
  - Violence
  - Insubordination
  - Sabotage and negligence
  - Theft
  - Confidential information
  - Ethics
  - Attendance and punctuality

- Use of employer equipment
- Use of personal telephone or computer
- Use of employer vehicles
- Dress code
- Records maintenance and worktime cards/reporting
- Performance evaluations
- Progressive discipline
- Employment termination
- Payday and paychecks or direct deposit
- Expense reimbursement
- Holidays and vacation time off (paid and unpaid)
- Leaves of absence
- Drug-free workplace and drug testing
  - Employee healthcare benefits
  - Employee assistance program benefit
  - Employee expectations of privacy

There are often other subjects included as well. Some are the personal preferences of the organizations that explain "the way we do things around here." Some are cultural issues reduced to writing. There was a time when male employees of IBM all wore white dress shirts and ties. Colored shirts were not acceptable. The dress code was clear and in writing.

Whenever someone joins the organization as a new hire, a copy of the employee handbook should be provided to him or her in the new-employee orientation session. At that time, other actions should be taken to complete payroll forms (for example, W-4 and I-9), benefit election forms for insurance coverage, and so forth. It is at that time all policies should be reviewed with the new hire. Everyone should have the advantage of knowing what the rules are before they begin their employment.

Common Employee Policies

Almost all legal advisors recommend that employers have a written set of work rules that lay out expectations for employee behavior. Table 8-1 lists common topics employers should cover.

Health and Safety Policies

Employers often have a significant portion of their employee handbook or a completely separate manual dedicated to health and safety policies. Workplace policies are the primary vehicle in which employees receive information about what the organization expects. Health and safety are important for any organization, and such policies help prevent costly or life-threatening injuries or accidents from occurring. They are even more important for organizations that provide services with a high risk of injury or illness, such

PART II

Topic	Subjects Often Included
Personal appearance	Sometimes called a *dress code*, this can specify the expectations of an employer and reduce confusion about employee clothing and other adornments. This category can include clothing, uniforms, headwear, jewelry, hair styles, tattoos, piercings, and other appearance considerations.
Use of company communication/ computer equipment	If an employer allows workers to use company equipment for personal use, this is where these permissions will reside. If an employer wants to ban personal use of organization-owned equipment, this is the place where these rules can be outlined. Included in this category, you usually find telephone equipment (including cell phones, smart phones, tablets, pagers, and walkie-talkies), office computer equipment, private television circuits, and company accounts for Internet services such as Skype and My Meeting.
Moonlighting	Some employers object to workers having more than one job. Moonlighting is the practice of holding more than one job at a time. Objections include employee fatigue, loss of concentration, and safety concerns. Other employers don't mind as long as the employee is able to perform the work as assigned and be prompt for each day's schedule.
Gifts and tipping	Allowing employees to receive gifts or tips from vendors or customers can be sensitive in some work groups. If the employee has a relationship with the vendor or supplier, for example, gifts or tips could be perceived as bribes for purchasing more product or service from the vendor. If that is objectionable, then this is the place to specify its prohibition.
Smoking	Smoking is receiving a great deal of attention in many parts of the country. There are many public facilities (airports, hospitals, restaurants, and sporting venues, for example) where smoking has been banned altogether. Some states have prohibited smoking in the workplace. Others leave the decision up to the employers. Here is where the policy on smoking can appear to communicate those expectations to the employee body.
Conflict of interest	Akin to gifts and tipping, conflict of interest can embrace any condition that might suggest the possibility of undue influence over the decisions an employee is required to make in the course of his or her employment. That could apply to purchasing agents but also to janitors who have authority to recommend certain products. If there is a personal financial interest or potential financial gain from activities performed in the course of doing a job, the employer has a right to prohibit an employee from participating in those activities.
Political contributions	In some jurisdictions, it is not permissible for employers to make political contributions. If it is, the employer has a right to control how its name and resources are used in any political context. If there are rules, they should be included in the code of conduct.

Table 8-1   Common Topics in an Employee Handbook (*continued*)

Topic	Subjects Often Included
Work time and time records	Payroll depends upon accurate work time recordkeeping. If an employee is permitted to make or change work time records for himself or herself or a co-worker, that should be explained in the code of conduct. Likewise, if making changes is not permitted, that should also be explained. Of course, it is a good idea to specify that falsifying time records is cause for disciplinary action.
Time and attendance	To assure that work gets completed on time and customers are satisfied, it is important to create guidelines regarding how much advance notice is needed if an employee is going to be absent or late. This helps give the company adequate time to find a replacement for the work. Many policies also outline a progressive discipline policy for excessive unexcused absences or tardiness.
Expenses	Some jobs require a great deal of travel. Companies also frequently cover the cost of offsite training programs for employees. Expense reimbursement policies cover the details associated with reimbursing things such as airfare, mileage, hotel expenses, meal expenses, and training costs. The more detailed this policy, the better for the company. For example, clearly stating a maximum daily meal reimbursement or that only economy airfare will be reimbursed can help the company stay in budget.
Personal behavior	Unacceptable personal behavior includes arguing, fighting, threatening, and harassing. Acceptable behavior includes working a full day with appropriate effort to accomplish the job assigned. It includes getting along with co-workers and others with whom the employee interacts routinely.
Safeguarding organizational property and funds	Every employee has a responsibility for safeguarding organization property. Even if the employee is a copy clerk, the reproduction equipment is expensive and should not be abused. Managers and supervisors have responsibility for properly using employee resources by scheduling work appropriately and not allowing resources to be used for things other than organizational business. Personal expense accounts, office cash funds, checking account transactions, receivables, and other financial instruments are obvious targets of policy protection. Employer property, including note pads, pencils, and batteries, should never be taken for personal use.
Integrity and ethics	Working up to the best possible performance should be everyone's responsibility. Ethics means employees should not solicit or accept any payment, gift, commission, service, or favor in the transactions performed on behalf of the employer. It also means personal issues should not interfere with responsibilities to the employer for honest performance of the job. Honesty should prevail in all activities.
Workplace violence	Ensuring a workplace free from violence is everyone's responsibility. Employees should be clearly instructed to not bring weapons into the workplace and that the employer has zero tolerance for statements, gestures, or expressions that communicate a direct or indirect threat of physical harm. Threats of violence that might come from outside customers or vendors should also be reported to management.

Table 8-1   Common Topics in an Employee Handbook

as construction. Before reading further, it is wise to review Chapter 2 and Chapter 4 in this book to refresh your knowledge of the safety and security requirements in the workplace.

It is a good idea to create workplace safety programs in partnership with the safety director or whomever at the organization oversees this function. A secondary review by an attorney or risk management consulting firm is also helpful to be sure all state and federal laws, labor codes, or industry-specific requirements are covered. For example, drivers subject to Department of Transportation requirements have a different set of drug testing requirements.

Table 8-2 reviews workplace health and safety programs that should be covered in an employee handbook or policy manual.

Occupational Safety and Health Act (OSHA)	With the Occupational Safety and Health Act, Congress created the Occupational Safety and Health Administration to assure safe and healthful working conditions for workers by setting and enforcing standards and by providing training, outreach, education, and assistance. Workplace policies that focus on required safety training, accident reporting, hazardous materials, and personal protective equipment support compliance with OSHA.
Workers' Compensation	Workers' compensation is insurance purchased by employers to provide medical benefits and wage replacement to employees injured on the job. Workplace policies about workers' compensation should include the protocol for reporting accidents, post-accident drug testing if required, and information on doctors and medical facilities covered by the program. An employer's workers' compensation insurance carrier is also a valuable resource that manages nearly all of the worker's compensation claim process and regularly reports back to the employer.
Emergency Response	There are many types of emergencies that can occur in the workplace. From an active shooter to an earthquake, it is important to work closely with your safety director to think critically about emergencies that may arise and what the protocol will be if they happen. A policy addresses all of the action steps that will be taken if an emergency occurs, including if and when to call the police. It is even more important to regularly train employees on the policy so the entire team is aware of their individual responsibility and can act quickly in the event of an emergency.
Disaster Recovery for Business Continuity	It is wise to review the "Disaster Recovery" section in Chapter 4. In many ways, disaster recovery covers the action items after the immediate threat of an emergency has passed. Who is assigned to handle media requests? Where can displaced employees go? What aspects of the organization can remain open and which cannot? There are many questions to be answered in a policy like this.
Substance Abuse	Most employers have a policy prohibiting using illegal drugs and consumption of alcohol in the workplace. Good policies also extend to possessing, distributing, selling, purchasing, manufacturing, or being under the influence of drugs and alcohol. Misuse of prescription drugs should also be addressed, especially in safety-sensitive positions.

Table 8-2 Workplace Health and Safety Policies (*continued*)

Data Security and Privacy	Policies that protect both customer and company information are imperative in the digital age. The Federal Trade Commission enforces penalties against companies that have neglected to ensure the privacy of a customer's data. Some key items to address are confidentiality, handling remote access, virus detection software, acceptable use of technology, account and e-mail monitoring, and responding to incidents.
Legal Postings	Subscribing to the Society for Human Resource Management (SHRM) daily bulletins or the OSHA Quick Takes Newsletter is a good idea to stay up-to-date on legal requirements associated with safety. There are many postings mandated by federal and state law. Postings should be easily accessible to all employees. This might also mean versions in other languages should be posted if you have a large population of employees who do not speak English. Also, consider that an employee in a wheelchair might not be able to read postings unless they are located at his or her eye level.

Table 8-2 Workplace Health and Safety Policies

Disciplinary Action

In small organizations, discipline and termination are handled without many written procedures. The "boss" simply tells one of the employees that they are being disciplined because of a specific infraction. In larger organizations, the procedures for disciplinary action are written down in a step-by-step format and followed by managers.

Usually, discipline and termination are a multistep process. It doesn't have to be a formal process, but it can be. Here are the typical steps in that process:

- **Oral warning** Observing the employee violating a policy, procedure, or instruction. In a personal discussion with the employee, the boss explains the problem and issues a verbal warning that the problem should not happen again.

- **Written warning** Observing the employee doing the same behavior for which he or she received the oral warning. This is an "escalation" of discipline to the next step. A warning in writing should explain the infraction and why it is unacceptable. It should also explain the consequence of the same thing happening again.

- **Suspension** Although this step is not always included in the process, it is available for use to emphasize to the employee how serious the behavioral problem is. In most cases, a suspension will be unpaid time off. It can last from a day to several weeks. The length of time should be dependent upon the seriousness of the problem and the employee's length of service. A suspension may also be used as an investigative tool. At some workplaces, employees are placed on suspension following an allegation of a serious workplace problem, and the suspension time period is used to investigate the problem and determine a resolution.

- **Termination** The final stage of the disciplinary process is removing the employee from employment. Using this step acknowledges that the employee cannot be salvaged.

NOTE Whatever disciplinary procedures you elect to use in your organization, they should be applied consistently in similar situations. It is not a good idea to treat people differently when their situations are similar. That will surely land you in court or present you with a union grievance.

Employers can avoid locking themselves into strict disciplinary procedures if they provide a policy for discretionary disciplinary decisions based on the circumstances of a situation. Hard rules about steps to be used in the process can prevent flexibility and discretion.

Background Investigations

For decades, legal advisors have been telling their employer clients to conduct background checks on every new employee. These investigations have helped detect inaccuracies on application forms and resume's.

Typically, background investigations involve verification of employment history and educational achievements. Occasionally they will also delve into personal references and professional references. These are often less than helpful, however, because a job candidate will only list references that are known to provide good comments if asked.

In 2012, the Equal Employment Opportunity Commission (EEOC) published its guidelines on use of arrest and conviction records in employment decisions.[5] These guidelines are not legal requirements but will be considered if complaints of illegal discrimination are filed against an employer. Basically, the guidelines say that disparate impact against Hispanics and Blacks results from consideration of criminal records because there is a higher percentage of those races/ethnicities represented in the prison and ex-convict population. There have been many voices raised against this position, yet the guidelines remain. There are exceptions allowed by the guidelines for a direct link between job requirements and the reason for conviction. The guidelines prohibit use of any conviction or arrest record if it is not specifically job related.

Credit Checks

Credit checks are another area of controversy in the employment world. It has been common for employers to use credit checks in their employment decision-making based on the premise that someone with bad credit would constitute a bad risk on the job. Without specifics, however, the relationship between job requirements and credit history wasn't generally made.

The Fair Credit Reporting Act (FCRA) (see Chapter 2) requires employers to obtain a job applicant's permission to seek a credit report from one of the major credit reporting agencies. It also requires the information obtained be maintained as private and confidential. If a negative decision is made based on the credit report information, the candidate (or employee) must be given a copy of the credit report that was used in making the employment decision.

Documentation Techniques and Guidelines

There are many reasons for creating documentation. Often, conversations with employees are held to provide feedback on job performance or to discuss behavioral problems that have led to disciplinary decisions. Documentation is especially important to support the topics we discussed in previous sections in this chapter. Other types of documentation relate to projects, proposals, or other employment issues. Whatever the reason for creating documentation, it should contain answers to these questions:

- Who?
- What?
- When?
- Where?
- Why (if employee discussions provide this information)?

Documentation should not include guesses, suppositions, assumptions, or other non-factual information. Opinions belong in documentation only if they are labeled as opinions. They should never be unlabeled and presented as facts. Documentation should contain a date identifying when it was created and a name to indicate who created it. If a document is created some time after the event it describes, it should be dated on the day it was created, not predated to the time of the event.

Documentation of employee conversations does not ordinarily need to be signed by the employee. Exceptions to that include requirements of union agreements or employer policy to the contrary. Remember to follow the basic rule that any time an employee signs a document of any type, a copy of that signed document should be given to the employee. It is a requirement in some states that those copies be provided. Otherwise, depending again on your legal jurisdiction, documents about employee conversations can be considered the property of the employer.

Performance Management

Managing employee performance is a key part of employee and labor relations. Performance management gives you the ability to gauge individual and organizational efficiency, determine who high performers are, understand gaps that need to be filled by training, and get insight on other areas of improvement needed in the organization. Human resource professionals are tasked with the responsibility of clearly communicating performance expectations and working with employees and supervisors to ensure they are met. Before reading further in this section, reviewing Chapter 6 in regard to the topic of performance management and performance management methods is recommended.

Performance Reviews

Most organizations conduct performance reviews on a regular basis. The frequency of reviews depends on the organization, but common time frames are at the 90-day mark for newly hired, transferred, or promoted employees and on an annual basis. There are varying opinions in regard to the benefits of performance reviews, but many of the benefits tie back to the employee relations function. Here are a few of these benefits:

- Provide honest feedback to employees
- Improve organizational and departmental communication

- Make employees feel valued
- Clearly define performance expectations
- Resolve grievances
- Document poor performance
- Set goals and refocus the team

Whatever the reason for doing a performance review, it is important to remember that all performance review documents should be reviewed by a human resource professional before being presented to an employee. A minor wording mistake or large fluctuation in ratings between review cycles may lead to legal issues for an employer. For example, stating that an employee needs to be more "energetic" might lead to an age discrimination claim if only the oldest worker in the department received this feedback. Or terminating an employee for poor performance after she has received a glowing performance review a few months prior would likely receive some criticism from a judge during a wrongful termination case.

Promotions

To avoid legal pitfalls, it is important that opportunities for advancement or promotion are offered fairly to employees. Performance reviews are a great way to gauge and compare employee performance to determine the best candidate for selection. An internal job posting process can also be helpful. This type of process offers the opportunity to file an application for a promotional opportunity to internal employees before external employees. Some employers even have sections in their human resource information system that allow employees to self-report career goals, skills, and interests. With this information, employers may be less likely to pass on an internal candidate for promotion that may have the interest and/or the skill set desired. But beware, if any of these tools are not used or administered consistently, there is a risk in violating a slew of employment laws. In the employee relations world, fairness and consistency with past practice are the golden rules.

Coaching

Like the coach of a sports team who is tasked with motivating team members to perform at their best, the coaching process strives to achieve the same goal. Sometimes coaching is also included as the first step in the disciplinary action process. It can be especially helpful when trying to correct employee performance deficiencies when performance reviews are conducted too infrequently.

Creating an organizational culture where employees feel valued rests a great deal on how employers communicate, especially relative to negative feedback. No one likes to be told they are not doing a good job. In the coaching process, the goal is to clearly communicate a performance deficiency to an employee and provide the employee with the resources and support to improve. Support for improvement might be through a goal setting process, regular meetings with an organizational supervisor or mentor, or additional training.

Performance Improvement Plan

If the coaching process is unsuccessful, the next step to improve poor employee performance is often a *performance improvement plan* (PIP). A PIP outlines areas where performance improvement is needed, the expected timeline for improvement, and resources and support for improvement. Employees are often placed on a PIP for a certain period of time. During this time period, generally 60 or 90 days, job performance is monitored closely. Employees are expected to make noticeable performance improvements and make use of the resources assigned to or made available to them. If an employee does not successfully complete a PIP, involuntary termination is generally the next step.

Before issuing a PIP to an employee, it is wise to obtain a legal review of the document. Because PIPs are generally the final document that supports a termination decision, there will be much scrutiny of the document if the employee sues the organization after termination. Some attorneys may even provide a template for future use that can be catered to other employees being placed on a performance improvement plan.

Terminations

Sometimes relationships must come to an end. Employment relationships are no different. We discussed employment at will earlier in this chapter. *Employment at will* means that the employment relationship can be terminated at any time, either by the employer or by the employee. As a reminder, employment at will exists in most states in the absence of an employment contract. However, it is important to check your state's regulations to determine whether they affect the ability to make termination decisions. Whether or not the employment-at-will doctrine applies does not change the fact that terminations will happen; it only affects the legal risks that may result from mishandling terminations.

There are several types of terminations:

- **Voluntary terminations**   These occur when an employee decides to leave an organization. Voluntary terminations may be in the form of resignation or retirement. It is a generally accepted practice for employees to provide at least two weeks' notice for voluntary terminations. This gives an employer time to hire and train a replacement.

- **Involuntary terminations**   These are initiated by the employer. This type of termination results from repeated policy violations, poor performance, or gross misconduct such as theft or harassment. The reasons for an involuntary termination are endless. What is most important is that involuntary termination decisions are made on the basis of fact and include supporting documentation to ensure that decisions were made fairly and legally.

- **Job eliminations**   These occur when the organization no longer has a need for a certain job. For example, enhancements to technology may result in replacing a certain position at an organization with a software program. However, it is important to remember that a job elimination applies to all jobs that are affected by the organizational change. It does not mean that an organization can decide to keep the top-performing employees in a certain job and eliminate the others in the same job. That is not a true job elimination and can put the organization in some legal trouble.

- **Reductions in force**   These are also known as layoffs. They generally apply to a larger component of the organization than a position elimination. Employers sometimes have a policy outlining how employees will be selected if a reduction in force occurs. Union contracts almost always include this language. Many union contracts require the method of "last in/first out" when faced with a reduction in force decision. This means that layoff selection is entirely based on seniority. Employees with the least company seniority are selected for layoff first. As a reminder, the Worker Adjustment and Retraining Notification (WARN) Act outlines specific requirements for large reductions in force. Chapter 2 reviews this act in more detail.

In the Trenches

From Employee to Ex-Employee in Five Minutes

Gerald was upset about the merit rating he received from his supervisor. When his boss's boss came to the office, Gerald was ready with his list of grievances and was going to let the executive have it right between the eyes.

Gerald got the attention of his senior manager and began with his statement explaining how upset he was about the situation. He was threatening in his tone. Muriel, the executive, said to him, "Gerald, please lower your voice and change your tone. We can't have a discussion until you are more reasonable in your approach." Gerald continued with his rant.

Muriel said, "Gerald, I'm warning you that you must change your tone or there will be consequences." Gerald continued.

Muriel said, "Gerald, I'm giving you an oral warning that you will be suspended for two days if you don't stop threatening me." That didn't even slow him down.

Muriel said, "Gerald, you are now suspended for two days without pay. You should go home and give some thought to how people need to communicate in the workplace."

Did Gerald stop? It only made him more angry. His rant continued.

Muriel said, "Gerald, you have already been suspended for two days without pay. If you don't stop right this minute, you will be risking your job. I will terminate your employment if you continue your behavior."

Gerald was so worked up that he could only see that he was not getting his message across. So he raised his voice and volume for the next few sentences.

Muriel said, "Gerald, it is with sadness that I tell you that you are being terminated. I will have your final paycheck ready for you in 30 minutes. Please gather your personal things and prepare to leave the building."

That's progressive discipline in action, from caution to dismissal in five minutes.

Employee Relations Programs and Organizational Culture

While laws help drive decisions, HR is ultimately about people. Employee relations focuses on the relationship between supervisors and subordinates in an employment organization. As reviewed in Chapter 3, several concepts such as organizational behavior and levels of emotional intelligence roll up into a company's overall culture. Company culture can be a vague term that is not widely understood. There is much academic research on the topic but no widely accepted definition of company culture. It includes a variety of elements, including work environment, company mission, values, ethics, expectations, and goals. According to the Society for Human Resource Management, organizational culture is based on a company's assumptions about the following topics:[6]

- **Human nature**   Are people inherently good or bad, mutable or immutable, proactive or reactive? These basic assumptions lead to beliefs about how employees, customers, and suppliers should interact and how they should be managed.

- **The organization's relationship to its environment**   How does the organization define its business and its constituencies?

- **Appropriate emotions**   Which emotions should people be encouraged to express, and which ones should be suppressed?

- **Effectiveness**   What metrics show whether the organization and its individual components are doing well? An organization will be effective only when the culture is supported by an appropriate business strategy and a structure that is appropriate for both the business and the desired culture.

Organizational culture is often defined by employees, at least in part by the type of employee relations programs that exist. We are talking about structured programs that are designed to help employees feel like they are part of the organization in positive ways. Creating a positive culture is not a simple matter and is an essential influential factor for recruiting and retaining talent. HR devotes much effort and time to champion a positive culture with effective employee relations programs. The human resources department also serves as an employee advocate. Culture is defined by the way an organization treats its employees, customers, and others. It is also influenced by the way power is distributed within the organization and the amount of power employees sense they have. What follows is an overview of different types of employee relationship programs.

Recognition

The larger an organization grows, the greater the likelihood that its recognition programs will be structured. In small organizations, recognition can be given in many forms, often as events unfold and accomplishments are achieved.

Employee recognition can include service anniversary awards (watches, clocks, plaques, certificates, pins), employee-of-the-month awards (designated parking space, plaque or bulletin board posting, special benefit like a dinner gift certificate), cost savings suggestions, sales achievement awards, team achievement awards, or individual achievement awards. Obviously, that is not an exhaustive list. You can add others and apply them as your organization finds a fit between the recognition and the accomplishment.

Nonmonetary Rewards

Nonmonetary rewards are often given because they are effective and do not impact the budget. Monetary rewards are such things as merit pay increase, bonus payment, or other cash payment. Nonmonetary rewards can include such things as a day off, picnics, recognition of birthdays, free lunches, restaurant gift certificates, plaques, designated parking space, or company jackets reserved for special performers. Chapter 7 has more information on nonmonetary compensation.

Still, the most effective and least expensive form of nonmonetary reward is a sincere "thank you" from the boss. Done publicly, with detailed explanation of the employee's accomplishments, it can be even more effective.

Special Events

Taken in context as employee relations programs, special events can include free pizza Fridays, after-hours beer parties, company day at the county fair, or political rallies with presidential candidates. It can also involve the organization and its employees in news coverage of its products or services being used in historical situations like the moon landings. Special events can embrace new product introductions and unveiling of innovative service offerings. Events involving employees in activities that contribute to a sense of pride in the organization and for being a member of the employment family would qualify in this category of employee relations programs.

Diversity and Inclusion Programs

If the foundation of employee management is equal employment opportunity (EEO) and a tool for ensuring organizations meet those EEO obligations is affirmative action, then diversity and inclusion are the next step in ensuring that human contributions come from all sectors of the employee population. Diversity and inclusion (D&I) is based on the premise that all employees have contributions to offer based on their experiences and that different experience histories can make a collective group of employees more effective in addressing organizational problems, including production and revenue generation.

D&I is present in recruiting programs, internal employee programs, training, advertising, and customer appreciation programs and is critical to ensuring compliance with legal requirements and company goals. Managing people from extremely different cultural backgrounds and with different generational representation is a challenge that can be addressed through a good D&I program. While it may be human nature to feel most comfortable with people like ourselves, it is going to be more and more necessary to push that comfort boundary and include people unlike ourselves if we are to be successful as an organization.

PART II

Common employee activities in a D&I program are employee resource groups (Black engineers, Hispanic professional women, Veteran employees). These groups are endorsed by employers in many cases and are sometimes provided with facilities in which to conduct meetings or informal gatherings. These programs do much more than help comply with federal laws and regulations such as affirmative action. When employees have an opportunity to meet with people like themselves and discuss issues associated with succeeding in the workplace, they can adjust more readily and feel better about their employer and themselves.

Some employers schedule special events or celebrations based on specific cultural groupings, such as International Food Day, unique cultural celebrations exhibits, or Gay Pride Day. Almost anything that recognizes and supports differences between people and cultures can expand individual employee tolerance and add value to decision-making processes.

Corporate Responsibility

Celebrating diversity and inclusion in the workplace has expanded to a broader topic called *corporate responsibility*. Corporate responsibility is when organizations set concrete goals to comply with legal requirements and make strides to improve the society around them. Supporting activism that aligns with the company's values, setting targets for a greener workplace, supporting a community outreach program for underprivileged children, or engaging in charity work are just a few examples. Rather than simply putting an affirmative action plan on paper or creating a policy about equal employment opportunity, attending a rally to support equal pay in the workplace or sponsoring a fundraiser for veterans helps turn words into actions.

In the Trenches

Tapping the Riches of Global Diversity

Susan Farwell, President, The Executive Communicator, LLC, New York City sf@executivecommunicator.com

Although today's workplaces often consist of bland-looking cubicles and rows of uniform offices, if we take an aerial view, we will see a rich tapestry of color, culture, custom, and belief in the employees working in those spaces. Organizations equipped to tap into the vibrancy of this diversity will draw from a larger pool of ideas and experiences and will increase their ability to stay competitive well into the future.

(continued)

There is greater opportunity for cross-cultural interaction in business today than in just about any other place in the world. In cities, neighborhoods, and villages around the globe people still often gravitate into culturally familiar groupings. This is no longer an option in the business world. Employees in today's global business environment are collaborating and negotiating with others whose ancestry, religious beliefs, leadership, and communication practices are often quite dissimilar to theirs.

I worked with a senior team that consisted of division leaders from Britain, Thailand, Egypt, and the United States. The team was encountering considerable difficulty communicating and resolving conflict, and yet they had not considered their cultural differences as having any impact on this dysfunction. When I broached the subject of culture with the team, the executive in charge dismissed it by saying, "All of us have had many years of international work experience, so I don't see how we can still be influenced by the country we grew up in."

We learn our culture's values and communication practices early on, consciously through adults who praise, criticize, and give instructions nonverbally and verbally and unconsciously by observing adults who are acting in consistent ways. Because communication practices are adopted from birth, they are held in the subconscious, and they just seem right; they are common sense.

So, for the Brit on this team, it felt right to employ clever quips and to practice understatement; for the Egyptian, it was right to speak passionately and to defend his team's "honor." The Americans were expected to say what they meant and not beat around the bush, while for the Thai member of the team, it was common sense to "save the face of others" by being selective and implicit in communication style.

Each of these approaches is valid in the individual's country of origin, but on this team the behaviors collided. Of course, we can't assume that all communication choices the team members were making were culturally derived; however, once the topic of culture was discussed, the dynamics on the team changed, and respect grew. Team members were able to then agree on a set of communication ground rules that they practiced going forward. In my experience facilitating diversity dialogues, leading intercultural workshops, and coaching global leaders and teams, I have had the opportunity to see firsthand how openly discussing diversity enriches interaction and creativity.

Globalization and the seismic shift in workforce demographics are two megatrends that drive the confluence of diverse peoples, values, beliefs, and practices. Success in today's business world dictates the need for increased cultural awareness and agility, an essential role that the HR professional holds.

Self-Directed Work Teams

In organizations that do not have labor unions (and in a few that do), self-directed work teams are used to tackle projects or problems when multiple disciplines are needed for the effort. This is a common approach in the high-technology industry. It is even found in some old-line manufacturing companies when adapting and implementing new technologies on the production line. The automobile industry is a prime example of a long-established, union-represented industry that uses work teams to tackle quality problems.

When an issue is systemic in its nature, gathering representatives from all the affected functional disciplines can bring the appropriate talent to bear on finding a solution to the problem. Such teams can work without designated leaders or can appoint their own leaders when necessary. They work independent of management oversight except for their accountability for the end result of their efforts. Once the problem has been solved, the team disbands, and people return to their normal job assignments.

Employee-Management Committees

The National Labor Relations Board has issued decisions in several cases over the past two decades that have both criticized and endorsed different forms of employee-management committees.

The board has held illegal committees that were charged with suggesting policies or courses of action to management that would subsequently decide whether to accept the committee recommendations. The board said that such a committee was engaged in issues of working conditions.[7]

Later, the NLRB decided that committees that were assigned management authority to oversee certain aspects of the business with limited power were not negotiating groups, but management agencies. In that format, such committees are legal, said the board.[8]

 NOTE Employee-management committees are becoming increasingly popular as a method of involving workers in the management of an enterprise. Given the rocky experiences in front of the NLRB on this issue, it would be wise to seek the advice of your labor attorney before implementing any program of this nature. The same is true of employee brainstorming committees and suggestion box offerings.

Labor Leadership Concepts and Applications

In both the public and private sectors, the movement toward a more cooperative and collaborative labor-management practice is in force. Efforts are characterized by the following:

- Increased willingness to share power
- Candid sharing of more information
- Joint decision-making on issues of common concern

- Win-win-win bargaining techniques (organization/union/customer)
- Shared accountability of results and responsibilities

Employee Complaints and Grievances

Several conditions impact how employee complaints and grievances are handled within an employer's organization. One large determining factor is whether the employer has labor unions involved in the workplace. Labor agreements/contracts (or a memorandum of understanding) will usually contain a structured method for dealing with employee grievances. Those agreements designate steps for handling complaints about working conditions or other provisions of the labor union contract. Complaints about issues outside working conditions are not usually addressed within the confines of a labor union contract. Those are handled by other employer policies.

Using Employee Input to Prevent Complaints

There are many methods for gathering employee input regarding organizational changes and how they would react to those changes. Some techniques are formal employee focus groups (facilitated discussions describing certain programs or conditions and gathering employee reactions to those ideas), employee surveys (written or computer-based gathering of employee responses to multiple-choice or narrative alternatives in designated situations), or individual interviews (one-on-one sessions to ask for specific feedback about specific proposals).

Taking employee thoughts into consideration before implementing changes is one way to help prevent complaints later. Organizational changes that can evoke strong employee reactions include organizational structure modifications (new divisions, departments, or hierarchy), employee benefit programs (changes to existing benefit programs, proposed new benefit programs, or elimination of benefit programs), or alterations to employee development programs (training opportunities, temporary assignment opportunities, or advanced education sponsorship programs).

NOTE When employees have the opportunity to review and comment on proposals for change, they will have a higher level of acceptance for whatever decisions are made about those proposals. Presenting decisions as a *fait accompli*, or a done deal, can result in bruised feelings, resentment, and sometimes passive sabotage.

Conflict Resolution

Some amount of conflict will always be present in the workplace. The fact that it exists is not necessarily an unhealthy thing. When it is resolved quickly and effectively, it can lead to personal and professional growth. In many cases, effective conflict resolution can make the difference between positive and negative outcomes. The Leader's 5-Step Guide to Conflict Resolution[9] recommends five steps in the conflict resolution process:

- **Affirm the relationship**   "I am here because I value your friendship more than I value the discomfort of confronting my hurt feelings."

- **Seek to understand**   Stephen Covey's thoughts on listening are worth their weight in gold, teaching one to seek the other person's feelings, thoughts, and perspectives first.

- **Seek to be understood**   After understanding, share one's feelings, thoughts, and perspectives, not in an attacking mode, but in an effort for the other party to see one's views.

- **Own responsibility by apologizing**   Seek to see where any, if not all, of the conflict is one's responsibility, learning to respond differently in the future. A genuine apology not only affirms the relationship but can do wonders in releasing hurt feelings.

- **Seek agreement**   After both parties have apologized, accepting responsibility for their parts in the conflict, seeking agreement means reuniting on the common vision that drew both sides together in the first place, agreeing that the cause is bigger than the conflict is for both parties.

Complaint/Grievance Handling

Employee grievances can relate to any subject but always indicate a feeling of upset or discontent about something going on in the workplace…the way they are being treated, organizational policies, and the big category of "fairness."

In union-represented organizations, the union contract (memorandum of understanding) will usually explain what steps exist in the grievance procedure. They are designed to permit union members the opportunity to formally protest application of any contract provision. Most will deal with working conditions such as hours of work, how shifts are assigned, or seniority practices.

In nonunion organizations, employee handbooks will often detail the steps for submitting and processing an employee complaint. Moreover, a good antidiscrimination and antiharassment policy at an organization will outline a specific process for complaints to ensure that employees understand their rights and how to best address instances of perceived discrimination or harassment.

NOTE   Rarely will such complaints be called *grievances* in nonunion groups. That is usually a term reserved for union contracts.

Here are the typical grievance handling steps you will find in most organizations:

- **Submit a written complaint**   The employee describes in writing what is causing the upset or discontent.

- **Supervisor-level discussion**   The employee's supervisor (or another group's supervisor) will discuss the complaint with the employee, reviewing facts and reasons for the decision that resulted in the complaint. If the explanation is sufficient, the grievance ends here. If the employee presents information that causes the decision to be changed, the grievance can also end here.

- **Management- or HR-level discussion**   If the supervisor and employee can't agree, the next discussion is with a management person and/or the human resource department. If an agreement is reached, the matter is settled. If not, it can go to a final step with senior management.

- **Senior management**   The final step is usually with a senior management official. Sometimes that is the chief executive officer, but it can be with any other designated official who has authority to make any adjustments or decisions deemed appropriate in settling the grievance. If no agreement is reached at this step, the employee will have to either drop the complaint or seek legal advice in a potential civil suit.

Conducting Unbiased Investigations

Investigations are appropriate in several circumstances within an employer's organization. They can be helpful in a grievance-handling effort and are essential in determining the validity of discrimination complaints. Whenever there is a need to determine facts surrounding a complaint, an investigation should be conducted.

Internal HR professionals are almost always given authority in state and federal law to conduct an investigation on behalf of the employer. If the organization wants to have an external investigator handle the fact finding, there are some limitations imposed by certain state laws. In California, for example, external investigators who are not licensed attorneys must be licensed private investigators. Other states have different requirements.

Legal advisors suggest that internal attorneys are not the best people to conduct investigations because they could be placed in the position of having to testify to their investigative activities while still providing legal advice to their employer.

Whoever is designated as the investigator should normally follow these steps:

- **Obtain a written complaint**   The employee should write a complaint that states he or she was treated differently from others in similar situations based on a legally protected category and identify that category. If the employee can do this, he or she will have provided a *prima facie* case, which means it sounds good on its face.

- **Interviews**   Next it is necessary to interview the complaining employee, the supervisor or management person who is named as the offending decision-maker, and any witnesses the employee says were there at the time. Sometimes it is a peer who has been the offending party. When that is the case, at least one interview of the offending party should be scheduled. The investigation should follow whatever leads are uncovered until the investigator is satisfied that all the facts have been uncovered that can be uncovered. Each step of the process should be documented in writing and maintained in a complaint investigation file.

- **Determination**   Once the facts have been determined as best as possible, a determination should be made about the validity of the complaint. If the complaint is valid, a remedy should be sought based on both legal and reasonable requirements. If the complaint is determined not to have valid grounds, that will be the determination. The decision should be documented in writing and included in the investigation folder.

- **Feedback**   The employee who filed the complaint should be given feedback about the investigation results and any decisions made as a result. It may or may not be advisable to provide specific information about disciplinary action taken against an employee. Your legal advisor can give you guidance about that in your specific circumstances.

Using Surveillance as an Investigative Tool

With the advent of technology, employers continue to become more adept in their ability to conduct a thorough investigation. For any human resource professional who has investigated a workplace issue, it is all too familiar that there are at least two different sides to any story. Differing views or interpretations of situation have long complicated the investigative process. Surveillance is a tool that can help. When a workplace uses surveillance technology, it is possible to "see" the workplace issue in question unfold and develop a strong, fact-based recommendation to resolve the issue.

While surveillance is a powerful tool for investigations, it is important to remember that certain areas where privacy should be protected, such as restrooms or employee changing areas, should not be under surveillance. We talked earlier in this chapter about invasions of employee privacy. While employees should generally not have an expectation of privacy while in common areas of the workplace, rules differ for private- and public-sector employers.

Internal vs. External Complaints

Internal complaints can run the gamut from "it isn't fair" to "I was discriminated against illegally." Especially in nonunion organizations, it is important to let employees know that their complaints are taken seriously. Each one should be handled in a way that conveys that message. If necessary, the four steps of an investigation should be followed as just outlined.

Internal complaints give an employer the opportunity to resolve issues with employees before they fester further and generate formal external agency complaints. Wise HR professionals will make every effort to encourage employees to file complaints internally so they will have the opportunity to investigate and resolve them. Dealing with issues internally is always preferable to having them registered with third-party law enforcement agencies and much less costly.

External complaints are those filed with state or federal fair employment practices agencies (for example, Equal Employment Opportunity Commission), wage and hour enforcement agencies (for example, U.S. Department of Labor, Wage and Hour Division), or safety enforcement agencies (for example, Organizational Safety and Health Administration or Mine Safety and Health Administration). When a formal complaint is filed with an external agency, it is often a signal that the employer may no longer speak with their own employee about that issue. All discussions with the employee after a complaint is filed must be handled through the enforcement agency. As a practical matter, that means the employer will face some limitations.

Before a response can be prepared explaining what happened and why, the employer will need to conduct an investigation to determine whether the complaint has merit. Based on that result and with the help from legal counsel, a formal response can be prepared explaining the employer's position.

Remember that these are law enforcement agencies with authority to require employers to take certain actions to remedy complaints if that is warranted. Your legal advisor is always your best ally when working with external agencies. There are usually complaint filing deadlines, designated response deadlines, and deadlines for implementing remedies. Those will vary depending on the agency involved and provisions of the relevant laws.

Mediation and Arbitration (Alternative Dispute Resolution)

Mediation and arbitration are alternative methods for dispute resolution. Some employers require one or the other in lieu of lawsuits to resolve employment problems with workers. Each requires certification by a national or state board and also requires compliance with strict ethical standards.

Mediation is the less formal of the two problem-solving methods. Since 1995, the American Arbitration Association (www.adr.org) has used a due process protocol that requires fair hearing of an issue. Mediation is usually not binding on the parties involved. That means employers and employees can go through the process, arrive at a conclusion, and still not accept it, though why that would happen seems odd.

Arbitration is a stricter alternative. It is usually binding on the parties because they accept that condition before the process begins. Arbitration is nearly always conducted by an arbitrator who is a neutral party and a member of the American Arbitration Association. Binding arbitration is sometimes used as an alternative to lawsuits because the expense is considerably less than court and attorney costs, and it can be quicker.

Cost of mediation or arbitration is often split equally by the parties, although it is possible for the employer to agree to accept responsibility for paying all costs involved. In union contracts there is frequently a provision that costs will be split between the union and the employer. The method for selecting an arbitrator is usually specified in a union contract when that step is included in the grievance-handling process.

Using External Experts

There are many different types of external experts who can be resources when appropriate. They include lawyers, consultants, investigators, educators, or trainers. The key to using external experts is to determine there is a benefit to be gained over performing the required tasks using internal personnel. The benefit might be a cost reduction or simply relief of the workload being carried by internal people. Sometimes it doesn't make sense to have a special talent or resource on the payroll because the frequency at which it is used seems so low. When the "growing your own" internal resource isn't practical, calling upon external resources is the next best thing. They can be used for the project, and then the expense can end.

Expert witnesses are sometimes hired by employers and their legal representatives to support their position in lawsuits. When that happens, the people hired as experts offer knowledge and experience that fits the issues being disputed.

HR's Role in the Litigation Process

Employee and vendor lawsuits are quite common—much more than employers would like. The question here is, "What is the role of HR management in that litigation process?" The answer is, "Several roles come to mind."

- **Preserving documentation**   Once a lawsuit has been filed, your employment attorney will notify you and instruct everyone in the organization to preserve all records related to that suit. Because the HR department has custody of most employment-related records, a bulk of the responsibility for record preservation rests with the HR professionals. Preservation means records may not be destroyed or altered. Records may be in hard copy, on computer files, or in archive form somehow. It is necessary that they all be flagged in some way to indicate that they may not be destroyed until a release is provided by the organization's attorney.

- **Gathering witness information**   With help from the organization's attorney, HR professionals should identify appropriate witnesses in the lawsuit. Those people should be contacted to be sure they are aware that they may be called to testify. Any records they have about the issue at hand must be preserved until the matter is settled.

- **Identifying others involved**   This includes the complaining employee's supervisor, the decision-maker, co-workers who were present at the time, and other employees who are in similar situations as the complaining employee.

- **Communication with involved employees**   Notify all employees involved in the lawsuit that they may not discuss it with the complaining employee or with that employee's legal counsel. They should report to HR or the legal department any attempt by the complaining employee or a lawyer to contact them to discuss the case.

Collective Bargaining

Collective bargaining is a process of negotiation that is required by the National Labor Relations Act (NLRA) (see Chapter 2). Once an election has resulted in a union being certified as the representative of a work group, the next step is to develop a written contract that will lay out all the working conditions appropriate to the relationship and the work group requirements. That process of contract development is called *collective bargaining*.

Governance of the Union-Employer Relationship

The National Labor Relations Act was passed by Congress in 1935 to encourage employers and employees to work together through collective bargaining. It protects the rights of employees and provides procedures for establishing and eliminating bargaining units from the employment relationship. Union representation is always conducted under written contract with employers. Because represented employees have a written contract for their employment, they are no longer considered employment-at-will employees.

Contract Negotiation

Negotiating a contract requires identifying the subjects to be addressed by the agreement. Then each party prepares its preferred position on each subject. Next, the process of comparing those positions begins. Often, dollars are attached to contract subjects. For example, the length of work shift, the amount of overtime to be paid, and the cost of healthcare benefits all can be represented by dollar values. If the union wants greater benefits for its members, a dollar value can be assigned to that increase. Employers argue budget restraint and use dollar values to justify their reasoning.

According to the Legal Dictionary, there are five core steps in the negotiation process.[10] Here is a list of the process step flow in contract negotiations:

1. **Preparation**   Choose a negotiation team and representatives of both the union and employer. Both parties should be skilled in negotiation and labor laws, and both examine available information to determine whether they have a strong standing for negotiation.

2. **Discussion**   Both parties meet to set ground rules for the collective bargaining negotiation process.

3. **Proposal**   Both representatives make opening statements, outlining options and possible solutions to the issue at hand.

4. **Bargaining**   Following proposals, the parties discuss potential compromises, bargaining to create an agreement that is acceptable to both parties. This becomes a "draft" agreement, which is not legally binding but is a stepping stone to coming to a final collective bargaining agreement.

5. **Final agreement**   Once an agreement is made between the parties, it must be put in writing, signed by the parties, and put into effect.

Establishing Contract Costs

Each component of a contract agreement can be assigned a cost in dollars. Adding all of those component costs can produce the total contract value. For example, health benefits will cost several hundreds of dollars each month to cover an employee and family members. The employer can agree to cover a percentage of that cost, with the balance being paid by the employee. A union will ask for more employer contribution to that formula. And should the employer agree, the increased contribution can be assigned an incremental cost increase value. Adding that to other cost increases, such as increased pay schedules and overtime rates, will produce a total increase of contract costs. Each time a new proposal is made or received, a cost analysis should be made to determine the budgetary impact. Some costs will be perpetual, such as an increase in pay rates. Other costs can be limited to one time only, such as special bonus payments. There are advantages and disadvantages to costs that will be contained to one period of time (year) versus continuing into future periods of time.

Administering Union Contracts (MOU or CBA)

The thought that only large employers have union contracts is a myth. Many small employers work with union agreements. That is often the case in the construction industry, for example. Operating Engineers, Teamsters, and Laborers, among other unions, will sometimes have agreements with governmental entities that only union-represented workers will be employed on projects funded by that entity. This is common practice for cities and counties, particularly in geographical areas where labor organizations are a strong political influence.

Memoranda of understanding and collective bargaining agreements are the written contracts between employers and unions. MOU is a term usually found in the public sector, and CBA is a term normally used in the private sector.

Whether the employer is large or small, someone in the organization must be assigned the responsibility for coordinating work through unions and ensuring the employer abides by all requirements of the union contract. Sometimes unions require that they process all job requisitions from their employer counterparts. Hiring through union "hiring halls" is the practice of notifying the union of a job opening and receiving a qualified union member as the new hire designee. It is a simple process that can provide staffing quickly, often with only one telephone call or e-mail with the employment requisition.

Large employers will have labor relations staff groups that are assigned responsibility for day-to-day interactions with labor unions, as well as carrying responsibility for contract negotiations. Small employers will rely on a part-time job duty assignment for the labor relations function because it doesn't require full-time attention. Small employers sometimes rely on their labor attorneys to fill the role of contract negotiator and grievance handler, while job requisitions are processed part-time by another company employee.

Unfair Labor Practices

The National Labor Relations Act explains that unfair labor practices can be blamed on either employers or labor unions (see Chapter 2). Common issues evoking such claims are those revolving around the process of union elections. Unions commonly claim the employer is blocking their organizing efforts, and employers claim that the union is harassing employees and electioneering using paid time. Another issue that generates great numbers of complaints is how management and union members behave during a work stoppage (strike).

Complaints of unfair labor practices are formally filed with the National Labor Relations Board. The NLRB will investigate the complaints and issue a determination along with any order for corrective action or limitation on activities of the offending party.

In some instances, when an employer believes there has been a violation of civil law requirements, it will go directly to court requesting an injunction against the union to prevent the behavior causing the problem. That is common when striking union pickets block access to parking lots, loading docks, or employee building entrances. Municipal laws in many locations govern how public access to property must be maintained and how public sidewalks and roadways can be used appropriately.

In other instances, unions can seek court assistance when employers are being accused of inappropriate controls on picketers. Use of physical force by private security guards could be an example.

In either situation, the remedy sought through the court is an injunction preventing the offending behaviors. With an injunction in hand, it is possible to request help from law enforcement bodies such as the police department or sheriff's department to enforce the injunction.

Strikes, Picketing, and Boycotts

Agreement is not always reached when negotiating the terms of a union contract. Bargaining impasses can reach the point of a deadlock that cannot be resolved. There are three arrows a union has in its quiver of actions to take against an employer. When negotiations break down, there are still some actions that can be taken. These are protected concerted activities under the NLRA.

Strikes

Work stoppages are the last resort of a failed negotiation process. When a union contract expires and the union and management are unable to reach agreement on terms of a new contract, the union can call a strike. When that happens, all union members are directed by the union to report for duty on the picket line and not to go to their normal jobs. Should a union member fail to report for picket duty as directed by the union, he or she may be fined by the union. Some laws govern the amount of notice that must be given to management or the public before a work stoppage can be implemented. Union leadership is obligated to get a majority agreement from its members on the advisability of a strike. A strike may be unlawful if its purpose or methods are illegal such as strikes in violation of a no-strike clause in an existing agreement. Federal employees do not have the right to strike, as doing so would not be in the public's interest and can be punished with felony charges and/or dismissal.

- **Economic strike**   Based on employee desire for more compensation or benefits.

- **Unfair labor practice strike**   Some labor practices such as overtime assignment procedures are disputed and not resolved in negotiations. The union can call a strike to stop work, putting pressure on the employer in an attempt to gain the union's objectives.

- **Wildcat strike**   An illegal, unsanctioned work stoppage by the union in reaction to some dispute with the employer.

- **Jurisdictional strike**   A work stoppage precipitated by two or more unions claiming jurisdiction in representation of the work group in question.

- **Sympathy strike**   A cessation of work by a second union in support of the first union that actually called an economic or unfair labor practice strike against the employer. If negotiations break down with one union, when that union calls a strike, it can seek support from other unions that it hopes will put additional pressure on the employer.

Picketing

There are two primary types of picket exercises. One is informational picketing. The other is work stoppage picketing. *Informational picketing* is a technique used by unions when they want to have the public learn about certain issues. Informational pickets usually carry signs or placards containing their message. *Work stoppage* (or *primary picketing*) occurs when the union has taken a strike vote and the majority of members want to exercise their right to strike. While employees are marching on the picket line, they are not working and, therefore, not being paid. Sometimes unions have amassed a strike fund that will provide sustenance-level support to members who need it. In most jurisdictions, strikers are not eligible for unemployment insurance while they are on strike. That is because they are without work by choice, akin to being barred from receiving unemployment insurance payments after resigning a job. Other types of picketing include the following:

- **Recognitional**   Picketing designed to get an employer to recognize the union as the official representative of employees in that work location.

- **Organizational**   Picketing designed to get workers to recognize the union as their representative.

- **Area standards**   Picketing used by unions to get an employer to accept standards used in the industry within the local area.

- **Common situs**   Illegal picketing of a construction site by a union because of a grievance against a single subcontractor on the worksite.

- **Consumer picketing**   Picketing by a union in an effort to get consumers not to patronize a given employer organization because of a labor dispute.

- **Bannering**   Use of large banners (sometimes up to 20 feet long) and passing out handbills usually on public sidewalks or streets. In those conditions, bannering is usually considered legal.

Boycotts

Primary boycotts are a form of protest that unions sometimes use to emphasize the strength of their beliefs. Boycotts are organized withholding of transactions from a target employer or group of employers. For example, in 2011, members of the Wisconsin State

Employees Union, AFSCME Council 24, circulated letters to businesses in southeast Wisconsin, warning that they would face a boycott if they didn't support collective bargaining for public employee unions.[11] Boycotts are sometimes called against companies that don't sell goods produced by union-represented workers. "Buy Union Labels" is a common theme. Unions have sometimes been known to call for members to boycott certain stores because they resist union-organizing attempts. Boycott International, a program of 1World Communication, called for unions around the country to boycott Walmart because the chain sold clothing made in Bangladesh where wages are low. What impact such actions have on employers is not known.

There are also secondary boycotts, which fall into the following categories:

- **Ally doctrine**   This is a boycott against a secondary employer because it is virtually indistinguishable from the primary employer—for example, the General Motors assembly plant and the General Motors painting facility next to the assembly plant. Another example is Dole fruit harvesting and Dole canning and packaging operations.

- **Single employer**   This is a boycott against a single employer or entities that operate so closely that they are treated as a single entity.

- **Joint employer**   Professional employer organizations (PEOs) fall into this category as a joint employer with the primary employer organization against whom the union constructs a boycott.

- **Alter ego doctrine**   This determines that two or more businesses are essentially the same business for the purposes of NLRA coverage. Four criteria were established by the U.S. Supreme Court to determine whether only one employer exists for labor relations purposes: interrelation of operations, central control of labor relations, common management, and common ownership.[12]

- **Double-breasting**   Usually this is used in construction where multiple corporate structures are created. One handles work performed under union agreements, and another performs work where workers are not union represented. A boycott against one is a boycott against all.

- **Straight-line operations**   This is a boycott against two separate business organizations that operate in the same industry doing the same type of work on the same or similar projects.

- **Hot cargo clauses**   This is an illegal boycott that involves the union coercing an employer not to do business with another firm.

Lockout

Lockouts can occur when management shuts down operations to prevent union employees from working. A lockout can occur when an organization is concerned about sabotage and can force the union to look again at its bargaining position. Employers may also have the right to transfer work to another facility, run the business with management personnel or people not associated with the bargaining unit, and protect their property from trespass.

Employment Legal Issues

Of course, there are many legal issues faced by employers. Those resulting from the acts of hiring and firing/layoff have special meaning in many states. These issues are usually defined and governed by state laws.

Negligent Hiring

This tort (legal injury) claim is brought against an employer when a person hired by the organization causes injury to someone inside or outside the organization in a way that should have been predicted by the employer had a proper background investigation been conducted. When a new hire gets angry and physically assaults another employee, it could represent negligent hiring if the employer could have determined that the new hire was dismissed from previous jobs because of anger issues. Failure to conduct proper background checks is usually the foundation for these types of claims. If a background check was conducted and the issue of violence was investigated with prior employers, the new employer could have a defense against such claims.

Preventing negligent hiring is a matter of conducting background investigations, probing for information relevant to the specific job requirements. Behavioral issues should always be on the list of subjects investigated. Misbehavior at previous employers should be a warning signal that future problems may exist if this individual is hired. Ignoring such information is always a risk.

Negligent Retention

A cousin of negligent hiring, this tort action can be brought against an employer for keeping someone on the payroll who is known to be a danger to others inside or outside the organization. When such a person then hurts a customer, another employee, or member of the public, the employer can be liable for the damages. These types of cases usually depend on an answer to the question, "Did the employer know, or should the employer have known, that the employee could be a threat to others?" If the employer knew, or reasonably should have known, that the employee was a possible threat, then the employer should have acted to remove the employee from employment through due process.

Liability for negligent retention can be controlled if managers and supervisors are trained to take appropriate disciplinary action when behavior problems occur. If a problem of violence arises, it may be appropriate to immediately dismiss the worker. When due process calls for progressive discipline, it should be implemented diligently and fairly. Similar problems should receive similar treatment. Accepting misbehavior is a recipe leading to liability.

Defamation

When an employer publishes (writes or says) something about an employee that it knows is not true, the employee may have recourse through a charge of defamation. Damage to the employee could include loss of reputation, loss of income, loss of employability, and more.

Sometimes these charges come up when an employer is asked for information about a former employee. If someone provides rumor, innuendo, or accusations that are untrue or hearsay, the employer could be "on the hook" for the damage it does to the former employee.

The way to prevent defamation charges is to train employees and management in how to handle requests for references from another employer. Directing these requests to one person can help reduce the risk that something inappropriate will be provided to the other employer.

Measuring Disparate Impact During Reduction in Force

You will recall that disparate impact is one of two types of illegal discrimination under the Civil Rights Act of 1964. It is usually proven statistically, involving groups of people rather than through comparison of individual treatment.

Proving illegal disparate impact is a deeply mathematical process involving large linear regression tables. That measurement requires a computer, and it is a legal process.

A less time-consuming, less accurate, but simple rule of thumb has existed since 1978. The Uniform Guidelines on Employee Selection Procedures (1978)[13] say that disparate impact occurs when the selection rate for a protected group falls below 80 percent of the selection rate for the most favorably treated group involved in the selection decisions. Sometimes called the *four-fifths rule* or the *80 percent rule* or *adverse impact test (impact ratio analysis* [IRA]), this level of analysis falls far short of proving disparate impact according to the U.S. Supreme Court.[14]

Nonetheless, HR managers will find it helpful to do rapid comparisons using the 80 percent rule when they look at data from hiring, promotion, termination, or training decisions. Sometimes what seems to be a neutral policy can actually result in illegal discrimination. The most famous of these seemingly neutral policies involved the use of height and weight requirements for the selection of firefighters. It was ultimately determined that the height and weight requirements had a statistically provable negative impact on females, Hispanics, and Asians. In recent times, it is rare to find height and weight requirements as part of the job hiring process. The 80 percent rule is our first line of defense against such problems.

 NOTE You will probably find questions about the adverse impact test or 80 percent rule on the PHR and SPHR exams. You should know how to compute the results and what they mean. Remember that they do not prove illegal discrimination but simply act as a red flag to indicate additional analysis should be done.

Table 8-3 provides an example of how the 80 percent rule can be applied.

Category	# Qualified Applicants	# Hires	Hiring Rate (Hires/Apps)	Impact Ratio
Male	141	67	67/141 = 48%	48/59 = 81% No
Female*	111	66	66/111 = 59%	Most favorably treated group
White	75	40	40/75 = 53%	53/64 = 83% No
Black/African American**	30	10	10/30 = 33%	33/64 = **52% Yes**
Hispanic**	45	20	20/45 = 44%	44/64 = **69% Yes**
Asian*	55	35	35/55 = 64%	Most favorably treated group

* This is the most favorably treated group. According to the Uniform Guidelines on Employee Selection Procedures (1978), White is not always the most favorably treated group, and in this example that is the case. Asians are the most favorably treated group because they have the highest selection rate (64%). In positive employment actions such as hiring and promotion, the most favorably treated group is the one with the highest selection rate. In a negative employment action, such as layoff or downsizing, the most favorably treated group is the one with the lowest selection rate.
** There is adverse impact because the impact ratio is less than 80 percent.

Table 8-3   Hiring Analysis

The results shown in our example indicate that more analysis should be done for Black/African American and Hispanic. Even though Hispanic is an ethnicity rather than a race under Title II, it is still treated like a race in these computations.

Additional Statistical Analysis
Beyond the 80 Percent Rule or Adverse Impact Test

Employers can use probability and standard deviation analysis as the next step in their investigation of statistical anomalies. The group "age over 40" can be added to the computations if needed to determine how a downsizing or layoff is affecting that group. It is a protected group under the Age Discrimination in Employment Act and should not suffer because of layoff decisions.

It is commonly accepted that results in excess of 2.0 standard deviations from the center of a bell curve distribution cannot have happened by chance. Said differently, results that fall out in the tails of the bell curve could not have happened by chance. Results within the "fat" part of the curve distribution might have happened by chance. The courts have said that employers will not be held accountable for illegal discrimination (disparate impact) unless it has been demonstrated to occur with statistical certainty. The only way to prove statistical certainty is with a multiple-regression analysis. For that you need to turn to statisticians.

In summary, if you want to use a rule of thumb, the 80 percent rule is a good tool. If you want to analyze data from your employment decisions to determine whether you may have a statistically significant problem, you will want to use standard deviations or probability testing as your tool.

Evaluating Program Effectiveness

Whenever an HR professional implements a new program, there should be a plan for how results will be measured. Without measurements, it is not possible to determine whether a program has been successful. Establishing measurements should be a key component of any new employee program throughout the employee life cycle, from hiring to exit.

Hiring Effectiveness

As reviewed in Chapter 5, the first stage in the employee life cycle is hiring. It would benefit you to refer to Chapter 5 to review key metrics such as hiring response time, recruiting efficiency, cost per hire, recruiting cost ratio, and recruitment yield ratio. These measurements are critical to determining the success of an organization's hiring process and potential areas of improvement. With the growth of technology, there are also many innovative ways for employers to navigate the hiring process more efficiently. For example, many recruiting options that use artificial intelligence are gaining popularity. There are artificial assistants that manage communication with candidates, programs that help sort through résumés and conduct telephonic interviews with candidates, and software that can analyze emotional intelligence in a video interview. Any of these tools can be helpful for an HR department to continuously improve the effectiveness of the hiring process.

Furthermore, individual programs can have a large impact on the cost of hiring and potentially result in increased engagement. Educational institutions often have an alumni program that includes a strong network of supporters for the institution. Not only do these individuals have a vested interest in improving the institution, financial or otherwise, they can be a helpful resource for hiring. Many organizations post positions on relevant alumni networks to reach candidates who have a desired skill set. For example, a school that specializes in engineering is a great place to find an engineer. Posting a job on an alumni website or reaching out to a network of alumni can be a free or low-cost way to promote a job to a group of individuals who possess the desired skill set, resulting in a quick and cost-efficient hiring process.

Similar to an alumni program is the concept of employee referrals. Like alumni, current employees understand the organizational culture and have a vested interest in making it a great place to work. Who better than a current employee to refer a new employee? Providing a financial incentive for referring a successful hire can also improve employee satisfaction and engagement.

Training Effectiveness

One area of the employee life cycle that often gets overlooked is onboarding training. Organizations invest a great deal of time and resources into the hiring process. Once the offer letter is signed and a quick company onboarding completed, employees are sometimes left to their own devices. The first few months of a new position is a key time for employees to learn their position and the dynamics within their new department.

Reviewing employee performance within the first three months of a new position is a helpful way to gauge how well employees are adjusting to their jobs. Consistently low performance scores may be an indication of poor onboarding training within the organization. The more interactive these performance conversations are, the better. New employees offer a fresh perspective on the organization and can provide valuable feedback about what is going well and what is not.

As reviewed in Chapter 6, learning and development help to enhance the employee experience. Obtaining feedback after a training course through a standard survey helps provide concrete measurements for the areas of training strength and weakness. Most importantly, HR should always be on the lookout for ways to enhance organizational effectiveness through training. For example, several employees not following a certain policy, poor communication among a certain work group, or poor customer service signal the need for training. In these circumstances, training is not only the first step to problem resolution but shows the organization is taking accountability for fixing the issue and clearly communicating expectations. If problems continue, the root cause of the issue can be discovered through further investigation. Training can be worth its weight in gold in these circumstances if one training course helps avoid a costly problem.

Development is also often at the individual level. An employee selected to participate in a succession plan may need to hone certain skills to move into the new position. Furthermore, all industries continuously grow and develop. From new products to new technology, industry training can help enhance individual skill sets and bring innovative ideas back to the organization. While the cost of some individual development programs varies, organizations should look at the return on investment. There could be revenue-building or cost-savings ideas as a result of training or a reduction in external recruiting costs as a result of developing a needed skill set in an employee.

Turnover Rates

If a program results in employee turnover that exceeds expectations, it could be a serious problem for the employer. Turnover is expensive, and if people begin finding jobs elsewhere if you change your vacation policy or decide to freeze wages for the coming year, the cost of recruiting and training new workers could exceed the savings from the new program or policy.

These effects can happen when implementing healthcare program changes or taking away benefits such as employee discounts, company contributions to educational expenses, or sabbatical leaves of absence. If employer contributions to employee healthcare or savings programs are reduced or eliminated, workers can get upset to the extent that they seek employment elsewhere.

One way to anticipate these types of reactions and reduce employee turnover is to conduct focus group discussions about alternatives being considered. Ask employees for their reactions to each alternative and test various explanations of the business reasons for the notion that certain employee benefits will have to be reduced or eliminated. Armed with knowledge about employee reactions, decisions can be made more intelligently by senior management, and it may be possible to contain the damage represented by employee turnover.

Employee Surveys

Employee surveys are a tool that wise employers use to constantly monitor the pulse of their workplace. A strong pulse can indicate employee satisfaction and cooperation with business objectives. A weak pulse can indicate employee upset or dissatisfaction that will result in higher turnover and greater cost to the enterprise.

Some employers, particularly smaller ones, will create and use their own employee surveys. There are off-the-shelf software packages that help construct survey questions and implement the survey. Some of them even allow surveys to be conducted on company intranet web networks.

There are some do-it-yourself survey services that charge fees for online surveys that can be used by employers to test employee satisfaction as well as things such as customer satisfaction. Survey Monkey (www.surveymonkey.com) is one such service with tutorials on creating unbiased survey questions.

Then there are consultants who will prepare survey questions and implement the survey process for a fee. These are often people with doctorate-level degrees who specialize in monitoring employee attitudes and analyzing the statistics that result from their survey efforts.

For surveys to deliver benefits, they should do the following:

- Guarantee anonymity
- Provide feedback on the results to the surveyed population
- Have a clear purpose defined and communicated

However you do it, keeping a monitoring system of some kind on the pulse of employee attitudes is a constructive human resource management effort. Surveys are one way to accomplish that and provide painful and brutally honest feedback.

Once survey results are tabulated, communicating these results helps to create mutual understanding in the organization. Employees are aware of the areas that need improvement in an organization and so are managers. With this awareness comes the ability to make strides toward improving areas of weakness. When these steps to improvement are communicated to employees and visibly undertaken, employees are more likely to have a more positive view of the organization and management. The old adage "with wisdom comes responsibility" rings true here.

Exit Effectiveness

It may be the last step in the employee life cycle, but like all other HR functions, the exit process should be handled with care. Many legal challenges can arise from the exit process, especially claims of wrongful termination. Whenever a termination is involuntary, or initiated by the employer, HR should ensure consistency with past practice, organizational policy, and adherence to all laws and regulations. Consulting with a legal advisor can be helpful, especially in complicated situations. A good way to gauge effectiveness in the exit process is reviewing the total number of legal issues associated with employee terminations. The fewer number of EEOC claims, lawsuits, or union grievances, the better.

Exit interviews are also a common way to obtain employee feedback. An exit interview is an interview conducted by HR with an employee in the last few days at the organization. The interview focuses on questions about the employee's position, supervisor, and the organization's strengths and weaknesses. When employees are leaving an organization, they are generally more comfortable providing candid observations and feedback. This feedback can be helpful to address areas of improvement in the organization and make it a better place to work for current employees.

Chapter Review

Employee and labor relations is a complex issue. The area often requires HR personnel to understand complex legal requirements and depends on talented and skilled management personnel to guide employees and the organization through all the requirements of day-to-day concerns. In today's employment world, HR professionals must have a great depth of legal knowledge because they will need to use that knowledge every day. In complement to the legal knowledge required are concepts such as workplace culture, employee relations programs focused on improving morale, and coaching and communication processes. The word *human* is the first word in the human resource function for a good reason.

Questions

1. Alysse is setting up the human resource systems for her newly formed organization. She wants to write a policy about employment at will but isn't sure what it is. How would you explain it to her?

   A. Employment at will means either the employee or the employer can end the relationship at any time for any reason.

   B. Employment at will means the employer can terminate an employee when necessary, but the employee must give two weeks' notice.

   C. Employment at will means the employee can quit at any time, even without notice.

   D. Employment at will doesn't exist anymore because of state and federal labor laws.

2. When Barack began his work with the AB Trucking Company, he established a process of sending engagement letters to all his new employees. Is he creating employment contracts by doing so?

   A. Probably. By laying out the amount of money he is going to pay them and when they will begin work, he is creating a contract agreement.

   B. Not at all. By specifying how much will be paid and the start date, there is no promise of continued work, so there is no contract.

C. Absolutely. By giving the new employee a chance to review the employee handbook and sign the engagement letter, there is a written contract for employment.

D. Maybe not. If the letter doesn't require a signature from the new employee, there likely isn't a contract being created.

3. Caladonia was interviewing with the HR manager of an organization she really wanted to work for. The HR manager told her that "the employer was really good about not laying off workers." They always found another way to deal with slow periods. Can Caladonia rely on that statement as an oral contract?

A. Perhaps. It was close to a promise that she wouldn't be laid off in the future.

B. Absolutely. There is no question that the HR manager made an oral contract with Caladonia.

C. Probably not. There really wasn't any promise made to not lay her off later.

D. Definitely not. The HR manager can say anything during an interview, and it can't be relied on as an oral contract.

4. _____ _____ _____ are contracts between a union and an employer.

5. Will seniority always be the determining factor in a union agreement?

A. Not always. Some union contracts will use education as the determining factor over ruling seniority in the process.

B. Seniority is used only by unions that have contracts or subcontracts with federal agencies.

C. Public agencies rely on seniority, and they are the only ones with those agreements.

D. Universally, unions will rely on seniority as the determining factor for all treatment under contract provisions.

6. Is it possible for employment policies (as laid out in the employee handbook) to take precedence over union contracts?

A. If there is a conflict between the union contract and the employer's policies, the contract will always win.

B. If a conflict arises, then the policy will always prevail.

C. Whenever there are different provisions in a union contract and employer policy, the differences must be arbitrated to resolution.

D. It is up to the manager of the unit involved to determine which will be applied in a given situation.

7. Dabney is the HR manager for his employer. He has been asked to write an employee handbook to provide all the organization's policies in writing. What will employees be able to assume about the handbook policies?

   A. Handbook policies are only guidelines, and they will offer general instruction about how to treat things like vacation and leaves of absence.

   B. Dabney should write the handbook so policies are acceptable to most employees. There will always be some exceptions to the rules.

   C. The policies are requirements. All managers and employees should use them consistently, or there can be complaints of illegal discrimination.

   D. With provisions for exceptions to be approved by senior management, Dabney can be confident that the handbook policies will be applied by all the managers in his organization.

8. Which of the following two items are elements of a performance improvement plan?

   A. Witness statements outlining the employee's performance issues

   B. Explanation of areas requiring performance improvement

   C. Consequences for not successfully completing the plan

   D. Section for the employee to waive rights to pursuing legal action

9. A union contract normally details the process called *progressive discipline*. How would you counsel nonunion employers to deal with the process?

   A. Progressive discipline is required only for union-represented organizations.

   B. There is no need for nonunion employers to have a progressive discipline process since they are probably at-will employers and can terminate employees any time.

   C. Progressive discipline is a good process for any employer. It offers due process to workers, and it satisfies the legal covenant called *good faith and fair dealing*.

   D. Employers can consider using progressive discipline, but absent a union contract, there is little motivation to use the process.

10. Elaine has attended an industry meeting with other HR professionals. She came back to her office with the idea that background investigations of new hires is something she ought to implement. What would you say to Elaine about that idea?

    A. The EEOC has banned background investigations in any form because they discriminate against Hispanics and Blacks.

    B. The EEOC has only recommended that background checks not automatically eliminate Hispanics or Blacks because of employment history.

    C. Background checks are still legal and should be conducted on applicants before a job offer is made to be sure there is no history of bad behavior that could bring liability into the new workplace.

    D. Finding anyone these days with no skeleton in the closet is going to be difficult. Background checks are not really worth the money or time they require.

11. Which of the following two employer policies are employee relations programs?

    A. Grievance resolution process

    B. Employee assistance program

    C. Employee suggestion program

    D. Internal application process

12. Mary received an anonymous complaint that an employee initiated a physical fight with another employee. After investigating the complaint and speaking to witnesses, she learned that the allegations made in the complaint were true. Mary has never before had an employee who caused a physical fight with another employee. The policy in her organization calls for progressive discipline. Mary isn't sure if she should just give the employee a warning or terminate him immediately. What would you recommend?

    A. This is the reason people should learn self-defense. When someone is defending themselves, there should be no reason for employer-imposed discipline. The aggressive employee should be given a written warning, though.

    B. It is hard for someone to start a fight by themselves. Both employees should be written up, skipping the oral warning step of progressive discipline.

    C. It depends on how other aggressive behavior has been treated in the past. Even though there have not been fights per se, the employee treatment should be guided by history.

    D. Violent behavior of any kind is justification for immediate dismissal. Even if there is no policy that says violence can result in immediate termination, that is how this situation should be handled.

13. An illegal, unsanctioned work stoppage by a union in reaction to some dispute with the employer is a _____ _____.

14. Woodrow has been awarded a paid day off because he delivered his product development project ahead of schedule. Does this mean every time someone delivers a job in advance of the deadline they should be given a paid day off?

    A. Maybe. If the situations are the same or very similar, the reward should be the same.

    B. Maybe. Assuming that the employees had the same amount of service and their projects were similar in difficulty, they should all be given a paid day off.

    C. Maybe. With an eye on illegal discrimination, the employer should err on the side of providing a day off with pay to anyone who completes work ahead of schedule.

    D. Maybe. However, if the employer can describe the reward as "special" based on the circumstances, it needn't create a precedent that must be followed in each future instance.

15. Harold has heard that it is necessary to have a diversity management program under some new federal law. What would you tell Harold about that requirement?

A. The new law won't be effective until a year after it was passed. So there is no immediate requirement for him to worry about.

B. There is no federal law requiring diversity management programs. Sophisticated employers are moving in that direction because it is the right thing to do and production results often improve.

C. There is no law requiring diversity management programs, and employers should not consider moving toward such programs unless they are federal contractors.

D. The new law will require diversity management programs only for employers who have federal contracts to provide goods or services to government agencies.

16. Gianna has been asked by her boss to develop a program for use of self-directed work teams in their organization. She has limited experience with that form of organization. How would you advise her on her project?

A. Self-directed work teams only work well in the high-tech industry.

B. Her program should have a method for determining how a leader will be appointed for each work team. There must be management control over all team efforts.

C. Gianna should review the experience of employers in the automobile industry to determine how to design her program.

D. She should place a sunset provision into her program so each work team is disbanded 12 months after it is formed. Everyone needs to return to their normal work group no later than that 12th month.

17. Which of the following two policies should be covered in a health and safety program?

A. State disability insurance

B. Background checks

C. Accident reporting

D. Emergency response planning

18. Emma has never had to manage a union contract before. As the HR manager, she is involved with the grievance-handling process as the third step in the process. At her first meeting with the union steward, the steward began yelling at Emma and telling her what she had to do to satisfy the union in this situation. Emma was stunned. What should she do?

A. She has little choice but to sit there and take it. She is the employer's representative, and if she gets upset, it will only make matters worse.

B. Emma should call a recess and ask for a management representative to join the meeting with her so she can have some backup in an unpleasant situation.

C. Emma should recess the meeting and tell the steward that she will not continue their conversation until the steward can conduct herself in a civil manner.

D. Once the steward has blown off all her steam, Emma should continue the discussion by explaining the employer's position.

19. Sophia makes it a practice to call each applicant's former employers to verify employment claims and determine if there were any behavioral problems in prior jobs. Her company is now being sued because a new hire had an automobile accident while on a delivery run. It turned out he had a history of reckless driving charges in his past two jobs. But she wasn't told about those when she talked with the former employers. Should Sophia be worried?

A. Yes. Almost certainly, Sophia will be blamed for negligent hiring. She has little defense. She should have found out about the new employee's previous employment issues.

B. No. She tried to get information from the previous employers, and they wouldn't talk to her. She made a good faith effort. She is off the hook.

C. Yes. Sophia is going to have to explain to her attorney why she hired this person when there was such a bad history of workplace behavior.

D. Yes. In this instance, she should also have conducted a search of his driving record before hiring him into a job that required driving for deliveries. She shouldn't have relied on only former employer input.

20. Olivia believes that it is a good idea to conduct an employee survey each year to get input about employee attitudes. Her vice president thinks that employee surveys cost too much money and don't provide much value in the end. What should Olivia tell the vice president?

A. A well-constructed employee survey can provide information about the types of employment benefits employees would find attractive, how they feel about their managers, and if they believe they are being treated fairly. All of these feedback categories can be assigned dollar values and can be compared over time as budget impacts.

B. Because the professional HR community is suggesting that employee surveys be conducted each year, it would be wise for Olivia's organization to do that also.

C. The organization Olivia worked at before did an employee survey, and she thinks it would communicate to employees that the employer is willing to listen to them.

D. In the modern workplace, employee attitudes are controlling factors. Surveys will help managers regain control of the workplace.

Answers

1. **A.** Either party can end the relationship with or without notice subject to some limitations on the employer created by various laws barring illegal treatment.

2. **B.** Employment contracts require a promise to do something in return for a consideration such as work. Even if an offer is made and accepted, the letter would need to contain a promise of retention for a certain period of time to overcome the employment-at-will status.

3. **A.** Caladonia wasn't promised a job forever. But she was told the employer always found another way to deal with slow periods. In many jurisdictions, she can rely on that as a contract.

4. **Collective bargaining agreements**

5. **D.** We have yet to see a union contract that didn't use seniority as the determining factor for contract provisions.

6. **A.** Contract provisions are policy. So contract provisions will prevail.

7. **D.** There will always be someone wanting an exception to a policy. Requiring senior management review and approval for each exception is key to making sure there are legitimate business reasons supporting each request. Otherwise, all managers should apply handbook policies consistently.

8. **B, C.** Performance improvement plans outline expected areas of performance improvement, timeline for improvement, resources available to assist the employee, and consequences for not meeting plan expectations.

9. **C.** Due process is the effort made by employers who want to convey that they are treating employees fairly. It demonstrates that the employer is abiding by the covenant of good faith and fair dealing.

10. **C.** Background checks are still legal. The EEOC simply recommends making sure they are job related and that conviction records not automatically disqualify candidates. Using background checks to help prevent claims of negligent hiring is a good idea.

11. **A, C.** While an employee assistance program and internal application process may have employee relations benefits, they are not true employee relations programs. An employee assistance program is part of an organization's benefits packet, and an internal application process is part of the talent acquisition process.

12. **D.** It is hard to be absolute in any recommendation, but this situation sounds like it should result in the immediate termination of at least the aggressive employee. It may be appropriate to also discipline the other employee depending on the outcome of an investigation.

13. **Wildcat strike**

14. **D.** It is not a requirement that each person who completes their project ahead of schedule be given a paid day off. However, if you create a situation where people in similar circumstances are treated differently based on membership in a protected class, you could face a claim of illegal discrimination.

15. **B.** Diversity management programs are not a new idea, and they are not a legal requirement. More and more employers, however, are implementing them because they help with employee satisfaction and marketplace perceptions.

16. **C.** The best way to ensure success of a new employment program is to study those that have already been successful. The automobile industry has achieved a great deal of success with this method of addressing work problems. It makes sense to study their efforts and consider using some of their methods.

17. **C, D.** Background checks are completed prior to hire or transfer into a new position and not for health or safety reasons. Long-term disability is part of the employee benefit package and should not be confused with workers' compensation for work-related injuries.

18. **C.** Emma does not have to sit there and take abuse from the steward. If the steward cannot behave civilly, the meeting should end. Only when the steward can control herself should Emma agree to continue. It might also be a good idea to provide some feedback to the union president about what has happened in the meeting.

19. **D.** A background check should be tailored to the situation. For a job that requires driving, a check of DMV records and history of insurance claims should be routine. Had Sophia conducted such a check, she surely would have uncovered this history and been able to change her hiring decision.

20. **A.** In fact, each category of employee feedback can be assigned a dollar value, and those can be tracked over time as budget impacts. Benefits are only one segment of the employee experience at work. Interpersonal relations with supervisors and managers is another big issue. Generally speaking, employees who feel well treated will be better performers, which also impacts the financial results.

Endnotes

1. Seymour Moskowitz, *Employment at Will & Code of Ethics: The Professional Dilemma*, 23 Val. U.L. Rev. 33 (1988). Available at http://scholar.valpo.edu/vulr/vol23/iss1/7.

2. http://www.nrtw.org/right-to-work-frequently-asked-questions/

3. *Harris v. Quinn* (S.Ct. No. 11-681), June 30, 2014, http://www.supremecourt.gov/opinions/13pdf/11-681_j426.pdf.

4. *Janus v. AFSCME* (S.Ct. No. 16-1466), June 27, 2018, https://www.supremecourt.gov/opinions/17pdf/16-1466_2b3j.pdf.

5. "Consideration of Arrest and Conviction Records in Employment Decisions Under Title VII of the Civil Rights Act of 1964," www.eeoc.gov/laws/guidance/arrest_conviction.cfm.

6. The Society for Human Resource Management. "Understanding and Developing Organizational Culture". https://www.shrm.org/resourcesandtools/tools-and-samples/toolkits/pages/understandinganddevelopingorganizationalculture.aspx

7. *National Labor Relations Board vs. Electromation, Inc.*, 309 NLRB 990 (1992), enf'd., 35 F.3d 1148 (7th Cir. 1994).

8. *National Labor Relations Board vs. Crown Cork & Seal Company*, 334 NLRB No. 92 (July 20, 2001).

9. The Center for Social Leadership, http://thesocialleader.com/leaders-5-step-guide-conflict-resolution/.

10. The Legal Dictionary, https://legaldictionary.net/collective-bargaining/.

11. Milwaukee, Wisconsin *Journal Sentinel,* March 31, 2011, www.jsonline.com/news/statepolitics/118963234.html.

12. *Radio Union vs. Broadcast Services Inc.*, 380 U.S. 255 (1965).

13. 41 C.F.R 60–3.

14. *Griggs v. Duke Power Co.*, 401 U.S. 424 (1971); *Wards Cove Packing Co., Inc., et al. v. Atonio, et al.*, 490 U.S. 642 (1989).

PART III

SPHR Body of Knowledge Functional Areas

■ **Chapter 9**   Leadership and Strategy
■ **Chapter 10** Talent Planning and Acquisition
■ **Chapter 11** Learning and Development
■ **Chapter 12** Total Rewards
■ **Chapter 13** Employee Relations and Engagement

Leadership and Strategy

This chapter is focused on senior human resource management skills. It is massive in terms of its impact and weight in the certification exam. Leadership and Strategy carries a 40 percent weight on the Society for Human Resource Management (SHRM) exam. We recommend you spend a considerable amount of time assuring you have mastered this information prior to the exam.

Responsibilities

- Develop and execute HR plans that are aligned to the organization's strategic plan (for example, HR strategic plans, budgets, business plans, service delivery plans, HRIS, technology)

- Evaluate the applicability of federal laws and regulations to organizational strategy (for example, policies, programs, practices, business expansion/reduction)

- Analyze and assess organizational practices that impact operations and people management to decide on the best available risk management strategy (for example, avoidance, mitigation, acceptance)

- Interpret and use business metrics to assess and drive achievement of strategic goals and objectives (for example, key performance indicators, financial statements, budgets)

- Design and evaluate HR data indicators to inform strategic actions within the organization (for example, turnover rates, cost per hire, retention rates)

- Evaluate credibility and relevance of external information to make decisions and recommendations (for example, salary data, management trends, published surveys and studies, legal/regulatory analysis)

- Contribute to the development of the organizational strategy and planning (for example, vision, mission, values, ethical conduct)

- Develop and manage workplace practices that are aligned with the organization's statements of vision, values, and ethics to shape and reinforce organizational culture

- Design and manage effective change strategies to align organizational performance with the organization's strategic goals

- Establish and manage effective relationships with key stakeholders to influence organizational behavior and outcomes

Knowledge Of

- Vision, mission, and values of an organization and applicable legal and regulatory requirements
- Strategic planning process
- Management functions, including planning, organizing, directing, and controlling
- Corporate governance procedures and compliance
- Business elements of an organization (for example, products, competition, customers, technology, demographics, culture, processes, safety and security)
- Third-party or vendor selection, contract negotiation, and management, including development of requests for proposals (RFPs)
- Project management (for example, goals, timetables, deliverables, and procedures)
- Technology to support HR activities
- Budgeting, accounting, and financial concepts (for example, evaluating financial statements, budgets, accounting terms, and cost management)
- Techniques and methods for organizational design (for example, outsourcing, shared services, organizational structures)
- Methods of gathering data for strategic planning purposes (for example, strengths, weaknesses, opportunities, and threats [SWOT] and political, economic, social, and technological [PEST])
- Qualitative and quantitative methods and tools used for analysis, interpretation, and decision-making purposes
- Change management processes and techniques
- Techniques for forecasting, planning, and predicting the impact of HR activities and programs across functional areas
- Risk management
- How to deal with situations that are uncertain, unclear, or chaotic

Leadership and Strategy Responsibilities

It doesn't matter what portion of an organization is involved, nothing gets done without stimulation from a competent leader. If you want to perform as a senior HR professional, you will encounter the need to act in a leadership capacity at least some of the time.

If your actions inspire others to dream more, learn more,
do more, and become more, you are a leader.

—John Quincy Adams, U.S. president

Develop and Execute HR Plans That Are Aligned to the Organization's Strategic Plan

The purpose of aligning HR's initiatives and objectives with the organization's objectives is to ensure that the functions and responsibilities HR is accountable for are in alignment with the organization's plans and are helping move the organization toward its vision. This is the "big-picture" view that we've been referring to in this book and is expressed in the "In the Trenches" sections. Having the right number of people with the right capabilities at the right times and in the right places engaged and motivated to do the right things is HR's primary support role for the organization. Basically, HR is charged with aligning the human capital with the organization's strategy plans. For example, recruitment initiatives must correlate with plans for opening a new facility. Retention incentives such as compensation and benefits would fit into the organization's plans for holding on to key employee groups. Or culture-creating initiatives to heighten the engagement of the workforce could involve HR policies and procedures. It is the human capital in an organization that actually produces the desired results from a strategic plan, and HR is a gatekeeper of the human capital.

HR Strategic Plans

What will the human resource department's contribution be to the enterprise strategic plan? Here are some things that are fairly common:

- Cost containment
  - Payroll costs
  - Benefit plan costs (e.g., health insurance, life insurance, disability insurance, vacation and PTO policies)
  - Union contract provisions
  - Recruiting expenses
- Departmental support
  - Recruiting
  - Training
  - Coaching for supervisors and managers
  - Safety program planning and implementation
- Data management
  - HRIS
  - Reporting service (e.g., safety, recruiting and hiring, employee service reports, retention)

Budgets

Budgeting is the process of estimating the amount of income and expenses that will occur within a given period of time. It is usually done on an annual basis, although budgets can be created for multiple years and for shorter periods of time such as months and quarters.

PART III

The accuracy of budgeting can be improved when there is some historical data on which to rely. Generally speaking, budgets in the short term can be easier to construct and are usually more accurate than long-range budgets. The reason, simply, is that many unforeseen influences can enter the long-range picture. Fewer unpredictable influences tend to occur in shorter periods of time. Figure 9-1 illustrates the basis of budgeting.

In some organizations, HR budgets are allocated to departmental client organizations. So based on the services used, departments will "pay" for the HR expenses they incur. If the production department uses more recruiting and hiring services than any other department, they will pay more based on that usage. This requires HR tracking the expense by units of use. For new hires, that may be head count. For recruiting, that may be the number of applicants or job candidates.

Departments can be allocated prorated shares of benefit expenses, training expenses, and database management expenses. Naturally, the client departments will want those expenses to be as low as possible because those expenses will directly impact the operational budgets of those organizational components. "Pay for what you use" is a concept that has been gaining traction in companies around the country. It is quite common for this approach to be used where HR is a centralized function serving the parent company and numerous subsidiaries. It can prevent duplication of services and the expenses associated with those services.

Where HR expenses are not allocated to client departments, they influence the organization's "bottom line." Individual department executives may not be as sensitive to the cost of HR support for their groups, but it is hard to escape the interest your chief executive officer (CEO) and chief financial officer (CFO) will have in the topic.

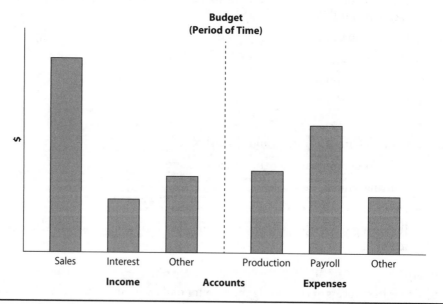

Figure 9-1 Budget chart

Why is it not a good idea to spend money that wasn't planned in the budget? What is a budget anyway, and how do you get one? These are basic business issues that HR professionals must be able to master, particularly at the senior level. What would an initial public offering (IPO) mean to the HR department's budget? How will due diligence regarding an international expansion impact the HR department's budget?

Budgets begin with an estimate of expenses that will be necessary during the coming calendar period, be it a calendar year, fiscal year, month, or quarter. How much money will your department need for payroll (the full-time equivalent head count in each compensation level)? Here are some other budget items you may want to consider. There are many more that you will discover as you begin your budgeting experience.

- Payroll (FTE)
- Payroll taxes
- Cost of the work space (office or construction site)
- Furniture expense (desks, chairs)
- Equipment purchases (office copy machine)
- Equipment rentals (letter mailing equipment for open enrollment season)
- Telephone expenses
- Fax expenses
- Computer expenses (purchase/rental, technical support)
- Internet expenses
- Web site maintenance for job posting
- Software subscriptions (applicant tracking, security, HRIS)
- Participation in recruiting fairs and college campus recruiting visits
- Printing expenses (letterheads, forms, orientation materials)
- Training (materials, classroom expense, Internet self-serve expenses)

Business Plans

Business plans are expressions of opportunities and challenges along with benefits to be gained and action plans for reaching them. To obtain funding, almost every business enterprise must provide a business plan that explains what the money will be used for and how it will be earned back. This rule generally applies to any business, large or small. Even public-sector organizations use business planning to identify their constituents, the needs to be served, and how success will be measured. Oh, and don't forget the budget dollars it will require to achieve those accomplishments.

HR departments should be expected to generate their own business plans, regardless of their membership in a private- or public-sector organization. The HR business plan should answer questions such as "What is the opportunity or challenge?" and "What is the expected benefit?" and "How much will it cost?" and "How much revenue will it generate?" and "How long will it take?" Answering these questions will allow a written compilation of information that justifies moving forward with the effort. For example, your HR department is considering the purchase of a new human resource information system (HRIS). A business plan would include researching options (existing software versus creating software), identifying costs and benefits of each option, and identifying implementation requirements of each option, including the time it will take to get the system up and running. You can think of many more questions to ask in creating this business plan. As a senior HR professional, it is your role to create these planning documents and use them as blueprints for your projects.

Service Delivery Plans

There is a published standard for developing service delivery plans.[1] The National Occupational Standards (NOS) organization in the United Kingdom has developed that standard. "This standard is about designing and developing specific services within the strategy for service provision and access, and determining how these services will be delivered cost effectively. It is also concerned with scoping and defining the services or mix of services required to meet the needs of specific customer groups with particular needs, e.g. services for students, researchers, business communities, children, disadvantaged groups, etc. This standard is applicable to people in management and practitioner roles who contribute to the planning and design of services and who will be responsible for and/or actively engaged in service delivery and the definition of customer needs. It is also applicable, in part, to people in operational roles who can contribute to service design from the perspective of delivering front line services."

The American National Standards Institute (ANSI) has published standards for service delivery.[2] Three of them that have influence on the HR profession are as follows:

- **ISO 10001:2018**   Quality management - Customer satisfaction - Guidelines for codes of conduct for organizations

- **ISO 10002:2018**   Quality management - Customer satisfaction - Guidelines for complaints handling in organizations

- **ISO 10004:2018**   Quality management - Customer satisfaction - Guidelines for monitoring and measuring

When you next prepare a service delivery plan, it would be wise to follow these standards and refer to them in your plan description.

HRIS

An argument could be made that suggests nothing is more important in running an organization than data. Data is the life blood of what gets done. It can be marketing data, product data, repair data, customer data, or employee data. Only small employers are still using manual means of tracking employee data these days. Paper records have been surpassed by Microsoft Excel spreadsheets at the least. Once an employer has reached the workforce size that it requires a human resource professional, chances are that it is time to begin considering investing in a purpose-designed human resource information system.

Payroll providers such as ADP and Paychex often offer an HRIS component as an additional-cost option to their employer clients. Other organizations have built their entire business on serving the HRIS needs of client organizations.

There are three types of information systems for tracking employee data:[3]

- **Human resource information system**   Usually includes the following: core HR information, benefit administration, attendance management (absence management), compensation, training, safety incidents, self-service options, system reporting

- **Human capital management**   Usually includes the following: all of the HRIS content plus performance data, succession planning, compensation planning, global considerations, data analytics in addition to reporting

- **Human resource management system**   Usually includes the following: all of the HRIS content plus the HCM content plus payroll records, history of time, and labor data

With each expansion of the data tracked and the capacity for data history, the cost will rise. To determine what type of system you need, we suggest starting with two types of output requirements and then building your data gathering around those. These output requirements are the following: What type of senior management reporting do you need? What type of departmental manager reporting do you need? What type of governmental reporting do you need?

For example, your payroll system needs to be able to generate reports for the government (e.g., W-2, 1099). Those reports become minimum requirements or criteria for your system selection process. Your HRIS has minimum requirements also. These can include annual EEO-1 reporting, departmental and job group reporting, and accident reporting.

Technology

Technology plans for human resource organizations vary as much as they do for any other department. Here are some questions to help you arrive at a description of your technology needs in your HR operation:

- Will records be stored locally or in the cloud?
- What record security provisions do you require?
- What backup system do you require?
- Will there be direct employee self-serve availability for their personal data?
- What remote access provisions will be necessary?
- What type of equipment will HR staff be using?

Add your own questions to the list to satisfy your specific needs. Then start answering those questions. The result will be a list of criteria you can use to make your technology selections.

Evaluate the Applicability of Federal Laws and Regulations to Organizational Strategy

Some of the expense undertaken by human resource departments is the cost of compliance with federal laws and regulations. These are often not single fees but ongoing compliance requirements that must be replicated each year. An example is the preparation of reports such as the EEO-1 or EEO-4 (Standard Form 100). The EEO-1 report must be filed each year by private-sector companies with 100 or more people on the payroll. Companies that service federal contracts for goods and services with 50 or more people on their payroll must also file the EEO-1 report. That means expenses for collecting the data, summarizing the data, and inputting the data on the government's web page. Other annual reporting expenses associated with compliance include the OSHA-300 report and affirmative action plan updates with all their analyses requirements.

Policies

Corporate policies can influence how expenses will be involved with government compliance. It is legal for companies to prepare voluntary affirmative action programs. The requirement is that these programs meet all of the requirements expected of nonvoluntary plans. So all of the data collection, analysis, and reporting requirements will be as costly for these employers as for those who are receiving federal contract revenues.

Another example is that the WARN Act requirements come into play when a policy decision is made to shutter a work location and move the jobs somewhere else. Notices must be provided to various parties, including impacted employees, and if 60 days' advance warning is not given to these workers, they must be paid the balance of the 60 days in wages. Policy decisions can create expense. It is the responsibility of senior HR professionals to introduce these considerations during the policy discussions and planning sessions. It is necessary for all of these considerations to involve cost analyses requirements. This way, executives can have all the information necessary when making their policy decisions.

Programs

Safety programs are mandated by the government. They are a compliance requirement, and they have budget impact. Personal protective equipment (PPE), safety training materials, and time and data tracking are all expenses that can be required in a safety management program. Affirmative action programs are mandated for many federal contractors. Family and Medical Leave Act–mandated time off may be an unpaid requirement, but there are expenses associated with tracking and replacing the incumbent during their absence.

Practices

Federal laws can influence your employment practices in many ways. Here are some of them:

- **EEO requirements** Data tracking, government reporting, complaint investigations, record security
- **Risk management** Safety requirements, safety reporting, workers' compensation programs, return to work practices

- **Work schedules and compensation** FLSA requirements for overtime eligibility, classification and overtime payments, records management, child labor restrictions
- **Work authorization practices** Form I-9 requirements, copies of justification documents
- **Benefits continuation after employment** COBRA benefit management
- **Job accommodation requests** Tracking of requests, responses, determinations
- **Job candidate screening** Validation of all screening devices used in employment selection processes

Business Expansion/Reduction

Strategic growth plans, or conversely, strategic reduction plans, have impact from government requirements.

- **Business expansion** Oftentimes corporate expansions can result in the relocation of facilities. When that happens, state and local jurisdictions will sometimes offer tax breaks and other incentives for relocating to their vicinity. Seeking out such benefits can be a good strategy when there is sufficient time available to plan and negotiate final arrangements.
- **Business reduction** When a private employer concludes that it must reduce its workforce at a given location by 50 or more people, the Worker Adjustment and Retraining Notification Act specifies both notice and pay requirements. Other governmental controls such as the Older Workers' Benefit Protection Act (OWBPA) and the Employee Retirement Income Security Act (ERISA) can become important for qualifying organizations that plan to undergo force reductions. Strategically planning the cost/benefit impact of such government requirements will permit the least negative financial impact on the organization.

Analyze and Assess Organizational Practices That Impact Operations and People Management to Decide on the Best Available Risk Management Strategy

Any attempt to manage risk successfully will be dependent upon the way your organization operates, the industry you are part of, and the types of risks that attach to your operations.

Risk Avoidance

Risk avoidance is eliminating the risk at any cost. For example, to avoid charges of negligent retention, any employee who gets into an argument with a customer will be immediately terminated. Erecting transparent barriers between visitor galleries and the production floor is a way of keeping visitors away from production equipment and possible injury. Risk avoidance is usually the most expensive of all risk management approaches.

Organizational practices such as using only full-time employees to control the number of people who must undergo safety training can incur extra expense. Strategically using part-time workers in those areas where less than full-time work is available can reduce payroll costs even though some extra training may be necessary. The costs may not be equal.

Risk Mitigation

Implementing actions that can control the costs of given risks will help positively impact the profit and loss statement. Roofers using safety harnesses to prevent falls from rooftops and implementing dual signature requirements on checks exceeding a certain amount are examples of mitigation efforts.

Acceptance

Acknowledging that the risk exists and accepting it is quite like self-insuring. The decision assumes that the risk of occurrence and/or impact is low. Carrying earthquake insurance in the San Francisco Bay Area is expensive. Accepting the risk of an earthquake is a decision to not buy insurance and accept statistical forecasts that nothing will happen to cause building damage within the coming few years. If the next few years go by without a damaging earthquake, the strategy would have succeeded.

Interpret and Use Business Metrics to Assess and Drive Achievement of Strategic Goals and Objectives

However beautiful the strategy, you should occasionally look at the results.
—Sir Winston Churchill, U.K. prime minister

This presupposes that you have a set of strategic goals and objectives. If not, it is your role as a senior HR professional to provide guidance to your executive team so these goals and objectives can be developed for your enterprise.

If your organization already has strategic goals, the next question is whether you have strategic goals for your HR organization that can be directly matched to the organizational objectives. Remember the rules about strategic goals and objectives: there should only be subordinate group goals and objectives that support the goals and objectives of the larger organization. If you have some goals and objectives that do not directly relate to the company goals and objectives, then you should ask, "Why?"

Key Performance Indicators

Some HR performance indicators include the following:

- Job requisitions filled by deadline
- Number of job requisitions with multiple candidates
- AAP placement-rate goals met for minorities and women
- AAP placement-rate goals met for disabled and veterans
- Number of injury accidents by department

- Number of managers and supervisors trained in required courses
- Number of employees trained in required courses
- Number of HR personnel attaining professional certification
- Turnover costs
- Turnover rates
- Retention rates
- Number of labor complaints
- Number of discrimination complaints, internal and external
- Mentorship program success rates
- Benefit program costs per employee for each benefit program
- Budget impact of each benefit program
- Union contract negotiation needs vs. concessions
- Union contract costs for incremental improvements in provisions
- Cost of union certification prevention effort

Financial Statements

Senior HR professionals need to understand how to read financial statements and then study them for their organization. Profit and loss (P&L) statements may not apply to public-sector groups, but there are certainly statements showing budget allocations versus actual spending that need to be digested. Private-sector groups will have P&L reports periodically compiled throughout the year and one at the end of the year. What expenses have been generated? What revenues were received from each source? How did the HR organization impact both revenues and expenses? What was the difference between revenues and expenses, a profit or a loss?

Do you understand depreciation of assets? What is an asset anyway? (It is something of value that was purchased or obtained by the business.) How does investing in a new computer system for HR impact the company balance sheet? How is stockholder equity created or altered? How are taxes computed and on what? These questions and more are separate study goals for every HR manager.

P&L statements explain income (revenues) versus expenses. Income can include sales revenue, grants, interest income, and refunds of prior purchases. Expenses can include payroll compensation, payroll taxes, cost of benefits, cost of employee training, COBRA benefit continuation vendor contract, and bottled water for the office. A complete list of both income and expense items should be developed during the planning process. Any strategic plans to accomplish specific goals in the coming period should be considered. Ultimately, individual expenses and individual revenues will be combined into summary categories such as customer software sales, hardware sales, or pro rata allocation of HR services reimbursements from departments. Expenses can be consolidated into categories such as office expenses, payroll expenses, health insurance benefit expenses, vacation expenses, and policy development.

PART III

Design and Evaluate HR Data Indicators to Inform Strategic Actions Within the Organization

Certain HR activities have great importance in both budgeting and strategic accomplishments of the organization. The following are three common indicators that should be closely monitored.

Turnover Costs

You have already seen in Chapters 5 and 8 that employee turnover can be expensive. The opposite of retention, turnover measures the rate of employee loss.

This section explains one formula you can consider to measure employee turnover.

Determine the examination period (month, quarter, year). For that period, do the following calculation:

Cost of Hiring (Recruiting, Interviewing, Processing) + Cost of Unemployment Insurance for Departed Employees + Workers' Compensation Insurance Cost for Departed Employees + Cost of Training a Replacement + Other Expenses

Divide these total dollars by the number of employees who left during the same period. The result is your turnover cost. For example, here are the cost figures for six middle managers:

Cost of Hiring	$38,000
Cost of UI – previous EEs	$12,000
Cost of WC for 1 EE	$24,000
Total Cost	$74,000

Turnover Cost per Employee = $74,000 / 6 = $12,333

Turnover Rates

Turnover rate refers to the percentage of employees leaving an organization during a certain period of time. It can be determined by dividing the number of employees who left by the number of employees on the payroll. This can be done based on various time segments (month, quarter, year), by organizational increment (department, division, company total), or by project. Here's an example:

Total Employees (EEs)	267
# Separations	18

Turnover Rate = 18 / 267 = .067 = 6.7%

Cost per Hire

You will find the formula for computing cost per hire in Chapter 5.

Recruiting Cost

You will find the formula for calculating recruiting costs in Chapter 5.

Retention Costs

Retention rate speaks to how long new employees remain on the job after they are hired. If you spend a lot of money to recruit and hire new workers and they leave within two months, there is a rather expensive revolving-door staffing requirement for that job opening. Aside from why people are leaving so soon, the first step is to determine what the retention rates are for key jobs or job categories. Perhaps you want to look at your entry-level engineers, for example.

Identify how long (months, years) you need people to remain on the job at a productive level to pay back the expense of their hiring. Productivity can be measured by the amount of output from the job in terms of dollars minus the cost of hiring, payroll, and benefits. Here's an example:

Engineer I – 1 Position
Cost of Hiring	$12,000
Cost of Payroll (1 year)	$65,000
Cost of Benefits (1 year)	$16,250
Cost of 1 Incumbent for 1 year	$93,250
Value of 1-year productivity	$650,000

$93,250 / $650,000 = .143 = 14.3% Cost factor
100% – 14.3% = 85.7% Productivity margin
52 weeks × 14.3% = 7.4 weeks break-even point

If an engineer leaves before 7.4 weeks have passed, you lose money. If the engineer stays longer, you have recouped the costs associated with placement.

Retention Rates

Once you know the breakeven point on your new hire retention, in this example 7.4 weeks, you are able to compute the retention rate for all your new Engineer I incumbents.

Number of Engineer I hired this year	160
Number of new hires remaining 7.4 weeks	153

Retention rate for 7.4 weeks = 153 / 160 = .956 = 95.6%

Take the same situation and consider how you have done over the course of a year.

Number of Engineer I hired this year	160
Number of new hires remaining 1 year	140

Retention rate = 140 / 160 = .875 = 87.5%

With that information you can set some targets for the future. What rates of retention do you want to achieve as you move into your next year? What retention rate would it take to support the strategic goals of the company?

Evaluate Credibility and Relevance of External Information to Make Decisions and Recommendations

There are many external information sources you can use to help manage your HR responsibilities. If you are involved in union contract negotiations, you will have an interest in the terms that appear in recently agreed-to contracts your union has made with other employers. If your compensation program depends on the consumer price index (CPI), you will want to track that through the U.S. Bureau of Labor Statistics.[4] Sometimes, external salary survey data is important to your compensation planning.

Salary Data

It used to be a common practice to inquire about prior salary/wage rates from job candidates. Now, 11 states ban the practice of considering such pay history. Nine additional states have local laws that ban the practice.[5]

Management Trends

Policies change from time to time. For example, the executive committee may believe it is important to have a 65 percent salary/wage versus 35 percent benefit value when benefits only used to make up 20 percent of the total compensation package. That can happen if new factors surface for consideration such as bonus programs, employee stock ownership programs (ESOPs), and profit-sharing programs. When those shifts take place, employees need advanced warning that such changes will be made to adapt industry patterns or to adjust to other motivators.

Published Surveys and Studies

Many industries conduct and publish salary surveys for employers in their type of work. Some organizations make a business out of compiling and selling compensation data.[6] The single most important thing to remember about using salary surveys is that you must check the duties of the title, not just the title. If the job contents don't match your job, the compensation data may have little or no value to you. Also, remember that geography, time in title, and other factors may impact your compensation rates.

Legal/Regulatory Analysis

Each year some employers are subject to minimum wage adjustments imposed by their states. Others are subject to minimum wage adjustments imposed on federal contractors by the U.S. Department of Labor's Wage and Hour Division. It is important to know where you stand in the regulated community and what rules to follow so you won't be caught unaware. Remember, it is up to the employer to stay on top of these requirements. It is not up to the government to give you constant updates and reminders.

Contribute to the Development of the Organizational Strategy and Planning

Senior HR professionals should be ready to participate in the strategic planning process with other company officials. They should help senior executives reach decisions about vision, mission, values, and ethical conduct expectations. They should also be able to guide their own HR organization to determine vision, mission, values, and ethical conduct expectations for their group. The latter must support the former. Chapter 4 has more discussion about these issues.

Vision

What does the organization want to be in the future?

Mission

What will be achieved by organizational success? How might that change over time?

Values

What gets rewarded? What behavior is important to the organization? How does the organization want to be known? Is quality really important?

Ethical Conduct

Do people get rewarded for ethical behavior? Or is it more important to get to the objective even if you have to cheat?

Develop and Manage Workplace Practices That Are Aligned with the Organization's Statements of Vision, Values, and Ethics to Shape and Reinforce Organizational Culture

Good communication between HR and the general employee body is critical to achieving a smooth understanding of the employer's expectations. Helping employees understand the vision for their employer and work unit within that enterprise becomes a lead-in to discussions about values and the things that may be unintended reinforcements that should be addressed. Ethics cannot be overlooked. People need to know that there are lines over which one does not cross. Managers and executives need to know how to work with people to be sure those lines are not crossed.

Workplace practices involve maintaining assigned work schedules, performing a full day of work for a full day of pay, supporting the work team however needed, and abiding by the code of conduct while doing it.

Design and Manage Effective Change Strategies to Align Organizational Performance with the Organization's Strategic Goals

Here are some key elements of effective change strategy:[7]

- *Conduct a needs analysis.* Identify what gaps there are between the organization's strategic goals and the current approach to goal achievement. This is often an unpopular exercise because you will be identifying specific groups that have deficiencies in their achievement of goal contribution. Nonetheless, it must be done.

PART III

- *Conduct an analysis of factors needed to create the change.* How fast must the change be made? Who or what is likely to resist the change? How will that resistance take place? Who has information that is essential to making the change? What is the relationship of the change instigator with others that will be involved in making the change? How can this group better contribute to the organizational strategic goals?

- *Develop an action plan.* Specify what must be done, when it must be completed, who will be responsible, and what groups will be needed in support. What organizational strategic goals will be improved as a result of this action plan?

- *Monitor the implementation process.* Design modifications in the change based on unexpected problems that will occur. Track the action plan progress and how effectively each person is contributing to their task or assignment. Identify the impact the change has had on organizational strategic goals.

Establish and Manage Effective Relationships with Key Stakeholders to Influence Organizational Behavior and Outcomes

One of the key responsibilities of senior HR professionals is to monitor and continually work to improve organizational achievements. To do that, maintaining relationships with key people is a necessity. Internal customers (employees, departmental managers and supervisors, senior executives), external business contacts (HRIS vendors, suppliers), and even enforcement agencies (EEOC, OFCCP, NLRB) are all groups with which positive relationships should be cultivated. Everything HR managers do with these key stakeholders should contribute in some way to the achievement of organizational goals.

Leadership and Strategy Knowledge Requirements

Being involved in achieving strategic objectives is dependent on first knowing what they are. Leading people to achieving strategic objectives is also dependent on understanding both the objectives and the necessary HR impact for accomplishing those objectives.

Outstanding leaders go out of their way to boost the self-esteem of their personnel. If people believe in themselves, it's amazing what they can accomplish.

—Sam Walton, founder, Walmart and Sam's Club

Vision, Mission, and Values of an Organization and Applicable Legal and Regulatory Requirements

Any law-abiding organization will keep in mind the legal requirements and regulatory compliance necessary for that organization to thrive. Once legality has been determined, it is up to the organization to establish its vision, mission, and values so it can accomplish the goals it has set in a way it determines appropriate.

There are certain legal and regulatory overlays that law-abiding organizations may not ignore. They include EEO, child labor restrictions, interstate commerce regulations, WARN staff reduction notifications, payroll payment requirements, and countless others.

The covenant of good faith and fair dealing hovers as an expectation over all employers. No employer organization may ignore these requirements when creating vision, mission, and values without being considered an illegal actor.

Strategic Planning Process

What is important to your organization? Here are the basics to follow when creating a strategic plan.[8] Leaders will be creating these opportunities from day one.

- *Establish your mission.* What is the organization's core purpose?
- *Establish your values.* What are your organization's core beliefs?
- *Establish your vision.* What will your organization look like in five years?
- *Define your competitive advantages.* What is your organization's unique position in the marketplace?
- *What are the organization-wide strategies for getting there?* How will you succeed?
- *Develop a three-year framework of six or fewer objectives.*
- *Develop a three-year financial projection.*

Management Functions, Including Planning, Organizing, Directing, and Controlling

A good HR leader will practice good management. Remember, the basic management functions are planning, organizing, directing, and controlling. There is more information about them in Chapter 4.

Corporate Procedures and Compliance

There has to be a strong link between corporate procedures and compliance with government requirements. It is not possible, for example, to have a set of procedures that ignores payroll withholding and reporting requirements. The law requires employers to perform those tasks, and corporate procedures must link to their completion. As we have seen, there are any number of compliance requirements for employers. Accounting, payroll, EEO, affirmative action, safety, and more are included in the subject group.

Even corporate social responsibilities have some compliance obligations. Being involved in certain activities is not necessarily a requirement, but once involved, how that happens is quite frequently a compliance issue.

Corporate social responsibility (CSR) reflects how the organization integrates and aligns with its communities as a helping hand for sustaining economic prosperity, social equity, and environmental protection. CSR is composed of the following philosophies and programs:

- Approaches to community inclusion and engagement (e.g., representation on community boards, joint community projects, employee volunteerism).
- Creating shared value (e.g., definition, best practices).

- Developing CSR-related volunteer programs (e.g., recruiting and organizing participants).

- Organizational philosophies and policies (e.g., development, integration into the organization).

- Principles of corporate citizenship and governance.

- Steps for corporate philanthropy and charitable giving (e.g., selecting recipients, types, donation amounts).

When the Society for Human Resource Management (SHRM) weighs in on the issue, it suggests the following list of responsibilities for senior HR professionals. Senior HR professionals should do the following:

- Serve as a leader in community-based volunteer and philanthropic organizations

- Develop CSR strategies that reflect the organization's mission and values

- Ensure that the organization's CSR programs enhance the employee value proposition and have a beneficial impact on HR programs (e.g., recruitment and retention) and/or contribute to the organization's competitive advantage

- Create CSR program activities that engage the organization's workforce and the community at large

- Coordinate with other business leaders to integrate CSR objectives throughout the organization

- Coordinate with other business leaders to develop and implement appropriate levels of corporate self-governance and transparency

Business Elements of an Organization

Remember that each of the following elements contribute to the business effectiveness of your organization: products, competition, customers, technology, demographics, culture, processes, and safety and security. Chapter 4 has more information about each of these.

Third-Party or Vendor Selection, Contract Negotiation, and Management, Including Development of Requests for Proposals

Overseeing these processes is the senior HR professional's job. Remind yourself of their definitions and importance by reviewing them in Chapter 4.

Project Management

"Although there is an expectation for project managers to be leaders, project management and leadership are two different things. Being a successful project manager, delivering successful projects consistently, does not mean that one is a successful leader. Successful project managers develop project management skills through knowledge of the standard project management framework and through experience in utilizing best practices in implementing project management methodologies. Successful leaders are innovative and creative individuals who continuously develop new skills to integrate with their current capabilities. Effective leaders integrate leadership skills with project management skills, developing new leadership skills to complement their project management skills."[9]

> *The greatest leader is not necessarily the one who does the greatest things.*
> *He is the one that gets the people to do the greatest things.*
> —Ronald Reagan, U.S. president

Goals

Setting objectives for the organization to follow is a leader's responsibility. Managers target accomplishments that will keep the organization afloat and in business. Leaders target accomplishments that will stretch the organization in new ways that require innovation.

Timetables

Managers usually think short- to mid-term in terms of things that must be done. Leaders think in the long term, seeking distant objectives that can help position the organization along strategic lines.

Deliverables

Leaders will always try to innovate new deliverables. They will identify unique targets that can take advantage of environmental or competitive voids. Ruth Stafford Peale, wife of the Rev. Norman Vincent Peale, coined the phrase, "Find a need and fill it."[10] Leaders look for those unfulfilled needs. Leaders also look for new strategies that can help achieve those needs.

Procedures

Procedures are created for processes that will be recurring. If you need to do something only once, there is no need to document a formal procedure, unless you need to show that you have actually done the work. Usually, when processes happen in a repeated fashion, formal procedures are a good idea. They can be called *protocols, procedures,* or *methods.* They become important for the organizations that have production groups making product, accounting groups entering revenues and expenses in the accounting records, or HR people updating the HRIS records for employees.

Employment policies often have procedures associated with them so everyone can experience the same outcomes for the policies. An example is benefit administration and eligibility. For calendar-year benefits plans, each year around September and October a window of time opens that is called Open Enrollment. That window is a time period for employees to enroll in or change their enrollment for health insurance benefit programs. If you want to change from Kaiser to Blue Cross, that is the time to do it without penalty. Making an enrollment change at any other time during the year can sometimes result in penalties such as delays in benefit eligibility. Procedures assure everyone of the same experience.

PART III

Technology to Support HR Activities

Without computers, much of what we know of the HR functions today would not be possible. At least, they would be much more difficult to accomplish. Computers help us to track employee information in the HRIS. They permit us to track employee benefit enrollment decisions, workers' compensation cases, employee training needs and completions, and complaint cases. Employee demographics such as race, sex, disability, and veteran status are key ingredients in most HR reporting and analysis. Computer technology permits us to do those analyses.

There are still some software companies that sell desktop programs. But, more and more, vendors are migrating to renting software-as-a-service. These offerings are almost always located in "the cloud." Even data is not maintained locally anymore. And that raises some serious data security concerns.

It is important for HR professionals to work closely with the information technology (IT) department to address those security concerns. Playing fast and loose with employee data is a recipe for disaster. Believing that software vendors have your best interests in mind and that they will never permit any data disclosure is a cavalier approach that can get you into trouble. We are responsible for conducting due diligence to determine what protections they offer and what invasions they have had in the past. Think about the disaster that happened when Equifax was hacked and lost personal and confidential information on more than 43 million customer records. Equifax is one of the "big three" credit monitoring bureaus in the country. If it can happen to them, it sure can happen to you.

Budgeting, Accounting, and Financial Concepts

Budgeting is the process of estimating the amount of income and expenses that will occur within a given period of time. It is usually done on an annual basis, although budgets can be created for multiple years and for shorter periods of time such as months and quarters.

Evaluating Financial Statements

HR professionals must be able to analyze their organization's financial statements. Whether private or public sector, understanding financial statements is essential. Please review the "Financial Statements" section, which covers P&L statements, as they are also key parts of accounting concepts and outputs.

Budgets

The accuracy of budgeting can be improved when there is some historical data on which to rely. Generally speaking, budgets in the short term can be easier to construct and are usually more accurate than long-range budgets. The reason, simply, is that many unforeseen influences can enter the long-range picture. Fewer unpredictable influences tend to occur in shorter periods of time. Figure 9-1 illustrates the basis of budgeting.

There are two primary types of budgeting:

- **Incremental** Uses actual experience and budgets from previous time periods to identify how much will be allotted for the coming period. It adds any increases, such as CPI adjustments to compensation amounts and vendor increases in service contracts. Since this practice depends on the amount actually spent in the previous period, there is a tendency for this to create a "use it or lose it" mentality. What isn't spent in the previous period will result in a decrease of allocation for the future period.

- **Zero-based**   Each period the budgeting process begins with zero dollars allocated to each budget line item. That means budget requests (estimates) from stakeholders are the primary input. Requests must be accompanied by justifications for the amounts requested (e.g., special project coming up, CPI increases in compensation, inflationary increase in cost of office supplies). Since there is no dependency on how much was spent in the previous period, there is no tendency to spend everything just to protect future allocations. Each year, future allocations are based on the business case analysis of needs.

Accounting Terms

Thousands of terms can be associated with the accounting of funds in an employer's organization. Here are some of the most common. (This is not nearly an exhaustive list. Please see the glossary for a more detailed list of HR-related terminology.)

- **Accounts payable**   Money that is due (e.g., to vendors and suppliers) for purchase orders you have issued. Vendor invoices are received and processed for payment. Between the time the invoice is received and the time it is paid, the amount is considered an "account payable."

- **Accounts receivable**   Money that is due to you as a result of work performed and billed to a customer or client. Dollars that are represented by your invoice that has been sent to the customer but not yet paid is known as an *account receivable*.

- **Asset**   Any owned tangible or intangible object having economic value useful to the owner.

- **Bonds**   Long-term promissory note considered a liability by the issuing organization.

- **Book value**   The value of a security or asset as entered in a company's books.

- **Bylaws**   Collection of formal, written rules governing the conduct of a corporation's affairs (such as what officers it will have, what their responsibilities are, and how they are to be chosen). Bylaws are approved by a corporation's stockholders, if a stock corporation, or by other owners, if a nonstock corporation.

- **Cost accounting**   Detailed accounting of expenses and revenues at the product or project level.

- **Credit**   An increase in a liability or decrease in value of an asset.

- **Current asset**   An asset that can reasonably be expected to convert to cash within a year if that is desired.

- **Debit**   An increase in an asset or decrease in credit balance.

- **Earnings per share** Net earnings divided by the number of outstanding shares of stock.
- **Goodwill** An intangible asset representing market image, brand value, and other similar premium values for the organization.
- **Liability** A debt or obligation payable to someone else.
- **Owner's equity** What remains after deducting liabilities from asset value.

Cost Management

One of the more challenging tasks in any employer organization, cost management is the process of controlling the expenditures needed to generate the product or service for which the organization is in business. What do you do when someone spends money that has not been allocated in their budget? What do you do when legitimate expenses escalate to unanticipated levels? What do you do when a new union contract boosts compensation to unplanned amounts?

Procedures for authorizing expenses are often used to help control costs. Pre-approval can be required if need be so people don't just spend money that hasn't been allocated in the budget. Sometimes organizations engage in identifying authorization amounts according to the management level of the individual. If an amount is sufficiently large, it may require CEO or board of directors approval before the money can be spent.

Techniques and Methods for Organizational Design

Aligning the way parts of an organization relate to one another is considered the organizational structure. HR professionals need to be familiar with organizational structures so they may act as a guide for management in the selection and determination as to which structure would be best to gain the best performance.

Outsourcing

Outsourcing is shifting a workload out of the organization through a contract with another employer organization, either here in this country or somewhere else in the world. Managed service providers (MSPs) offer to manage functions as part of a strategic decision to move operations or support functions out of an employment organization to a vendor that can perform them less expensively. Such a decision is designed to allow the client company to focus on key activities within its core business while a vendor handles support activities for the client.

Shared Services

Organizations can be self-sufficient or interdependent.

- Self-sufficient organizations will have all of the administrative support groups contained wholly within the group. So a production department and a marketing department could have independent HR staff and IT staff within the department. They would not necessarily talk with one another or interact in the performance of their duties. Each department would absorb the total cost of staff support it needs to perform its mission.

- Interdependent organizations are those that share staff support expenses. One HR staff and one IT staff serve the needs of all departments. Cost of that support is prorated or allocated based on usage. Each department pays for its share of the administrative support it uses.

Methods of Gathering Data for Strategic Planning Purposes

When developing a strategic plan, leaders need to understand and know what is going on in their organization's industry, the market it serves, and the organization itself. They need to be acutely aware of risks such as technological advances and how that may impact the organization or its business. The framework to collecting, analyzing, and interpreting relevant information of threats and opportunities is known as *environmental scanning*. It's not always easy to define what is going on outside an organization, yet it is vitally important for the outcome of strategic planning.

The following factors will shape an organization's external environment and need to be considered when doing environmental scanning:

- Demographic factors, such as age, gender, ethnicity, generations, shifts in population, education trends, and labor force, need to be considered.

- Economic factors can be a host of things such as the current-day recession, rising health and retirement costs, and emerging global economies—just to name a few. The gross domestic product (GDP), consumer price index, interest rates, and inflation all can have an immediate and direct effect on financial planning, which includes wage increases, benefit costs, and retirement notices.

- Political factors must weigh in because one thing that U.S.-based organizations can count on is an ever-fluid regulatory and legislative government arm continually being enacted at the federal, state, and local levels.

- Employment factors are looked at in environmental scanning. Retention, turnover, skilled labor competition, unions, immigration, and even attitude and generational trends and realities are determined.

- International factors are interwoven into the environmental scanning because of the nature of our growing global connections as a world. Trade agreements, offshoring, and international labor laws may impact the organization or its industry.

- Social factors have a place in the scanning review and research. For example, the prominence of single parents in the workforce and a generation that is working past normal Social Security retirement age will necessitate planning and consideration.

- Forever increasing in their speed of change are technological factors. The advances we have seen in just the past five years are astounding when it comes to information access and the speed of that access. The awareness of technological skills and the training to keep workforces up to speed on ever-changing software programs and equipment are required. A digital divide has been created, in much the same manner as the divide created during the first years of automobile ownership in the early 1900s. The haves and have-nots are apparent again in terms of broadband access.

PART III

Strengths, Weaknesses, Opportunities, and Threats

SWOT stands for strengths, weaknesses, opportunities, and threats. Strengths and weaknesses are looked at as internal factors within the organization that can be managed. Opportunities and threats are controlled by external forces. It is a long-standing simple process used in strategic planning for collecting information about an organization's current state. Four foundational questions are posed:

- **S** What are the organization's strengths?
- **W** What are the organization's weaknesses?
- **O** What external opportunities might help the organization to progress toward its vision?
- **T** What external threats could foil the organization's plans and business?

Assessments are helpful in SWOT analysis, including customer focus groups or surveys, current employee attitude surveys, and exiting employee interviews. It's important to ask these groups open-ended questions such as the following:

- What's going well and right with the organization?
- What would be more ideal with the organization?
- What needs improvement or is not working so well?

Political, Economic, Social, and Technological

PEST stands for political, economic, social, and technological factors. PEST analysis is also referred to as STEP analysis—they are the same tool used within the SWOT process. The PEST process is focused on the external scanning and gathering of information. Today, software has been developed to use the PEST process, which is widely helpful in reducing the amount of time for research, in particular with opportunities and threats. An additional way to obtain information from the organization's marketplace is through a third-party consulting firm. Those firms have collected vast amounts of data and information, including data about trends and other predictions of information.

Porter's Five Forces

This is another analytical tool created by a Harvard Business School professor, Michael E. Porter. Porter asserts in his book *Competitive Strategy: Techniques for Analyzing Industries and Competitors*[11] that there are five forces found in all industries—competitors, suppliers, buyers, alternative products for consumers, and type/level of competition in the industry. Porter's model of analysis targets the specific issues of the industry in which the organization operates, keeping an eye on the horizon and futuristic events. Five questions are posed:

- What new competition might enter the organization's market?
- What level of reliance does the organization have with its suppliers?

- What is the diversity of the organization's customer base?
- What substitutions as a more reasonable cost to the customer might pop up?
- What is the level of competition in the current marketplace?

Qualitative and Quantitative Methods and Tools Used for Analysis, Interpretation, and Decision-Making Purposes

As you learned in Chapter 3, qualitative and quantitative methods and tools used for analysis, interpretation, and decision-making purposes are considered core knowledge for HR professionals. So that becomes our foundation on the topic.

Qualitative Data Gathering and Analysis

It may sound simple, but collecting information that is not initially quantifiable can require some serious effort. Here are some characteristics of qualitative data gathering and analysis:[12]

- Collecting and analyzing data is highly labor-intensive (e.g., interviews, focus groups).
- It allows probing "why" and "how" questions.
- Data is "soft" (e.g., text, images, artifacts, narratives).
- It's flexible enough to permit adjustments during data collection (e.g., supplementary questions, follow-up probing).
- It provides huge amounts of data that must be summarized and interpreted.
- Analysis can begin before all data has been collected.
- It focuses on meanings of events and actions as perceived by the participants.
- Some analysis may be performed by computer.

Quantitative Data Gathering and Analysis

Anytime you can count something, it is easier to collate information, as long as the data sets are referencing the same items. Even comparing quantities of differing items is possible using this approach. Here are some characteristics of quantitative data gathering and analysis:[13]

- Collecting and analyzing data is usually straightforward (e.g., counting, measuring).
- It's helpful in answering questions of "who," "where," "how many," "how much," and "what is the relationship between specific variables."
- It involves hard data (e.g., counts, numbers, amounts, sizes).
- Following the collection of all data, the analysis can be done.
- It's not flexible, and follow-up is usually difficult.
- Some analysis may be performed by computer.

Change Management Processes and Techniques

Change management is a structured approach for ensuring that changes are thoroughly and smoothly implemented and that the lasting benefits of change are achieved.[14]

Managing change is the largest driving force behind employee relations. Change is a process that people and organizations undergo as a response; it is a transformation toward flexibility. HR is involved in managing of people issues resulting from change, either planned changed or a reactive change, such as something occurring from an external source (for example, an employment-related law that regulates behavior in the workplace).

Helping both employees and management in an organized process through the roller-coaster ride of change, as identified by Elisabeth Kubler-Ross in her book *On Death and Dying*,[15] is an emotional intelligent (EQ) competency skill for HR professionals and leaders. First, shock and denial about the change are awakened within people. Anger is the next response. Depression eventually sets in about the "loss" of status quo resulting from the change. Then movement toward bargaining and dialogue occurs related to the change. Finally, the roller-coaster ride ends as employees reach a level of acceptance about the change. The key knowledge is in understanding the change and the management of the anticipated reactions.

Donald Kirkpatrick's *How to Manage Change Effectively*[16] discusses a model with the following seven basic steps in the change management process to be followed by HR and organizations:

- Determining the need or desire for change
- Preparing the tentative plans for change
- Discussing alternative and probable reactions to the change
- Making a final decision about the change
- Establishing a project plan and associated timetable
- Communicating the change
- Implementing the change and evaluation

Techniques for Forecasting, Planning, and Predicting the Impact of HR Activities and Programs Across Functional Areas

These same tasks are found in a lesser form as part of the PHR requirements. SPHR-level HR professionals do the same things but at higher levels of responsibility and organizational impact.

These are the PHR tasks:

- Forecasting the workforce needs of client departments
- Planning the steps and resources needed for recruiting job candidates for the forecasted job openings
- Predicting the participation rates for new employee payroll savings plans

These are the SPHR tasks:

- Forecasting the organizational structure changes necessary as the company moves into new geographies or internationally
- Planning the steps and resources needed for international compliance requirements related to workforce needs
- Predicting the strategic goal achievement for new union contract negotiations

Risk Management

Today risks can be salient in financial regulation, markets, and products. There are also risks in employee management, industry evolution, and technological advances. Offering opportunities to lead an organizational effort to address one or more of these risks can result in skill enhancement. You will find much more about risk management in Chapter 4.

How to Deal with Situations That Are Uncertain, Unclear, or Chaotic

"A critical planning task is recognizing and addressing uncertainty. Actual problems vary in uncertainty over means and ends. If people agree on what they want and how to achieve it, then certainty prevails and planning is rational application of knowledge. If they agree on what they want but do not know how to achieve it, then planning becomes a learning process; if they do not agree on what they want but do know how to achieve alternatives, then planning becomes a bargaining process; if they agree on neither means nor ends, then planning becomes part of the search for order in chaos. Each prototype situation suggests a particular range of planning styles. Planners should tailor their styles to problem conditions. By acting contingently they can use reason to cope with uncertainty."[17]

Chapter Review

This chapter has concerned leadership and strategy at the senior levels of HR requirements. Advanced management skills are required to anticipate organizational needs and contribute to strategic planning and goal achievement. Senior HR professionals are key players in mergers, acquisitions, and international expansion. Essentially, senior HR professionals carry the burden of identifying how the HR staff can support organizational strategic goals. What HR strategies will be needed to make those contributions?

You learned about compliance with laws and regulations through organizational design, job design, and leadership skills. Creating HR indicators that inform strategic actions will support the executive team in its quest for strategic goals. Additionally, you learned that understanding business is a requirement of being a senior HR practitioner.

Questions

1. Which of the following is not an HR data indicator?

    A. Turnover rates

    B. Retention rates

    C. Production rates

    D. Cost per hire

2. Risk management strategy can include:

    A. Avoidance, mitigation, acceptance

    B. Acceptance, non-acceptance, insurance

    C. Insurance, FEMA support, industry support

    D. OSHA endorsement, insurance, risk assessment

3. Vision, mission, and values are part of an organization's _____ _____ process.

4. Which of the following are budgeting, accounting, and financial concepts? (Choose two.)

    A. Outsourcing

    B. Government contracting

    C. Competitive advantage

    D. Shared services

5. Which of the following are methods of gathering data for strategic planning purposes? (Choose two.)

    A. EFOS

    B. SWOT

    C. PEST

    D. RIDS

6. HR strategic plans should always:

    A. Provide for a 2 percent growth in staff

    B. Give more responsibility to the HR director

    C. Provide for an annual planning session retreat

    D. Contribute to the enterprise strategic plan

7. The primary responsibility of HR in its support of enterprise strategic plans is to:

    A. Align human capital with the larger organization's strategic plans

    B. Set goals that the board of directors tells HR to set

    C. Set goals that the CEO tells HR to set

    D. Align human capital (head count) with the approved budget

8. A budget is:

    A. An allocation of money that may not be exceeded

    B. An estimate of income and expenses that will occur in a given time period

    C. A statement of actual expenses incurred in the most recent time period

    D. A guess about the cost of participation in professional organizations and events

9. _____ _____ are expressions of opportunities and challenges along with benefits to be gained and action plans for reaching them.

10. Which of the following publishes standards for developing service delivery plans? (Choose two.)

    A. United Nations Standards Publishing Organization (UNSPO)

    B. Universal Business Standards Development Organization (UBSDO)

    C. National Occupational Standards (NOS)

    D. American National Standards Institute (ANSI)

11. The three types of information systems used for tracking employee data are:

    A. HRIS, UEDE, HRQM

    B. HRIS, EDRS, QMEE

    C. HRIS, BCOP, HCTD

    D. HRIS, HCM, HRMS

12. Strategies must support a commitment to:

    A. Meeting legal requirements

    B. Meeting industry requirements

    C. Meeting competitor requirements

    D. Meeting payroll requirements

13. When considering business expansion, it is wise to explore the potential _____ _____ offered by various jurisdictions.

14. Business metrics can include which of the following? (Choose two.)

    A. Turnover rates

    B. Financial statements

    C. Planning session attendance

    D. Remedial staffing indicators

15. Turnover measures:

    A. The amount of time it takes to interview all job candidates in a selection pool

    B. How quickly the budget can be approved

    C. The number of people in a training program

    D. The rate of employee loss

16. Retention rates measure:

    A. The amount of time trainees retain the knowledge from class

    B. How long new employees remain on the job after they are hired

    C. How many people remain in the candidate pools for consideration

    D. The number of people who are not qualified for the job in question

17. External information sources used for HR decisions and recommendations can include:

    A. Salary data surveys and management trends

    B. Legal analysis and CEO expectations

    C. Candidate compensation expectations and salary history

    D. Industry data survey and published national affirmative action plan summaries

18. The covenant of good faith and fair dealing means:

    A. A religious obligation

    B. An employer's obligation to be honest in employee interactions

    C. An employer's obligation to give the employees what they want

    D. A requirement stemming from the Renaissance

19. Corporate social responsibility (CSR) reflects how the organization integrates and aligns with its communities as a helping hand for sustaining economic prosperity, social equity, and _____ _____.

20. A zero-based budget is:

    A. A result of subtracting expenses from revenues to get zero

    B. Providing zero compensation for projects submitted after the budget is finalized

    C. Based on a fresh start each year with no carryover from previous years

    D. Using a foundation of zero additions to head count before new requirements

Answers

1. C is correct. Production rates are not an HR data indicator. Turnover rates, retention rates, and cost per hire are common HR data indicators.

2. A is correct. Non-acceptance, insurance, FEMA support, industry support, OSHA endorsement, and risk assessment are not risk management strategies.

3. Strategic planning

4. A, D. Government contracting and competitive advantage are not considered budgeting, accounting, or financial concepts.

5. B, D. RIDS and EFOS do not exist.

6. D. HR strategic plans should always support the enterprise strategic plan. The other answers may be correct only under very narrow circumstances and therefore are not appropriate answers for this question.

7. **A.** HR must always support the larger organization's strategic plans. The other three options do not suggest that HR is involved in the larger organization's strategic planning process.

8. **B.** It is an estimate for the future. A is incorrect because an estimate is not a firm allotment. C is incorrect because a budget looks forward; a statement of actual expenses is a report, not a forecast. D is incorrect because professional group membership and participation is likely only one line item in an HR budget.

9. **Business plans**

10. **C, D.** NOS is British. ANSI is American. The other two options do not exist as organizations.

11. **D.** All three are valid data systems. A, B, and C are incorrect because, aside from HRIS, the other data systems do not exist.

12. **A.** All legal requirements must be included when setting strategic goals. B and C are incorrect because they are narrow and do not include all legal requirements. D is incorrect because payroll requirements are just part of the legal requirements.

13. **Tax incentives**

14. **A, B.** Turnover rates and financial statements are both business measurements. Planning staffing attendance and remedial staffing indicators are not business measurements.

15. **D.** Turnover measures the rate of employee loss. The other answers are incorrect because they do not have anything to do with employee loss.

16. **B.** Retention rates relate to new employees. How long they stay in the job after being hired is the measurement. The other answers do not have anything to do with new employees remaining with the company.

17. **A.** Both salary data surveys and management trends are valid external information sources for decision-making. Legal analysis is also a valid input. However, CEO expectations are internal, not external. Candidate compensation may be valid, but salary history is now outlawed in many jurisdictions. Industry data survey information may be a valid source, but there are no published national affirmative action plan summaries.

18. **B.** The expectation is that the employer and employee will deal with each other honestly, fairly, and in good faith. It is not a religious obligation. It is not an obligation to give employees whatever they want. And it is not something stemming from the Renaissance.

19. **Environmental protection**

20. **C.** Zero-based budgets start fresh each year. Simply subtracting expenses from revenues to get zero would work fine in a public-sector organization but not in a for-profit company. Refusing to accommodate projects that come up after a budget is finalized means there can be no flexibility in the organization's response to new needs. And it has no relation to head count except that head count translates to expense dollars, only one part of the budget.

Endnotes

1. https://www.sqa.org.uk/files/aq/HA5H04.pdf

2. https://blog.ansi.org/2018/07/customer-satisfaction-iso-10002-quality/

3. https://www.financialforce.com/blog/types-of-hr-technology-systems-hris-hcm-hrms/

4. https://www.bls.gov/cpi/

5. https://www.hrdive.com/news/salary-history-ban-states-list/516662/

6. https://compensation.blr.com

7. https://hbr.org/2008/07/choosing-strategies-for-change

8. https://onstrategyhq.com/resources/strategic-planning-process-basics/

9. Kumar, V. S. (2009). Essential leadership skills for project managers. Paper presented at PMI Global Congress 2009—North America, Orlando, FL. Newtown Square, PA: Project Management Institute. https://www.pmi.org/learning/library/essential-leadership-skills-project-managers-6699

10. http://whartonmagazine.com/blogs/fanafi-why-entrepreneurs-should-find-a-need-and-fill-it/#sthash.GAPEISuD.dpbs

11. Porter, Michael E., *Competitive Strategy: Techniques for Analyzing Industries and Competitors* (Free Press, 1980)

12. https://www.researchgate.net/publication/278961843_Qualitative_Data_Analysis_and_Interpretation_Systematic_Search_for_Meaning

13. Ibid

14. https://www.mindtools.com/pages/article/newPPM_87.htm

15. Kubler-Ross, Elisabeth, *On Death and Dying: What the Dying Have to Teach Doctors, Nurses, Clergy and Their Own Families*, Scribner, https://www.amazon.com/Death-Dying-Doctors-Nurses-Families/dp/1476775540

16. Kirkpatrick, Donald L., *How to Manage Change Effectively: Approaches, Methods, and Case Examples,* Jossey-Bass Management Series, https://www.amazon.com/How-Manage-Change-Effectively-Jossey-Bass/dp/0875896596/ref=sr_1_1?ie=UTF8&qid=1536259371&sr=8-1&keywords=How+to+Manage+Change+Effectively

17. https://www.tandfonline.com/doi/abs/10.1080/01944368508976801

CHAPTER 10

Talent Planning and Acquisition

In Chapter 5, we stressed the importance of the Talent Planning and Acquisition function for the Professional in Human Resources (PHR) exam. The importance of this function does not change for the senior human resource professional. Talent planning and acquisition lays the groundwork for the other human resource topics we discuss in this book. Material from Chapter 5 will likely be included on the SPHR exam, so it should be considered a complement to this chapter. Talent planning and acquisition makes up 16 percent of the Senior Professional in Human Resources (SPHR) exam.

The official HR Certification Institute (HRCI) Talent Planning and Acquisition functional area responsibilities and knowledge statements for the SPHR exam are as follows:

Responsibilities

- Evaluate and forecast organizational needs throughout the business cycle to create or develop workforce plans (for example, corporate restructuring, workforce expansion, or reduction)
- Develop, monitor, and assess recruitment strategies to attract desired talent (for example, labor market analysis, compensation strategies, selection process, onboarding, sourcing, and branding strategy)
- Develop and evaluate strategies for engaging new employees and managing cultural integrations (for example, new employee acculturation, downsizing, restricting, mergers and acquisitions, divestitures, global expansion)

Knowledge Of

- Planning techniques (for example, succession planning, forecasting)
- Talent management practices and techniques (for example, selecting and assessing employees)
- Recruitment sources and strategies
- Staffing alternatives (for example, outsourcing, temporary employment)

- Interviewing and selection techniques and strategies
- Impact of total rewards on recruitment and retention
- Termination approaches and strategies
- Employee engagement strategies
- Employer marketing and branding techniques
- Negotiation skills and techniques
- Due diligence processes (for example, mergers and acquisitions, divestitures)
- Transition techniques for corporate restructuring, mergers and acquisitions, offshoring, and divestitures
- Methods to assess past and future staffing effectiveness (for example, cost per hire, selection ratios, adverse impact)

Workforce Planning

Workforce planning is a process that ensures the organization's goals are aligned with the activities and makeup of the workforce. For an organization to be productive, it is important that everything the organization hopes to achieve is being cascaded to and carried out by its people. For example, organizational goals such as customer service metrics and production targets are all heavily affected by the performance and output of an organization's employees. For goals to be met, the right number of employees need to be on the payroll and in the right departments.

Although organizations spend a great deal of time focused on the strategic planning process each year, some level of uncertainty always exists in business operations. Regular forecasting of business needs and heavy involvement of senior human resource professionals in the workforce planning process helps ensure an organization is adept at making changes when necessary. Many internal and external factors affect the workload required in the organization and the number of people available to complete the work. Here are a few examples:

- Organization A experiences a merger that leads to both an increase in the workload and an expansion of the workforce. To support these changes, new corporate management positions are also created to oversee new lines of business and help manage organizational changes.

- Organization B is not meeting revenue targets and decides to reduce the workforce. Employees who are not laid off are required to take on more responsibility to support the workload.

- Organization C employs a large number of long-term employees. Sixty percent of this group decides to retire in 2018. Until new talent is hired, the organization must hire temporary labor and adjust the responsibilities of a few positions to make ends meet.

- Organization D outsources call center operations to another country to reduce labor costs in the department.

Forecasting

Forecasting is one of the major activities involved in workforce planning. This activity is best done in partnership with the organization's finance director. It starts with a high-level review of the organization's current budget, anticipated future revenue and expenses, and plans for growth or downsizing. Any major change in these factors will have an impact on staffing requirements. For example, startup organizations often have to do more with less until they can afford to hire a larger team.

Once budgetary factors are determined with the aid of the finance department, full-time equivalent (FTE) calculations are developed to align the workload with the budget. As a reminder, the number of full-time equivalent people (FTE) required is equal to the total functional workload divided by the workload handled by one person. For a review of how to calculate FTEs, please see Chapter 5.

After determining FTE needs for each department and division in the organization, the total number of internal employees should be reviewed to determine the needs for future staffing or downsizing. For future staffing needs, a recruitment plan is the next step. A recruitment plan details the steps the organization plans to take for both internal and external sourcing of applicants for a new position. There are many effective options for sourcing, especially with the growth of the Internet and social media.

Succession Planning

Succession planning identifies top internal candidates for managerial or executive positions and the developmental steps necessary for them to become qualified for the higher-level job when an opening occurs. Good succession planning takes time and is a wise undertaking for any organization. Unplanned turnover can create chaos for an organization and have dire consequences for operations. A successful succession plan will prevent uncertainty and costly delays in searching for qualified job candidates. It also ensures the organization's goals are aligned with the skill set of the staff members who carry them out.

It is common for senior HR managers to be involved with succession planning. These planning documents are extremely sensitive and carefully guarded. HR professionals, even at the highest level, may not be permitted to be part of the succession planning process for senior executives. Excluding HR is more of a parochial view these days, but you may still encounter it in some organizations. Premature release of any such senior executive information may result in violations of Securities and Exchange Commission rules. This could impact stock prices, up or down, depending on the public perception of the information released. Two words associated with succession planning are often sacred and secret. Sometimes, individuals are not even aware that they are named on a succession plan.

A succession plan should contain an assessment of each employee, detailing whether that person is "Ready now for promotion," "Ready in the future for promotion," "Best to remain in current position," and "On performance improvement program."

- *Ready now for promotion* means the employee could move into a specific higher position and be successful without further developmental activities. The employee currently has all of the knowledge, skills, and abilities required of the higher job.

- *Ready in the future for promotion* means that there is some specific knowledge, skills, or abilities the employee must attain before being ready for the higher-level job. There may be specific plans to send the individual to training programs or to move them into other specific jobs for experience needed before being ready for the promotion. Other developmental activities might include assignment to specific task force groups or additional education in certain university programs. If an advanced degree is needed, that should be identified (for example, a master of business administration).

- *Best to remain in current position* means the employee has a satisfactory or better job performance rating in the current position. Performance appraisals indicate that there is not a high chance of success if promoted. It might be that the individual participated in a formal assessment program and was judged unlikely to succeed if promoted. In any event, remaining in the current job is the best for both the employee and the organization.

- *On performance improvement program* means anyone who is less than satisfactory in their current job should be provided with a specific plan for development of the deficiencies so he or she can be successful. If the improvement program does not help generate successful knowledge, skills, or abilities, the employee should be moved into a job where existing skills would be adequate, or the individual should be terminated.

Once the inventory of employees has been completed, identification of likely internal candidates for each executive position can begin. It is important to note that annual inventory regulations for disabled affirmative action require an annual review of employee skills, training needs, and preparation for promotion. It applies only to disabled employees. Since "nondisabled" is not a protected category, employees who are not disabled have no basis for a discrimination complaint because they are omitted from such a skills review. However, including all employees in the review makes good business sense because it can identify everyone the employer believes to be ready now for promotion and worthy of including on the succession plan. Usually, three people are identified as potential successors for each executive job. When doing so, first identify those who are "ready now" and then those who still need some developmental work.

When you are done, a chart of positions and likely successors can be created and published. Distribution of such plans is normally tightly controlled. There are many reasons for exercising restraint in distribution of succession plans:

- If incumbents know they are identified as the possible successor to an executive, contractual expectations could be created that would raise legal liability problems.

- People who are identified as successors might conclude that they no longer need to produce at exceptional levels in the current job.

- People who are not identified as successors can experience a decrease in morale, resulting in production issues.

Those not identified as successors may leave the organization, and the resulting turnover could reach unacceptable levels. Each departure results in the loss of institutional knowledge that cannot immediately be regained, even if replacements are found quickly. In summary, succession plans are important when disaster strikes an employer's organization or when large numbers are expected to retire, causing a gap in skills and knowledge, which is what has been predicted with the Baby Boomer exodus. Succession plans typically involve plans for filling vacancies at the most senior levels of management. However, it is possible to expand the coverage to any level of management. They can ensure trained, experienced people ready to take over a more senior job once the job becomes vacant.

In the Trenches

Surprise Resignation

It was Tuesday morning, and Sarah, the human resource director at a small firm, just arrived at the office. While filling her coffee cup, she noticed a note on her desk. The note was from Leslie, the firm's accounting manager, and read, "I found another job. This note serves as my immediate resignation." Sarah nearly spilled her coffee. Although she interacted closely with Leslie, the resignation came as a complete shock. The firm's chief financial officer (CFO) position was already vacant because of a planned retirement, and Sarah was in the final stages of the interview process with three candidates. Until yesterday, Leslie was the most senior person on the accounting and finance team. Not only was Leslie the only person at the firm who knew how to process payroll, but the firm was also in the middle of its annual audit and preparing annual tax filings. Not to mention, Tuesday was payroll processing day.

Sarah sat at her desk, in a state of panic. Why did she leave? What did we do wrong? How will we pay our employees this week? How will we finish our audit and tax processing efforts? What company property is in Leslie's possession? How do we access our financial system and bank accounts? How will we train the CFO? How will we fill Leslie's position in the short term? How long will the recruiting process take for a permanent replacement? The questions were endless, and Sarah's state of helplessness prevailed. Although she was asked to train the receptionist on a few accounting duties, Leslie always had something more important to do. After all, she was also the acting CFO. She did a great job, and no one wanted to stress her out by adding another task to her plate. Leslie could "do it all." Up until now, at least. Now all that was left was a large void with serious financial and operational risks for the firm.

Sarah picked up the phone to make the first of many phone calls that day. To Leslie. To an executive staffing firm. And to the firm's financial system provider so Sarah could learn how to process payroll—a task she never imagined she would be doing.

Selection Strategies

Although employers might be subject to different requirements regarding job posting, job posting processes are nonetheless part of a selection strategy. For example, employers subject to affirmative action requirements must list their job openings with the employment service veterans' representative to provide veterans with a 72-hour advance opportunity to respond to the opening if they are interested and qualified. After the three days have passed, the employment service will post the job opening on its general job board. Although it is perfectly legal to discriminate in favor of otherwise qualified veterans, just as it is legal to discriminate in favor of otherwise qualified disabled candidates, employers not subject to these requirements may find it possible to employ a completely different selection strategy.

Generally speaking, there are four key components of recruiting strategies that every organization should employ:

- **Identifying your brand**   If you are the leading company in a specific arena, let people know that.

- **Targeting specific candidate sources**   Identify the most likely sources for the type of candidates you seek. If you want professional engineers, look in engineering associations and college institutions. If you want electricians, look at the union organizations in the locations where your need exists. Target the specific sources you know will be able to give you the qualified candidates you need, including the gambit of social media platforms that link to professional organizations in this day and age.

- **Working with your key sources**   When you find organizations that have job candidates that can fill your needs, cultivate positive relationships with them. Give them tours of your facilities and stress how it is possible for you to work together to reach mutually satisfactory goals and objectives. Federal contractors have obligations to foster these types of relationships with sources of veterans and disabled job candidates in addition to those serving the female and minority job seekers.

- **Preparing your sales pitch**   Be prepared to sell your best job candidate on the benefits of working for your organization. Explain the environment, the working conditions, the side benefits, and the culture in a way that entices the job candidate to want to accept your job offer.

Branding and Marketing the Organization

Branding is a key recruiting strategy that differs from marketing. Branding is a strategic exercise, whereas marketing is a tactical process. Branding is also a method of conveying key organizational values, while marketing is a process of encouraging people to purchase the organization's product or service. Branding statements help explain to a prospective hire what the company culture is like. For example, "Here are the things we value as an employer." "Here is the way we do things around here." "Here we have a culture that values _____." In contrast, when we hear things like, "We can provide that solution for you with our product/service," we know we are hearing a marketing statement. It says "buy me." It is more direct and pointed than a branding statement. They are often confused simply because they are so closely related.

An organization's branding and marketing efforts have important implications for HR. The old adage "actions speak louder than words" rings true. It is helpful and informative to communicate an organization's products and services, but if that organization's branding statements conflict with its actions, that is an easy way to lose the trust of current and prospective employees. Senior HR professionals are responsible for ensuring the organizational values defined in strategy meetings are actually a reality in the workplace. Here are a few examples of how this works:

- **Recruitment strategies**   Does an organization boast that it is "locally owned and operated for 50 years" in its marketing materials? The organization's recruitment strategy can help ensure there is true alignment with this statement. For example, are recruiting sources focused locally? What if the organization hosts a job fair solely for small, local businesses in an effort to boost local employment? These are great ways to turn words into actions. The same branding strategy and job fair program can also be advantageous to veteran or disabled job seekers by representing a core part of an organization's diversity and inclusion program.

- **Compensation**   "We offer the best-in-class benefits! Employees and their families are our top priority!" A compensation plan will either support or oppose these taglines. Compensation is a key factor in talent acquisition and retention. A plan should be carefully crafted to align with an organization's values. Some organizations might also offer a unique total rewards package to support the unique brand and culture of the organization.

- **Onboarding**   A welcoming atmosphere during an interview does not always translate to the same environment on the first day of the job. Providing consistency in this area goes a long way to create the culture an organization strives for. Training and mentoring programs geared toward new hires will help support a seamless transition to a new job and improved retention rates.

Emotional Intelligence in Interviewing

In Chapter 5, we reviewed several different types of employment testing techniques, with interviewing being one of the more common forms of employee selection. While it is easy these days to search the Internet for questions to ask a candidate during an interview, emotional intelligence during an interview is a concept that sometimes gets overlooked. It is just as important as the questions you ask. As a reminder, emotional intelligence refers to the ability to perceive, control, and evaluate emotions. What better time to use this skill than during an interview?

Asking the right questions that allow you to get to know a candidate on a more personal level and develop a sense of ease and trust is the goal during this process. The Society for Human Resource Management (SHRM) created some sample interview questions for the emotionally intelligent interviewer.[1] These are included in Table 10-1.

Question Type	Interview Question
Opening question	"Tell me about your job search up to now. What's motivating you to look for another opportunity, and what have your experiences been as a candidate in the open market?"
Opening question	"Before we launch too deeply into your career experience and background, as well as what we're looking for in our next hire, tell me what criteria you're using in selecting your next role or company. What's really important to you at this point in your career?"
Opening question	"As a hiring manager yourself, what do you look for when interviewing candidates in terms of their background, experience, and overall style? What do you like or dislike about hiring candidates from your side of the desk?"
Core question	"Walk me through your career progression, leading up to how you landed your current role at your present company."
Core question	"What's one thing about your career at this point that's guaranteed to make you smile?"
Core question	"What would be your next career move if you remained with your current employer, and how long would it take you to get there?"
Core question	"Based on your understanding of the role so far, why would this position make sense at this point in your career in terms of building your resume?"
Core question	"If you were to accept this position, how would you explain it to some prospective employer five years from now in terms of serving as a link in your career progression?"
Core question	"Based on what your most respected critic would say, what's the greatest asset you will bring to our company? What areas for career development and personal improvement are you focusing on at this point?"
Closing question	"Not to limit you in any way, but are you further down the road with any other companies at this point? In terms of your sense of urgency in finding a new opportunity, when would you accept an offer, and when would you reject one?"

Table 10-1   Emotionally Intelligent Interview Questions

Executive Recruiting Alternatives

When hiring executive staff, there is generally a smaller talent pool available for the job you are trying to fill. It takes years and often an array of educational accolades to develop the skills and experience needed in an executive role. Also, these individuals are not necessarily equally distributed across the United States, or even globally. There may be a need to hire an executive from a different location and coordinate a transition package to the new location. For these reasons, organizations sometimes employ different recruiting strategies when hiring executives.

If an unexpected departure arises in an executive position and a succession plan is not ready for execution, organizations sometimes turn to temporary or contract help in the form of a consultant who specializes in the gap areas needed. For example, the departure of an organization's marketing director might result in skill gaps within the organization's advertising, marketing, public relations, and internal communications functions. Employing an executive recruiting or "headhunting" firm to fill this need is a strategy that gives the organization time to fill the key position with less adverse impact on the organization's operations. These firms maintain regular communication with executives in their industry of specialization (for example, hospitality, finance, etc.) so they have an available pool of talent if they are contracted to fill a hiring need. The term *headhunting* comes from the concept that regular communication with the talent pool may lead the firm to transitioning someone who is currently employed but expressing dissatisfaction with his or her current job to a new job without any period of unemployment. These firms can supply available talent in the form of temporary or permanent job placements.

Negotiation Skills and Techniques

Especially when hiring employees for senior-level positions, effective negotiation becomes a more significant element in the hiring process. With a narrow talent pool for a skill set in high demand, the total rewards package of one position is often compared to that of another position a candidate may be considering. The organization and the job candidate need to negotiate to determine whether the open job is the right fit for both parties. Some helpful tips for hiring managers in the negotiation process are outlined here:[2]

- *Know your options.* It is important to start the negotiating process by evaluating the costs and benefits of making the hiring decision or not closing the deal. As an employer, if this is the only qualified candidate for the position but you have some reservations, how does hiring this candidate compare to your other alternatives? How costly or impactful to operations would it be to wait another month or three months to find the right fit? If a candidate asks for a higher figure than you've offered, consider how difficult and time consuming it would be to begin your search again. You have three options: agree, make a counteroffer, or stand firm.

- *Offer noncash compensation.* Don't get stumped if you can't match a candidate's salary request. Consider revisiting other parts of the compensation package, such as flexible scheduling or additional vacation days. Applicants often compromise on base salary if the total compensation package is attractive.

- *What is your ceiling?* Consider the existing pay levels for similar positions in your company. If you agree to a higher salary to win a stellar candidate, you risk lowering morale or even losing current staff if they find out a new hire is making more money than they are.

- *Know when to walk away.* If your candidate becomes evasive or difficult to reach, they may be waiting for another offer to come in or using your offer as leverage for a different position. If you feel like the candidate is playing games or if you aren't getting anywhere, thank the candidate for his or her time and then move on.

Employee Engagement Strategies

Employee engagement is a broad term. In any step of the business or human resource life cycle, there are opportunities to engage employees. In hiring, current and prospective employees may become more engaged in the organization simply by the way programs are rolled out. For example, soliciting feedback on an onboarding program from a focus group of entry-level employees prior to launch will help these employees feel engaged in the process and empowered that their feedback affected the program. Or creating an internal job posting policy that gives internal employees the opportunity to express interest in a job before external candidates may contribute to a feeling among employees that the organization cares about their career development and interests.

Managing Culture During Organizational Changes

Employee engagement becomes even more important during times of organizational change. When an organization experiences growth, such as during a merger and acquisition or global expansion, an organization experiences an integration of multiple companies and, potentially, employees from entirely different countries with different societal and cultural norms. In these circumstances, failing to carefully manage the integration might lead to a culture clash. An article by Bain and Company describes this problem in simple terms: "In a culture clash, the companies' fundamental ways of working are so different and so easily misinterpreted that people feel frustrated and anxious, leading to demoralization and defections."[3] Symptoms of a culture clash might include decreased morale, key employee resignations, poor communication…the list goes on.

Successfully managing a cultural integration starts from the top. Top executives, often with leadership from the senior HR professional at the organization, need to define what they want the organizational culture to be. Questions like the following help determine the direction the organization wants to go in: What behaviors do we want employees to exhibit? What do we like about each company culture now? What do we dislike? What do we want to keep? What do we want to change? An array of helpful tools can be used to determine the answers to these key questions. The following are some common ones:

- **Employee opinion surveys** are a quantitative way to gauge current strengths and weaknesses and determine attitudes toward the change. Feedback is also anonymous, which often results in greater employee participation and more honest responses.

- **Organization charts and work flow outlines** help visibly describe the makeup of each company and department and the way in which work gets done. These diagrams can be a simple way to describe the structure of a company and visibly outline redundancies or areas of needed improvement.

- **Management interviews** allow for a detailed picture of the current company landscape and management styles. For best results, interview questions and selection criteria for manager interviews should be consistent. This allows for greater generalization of results to the entire population.

- **Employee focus groups** can provide information about attitudes, opinions, and perceptions regarding changes by gathering data from a small subset of the population.

Focus groups can be a great supplement to employee opinion surveys because they help enhance results. To help keep these discussions targeted and obtain valuable results, it is important to have a neutral facilitator for the session, create a statement of purpose and outline for the meeting, and keep the group small. Five to ten participants is a good rule of thumb. It is also helpful to use more than one group to better generalize findings.

- **Customer surveys and interviews** are a way to obtain data from a different perspective. While an organization may have a sense of what is going on inside its walls, what do outsiders see? It is important to gauge the effects of organizational change on customers to determine areas of strength and weakness and devise a plan for improvements if necessary.

Once an organization has gathered enough data from these tools, a plan to merge the company cultures can be created. This plan will include specific process steps to achieve the desired outcomes. For example, if the organization decides that it wants its culture to be "people driven," there needs to be a road map to reach that goal. Maybe this road map would include the development of employee task forces to help make decisions, programs that are more customer-centric, or training that focuses on improving customer service.

Special attention should also be given to onboarding programs. We've all heard the saying "first impressions are the most lasting." When undertaking a merger and acquisition, a new organization is essentially being created. How you introduce employees to this new organization will help set the stage for their opinions and perceptions of the changes. Onboarding should tie back to the culture and values the organization has established and be engaging, fun, and informative to provide a sense of excitement about the new organization and help restore trust that may have been lost.

The Impact of Total Rewards on Recruitment and Retention

Compensation and benefits are, among other things, tools for recruiting and retaining quality employees. An employer can't hope to recruit top talent unless it is willing to pay a wage or salary that is competitive in the marketplace. Benefits take on a similar role and help with recruiting and retention. Senior HR professionals are involved at the policy level for each of these compensation elements. They need to research and recommend to the executive team policy changes or adoptions. A complete business plan should be used for the presentation.

Recall that there are no legal requirements that demand employers provide paid vacation time to employees. Vacation is an invention that comes through either union agreements/contracts or from the need to be competitive in the employment market. Imagine a company trying to hire people today if it did not offer some competitive number of paid vacation days. Not many people would like to work at that place if vacation weren't part of the employment package. So, by policy, employers offer paid time off to their workers. Other benefit programs that add to the employment enticement package include retirement programs, savings plans, medical benefits, employee cafeterias, employee spas, rest and recovery centers, and pizza Fridays.

All of the benefits can be quantified and their contribution to employment and retention efforts can be computed. There is no doubt that an employer's total rewards program is a major factor in its efforts to attract and retain talent on its payroll.

Diversity Management

Diversity and inclusion (D&I) are no longer just topics of interest; they are essential components of any large organization's strategic planning process. If the foundation of employee management is equal employment opportunity (EEO) and a tool for ensuring organizations meet those EEO obligations is affirmative action, then diversity and inclusion are the next step in ensuring that human contributions come from all sectors of the employee population. D&I is based on the premise that all employees have contributions to offer based on their experiences and that different experience histories can make a collective group of employees more effective in addressing organizational problems, including production and revenue generation. Policy development, outreach and recruiting program design, and brand management are all part of the senior HR professional's role.

At the most basic level of D&I program measurement are the demographic comparisons between incumbents and computed availability. Ensuring diversity in employee recruiting programs is another first-stage effort. Advanced D&I management will include executive-level diversity (including board of directors membership) and an active focus on D&I in advertising programs and customer appreciation programs. Focus groups, climate surveys, and employee opinion monitoring will all play a role in advanced diversity management. Management training will be essential for the success of serious D&I programs. Managing people from extremely different cultural backgrounds and with different generational representation will be a challenge into the future. In several states currently, there is no racial majority group. All racial groups are in the minority. That means any employer organization will be required to hire, train, and tap into the various talents and cultural assets of a human pool with multiple levels of sophistication. While it may be human nature to feel most comfortable with people like ourselves, it is going to be more and more necessary to push that comfort boundary and include people unlike ourselves if we are to be successful as an organization.

Staffing Effectiveness Assessment and Metrics

When considering staffing metrics specifically, there are actually two types of staffing to consider measuring: staffing of the overall employer organization and staffing for the HR organization within the larger employer group.

Effectiveness of staffing in HR is usually measured by the ratio of HR workers to the total organizational head count. It used to be that executives expected one HR person for every 100 employees. Today, those ratios are influenced by more sophisticated considerations having to do with strategic planning (succession planning, training, and development) and implementation of special programs (mergers and acquisitions with large cultural differences). "Cheap" isn't always the most effective route to success.

Overall staffing success can be measured through the consideration of turnover rates (before and after mergers and acquisitions), the level of professional staff remaining after a raid by a respected research university, or the quantity of employees who remain on their job for at least 12 months after being hired.

Each organization must devise its own measures for staffing effectiveness. Identify the factors that affect staffing and retention. Isolate those factors that are unique to the organization because of special conditions. Create measurements for normal conditions and a separate set of measurements for the unique conditions. Complete the statement for each condition, "I know our staffing programs have been successfully effective because they _____."

NOTE   Remember, cost per hire will likely be tested on the PHR and SPHR exams. Cost per hire is calculated dividing the sum of internal and external recruiting costs by the total number of hires in a time period.

$$\text{Cost Per Hire} = \frac{(\text{S(External Costs)} + \text{S(Internal Costs)})}{(\text{Total Number of Hires in a Time Period})}$$

Adverse Impact

As discussed in Chapters 5 and 8, adverse impact, or disparate impact, refers to employment practices that appear neutral but have a discriminatory effect on a protected group. You should be acquainted with the *80 percent test*, which is sometimes called the *four-fifths rule*. Simply said, if any protected group is selected at a rate (percentage) that is less than 80 percent the selection rate of the most favorably treated group, there is sometimes a problem. The 80 percent test is almost never used anymore because it has been replaced by statistical analysis techniques that are much more accurate. Nonetheless, you should know how to use the 80 percent test. It will likely be on the exam.

Because it often happens unknowingly, when an organization has a job requirement for a certain level of education or physical ability, it is important for HR to question whether the organization is screening for a relevant job attribute and whether it may lead to adverse impact. For example, does a pre-employment test for physical ability screen out a high proportion of women and not men? In this case, HR must question whether the selection procedure is job-related and the ability tests are necessary for business operations or job safety.

NOTE   Reacquaint yourself with adverse impact calculations from Chapter 8. Selection ratio is the number of individuals hired from a group divided by the number of applicants from a group. Impact ratio is the selection ratio for a group divided by the highest selection ratio for a group. The 80 percent test is conducted by analyzing the impact ratio for each group.

PART III

Analysis of Labor Market Data

Labor market data can be used in a couple of important ways within the recruitment process. First, it offers demographic data on race and sex that can be used in affirmative action plan preparation. Occupational categories are available in the U.S. Census American Community Survey, and each occupational category has a count of sex and race/ethnic representation. This data is used to create affirmative action benchmarks in computing the availability of qualified workers. A visit to the Census Bureau's website can yield a wealth of information.[4]

The second type of labor market data application is in the function of compensation management. Market studies by geography can be helpful in determining how much money people in designated job titles are earning. This can support both calculation of internal compensation ranges and new hire salary offers.

Organizational Exit

Everyone will eventually leave an employer. The question isn't "If?" but "How?" Some departures are voluntary; some are involuntary. Some are performance-related, and some are for retirement. Sadly, people also become disabled and die. Especially during downsizing, restructuring, off-shoring, or a divestiture, employees often experience a change in their employment relationship. Some employees may be laid off, and some may be exiting to an entirely new organization. Such changes can have a lasting effect on the organizational culture if not handled with care.

Senior HR professionals are tasked with creating the policies associated with organizational exit. These are some key topics that are covered in these policies:

- **Notice requirements**   Whenever possible, two weeks' advance notice prior to voluntary resignations is helpful in the recruitment and training replacement process.

- **Final paycheck procedures**   How and when final paychecks are presented often depends on state laws.

- **Separation clearance procedures**   What needs to be returned to the employer upon exit is often presented in the form of a checklist to ensure nothing falls through the cracks.

- **Benefits termination and COBRA**   COBRA communications address the exiting employees' options for continuing benefits. We'll talk about this more later in the chapter.

- **Reference checks**   If the organization is contacted by a prospective employer for a former employee, it is helpful to outline what will and will not be shared in a reference check. Often, organizations have a policy of only communicating dates of employment, job title, and eligibility for rehire. The answer to the question "Is this employee eligible for rehire?" is generally as simple as yes or no. Employers should be careful that they have job performance records that support whatever job performance they communicate to prospective employers.

Involuntary Separations

People sometimes have their employment status terminated despite not wanting to lose their job. Individual separations can happen because of performance deficiencies. They can happen because of an employee's inability to maintain a satisfactory attendance record. When work goes away, however, both individuals and groups of people can be affected at once. If no work is available for which they are qualified, employees are usually laid off. The absence of work in the engineering department can result in the loss of one FTE position, also known as a *position elimination*. At the same time, the loss of a customer contract can result in a need for many fewer delivery drivers. The term *reduction in force* (RIF) is used to describe both circumstances. It represents a cutback in employee headcount. See the following section, "Reductions in Force."

Sometimes layoffs happen with a "separation allowance" based on length of service or the boss's generosity. Sometimes there is no financial benefit provided to laid-off employees.

Involuntary separations are governed by union contracts where they exist. Nearly always, when unions are involved, separations are determined based on inverse seniority for people in the affected work groups. This means that the employees with the shortest length of service are selected for layoff first. Seniority lists are sometimes used even when there are no unions representing workers. Determinations can also be made based on performance evaluation ratings, area of specialty or expertise, or the length of time employees have been in the workgroup.

Reductions in Force

When workloads fall, sales take a tumble, or contracts are canceled, then staffing needs suddenly shift. It is sometimes necessary to reduce force by large amounts that will involve layoffs.

A reduction in force can happen to one person or to a group of people. Outsourcing functions performed by our jobs can reduce the need for employees. When the job goes away and there is no more work to be done in that function, the individual is removed from the payroll as a reduction in force. If there are multiple branches at the organization that employ the same position and all are outscored, this is a position elimination.

If the entire painting function is subcontracted out to a vendor who can do it cheaper, the group of painters who used to do that work in-house will be surplus employees and subject to a reduction in force.

HR professionals should be particularly careful to avoid removing individuals from the payroll claiming a position elimination RIF when the real reason for payroll separation is performance deficiency. That type of action can cause complaints of illegal discrimination. When the RIF or position elimination is pretext for discrimination, nobody wins.

You already know that state and federal laws come into play when groups of people are going to be separated from the payroll at a single location. Chapter 2 has information about the Worker Adjustment and Retraining Notification (WARN) Act, which governs layoffs for employers with 100 or more workers.

Needless to say, the determination of who gets a separation notice should not be based on any protected category membership. It is even advisable to forecast who will be separated and conduct some disparity analyses to determine if any protected group (people over 40 years old, women, disabled, and so on) will be experiencing higher-

Qualifying Event	Minimum Required Duration of COBRA Availability to Employee
Termination of employment (voluntary or involuntary)	18 months for coverage of employee, spouse, and dependent child
Reduction in work hours	18 months for coverage of employee, spouse, and dependent child
Employee's Medicare entitlement begins	36 months for coverage of spouse and dependent child
Divorce or separation (of employee and spouse)	36 months for coverage of spouse and dependent child
Death of employee	36 months for coverage of spouse and dependent child
Loss of dependent child status	36 months for former dependent child
Qualified disabled beneficiaries (those disabled within the first 60 days of COBRA coverage become eligible for an additional 11 months of coverage in addition to the basic 18 months)	29 months total for disabled person

Table 10-2   COBRA Coverage Provisions

than-acceptable rates of separation. COBRA-qualifying events are the triggers for making COBRA benefits available to employees. The type of qualifying event will dictate the maximum number of months the employee may retain coverage of health insurance using COBRA. Table 10-2 provides an easy reference about COBRA availability periods; this information has a high probability of showing up on the PHR/SPHR exams.

COBRA coverage gives employees the right to continue health insurance coverage by paying 100 percent of the premiums required for the coverage. How much of the premium was paid by the employer prior to the qualifying event is irrelevant in computing the amount of COBRA cost to the employee. Unless the employer offers to voluntarily pay for a portion of COBRA premiums, the employee is obliged to assume all of the cost of continued health plan coverage. COBRA just means the coverage may not be taken away during the entitlement period if the employee wants to pay for continuation.

In the Trenches

Equity Theory

A medium-sized employer with about 250 employees encountered severe financial difficulties. The trouble was, a rumor got out that there were problems and the company might be looking at layoffs or even shuttering the business. This was an engineering and construction company. It did design-build projects such as commercial building construction and retail store center construction.

(continued)

Once the employees got wind of the rumor, they decided that, true or not, they would secure their own compensation for all the years of service that were expected to end soon. The company didn't respond to the rumors. The "old man" was too devastated at losing his business to be able to address his employees' concerns.

So in exchange for losing their jobs, employees began taking home the company tools. Hand tools, small power tools, and even wheelbarrows, rakes, shovels, and hoes disappeared. Soon there were no more drills, sanders, or levels left on the shelves.

Known as the *equity theory*, employees sensed that the scale of the loyalty relationship was tilting away from them. Their stealing was an attempt to rebalance the scales so they "got theirs" and didn't walk away empty-handed. Illegality and ethics weren't even considered.

Unusual? You would be surprised. Equity theory is at work every day. Employees don't like to feel they are getting the short end of the stick.

Voluntary Separations

Under some circumstances, people willingly leave the payroll. This can happen if an employee receives a better job offer, the employee's spouse gets a job out of town, the employee must relocate because of their child's health, or the employee has finally made it to retirement. Sometimes voluntary resignations can be predicted. Sometimes they cannot. It is up to HR to react appropriately to the staffing need left by a resignation.

During large workforce reductions it is common for "separation packages" to be offered to certain qualifying groups of employees as an enticement that can prevent involuntary reductions. These are strategic and policy decisions the senior HR professional should be involved with from the start. It is essential to work with legal experts and the accounting team to build a program that will fit the need. These enticement packages can include cash incentives based on length of service, additional retirement benefits, continuing health benefits, and about anything else you can imagine. If enough employees accept the offered separation packages, then involuntary layoffs can be cut back. Ideally, the head count reduction goal can be met by voluntary means and no layoffs will be required. Separation packages are normally accompanied by a waiver that asks employees to waive their rights to sue the company or file discrimination complaints in exchange for the separation payment.

Another consideration is the Older Workers Benefit Protection Act (OWBPA), which is an amendment to the Age Discrimination in Employment Act (ADEA). Please refer to Chapter 2 for more detailed information about each of these laws. The OWBPA requires that voluntary waivers of rights or claims under the ADEA are valid only when they are "knowingly and voluntarily" made. OWBPA requires the following:

- The waivers must be in writing and signed.
- The employee must receive severance payments or something else of value they would not otherwise receive.
- The employee must be advised in writing to consult an attorney before signing the waiver.
- The employee must be given 21 days to consider the terms (45 days if more than one employee) and be able to revoke the agreement for up to 7 days after.
- Employees must be given (when more than one employee) certain disclosure information designed to allow the employee or his/her attorney to determine whether the terminations will have an adverse impact on older workers.

Exit Interviews

An exit interview is a tool used to seek feedback from employees who are leaving the payroll. There are times when employees resign unexpectedly and the employer would like to know why that happened. Exit interviews are the tool to help discover those things. Senior HR professionals can use the information disclosed in exit interviews to address workplace issues and improve employee programs. Employees often feel more comfortable disclosing information as they walk out the door, and it is not uncommon for an exit interview to result in the investigation of a previously unaddressed workplace problem.

Often, exit interviews seek information and opinions from the departing employee about supervision or management. How did they feel they were treated? What would they like to have had their supervisor or manager do differently? How were the working conditions? What did they think about their co-workers? Did they feel appreciated on the job for their work? Almost anything is "fair game" for probing and discovery.

Unfortunately, not every departing employee will be willing to participate in an exit interview. It is up to HR to try to convince an employee that it will help the organization get better.

International Workforce Management

More organizations each day are finding that they have needs related to multinational employment. And it's not just the private sector that is experiencing these added workforce management issues. Many governmental organizations are finding that they have overlapping responsibilities that embrace international issues.

International Workforce Planning

Labor laws are significantly different in other countries. Not only is it necessary for international organizations to understand and abide by those rules, but it is essential that they understand the customs and expectations of people in any new remote location in which they want to establish new operations.

Types of International Workers

It is necessary to understand the types of worker classifications that appear on the international stage. There are people who originate in the home country, people who originate in the remote country, and people who come from some other country altogether.

Parent-Country Nationals

These people are expatriates or parent-country nationals (PCNs). They come from the country where the employer is based at the corporate level. Royal Dutch Shell is based in the Netherlands. Nestle is based in Switzerland. General Motors is based in the United States. Each of them is an international enterprise. Anyone sent from the country where headquarters is located to another country is a PCN.

Third-Country Nationals

It is common for an international organization to have PCNs assigned to remote countries. When the organization wants to open operations in a new location in some other country, it can move third-country national (TCN) staff from the first remote location to the new remote location. These people become third-country nationals. When Shell wants to build a refinery in Chile, it might move key management people from its refinery in the United States to work on establishing the new facility in Chile. They become TCNs. They do not originate from the country where headquarters is located (the Netherlands), and they do not originate from the host country (Chile). They have been moved from a third country (the United States).

Host-Country Nationals

Also called local *nationals,* host-country nationals (HCNs) originate in the country where the remote location is being established. When General Motors wants to build a new manufacturing facility in Mexico, for example, it can hire Mexican nationals to run that facility. They are HCNs.

Expatriates

Sometimes these people are referred to as *expats,* probably because we love to shorten words by removing syllables. Expatriates are people who are working in a country other than the one of their origin. They are expatriates of the country in which they originated. International relocation expenses can be extremely high, so it is usual to only see professionals and managerial people moved internationally. It is often less expensive to obtain lower-skilled workers who are already in the host country.

Inpatriates

These are people who are working at corporate headquarters who originated in another country. Transferring management people to headquarters on a rotational assignment is commonly used for career development. Later, inpatriates can return to their home country or be assigned to another position elsewhere.

Repatriates

When employees return to their home country from a foreign assignment, they are repatriates. They are said to have been *repatriated*.

Organizational and Staffing Approaches to International Business

Not only are there different laws and customs to be considered, but there are definite differences in the possible approaches to staffing a remote international organization. Here are the primary strategies for international staffing strategies. Immigration policies of the countries involved in international staffing methods will have a profound impact on the level of success that can be achieved with any of the following policy types.

Ethnocentric

This policy provides for all key management positions to be filled by expatriates. If all management personnel are from the headquarters organization, they know what is expected by the corporate office. Communications can be expedited because there are no language or idiom barriers to overcome when every manager in the remote location is from the home office.

Polycentric

When corporate headquarters positions are staffed with inpatriates (people from other countries) and remote locations are staffed with expatriates (people from the headquarters country), they are engaging in a multiple-centered staffing practice known as *polycentricism*. This policy can reduce corporate and cultural myopia because it "mixes things up" and forces integration of cultures.

Regiocentric

Staffing and planning organizational issues around regionalization is what we find with *regiocentric* organizations. We think of examples such as European, Asian, or South American. They become extensive, multinational organizations that are adapted to the cultural, economic, and sometimes language commonalities of a given region.

Geocentric

This type of staffing policy seeks to place the best qualified individuals into job openings regardless of their country of origin.

Types of International Assignments

Many different types of assignments are possible when international staffing is involved. Table 10-3 outlines typical international assignments.

Type of Assignment	Definition
Short-term assignees	Relocation from one country to another for the duration of the assignment, lasting from six months to one year.
Long-term assignees	Relocation from one country to another for the duration of the assignment, lasting more than one year.
Sequential/rotational employees	Workers who move laterally within an employer organization to a different job title or department with the objective of building new skills or enhancing professional development.
International commuting employees	Employee works in one country of assignment and commutes frequently to the home country.
Frequent flyers/extended business travelers	Employee does not relocate but travels regularly to the assignment location.
Stealth expats/stealth pats/stealth assignees	Employees who are working in other countries outside the employer's formal global mobility program without the knowledge of human resources.
Local hires	People who are hired within the vicinity of the work location.
Localized transfer	Cross-border move in which employee is ultimately moved to permanent local status.
Permanent assignees	Employees who are assigned to a work location on a permanent basis.
Interns/trainees	People who are in a training status that may or may not lead to a regular job assignment.
Returnees	People who are enticed to return to their home country to work for the same or a different employer.
Virtual employees	Workers who are not physically present at the workplace.
Retirees	Workers who have left employment on a formal or informal program of retirement.
Part-time employees	Workers who work less than a designated number of hours per week or per month, as established by the employer. Typically less than 40 hours per week, which is usually considered to be full-time status.
Temporary employees	Employees who have been hired for a designated task that is expected to last for a short period of time, usually less than six months.
Temp-to-hire employees	Workers who are engaged through a temporary service agency for a specific assignment and converted from nonemployee to regular employee status. These are usually noncompetitive new hires.
Outsourced employees	People who work for another employer who are assigned tasks otherwise performed by employees at the outsourcing organization. Work is performed by the vendor organization under contract, so the vendor's employees are not on the outsourcing organization's payroll. Employment taxes, employee benefits, and other employment issues are managed by the vendor.

Table 10-3   Types of International Assignments

PART III

Chapter Review

As we have reviewed in this chapter, workforce planning is the basis for managing a good talent acquisition function. Selection practices should not be determined at random. Employing a strategy for selection will help avoid unnecessary legal trouble and help target better candidates. Selection strategies may also differ when hiring senior-level staff members, and using emotional intelligence in an interview can allow an interviewer to better understand whether a job is the best for the candidate and the organization. You also learned that times of change for an organization, including divestitures, restructures, offshoring, mergers, and acquisitions, require a top-down approach to creating and managing company culture. Employee engagement strategies and human resource programs should complement company culture. We closed the chapter by reviewing termination approaches and key topics in international workforce management.

Questions

1. Harriet has just taken over for the HR manager in her group, and her boss is asking for an update on the succession plan. He wants to see the employee skill inventory as soon as possible. Harriet didn't even know there was a succession plan. What should Harriet be looking for in her files?

   A. A confidential record that lists each employee's skills and abilities

   B. A list of only the top-rated people in the group who have computer skills

   C. A list of everyone in the group identifying each person's skills and whether they are currently ready for promotion

   D. A list of people showing what individuals are capable of doing now, without regard for any future assignment

2. Match the workforce analysis technique to its definition.

   A. Gap analysis technique

   B. Delphi technique

   C. Linear regression

   D. Turnover analysis

   (1) Tool to compare relationships among several variables

   (2) Measuring the distance (or difference) between where you are and where you want to be

   (3) Analyzing trends with regard to the reasons employees leave an organization

   (4) Determining the future outcome and then manipulating a group to reach that conclusion or goal statement

3. AB Trucking has had a policy that nobody will be hired unless they complete the company's job application. Now, all of their job applications are being processed online, and some applicants want to submit their résumés instead of a job application form. What can AB Trucking do about the résumé versus application controversy?

   A. It is entirely up to the company how it wants to handle the policy. Application forms are not a legal requirement, but using them is generally considered a best practice in the employment arena. Job candidates can be forced to go through the company's process of completing an application form, online or offline.

   B. The government has set up regulations that say employers have to accept résumés if they are submitted in a job search. The company doesn't really have any choice but to accept them.

   C. Job applications are old-school. Almost no employer uses them these days. The company should change its policy and use only résumés in the future.

   D. Résumés don't have all of the information that can be gathered on a job application, and people lie on résumés anyway. That alone is reason for the company to continue using its job application forms.

4. An employee in Cortez's organization came to him and suggested that she and her co-worker could consolidate their duties into one job and each work part-time, sharing the 40 hours each week so the work got done as always. What would you say if you were Cortez?

   A. Unfortunately, the Fair Labor Standards Act and the Unified Job Consolidation Act say that sharing jobs is not permitted because it would violate union agreements.

   B. There is no reason that it couldn't work if Cortez believes the two people are capable and want to make it work.

   C. Having more than one person and one Social Security number on one job assignment won't work. It makes tax reporting impossible.

   D. It's not a good idea because it doubles the liability for workers' compensation and unemployment insurance.

5. The local county's workforce has been decimated in recent months because the pension plan is changing and folks wanted to get their higher-level calculation before the changes cut that formula. The result, however, has been that a great deal of organizational intelligence walked out the door. The senior staff are suggesting you hire back some of the key personnel as temporary workers until you are able to get replacements trained. Is that a good idea?

   A. Hardly ever. It gives the newly retired people a way to "double dip" and make more money than they would have if they had stayed on the job without retiring.

   B. Sometimes. If the temporary period is truly used to train a replacement, it could get the organization across the institutional knowledge gap, passing along that information to someone new.

C. Always. There is no downside to bringing back retirees as temporary workers. So what if they make a bit more? The work gets done without interruption.

D. Maybe, if there is a limit of six months on the temporary assignment in compliance with the Fair Labor Standards Act.

6. Abel has been having trouble selecting quality accounting people. Everyone claims to be able to use Excel spreadsheets, but few actually can once they get on the job. In the end, he has had to terminate people because of poor performance. He is thinking he will use a test he saw at the local office supply warehouse. If you were the HR manager in Abel's organization, what advice would you give him about his plans for testing?

A. It sounds like a good idea. It certainly could control the cost of turnover. We should try it.

B. It sounds like a good idea. Will he be able to show that the test actually predicts success on the jobs he wants to use it for? If not, he should find a different screening tool.

C. It doesn't sound like a good idea. With everyone talking about the liability of written tests these days, we can't take that risk for any job.

D. It doesn't sound like a good idea. It is going to create more paperwork for HR, and we can't stand any workload increase.

7. Jo is trying to standardize the selection system for instructors in her training group. Having one procedure to screen candidates should yield both consistency and accuracy. What she hasn't decided is whether she should use an objective or subjective system. What would you tell her?

A. Only objective systems are able to "slice and dice" candidates effectively. Jo should use numeric devices only.

B. It is so hard to pin down clear delineations of skill using a numeric system. Jo should rely on a subjective process that gives her greater flexibility in grading candidates.

C. There is no way to quantify everything about an instructor's job. Therefore, it is impossible to use a quantitative system for that job set. Go with the subjective.

D. Both subjective and objective approaches can be used on instructor jobs as long as they both have been validated according to the Uniform Guidelines.

8. _____ are people who are working at corporate headquarters who originated in another country.

9. Which of the following are requirements of voluntary waivers or claims to comply with the Older Workers Benefits Protection Act (OWBPA)? (Choose two.)

A. The waivers must be signed by the CEO of the organization.

B. The employee must receive severance payments or something else of value they would not otherwise receive.

C. The employee must be advised in writing to consult an attorney before signing the waiver.

D. The employee must be given 30 days to consider the terms and be able to revoke the agreement for up to 10 days after.

10. Siena is the operations manager for a startup. Senior management is interested in the cost per hire of the 12 customer service representatives who were just hired. The total job posting fees were $680, it cost $1,200 to upgrade the office space to accommodate the new employees, and it cost $520 to purchase new uniforms for the staff. The cost per hire is _____.

11. The hotel Steve works at is closing two restaurants. Both restaurants are staffed by union servers and kitchen staff, as well as nonunion management staff. Steve needs to plan a reduction in force (RIF) for all servers and half of the restaurants' management. Kitchen staff will be moved to another restaurant at the hotel. How should he select staff for the RIF?

A. Steve should select all staff based on inverse seniority.

B. Steve should select all staff based on recent performance evaluation scores.

C. Steve should follow the collective bargaining agreement for reducing union staff and reduce management based on recent performance evaluation scores.

D. Steve should follow the collective bargaining agreement for reducing union staff and reduce management based on organizational policy.

12. Which of the following is *not* correct about COBRA availability periods after a qualifying event?

A. In the event of an employee death, 36 months of COBRA coverage is available for the employee's spouse and dependent child(ren).

B. Upon an employee's termination of employment, 18 months of coverage is available for the employee, his or her spouse, and dependent child(ren).

C. If an employee's work hours are reduced to the point that he or she no longer qualifies for benefits, 16 months of coverage is available for the employee, his or her spouse, and dependent child(ren).

D. A qualified disabled beneficiary is allotted 29 months of COBRA coverage after a qualifying event.

13. _____ is a process that ensures the organization's goals are aligned with the activities and makeup of the workforce.

Questions 14, 15, and 16 apply to the following scenario:

Lucky Mart has been struggling over the past few months to hire quality candidates. They have changed their interview process to include a pre-employment skills test that screens candidates for their understanding of bagging procedures in English, the native language at Lucky Mart's headquarters. The store has also begun posting on different online job boards to attract a wider candidate pool and is requiring applicants to submit résumés instead of applications.

14. There are 500 applicants for Lucky Mart's most recent job posting. Two hundred applicants are White (not Hispanic or Latino), and 5 are selected. The other 300 applicants are Hispanic or Latino, and 3 are selected. What is the selection ratio of the Hispanic or Latino group?

    A. .01

    B. .1

    C. .25

    D. .025

15. Lucky Mart is concerned that fewer Hispanic or Latino applicants were selected than White (not Hispanic or Latino) applicants. Should Lucky Mart be worried about adverse impact?

    A. Yes. The impact ratio for Hispanic or Latino applicants is .06 (60 percent) and less than the two-thirds rule. Additional analysis should be done to see whether there really is adverse impact.

    B. No. The impact ratio for Hispanic or Latino applicants is .07 (70 percent) and more than the two-thirds rule. This means there is no adverse impact.

    C. Yes. The impact ratio for Hispanic or Latino applicants is .04 (40 percent) and less than the four-fifths rule. Additional analysis should be done to see whether there really is adverse impact.

    D. No. The impact ratio for Hispanic or Latino applicants is .09 (90 percent) and more than the four-fifths rule. This means there is no adverse impact.

16. If you were the HR director at Lucky Mart, which of the following procedures would you evaluate first to avoid the potential for adverse impact in selection?

    A. The new pre-employment skills test

    B. The job boards the positions are being posted on

    C. The new procedure of submitting résumés instead of applications

    D. All of the above

17. Which of the following are the best two options to close a job offer with a high-potential candidate for manager position?

    A. Offer her extra vacation days.

    B. Build her a larger office space.

    C. Offer her a signing bonus.

    D. Offer her a salary above the maximum pay rate for the job.

18. When all key management positions are filled by expatriates, this is a(n) _____ global staffing approach.

19. Malea is leading the organization's restructure project and has to reduce the workforce. To affect the least number of employees, Malea decides to eliminate the same accounting position across the organization. What is the best way for her to do this?

A. Select employees for separation based on their performance.

B. Separate all employees in this position, regardless of their performance.

C. Select half of the employees for separation because they have the most recent hire date and move the other half to new positions.

D. Communicate to the employee group that the position will be eliminated in advance, give the group an opportunity to transfer open positions in the organization if they are qualified, and separate all employees not selected for a new position.

20. Which of the following is *not* a type of international work assignment?

A. Indirect assignee

B. Stealth expatriate

C. Returnee

D. Outsourced employee

Answers

1. C. The list should show what skills each person has now and whether they are ready for promotion now or need further experience or training before being ready for promotion.

2. A2; B4; C1; D3.

3. A. The company is not constrained by the government on how it designs its job application process. If it wants to have a certain form completed, it can establish that policy. A decision should be made about what documents it will accept from job applicants. Consistency in how the process is applied is critical in avoiding complaints of bias.

4. B. Sometimes using part-time workers to accomplish one job is a good solution. A great deal depends on the reliability of incumbents.

5. B. One reason these arrangements sometimes fail is that they go on and on and on. There is no real replacement training going on. The retired employee is doing the same work as before they retired, and nobody is being transferred, promoted, or hired into that job as a replacement.

6. B. The test should measure Excel skills because those are the predictors of success for Abel's accounting positions.

7. D. There is no reason that both objective and subjective selection systems cannot be used together in sorting candidates for instructor jobs.

8. Inpatriates

9. B, C. All waivers must be in writing and signed, but it is not a requirement that they be signed by the CEO of the organization. The employee must be given 21 days to consider the terms (45 days if more than one employee) and be able to revoke the agreement for up to 7 days after.

10. $200. Cost per hire = (($680) + ($1,200 + $520)) / 12

$$\text{Cost Per Hire} = \frac{(\text{S(External Costs)} + \text{S(Internal Costs)})}{(\text{Total Number of Hires in a Time Period})}$$

11. D. While selecting staff for an RIF based on inverse seniority or performance evaluation scores are common tactics, union and nonunion employees cannot always be treated the same. The collective bargaining agreement should be consulted for all employment decisions regarding union staff, and the organizational policy should be consulted for nonunion staff. In the absence of a clear policy, Steve has more control over how RIF determinations are made.

12. C. Eighteen months of coverage is available for employees and their dependents in the event of a termination or reduction in work hours.

13. Workforce planning

14. A. The selection ratio is determined by dividing the number of applicants hired from a group by the total number of applicants from that group. For the Hispanic or Latino population, 3 selected applicants divided by 300 in the total population is .01 or 1 percent.

15. C. First, let's calculate impact ratios to see whether there is adverse impact. This is done by dividing the selection ratio for a group by the selection ratio for the highest group. We know the selection ratio for Hispanic or Latino applicants is .01. The selection ratio for White applicants is as follows: 5 selected applicants / 200 total population = .025 or 2.5 percent. This means the impact ratio for Hispanic or Latino applicants is as follows: .01 / .025 = .4 or 40 percent. This is less than 80 percent, which means additional analysis should be done to see whether there really is adverse impact.

16. A. The pre-employment skills test is a concern because it is in English. The native language of Hispanic or Latino applicants may not be English, and it may be more difficult for this group to perform well on the test because of language barriers. The job boards and new process of submitting résumés are not a foremost concern because the Hispanic or Latino applicant population is higher than the White population.

17. **A, C.** Extra vacation days or a signing bonus are great ways to sweeten the total rewards package. Decisions that might result in inequity compared to other employees are not a good idea.

18. **Ethnocentric**

19. **D.** This approach is the best way to help maintain goodwill with employees. The change is not a surprise, and employees are given the opportunity to find a position in another part of the organization. All employees who are not transferred are separated because the position is being eliminated.

20. **A.** An indirect assignee is not an international work assignment.

Endnotes

1. Society for Human Resource Management, *The Emotionally Intelligent Interviewer: A Smarter Questioning Strategy.* https://www.shrm.org/resourcesandtools/hr-topics/employee-relations/pages/good-interviewing-techniques.aspx

2. Robert Half, *Negotiating Salary: A Guide for Hiring Managers.* https://www.roberthalf.com/blog/compensation-and-benefits/negotiating-salary-a-guide-for-hiring-managers

3. Bain and Company, *Integrating Cultures after a Merger.* https://www.bain.com/insights/integrating-cultures-after-a-merger/

4. U.S. Bureau of the Census, www.census.gov

PART III

CHAPTER 11

Learning and Development

Remember that all of the Senior Professional in Human Resources (SPHR) requirements are built upon the competencies of Professional in Human Resources (PHR) professionals. That said, be sure you are fully acquainted with the content of Chapter 6. Learning and development is the only subject area that appears in both the PHR and SPHR Exam Content Outline. Everything in Chapter 6 is likely to appear on the SPHR exam just as is the material in this chapter. Learning and Development carries a 12 percent weight on the SPHR exam.

Responsibilities

- Develop and evaluate training strategies (for example, modes of delivery, timing, content) to increase individual and organizational effectiveness
- Analyze business needs to develop a succession plan for key roles (for example, identify talent, outline career progression, coaching and development) to promote business continuity
- Develop and evaluate employee retention strategies and practices (for example, assessing talent, developing career paths, managing job movement within the organization)

Knowledge Of

- Training program design and development
- Adult learning processes
- Training and facilitation techniques
- Instructional design principles and processes (for example, needs analysis, content chunking, process flow mapping)
- Techniques to assess training program effectiveness, including use of applicable metrics
- Career and leadership development theories and applications
- Organizational development (OD) methods, motivation methods, and problem-solving techniques

- Coaching and mentoring techniques
- Effective communication skills and strategies (for example, presentation, collaboration, sensitivity)
- Employee retention strategies
- Techniques to encourage creativity and innovation

Federal Laws That Apply to This Body of Knowledge

The laws listed in Figure 11-1 are the same ones listed in Chapter 6. What is different here is the level of skill and strategic involvement to be found in senior-level responsibilities. Developing policies related to training and creating strategies for its use are the purview of senior HR professionals. Design and development of training is something the senior HR professional should oversee. Of course, measurement of training effectiveness is also a responsibility of the senior HR professional.

Training Program Design and Development

Employee training programs exist for only one reason: to make the employer organization more effective in the achievement of its organizational objectives. Training helps people do their jobs better or prepares them for new jobs and assignments. Basic employee training can help people deal with "the way we do things around here" based on company policies and requirements. More advanced training can be specifically directed at customer project requirements, government reporting needs, or skill development aimed at career development. Management skills training can effectively provide growth opportunities to managers and supervisors so they can be more effective in their supervision of others.

Chapter 6 shows more detail for each of the following components of the process:

- **Identifying training needs** What skill or knowledge is lacking that can be enhanced through training? What is the target population?

- **Selecting a training program: purchase or develop?** Are there existing training programs that can address the specific need? If not, what is the cost-effectiveness of developing a new program?

- The Copyright Act (1976)
- The Trademark Act (1946)
- Uniform Guidelines on Employee Selection Procedures (1978)
- Age Discrimination in Employment Act (1967)
- The U.S. Patent Act
- Title VII of the Civil Rights Act (1964)
- The Americans with Disabilities Act (1990)
- Uniformed Services Employment and Reemployment Rights Act (1994)

Figure 11-1   Federal laws that apply to human resource development

- **Selecting the trainer**   Do you need an instructor, facilitator, or both?

- **Implementing the training program**   First, pilot the program to see whether it will meet your expectations; then, "roll out" the program on an implementation schedule for the target population.

- **Evaluating the training results**   Use previously defined measurements to identify the effectiveness of the training program.

In the Trenches

Keep an Eye on the Horizon: Knowledge Transfer

Rob Hyde, HR Business Partner, Kaiser Permanente

How many generations are represented throughout your workforce? Are your new employees ready to take the reins from the generation that is retiring and to continue growing the organization beyond what it is today? These are questions whose answers are self-evident. "Several" and "I really don't know" are the answers for most organizations, and that likely includes yours. So, now what do you do about it? The answer might lie in the success of one of our most established and what some call *old-line* industries.

Over the past decade or more, the defense industry has been faced with a generational talent drain that's likely greater than anything you've seen in your company or your industry. You see, the Baby Boomers, that generation of engineers and technologists who literally won the Cold War, are now retiring in droves. So how is that industry coping, retaining that basic technological know-how and passing on the whys, the errors, and the lessons learned from five decades of success that provided our nation's security? The answer is they've embarked on a program of knowledge transfer. They are replicating the passing down of knowledge that began millennia ago and has seemingly become a forgotten art. Rebuilding that art form that began at the proverbial ancient campfire and applying it to the modern office was an answer so self-evident as to be simple.

What is knowledge transfer? Mimicking those ancient councils, it starts with a partnership between the elders and the new. It has to be part of job descriptions, performance evaluations, and daily routine. In the past, failing to learn resulted in a hungry family; now it equates to career stagnation and perhaps a hungry family as a result. It includes lessons on where to find the dusty data that might be the answer to tomorrow's puzzle, lists of who to call for different types of inquiries, the obscure reference material and where it can be found, and (of course) those wonderful undocumented shortcuts that have been learned the hard way. At the core of the program, however, is a system to learn specific tasks and demonstrate a capability in performing them. The list of things that need to be known has to be robust and the demonstrations of capability rigorous.

(continued)

Managers must be engaged in reviewing these demonstrations and responsible to only open the gate to the "next step" when satisfied the knowledge and skill set that are going to depart have been replicated. Remember, things haven't changed all that much—if the student can't bring home the game, then the village starves. That's still true.

Done right, a knowledge transfer regimen can be interesting, challenging, and profitable. Without one, you might be on the road to yesterday without a tomorrow to look forward to.

Training Program Design

Program design is a broad category of activities that eventually result in a training program that can be implemented in the classroom, on the Internet, or via a kiosk terminal in the workplace. Here is a summary of the tasks that are involved in creating a training design.

Needs Assessment

There are many different types of needs that can be addressed by training programs. The three most common are as follows:

- **Employee needs**   Current skill and knowledge needs of the existing workforce. These needs can be identified by using employee surveys, focus groups, interviews, and performance results.

- **Job needs**   Clarification or expansion of job requirements. Determining what jobs require can be determined through use of observation of job performance, results versus benchmarks, and focus groups or interviews.

- **Company needs**   Organization-wide deficiencies that could use a training solution. These are often pointed out through use of HR audits, review of HR measurements such as turnover, recruiting and placement, tardiness and absenteeism rates, and employee complaint rates.

Needs Analysis

Once you have identified the needs you believe training can address, it is time to analyze those data so you can be sure there is a way forward through training to the organizational improvement you want to see.

Motivation Assessment   If you elect to use a training solution to the problem of some deficiency, it is first necessary to answer the question your employees will be asking, "What's in it for me?" Why should employees spend their mental and physical effort to complete a training program if a benefit for them can't be articulated? What is the employee benefit for working through the training program?

The Hawthorne Effect[1] is important to note when thinking about employee motivation. In 1924, Western Electric Company (an American Telephone and Telegraph subsidiary) in Cicero, Illinois, commissioned a study that lasted until 1932. The question they asked was, "Could changes in factory lighting affect the production of workers?" The study was expanded to include the impact working hours and break times would have on production levels.

During the study, each time the light levels were changed (up or down), production went up. When the study ended, production levels fell. It wasn't until 1958 that Henry A. Landsberger looked at the data that had been collected during the study that he discovered the real impact on production wasn't the light levels, break times, or work schedules. It was because the company was paying attention to the test group. Being observed and being the center of attention had its impact on production levels.

HR professionals should be cognizant of the possibility that just participating in a training program can increase employee motivation. That may not last long, however, if the company ends its recognition of employee contributions after the training ends.

Operant Conditioning   A psychologist named B.F. Skinner is considered the father of operant conditioning. *Operant conditioning*[2] is a method of learning that occurs through rewards and punishment for behaviors. Skinner used rats in his experiments, rewarding them with food pellets when their response was correct and punishing them with electric shock when their response was incorrect.

Toward the close of World War II, Skinner was asked by the Army Air Force to create a guided bomb. He used pigeons in the effort.[3] He taught the pigeons to recognize photographs of the bombing target that would be destroyed. Then he taught the pigeons to peck at rudder controls so the bomb would go right or left, always staying in the center of the live picture of the ground below, showing the target. There was some modicum of success in the experiment, but the war ended before the idea could go into production. It was an ingenious idea, even if it was a little hard on the pigeons in the end since they were passengers in the bombs.

Operant conditioning is a technique applied to modern training programs and many management skills efforts. Positive reinforcement in response to good behavior is now recognized as a method for getting employees to repeat the desired behavior. Punishment is a way to extinguish undesired or unwanted behaviors. In terms of duration, positive reinforcement lasts longer than punishment when reinforcement is ended.

So building in motivational methods to the training program is a way to increase the impact that training will have on the participants, even after training ends.

Training Design

Training design is the development of a table of contents for a training program's significant components. As a senior HR professional, it is up to you to identify the strategic value of each training program. How will each program help achieve the enterprise's strategic goals? If you have training development experts on staff, you can rely on them to build programs that meet the objectives you have identified for training participants.

If you don't have that resource, then either you will have to hire an outside vendor to do the development work or you will have to do it yourself.

Training design involves the following:

- List of objectives for training participants to meet by the end of the training program
- Table of contents for the program
- Delivery method that has been selected for this training program (for example, instructor-led classroom, instructor-led online classroom, facilitator-led study group, self-paced program, self-study guide)
- Training techniques that will be built into the program and those that will rely on instructor or facilitator skill (for example, visual aids, small group exercises, large group discussion, problem-solving exercises)
- Business case analysis to demonstrate cost-effectiveness of the problem and its solution

Training Program Development

Once the design choices have been made, it is essential to create a training program out of those provisions.

- An instructor-led program will need to have participant materials and instructor materials. The instructor needs information about how to deliver the content, prepare participants for the exercises embedded in the program, and debrief the experiences participants will be having. Whether the program is delivered in a physical classroom or a virtual classroom doesn't matter. All of those materials will be required. They include PowerPoint materials, other audio/visual content, handouts, answer sheets, and evaluation sheets.
- A facilitator-led program can be presented at one physical location or online to a virtual group. The facilitator is responsible for leading the group to discover for itself the learning points, to develop its own objectives beyond those in the training program, and to take responsibility for using the skills and knowledge gained in training once back on the job.
- Coach-led training programs place most of the responsibility for learning on the participants. Coaches are available to help get people over the rough spots, to untangle issues that may be blocking progress, and to be sure the direction participants move in is the proper one for the program.
- Self-study programs are totally dependent upon the learner. Without an instructor or coach, the self-study program is both self-paced and self-motivating. Content must be totally self-supporting. This book is an example of that approach. We are supporting your interest in passing the PHR or SPHR certification exam. Sometimes, self-study guides are used as aids in study groups.

- Study groups are small gatherings of people with the same objective: to learn something that will provide them with a common set of benefits. In the example of PHR and SPHR certification, the common benefit is to successfully pass a certification exam. Group members support one another in their study efforts. They use a common study guide, such as this book.

Beta Testing Training Program

Once the development has been done, it is important to "try out" the training on a group of typical target audience participants. Does the training really work? Does it help participants reach the training objectives? The developer should sit in the back or monitor online, taking notes about what works and what doesn't work. Those notes can be helpful in rewriting any portions of the program that need improvement. This is a fine-tuning process that will assure the program will perform as desired when released for use by the general target population.

Rewriting Training Content

Beta testing is designed to provide the training development staff with the opportunity to see what works and what doesn't work. Once that is determined, changes should be made to the program so it will go smoothly when implemented with the target population.

Training Program Publication

Once the development has completed, the beta testing has concluded, and rewrites have been done, it is appropriate to publish the training program for use with its target audience. That is when the program "goes live" and becomes part of the catalog of training program offerings in your organization.

Training Program Implementation

Once development has concluded, implementation begins. It's not a simple matter of sticking the program on the shelf and having people come along and select it for their use. Depending on the delivery method, there are other prerequisites to getting participants involved with the course materials.

Instructor-Led Programs

Whether classroom or online group, instructors must be identified and selected for your program. They must be trained in the course materials and given a chance to run a beta group of their own during which they can be observed and given feedback about their handling of the training materials.

Self-Paced Programs

The course must be entered into the proper catalog and announcements made about its availability. The target audience must be made aware of its availability. If this is a mandatory program, there must be a tracking system that permits the employer to identify who has participated in the program. Computer-based training programs will need a way to communicate logon procedures and instructions on how to use the program.

Will users be able to access the training from their smart phones and tablets, or must a PC be used? Can training programs be accessed from company kiosks located throughout the work location?

Training Evaluation Methods

It is time to look at the ways in which a senior HR professional can evaluate training programs. After all, training is part of the strategic HR plan, and results should be reported to senior management and perhaps to the board of directors as well.

Donald Kirkpatrick's Four-Tier Model

There is one widely known model that explains how to evaluate training and HR programs. Donald Kirkpatrick's model focuses primarily on evaluating the effectiveness of the training presented (Figure 11-2).

1. The first level measures the **reaction of the participant**. A survey given at the conclusion of the training is the most common method. Participants detail how they liked the training and their thoughts as to its applicability. This, however, measures the immediate reaction about the training delivery and its environment rather than their level of learning.

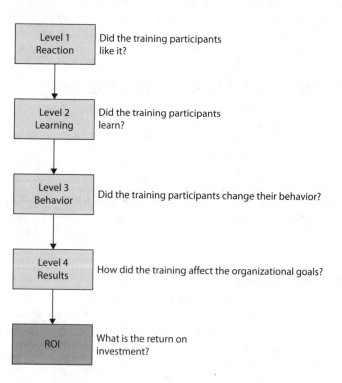

Figure 11-2 Kirkpatrick's four levels of evaluating training

2. The second level measures **how well participants in the training learned** facts, concepts, theories, and behaviors. Using this measure normally requires HR professionals or consultants who are trained in statistics and studies to interpret the results. Pre- and post-training measurements are conducted, and control groups may be involved. The results will indicate the effectiveness of the training.

3. The third level deals with the **measurement of behavior** and is more difficult to measure than the previous two levels because it can be difficult to determine whether behavior changed solely because of the training program; other outside influences could be involved. In this measurement, observations, interviews, 360-degree feedback instruments, and simulations can be used. Critical incidents performance by the trainee's supervisor might be employed.

4. The fourth level deals with the **measurement of results** to determine whether the planned effectiveness of the training delivered the desired results. The difficulty with this measurement is with determining whether the training was the sole factor affecting the results. Typically, a cost-benefit of return on investment (ROI) follows to substantiate the fourth-level results.

When evaluating a training program's effectiveness, it is important to achieve an objective viewpoint. Solicit information from all affected sources—not just the training participants and presenter but also the sources affected by the training, which could be other departments, management, and even customers.

Using Metrics for Training Evaluation

Sometimes, it is helpful to have standardized measurements that everyone can understand and that will show trends over time.

Employee Survey Results   Employee satisfaction ratings (for example, on a scale of 1 to 5 or 1 to 10) indicate their experience in the training program. That can include instructor engagement, facilities used, materials used, and impact on their job. You can lump them all together into a single rating, or you can break them out individually for more specific rating data. Rating scales allow you to convert subjective feelings and beliefs into objective scores.

Job Impact Results   Supervisor feedback or ratings indicate what impact the training program had on the employee's performance results. This data may be gathered in survey form or through interviews with supervisors.

Training Costs   What is the cost per student (total training program cost divided by number of students)? What is the cost of each training program component (for example, classroom, instructor, printed materials, programming of content, or audiovisual programs created or obtained from others)? What is the cost savings by job performance improvement? What are dollar savings from reduced accident rate, reduced turnover, reduced absenteeism, or improved quality results?

Facilitator Evaluation

Facilitators and instructors are not necessarily the same type of critters. Facilitators are guides. They don't deliver instruction, other than about the process to be followed in the session. Facilitators will lead discussions, ask questions, write down responses, and help the group reach its own decisions and plans. This form of group assistance is often used in strategic planning sessions. The facilitator has no personal interest in the outcome of the session other than to assure the group arrives at the best possible destination by the end of its session.

Evaluating facilitators should be done by asking session participants to rate the facilitator using questions such as these:

- How effective was the facilitator in outlining the purpose of the session?
- How effective was the facilitator in leading discussions?
- How accurate was the facilitator in logging input from the group, exactly as it was offered?
- How effective was the facilitator when challenging the group to go beyond its self-imposed limits?
- How valuable was the end result of the session?
- How realistic will the application of our conclusions or plans be once we are back on the job?

Coaching and Mentoring

More organizations are realizing the advantages of having coaching and mentoring programs as part of their overall career management strategy. These programs are advantageous for HR for their effectiveness in working one on one with individuals, allowing HR the ability to maintain an unbiased position.

Coaching

Coaching involves one-on-one discussions between the employee and a "coach." The coach can be internal or external. An internal coach could be a member of the HR team or a line manager. Coaching can involve ongoing activities with a direct supervisor or HR professional who provides discussions focused on the career objectives of an employee, including perspective assessments such as poor job fit or potential growth tracks. External coaches are professionals hired at the organization's expense who typically work on the development of an employee in a particular area—for example, presentation or communication—or to hone and shift leadership skills. This type of coaching is focused solely on the employee and is confidential and private. At the level of executive coaching, which is more prevalent in organizations of all sizes, a third-party certified executive coach is utilized to allow executives the freedom to discuss aspects of career-life balance with a high level of trust and nondisclosure.

Mentoring

Mentoring is an action-oriented relationship between two people within the organization, usually a senior and junior colleague.[4] It involves advising, providing opinion and perspective, role modeling, and sharing contacts and networks, along with support. The mentee receives career support and learns the ropes in the organization, and the mentor has the opportunity to share knowledge and perhaps pass the baton of job responsibilities on to afford the mentee a chance to move out of the current role. Mentorships can occur at all levels in an organization. They can be formally designed by HR, such as part of the onboarding orientation process, or they can be part of a succession planning program.

Succession Planning

Any organization larger than a single entrepreneur will have multiple leaders and multiple key personnel. Obtaining key personnel insurance is something normally done by the chief financial officer, but sometimes human resources is involved. It is a business function.

Succession planning comes into play when the organization has grown sufficiently that it can be expected some of its key leaders will leave their positions. They may die, find a better job elsewhere, or quit in a huff. Whatever the reason for their leaving, it becomes necessary to find a replacement. Key player positions cannot remain open very long without doing damage to the organization.

Executive and Senior Manager Succession

It is often the case that the chief financial officer (CFO) and the chief executive officer (CEO) work with the board of directors and plot succession plans. Sometimes when that happens, the people identified as successors don't even know they have been designated as such. And human resources is not included in the process.

With the importance of HR growing and senior human resource officers (SHROs) taking on executive-level responsibilities, they also take on responsibility for succession planning in the executive ranks.

Mid-Level and Supervisor Succession

It is quite common for HR managers to be involved in the succession plan development for first and mid-level management positions. It begins with the identification of individual skills and abilities, developmental needs, promotional interests, and educational needs. Based on all those factors and more, people are slotted to succeed more senior people should they leave their jobs. There may be two or three successor candidates for each job. It is a plan after all. HR professionals are charged with maintaining the plan content and periodically offering it to senior executives.

Usually succession plans, regardless of the levels involved, are considered extremely confidential. They can even be considered proprietary and competitive information. Imagine what competitors would do to get their hands on your succession plans—what a recruiting aid that would be for them!

Impacts on Communication

Multicultural workplaces are more the norm these days than the exception. That means managers, and especially HR managers, should be leading the development of intercultural understanding at work.

Cultural Sensitivity

Being sensitive to cultural differences among co-workers can increase communication effectiveness and everyone's sense of inclusion in the organization. Here are a few suggestions that may help increase cultural sensitivity in your organization:[5]

- **Prepare yourself**   Read about and listen carefully for culturally influenced behaviors.

- **Recognize your fears**   Recognize and face your own fears of acting inappropriately toward members of different cultures.

- **Recognize differences**   Be mindful of the differences between yourself and those from other cultures.

- **Recognize differences within the group**   At the same time that you recognize differences between yourself and others, recognize that there are often enormous differences within any given cultural group.

- **Recognize differences in meaning**   Words don't always mean the same thing to members of different cultures.

- **Be rule-conscious**   Become aware of and think mindfully about the cultural rules and customs of others.

Body Language

We have all heard that body language is sometimes louder than the spoken word. Perhaps you have experienced that in your own professional life. Here are some key body language expressions you can begin noticing in yourself and others, if you don't already:[6]

- **Facial expression**   We experience in our own body what the other person is expressing. A smile from someone else will bring a smile to our own face. A scowl will elicit the same from the other person. Either way, you will have impacted the conversation.

- **Eye contact**   Making and holding eye contact with the person you engage in conversation will convey to that person the authenticity of your message. This is particularly important if you are giving feedback.

- **Posture**   Sitting straight or slouching, arms folded or relaxed at your side, turned toward the other person or angled away from them, or looking over their shoulder or directly at them—each of these comparisons can influence the effectiveness of your communication.

- **Attention**   Are you reading your mail while someone is trying to talk to you? Do you permit phone calls to interrupt your conversation? If we naturally find ourselves spending up to half of our mental effort thinking about what has happened and what might happen next, it is sometimes difficult to hold attention to what is going on now. Attention is not only the most effective way to get and give information, it is the courteous way to acknowledge that the person communicating with you is valuable, too.

- **Breathing**   Stressed or angry? Your breathing will be more shallow and rapid. Hyperventilation can follow. Exasperated or tired? You're more likely to audibly sigh. If the person we are talking with sighs a lot, we may think they are annoyed at us. If you know the conversation you have coming up will be stressful, calm yourself in advance by taking a series of slow, deep breaths and allow yourself to relax. When you go to your meeting, you will be better prepared for that conversation because you will be calm.

Presentation Success

With a few focused moments of attention and a little thought, you can craft a presentation that will be successful in all the ways you want. Senior HR professionals will need to be capable of making presentations to senior executive groups, even the board of directors at times. They will also be required to present information to large groups of employees, serve as facilitator in employee-listening sessions, and handle small-group discussions following a presentation of policy updates.

Presentation Outline

Give considerable thought to what your presentation will contain. Answer these questions: Why am I doing this? What is the message? What do I want the audience to be able to do when the presentation is over? Who will be involved during and after the presentation?

Follow this simple rule: Tell them what you are going to tell them (review the outline and objectives up front). Tell them (review the presentation content with the group). Then, tell them what you told them (review the outline and test each objective to be sure it was met).

Presentation Skills

There are some key elements to success as a presenter. Here are three of them:

- **Voice projection**   Your message will not get across to the group if they can't hear you. If you have a microphone, use it. If you are uncomfortable speaking into a microphone, find a way to use a facility with one and practice in the empty room using the audio equipment. Get used to it. Avoid comments like, "I hate these things…," or "I don't need this…." Chances are good that you actually do need to use the microphone. Learn how to speak into it, where to hold it near your mouth (not down at your belt level), and how not to chew on it (some people seem to want to put it into their mouth).

If you don't have a microphone available, you will need to rely on your voice projection to get the message to the folks in the back of the room. Pick out someone in the last row and talk to that person. You can even ask if that person can hear you. Then keep it up. Don't allow your voice volume to drop as your presentation goes on. The last row must be able to hear everything you say all through the presentation. This takes practice, like using a microphone takes practice. When you practice giving your presentation, do it in a room that is about the size of the one you will be in for the live performance. Speak to the back of the room.

- **Gestures**   Hand and arm gestures can be helpful in emphasizing key points in your presentation. The danger is that you will overuse them. Use the same gesture over and over again, and people will begin focusing on that to the distraction of their attention on what you are saying. Practice your gestures. Plan to use them at certain points in your presentation and consciously hold yourself back from using them at other times. Remember, too much of a good thing is too much of a good thing.

- **Scanning the group**   Everyone in the group likes to be included, even if that only means the speaker looks at them occasionally. Be sure you move around from one side of the room to the other while you are talking. (Don't fall off the stage or trip over your microphone cord.) If you can't move because the microphone is attached to the lectern, move your gaze around the room, left to right and front to back.

Presentation Aids

Few people have the charisma to capture and hold an audience with their voice alone. Others of us need to use some presentation aids to help reinforce the message we are communicating.

Audiovisual Aids   PowerPoint is an example of an audiovisual aid. It permits the presenter to project content on a large screen so the entire group can follow along with the points being made. Sometimes presenters use a laser pointer to help emphasize key elements of the slides. Rarely does this work well. A laser pointer projects a dot of light, usually red or green, and it cannot be held still. It wobbles because the person's hand holding it makes small movements that are exaggerated across the distance to the screen. Pretending the laser dot can underline a word or sentence is only going to make the dot move in circles or swipe back and forth. Placement at a specific spot on the screen is almost always difficult to achieve. Movement of the dot is going to be distracting to your audience and is best not used at all. Leave your laser pointer at home. Rather, call your audience's attention to the element you want to highlight by saying, "Look at item 3 for a moment."

Handouts   If you use PowerPoint slides in your presentation, make printed copies of them available for your audience members. If the audience is too big or disbursed around the country in an electronic hookup, make an electronic copy available for them.

Make sure they know up front that they will get these materials so they don't have to take down the information that will be on the slides. If you have other handout materials that are part of the presentation, distribute them in advance. It's okay if people look them over before you begin. At least they will be able to follow along when you get to that part of the presentation.

Easel Charts/Blackboards/Whiteboards   In some cases you will want to write notes on an easel chart or blackboard (whiteboard). Make sure they are short notes. Don't try to write the entire presentation on the chart. Use the key words only. At the end, you should promise to have the easel contents transcribed and distributed if it is appropriate.

Communication Skills and Strategies

Workplace effectiveness, by any measure, is dependent upon effective communications between and among workers at all levels. Managers must be particularly careful about the messages they send. Message accuracy and clarity are two requirements everyone should strive to achieve.

Communication Cycle

Chapter 4 introduced the topic of the communication cycle. You should review that information and then assess your own effectiveness in achieving the clarity necessary in your messages. Do you always ask for feedback to be sure your message has been received as you intended? If not, do you take a different approach or use different examples to strengthen the message and then test again with feedback requests?

Getting the communication cycle right is the foundation of your effectiveness in your organization. Well, the same principles apply in your personal life, too. Testing for understanding is the additional step that is often left out. It takes only a few extra moments, but it can cement the proper message being sent and received.

If you elect to use communication strategically, be sure you include the final step in the process. There is no communication success to be had without it.

Presentation

How you choose to deliver your message is an important decision. Will you use an oral or written approach? Remember, either way there is likely to be a recording of your thoughts and comments. Those recordings last indefinitely in this age of electronics and social media. HR practitioners should operate with the belief that everything they say and do is going to be recorded and can come back for replay later. You should have no expectation of privacy in any of your communications, even if using a private and secure network. Your messages may be discoverable as evidence in a lawsuit later.

Written Communication

There are many media that can be used. Social media offers a host of services that can be used to pass written messages back and forth between and even among groups of people.

PART III

There are e-mails, tweets, LinkedIn messages, Facebook messages, WhatsApp, WeChat, Skype, and Snapchat all offering to provide you with a platform for your communications. And all of them archive the messages sent on their systems.

Lest we forget, there are still people who prepare letters on stationery and sometimes even plain paper. Those letters can be handwritten or run through a computer printer. Signing a document gives a personal touch that is often missing with electronic communication methods. Putting a stamp on an envelope and mailing a letter is still a technique preferred by many people.

Oral Communication

By far the most common form of oral communication is the personal one-on-one talking that we all do every day. But there are other oral communication methods (Figure 11-3).

A key strategic skill within oral communication is called *active listening*. Here are some tips on how it is done:

- Try to find a location that won't allow for interruptions.
- Focus on being interested, not interesting.
- Use body language to indicate you're receiving the message (nod, smile, tilt of your head).
- Use verbal encouragement to keep the other person talking ("Um-hum," "Okay," "And…").
- Paraphrase what the speaker says ("You are saying…," "I'm hearing…," "What happened was…").
- Validate the speaker's emotions ("You're angry because…," "It's easy to see your excitement…").
- Agree on any action to be taken (confirm the agreement).

Collaboration

"Collaboration and communication involve being able to read the vast number of verbal and nonverbal cues that we all use to communicate our ideas and emotions. People need to learn to build shared understanding, negotiate outcomes, and cultivate trust to work together to solve the problems that no one can solve alone."[7]

• One-on-one interaction	• Small group presentation
• Large group presentation	• Classroom presentation
• Webinar	• Storytelling
• Meeting participation	• Radio/TV broadcast

Figure 11-3   Common methods of oral communication

HR professionals are especially dependent upon collaborative relationships. Only when successfully working with others (employees, managers, supervisors, executives, board of directors) can strategic targets be attained.

Here are six steps to a more collaborative workplace. Strategically speaking, these can help you in your HR job.

Six Steps to Workplace Collaboration[8]

- **Communicate company expectations**   What are the company's strategic goals? How can each element of the company contribute to achieving those goals?

- **Set team goals**   Be sure that individual organizational groups are making a conscious effort to contribute to the company efforts.

- **Foster a creative atmosphere**   Be willing for people to try new ideas and to fail sometimes. They will also succeed sometimes.

- **Build cohesion**   People feel good when they are included in decision-making. Expand the process to include as many people as reasonable.

- **Know one another**   Get team members to discuss their preferences for communication approaches, contribution methods, and team interactions. Then discuss how all those preferences can be effectively combined into the team effort.

- **Leverage team member strengths**   Knowing team member strengths can help with work assignments. Assign people tasks that play to their strengths. That will improve your team success rate.

Sensitivity

Sensitivity is never more important than when disciplining employees. Sometimes discipline may be required as the first step in an employee's development plan. Often, supervisors, and even HR managers, will be accusatory in their approach to the employee. The result is not just a damaged relationship with that employee; it could introduce enough emotion to cause a violent response from your worker. Workplace violence has stemmed from such reactions to discipline and termination. Why is it that HR managers are targets of such violence? Simply said, they may not have fulfilled their role as protector of the employee's self-esteem.

Protecting Others' Self-Esteem

It is entirely possible to address the need for discipline without blaming the employee. Protecting the employee's self-esteem will permit that person to walk out of the disciplinary meeting with his or her head held high. Even though they have been punished for some infraction, they have their core self-worth intact. Nobody likes to be told they are worthless or anything along that end of the personal value spectrum. We all like to believe we have value to the world. If we don't have self-worth, what is there in life that can be nice?

- *Express appreciation* for the employee meeting with you.
- *Explain the nature of the problem* (e.g., failure to meet goals in a performance improvement program by continuing to arrive late each day).
- If appropriate, *express appreciation* for the employee trying to reach the objectives.
- Explain that we have *reached the point where we must end the employment relationship.*
- If it is appropriate, *tell the employee you will be glad to provide a reference* for the good things they have accomplished (good work product, good relationships).
- Explain that the results have brought us to the point where we have to part ways. *Effective today, the employee will be removed from the payroll.*
- Provide the final paycheck if required and *thank the employee for all she has done.*

Your employee will leave the meeting without a job but will have her self-esteem intact.

Figure 11-4   Guidelines for conducting a termination discussion

Assume you have an employee who just can't get to work before noon every day. She is supposed to arrive at 8 a.m. There is a different excuse every day. Something is always getting in the way of her arriving on time. Her work is good when she is here. Her relationships with the work group are beginning to suffer because they are having to pick up her slack. Her performance is impacted because she doesn't put in a full day. Here is how you might conduct the separation interview with this employee (Figure 11-4).

Learning and development is broad enough to encompass these disciplinary discussions. HR professionals, particularly at the senior levels, need to be able to handle these types of interactions with poise and confidence. Mastering these interactions while protecting the employee's self-esteem is a requirement of SPHR certification holders.

Cultural Sensitivity

As international business activity expands, there is greater interaction between people of the United States and other countries. When you are involved in such interactions, it is important to be sensitive to the cultural differences you will find in the other country. Here is a brief guide to cultural sensitivity in communications.

Guidelines for Cultural Sensitivity in Communications[9]

- **Prepare yourself**   Study the culture you will be visiting. What are the expectations for physical and verbal communication? (In Asia, give and receive business cards using two hands.)
- **Recognize your fears**   Identify what you may be worried about in upcoming interactions (such as acting inappropriately during your talks).
- **Recognize basic cultural differences**   What are the differences that exist between your two cultures? (Is a suit and tie required versus informal wear?)
- **Recognize differences within the group**   What cultural differences exist within your own workgroup? (Examples are national backgrounds, religious differences, and educational differences.)

- **Recognize differences in meaning**   Words can be used differently by various cultures. (*America* can mean homeland both in the United States and in South American countries. *Gypped* means cheated in the United States. In some other countries, it is a racist slur meaning the stereotype that nomadic Roma are thieves. A *banger* can be either a sausage or a decrepit automobile.)

- **Be rule conscious**   Study the other culture's rules and expectations. Be prepared for the basic interactions when you first meet with folks from the other country.

Employee Retention Strategies

Once you have recruited a new employee, you want to keep them. Developing strategies for doing that is the responsibility of the SPHR. But remember what Winston Churchill once said, "However beautiful the strategy, you should occasionally look at the results."

Retention is the collection of programs and techniques that result in good employees staying on the job. Retaining employees means the employer does not have to undertake the expenses involved with recruiting, hiring, and training new workers.

Retention Metrics

Measuring retention is fairly easy. Depending on what you really want to know about your programs, you can include these measurements:

- Number of new employees on the payroll at the end of a year

- Cost of recruiting by job level, job title, and compensation grade

- Number of new employees on the payroll by department and by reporting period

- Turnover rate by job title, department, and work location

Retention Strategies

Using retention metrics can help you understand if there are any issues regarding retention. If there are, you should define the problem (using problem-solving techniques) and determine the breadth of the problem. Is it something that is systemic for the organization? Is it something that is a problem in only one department or division?

You should identify the cause of the problem using employee surveys, exit interviews, and management interviews. Depending on the cause, the strategy for handling it will vary.

Here are some actions and programs that can be used strategically to improve employee retention.

How to Improve Employee Retention[10]

- **New employee orientation and onboarding**   First impressions really do matter. It is the first day of work for the new employee that will set the stage for the remaining employment experience. Do you make people feel welcome? Are there more smiles than frowns among the work group members? How is the new employee made to feel when meeting her or his new team members? What does the boss say when meeting the new worker, not as a job candidate but as a new employee? What does HR do to make the employee feel comfortable?

- **Mentorship programs** Take the time to analyze the new employee's abilities and needs and then match him or her up with another worker who can provide guidance and counsel along the employment path. This buddy system not only helps retain workers but also facilitates higher levels of personal satisfaction with the work and with the organization.

- **Compensation programs** The total compensation package is important for retention results. The current labor market is strong, and workers are hard to find for open positions. It wasn't that way just a short time ago when there were more workers than jobs. Wages/salaries plus bonuses, profit sharing, insurance benefit programs, paid time off, educational support, professional development sponsorship, and retirement plans all make it easier for the employee to stay rather than go.

- **Work-life balance** Policies that support parental needs, educational efforts, and social involvement will contribute to positive employee attitudes. Recognize that work is only part of a person's life. Family and entertainment also play a part.

- **Training and development** Employers that offer employer-sponsored professional development opportunities will support employee satisfaction. And assuring that each person has had the proper training so they can perform their job properly is critical for that satisfaction.

- **Communication and feedback** Employees who are informed about what is happening with the company are happier than those who are deprived of such information. People may not want to participate in the decision-making, but they do want to know what is going on. And they want to know what impact those decisions will have on them and their job. Supervisors and team leaders need to be constantly providing feedback about the work done by each individual. "Thank you" is a simple type of feedback and effective in retention efforts.

- **Dealing with change** Being personally involved as the HR professional in big changes like mergers and acquisitions is nice, but that personal involvement must extend to the employee body. Communication with employees about what is happening and how it will impact them and their jobs is going to prevent panicked messages in the rumor mill. Give them the truth before they invent ideas about worst-case outcomes.

- **Fostering teamwork** When everyone understands the team objectives and how they can contribute to achieving those objectives, morale will not fall. When possible, HR professionals should help eliminate roadblocks to those achievements. When people feel they are a member of the group, accepted, and appreciated, they will do their best to add their contributions to the effort.

- **Team celebration**   When milestones are reached on a project, acknowledge it by bringing in pizza and soft drinks. When a team member achieves a professional certification, celebrate by acknowledging that achievement in a group meeting. Every time you make the individuals and the team feel that their accomplishments are appreciated, they will come back to do more.

Finally, retention programs should be reviewed at least annually. If you don't monitor the compensation rates in your industry or geography, you can be sure the employees are doing the monitoring themselves. If things get too far from what other employers are paying for the same type of work, you will discover people abandoning your organization for another that has better compensation. Employee loyalty is not what it was 50 years ago. In that time, people had an expectation that they would work for an employer for their entire career. Through thick or thin, the employee-employer relationship would weather any storm. In the end, there would be a nice retirement because of the fully funded pension program. Those same conditions do not exist any longer. Employers must work at keeping workers within the organization. That means spending effort and, yes, budget on that effort.

Creativity and Innovation

With the pace of business today, finding new ways to solve problems is critical. Here are some ways you can encourage creativity and innovation in your employee body.

Encouraging Creativity and Innovation Among Your Employees

- **Reward innovation**   Whether ideas are generated individually or through group gatherings, be sure you acknowledge any that are accepted as workable. The reward can be based on the impact the idea will have on your company. If it saves you a million dollars, perhaps a percentage would be a nice reward. If it improves the flow of work through a processing center, perhaps a weekend getaway for two would be nice. A gift card to Starbucks or a dinner out could also qualify as desirable rewards. If the entire team was responsible, then a reward for all team members should be provided. Make the reward fit the circumstance and let its perceived value guide your generosity. A chintzy reward will be met with employee belief that the employer didn't really think much of their effort.

- **Allow project ownership**   If it is the idea of a single employee, invite that person to take the lead in implementing the idea. If they aren't interested in the leadership spot, acknowledge their contribution in the company newsletter or CEO bulletin to employees.

- **Encourage risk-taking**   People should be given the opportunity to stretch in their thinking and their problem-solving. Any solution to a problem is a good solution if it works. Sometimes, we don't know if it will work until we try it. So try some solutions that seem like they will be good ones. Give them a fair shot. Some of them will prove to be good ideas because they will work. Others will not work well and must be discarded. That is particularly difficult when it takes a long time to determine whether the solution will be acceptable. For example, in the medical research industry, lines of inquiry can be pursued for decades before discovering that they won't work.

- **Embrace failure**   The pharmaceutical companies have this problem from time to time. One researcher, when asked what he would do after 25 years working on research that didn't prove workable, said, "I guess I'll try something else tomorrow." Organizations that permit such failure will eventually find large returns on something no one expected to have work. Thomas Edison said about his 3,000 failed attempts to create an electric light bulb, "I now know 3,000 ways *not* to make it work." Each attempt, successful or not, added to his database.[11]

Chapter Review

In this chapter, you explored some strategic elements of learning and development. Senior human resource professionals are responsible for developing and evaluating training strategies. To do that, they need to understand adult learning concepts, program design, implementation techniques, and evaluation methodology. Communication strategies, succession planning, and employee retention strategies are all part of the senior HR manager's chart of responsibilities. All of Chapter 6 material is considered the foundation for this chapter's additional study materials.

Questions

1. Which two of the following laws impact employee learning and development?

    A. Sherman Antitrust Act

    B. Civil Rights Act of 1964

    C. Age Discrimination in Employment Act

    D. Sarbanes-Oxley Act

2. Content chunking is a concept that has particular application in what type of training?

    A. Internet based

    B. Classroom based

    C. Self-paced books

    D. Job based

3. The first step in the training process is to:

    A. Select the instructor for the pilot program

    B. Identify the training developer

    C. Establish a budget for the training program

    D. Identify the training needs

4. Finally, every training program should include an _____ of training _____.

5. The Hawthorne Effect pointed out:

    A. A greater amount of light in a work space created motivation.

    B. Less light in a work space didn't impact motivation.

    C. The amount of light in a work space wasn't a prime motivator.

    D. Motivation came from being able to see the work bench.

6. Operant conditioning was a creation of:

    A. Herzberg

    B. Skinner

    C. Maslow

    D. Freud

7. Operant conditioning suggests:

    A. Motivation comes from levels of personal responsibility.

    B. Motivation comes from ego needs.

    C. Motivation comes from self-actualization.

    D. Motivation comes from positive reinforcement.

8. The first thing to do when designing training is to:

    A. Establish the training objectives

    B. Establish the format for training delivery

    C. Establish the program length

    D. Establish the program location

9. Adult students are generally more _____ _____ _____ than younger students.

10. Which of the following is not a commonly accepted training program design?

    A. Instructor led

    B. Facilitator led

    C. Self-study

    D. Sleep messaging input

11. At the end of each training session, it is important to review the _____.

12. Training can be used as a strategic tool to do what? (Choose three.)

    A. Raise employee interpersonal skills

    B. Improve job performance

    C. Adjust prior quarter results

    D. Adjust to industry advancements

13. Cultural sensitivity requires:

    A. Other people adjusting to your background

    B. Your willingness to expand your acceptance of other people's background

    C. Other people explaining how you need to change your attitude

    D. Your learning new languages

14. Active listening is used to:

    A. Keep pace with the speed of the conversation

    B. Keep the other person talking to extract more information

    C. Whisper sensitive information from mouth to ear

    D. Give the impression that you aren't planning your next comment

15. What do presenter platform skills include? (Choose two.)

    A. Projecting your voice

    B. Reading the training script

    C. Scanning the group looking for nonverbal clues to responses

    D. Having people read the PowerPoint slides for themselves

16. Successful communication always includes:

    A. Feedback to the sender

    B. Projection to the receiver

    C. An easy message to understand

    D. A deadline for action

17. Collaboration is a process of:

    A. Blending a dominant group with a submissive group

    B. Establishing leader dominance first and foremost

    C. Working together to accomplish a common set of goals

    D. Collaring the most brilliant employee as a team member

18. Disciplinary discussions should always:

    A. Be conducted on a Friday afternoon

    B. Be conducted by the second-line supervisor

    C. Protect the employee's self-esteem

    D. Protect the HR manager from involvement

19. Employee retention programs can:

    A. Save money

    B. Eliminate the need for exit interviews

    C. Prevent competitors from stealing our workers

    D. Encourage managers to expand work objectives

20. Which of the following are strategies for improving employee retention? (Choose two.)

   A. On-time paychecks

   B. Mentorship programs

   C. Supporting work-life balance

   D. Preventing managers from dismissing anyone without HR approval

Answers

   1. B, C. The Civil Rights Act of 1964 prohibits discrimination in treatment based on race, sex, national origin, religion, or color. This applies to selection for participation in training programs as well as hiring and firing. The Age Discrimination in Employment Act protects against discrimination based on an employee's age (over 40). Training participation decisions may not be made on that basis.

   2. A. Chunking is particularly helpful in Internet-based training programs where students can participate in a course in small time increments.

   3. D. Identifying the training needs is primary. Everything else is based on the results of that determination.

   4. Evaluation of training **results**

   5. C. The amount of workspace light during the Hawthorne study had no correlation with productivity levels. It was having the company pay the workgroup some attention that caused production to rise.

   6. B. B.F. Skinner was the father of operant conditioning.

   7. D. Motivation comes from positive reinforcement.

   8. A. The training objectives are the focus for every piece of training program content. If it doesn't help achieve the training objectives, it should not be in the training program.

   9. Ready to learn

   10. D. Training during employee sleep is not a common form of training program design.

   11. Objectives

   12. A, B, D. Training can raise employee interpersonal skills, improve job performance, and adjust to industry advancements. It cannot adjust prior quarter results. History cannot be changed by training today.

   13. B. Cultural sensitivity requires a willingness to accept other people's background.

   14. B. Active listening is used to keep the other person talking.

   15. A, C. Voice projection and scanning the group looking for nonverbal clues to responses are two presenter platform skills.

16. **A.** Successful communication always includes feedback to the sender from the receiver.

17. **C.** Collaboration is working together to accomplish common goals.

18. **C.** Protecting the employee's self-esteem is essential in every employee discussion.

19. **A.** Retention programs will save money.

20. **B, C.** Improving employee retention can be accomplished through mentorship programs and supporting work-life balance.

Endnotes

1. https://en.wikipedia.org/wiki/Hawthorne_effect

2. https://www.simplypsychology.org/operant-conditioning.html

3. https://www.smithsonianmag.com/smithsonian-institution/bf-skinners-pigeon-guided-rocket-53443995/

4. Murray, M., *Beyond the Myths and Magic of Mentoring: How to Facilitate an Effective Mentoring Process*, 2nd edition, Jossey-Bass/Wiley, San Francisco, CA 2001.

5. http://tcbdevito.blogspot.com/2011/10/communication-strategies-cultural.html

6. https://www.psychologytoday.com/us/blog/feeling-it/201704/8-ways-your-body-speaks-way-louder-your-words

7. http://www.learnwithtworivers.org/collaboration--communication.html

8. https://www.americanexpress.com/us/small-business/openforum/articles/fostering-collaboration/

9. http://tcbdevito.blogspot.com/2011/10/communication-strategies-cultural.html

10. https://www.roberthalf.com/blog/management-tips/effective-employee-retention-strategies

11. https://www.quora.com/How-many-times-did-Thomas-Alva-Edison-fail-before-he-invented-the-light-bulb

CHAPTER 12

Total Rewards

An organization's total rewards package is a critical tool for employee retention, attraction, and motivation. While previous chapters have laid the groundwork for executing total rewards, senior human resource professionals should concern themselves with the development and analysis of total rewards programs, as well as the implication these programs have on the organization's strategic plan and culture. Material from Chapter 7 will likely be included on the SPHR exam, so it would be wise to review it in concert with this chapter. The Total Rewards functional area makes up 12 percent of the SPHR exam.

The official HRCI Total Rewards functional area responsibilities and knowledge statements for the SPHR exam are as follows:

Responsibilities

- Analyze and evaluate compensation strategies (for example, philosophy, classification, direct, indirect, incentives, bonuses, equity, executive compensation) that attract, reward, and retain talent
- Analyze and evaluate benefit strategies (for example, health, welfare, retirement, recognition programs, work-life balance, wellness) that attract, reward, and retain talent

Knowledge Of

- Compensation strategies and philosophy
- Job analysis and evaluation methods
- Job pricing and pay structures
- External labor markets and economic factors
- Executive compensation methods
- Noncash compensation methods
- Benefits program strategies
- Fiduciary responsibilities
- Motivation concepts and applications
- Benchmarking techniques

Strategic Objectives of Total Rewards

As a reminder, *total rewards* includes compensation (direct compensation) and benefits (indirect compensation). Total rewards programs significantly impact all the other HR functions, including staffing, performance evaluations, training and development, and employee relations, and these HR functions likewise influence total rewards programs. Compensation and benefits also affect organizational processes, job satisfaction, productivity, and turnover. Offerings must be viewed not only on the basis of what is legal and motivating but also on the ethical basis of what is fair and just.

Organizations want to attract and retain good, qualified workers who are motivated to a degree of high productivity, but organizations must make total rewards decisions with competing pressures. Simply paying more or providing better benefits may make some employees happy but will, in the long term, raise labor costs and may make the company less competitive. Developing a total rewards strategy helps an organization avoid making quick decisions that might be harmful long-term. Strategies are generally developed by a small group of senior professionals in an organization, including the top operations, finance, and human resource executives. Each respective department head can provide insight on key variables that affect the strategy. For example, the finance executive can speak to the organization's financial projections, the operations executive to business demand, and the human resource professional to the nuances of the workforce and competitive labor pressures in the market.

In the total rewards design phase, it is important to ask key questions like the following:

- What funding do we have available for the program?
- Which employee classifications and positions should be eligible for certain programs (e.g., commission programs or benefits offerings)?
- What values are important to our organization and to our employees? Which values do we want to reward?
- What kind of rewards will work best for our employee population?
- How should we involve current employees in designing the rewards system?

Developing a total rewards strategy is ultimately a fine balance between aligning with organizational strategy and remaining competitive in the market. Let's look at an example.

If a fitness studio learns that a direct competitor (who happens to offer a great employee total rewards package) is opening a gym in the same shopping center, the fitness studio would likely be concerned about the threat of the competing gym. The fitness studio does not offer employee benefits and may lose valued employees to the competing gym if it does not develop a good retention strategy. So the organization decides to pay all employees an extra dollar per hour. The simple introduction of a "threat" (see Chapter 9) can have a drastic effect on an organization's compensation decisions.

If we expand this example to include a new tidbit of information about the fitness studio's strategic plan, the results may be different. If, like the previous example, a competing gym was opening in the same shopping center but the fitness studio's new strategic plan was focused on virtual fitness classes and online memberships, the success of their brick-and-mortar studio might not be as important. The fitness studio may already be considering downsizing its number of physical locations and allowing current employees to work remotely, offering more flexibility and a better quality of life. The extra dollar per hour may not be as important for employee retention and be an unnecessary cost. As this example demonstrates, it is important to consider many factors in total rewards decisions.

In the face of competitive pressures, all decisions should

- **Be legal**   Must be consistent with numerous federal, state, and local laws. Laws such as the Equal Pay Act (EPA), Lilly Ledbetter Fair Pay Act, Fair Labor Standards Act (FLSA), prevailing wages under the Service Contract Act, and several other laws related to total rewards will be covered on the SPHR exam. Chapter 2 includes a complete listing of these laws.

- **Align with strategy**   Must be aligned with the organization's goals and overall compensation strategy.

- **Be adequate**   Be large enough to attract qualified employees to join the organization and stay.

- **Be motivating**   Should provide sufficient incentives to motivate employees to perform efficiently.

- **Be equitable**   An employee should think that his or her compensation is internally equitable relative to other employees in the organization and externally equitable relative to employees doing similar work in other organizations. Engaging in job evaluation and job pricing helps ensure consistency between jobs in an organization. Salary grades and ranges help expand a compensation system's equity to all jobs in an organization. Benchmarking techniques gauge external equity. Chapter 7 explains these processes in more detail.

- **Provide security**   Employees want to feel that their monthly income is secure and predictable. They need to feel that their pay is somewhat insulated from changes in employment, profitability, individual performance, and personal health.

- **Be cost-benefit effective**   The organization must administer the compensation and benefits system efficiently and have the financial resources to support it on a continuing basis. Forecasting long-term financials helps ensure the right mix of total rewards can be offered for several years.

Employee Motivation Concepts and Application

As reviewed in Chapter 6, there are several popular theories associated with employee motivation. Whichever theory you choose, each helps explain employee motivation in some fashion. Because total rewards are a key employee motivation tool, these theories are pretty important to consider when designing a total rewards package. Taken together, there are commonalities between each theory that inform the makeup of a good total rewards package. They are summarized in Table 12-1.[1]

Employee Motivation Concept	Examples of Total Rewards Programs That Apply to This Concept
Employee Needs Employees have needs based on their values and desire a sense of satisfaction. These needs depend on each employee's current and desired economic, political, and social status; career aspiration; the need to balance career, family, education, community, religion, and other factors.	• Base pay • Paid time off • Health and welfare benefits • Retirement plans • Paid leaves • Flexible work arrangements • Training and career development opportunities • Childcare • Wellness programs
Job Responsibilities If an employee feels competent to perform in a more challenging capacity and has demonstrated the competence to advance, an employee may seek additional responsibilities and will expect to be rewarded in a fair and equitable manner.	• Opportunities for advancement • Job evaluation process • Salary grades and ranges
Work Environment Employees want to work in an environment that is productive, that is respectful, and that fulfills employee needs.	• Job design • Workplace amenities • Work-life balance
Fairness, Equity, and Effort Employees want to be treated and rewarded in a fair and equitable manner. Employees also expect to be rewarded for more output and higher levels of performance.	• Merit pay • Productivity-based pay • Pay differentials • Commissions • Bonuses
Feedback Employees prefer to have timely and open feedback from their supervisors.	• Recognition programs

Table 12-1   Key Motivation Concepts and Application to Total Rewards Programs

External Factors Affecting Total Rewards

Senior HR professionals are required to make informed decisions on a daily basis. To make informed decisions, it is important to stay up-to-date on state and federal law and emerging case law, to review human resource publications, and to stay abreast of any outside factors that may affect employees. There are always external factors at play that can affect an organization's total rewards program. Here are a few examples:

- **Fluctuating unemployment levels** often cause employers to examine their total rewards strategies. In times of low unemployment, there are more job opportunities available to choose from. It is important to have a total rewards package that keeps employees on the payroll. Even during times of high unemployment, there is always a risk of losing high-performing employees who possess a skill set in high demand.

- **High market demand** for a certain skill set means that organizations are willing to pay more to have someone on their payroll with the skill set in high demand (for example, project management certification, technology skills such as mobile application development, advanced degrees, etc.). Compensation data sources often include adjustments for certain levels of education, skills, or years of experience to assist with these benchmarks. When a high-potential employee attains a certification or masters unique skills, it is wise to reconsider that employee's compensation through a new job evaluation and updated job price to account for the job's value to the organization. Doing so helps ensure that compensation is fair and provides the added benefit of retaining a helpful skill set within the organization.

- **External competitors** can provide a direct or indirect threat to business success and, to make the situation worse, poach employees with an enticing compensation and benefits package. Senior HR professions should ask, "What makes the company a desirable place to work compared to competitors?" If the answer to this question is not top of mind, conduct an employee opinion survey and employees can help. Benchmarking tools such as compensation and benefits surveys can also provide a wealth of helpful information regarding competitor plans and market offerings.

- **Cost of living** in certain areas can have a profound effect on the desirability of the work location. Wages should be compared to market rates using pay surveys and adjusted using a cost-of-living indicator to be certain pay is competitive.

- **Emerging total rewards trends** are the topic of regular discussion in human resource publications. All employers want to know the best ways to keep employees on the payroll. Remaining educated on popular trends and their applicability to the organization is a great way to stay innovative and provide new and exciting benefits offerings to employees.

Benefits Needs Assessment

Employee benefits represent a significant financial investment on the part of an employer. An employer's total benefits program must be cost-effective, meet their stated purpose, must be affordable for both the employer and the employee, and must comply with local, state, and federal law. To accomplish these objectives, data must be collected and analyzed to determine whether the employer's benefits program actually meets its objectives. This process is known as a *benefits needs analysis*.

A benefits needs analysis consists of several steps that include data collection and analysis culminating in a report called a *gap analysis*. This process is as follows:

- **Reviewing the organization's overall culture and strategy** The results of this effort will determine the potential coverage and scope of benefits programs.

- **Collecting and analyzing the employer's workforce demographics** This data is key to determining potential benefits needs.

- **Analyzing the utilization and costs of existing benefits plans and programs**
  The results of this data, coupled with the demographics data, will help determine the nature of coverage desired.

- **Determining potential benefits coverage and costs**   This analysis will be an important factor for comparison with the demographics and benefits utilization data.

The final step is to compare the organizational needs and budget with employee needs and any existing benefits coverage. The end result is a gap analysis, a document that will indicate what a benefits package should and should not include.

In the Trenches

Employee Benefits: It's All About Strategy!
Fredi Foye-Helms, Vice President, Employee Benefits, EPIC

Managing employee benefit plans used to be routine and predictable. Employees assumed a comprehensive benefit package was a right of employment. Employers viewed employee benefit plans as an important tool to attract and retain employees, but for many, the benefits program was reviewed annually, and the results were shared with employees at open enrollment. Once done, it was put to bed for another year, and HR moved on to other priorities. Well, those days are gone. With healthcare costs rising and the burden of complying with numerous provisions of the Affordable Care Act, benefit plans are front and center in HR strategy discussions, and the savvy HR professional needs to be ready for it.

We've all heard the statistics report that employees spend less than 20 minutes a year on benefit decisions. We also understand that more frequent and relevant employee education about company-provided benefit plans will foster job satisfaction and influence employee loyalty. The biggest opportunity surrounding employee benefits continues to be well-crafted communications and a focus on basic strategies, such as the following:

- **Engage**   Determine what communication method works best for your workforce. Use tactics that your group will respond to, based on their demographics, such as age, comfort with technology, work locations, language, and specifics of your firm or industry.

- **Educate**   Make your communications simple and relevant. Include family members in the education effort. Provide education when and where they want it. Recorded webinars, videos, and podcasts are replacing in-person meetings in today's environment.

(continued)

- **Innovate**   What is your company's road map for employee benefits over the next three to four years? Assess the company priorities and lead toward that direction in your plan design and employee communications. Clarity of the long-term goal helps employees engage and begin taking the steps to reach that goal.

- **Measure**   Measuring the impact of each benefit program will allow you to determine which benefits provide the most value to employees and the company, and this information will help you allocate future resources wisely, using the resulting data.

We all love choice, and the benefits arena is no different. With the health insurance marketplace, public and private insurance exchanges, and increasing enrollment in high-deductible health plans, employees today have an increasing number of options for coverage. Recent surveys indicate that employees want more personalized benefits geared toward differing age groups. Employers and employees are being asked to become consumers of healthcare services, and the technology and tools are advancing rapidly to support this ownership approach to healthcare services. Strategic-thinking HR professionals will stay on top of emerging programs, tools, and resources.

It is a challenging time in employee benefits, but it is an exciting time that allows HR to empower employees to learn and take control of their healthcare and benefit decisions. The HR professional who uses creative tools and resources to communicate, engage, educate, and innovate will help provide a more positive employee experience and in turn demonstrate HR's ability to develop strategic solutions and act as a valuable partner to support company goals.

Incentive Pay

Incentive pay is pay designed to promote a higher level of job performance than otherwise included in the basic design of the job. Incentive pay programs are popular because motivating individual or group job performance generally has a direct result on the organization's financials. When employees perform better, the organization does too. Some incentive measures include profits (organization-wide), organization performance, business unit/function/group rewards, and nonfinancial incentives such as customer satisfaction. Incentive pay programs are highly regulated; as such, legal and accounting expertise should be consulted during the development phase.

Requirements

Organizational requirements include the following:

- **A stable base pay plan**   These kinds of plans must be fair and equitable with long-term stability. Staff must be compensated competitively. An incentive plan will not support a base compensation system that is internally or externally inequitable.
- **An existing strategic plan**   Long-term organizational goals, as expressed in the organization's strategic plan, must be clear, consistent, and measurable. There must be stability as measured through the organization's sales volume, expenses, profitability, and customer satisfaction.
- **Complete commitment**   A great deal of effort goes into creating an incentive plan. The plan must be accepted at all levels of management. Continued coaching and training are necessary for long-term stability. Learning must be reinforced by strong support and commitment to achieve desired results using measured output to evaluate performance.

Plan Criteria

The plan must meet the following criteria:

- *It must fit with other programs.* For example, individual sales reward programs must be compatible with larger team recognition and reward programs.
- *It must be in the employee's "line of sight."* Job performance measures should reflect the results the employee actually controls. For example, a laboratory technician's zero-defect completion of a prescribed number of test results within a specified period of time would be a "line-of-sight" accomplishment.
- *It must have a "sunset clause."* The incentive plan should be in effect for a specific time period with an identified end date for tracking and measurement purposes.
- *It must incorporate both short- and long-term perspectives.* It should be structured to reward short-term goals (e.g., increased production capacity), as well as long-term results (e.g., achieving a strategic growth objective). The short-term perspective may be easier to visualize and achieve, but that may not encourage employees to think about long-term results.

Required Internal Processes

In addition to the plan criteria, an organization must consider its internal processes.

- *Good communication is required.* Incentive programs break down when there are barriers to good communication, such as a lack of teamwork, personal grievances, low morale, and other management failures. Good communication must be constant and ongoing. Management will need to share information relative to the organization's overall performance and how performance is rewarded. Employees need to understand their role in their organization's operations.

- *A reliable measurement system is required.* Both management and workers must be able to understand the results achieved and be committed to behaviors that will achieve an incentive plan's established goals.

Types of Incentive Programs

There is no "one size fits all" when it comes to incentive plans. In fact, an effective incentive plan is designed specifically to fit the culture of the organization it supports. Incentive plans can be broken down into three categories: individual programs, group programs, and organization programs.

Individual Incentive Programs

The objective of an individual incentive program is to improve job performance. As such, the individual incentive program must be available to all employees in a particular group. An individual incentive program must be clearly designed and implemented as an incentive separate from an individual's base pay. Individual incentive programs can be either cash-based or non-cash-based.

Cash Awards Cash award programs reward performance with extra pay based on job performance. The rewards are usually lump-sum rewards such as discretionary bonuses based on the judgment of a supervisor or manager, a performance-based bonus based on predetermined performance criteria, and formula-based bonuses based on a percentage of profits or other pre-established measurement.

Noncash Awards Noncash awards include prizes, gifts, recognition awards, and other similar noncash items of value to the recipient. Sometimes these awards can be for length of service or contributions in addition to job performance.

 NOTE Although giving cash and noncash awards appears to be pretty straightforward, in fact, it can be more complicated than circumstances suggest. Some awards have tax implications, so advice might be required from accounting or legal counsel as part of developing a cash or noncash incentive program.

Group Incentive Programs

Incentive programs designed for groups of employees have the objective of rewarding the job performance of a group considered necessary to accomplish a unit of work or when the desired result requires a team approach to the work. Group incentive programs can reward both short- and long-term work effort. Often, these programs include financial and nonfinancial measures as criteria for success. Group incentive programs include profit-sharing plans, gainsharing plans, and group performance incentives—for example, employee stock ownership plans (ESOPs).

Profit-Sharing Plans Profit sharing refers to various incentive plans that provide direct or indirect payments to employees who depend on a company's profitability. These payments are in addition to the employees' regular salary and bonuses. In profit-sharing plans, the employer has the discretion to determine when and how much the company will pay into the plan. The contribution and any investment earnings accumulate in the plan on a tax-deferred basis. The IRS taxes these benefits only when employees receive distributions from the plan. A profit-sharing plan can be set up where all or some of the employee's profit-sharing amount can be contributed to a retirement plan. These are often used in conjunction with 401(k) plans.

Gainsharing Plans   Gainsharing plans are similar to profit-sharing plans except that gainsharing plans measure the gain achieved from one performance period to the next, while profit-sharing plans measure the profit to be shared from period to period. In a gainsharing plan, each member of the unit receives the same reward. Gainsharing measures usually apply to productivity terms, while profit-sharing plan measures typically apply to profitability. Three types of gainsharing plans are the Scanlon Plan, the Rucker Plan, and the Improshare Plan.

- **The Scanlon Plan**   The Scanlon Plan is the oldest and most widely used type of gainsharing plan. It's based on the historical ratio of labor cost to sales value of production. And because it rewards labor savings, it is most appropriate for companies that have a "high touch labor" content. The distinctive characteristics of the Scanlon Plan are its philosophy of participative management, administration by a committee of employees and management, and its percentage method of payment. A distinguishing characteristic is that the organization does not have to be profitable for workers to receive an incentive.

- **The Rucker Plan**   The Rucker Plan is based on the premise that the ratio of labor costs to production value is historically stable in manufacturing. The Rucker Plan tracks the value added to a product as a measure of productivity. In the Rucker Plan, a ratio is calculated that expresses the value of production required for each dollar of the total wage cost.

- **Improshare Plan**   Improshare measures change in the relationship between outputs and the time required to produce them. This plan uses past production records to establish base performance standards. A standard is developed that identifies the expected number of hours to produce something. Any savings between this standard and actual production are shared between the company and the workers. The organization and its employees share 50/50 in all productivity gains. It is minimally affected by changes in sales volume, technology and capital equipment, product mix, or price and wage increases. It's the easiest of the gainsharing plans to understand and install.

Employee Stock Ownership Plans

An employee stock ownership plan (ESOP) is a retirement plan in which the company contributes its stock (or money to buy its stock) to the plan for the benefit of the company's employees. The plan maintains an account for each employee participating in the plan. Shares of stock vest over time before an employee is entitled to them. With an ESOP, you never buy or hold the stock directly while still employed with the company.

If an employee is terminated, retires, becomes disabled, or dies, the plan will distribute the shares of stock in the employee's account.[2]

Executive Incentives

Executives form the highest level of management within their organization. In addition to their substantial management responsibilities within their organizations, they develop relationships with people outside their organization with the purpose of improving organizational growth opportunities. Their scope of activities and responsibilities impacts their compensation plans in two ways. First, their total compensation package includes their annual cash compensation plus the value of long-term incentives that usually accounts for the larger share of their total package. Second, their incentives are generally linked to the performance of the entire organization's profitability and, in some cases, other nonfinancial measures such as customer satisfaction and/or meeting certain other strategic objectives.

While there is no single compensation package designed for executives, their pay usually consists of a base salary that is "guaranteed," with other forms of variable (incentive) compensation dependent on performance factors.

Perquisites Special privileges for executives are referred to as *perks*. These privileges include club memberships, company cars, reserved parking, and a host of other noncash benefits. The 1973 Tax Act greatly diminished these perks, but they can sometimes remain a substantial element in an executive's compensation package.

Golden Parachutes These are provisions included in executive employment contracts that provide special payments or benefits to executives under certain adverse conditions such as the loss of their position or if they are otherwise adversely impacted by organizational changes. Most often, these impacts are the result of an organizational merger in which there is a change of control that displaces a senior executive. These "golden parachutes" may provide for accelerated payments or early vesting in nonqualified retirement plan options, among other possibilities.

Long-Term Incentives

Long-term incentive plans reward employees for attaining results over a long measurement period. For this purpose, *long-term* generally means more than one year and typically is between two and five years. Tax-deferred compensation plans, long-term cash plans, and certain stock-based plans are all considered long-term incentives.

The form of payment from a long-term incentive plan is typically cash or equity. An employer might choose one or the other based on the goals of the plan, the recipients of the awards, and the availability of cash or equity for payment.[3]

Incentive Stock Options

There are several varieties of stock options, all of which share some basic characteristics. A stock option is a right to purchase a share of stock in the future at a price determined at the grant (or based on a formula defined at the grant). Incentive stock options (ISOs) are a special subset of stock options, satisfying certain criteria promulgated by the Internal Revenue Service and discussed in Internal Revenue Code Section 422.[4]

One of the primary restrictions is that an ISO can be granted only to an employee—ISOs cannot be granted to outside directors, independent contractors, consultants, or any other nonemployees. Also, the recipient must exercise the ISO within three months of terminating employment.

Employee Stock Purchase Plans

An employee stock purchase plan (ESPP) is a company-run program in which participating employees can purchase company shares at a discounted price. Employees contribute to the plan through payroll deductions, which build up between the offering date and the purchase date. At the purchase date, the company uses the accumulated funds to purchase shares in the company on behalf of the participating employees. The amount of the discount depends on the specific plan but can be as much as 15 percent lower than the market price.

Depending on when you sell the shares, the disposition will be classified as either qualified or not qualified. If sold two years after the offering date and at least one year after the purchase date, the shares will fall under a qualified disposition. If the shares are sold within two years of the offering date or one year after the purchase date, the disposition will not be qualified. These positions will have different tax implications.[5]

Phantom Stock Plan

A *phantom stock plan* is an employee benefit plan that gives selected employees (senior management) many of the benefits of stock ownership without actually giving them any company stock. This is sometimes referred to as *shadow stock*.

Rather than getting physical stock, the employee receives "pretend" stock. Even though it's not real, the phantom stock follows the price movement of the company's actual stock, paying out any resulting profits.[6]

Restricted Stock Unit

A *restricted stock unit* is compensation offered by an employer to an employee in the form of company stock. The employee does not receive the stock immediately but instead receives it according to a vesting plan and distribution schedule after achieving required performance milestones or upon remaining with the employer for a particular length of time. The restricted stock units (RSUs) are assigned a fair market value when they vest. Upon vesting, they are considered income, and a portion of the shares are withheld to pay income taxes. The employee receives the remaining shares and can sell them at any time.[7]

For example, suppose Madeline receives a job offer. Because the company thinks Madeline's skill set is particularly valuable and hopes she will remain a long-term employee, it offers part of her compensation as 500 RSUs, in addition to a generous salary and benefits. The company's stock is worth $40 per share, making the RSUs potentially worth an additional $20,000. To give Madeline an incentive to stay with the company and receive the 500 shares, it puts them on a five-year vesting schedule. After one year of employment, Madeline will receive 100 shares; after two years, another 100; and so on; until she has received all 500 shares at the end of five years. Depending on how the company's stock performs, Madeline may actually receive more or less than $20,000.

Thus, the RSUs give Madeline an incentive not only to stay with the company long term but to help it perform well so that her shares will become more valuable. In fact, Madeline decides to hold the shares until she receives all 500, at which point the company's stock is worth $50 and Madeline receives $25,000, minus the value of the shares that were withheld for income taxes and the amount due in capital gains taxes. However, if Madeline had left the company after 18 months, she would have received only the 100 shares that vested after the first year. She would have forfeited the remaining 400 shares to the company.

Performance Grants

Public companies can also benefit from linking stock-based compensation to organizational performance. If done properly, such an arrangement can qualify as performance-based compensation, which avoids the deduction limits that can be imposed under Internal Revenue Code Section 162(m). Such arrangements can also motivate recipients to achieve goals that are valuable to the organization and its shareholders. The accounting consequences of such arrangements can be tricky, and care should be taken to get the views of the organization's accountants.[8]

Sales Personnel Incentive Programs

There are several ways to compensate personnel who are responsible for sales, depending on the circumstances surrounding the sales activities. Compensation usually is both *direct,* that is, paid by cash or by cash and incentives (in turn, incentives can be cash-driven—for example, bonuses and commissions), or *indirect,* that is, paid through perks and entitlements (for example, cars and expense accounts, club membership, and allowances).

Factors that influence the design of a salesperson's compensation plan include the following:

- The time involved servicing the account as compared to the time spent in the sale of goods or services
- The ability to objectively measure the sales activity
- The nature of the sales activity is difficult to distinguish from the activity spent providing support services
- The degree and type of motivation associated with the sales activity
- The significance of the sales cost involved in the transaction
- The comparative marketplace practice

Three types of compensation plans are most commonly used:

- Straight salary plans
- Straight commission plans
- Salary plus commission plans

Straight Salary Plans Of the three types of plans, the straight salary plan is the least used, but it more than likely will be found in situations where most of the time involved is spent servicing the account rather than selling the account. It is also more likely when sales costs would otherwise be higher than acceptable to management and finally when, by comparison, the marketplace is more likely to compensate sales on a straight salary basis.

Straight Commission Plans This is the other extreme of the sales compensation spectrum. In this case, a person's entire salary is paid by commission. This most often occurs when the ultimate objective is the increased sales volume with less emphasis or need for service, as well as when the marketplace approach is also to compensate by way of a straight commission plan.

In some cases, organizations that use a straight commission form of compensation will provide what is called a *draw* for novice or entry-level sales personnel. Typically, the draw consists of a nonrecoverable or guaranteed commission for a defined period of time, usually not more than one year. If, during this period, a salesperson does not earn a commission equal to or exceeding the draw, the salesperson does not owe the organization the difference. The period of time the draw is in place usually conforms with the organization's experience in developing the salesperson's selling capabilities to a point the individual is able to earn at least as much or more than the draw provides.

Salary Plus Commission Plans In a salary plus commission arrangement, a portion of the total salary is a fixed salary; the remainder is commission. This is the most popular form of sales compensation in that it incorporates parts of both the fixed salary (and thus some stability with the individual's income flow) and the commission or the reward for sales success (thus the incentive for greater future success).

Fiduciary Responsibilities

Although a human resource executive may delegate the responsibility for administering an organization's benefits plan to someone else on the HR team, the HR executive may ultimately have *fiduciary responsibility,* or legal and ethical responsibility, for the benefits program. If not the HR executive, this responsibility is often assigned to the finance executive within an organization. The Department of Labor ascribes the fiduciary responsibilities created by the Employee Retirement Income Security Act (ERISA) relative to those people or entities who exercise discretionary control or authority over plan management or plan assets, have discretionary authority or responsibility for the administration of a plan, or provide investment advice to a plan for compensation or have any authority or responsibility to do so.

The primary responsibility of fiduciaries is to run the plan solely in the interest of participants and beneficiaries and for the exclusive purpose of providing benefits and paying plan expenses. Fiduciaries must act prudently and must diversify the plan's investments to minimize the risk of large losses. In addition, they must follow the terms of plan documents to the extent that the plan terms are consistent with ERISA. They also must avoid conflicts of interest. In other words, they may not engage in transactions on behalf of the plan that benefit parties related to the plan, such as other fiduciaries, services providers, or the plan sponsor.[9]

Communicating Total Rewards Programs

In the words of George Bernard Shaw, "The single biggest problem in communication is the illusion that it has taken place."[10] Communication, whether verbal or written, is the primary way in which humans interact. For employees to understand the equity inherent in a total rewards program and the value of rewards, organizations must be transparent about rewards.

Each reward program that is implemented should include a communication plan. Without a communication plan, employees may not understand the value of the program or be confused by it. All of the time put into the design and development of the program needs to be supported by a good program execution. To develop a communication plan, consider the following:

- **Who is the audience?** Does it apply to all employees or only one department? Even if the program applies to only one department, would it be beneficial to communicate this program to the whole company to ensure transparency and build support for the program?

- **What are the best ways to reach the target group of employees?** Which communication mediums are available, and which will be most effective? Is it easy to gather the group together for a meeting? Does the group have access to email? Does the group read their emails? Can a webinar be created?

- **How do we explain the value of the reward?** Is it a complicated program that requires a group meeting to explain it? Is the reward relatable on an individual level?

- **Who will communicate the program?** Is messaging more powerful if it comes from the chief executive officer (CEO)? Will supervisors need to cascade communication to their teams? Do supervisors need a communication toolkit to maintain messaging consistency?

- **When should we communicate the program?** How much time is needed to prepare before program launch? Is more time needed because this is a big change for employees? Is a transition period needed from the previous version of the program?

- **How many times should we communicate the program?** This might depend on how employees are adapting to the program. Do employees need to be reminded about the program regularly? Will posting the program on the company intranet allow for greater exposure to it?

Once a senior HR professional has answered these questions, there are some best practices[11] that can help ensure the program is well received:

- Make more information about the total rewards system available to employees, especially details about how the system operates. Use different mediums of communication to support different learning styles. Real-life examples are also helpful in explaining complicated programs.

- Personalize total rewards by creating a statement for each employee detailing the rewards he or she has received. There is no better way for an employee to understand the value of a program than by seeing how the entire total rewards program affects his or her personal earnings.

- Minimize the use of traditional communication vehicles, such as policy statements, to announce or explain rewards. Let's face it, policy statements are not the most exciting read. Using a different medium to explain a program, or a variety of mediums, helps to increase the likelihood that employees will take an interest in the information and digest it.

- Encourage one-on-one conversations between supervisors and employees about total rewards. Supervisors are the primary point of contact with employees on a daily basis and where much of the information exchange occurs. Supervisor opinions inform employee opinions. Providing supervisors with a communication toolkit about the program is a helpful way to ensure consistent messaging.

- Provide more interactive communication through the company website or intranet. Offering more engaging means of communicating a program is a great way to build support and understanding for total rewards programs.

In the Trenches

Communication Breakdown

Tyrone was celebrating 25 years in business. Up until recently, he had run a successful ticket resale business. Unfortunately, the past year had been tough on Tyrone. Ticket sales were well below projections each month. Tyrone thought it would be a good idea to ask his employees for feedback about recent sales challenges, so he conducted a few focus groups.

In the focus groups, employees shared that they were less motivated to pursue new ticket sales partnerships because new accounts were much harder to close because of market competition. Tyrone decided that it would be a good idea to create a new commission program to incentivize sales employees to seek out new leads. He asked his operations manager, Cindy, to communicate the program and felt good about the changes being made.

Cindy decided to communicate the program over email because that was the best way to reach sales employees who were regularly in the field. Caught in the midst of another busy day of operations, Cindy unknowingly sent the email about the commission program to the administrative team, not the sales team. The administrative team left work that day on cloud nine; they were getting commission for all new accounts. The sales team continued business as usual.

(continued)

At the end of the first month of the program, commissions for new sales were included in sales team member earnings. A few members of the sales team shared their mutual confusion about the new commission in the break room. A member of the administrative team overhead the conversation in the break room and noticed commission was not included in his paycheck. Word spread quickly throughout the administrative team; they were angry and approached Cindy and Tyrone. Cindy realized she made a mistake and apologized to the administrative team, saying the extra commission was intended for the sales team.

The administrative team continued to harbor frustration about the mix-up and became less motivated to do their work because of the feeling of inequity and loss of a reward, even if it was a mistake. "We work so hard and never get recognized. Management obviously appreciates the sales team more than us," the administrative team grumbled. Shortly after the mix-up, a few key administrative team members stopped turning down the job offers from competing resellers and accepted them. After all, there was no reason for them to stay loyal to an organization that did not seem to appreciate them. Now Tyrone had serious gaps in his administrative team and a loss of institutional knowledge in addition to his sales problem, all because of a simple communication mistake.

Measurements and Analysis

Management may think a total rewards program is great, but how do you quantify "great"? What if employees don't share the same sentiments about the program? Senior HR professionals are responsible for knowing whether an organization's total rewards program is effective. If not, responsibility lies in making necessary improvements until the total rewards program is effective.

The following are measurements and analysis needed to determine whether an organization's compensation and benefits program is meeting its stated goals and objectives. These are also explained in Figure 12-1.

- Is the system legally compliant?
  - Does the system meet ERISA nondiscrimination requirements?
  - Is there adverse impact on protected groups?
  - Are the organization's EEO and affirmative action objectives supported?
- Is the system compatible with the organization's mission and strategy?
  - Does it meet the organization's mission, goals, and objectives?
  - Are changes made to the program as a result of changing needs?
- Does it help the organization attract and retain employees?
  - Does it motivate employee performance?

- Does the system fit the culture? Is it appropriate for employees?
  - Is the organization entitlement-oriented (e.g., expecting pay increases at a certain frequency based on seniority)? Or is the organization contribution-oriented (e.g., do employees expect pay increases to be based on their contributions or performance)?
  - Does the system support the organization's orientation?
  - Does the system have programs that meet employee lifestyle needs?
- Is the system internally equitable?
- Does the mix (fixed versus variable, cash versus benefits, retirement versus health/welfare) fit?
- Do employees perceive the system to be fair and adequate?
- Is the system externally competitive?
- How does this system compare to the competition?
- Are dollars spent generating a meaningful return?
- Is the program well-communicated?
- Do the employees understand the system?

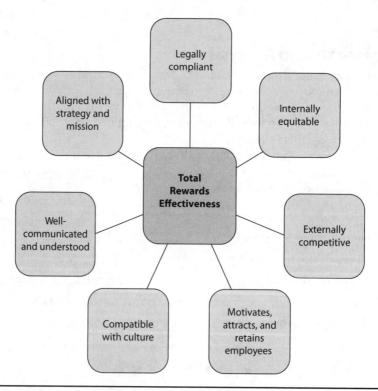

Figure 12-1 Total rewards effectiveness

Once a senior HR professional can answer these questions, gap areas can be determined and program changes can be developed and implemented. Whichever gap areas are addressed, it is helpful to maintain regular communication with employees about the problems identified and the remedy for those problems. When an organization makes improvements to total rewards programs, this can generate a lot of goodwill and respect among employees. So communicate, communicate, communicate!

Compensation and Benefits—International Employees

Compensation and benefits are a critical element in an organization's strategic goals and plans. This principle is even more true when an organization is involved with international operations. The nature and complexity of international operations add to the complexity of the design features of international compensation and benefits, as well as to the administration of international compensation and benefits plans. This section addresses some of the principles and issues international organizations face.

For the purposes of understanding types of employees involved in an organization's international operations, it is important to recognize the following international employee categories:

- **Expatriates** Traditionally applies to people who move from one country to another and are employed by an organization based in another country

- **Inpatriates** Describes employees brought in from another country to work in the headquarters country for a specified period of time

- **Repatriates** Refers to employees who have returned home from an international assignment

- **International assignee** An umbrella term that describes anyone who is assigned to an international location

Generally, organizations are reducing the number of long-term international assignments while increasing the number of local hire employees. In many cases, local nationals fill cross-border assignments on both short-term and permanent assignments.

This assignment pattern creates additional complexity in determining competitive terms and conditions of labor markets in other countries. The terms and conditions may vary widely from country to country based on local norms and customs related to each country's culture, driven by its history, laws, rules, and regulations. The following is a list of issues that HR must keep in mind as part of developing international compensation and benefits programs:

- **Standardization vs. localization** While strategies are typically standardized consistent with the organization's overall compensation and benefits strategy, specific practices tend to be localized to fit the context of the country, region, or local conditions.

- **Culture** Cultural differences that result from different local, regional, and national backgrounds add challenges to creating an understanding of applicable compensation and benefits programs. Benefits highly valued in one country may be almost meaningless in another. Differences are often the result of deeply entrenched beliefs, values, and attitudes.

- **Competitive labor market** The purpose of an effective compensation and benefits program is to attract and retain talent. The effectiveness of the program is mostly determined by the competitive demand for the talent. The competition for talent will vary from country to country, often driven by type of talent sought, geographic scope of available talent, the industries in which talent can be found, and a variety of compensation elements.

- **Collective bargaining, employee representation, and government mandates** In most parts of the world, employees are legally protected from actions that might impact their wages and employment conditions, although the extent of these protections vary widely from country to country. Decreasing an employee's salary is illegal in most countries, particularly in Latin America and Europe. In some countries, unions play a powerful role, sometimes including provisions for management as well as workers. Work councils (not to be confused with unions) also offer worker protections.

- **Economic factors** Countries have a wide range of economic differences in terms of internal politics, the distribution of wealth, and rapidly changing events such as rates of inflation, currency valuation, and so on.

- **Taxation** Tax regulations vary widely from country to country. While some countries have no income tax, others have income tax in excess of 50 percent. Benefits in some countries are taxable, while in others they are not.

- **Laws and regulations** There are significant differences in the legal protections from one country to the next: laws that affect work hours and compulsory time off, minimum wage, overtime, compulsory bonuses, employment at will, and acquired rights of employment.

Assignment Compensation Terms

Creating an international compensation plan is more complex than a domestic plan. Whereas a typical domestic compensation plan usually relies on pay level and ranges, the same cannot be effectively applied in an international situation. Because international assignments may involve high-cost locations as well as low-cost locations, the compensation and benefits portion of an effective compensation plan must be designed to respond to each international location's specific characteristics. To meet these characteristics as well as the objectives of both multinational assignees and local hires, various approaches have been developed. The following text examines some key concepts for international assignment lasting longer than one year and involving the relocation of the employee and his or her family to the host country. Common international assignment approaches include those discussed in the following sections.

Negotiation/Ad Hoc

Negotiation is typically used when the first few assignees are sent from headquarters to other countries and evolves to meet the needs of each individual assignee. Terms are negotiated on an ad hoc basis. The advantage of this approach is that it does not require long-term planning because its terms are negotiated on an individual basis. The disadvantage is inconsistency that develops over time.

Pure Localization

Of the different approaches, pure localization is the most straightforward. The assignee is paid exactly what local nationals in equivalent positions in the host country are paid. The advantage of this approach is that it is simple to communicate and administer. It works best when assignees are located from a low-salary country to a high-salary country. The disadvantage is that it is inappropriate for assignments from a high-salary country to a low-salary country. In some cases, allowances can help offset the disadvantage of an assignment from a high-salary country to a low-salary country.

Higher-of-Home-or-Host-Country

Higher-of-home-or-host-country is a variation of a localization strategy that is essentially founded on which location is the high-salary location and pays on that basis. It is simple to communicate. Its disadvantage is that it will usually require allowances and adjustments for differences in individual expenditures.

Home-Country-Based Balance Sheet

The employer in the home-country-based balance sheet approach pays a differential between home-country costs and assignment costs. In this approach, assignees maintain their home-country standard of living as they move from one country to another. This preserves an assignee's purchasing power at a fixed level; it eliminates the disincentive to repatriate because of a loss of purchasing power. A disadvantage is that it may create a perception of inequities among assignees of different nationalities working in the same host country.

Headquarters-Based Balance Sheet

The headquarters-based balance sheet is similar to the home-country-based balance sheet but calculates the compensation package only for the typical headquarters-based employees. It ensures that the same level of salary and allowances given to the headquarters country is given to assignees from other home countries. This approach maintains the purchasing power of assignees from the headquarters country. It is easy to communicate and administer. The disadvantage is that it often translates to high costs for the organization, especially for assignees from low-salary countries. This can make it difficult to repatriate assignees back to their home county.

Lump Sum

With a lump-sum approach, the employer pays a lump sum instead of allowances and differentials. This provides maximum flexibility for the assignee. A disadvantage is that this approach may lead to the loss of certain tax advantages, particularly with host-country housing.

PART III

Cafeteria

With the cafeteria approach, the employer establishes several benefits options and offers these options to the employee subject to an overall limit. This provides a degree of flexibility for the assignee. A disadvantage is that some of the options may be inappropriate for some assignees from some countries.

International Benefits Variations

International benefits decisions can be a particular challenge for the international employer. Issues unique to international assignments include differences in what government taxes cover and what employees expect. The structure and administration of a benefits program is generally dictated by extensive but widely varying regulations in each country. Differences from country to country and, in particular, differences between other countries and the United States significantly complicate the choice of benefits. For example, the governments of many countries provide healthcare coverage, but in the United States most health benefits have been employer-sponsored with the exception of Affordable Care Act marketplace plans. The following are common country variations outside of the United States:

- **Government-provided benefits**   These benefits are administered and provided directly by the government, usually paid for through taxes.

- **Government-mandated benefits**   These benefits are provided by employers by government mandate.

- **Benefits that are discretionary or market practice**   Benefits are voluntarily provided by the employer but may not be entirely discretionary since the employer may be under the pressure of competitive practice.

Nonsalary International Benefits

Reflecting the wide range of different approaches to compensation and benefits, nonsalary benefits also vary widely among countries.

- **Paid time off**   Vacation and other paid time off often are determined by legislative mandate or collective bargaining. Generally, time-off programs are strongly based in culture and tradition. Many countries have paid-time-off programs that reflect these influences and result in significant time off.

- **Healthcare**   In many countries, healthcare is paid for through taxes or a form of social insurance. In some cases, healthcare is funded by employers, employees, general taxation, or some combination of these sources. In most cases, individuals are covered, at least partially, by some form of government-supported healthcare.

- **Disability**   Generally, disability is treated differently depending on whether it is short- or long-term. The approach differs from country to country.

- **Life insurance**   Generally, life insurance that is payable upon a person's death is covered by some form of social security. Some countries mandate that employers provide this life insurance, although most employers voluntarily provide this benefit. Many countries allow an employee to purchase some form of supplemental coverage under their employee-sponsored group plan.

- **Social security**   Social security benefits vary widely typically, reflecting the culture and political history of each country. In some countries, social security benefits are generous, while other countries barely provide coverage. Beginning in the 1970s, the United States established a network of bilateral social security agreements that coordinate the U.S. Social Security program with comparable programs in other countries. These agreements, often referred to as *totalization agreements,* have two objectives:

  - Eliminate dual social security taxation, a situation that occurs when a person works in another country and is forced to pay taxes in both the United States and the other country at the same time.

  - Help fill the benefit protection gaps of workers who have spent part of their career overseas on international assignment and part of their career in the United States; in some cases, they are therefore not eligible for social security coverage in either nation.

- **Severance**   Payments associated with terminations of employment, whether voluntary or involuntary, can be complex. Local laws may dictate the conditions under which an employee can be terminated and the amount of payment the employee is entitled to receive.

- **Retirement**   Retirement options vary country to country. In some cases, they are mandated by the government and often paid for with employee and employer contributions. Defined benefit plans are often used to provide retirement funds. Differing cultural expectations, local and country laws, and taxes create significant differences in how retirement is approached.

Chapter Review

With total rewards being a major factor in the attraction, motivation, and retention of employees, the development and analysis of these programs is an important part of a senior HR professional's role. This chapter covered compensation and benefits philosophies and how to align total rewards decisions with an organization's strategic goals. The chapter also reviewed employee motivation concepts and resulting total rewards programs to align with these concepts, as well as incentive pay and executive compensation. Key foundational questions and best practices for communicating and evaluating total rewards programs were also discussed. This chapter closed with a review of key factors in implementing a compensation and benefits plan for an international employer.

Questions

1. The purpose of a gap analysis is to:

   A. Determine which employees are underinsured

   B. Revise benefits that are not meeting employee or organizational needs

   C. Eliminate benefits that are too costly

   D. Ensure that all employees receive the same benefits

2. Lydia finds that her job descriptions are all written and current. Now, she wants to use them to be sure each job is properly assigned to a compensation level. She doesn't want to get caught in an OFCCP audit with the government telling her she needs to make large adjustments all at once. How should Lydia's organization be evaluating their jobs for compensation levels?

   A. Lydia should call one of the job evaluation consulting firms to have them review all the jobs in her organization.

   B. She can create her own point system and arbitrarily set compensation levels wherever she wants.

   C. A point system is not necessary for determining what similarities exist between job content descriptions. She can assign compensation groups based on her assessment of those similarities and differences in the level of job responsibilities.

   D. Lydia should avoid any type of job evaluation program if it hasn't been statistically proven to be 100 percent accurate.

3. According to USERRA, employees called to active duty are entitled to:

   A. Higher limits for salary deferral contributions

   B. Credited service for retirement plan purposes

   C. Lower co-payments and deductibles for continued family benefits

   D. An early vesting schedule for retirement benefits

4. Which of the following is a common action taken in the United States to lower budgets that would most likely violate compensation laws in other countries?

   A. Reduce base salary levels

   B. Offer early retirement packages

   C. Delay or not fill open positions

   D. Downgrade job titles

5. An organization establishes an ESOP by doing which of the following?

   A. Deducting a small amount from the individual's pay for the purchase of stock

   B. Using stock as collateral to borrow capital from a financial institution

   C. Providing upper management with a bonus

   D. Having its profits distributed with favorable tax treatment

6. _____ is the right of employees to receive benefits from their retirement plans.

   A. Transference

   B. Portability

   C. Social Security

   D. Vesting

7. Under the Service Contracts Act, a company with a federal service contract exceeding $2,500 must pay:

   A. The wage established by the contract

   B. Union wages

   C. 125 percent of the maximum wage

   D. The local prevailing wage

8. The _____ plan is a gainsharing plan based on the historical ratio of labor cost to sales value of production.

9. Alonzo is developing a communication plan to accompany his organization's new safety incentive program. Which of the following actions should Alonzo take first in developing the plan?

   A. Determine the timing of communication

   B. Determine the audience for communication

   C. Determine the cost of communication

   D. Determine the content of communication

10. Pradeep's organization recently conducted an employee opinion survey. Results indicated that the work environment needs improvement. Based on employee motivation concepts, which two rewards programs should Pradeep consider implementing to improve the work environment?

   A. New workplace amenities

   B. Bonus program

   C. Program to enhance work-life balance

   D. Recognition program

11. Cecilia just graduated from college and is starting her first job in sales at XYZ Pharmaceutical Sales. XYZ Pharmaceutical Sales normally pays sales employees 100 percent commission but has created a new compensation plan for Cecilia that calculates commission for closing new sales accounts, with less risk to her total compensation in her first year of employment. Which type of sales incentive plan has XYZ offered Cecilia?

    A. Straight salary plan

    B. Salary plus commission plan

    C. Straight commission plan

    D. Straight commission plan with a draw in Cecilia's first year of employment

12. Which of the following steps are part of a benefits gap analysis? (Choose two.)

    A. Reviewing the benefits offered by competitors

    B. Reviewing how many employees have individual or family coverage

    C. Analyzing which benefits plans are most utilized by employees and which are least utilized

    D. Reviewing how many sick days employees use per year

Questions 13 and 14 apply to the following scenario:

Yasmine is the new HR director for a small technology startup company with 10 employees. The company is forecasting rapid growth with plans to grow to 100 employees in the next year. The company currently does not have a total rewards strategy in place. Yasmine has been tasked with developing a total rewards program. Each of the current employees, both male and female, are paid based on their desired salary expressed at the time of hire.

13. What should Yasmine's first step be in developing a total rewards strategy?

    A. Analyze the current benefits offerings and evaluate the best options for the company

    B. Conduct a strategic planning session to determine the organization's goals for compensation and benefits

    C. Conduct an employee opinion survey to evaluate employee opinions about compensation and benefits plans

    D. Meet with the finance director to determine the total budget for compensation and benefits

14. Which potential legal problems should Yasmine be worried about, based on the company's current compensation methods?

    A. Violating the Equal Pay Act (EPA)

    B. Violating the Copeland "Anti-Kickback" Act

    C. Violating the Service Contract Act

    D. Violating the Age Discrimination in Employment Act (ADEA)

15. A _____ _____ international compensation plan works best when an employee is moving from a low-salary country to a high-salary country.

16. What is the compa-ratio of an employee's salary if she is paid $60,000 per year and the midpoint of the salary range for that position is $65,000 per year?

    A. 1.08

    B. 1.02

    C. 0.92

    D. 0.96

17. Which of the following are ways that organizations can help lower healthcare costs? (Choose two.)

    A. Implement an age-risk assessment program

    B. Increase deductibles

    C. Join a Health Insurance Purchasing Alternative

    D. Require generic drugs in their prescription plans

18. Which of the following does *not* apply to an incentive stock option (ISO)?

    A. ISOs can be granted only to employees.

    B. Employees must exercise the ISO within three months of terminating employment.

    C. ISOs are governed by Internal Revenue Code Section 422.

    D. ISOs are not permitted in the financial industry.

19. Which of the following apply to a restricted stock unit (RSU)? (Choose two.)

    A. RSUs are assigned a fair market value at the time of contract negotiation.

    B. RSUs are received according to a vesting schedule.

    C. Upon vesting, a portion of the RSUs is withheld to pay for income taxes.

    D. RSUs are considered indirect compensation.

20. Which of the following laws cover both whistle-blower protection and notice requirements for defined contribution plans?

    A. ERISA

    B. Sarbanes-Oxley Act

    C. False Claims Act

    D. Privacy Act

PART III

Answers

1. **B.** A gap analysis compares the organizational needs, the employee needs, and the existing set of benefits to determine what the organization's benefits package should and should not include.

2. **C.** It isn't necessary to use a point system to evaluate job content for compensation purposes. Making comparisons of responsibility levels can be done and compensation levels determined based on those comparisons. Lydia should attempt to be consistent in how she makes those comparisons so the compensation decisions will be consistent.

3. **B.** USERRA gives employees on military leave the same seniority-based benefits, including retirement rights, as they would receive if they had not taken leave.

4. **A.** Decreasing an employee's salary is illegal in most countries, particularly in Latin America and Europe. It is legal in the United States.

5. **B.** An employee stock ownership plan (ESOP) is an employee-owner method that provides a company's workforce with an ownership interest in the company. In an ESOP, companies provide their employees with stock ownership, often at no up-front cost to the employees. ESOP shares, however, are part of employees' remuneration for work performed. Shares are allocated to employees and may be held in an ESOP trust until the employee retires or leaves the company. The ESOP can borrow money to buy shares, with the company making tax-deductible contributions to the plan to enable it to repay the loan.

6. **D.** Vesting is the absolute right to an asset that cannot be taken away by any third party, even though one may not yet possess the asset. The portion vested cannot be reclaimed by the employer, nor can it be used to satisfy the employer's debts. Any portion not vested may be forfeited under certain conditions, such as termination of employment.

7. **D.** The Service Contract Act requires contractors and subcontractors performing services on federal prime contracts in excess of $2,500 to pay service employees in various classes no less than the wage rates and fringe benefits found prevailing in the locality where work is performed.

8. **Scanlon**

9. **B.** Determining the audience for communication is the first step. The audience will help inform the content of the communication, timing, and cost.

10. **A, C.** A bonus program helps improve the perception of fairness, equity, and effort, and a recognition program helps improve organizational feedback.

11. **D.** Based on XYZ's past practice of 100 percent commission compensation plans for sales employees, Cecilia would receive straight commission with a draw in her first year of employment. A draw consists of guaranteed commission for a defined period of time. If, during this period, a salesperson does not earn a commission equal to or exceeding the draw, the salesperson does not owe the organization the difference.

12. **B, C.** A benefits gap analysis is intended to review an organization's current benefits offerings and determine what needs are not being met. As such, it is important to review workforce demographics and current plan utilization. A competitor's benefits plan and sick time usage might be helpful to review, but these actions are not part of a benefits gap analysis.

13. **B.** While all the answer options are important for developing a total rewards strategy, a strategic planning session should be the first step to ensure that future total rewards decisions are aligned with the company's goals, mission, and company culture.

14. **A.** Since we know that the company currently pays employees based on their desired salary, there is a potential for discriminating on the basis of sex by paying wages to employees at a rate less than the rate paid to employees of the opposite sex for equal work on jobs requiring equal skill, effort, and responsibility. We do not know if the company is a federal contractor (or subcontractor), so the Service Contract Act may not apply to the company. We also do not have information on the ages of company employees with regard to the Age Discrimination in Employment Act.

15. **Pure localization**

16. **C.** Compa-ratio is calculated using this formula: Pay rate / midpoint; 60,000 / 65,000 = 0.92.

17. **B, D.** Increasing deductibles and requiring generic drugs in prescription plans are common ways to reduce healthcare costs. Health-risk assessment programs and Health Insurance Purchasing Cooperatives (HIPCs) are also common. Implementing an age-risk assessment program sounds like possible discrimination.

18. **D.** There is no industry restriction on ISOs. All of the other answer options are correct.

19. **B, C.** RSUs are received according to a vesting schedule, and a portion is used to pay for income taxes at the time of vesting. Additionally, RSUs are assigned a fair market value when they vest and are considered direct compensation.

20. **B.** The Sarbanes-Oxley Act protects whistle-blowers who expose security violations and also requires administrators of defined contribution plans to provide 30 days' notice of a blackout period.

Endnotes

1. "A Review of Employee Motivation Theories and their Implications for Employee Retention within Organizations," Sunil Ramlall, Ph.D. The Journal of American Academy of Business, Cambridge.

2. "ESOP (Employee Stock Ownership Plan) Facts," The National Center for Employee Ownership (NCEO) (www.esop.org/)

3. "Understanding and Using Long-Term Incentives," William H. Coleman and Keith E. Fortier, CCP, Salary.com, Inc.

4. U.S. Government Publishing Office, Internal Revenue Code 422, https://www.gpo.gov/fdsys/granule/USCODE-2010-title26/USCODE-2010-title26-subtitleA-chap1-subchapD-partII-sec422/content-detail.html

5. "Employee Stock Purchase Plan – ESSPP," www.investopedia.com/

6. "Phantom Stock Plan," www.investopedia.com/

7. "Restricted Stock Unit (RSU)," www.investopedia.com/

8. "Performance Grants," Society for Human Resource Management, 2013 SHRM Learning System, Module 4, Compensation and Benefits, Section 4-4, pp. 4–118

9. "Fiduciary Responsibilities," United States Department of Labor Website, www.dol.gov/, Health Plans and Benefits

10. George Bernard Shaw, Wikiquote.org, https://en.wikiquote.org/wiki/George_Bernard_Shaw

11. "Implementing Total Rewards Strategies," SHRM Foundation's Effective Practice Guidelines Series, https://www.shrm.org/hr-today/trends-and-forecasting/special-reports-and-expert-views/Documents/Implementing-Total-Rewards-Strategies.pdf

Employee Relations and Engagement

Senior HR professionals are ultimately responsible for the organizational strategies that drive employee and labor relations, employee satisfaction, performance management, and risk management. This chapter covers these topics in detail and also builds upon many of the topics covered throughout this book. The Employee Relations and Engagement functional area makes up 20 percent of the Senior Professional in Human Resources (SPHR) exam, but your study plan should include content from Chapter 8 as well.

The official HR Certification Institute (HRCI) Employee Relations and Engagement functional area responsibilities and knowledge statements for the SPHR exam are as follows:

Responsibilities

- Design and evaluate strategies for employee satisfaction (for example, recognition, career path) and performance management (for example, performance evaluation, corrective action, coaching)
- Analyze and evaluate strategies to promote diversity and inclusion
- Evaluate employee safety and security strategies (for example, emergency response plan, building access, data security/privacy)
- Develop and evaluate labor strategies (for example, collective bargaining, grievance program, concerted activity, staying union free, strategically aligning with labor)

Knowledge Of

- Strategies to facilitate positive employee relations
- Methods for assessing employee attitudes, opinions, and satisfaction
- Performance management strategies
- Human relations concepts and applications
- Ethical and professional standards

- Diversity and inclusion concepts and applications
- Occupational injury and illness prevention techniques
- Workplace safety and security risks, and strategies
- Emergency response, business continuity, and disaster recovery strategies
- Internal investigation, monitoring, and surveillance techniques
- Data security and privacy
- The collective bargaining process, strategies, and concepts (for example, contract negotiation, costing, administration)

Employee Relations and Engagement Strategies

When you consider that employees spend approximately 2,000 hours per year at work, more of employees' waking hours are often spent in the workplace than in their homes. For employees to be productive, there needs to be a certain degree of satisfaction. Employee satisfaction results in better employee performance and retention rates. In simpler terms, happy employees perform better and are more likely to stay with an organization long-term. After all, even despite advances in technology, there is still human capital fueling an organization's business success. Products are often not made by hand in this day and age, but there are people developing the technology to make products, running quality assurance tests on the new technology, or marketing the organization's new technology to prospective clients.

Employee satisfaction is dependent upon managing legal obligations and mediating risk. After all, it is unlikely that employees will stay with an organization long-term if claims of harassment, discrimination, or risks to employee health and safety are not managed appropriately. Senior HR professionals are responsible for developing policies and programs to achieve stated employee relations and engagement goals and also determining approaches for managing compliance with these programs across the organization, including the need for corrective action or coaching programs. Employees sometimes mistakenly see this as HR being both the "good cop and bad cop," but the intention is always to meet organizational objectives and ensure employees are being treated fairly.

Ultimately, an employee relations and engagement strategy should be aligned with an organization's mission, vision, and goals. These are the values that define the organization, and they should mirror the values articulated to employees. A strategy should also consider how employee programs will reinforce desired behaviors. If an organization has zero tolerance for errors and employees are terminated for a first infraction of any policy or procedure, there is possibly a problem. While this approach may make sense for policies such as antidiscrimination or antiharassment because of legal obligations and organizational values, the proper amount of training and development needs to be allotted to other areas to best nurture employee success. There is no "one-size-fits-all" strategy. Instead, a good employee relations and engagement strategy should be based upon the following pillars:

- **Federal and state legal requirements**   Meeting legal obligations should always be the first step. The intention of these requirements is to ensure fair and ethical workplace behavior.

- **Past practice**   While state and federal legal requirements may dictate a number of policies and procedures, how the organization has previously handled situations not dictated by law is important. For employees to be treated fairly and equitably, historical situations should be evaluated with care. Enforcement bodies and attorneys are also generally quite interested in how employment decisions align with past practice.

- **Organizational vision, mission, and values**   Employees and the organization are ultimately more successful when they understand and strive for the same metrics of success. For example, a core value of "honesty" may not be relatable to employees if there is not a performance evaluation program founded in honest employee/supervisor feedback or mediums for reporting employee concerns such as an open-door policy or an option for anonymous reporting of serious breaches of organizational policy.

- **Organizational behavior and culture**   What is unique about the organization? Why do employees enjoy working there? How can these unique traits be leveraged to create programs that motivate and retain employees? Regularly monitoring employee feedback helps determine employee programs that are the right "fit" for the organization. Gap areas can also quickly become a major liability if left unaddressed.

Communicating Values and Expectations

Senior HR professionals are responsible not only for contributing to the development of an organization's vision, mission, and values but also for modeling and communicating the required behaviors and expectations to align with these values. Organizational policies are a common way that programs and values are communicated. There are a few steps[1] required to develop a new policy for an organization:

1. **Policy need**   Policies are needed for various reasons. For a growing organization, new policies may be needed to comply with legal obligations for employers above a certain size. Policies are also often created to define required behaviors and expectations. A good clue that a policy is needed is if there is confusion about a certain organizational protocol among employees or a history of inconsistent decision-making in regard to a topic. A policy helps clarify expectations and ensure fairness across the organization. A policy should not be created for every single scenario that occurs in an organization, but to provide direction about common or important topics. If every scenario was documented in a policy, the resulting thousand-page policy manual would be hard for anyone to digest, let alone model the required behaviors in the workplace.

2. Draft the policy When drafting a policy, the goal is to create content that fills the need determined in step 1 using clear and simple language. The goal is for employees to model the behavior communicated in the policy, so using simple language helps make content easier to understand. Policies usually have three sections: a statement of purpose, the policy, and the procedures associated with the policy.

3. Double-check the wording Each word in a policy should be crafted carefully. Saying an employee "may be" or "will be" terminated for doing something are very different. The words used will also have legal implications. For example, if the verbiage "All employees will be terminated for sleeping on the job" is included in a policy and not everyone is terminated for sleeping on the job, anyone terminated for this reason may have cause for a wrongful termination lawsuit.

4. Obtain feedback and support Sometimes organizational policies address a welcome change for employees, and sometimes they do not. If an HR manager learns of regular noncompliance with a particular activity, a new policy may help address the consequences for noncompliance. Previously noncompliant employees may not like that. This is why policies should not be created in a vacuum by HR. It is wise to obtain support and feedback about a policy from supervisors before it is implemented. Supervisors can provide good insight and offer feedback on current operations, employee perceptions, and desired behaviors. This feedback can help improve the policy, and supervisor support can help improve the success of the policy when it is communicated to employees. If supervisors are passionate about a topic, they will do a better job modeling that behavior, and in turn, so will employees.

5. Obtain a legal review In addition to the slew of federal laws we cover in this book, there are various state laws that apply to policies. To double-check that all areas of compliance are covered, it is important to obtain a legal review of a policy before implementation.

6. Communicate the policy For employees to feel engaged, they need to understand the reasons why certain things happen. Communicating a policy should start with the reason behind the policy and the need for it. It is also important to create a form of acknowledgment that employees can sign for major policy changes. This ensures there is documentation that employees have received and read policy changes. If there is ever an issue of noncompliance with a policy, this acknowledgment would be the first document to look for in an employee's file. Before holding someone accountable for noncompliance, there must be assurance that the employee knew about the policy in question.

7. Monitor Policies are in a frequent state of flux. Laws change regularly, as do organizational needs. For this reason, policies should be reviewed at least on an annual basis. Once a policy is implemented, a senior HR professional should also check in with supervisors on a regular basis to see how the policy is being interpreted and carried out. There may be a need to revise certain aspects of the policy if it is not meeting its stated purpose.

In the Trenches

Shaping Culture Through Policy Development

Christina Nishiyama, MBA, SPHR, EVP/Human Resources Consultant

The policy development process is your opportunity to shape the work environment. Gone are the days of the dreaded personnel encyclopedia; make it a map of the culture!

Although this policy mantra is clear to me now, it was not so clear upon my initiation into policy development. On my first day at a new job, in a new industry, I vividly remember walking away from a brief meeting with a 1,000-page collection of reference materials and a daunting number of employment law acronyms scribbled on a notepad.

I began the policy development process with a laser focus on legal compliance and a vast amount of research. Although important, the hours I put in hunched over a computer, assuring that every word was carefully phrased and thoughtfully evaluated, are not what made my experience with policy creation successful. In taking a step back and thinking about how critical a policy manual was, I learned how to draft it not merely as a document that should be read once and strewn aside but as an opportunity to shape the organization's culture.

No two organizations are alike, and whether from a written or administrative perspective, neither are the policies that shape them. For a small organization with mostly exempt staff, an attendance policy may be much less critical than it is for the 800-employee casino across the street. Furthermore, a dress code may not be quite so "standard" across an organization with a technical operation in one state and a retail operation in another.

When granted the opportunity to create policies, it is important to begin the process by evaluating the culture of the organization—what are the mission, vision, and core values? How do staff and department heads view the organization in its current state, and where do they want it to be? Policies serve as a reference for decision-making across the organization. The verbiage you place in a seemingly simple corrective action procedure may change how the entire organization views the training, coaching, and performance management processes.

As you ascertain that each policy is compatible with legal requirements, conduct thoughtful research of policies at comparable organizations, and confirm that all relevant topics are covered in the manual, take your assignment a step further and think about actually implementing each policy in the workplace. Do staff members thrive on immediate recognition? If so, maybe the standard employee-of-the-quarter program is not right for the group. Do staff members

(continued)

struggle with communicating grievances through the right avenues? Think about a way to communicate the grievance procedure in a manner that is relatable to staff and tie it back to your founding principles. Taking the time to thoughtfully research innovative communication practices targeted to the workplace demographic may entirely change the way the policy manual is viewed. Finally, keeping language simple, clear, and easy to follow will make policies a useful resource for both supervisory management and employees to adhere to.

Developing Employee Relations and Engagement Programs

As we learned earlier in this chapter, a primary goal of the Employee Relations and Engagement functional area is to ensure employee satisfaction. A good way to keep employees satisfied with their jobs and the work environment is to develop programs geared toward employee satisfaction. All employee programs should be tied to the core values and the strategic plan of an organization. If they are not, there is a lack of alignment between the stated organizational objectives and the programs actually being communicated to employees. Developing an employee program very similar to developing a policy. To develop an effective employee program, senior HR professionals must do the following:

- Identify the need or reason for the program. Is performance improvement needed in a certain area? Are sexual harassment claims higher than normal?

- Assure the program is aligned with the strategic plan and organizational values. Are we, the organization, "doing as we say"?

- Determine the right timing for the program. For example, having a costly employee picnic a few months after a layoff will likely not be well received.

- Obtain support for the program. Ask supervisors and employees for their thoughts on the program. Not only will this feedback improve the program, but it will create a group to support and champion the change being implemented.

- Communicate the program. Is this program better communicated in person, via e-mail, or on the company intranet? What is the best way to reach the audience and generate engagement for the program?

- Measure program effectiveness. Is the program meeting established goals? Do employees like the program? If not, maybe the program needs to be revamped. We will discuss more specific methods for evaluating program effectiveness later in this chapter.

Diversity and Inclusion Programs

Diversity and inclusion (D&I) programs not only help organizations achieve legal requirements such as equal employment opportunity (EEO) and affirmative action; they help make an organization more effective by employing individuals with diverse backgrounds and experience. Senior HR professionals are generally involved in the development and implementation of D&I programs. According to the Society for Human Resource Management (SHRM), there are several steps associated with creating a D&I program:[2]

- **Step 1: Compile data on current employee demographics** For example, data such as employee age, disability, gender, veteran status, and race can help an organization better understand the diversity of its employees and identify any areas of concern or trends. Some of this information is available in an organization's human resource information system (HRIS), and some may be acquired thorough an anonymous, voluntary, self-identification survey sent to employees.

- **Step 2: Identify needs or areas of concern** Once all the data is collected in step 1, HR can do a review of demographics and determine which areas are underrepresented. Additionally, recent employee opinion survey results may also be used to illustrate areas of concern or weakness for the organization. For example, how employees answer the question "On a scale of 1 to 5, how much does my organization value diversity?" may inform how a D&I program is structured and communicated to employees.

- **Step 3: Address policies or practices affecting diversity** Sometimes, there can be organizational programs that result in poor diversity or underrepresentation by accident. For example, Harvard University launched Project Implicit[3] to spread awareness for *unconscious bias*. Unconscious bias[4] is stereotyping certain groups of people that individuals form outside their own conscious awareness. For example, a manager may have a form of unconscious bias if his or her department is significantly less diverse than other departments. In addition, seemingly harmless activities like political talk at work or certain religious beliefs among management may result in employee selection that is biased toward management's values.

- **Step 4: Identify business objectives and obtain buy-in** To best achieve D&I goals, they need to be embedded into business objectives and aligned with strategic goals. This helps ensure everyone is working toward the same goals. Additionally, the more senior management is involved in a D&I initiative, the more employees will believe the organization is taking the initiative seriously. For example, visibly seeing the CEO of the organization host a career development workshop for veterans shows that the organization is actively focused on veteran career development and workforce representation. Also, it is important to cascade this involvement to all levels of management in an organization. Supervisors should have open and honest conversations with their direct reports about D&I initiatives. D&I goals might even be tied to HR or management performance measurements to encourage participation.

- **Step 5: Implement** Like any policy or program, a plan of implementation should be created that describes what is being implemented, who is responsible, what actions are involved in implementation, and when program implementation is targeted for completion.

PART III

- **Step 6: Communicate the program**   As discussed in previous chapters, the more mediums of communication, the better. A variety of communication options creates opportunity for employees to have multiple touch points for the information and more opportunity for retaining the information.

- **Step 7: Measure outcomes and adjust the program if necessary**   To determine whether a program is actually working, organizations should measure key factors associated with D&I program success. Some examples are increased employee representation of certain groups, better employee opinion survey scores, or employer awards associated with D&I programs. A robust communication plan should also be created to spread awareness for program impacts. If impacts are not reaching expected levels, the program can be adjusted to better meet desired targets.

Recognition Programs

Employee recognition programs are a common way to engage employees and improve retention. Receiving direct praise makes people feel good and generally motivates people to perform at a higher level. Additionally, employee events allow employees to engage outside of the workplace and help improve camaraderie.

One of the challenges with recognition programs is making them effective and valuable to diverse groups of employees. This is because a reward can have different value to different people. For example, an employee of the month prize for a Disneyland vacation has a much different value for employee #1 who does not like amusement parks and employee #2 with three children who love Disneyland. Another example might be hosting an employee event at a water park and failing to realize that many employees are unable to swim or are uncomfortable wearing swim attire in public.

One of the ways organizations have improved the value perception issue is by allowing employees to choose their reward for different programs. For example, employees who achieve a certain milestone for years of service can choose from several different award options out of an online catalog. Additionally, managers who take the extra time to engage in friendly conversation with employees can learn a lot about their values. These managers can use this knowledge to select a reward that may cost the same amount in the budget but be exponentially more valuable to the recipient.

To be certain that a recognition program is achieving its goals, the program should be monitored and measured. Program success can be measured through employee feedback, employee performance, and whether a program positively or negatively affects employee conduct. For example, some organizations have stopped sponsoring holiday parties because the relaxed atmosphere and libations result in too many reported claims of misconduct.

Career Path Programs

Early in the twentieth century, employees spent most of their career in the same organization. Various economic factors over the years such as a decline in unionization, economic downturns, and a desire for more flexibility in the workplace have resulted in individuals changing jobs multiple times in their career. Career path programs keep high-performing employees from leaving the organization by increasing engagement and loyalty.

Senior HR professionals are responsible for developing career path programs and implementing related programs that support them. Various types of career path programs are covered in detail in Chapter 6, but supporting programs to consider are formal opportunities for employee/supervisor feedback that is focused on career goals, an employee skill set and career goals database in the HRIS system, development plans for employees interested in promotion, or even a "goals coach" for employees to support personal and professional goals (from running a half-marathon to becoming a manager).

Performance Evaluation

Performance evaluation is one of the primary mechanisms for feedback between supervisors and employees. Chapter 6 shared different types of performance evaluation and the advantages and disadvantages of each. Regardless of the program selected, senior HR professionals are responsible for spearheading the performance evaluation program for an employer's organization. These programs require a great deal of HR oversight because there is potential for legal risk as a result of poorly worded evaluations or rating bias. HR can help ensure the actions carried out by supervisors as a result of the program actually improve organizational effectiveness.

To effectively develop and manage a performance evaluation program, the following should be considered:

- A performance evaluation should effectively measure job duties and responsibilities and relate to core values. Otherwise, it is not a valid or effective tool. Performance metrics should ultimately relate to the factors that make the organization successful.

- Supervisors responsible for rating employee performance should be trained on appropriate verbal and written commentary to use during employee performance conversations. Performance ratings should never come as a shock to an employee. If so, this means the supervisor has likely not provided enough feedback prior to the evaluation or did not effectively share it in the performance evaluation meeting.

- Employees being reviewed should be encouraged to engage in the process so there is effective two-way feedback between supervisor and employee. Initiating employee engagement through a self-evaluation on the same performance metrics is a common way to do this.

- HR should review performance evaluations prior to presenting them to employees and analyze overall evaluation scores to determine whether any bias exists. This review helps avoid legal pitfalls and can be a helpful coaching opportunity between HR and supervisors.

Corrective Action and Coaching

Corrective action and coaching are different tools for managing employee performance. It depends on the person, but negative feedback can be difficult for some employees to process. Although it is necessary to keep employee performance aligned to expectations, negative feedback can result in decreased morale and performance if not handled appropriately.

Often supervisors are responsible for issuing corrective action to employees, and senior HR professionals play an important role as an organizational coach with respect to this process. There are several ways senior HR professionals can support this process:

- HR should be a respected advisor within the management team. HR can build that level of trust by checking in with supervisors on a regular basis and assisting with operational challenges that arise. After all, most operational challenges almost always involve people.

- Supervisors should be encouraged to build trust with employees from the start. Employees are more likely to respond positively to negative feedback from someone they trust.

- Regular feedback between supervisors and employees should be encouraged. The more irregular the feedback, the more likely the employee will be shocked or frustrated by it.

- Negative feedback should be timely. While it can be uncomfortable for some supervisors to deliver negative feedback, if it is not timely, it is not as effective in improving behavior. From parenting to psychology, this is a phenomenon widely observed and studied.

- The supervisor should remove himself or herself from the situation personally before reacting. This is where HR can serve as a good counselor, allowing a supervisor to share the details of the situation with HR first. When caught in the moment, it is easy for anyone to overact and say something inappropriate.

- The supervisor should participate in the performance improvement process after the conversation has happened. The supervisor is almost always the main source of support for improving performance. He or she should set time aside to check in with the employee and offer positive reinforcement for improvements that are made.

Methods for Assessing and Monitoring Employee Programs

Any organizational change, large or small, can affect employee opinions. Regularly assessing and monitoring employee attitudes and opinions helps an organization understand its workforce and make the right decisions to improve employee satisfaction.

A common tool for measuring employee satisfaction is an employee opinion survey. Chapter 8 can provide a refresher on this tool. There are also other tools for measuring the effectiveness of employee relations and engagement. Here are a few examples:

- **Values alignment** Are employees required to identify their job's core values during their first 90 days of employment? Is so, how well do employees perform on this task? Are core values tied to recognition programs? If so, how many employees receive awards for each respective core value? Which core value is least represented and why?

- **Employee complaints**   How many internal complaints are there this calendar year versus last calendar year? How long does it take to respond to internal complaints? How many cases are resolved each month? How many complaints require HR intervention, and how many do not? Less HR intervention may mean supervisors have become more skilled at dealing with employee issues.

- **Organizational communication**   How many times per week do supervisors have formal opportunities to communicate with their teams? How many times per month does senior management communicate with employees? How effective are these meetings? Consider asking employees for their opinion at the close of the meeting on an anonymous survey. Does each meeting agenda include a stated objective? Has that objective been met by the end of the meeting?

- **Performance evaluation**   What are average performance evaluation scores within the organization and within each department? What are the greatest areas of strength and weakness?

- **Corrective action**   How many employees are placed on performance improvement plans each year? How many employees successfully complete performance improvement plans each year? What policy violations most frequently result in corrective action within the organization and within each department?

Risk Management Program Strategy

Safety programs are mandated by the government and are a compliance requirement. However, a broader risk management strategy includes topics such as safety, security, employer liability insurance plans, and the general management of risk at the organization. A portion of the risk management strategy is dictated by compliance requirements and a portion by the organization's philosophy about risk. Chapter 9 can provide a refresher on the philosophies of risk avoidance, risk mitigation, and acceptance.

Depending on the risk strategy chosen, policies and procedures should align with that decision. For example, a risk avoidance strategy would include the most risk-averse policies and procedures, more robust distinctions in regard to building access, regular communication of safety hazards, and strict disciplinary procedures for safety or security violations. As long as compliance requirements are met, the key for employers is determining which programs are best for the organization and effectively managing the unique risks that may be present.

Risk Management Program Evaluation

Evaluating a risk management program's success ultimately comes down to whether a program makes sense for the organization and an analysis of the value the program provides. Mitigating and insuring against risk generally does not translate to profit on an organization's income statement, but it provides tremendous value in the event of a catastrophe. Quantifying this value is not always easy. Organizations often ask questions like the following to measure the success of a risk management program.[5]

- Is the safety or security program fully compliant? When was the last time a review of the program was completed by an outside consultant?

- Do the outcomes of the risk management plan match the objectives? Are employees using safety equipment? Is there a related decrease in accidents?

- What safety and security problems have occurred in the organization in the past year? Does the risk management plan effectively address these problems? If not, how should the plan be changed to address problems?

- What safety and security problems more commonly occur nationally or even globally? Is the organization prepared for those potential risks? For example, active shooter training is much more prevalent in organizations than it was 10 years ago.

- Are all activities in the plan effective? For example, is the emergency response plan thorough enough? Are there steps missing? Are any roles or responsibilities in the plan assigned to employees who no longer work for the organization? Are there any new roles that should be developed?

- Are there any key organizational factors that affect the plan's effectiveness? For example, are employees involved in less hazardous activities because of a change in business philosophy? Does this result in a change to safety policies?

- Is there a lack of clarity regarding certain policies in the organization? Is more training or communication needed? Does the policy need to be more detailed?

- Are insurance plans appropriate? Have employee responsibilities changed enough to result in an overall decrease in the cost of the workers' compensation plan? Did the organization's headquarters move to an area less prone to environmental hazards? Does this change make it appropriate to review or change aspects of the general liability coverage in relation to natural disasters or flooding risks?

Developing and Implementing Strategies to Maintain a Union-Free Environment

In the "old days," even before there were HR departments, there were labor departments in larger employment organizations. Remember that the first half of the twentieth century was a boom time for labor unions in the United States. Employers who didn't have union-represented workers often wanted to maintain their union-free environments. The process of gaining representation in a workforce is a strict legal process. Therefore, labor-management attorneys and law firms are often involved in guiding employers through the election process and negotiating contracts with successful unions. When employers want to prevent a union from gaining employee approval for representation, they often call on their labor attorneys for help. Senior HR professionals are also involved in this process.

NLRB Procedures for Recognizing a Union

Among other responsibilities, the National Labor Relations Board (NLRB) is responsible for supervising union elections under the National Labor Relations Act (NLRA), both in the United States and internationally. The NLRB has formal procedures for union recognition.

1. The NLRB receives a petition from a labor organization for specific bargaining unit certification. The union petition must demonstrate a "show of interest" from at least 30 percent of employees to organize into a collective bargaining unit. This show of interest is usually in the form of authorization cards the union asks employees to sign saying they would like that union to represent them.

2. If accepted by the NLRB, the employer may consent by voluntary agreement or request a hearing and election.

3. The NLRB conducts a hearing to determine the legitimacy of the election request. It determines the scope of the voting unit and whether that is a reasonable and appropriate group for collective bargaining. A *bargaining* unit is an employee group that shares a community of interest. Factors impacting that community of interest can include the following:

   - Common supervision

   - Similar wages, benefits, and working conditions

   - Similarity of skills

   - Business operations in common

   Each side (employer and union) may call or subpoena witnesses to testify during the hearing.

4. Next comes a pre-election campaign by the union and employer. A period of 25 to 30 days is normally allowed after the hearing decision for each side to try to convince employees of its viewpoint. The employer must provide to the NLRB an alphabetized list of employee names and home addresses who will be eligible to vote in the election. The agency will forward that list to the union so it can contact employees if it chooses to do so. That list is called an "Excelsior List" based on the NLRB case that first required employers to offer it. Employers may actively campaign against union representation, even using company time and facilities to do so. Employers are not required to provide union representatives with an opportunity to attend those sessions, nor even access to company property to refute these employer meeting presentations. All campaigning must end at least 24 hours prior to the election date as required by the NLRB 24-hour rule.

5. "Blocking charges" can be filed by either side. Charges of unfair labor practices can be filed with the NLRB by either the union or the employer. The pre-election process will be suspended while NLRB investigates and rules on the charges. Once charges are resolved, the pre-election campaign clock can begin ticking again.

6. The NLRB conducts the election. All managers and supervisors must stay away from the location where voting takes place on election day. They are not permitted to intimidate employees during the election process. People permitted at the voting location include the NLRB agent conducting the election, employee voters, one or more nonsupervisory observers chosen by the employer, and the same number of observers chosen by the union. Only employees who are determined to be in jobs within the bargaining unit are eligible to vote.

7. The union is elected to represent the bargaining unit or it is not (union election requires 50 percent plus 1 vote). The NLRB counts the votes and makes its announcement about the outcome.

Employer Reactions to Union-Organizing Efforts

Union-organizing efforts result in an array of different reactions from employers, from immediate acceptance to obstinate resistance, and everything in between. Three of the most common employer reactions to union representation are the following:

- **Voluntary agreement** Employers may agree voluntarily to recognize a union without a formal NLRB election. The union must still show that a majority of employees want to be represented by that union. Voluntary agreements are sometimes called *neutrality agreements,* where employers agree to remain neutral during the union campaign, even permitting union organizers access to employees and opportunity to address groups of workers. *Card check* is a process where a majority of employees in the bargaining unit sign a card saying they want representation from the specific union and the employer accepts that without an election.

- **Acceptance because of a requirement under the successorship doctrine** If an employer merges or acquires another employer and assumes the former union-represented workforce, it can be required to accept the union representation and its contract with the former employer.

- **Opposition to union-organizing efforts** Includes such actions as employee meetings, suggestion boxes, dispute resolution policies and procedures, exit interviews, open-door policies, and other employee-involvement programs. The key to any employer success is the proper training of managers and supervisors. There are two training objectives for supervisors: (1) instructions for prevention of unfair labor practices and (2) reinforcement of policies and procedures for employee communication of all types.

Decertification or Deauthorization of a Union

NLRB rules give new unions a full year before they are subject to decertification efforts. Once past that year, any union can be decertified if the proper procedures are followed.

What's the Difference?

Decertification of a union Removal of the union as the exclusive bargaining representative of the employees.

Deauthorization of a union Removal of "union security" (forced unionism clause) from the contract. The union remains as the exclusive bargaining representative and the collective bargaining agreement remains in effect, but employees are not forced to be members or pay dues to the union.

Decertification begins with at least 30 percent of the employees within the bargaining unit signing cards or a petition asking that the NLRB conduct an election to remove the union. (There can be additional restrictions during the first three years of a contract existence, particularly in the healthcare industry.) A majority of votes will determine whether the union stays or goes.

Common Employee Relations Strategies

Employees who feel they are well treated and included in what is happening in the workplace are not very likely to seek out union representation. Inversely, those workplaces where employees are feeling mistreated have a higher chance of seeing workers attempting to gain union representation. Unions are seen as a tool to force management to conform to certain rules of employee treatment. Preventing unions from gaining a foothold in the workplace can be accomplished by keeping the workplace satisfied with working conditions.

The following are strategies for preventing unionization efforts in the workplace:

- **Thorough management training in management skills** There is a mistaken belief that promoting someone to a management position will automatically result in their understanding all that is necessary for their success in the new role. Management depends on the successful use of a specific skill set. Included in that group of skills are leadership skills, communication skills, decision-making skills, perception skills, team-building skills, and more.

- **Thorough management training on organizational policies and disciplinary procedures** Consistency of treatment is critical for employees to believe they are getting a "fair shake." Once they begin believing they are being mistreated, all is lost.

- **Training managers and supervisors to recognize the signs that employees are starting to think about pursuing union organization in your workplace** Early detection is necessary for a successful effort at preventing the union's success. Signals are different depending on the employer, but an increase in uncharacteristic behavior and activity, such as employees gathering in unusual places to discuss topics privately, inquiries about employee benefits or company policies that is more extensive than usual, or strangers and former employees spending more time around the work site, may be telltale signs.

- **Monitoring employee benefit programs**   Monitor benefit programs such as vacations, medical insurance, retirement programs, and other policies to be sure that employees are receiving benefits comparable to what they would get if they worked for similar employer organizations elsewhere.

- **Monitoring employee attitudes constantly**   Use focus groups, employee surveys, and management discussions to help monitor how employees are feeling about their work environment and their treatment. When problems are detected, take action to resolve them.

- **Encouraging employees to present their complaints and irritations to their managers or to human resources officials**   This type of employee communication enables managers and HR officials to investigate and resolve issues. The time spent on such efforts will likely result in significant savings of time later.

Prevention of employee relations problems depends on strong and open communication channels within the organization. Successful organizations encourage employees to present their complaints so they can be addressed before they reach the level of a formal complaint or legal issue. Once a complaint goes outside the organization to an enforcement agency or court, the costs to an employer will escalate exponentially. It makes good business sense, and is substantially cheaper, to handle employee complaints internally. And the sooner the better. Left to fester, employee complaints can cause thoughts of union organizing and worse.

Identifying and Addressing Union Interests in Your Workplace

When a union shows interest in organizing, they won't come to the door and announce that fact. Identifying union interests requires alertness to what is going on with employees. It may be that union organizers are seeking employment so they will have access to other workers and can "talk up" advantages of union membership and representation. Union organizers may also take up positions at the front door to talk with employees as they come and go from work facilities. It may be that the union is handing out flyers or informational packets to employees in the parking lot. Staying alert helps detect these initial signs of union organizing.

Unions will "play up" their ability to act on behalf of employees who are being treated unfairly. They can emphasize their ability to structure overtime practices and take away the pain employees are feeling because of unfairly assigned work schedules. Whether or not these things are true, the union will attempt to get workers to believe that problems (true or imagined) can be solved by getting a union to represent them. Union-organizing efforts can involve unpleasant and distasteful claims by organizers. They can also test the employer's resolve to maintain order in the workplace.

If there is one key issue being pushed by union organizers, addressing that issue can take away the reason for the union to succeed in the organization. For example, if work schedules are assigned based on a first-come claim to the most desirable schedules, changing to assignment based on seniority could dull the point of union organizers' efforts.

There are law firms in the country that specialize in helping employers work their way through the process of resisting union-organizing efforts. If you experience such union efforts and would rather not have a union represent your employees, contacting one of these law firms might be a good business decision.

In the Trenches

HR Prevention: More Effective and Less Expensive Than Union Avoidance
Jim Foord, SPHR

Anyone attending a regional or national HR conference has undoubtedly been bombarded with the ever-increasing negative sentiment toward unions. It is, therefore, no surprise that the law firms and consultants that work with organizations to assist them in staying union free have become big business—so big, in fact, that the industry now has its own designation: *union avoidance.*

It is my opinion that HR's adversarial posture toward unions is not going to help it accomplish a key organizational goal: retaining a union-free workplace. In fact, I posit that organizations focused on avoiding unions are more likely to see a union form in their workplace. For it is not unions that make cultures bad; it is poor leadership that leads to bad cultures, which are a potent breeding ground for union organizing.

The basis for this argument is fairly simple. By focusing on keeping unions out, HR is probably not doing the basic HR work that, if done in a timely fashion, would naturally keep them union free. The old adage that an ounce of prevention is worth a pound of cure is spot on here. Unfortunately, many organizations wait until their workplace is in such disarray that workers are motivated to look elsewhere for remedies that should be coming from within, and it is this waiting that the union avoidance industry is poised to leverage.

We need to focus on the work of ensuring that our workplaces are keeping pace with the needs of today's workers. As a society we have fought hard to keep our economy as efficient and "free" as possible. Think, then, of the work of staying union free as a free market opportunity, an opportunity to develop and maintain a workplace where the workers have no desire to seek outside assistance. Instead of spending our valuable time and resources on a "pound of cure" type of solution provided by the union avoidance industry, let's redirect our efforts internally. These "preventive" internal efforts are bound to be in better alignment with our organization's strategic goals, and they also cost less to implement. They provide a much better value in the long run.

Recognizing Union-Organizing Efforts

Unions commonly request that employers accept the result of the show of interest cards without a formal election. That can represent a showing of anything over 30 percent of employees. Called *card checks,* these are shortcut recognition requests.

Another common tactic used by unions is known as *salting.*[6] It can take several forms:

- **Salting union members without identifying them as union members**   After they are hired, they usually violate employer policies until they are terminated, upon which the union files unfair labor practice charges against the employer.

- **Salting using union members wearing union clothing or other identifiers**   If the individuals are not hired, the union files unfair labor practice charges against the employer.

Unions will also demand to use employer facilities to address groups of workers during work time. They will try to get employer agreement to access employees while they are at work. It is simpler for them than having to contact each individual at their home. Employers have no obligation to permit union access to the organization's property or to provide even non-work-time access to employees at work.

Strategies for Maintaining a Union-Free Environment

Senior HR professionals are a key link in the chain an organization can forge to prevent union organizations from making inroads into the employer's group. Here are some key action steps that can help prevent a successful union-organizing campaign:

- **Maintain a written policy**   Explain why you want to remain union-free. Explain the advantages already provided by the company and that there are no additional advantages a union could provide.

- **Provide thorough communication**   Use employee meetings, newsletters, e-mails, and webinars to provide information to employees on a regular basis. Let them know what the company is doing and where it is headed. Keep employees up-to-date on the latest sales successes, and spotlight key people who are good performers. Offer an equally wide spectrum of ways employees can provide the employer with feedback. Those should include employee surveys, supervisor and management access, and written feedback systems. Publish survey results and explain what actions will be taken to follow up on those results. Use skip-level interviews to reach employee groups directly, soliciting their feedback about current conditions and key issues. Again, take action on the input received, particularly if there are problems to be addressed.

- **Be honest**   Always respond with honesty. If you can't comment on a particular issue, that can be acceptable to employees. If you lie to them, they will know it, and your case for a union-free environment will be substantially weakened.

Chapter Review

This chapter focused on HR responsibilities associated with the strategy, development, and monitoring of employee programs. Taking the time to thoughtfully plan the strategy and development phase of programs is a helpful exercise that creates better program alignment with core values, happier employees, and less risk of unionization in the workplace. This chapter started with a review of employee relations and engagement strategies, key programs targeted to employee satisfaction and performance management, and suggestions for evaluating program effectiveness. Risk management program effectiveness was also addressed. Remember, there is no "one-size-fits-all" employee relations, employee engagement, or risk management strategy. After meeting compliance requirements, programs should be targeted to an organization's needs. Lastly, the chapter covered labor relations, union avoidance, and strategies to manage union representation in the workplace.

Questions

1. Dabney is the HR manager negotiating a renewal of the contract his organization has with an international union. Because the union is international, he isn't sure if the National Labor Relations Act applies to his situation. What would you tell him?

   A. He's right to be concerned. It is the International Labor Relations Act (ILRA) that governs his situation with the union.

   B. When the union is an international organization, it can choose between the governance of the ILRA and the NLRA.

   C. The NLRA governs all union interactions regardless of the union's scope of involvement.

   D. If Dabney's organization is negotiating in good faith, there is no law that will tell him what to do. Only if he isn't willing to negotiate will the NLRA take effect.

2. If a union's collective bargaining agreement remains in effect but employees are not forced to be members or pay dues to the union, the union has been
_____.

3. Gwen has just been promoted to HR manager and has no background in that area of the business. She has always been in engineering. Her boss wants her to establish an employee-management committee that he can chair. How would you advise Gwen under those circumstances?

   A. Gwen should explain to her boss that the NLRB has ruled such committees to be in violation of the law if management controls them.

   B. There is nothing wrong with an employee-management committee as long as it has representation from both management and nonmanagement.

   C. Employee-management committees are legal only in organizations that have no union representation.

   D. When employees participate in management, they must be paid a differential to compensate for the higher-level responsibilities they are taking on.

4. Naji is wondering how he is going to describe the difference between his organization's employee grievance resolution process and the discrimination complaint–handling process. What would you suggest?

   A. There isn't any difference between them. The processes for handling them is the same.

   B. Employee grievances are often regarding workplace rules and work assignment processes. Discrimination complaints have more to do with equal employment opportunity issues.

   C. Grievances happen only in union-represented organizations, so Naji doesn't have to worry about that. He still has to explain how discrimination complaints can be handled in his organization.

   D. Handling grievances is not required by law, but handling discrimination complaints is a legal requirement under federal law.

5. When Lloyd was told that he couldn't take a personal leave of absence, he said to the HR manager that his boss was being unfair. Lloyd wants to file a complaint of discrimination because he is being treated unfairly. As the HR manager, what would you tell Lloyd?

   A. His boss has never made an unfair decision in his time with the company. It is unlikely he would be unfair in this situation.

   B. There can be discrimination only if someone else was given a leave of absence who was a different race than Lloyd.

   C. You will speak with Lloyd's boss to find out why the leave of absence was denied, and you will get back to Lloyd with some feedback about the reasons why.

   D. Fairness is not a protected or guaranteed outcome of every employment decision. Lloyd should just accept the decision and make other plans.

Questions 6 and 7 apply to the following scenario:

Charlene is the HR manager for her company. She opens her mail one day and finds a letter from the Equal Employment Opportunity Commission (EEOC) saying one of the company's employees has filed a charge of illegal discrimination.

6. How seriously should Charlene take this letter?

   A. This is a serious issue. Charlene should investigate the charge.

   B. This is a serious issue. Charlene has 90 days in which to get her response together.

   C. This is not serious. These things happen all the time. Charlene can talk it over with the complaining employee and try to get it resolved.

   D. This is not serious. There isn't much the EEOC can do even if the complaint has some merit. Charlene can set it aside and deal with it later when she gets time.

7. What should Charlene do before responding to the EEOC?

A. Go to the employee who filed the complaint and ask why.

B. Notify the employee's supervisor and explain that he or she cannot discuss the complaint with the employee. Conduct an investigation without talking to the complaining employee. Collect documentation that pertains to the complaint. Write the employer's rationale for the decisions and actions taken that resulted in the complaint.

C. Notify the employee that the notice of complaint was received and explain that we will be investigating to identify what happened and how to respond. Tell the employee she wants to schedule an interview to discuss what happened and what can be done to remedy the situation.

D. Tell the supervisor that she will have to explain this to the CEO and the senior legal counsel. Once they are aware of the complaint, she will get back to the supervisor with their reaction.

8. Which of the following two options are methods for assessing employee relations and employee engagement programs?

A. Volume of employee complaints

B. Total participation in a diversity and inclusion program

C. Annual cost of health benefits

D. Total number of employees requesting overtime

9. Mia has only been an HR manager for six months. She has been told by other HR professionals that she should have a policy that requires employees to go through arbitration rather than permit lawsuits. What should she do, if anything?

A. First, Mia should speak with her legal advisors to determine whether mediation or arbitration would fit into their employment culture. Not every employer is well suited to requiring all employees to use arbitration for the resolution of disputes in the workplace.

B. Mia should draft a new policy statement that can be forwarded to senior management for its approval. It should take advantage of mandatory arbitration to prevent the cost of employee lawsuits.

C. Never should a policy be drafted that doesn't already have the approval of senior management. A discussion about changing employee requirements related to dispute resolution should take place, and then a new policy should be drafted and implemented.

D. Once everyone in the organization understands the concept of mandatory arbitration and what it will cost each participant, the employer can proceed with a policy requiring it as the dispute resolution method to be used.

10. When Jacob's company experienced its first union-organizing effort, the union won the election, and Jacob was faced with having to negotiate his first union contract. Because it was his first time, what would you recommend Jacob do?

   A. He should be all right if he gets a copy of another contract to use as a model and then sticks to that language.

   B. Jacob would be well advised to invite his labor relations attorney to participate in the negotiation process. He will need advice at each stage of the process to be sure he makes only wise commitments for the employer.

   C. Jacob should turn the negotiations over to the labor attorney. He can do all the negotiating, and Jacob doesn't even have to be involved.

   D. Once the union provides its demands, the only thing Jacob needs to do is explain to the union what can be done and what can't be done.

11. Isabella is sitting at her desk in the HR department on the first day of a union strike. Picketers have assembled at the front gate and are blocking the sidewalk and not allowing anyone to enter the employer's property. As the HR manager, what should Isabella do?

   A. There is nothing she can do. The union has a right to picket outside the employer's gate. People will just have to wait for a break in the picket line so they can cross over and go to work.

   B. She can go out to talk with the picketers and ask them to allow people to cross over into work. She can also explain to the picketers that she will call the police if they continue to block public access to the employer's property. She should tell them she will get a restraining order if they don't open things up for people to move into the property.

   C. Without even talking with the picketers, she should call the police. There is no way they should be permitted to prevent people from entering the workplace.

   D. Isabella should fight fire with fire. She should organize a few management people with signs protesting the union blocking their entrance to the property and picket inside the gate. Their demonstration can counter any effect the union pickets might have.

12. Alex insists on taking all calls requesting employment verification for former employees. As the HR manager, he refuses to give any feedback about people who were poor performers, but for those who were good performers, he is willing to explain how well they had done. What do you think of Alex's approach to employee references?

   A. It sounds good. There should be no problem since he isn't saying anything bad about anyone.

   B. He should never give out any information about any former employee, good or bad.

    C. His approach to references will develop a reputation for the employer, and other employers will soon be able to know whether someone was a bad performer simply because Alex doesn't give them any feedback about performance. That in itself could constitute a poor reference and be cause for some upset among former employees. His approach is a risky one that could bring liability to the employer.

    D. Only if a former employee signs a release of liability should Alex give out information about poor performers.

13. What is the difference between corrective action and coaching?

    A. They are different steps in the disciplinary action process. Generally, corrective action is a first attempt to correct performance. Coaching involves more formal documentation if previous corrective action has been unsuccessful.

    B. Corrective action is for policy violations, and coaching is for performance issues.

    C. Corrective action applies only to the private sector. The public sector is required by law to use the term *coaching*.

    D. They are different steps in the disciplinary action process. Generally, coaching is a first attempt to correct performance. Corrective action involves more formal documentation if previous coaching has been unsuccessful.

14. _____ _____ are stereotypes about certain groups of people that individuals form outside their own conscious awareness.

15. Emilio has been tasked with developing a recognition program for his organization. What steps should he take to develop and implement the program?

    A. Review best practices in his organization's industry, draft the program, obtain management approval, communicate, and implement the program.

    B. Review recent organization-wide employee opinion survey responses, determine gap areas, draft the program, obtain management approval, communicate, and implement the program.

    C. Conduct a focus group in one department to find out what type of employee recognition program is valuable, and test the recognition program in that department. If it is successful, roll it out to the entire organization.

    D. Review the HRIS data of employee ages to determine what generations in the workplace are most prevalent, review published data about employee recognition programs and generations in the workplace, and develop and implement the most appropriate program based on the data.

16. Dora just completed performance evaluations for 10 direct reports. What should Dora do before she presents the performance evaluations to her direct reports?

   A. Ask her direct reports to complete self-evaluations, share her evaluations with HR for review, and review her performance ratings line by line with each direct report.

   B. Review her evaluations to be sure there is no rating bias, review her performance ratings line by line with each direct report, and mutually develop professional goals at the end of each meeting.

   C. Ask her direct reports to complete self-evaluations, share her evaluations with HR for review, and engage in two-way feedback with each direct report about the self-evaluation and supervisor ratings, mutually developing professional goals at the end of the meeting.

   D. Ask her direct reports to complete self-evaluations, share her evaluations with HR for review, and engage in conversation with each direct report, mutually developing personal and professional goals at the end of the meeting.

17. Christine is the HR manager at a supermarket that experienced vandalism. The police were nearby and caught the individuals engaged in vandalism. Christine learned that several former employees were involved. What should Christine do next?

   A. The vandalism is a safety risk. Contact the insurance carrier, file a claim, and begin repairing the area.

   B. Christine should write a new policy prohibiting vandalism and share it with all employees.

   C. If former employees are disgruntled, all employees might be disgruntled. Conduct an employee opinion survey.

   D. This demonstrates the start of a union-organizing attempt. Immediately hire a labor attorney.

18. Which of the following is *not* a factor that defines a bargaining unit?

   A. Common supervision

   B. Similarity of skills

   C. Similar values

   D. Business operations in common

19. When Ophelia had her weekend automobile accident, everyone in the office rushed to show her support. Now that she is confined to a wheelchair, she is asking her employer to support her by giving her a job accommodation so she can still do her job as the scheduling clerk. What should her employer do?

   A. They should listen politely and take her written request. There isn't anything they really have to do about an accommodation because it doesn't involve a workplace injury.

B. They should listen politely and take her written request. They should investigate other possible accommodations and give her some suggestions if those might be better than what she requested.

C. They should listen politely and take her written request. It is just a matter of time before they will have to approve the request because of the ADA requirements.

D. Because Ophelia is a member of the union that represents office workers, the contract will contain a specification explaining whether anyone in the workplace will be given a job accommodation and under what conditions.

20. _____ _____ is a process where a majority of employees in the bargaining unit sign a card saying they want representation from the specific union and the employer accepts that without an election.

Answers

1. C. The National Labor Relations Act has effect regardless of how large the union or employer may be. The key is that operations take place in the United States.

2. Deauthorized

3. A. Gwen should offer her boss the insight of *NLRB v. Electromation, Inc.* It prohibits employee-management committees that are controlled by management.

4. B. Labor relations issues are usually handled by grievance procedures, whereas discrimination complaints are considered EEO issues.

5. C. There may be a misunderstanding between Lloyd and his boss. You should speak with the boss to determine what the business reasons were for the decision to deny Lloyd's request. Feedback to Lloyd is critical to complete the communication.

6. A. The EEOC is a civil rights enforcement agency, so it is a serious matter. Charlene has 30 days to get her written response to the commission.

7. B. Once a formal complaint has been filed with the EEOC, an employer is prohibited from discussing it with the complaining employee. The employer will have to conduct its investigation without the benefit of the employee's input. That's why it is much better to handle complaints internally so everyone involved can participate in the investigation.

8. A, B. The volume of employee complaints can measure how well employee relations programs are operating, and total participation in D&I programs can provide insight on employee engagement. The annual cost of health benefits and total number of employees requesting overtime are helpful measurements but are not the best approaches for measuring these programs.

9. A. An examination of the pros and cons for mandatory arbitration should be made, and it should be reviewed with legal counsel before moving forward with a policy change. Not all employers will find that mediation or arbitration are the best methods for resolving conflicts in the workplace.

10. **B.** It is always a good idea to have a labor attorney involved with the negotiation process, but Jacob needs to be involved in the details so he can assign costs to each provision of the union requests. The bottom line is that there is always a budget constraint to be considered in the negotiation process. But Jacob doesn't want to make agreements that aren't required either. Paying for the attorney to participate is a wise decision.

11. **B.** Local and state laws will usually govern property rights and whether it is permissible to block entrance to private property. Law enforcement officials can be helpful to ensure access rights are not trammeled during a strike. If necessary, seeking a restraining order against the union may be necessary.

12. **C.** Providing references only about good performers will create a reputation that no reference means a bad reference. That could bring liability. It is best to provide references either for everyone or not for anyone. Your legal advisor can provide guidance.

13. **D.** Coaching is sometimes referred to as a verbal warning or counseling session in an attempt to correct workplace issues before they escalate into more formal corrective action.

14. **Unconscious bias**

15. **B.** While all of the options presented may be possible ways to achieve this task, B is the best answer. Employee opinion survey responses will be most applicable to the organization's needs. Also, some answer choices do not mention important steps such as determining gap areas, obtaining management approval, and communicating the program.

16. **C.** Ensuring HR has reviewed evaluations, engaging in two-way feedback, and mutually developing professional goals are best practices in the performance evaluation process. Performance evaluation meetings are not the most appropriate time to develop personal goals, since the conversation is focused on job performance.

17. **A.** Safety risks should always be considered first. Former employees may be disgruntled because of being involuntarily terminated. Current employees may not necessarily feel the same way.

18. **C.** Although it may make negotiations easier, having similar values is not a requirement of a bargaining unit. Similar wages, benefits, and working conditions make up the fourth requirement.

19. **B.** The interactive process requires employers to determine whether there might be other ways to accommodate the needs of their employee. Discussing those other possibilities will come next in the process.

20. **Card check**

Endnotes

1. How to Develop and Implement a New Company Policy, Society for Human Resource Management, https://www.shrm.org/resourcesandtools/tools-and-samples/how-to-guides/pages/howtodevelopandimplementanewcompanypolicy.aspx.

2. How to Develop a Diversity and Inclusion Initiative, Society for Human Resource Management, https://www.shrm.org/resourcesandtools/tools-and-samples/how-to-guides/pages/how-to-develop-a-diversity-and-inclusion-initiative.aspx.

3. Project Implicit, Harvard University, https://implicit.harvard.edu/implicit/.

4. Definition of unconscious bias, University of California San Francisco Office of Diversity and Inclusion, https://diversity.ucsf.edu/resources/unconscious-bias.

5. Evaluation of a Risk Management Plan, Management Study Guide, https://www.managementstudyguide.com/evaluation-of-risk-management-plan.htm.

6. NLRB Decisions: *Toering Electric Company*, September 29, 2007; *Oil Capitol Sheet Metal, Inc.*, May 31, 2007; *KenMor Electric Company, Inc.*, August 27, 2010. U.S. Supreme Court Decision: *NLRB vs. Town & Country Electric, Inc.*, 516 U.S. 85, 1995.

PART IV

Appendixes

List of Common HR Acronyms

AAP Affirmative Action Plan
ACA Patient Protection and Affordable Care Act (*see also* PPACA)
ADA Americans with Disabilities Act
ADAAA Americans with Disabilities Act Amendments Act
ADEA Age Discrimination in Employment Act
ADR Alternative Dispute Resolution
AFL-CIO American Federation of Labor and Congress of Industrial Organizations
AI Appreciative Inquiry
AIDS Acquired Immune Deficiency Syndrome
ALJ Administrative Law Judge
ANSI American National Standards Institute
AP Accounts Payable
APA American Psychological Association
aPHR Associate Professional in Human Resources
AR Accounts Receivable
ARRA American Recovery and Reinvestment Act
ASO Administrative Services Only Plan
B2B Business to Business
B2C Business to Consumer
BARS Behaviorally Anchored Rating Scale
BCP Business Continuity Plan
BFOQ Bona Fide Occupational Qualification
BLS Bureau of Labor Statistics
CBA Collective Bargaining Agreement
CBP Cafeteria Benefit Plan
CDC Centers for Disease Control
CEO Chief Executive Officer
CFO Chief Financial Officer
CFR Code of Federal Regulations
CHRO Chief Human Resources Officer
CO Compliance Officer

COBRA   Consolidated Omnibus Budget Reconciliation Act

COLA   Cost of Living Adjustment

CPA   Certified Public Accountant

CPH   Cost Per Hire

CPI   Consumer Price Index

CPM   Critical Path Method

CR   Corporate Responsibility

D&I   Diversity and Inclusion

DBA   Davis-Bacon Act

DMADV   Define, Measure, Analyze, Design, Verify

DMAIC   Define, Measure, Analyze, Improve, Control

DOL   U.S. Department of Labor

EAP   Employee Assistance Plan

ECPA   Electronic Communications Privacy Act

EE   Employee

EEO   Equal Employment Opportunity

EEOC   Equal Employment Opportunity Commission

EGTRRA   Economic Growth and Tax Relief Reconciliation Act

EI   Emotional Intelligence (*see also* EQ)

EO (or E.O.)   Executive Order

EPA   Equal Pay Act

EPLI   Employment Practices Liability Insurance

EQ   Emotional Intelligence (*see also* EI)

ER   Employer

ERISA   Employee Retirement Income Security Act

ESL   English as a Second Language

ESOP   Employee Stock Ownership Plan

ETA   U.S. Department of Labor, Employment and Training Administration

FACT   Fair and Accurate Credit Transactions Act

FAR   Federal Acquisition Regulations

FASB   Financial Accounting Standards Board

FCPA   Foreign Corrupt Practices Act

FCRA   Fair Credit Reporting Act

FES   Factor Evaluation System

FICA   Federal Insurance Contributions Act

FLRA   Federal Labor Relations Authority

FLSA   Fair Labor Standards Act

FMLA   Family and Medical Leave Act

FSA   Flexible Spending Accounts

FT   Full Time

FTE   Full Time Equivalent

FUTA   Federal Unemployment Tax Act

GATT   General Agreement on Tariffs and Trade

GDP   Gross Domestic Product

GINA   Genetic Information Nondiscrimination Act
GL   General Ledger
GPHR   Global Professional in Human Resources
GS   General Schedule
HSA   Health Savings Account
HCE   Highly Compensated Employee
HCN   Home-Country Nationals
HHS   Department of Health and Human Services
HIPAA   Health Insurance Portability and Accountability Act
HIPC   Health Insurance Purchasing Cooperatives
HITECH   Health Information Technology for Economic and Clinical Health Act
HIV   Human Immunodeficiency Virus
HMO   Health Maintenance Organization
HR   Human Resources
HRA   Health Reimbursement Accounts
HRCI   HR Certification Institute
HRCS   Human Resource Competency Study
HRD   Human Resource Department
HRIS   Human Resource Information System
HRM   Human Resource Management
ICE   U.S. Department of Homeland Security, Immigration and Customs Enforcement
IIPP   Injury and Illness Prevention Programs/Plans
ILO   International Labor Organization
INA   Immigration and Nationality Act
IRA   Individual Retirement Account
IRCA   Immigration Reform and Control Act
IRS   Internal Revenue Service
ISO   Incentive Stock Options
ISO   International Standards Organization
IT   Information Technology
JVA   Jobs for Veterans Act
KM   Knowledge Management
KSA   Knowledge, Skills, and Abilities
LMRA   Labor-Management Relations Act
LMRDA   Labor-Management Reporting and Disclosure Act
LMS   Learning Management System
LO   Learning Objectives
LOA   Leave of Absence
LTC   Long-Term Insurance Care
LTD   Long-Term Disability
M&A   Mergers and Acquisitions
MBO   Management by Objectives
MHPAEA   Mental Health Parity and Addiction Equity Act
MOU   Memorandum of Understanding

PART IV

MSDS   Material Safety Data Sheets
MSHA   Mine Safety and Health Act
MSP   Managed Service Provider
MSPB   Merit Systems Protection Board
NIOSH   National Institute of Occupational Safety and Health
NLRA   National Labor Relations Act
NLRB   National Labor Relations Board
NMB   National Mediation Board
OBRA   Omnibus Budget Reconciliation Act
OD   Organizational Development
OFCCP   Office of Federal Contract Compliance Programs
OJT   On Job Training
OPM   Office of Personnel Management
OSHA   Occupational Safety and Health Act
OWBPA   Older Workers Benefit Protection Act
P&L   Profit and Loss
PBGC   Pension Benefit Guarantee Corporation
PCAOB   Public Company Accounting Oversight Board
PCN   Parent-Country Nationals
PDA   Pregnancy Discrimination Act
PEO   Professional Employer Organization
PERT   Project Evaluation and Review Techniques
PEST   Political, Economic, Social, and Technological
PHR   Professional in Human Resources
PIP   Performance Improvement Program
PL (or P.L.)   Public Law
POP   Premium Only Plan
POS   Point of Service
PPA   Pension Protection Act
PPACA   Patient Protection and Affordable Care Act (*see also* ACA)
PPE   Personal Protective Equipment
PPO   Preferred Provider Organization
PT   Part Time
PTO   Paid Time Off
QME   Qualified Medical Examiner
RCR   Recruiting Cost Ratio
REA   Retirement Equity Act
RFID   Radio Frequency Identification
RFQ   Request for Quotation
RFP   Request for Proposal
RIF   Reduction in Force
ROI   Return on Investment
RSU   Restricted Stock Unit
RYR   Recruitment Yield Ratio

SAR Summary Annual Report
SBJPA Small Business Job Protection Act
SCA Service Contract Act
SCM Supply Chain Management
SHRM Society for Human Resource Management
SMM Summary of Material Modifications
SNAP Supplemental Nutrition Assistance Program (formerly known as the Food Stamp program)
SOX Sarbanes-Oxley Act
SPD Summary Plan Description
SPHR Senior Professional in Human Resources
SSI Supplemental Security Income
SSN Social Security Number
STD Short-Term Disability
STEEPLED Social, Technological, Environmental, Economic, Political, Legal, Ethics, and Demographics
SUB Supplemental Unemployment Benefits
SUTA State Unemployment Tax Act
SWOT Strengths, Weaknesses, Opportunities, and Threats
TANF Temporary Assistance to Needy Families
TCN Third-Country Nationals
TOC Theory of Constraints
TPA Third-Party Administrator
TQM Total Quality Management
UCA Unemployment Compensation Amendments Act
UGESP Uniform Guidelines on Employee Selection Procedures
UI Unemployment Insurance
ULP Unfair Labor Practice
URL Uniform Resource Locator (website address)
USC United States Code
USERRA Uniformed Services Employment and Reemployment Rights Act
VEVRAA Vietnam Era Veterans Readjustment Assistance Act
WARN Worker Adjustment and Retraining Notification Act
WC Workers' Compensation
WOTC Work Opportunity Tax Credit
WPE Workforce Planning and Employment

Federal Case Laws

Case Applications by Chapter

Chapter 4: Business Management—PHR

Year	Citation	Decision
1973	*McDonnell Douglas Corp. v. Green* (411 U.S. 792) http://caselaw .lp.findlaw.com/cgi-bin/getcase .pl?court=us&vol=411&invol=792	In a hiring case, the charging party has to show only that (1) the charging party is a member of a Title VII protected group, (2) he or she applied and was qualified for the position sought, (3) the job was not offered to him or her, and (4) the employer continued to seek applicants with similar qualifications. Then the employer must show a legitimate business reason why the complaining party was not hired. The employee has a final chance to prove the employer's business reason was really pretext for discrimination. This establishes the criteria for disparate treatment discrimination.
1991	*United Auto Workers v. Johnson Controls* (499 U.S. 187) www.law .cornell.edu/supct/html/89-1215 .ZO.html	The U.S. Supreme Court held that decisions about the welfare of future children must be left to the parents who conceive, bear, support, and raise them rather than to the employers who hire their parents.

Chapter 5: Talent Planning and Acquisition—PHR

Year	Citation	Decision
1971	*Griggs v. Duke Power Co.* (401 U.S. 424) www.law.cornell.edu/supct/html/historics/USSC_CR_0401_0424_ZS.html	When an employer uses a neutral test or other selection device and then discovers it has a disproportionate impact on minorities or women, the test must be discarded unless it can be shown that it was required as a business necessity; this was the first U.S. Supreme Court recognition of adverse impact discrimination.
1976	*Washington v. Davis* (426 U.S. 229) www.law.cornell.edu/supct/html/historics/USSC_CR_0426_0229_ZS.html	When an employment test is challenged under constitutional law, intent to discriminate must be established. Under Title VII there is no need to show intent, just the impact of test results.
1977	*Hazelwood School District v. U.S.* (433 U.S. 299) http://caselaw.lp.findlaw.com/cgi-bin/getcase.pl?court=us&vol=433&invol=299	An employee can establish a prima facie case of class hiring discrimination through the presentation of statistical evidence by comparing the racial composition of an employer's workforce with the racial composition of the relevant labor market.
1978	*Regents of University of California v. Bakke* (438 U.S. 265) http://caselaw.lp.findlaw.com/cgi-bin/getcase.pl?court=us&vol=438&invol=265	Medical school admission set-asides (16 of 100 seats) are illegal if they discriminate against Whites and no previous discrimination against minorities has been established.
1979	*United Steelworkers v. Weber* (443 U.S. 193) http://supreme.justia.com/cases/federal/us/443/193/case.html	Affirmative action plans are permissible if they are temporary and intended to "eliminate a manifest racial imbalance."
1982	*Connecticut v. Teal* (457 U.S. 440) http://caselaw.lp.findlaw.com/cgi-bin/getcase.pl?court=us&vol=457&invol=440	An employer is liable for racial discrimination when any part of its selection process, such as an unvalidated examination or test, has a disparate impact even if the final result of the hiring process is racially balanced. In effect, the U.S. Supreme Court rejects the "bottom-line defense" and makes clear that the fair employment laws protect the individual. Fair treatment to a group is not a defense to an individual claim of discrimination.
1987	*Johnson v. Santa Clara County Transportation Agency* (480 U.S. 616) https://supreme.justia.com/cases/federal/us/480/616/	The employer was justified in hiring a woman who scored 2 points less than a man because it had an affirmative action plan that was temporary, flexible, and designed to correct an imbalance of White males in the workforce.
1988	*Watson v. Fort Worth Bank & Trust* (487 U.S. 977) http://supreme.justia.com/cases/federal/us/487/977/case.html	In a unanimous opinion, the U.S. Supreme Court declared that disparate impact analysis can be applied to subjective or discretionary selection practices.

Year	Citation	Decision
2003	*Grutter v. Bollinger* (539 U.S. 306) http://supreme.justia.com/cases/federal/us/539/306/case.html and *Gratz v. Bollinger* (539 U.S. 244) http://supreme.justia.com/cases/federal/us/539/244/case.html	Diversity of a student body is a compelling state interest that can justify the use of race in university admissions as long as the admissions policy is "narrowly tailored" to achieve this goal. The University of Michigan did not do so for its undergraduate program, but the law school admissions program satisfied this standard.
2005	*Leonel v. American Airlines* (400 F.3d 702, 9th Circuit) http://cdn.ca9.uscourts.gov/datastore/opinions/2005/04/27/0315890.pdf	To make a legitimate job offer under the ADA, an employer must have completed all nonmedical components of the application process or be able to demonstrate that it could not reasonably have done so before issuing the offer.

Chapter 6: Learning and Development—PHR

There are no case laws that directly relate to this HRCI functional area.

Chapter 7: Total Rewards—PHR

Year	Citation	Decision
1974	*Corning Glass Works v. Brennan* (417 U.S. 188) http://supreme.justia.com/cases/federal/us/417/188/	Pay discrimination cases under the Equal Pay Act require the employee to prove that there is unequal pay based on sex for substantially equal work.
2000	*Erie County Retirees Association v. County of Erie* (2000 U.S. App. LEXIS 18317 3rd Cir. August 1, 2000) www.buypeba.org/publications/Eriecase.pdf	If an employer provides retiree health benefits, the health insurance benefits received by Medicare-eligible retirees must be at least equal to the health insurance benefits received by younger retirees.
2005	*IBP, Inc. v. Alvarez* (546 U.S. 21) www.law.cornell.edu/supct/html/03-1238.ZS.html	Time spent donning or doffing unique safety gear is compensable, and the FLSA requires payment of affected employees for all the time spent walking between changing and production areas.
2008	*LaRue v. DeWolff* (No. 06-856, 450 F.3d 570) www.law.cornell.edu/supct/cert/06-856	When retirement plan administrators breach their fiduciary duty to act as a prudent person would act in the investment of retirement funds, the employee whose retirement account lost money can sue the plan administrators.
2009	*Kennedy v. Plan Administrators for Dupont Savings* (No. 07-636) www.supremecourt.gov/opinions/08pdf/07-636.pdf	Retirement benefits were awarded to an ex-spouse even though she had agreed to disclaim such benefits, because the retiree had never changed beneficiary designation on the retirement plan. This points out the need for retirement plan administrators to pay attention to divorce decrees and qualified domestic relations orders.
2014	*Burwell v. Hobby Lobby Stores, Inc.* (S.Ct. No. 13-354) http://www.supremecourt.gov/opinions/13pdg/13-354_olp1.pdf	A closely held private corporation cannot be forced to pay for contraceptives as part of the Affordable Care Act if there is an objection based on religious beliefs of the business owners.

Chapter 8: Employee and Labor Relations—PHR

Year	Citation	Decision
1971	*Phillips v. Martin Marietta Corp.* (400 U.S. 542) www.uiowa.edu/~prslaw/courses/gender/cases/martinpdf.pdf	Employers may not have different policies for men and women with small children of similar age.
1974	*Espinoza v. Farah Manufacturing Co.* (414 U.S. 86) https://bulk.resource.org/courts.gov/c/US/414/414.US.86.72-671.html	Noncitizens are entitled to Title VII protection. Employers who require citizenship may violate Title VII if it results in discrimination based on national origin.
1975	*Albermarle Paper v. Moody* (422 U.S. 405) http://supreme.justia.com/cases/federal/us/422/405/	This requires employers to establish evidence that an employment test is related to the job content. Job analysis can be used to show that relationship, but performance evaluations of incumbents are specifically excluded.
1976	*McDonald v. Santa Fe Transportation Co.* (427 U.S. 273) http://supreme.justia.com/cases/federal/us/427/273/case.html	Title VII prohibits racial discrimination against Whites as well as Blacks.
1977	*Trans World Airlines, Inc. v. Hardison* (432 U.S. 63) http://supreme.justia.com/cases/federal/us/432/63/	Under Title VII, employers must reasonably accommodate an employee's religious needs unless doing so would create an undue hardship for the employer. The court defines hardship as anything more than de minimis cost.
1984	*EEOC v. Shell Oil Co.* (466 U.S. 54) http://supreme.justia.com/cases/federal/us/466/54/	The Supreme Court affirmed authority of EEOC commissioners to initiate charges of discrimination through "commissioner charges."
1986	*Meritor Savings Bank v. Vinson* (477 U.S. 57) www.law.cornell.edu/supct/html/historics/USSC_CR_0477_0057_ZS.html	This defined "hostile environment sexual harassment" as a form of sex discrimination under Title VII. It further defined it as "unwelcome" advances of a sexual nature. A victim's failure to use an employer's complaint process does not insulate the employer from liability.
1987	*Leggett v. First National Bank of Oregon* (739 P.2d. 1083) http://or.findacase.com/research/wfrmDocViewer.aspx/xq/fac.19870722_0041873.OR.htm/qx	The employer invaded the privacy of an employee when a company representative contacted the employee's psychologist (to whom the employee had been referred by an EAP—employee assistance program), inquiring about the employee's condition.
1987	*School Board of Nassau v. Arline* (480 U.S. 273) http://supreme.justia.com/cases/federal/us/480/273/case.html	A person with a contagious disease is covered by the Rehabilitation Act if they otherwise meet the definitions of "handicapped individual."

Year	Citation	Decision
1988	*DeBartolo Corp. v. Gulf Coast Trades Council* (known as DeBartolo II) (485 U.S. 568) https://bulk.resource.org/courts.gov/c/US/485/485.US.568.86-1461.html	The Supreme Court ruled that bannering, hand billing, or attention-getting actions outside an employer's property are permissible.
1989	*City of Richmond v. J. A. Croson Company* (488 U.S. 469) http://supreme.justia.com/cases/federal/us/488/469/	Affirmative action programs can only be maintained by showing that the programs aim to eliminate the effects of past discrimination.
1989	*Price Waterhouse v. Hopkins* (490 U.S. 288) http://caselaw.lp.findlaw.com/cgi-bin/getcase.pl?court=us&vol=490&invol=228	This decision relieved employers of liability if they would have made the same decision even if there had been no discrimination. Congress overturned the ruling providing that employers continue to have liability for injunctive relief, attorney fees, and costs even if they would have made the same decision in the absence of illegal discrimination.
1989	*Wards Cove Packing Co. v. Antonio* (490 U.S. 642) www.law.cornell.edu/supct/html/historics/USSC_CR_0490_0642_ZS.html	This decision made it more difficult for employees to prevail in employment discrimination cases. It was effectively overturned by Congress when it passed the Civil Rights Act of 1991.
1992	*Electromation, Inc. v. NLRB* (Nos. 92-4129, 93-1169 7th Cir.) www.leagle.com/decision/1994118335F3d1148_11017	The NLRB held that action committees at Electromation were illegal "labor organizations" because management created and controlled the groups and used them to deal with employees on working conditions in violation of the NLRA.
1993	*E. I. DuPont & Company v. NLRB* (311 NLRB 893)	The NLRB concluded that DuPont's six safety committees and fitness committee were employer-dominated labor organizations and that DuPont dominated the formation and administration of one of them in violation of the NLRA.
1993	*Harris v. Forklift Systems Inc.* (510 U.S. 17) www.law.cornell.edu/supct/html/92-1168.ZO.html	In a sexual harassment complaint, the employee does not have to prove concrete psychological harm to establish a Title VII violation.
1993	*St. Mary's Honor Center v. Hicks* (509 U.S. 502) www.law.cornell.edu/supct/html/92-602.ZS.html	Title VII complaints require the employee to show that discrimination was the reason for a negative employment action.
1993	*Taxman v. Board of Education of Piscataway* (91 F.3d 1547, 3rd Cir.) http://caselaw.lp.findlaw.com/scripts/getcase.pl?navby=search&case=/uscircs/3rd/961395p.html	Race in an affirmative action plan cannot be used to trammel the rights of people of other races.

Year	Citation	Decision
1995	*McKennon v. Nashville Banner Publishing Co.* (513 U.S. 352) www.law.cornell.edu/supct/html/93-1543.ZS.html	"After-acquired" evidence collected following a negative employment action cannot protect an employer from liability under Title VII or ADEA, even if the conduct would have justified terminating the employee.
1995	*NLRB v. Town & Country Electric* (516 U.S. 85) www.law.cornell.edu/supct/html/94-947.ZS.html	This Supreme Court decision is related to salting, which holds a worker may be a company's "employee," within the terms of the National Labor Relations Act, even if, at the same time, a union pays that worker to help the union organize the company.
1995	*PepsiCo, Inc. v. Redmond* (No. 94-3942 7th Cir.) http://caselaw.findlaw.com/us-7th-circuit/1337323.html	In this case, the district court applied the inevitable disclosure doctrine even though there was no noncompete agreement in place. An employee who had left his position in marketing PepsiCo's All Sport sports drink to work for Quaker Oats Company and market Gatorade and Snapple drinks was enjoined from working for Quaker because he had detailed knowledge of PepsiCo's trade secrets pertaining to pricing, market strategy, and selling/delivery systems.
1996	*O'Connor v. Consolidated Coin Caterers Corp.* (517 U.S. 308) www.law.cornell.edu/supct/html/95-354.ZS.html	To show unlawful discrimination under the Age Discrimination in Employment Act, a discharged employee does not have to show that he or she was replaced by someone outside the protected age group (that is under age 40).
1997	*Robinson v. Shell Oil* (519 U.S. 337) www.law.cornell.edu/supct/html/95-1376.ZS.html	Title VII prohibition against retaliation protects former as well as current employees.
1998	*Bragdon v. Abbott* (524 U.S. 624) www.law.cornell.edu/supct/html/97-156.ZS.html	An individual with asymptomatic HIV is an individual with a disability and therefore is protected by the ADA. Reproduction is a major life activity under the statute.
1998	*Faragher v. City of Boca Raton* (524 U.S. 775) www.law.cornell.edu/supct/html/97-282.ZO.html and *Ellerth v. Burlington Northern Industries* (524 U.S. 742) www.law.cornell.edu/supct/html/97-569.ZS.html	This distinguished between supervisor harassment that results in tangible employment action and that which does not. When harassment results in a tangible employment action, the employer is liable. Employers may avoid liability if they have a legitimate written complaint policy, it is clearly communicated to employees, and it offers alternatives to the immediate supervisor as the point of contact for making a complaint.
1998	*Oncale v. Sundowner Offshore Service, Inc.* (523 U.S. 75) www.law.cornell.edu/supct/html/96-568.ZO.html	Same-gender harassment is actionable under Title VII.

Year	Citation	Decision
1998	*Wright v. Universal Maritime Service Corp.* (525 U.S. 70) http://supreme.justia.com/cases/federal/us/525/70/	Collective bargaining agreements must contain a clear and unmistakable waiver if it is to bar an individual's right to sue after an arbitration requirement.
1999	*Gibson v. West* (527 U.S. 212) http://caselaw.lp.findlaw.com/scripts/getcase.pl?court=us&vol=527&invol=212	This endorses the EEOC's position that it has the legal authority to require federal agencies to pay compensatory damages when the EEOC has ruled during the administrative process that the federal agency has unlawfully discriminated in violation of Title VII.
1999	*Kolstad v. American Dental Association* (527 U.S. 526) www.law.cornell.edu/supct/html/98-208.ZO.html	Title VII punitive damages are limited to cases in which the employer has engaged in intentional discrimination and has done so "with malice or with reckless indifference...."
2001	*Circuit City Stores v. Adams* (532 U.S. 105) www.law.cornell.edu/supct/html/99-1379.ZS.html	A prehire employment application requiring that all employment disputes be settled by arbitration is enforceable under the Federal Arbitration Act.
2001	*Ronald Lesch v. Crown Cork and Seal Company* (334 NLRB 699) www.nlrb.gov/cases-decisions/board-decisions	This NLRB decision lifted some restrictions on the employer's use of employee participation committees.
2002	*EEOC v. Waffle House* (534 U.S. 279) www.law.cornell.edu/supct/html/99-1823.ZS.html	In this case, the Supreme Court ruled that even if there is a mandatory arbitration agreement in place, a relevant civil rights agency can still sue on behalf of the employee.
2002	*Phoenix Transit System v. NLRB* (337 NLRB 510) www.nlrb.gov/cases-decisions/board-decisions?volume=337&sort_by=case_nameSort&sort_order=ASC	This NLRB ruling struck down the employer rule prohibiting employees from discussing among themselves an employment complaint—in this instance, a complaint of sexual harassment—on the grounds that the prohibition was not limited in time and scope and interfered with a protected concerted activity.
2004	*General Dynamics Land Systems, Inc. v. Cline* (540 U.S. 581) www.law.cornell.edu/supct/html/02-1080.ZS.html	ADEA does not protect younger workers, even those over 40, from workplace decisions that favor older workers.
2004	*NLRB v. Weingarten, Inc.* (420 U.S. 251, 254 1975) http://clear.uhwo.hawaii.edu/weindecis.html Overturned by IBM Corp. v. NLRB (341 NLRB No. 148, June 9, 2004) www.nacua.org/documents/IBM_Corp_and_KennethPaulSchult.pdf	On June 9, 2004, the NLRB ruled by a 3–2 vote that employees who work in a nonunionized workplace are not entitled to have a co-worker accompany them to an interview with their employer, even if the affected employee reasonably believes that the interview might result in discipline. This decision effectively reversed the July 2000 decision of the Clinton board, which had extended Weingarten rights to nonunion employees.

Year	Citation	Decision
2004	*Pennsylvania State Police v. Suders* (542 U.S. 129) www.law.cornell.edu/supct/html/03-95.ZS.html	In the absence of a tangible employment action, employers may use the Ellerth/Faragher defense in a constructive discharge claim when supervisors are charged with harassment.
2005	*Smith v. Jackson, Mississippi* (544 U.S. 228) www.law.cornell.edu/supct/html/03-1160.ZS.html	ADEA, like Title VII, offers recovery on a disparate impact theory.
2007 and 2011	*Dana Corporation/Metaldyne Corporation v. NLRB* (351 NLRB 434) www.nlrb.gov/cases-decisions/board-decisions?volume=351&sort_by=case_nameSort&sort_order=ASC	An NLRB ruling that a recognition bar, which precludes a decertification election for 12 months after an employer recognizes a union, does not apply when the recognition is voluntary, based on a card check. This was overruled in 2011 in "Lamons Gasket," which restored the recognition bar for voluntary recognition but revised the prohibited time period from one year to a minimum of six months up to a year.
2007	*Ledbetter v. Goodyear Tire & Rubber Co.* (550 U.S. 618) www.law.cornell.edu/supct/pdf/05-1074P.ZS	A claim of discrimination must be filed within 180 days of the first discriminatory employment act, and the clock does not restart after each subsequent act (for example, issuance of a paycheck with lower pay than co-workers if based on sex). Congress overruled this decision with passage of the Lilly Ledbetter Fair Pay Act of 2009, which says the clock will restart each time another incident of discrimination occurs.
2007	*Oil Capitol Sheet Metal, Inc. v. NLRB* (349 NLRB 1348) www.nlrb.gov/cases-decisions/board-decisions?volume=351&sort_by=case_nameSort&sort_order=ASC	An NLRB decision that provides employers relief in salting cases by announcing a new evidentiary standard for determining the period of back pay; requires the union to provide evidence that supports the period of time it claims the salt would have been employed.
2007	*Syracuse University v. NLRB* (350 NLRB 755) www.nlrb.gov/cases-decisions/board-decisions?volume=351&sort_by=case_nameSort&sort_order=ASC	The NLRB found that an employee grievance panel did not violate the NLRA because the purpose of the panel was not to deal with management but to improve group decisions.
2007	*Toering Electric Company v. NLRB* (351 NLRB 225) www.nlrb.gov/cases-decisions/board-decisions?volume=351&sort_by=case_nameSort&sort_order=ASC	In this NLRB ruling, an applicant for employment must be genuinely interested in seeking to establish an employment relationship with the employer to be protected against hiring discrimination based on union affiliation or activity; creates greater obstacles for unions attempting salting campaigns.

Year	Citation	Decision
2009	*Ricci v. DeStefano* (No. 07-1428) www.supremecourt.gov/opinions/08pdf/07-1428.pdf	"…under Title VII, before an employer can engage in intentional discrimination for the asserted purpose of avoiding or remedying an unintentional disparate impact, the employer must have a strong basis in evidence to believe it will be subject to disparate-impact liability if it fails to take the race-conscious, discriminatory action."
2010	*KenMor Electric Co., Inc. v. NLRB* (355 NLRB 173) www.nlrb.gov/cases-decisions/board-decisions?volume=351&sort_by=case_nameSort&sort_order=ASC	The NLRB ruled that a system developed and operated by an association of electrical contractors violated the NLRA because it discriminated against individuals who were salts. The board held that an individual's right to be a salt is protected under the NLRA.
2011	*AT&T Mobility v. Concepcion* (S.Ct. No. 09-893) www.supremecourt.gov/opinions/10pdf/09-893.pdf	The Supreme Court ruled that some state statutes restricting the enforceability of arbitration agreements in a commercial context may be preempted by the Federal Arbitration Act.
2011	*Staub v. Proctor* (131 U.S. 1186) http://supreme.justia.com/cases/federal/us/562/09-400/	The Supreme Court applied the "cat's paw" principle to a wrongful discharge case, finding that an employer was culpable because the HR manager did not adequately investigate supervisors' charges against the fired employee.
2011	*Kepas v. Ebay* (131 S.Ct. 2160) www.ca10.uscourts.gov/opinions/09/09-4200.pdf	The Supreme Court refused to review a lower court decision that held in an employment case that a cost provision was severable from the balance of an arbitration agreement. The cost provision was unenforceable, but the agreement to arbitrate was enforceable.
2011	*Specialty Healthcare and Rehabilitation Center of Mobile v. NLRB* (15-RC-008773) www.nlrb.gov/case/15-RC-008773	The NLRB indicated that, in nonacute healthcare facilities, it will certify smaller units for bargaining unless the employer provides overwhelming proof of a community of interest.
2011	*UGL-UNICCO Service Company v. NLRB* (01-RC-022447) www.nlrb.gov/case/01-RC-022447	The NLRB re-established the successor bar doctrine, allowing unions a window of six months to one year of presumed majority support after the transfer of ownership of a business.
2012	*D. R. Horton, Inc. v. NLRB* (12-CA-25764) www.cozen.com/cozendocs/outgoing/alerts/2012/labor_011012_link.pdf	The NLRB ruled that requiring employees to agree to a class action waiver as a term and condition of employment violates Section 7 of the National Labor Relations Act.

Year	Citation	Decision
2013	*University of Texas Southwestern Medical Center. v. Nassar* (No. 12-484) www.law.cornell.edu/supremecourt/text/12-484	Retaliation claims brought under Title VII of the Civil Rights Act of 1964 must be proven according to principles of "but-for-causation," not the lesser causation test applicable to bias claims.
2013	*Vance v. Ball State Univ.* (No. 11-556) www.supremecourt.gov/opinions/12pdf/11-556_11o2.pdf	This case determined that an employee is a "supervisor" of another employee for the purposes of liability under Title VII of the Civil Rights Act of 1964 only if he or she is empowered by the employer to take tangible employment actions against the other employee.
2014	*Harris v. Quinn* (S.Ct. No. 11-681) http://www.supremecourt.gov/opinions/13pdf/11-681_j426.pdf	"The First Amendment prohibits the collection of an agency fee from [employees] who do not want to join or support the union." Essentially, this eliminates the agency shop.
2018	*Janus v. American Federation of State, County, and Municipal Employees, Council 31, et al.* https://www.supremecourt.gov/opinions/17pdf/16-1466_2b3j.pdf	This case decided that the state's extraction of agency fees for the union from nonconsenting public-sector employees violates the First Amendment.
2018	*Mount Lemmon Fire District v. Guido et al.* https://www.supremecourt.gov/opinions/18pdf/17-587_n7ip.pdf	The Age Discrimination in Employment Act of 1967 applies to all public-sector governments regardless of employee head count. The 20-employee threshold does not apply to government entities.

Chapter 9: Leadership and Strategy—SPHR

There are no case laws that directly relate to this HRCI functional area.

Chapter 10: Talent Planning and Acquisition—SPHR

See Chapter 5's PHR case law references.

Chapter 11: Learning and Development—SPHR

There are no case laws that directly relate to this HRCI functional area.

Chapter 12: Total Rewards—SPHR

See Chapter 7's PHR case law references.

Chapter 13: Employee Relations and Engagement—SPHR

See Chapter 8's PHR case law references.

PART IV

For Additional Study

The following are materials that can be helpful in your study for the Professional in Human Resources (PHR) and Senior Professional in Human Resources (SPHR) exams and for future reference as an HR professional. All of the materials in this appendix apply to more than one of the functional competency areas of the exams.

SHRM Code of Ethical and Professional Standards in Human Resource Management. Retrieved 2/7/2014 from www.shrm.org/about/pages/code-of-ethics.aspx.

"Models and Techniques of Manpower Demand and Supply Forecasting: A Strategic Human Resource Planning Model." Retrieved 2/7/2014 from http://corehr.wordpress .com/hr-planning/53-2/.

Becker, Brian E., Mark A. Huselid, and David Ulrich, *The HR Scorecard: Linking People, Strategy, and Performance*. Boston: Harvard Business School Press, 2001.

Benjamin, Steve. "A Closer Look at Needs Analysis and Needs Assessment: Whatever Happened to the Systems Approach?" *Performance Improvement* 28, no. 9, 12–16, Wiley Periodicals, Inc., 1989.

Bennett-Alexander, Dawn D., and Laura B. Pincus. *Employment Law for Business*. Chicago: Irwin Publishing, 1995.

Bliss, Wendy (Series Advisor). *The Essentials of Finance and Budgeting*. Boston: Harvard Business School Press, and Alexandria, Virginia: Society for Human Resource Management, 2005.

Blosser, Fred. *Primer on Occupational Safety and Health*. Washington, D.C.: The Bureau of National Affairs, 1992.

Carrell, Michael R., and Christina Heavrin. *Collective Bargaining and Labor Relations*, 3rd ed. New York: Merrill, 1985.

Cherrington, David J. *The Management of Human Resources*, 4th ed. Englewood Cliffs, New Jersey: Prentice-Hall, 1995.

Cofey, Robert E., Curtis W. Cook, and Phillip L. Hunsaker. *Management and Organizational Behavior*. Boston: Austen Press, 1994.

DeLuca, Matthew J. *Handbook of Compensation Management*. Englewood Cliffs, New Jersey: Prentice-Hall, 1997.

Denisi, A., and R. Griffin. *HR*, Mason, OH, Cengage Learning, 2011.

Doherty, Neil. *Integrated Risk Management: Techniques and Strategies*, New York, McGraw-Hill Education, 2000.

Feldacker, Bruce. *Labor Guide to Labor Law*, 3rd ed. Englewood Cliffs, New Jersey: Prentice-Hall, 1990.

Fitz-Enz, Jac. *How to Measure Human Resource Management.* 2nd ed. New York: McGraw-Hill Education, 1995.

Grant, Phillip. *Multiple Use Job Descriptions: A Guide to Analysis, Preparation, and Applications for Human Resources Managers.* Praeger, 1989.

Hayes, John. *The Theory and Practice of Change Management.* London, Palgrave Macmillan, 2010.

Herzberg, Frederick. *The Motivation to Work.* Somerset, NJ, John Wiley & Sons, Inc., 1959.

Jackson Lewis, LLP. *Employer's Guide to Union Organizing Campaigns.* New York: Aspen Publishers, 2007.

Kahan, Seth. *Getting Change Right: How Leaders Transform Organizations from the Inside Out.* San Francisco: Jossey-Bass, 2010.

Kirkpatrick, Donald L. *How to Manage Change Effectively.* San Francisco: Jossey-Bass, 1985.

Knowles, Malcolm. *The Adult Learner: The Definitive Classic in Adult Education and Human Resource Development.* Burlington, MA, Elsevier, 1973-2005.

Kushner, Gary. *Health Care Reform: The Patient Protection and Affordable Care Act of 2010.* SHRM/Kushner and Company, 2010.

Kutcher, David. "What Is an RFP, Where to Find RFPs, and are RFPs Relevant?" *Confluent Forms*, May 13, 2013. Retrieved 2/7/2014 from www.confluentforms.com/2013/05/requests-for-proposals-rfp.html.

Lawler, Edward E., III. *Strategic Pay: Aligning Organizational Strategies and Pay Systems.* San Francisco: Jossey-Bass, 1990.

Mantel Jr., S., J. Meredith, S. Shafer, and M. Sutton. *Project Management in Practice.* Somerset, NJ, John Wiley & Sons, 2010.

Mathis, R., J. Jackson, and S. Valentine. *Human Resource Management.* Boston, Cengage Learning, 2013.

Maslow, Abraham H. *A Theory of Human Motivation.* Martino Fine Books, 2013.

McGregor, Douglas. *The Human Side of Enterprise* (annotated edition). New York, McGraw-Hill Education, 2005.

Michaud, Patrick A. *Accident Prevention and OSHA Compliance.* Boca Raton, Florida: Lewis Publishers, 1995.

Milkovich, George T., Jerry M. Newman, and Carolyn Milkovich. *Compensation*, 7th ed. Boston: McGraw-Hill Education, 2002.

Porter, Michael E. *Competitive Strategy: Techniques for Analyzing Industries and Competitors*. New York: Free Press, 1980.

Richardson, Blake. *Records Management for Dummies*. Hoboken, NJ, For Dummies, 2012.

Rogers, Everett. *Diffusion of Innovations*. New York, Free Press, 2003.

Scott, Mark, JD, CFE. "Managing Risks in Vendor Relationships." The Fraud Examiner. March 2012. Retrieved 2/7/2014 from www.acfe.com/fraud-examiner .aspx?id=4294972428.

Tolbert, P., and R. Hall. *Organizations: Structures, Processes, and Outcomes*. New York, Pearson 2008.

Truesdell, William H. *Secrets of Affirmative Action Compliance*. Walnut Creek, CA: Management Advantage, Inc., 2016.

Ulrich, David. *Delivering Results: A New Mandate for Human Resource Professionals*. Boston: Harvard Business Review, 1998.

PART IV

About the Online Content

This book comes complete with TotalTester Online customizable practice exam software with complete practice exams for both the PHR and SPHR.

System Requirements

The current and previous major versions of the following desktop browsers are recommended and supported: Chrome, Microsoft Edge, Firefox, and Safari. These browsers update frequently, and sometimes an update may cause compatibility issues with the TotalTester Online or other content hosted on the Training Hub. If you run into a problem using one of these browsers, please try using another until the problem is resolved.

Your Total Seminars Training Hub Account

To get access to the online content, you will need to create an account on the Total Seminars Training Hub. Registration is free, and you will be able to track all your online content using your account. You may also opt in if you wish to receive marketing information from McGraw-Hill Education or Total Seminars, but this is not required for you to gain access to the online content.

Privacy Notice

McGraw-Hill Education values your privacy. Please be sure to read the Privacy Notice available during registration to see how the information you have provided will be used. You may view our Corporate Customer Privacy Policy by visiting the McGraw-Hill Education Privacy Center. Visit the **mheducation.com** site and click on **Privacy** at the bottom of the page.

Single User License Terms and Conditions

Online access to the digital content included with this book is governed by the McGraw-Hill Education License Agreement outlined next. By using this digital content you agree to the terms of that license.

Access To register and activate your Total Seminars Training Hub account, simply follow these easy steps.

1. Go to **hub.totalsem.com/mheclaim**.

2. To register and create a new Training Hub account, enter your e-mail address, name, and password. No further personal information (such as a credit card number) is required to create an account.

NOTE If you already have a Total Seminars Training Hub account, select **Log in** and enter your e-mail and password. Otherwise, follow the remaining steps.

3. Enter your product key: `50gt-267s-4mg6`.

4. Click to accept the user license terms.

5. Click **Register and Claim** to create your account. You will be taken to the Training Hub and have access to the content for this book.

Duration of License Access to your online content through the Total Seminars Training Hub will expire one year from the date the publisher declares the book out of print.

Your purchase of this McGraw-Hill Education product, including its access code, through a retail store is subject to the refund policy of that store.

The Content is a copyrighted work of McGraw-Hill Education, and McGraw-Hill Education reserves all rights in and to the Content. The Work is © 2019 by McGraw-Hill Education, LLC.

Restrictions on Transfer The user is receiving only a limited right to use the Content for the user's own internal and personal use, dependent on purchase and continued ownership of this book. The user may not reproduce, forward, modify, create derivative works based upon, transmit, distribute, disseminate, sell, publish, or sublicense the Content or in any way commingle the Content with other third-party content without McGraw-Hill Education's consent.

Limited Warranty The McGraw-Hill Education Content is provided on an "as is" basis. Neither McGraw-Hill Education nor its licensors make any guarantees or warranties of any kind, either express or implied, including, but not limited to, implied warranties of merchantability or fitness for a particular purpose or use as to any McGraw-Hill Education Content or the information therein or any warranties as to the accuracy, completeness, correctness, or results to be obtained from accessing or using the McGraw-Hill Education content, or any material referenced in such content or any information entered into licensee's product by users or other persons and/or any material available on or that can be accessed through the licensee's product (including via any hyperlink or otherwise) or as to non-infringement of third-party rights. Any warranties of any kind, whether express or implied, are disclaimed. Any material or data obtained through use of the McGraw-Hill Education content is at your own discretion and risk, and the user understands that it will be solely responsible for any resulting damage to its computer system or loss of data.

Neither McGraw-Hill Education nor its licensors shall be liable to any subscriber or to any user or anyone else for any inaccuracy, delay, interruption in service, error, or omission, regardless of cause, or for any damage resulting therefrom.

In no event will McGraw-Hill Education or its licensors be liable for any indirect, special, or consequential damages, including but not limited to, lost time, lost money, lost profits or goodwill, whether in contract, tort, strict liability, or otherwise, and whether or not such damages are foreseen or unforeseen with respect to any use of the McGraw-Hill Education content.

TotalTester Online

TotalTester Online provides you with a simulation of the PHR and SPHR exams. Exams can be taken in Practice Mode or Exam Mode. Practice Mode provides an assistance window with hints, references to the book, explanations of the correct and incorrect answers, and the option to check your answer as you take the test. Exam Mode provides a simulation of the actual exam. The number of questions, the types of questions, and the time allowed are intended to be an accurate representation of the exam environment. The option to customize your quiz allows you to create custom exams from selected domains or chapters, and you can further customize the number of questions and time allowed.

To take a test, follow the instructions provided in the previous section to register and activate your Total Seminars Training Hub account. When you register, you will be taken to the Total Seminars Training Hub. From the Training Hub Home page, select **PHR Practice Exam TotalTester** or **SPHR Practice Exam TotalTester** from the "Study" drop-down menu at the top of the page, or from the list of "Your Topics" on the Home page. You can then select the option to customize your quiz and begin testing yourself in Practice Mode or Exam Mode. All exams provide an overall grade and a grade broken down by domain.

New Question Types

In addition to multiple-choice questions, the PHR and SPHR exams now include a variety of other question types. More information about these questions is provided on HRCI's website. You can access example questions included with this book by navigating to the Resources tab and selecting **PHR Quiz** or **SPHR Quiz**. After you have selected the questions, an interactive quiz will launch in your browser.

Technical Support

For questions regarding the TotalTester software or operation of the Training Hub, visit **www.totalsem.com** or e-mail **support@totalsem.com**.

For questions regarding book content, e-mail **hep_customer-service@mheducation .com**. For customers outside the United States, e-mail **international_cs@mheducation .com**.

80% rule   The measurement known as a "rule of thumb" used to test for disparity in treatment during any type of employment selection decisions; also identified as *adverse impact*.

ADDIE   A five-step instructional design process: Analysis, Design, Development, Implementation, Evaluation.

administrative exemption   Exemption from overtime payment based on several qualifying factors, including minimum pay requirement and exercise of discretion and independent judgment performing work directly related to management of general business operations.

administrative services only plan   Health insurance programs in which all of the risk is assumed by the employer.

adult learning   The process of learning associated with people who are older than 18 and generally referred to as nontraditional learners; also identified as *andragogy*.

adverse impact   A legal category of illegal employment discrimination involving groups of workers and statistical proofs.

adverse treatment   A legal category of illegal employment discrimination involving individual treatment or "pattern and practice" treatment of groups of workers.

affirmative action   Use of special outreach and recruiting programs to ensure participation of qualified job candidates, vendors, or students in employment, employer purchasing programs, or college admissions.

aggregate stop-loss coverage   The health plan is protected against the risk of large total claims from all participants during the plan year.

aging   A technique used to make outdated data current.

andragogy   The study of how adults learn.

applicant tracking system   A method for retention of detailed information about job applicants, either manual- or computer-based.

assets   The properties an organization owns, tangible and intangible.

Associate Professional in Human Resources (aPHR)   An HR certification designed for professionals who are just beginning their HR career that focuses on knowledge of foundational human resource topics.

automatic step rate   Division of the pay range into several steps that can be advanced by an employee when time-in-job has met the step requirement.

average   Arithmetic average or mean arrived at by giving equal weight to every participant's actual pay; also, a number that is arrived at by adding quantities together and dividing the total by the number of quantities.

back pay   Payment of salary or wages that should have been paid initially, usually as a form of remedy for a complaint of discrimination.

background checks   Investigation of an individual's personal history, including employment, educational, criminal, and financial.

balance sheet   A statement of a business's financial position.

balanced scorecard   A big-picture view of an organization's performance as measured against goals in areas such as finance, customer base, processes, learning, human capital, and growth.

BARS   Behaviorally anchored rating scales used to rate job performance.

base-pay systems   Single- or flat-rate systems, time-based step-rate systems, performance-based merit pay systems, productivity-based systems, and person-based systems.

bell curve   Used to describe the mathematical concept called *normal distribution.*

benefits needs assessment or analysis   Collection and analysis of data to determine whether the employer's benefits programs actually meet their objectives.

bereavement leave   Paid or unpaid time off to attend funerals.

bill   A proposal presented to a legislative body in the U.S. government to enact a law.

boycott   A protest action that encourages the public to withhold business from an employer that is targeted by a union.

branding   The process of conveying key organizational values and associations.

broadbanding   Combination of several pay grades or job classifications with narrow range spreads into a single band with a wider spread.

budgeting   Forecasting income and expenses by category and subcategory.

business acumen   Knowledge and understanding of the financial, accounting, marketing, and operational functions of an organization.

business concepts   An idea for producing goods or services that identifies the benefits that can be achieved for prospective customers or clients.

business continuity   The ability to continue conducting business following an interruption of some sort.

business ethics   Generally accepted norms and expectations for business management behavior.

career development   A process involving individuals expanding their knowledge, skills, and abilities as they progress through their careers.

career management   Planning, preparing, and implementing employee career paths.

career planning   Activities and actions that individuals follow for a direction-specific career path.

case studies   Simulation of a real-world problem that demands some application of skill or knowledge to resolve problems or issues.

cash awards   Monetary rewards for exceeding performance goals, a formula-based bonus based on a percentage of profits or other pre-established measurement.

certification of a union   Formal recognition of a union as the exclusive bargaining representative of a group of employees.

change management   Transitioning individuals, groups, teams, and institutions to a desired future state.

change programs   Strategic approach to organizing and implementing specific changes (for example, policies or procedures) within an organization.

childcare services   Programs designed to help working parents deal with the ongoing needs of preschool or school-aged children.

code of conduct   An employment policy listing personal behaviors that are acceptable and required in the workplace.

code of ethics   Principles of conduct that guide behavior expectations and decisions.

cognitive learning   The refining of knowledge by adding new information thereby expanding prior knowledge.

collective bargaining   A formal process of negotiating working conditions with an employer for a work group represented by a union.

collective bargaining agreements   Union contracts for a represented group of employees and designated employers. A term usually used in the private sector.

combination step-rate and performance   Employees receive step-rate increases up to the established job rate. Above this level, increases are granted only for superior job performance.

communication skills   Verbal and written abilities that enable an individual to transmit and receive messages.

commuter assistance   Employer assistance programs designed to help defray public transportation costs associated with going to and from work.

compa-ratios   An indicator of how wages match, lead, or lag the midpoint of a given pay range computed by dividing the worker's pay rate by the midpoint of the pay range.

compensatory damages   A monetary equivalent awarded for pain, suffering, and emotional distress as a result of a legal proceeding.

competencies   Measurable or observable knowledge, skills, abilities, and behaviors critical to successful job performance.

competency-based system   When pay is linked to the level at which an employee can perform in a recognized competency.

compliance evaluation   Formal audit by the Office of Federal Contract Compliance Programs (OFCCP) of a federal contractor subject to OFCCP oversight.

computer employee exemption   Exemption from overtime payment based on several qualifying factors, including minimum pay requirement, job duties involving computer programming, software analysis, or software engineering.

computer-based testing (CBT)   Testing delivery method via computer in person at a testing center.

construct validity   The degree to which a test measures what it claims to measure.

consumer price index   The average of prices paid by consumers for goods and services.

content validity   The extent a test measures all aspects of a given job.

contract labor   Work performed under the terms of a legally enforceable contract.

contract negotiation   The process of give and take related generally to content details and provisions of an employment contract such as a union agreement or memorandum of understanding (MOU).

control chart   A chart that illustrates variation from normal in a situation over time.

controlling   A management function involving monitoring the workplace and making adjustments to activities as required.

cooperative learning   A strategy in which a small group of people working on solving a problem or completing a task in a way that each person's success is dependent on the group's success.

copyright   A legal form of protection for authors or original works.

core competency   A unique capability that is essential or fundamental to a particular job.

corporate governance   The mechanisms, processes, and relations by which corporations are controlled and directed.

corporate responsibility (CR)   Strategic goals achieved through local community relationships around social needs and issues.

cost containment   Efforts or activities designed to reduce or slow down cost expenses and increases.

cost of living adjustment   Pay increase given to all employees on the basis of market pressure, usually measured against the consumer price index (CPI).

cost per hire   The measurement of dollar expense required to hire each new employee.

cost-benefit analysis (CBA)   A business practice in which the costs and benefits of a particular situation are analyzed as part of the decision process.

credit report   Report obtained from one of the major credit reporting agencies that explains the individual's personal rating based on financial history.

criterion-related validity   Empirical studies producing data that show the selection procedure(s) are predictive or significantly related with important elements of job performance.

critical path method (CPM)   A sequence of activities in a project plan that must be completed on time for the project to be completed on the due date.

cross-functional work team   A group of people from different functions working together to generate production or problem resolution.

cultural blending   The blending of different cultural influences in the workforce.

culture   Societal forces affecting the values, beliefs, and actions of a group of people.

deauthorization of a union   Removal of "union security" from the contract. The union remains as the exclusive bargaining representative, and the collective bargaining agreement remains in effect, but employees are not forced to be members or pay dues to the union.

decertification of a union   Removal of a union as the exclusive bargaining representative of the employees.

defamation   Publication of something about an individual that the writer knows is untrue.

demand analysis   Estimation of what customers, clients, or patrons will want in the future.

demonstration   Showing students how something is done.

dental plans   Medical insurance programs that cover some or all of the cost of dental services for subscribers.

differential piece rate system   Employee receives one rate of pay up to the production standard and a higher rate of pay when the standard is exceeded.

direct compensation   Base pay, commissions, bonuses, merit pay, piece rate, differential pay, cash award, profit sharing, gainsharing.

directing   Managing or controlling people to willingly do what is wanted or needed.

disaster recovery plans   A set of procedures used to protect and recover a business from a natural or other disaster that has impacted the organization or employer.

discipline   Forms of punishment to assure obedience with policies.

diversity and inclusion   The practice of embracing differences of race, culture, and background and ensuring that everyone is a participant in workplace processes.

diversity programs   Methods for recognizing and honoring various types of employee backgrounds.

divestiture   The sale of an asset.

dual-ladder   A system that enables a person to advance up either the management ladder or the technical career development ladder in an organization.

due diligence   The first step in mergers and acquisitions involving a broad scope of research and investigation.

elder care   Programs to help employees deal with responsibilities for care of family elders.

e-learning   Internet-based training programs that can be instructor led or self-paced.

emotional intelligence (EQ or EI)   The ability of an individual to have understanding and sensitivity for another's emotions and control over their own.

employee assistance programs   Employer-sponsored benefits that provide a number of services that help promote the physical, mental, and emotional wellness of individual employees who otherwise would be negatively impacted by health-related crises.

employee complaints   Written or verbal statements of dissatisfaction from an employee that can involve charges of discrimination, lack of fairness, or other upset.

employee engagement   Where employees are fully absorbed by and enthusiastic about their work and so take positive action to further the organization's reputation and interests.

employee leasing   Contracting with a vendor that provides qualified workers for a specific period of time at a specific pay rate.

employee relations programs   Methods for management of the employer-employee relationship.

employee stock ownership plans   Retirement plans in which the company contributes its stock, or money to buy its stock, to the plan for the benefit of the company's employees.

employee stock purchase plans   Programs allowing employees to purchase company stock at discounted prices.

employee surveys   Tools used to gather opinions of employees about their employment experiences.

employee-management committees   Problem-solving groups of management and nonmanagement employees focused on specific issues within the workplace.

employer sick leave   Paid leave for a specified number of hours or days absent from work due to medical conditions.

employment affirmative action   Programs required by federal regulations for some federal contractors to implement outreach and recruiting programs when the incumbent workforce is significantly less than computed availability.

employment at will   A legal doctrine that describes an employment relationship without a contract where either party can end the relationship at any time for any reason.

employment policies   Rules by which the workplace will be managed.

employment reference checks   Verification of references, both personal and professional, provided by a job candidate on an application form or resume.

employment testing   Any tool or step used in the employment selection process. Commonly includes written tests, interviews, résumé review, or skill demonstration.

environmental footprints   The effect that a person, company, activity, and so on has on the environment.

environmental scanning   A process of studying the environment to pinpoint potential threats and opportunities.

equal pay   Providing equal compensation to jobs that have the same requirements, responsibilities, and working conditions regardless of the incumbent's gender.

equity   The difference between income and liabilities in a for-profit organization.

ethics   Principles and values that set expectations for behaviors in an organization.

ethnocentric   A policy calling for key management positions to be filled by expatriates.

evacuation plan   A written procedure for moving employees out of the work location to a safer location in case of fire or natural disaster.

evaluation   The ability to judge.

E-Verify   A government database that employers access to confirm a match between a new employee's name and Social Security number.

executive coaching   Coaching senior and executive-level management by a third party.

executive exemption   Exemption from overtime payment based on several qualifying factors, including supervision and minimum pay requirements.

executive incentives   Variable compensation additives for executive employees that may include company stock or use of company facilities, such as vacation timeshares. These are usually variable based on the profitability of the company.

exempt job   A job with content that is exempt from the FLSA requirement to pay overtime for work over 40 hours per week. Exemption is based on several designated factors.

exit interviews   Discussions with departing employees to explore how they feel about their experience as an employee and what recommendations they might have for the employer.

expatriates   Employees working in a country other than that of their origin.

external coaching   Coaching that is provided by a third party or by a certified coach.

extrinsic rewards   Rewards such as pay, benefits, incentive bonuses, promotions, time off, and so on.

factor-comparison job evaluation   A process that involves each job by each compensable factor and then identifying dollar values for each level of each factor to develop an actual pay rate for the evaluated job.

fast-track program   A career development program that identifies high-potential leaders for rapid career growth and organizational knowledge.

fee-for-service plans   Allows health plan members to go to any qualified physician, or other healthcare provider, hospital, or medical clinic, and submit claims to the insurance company.

fiduciary responsibilities   A legal and ethical relationship between two or more parties.

final warning   Last step in the disciplinary process progression prior to removing the employee from the payroll.

flat-rate or single system   Each worker in the same job has the same rate of pay regardless of seniority or job performance.

flexible spending account   Allows employees to set aside a pre-established amount of money on a pretax basis per plan year for use in paying authorized medical expenses.

floating holidays   Designated paid time off that can be used at any time during the year with the employer's approval.

flow analysis   How processes operate and how flows of products, data, or other items go through these processes.

forced choice   An evaluation method in which the evaluator selects two of four statements that represent "most like" and "least like."

frequency distribution   Listing of grouped pay data from lowest to highest.

frequency tables   Number of workers in a particular job classification and their pay data.

front pay   Payment of salary or wages that could have been earned had the individual continued to work on the job in question or had the person been employed for a future period of time.

full-time   Employees who work a designated number of hours per week, usually in the 30- to 40-hour range.

fully funded plans   Health insurance programs paid for entirely by the employer.

functional work team   A group of people from the same function working together to generate production or resolve problems.

gainsharing plans   Extra pay provided to individuals or groups of employees based on the gain in performance results in one measurement period over another period.

Gantt chart   A project planning tool that scopes and monitors the activities of a project, the time line, and accountability.

gap analysis   Measurement of the difference between where you are and where you want to be.

general duty clause   A provision in OSHA regulations that imposes a duty on all subject employers to ensure a safe and healthy working environment for their employees.

general pay increases   A pay increase given to all employees regardless of their job performance and not linked to market pressures.

geocentric   A staffing policy wanting to place the best person in the job regardless of their country of origin.

geographic-based differential pay   Adjustment to base pay programs based on cost-of-living requirements in various geographic locations where employees work.

geography   Adjustments to survey numbers based on geographic differences with original survey content.

glass ceiling   A discriminatory practice that has prevented women and other protected class members from advancing to executive-level jobs.

Global Professional in Human Resources (GPHR) A global competency-based credential validating the skills and knowledge of an HR professional who operates in a global marketplace.

golden parachute Provision in executive employment contracts that provides special payments or benefits to the executives under certain adverse conditions, such as the loss of their position.

graphic organizers Diagrams, maps, and drawings/webs as illustrations of learning materials.

green circle rates Pay at a rate lower than the minimum rate for the assigned pay range.

green initiatives Relationships around community and social issues.

grievances Formal employee complaints handled by a structured resolution process usually found in a union-represented workgroup.

gross domestic product (GDP) The total value of goods and services produced in a country.

group incentive program Pay to all individuals in a workgroup for achievement by the entire workgroup.

group term life insurance Provides lump-sum benefit to beneficiaries on the death of an insured.

halo effect Occurs when an evaluator scores an employee high on all job categories because of performance in one area.

harassment Persecution, intimidation, pressure, or force applied to employees by supervisors, co-workers, or external individuals that interferes with the employee's ability to perform the job assignment.

hazard pay Additional pay for working under adverse conditions caused by environment or due to specific circumstances.

health insurance purchasing cooperatives Purchasing agents for a large group of employers.

health maintenance organization Healthcare program where the insurer is paid on a per person (capitated) basis and offers healthcare services and staff at its facilities.

health reimbursement accounts Employer-funded medical reimbursement plans.

health savings accounts A tax-advantaged medical savings account available to taxpayers in the United States who are enrolled in a high-deductible health plan.

high-deductible health plans These programs help employers lower their costs and allow employees with set-aside money to pay for out-of-pocket medical and medical-related expenses.

histogram   A graphic representation of the distribution of a single type of measurement using rectangles.

horn effect   This occurs when an employee receives a low rating in all areas because of one weakness influencing the evaluator.

host-country nationals (HCN)   Employees originating in the country where a remote work location is being established.

HR business partner   HR staff who acts as an internal consultant to senior management.

HR Certification Institute (HRCI)   The certifying nonprofit professional organization for the human resource profession.

HR professional certification   Status awarded to HR professionals by a recognized certifying agency after satisfying qualifying requirements.

HRCI Body of Knowledge (BoK)   The description of a set of concepts, tasks, responsibilities, and knowledge associated with HRCI credentialing.

HRIS   Human resource information system. This is usually a computer-based collection of personal data for each employee.

human capital   The value of the capabilities, knowledge, skills, experiences, and motivation of a workforce in an organization.

human resource business professional (HRBP)   A global, competency-based credential designed to validate generally accepted technical professional-level HR knowledge and skills.

human resource development (HRD)   Systematically planned activities that help the organization's workforce meet the current and future job and skills needs.

human resource management (HRM)   The direction of organizational systems to ensure that human talent is used effectively and efficiently to accomplish organizational goals.

Human Resource Management Professional (HRMP)   Credential for those with mastery of generally accepted HR principles in strategy, policy development, and service delivery.

incentive pay   Pay designed to promote a higher level of job performance above the scope of the basic expectations of the job.

incentive stock options   Awards of rights to purchase company stock in the future at a price determined at the time of the grant.

indirect compensation   Social Security, unemployment insurance, disability insurance, pensions, 401(k) and other similar programs, healthcare, vacations, sick leave, and paid time off such as holidays.

individual incentive program   An offer to individual employees in a workgroup to receive extra pay based on achievement of clearly defined objectives.

Injury and Illness Prevention Programs (IIPP)   A written workplace safety program conforming to the specifications of OSHA.

inpatriates   Employees working at corporate headquarters who originated from a different country.

instructional methods   Approaches to training that are either teacher-centered or learner-centered.

internal coaching   Coaching by trained coaches who are employees in an organization or by supervisors and other leaders.

internal investigation   Gathering verbal and written information dealing with an issue that needs to be clarified.

intrinsic rewards   Rewards such as meaningful and fulfilling work, autonomy, and positive feedback that lead to high levels of job satisfaction.

investigation   A detailed search for facts involving records, witnesses, and other inputs.

investigation file   A collection of documents related to complaints or charges of discrimination, policy violation, or criminal behavior assembled by an employer about an employee or event.

involuntary separations   Individuals leaving the payroll for involuntary reasons, including such things as performance deficiencies, policy violations, or unauthorized absence.

item response theory (IRT)   Method used to pre-equate the difficulty level of questions on an exam.

job analysis   A process to identify and determine the particular job duties and requirements for a given job to fit into an employer's hierarchy of reporting relationships and compensation scales.

job application   A form used to gather information significant to the employer about an individual who wants to be employed by this organization.

job classification   Comparison of jobs to an outside scale with a predetermined number of grades or classifications.

job description   A document that contains a summary of duties and responsibilities of a given job assignment and a description of the physical and mental requirements of the job.

job enlargement   Broadening the scope of a job by expanding the number of tasks.

job enrichment   Increasing the depth of a job by adding responsibilities.

job evaluation   A systematic determination of the relative worth of jobs in an organization.

job evaluation method   Quantitative or nonquantitative programs allowing sorting or categorizing jobs based on their relative worth to the organization.

job ranking   Comparison of jobs based on each job's measurable factors.

job rotation   The process of shifting a person from job to job.

job sharing   Two or more employees who work part-time in the same job to create one full-time equivalent person.

judgmental forecasts   Projections based on subjective inputs.

judgment-based forecasting   Simple estimates, the Delphi technique, focus group or panel estimates, or historically based estimates used in human resource management.

knowledge   Facts and information gathered by an individual.

knowledge management   The way an organization identifies knowledge to be competitive and for the design of succession plans.

knowledge-based system   Pay that is based on the level of knowledge an employee has in a particular field.

K-W-L table   Display of what students know (K), what they want to know (W), and what they actually learned (L).

labor cost differentials   Adjustment to pay structures based on local competitive comparisons.

leadership concepts   The study of leadership styles and techniques.

learning management system (LMS)   A comprehensive system that tracks training content, employee skill sets, training histories, and career development planning.

learning objectives (LO)   Brief statements that define what will be expected to be learned.

learning organization   Organization that adapts to changes.

lecture   An oral presentation intended to teach or present information.

leniency errors   Occurs when ratings of all employees fall at the high end of the range.

leveling   Adjustments to survey numbers by an appropriate percentage needed to achieve a match with specific jobs.

liabilities   An organization's debts and other financial obligations.

location-based differentials   Adjustment to base pay programs based on work location remoteness, lack of amenities, climatic conditions, and other adverse conditions.

lockout Employer action that prevents workers from entering the workplace to do their normal jobs.

long-term care insurance Covers cost of long-term care at home, in an assisted-living facility, in a nursing home, or as an inpatient in a hospice.

long-term disability Begins where short-term disability ends. It covers some or all of an employee's income for up to a specified period, usually from six months to age 65 or an alternative number of years.

long-term incentives Rewards for attaining results over a long measurement period.

lump-sum increases Either a stand-alone performance bonus or part of an annual pay increase.

managed-care plans Insurance that provides plan subscribers with managed health-care with the purpose of reducing costs and improving the quality of care.

management by objectives (MBO) A method of performance appraisal that specifies the specific performance goals that the employee and manager identify.

management skills The abilities required to succeed at a management job. They include such skills as leadership, communication, decision-making, behavior flexibility, organization, and planning.

managerial estimates Projections based on managerial experience alone.

mandatory bargaining issues Issues that must be discussed by employer and union when negotiating a contract of representation.

market-based job evaluation Key jobs are measured and valued against the market, and the remaining jobs are inserted into a hierarchy based on their whole-job comparison to the benchmark jobs.

marketing The process of promoting the organization's products or services, including research, sales, and advertising.

mathematically based forecasting Staffing ratios, sales ratios, or regression analysis used in human resource management analysis of data elements.

mean (average) Arithmetic average or mean arrived at by giving equal weight to every participant's actual pay.

median The middle number in a range.

medical file A collection of documents related to medical evaluations or status of an employee.

memorandum of understanding (MoU) Union contracts for a represented group of employees and designated employers. This is a term usually used in the public sector.

mentoring   A career relationship with an experienced individual with another who has less experience.

mergers and acquisitions (M&A)   The joining together of two separate organizations (merger) or by acquiring of another organization (acquisition).

minimum premium plans   Health insurance programs paid for in part by the employer and in part by the employee.

mission statement   A statement describing what an organization does, who its customer/client base is, and how it will do its work.

mode   The most frequently appearing number in a range.

modified duty   Temporary alteration of job duties that can be performed by an employee who is medically restricted for a designated period of time.

motivation concepts   Notions about what motivates individuals that have come about as a result of scientific studies.

needs analysis   See *needs assessment*.

needs assessment   Determining through analysis what gaps exist between a standard or an objective and existing capabilities.

negligent hiring   A legal tort claim against an employer for injury to someone inside or outside the organization in a way that should have been predicted by the employer if a proper background check had been completed.

negligent retention   A legal tort claim against an employer for keeping someone on the payroll who is known to be a danger to others inside or outside the organization.

net assets   The difference between income and liabilities in a nonprofit organization.

new employee orientation   The process of welcoming and orienting new workers into the organization.

nominal group technique   Development of forecasts based on input from several groups of people.

noncash awards   Prizes, gifts, or recognition awards presented in recognition of service or production or other designated achievement.

nonexempt job   A job with content that requires payment of overtime for work in excess of 40 hours per week under the FLSA.

objective measurement   Impartial assessment of a result.

objectives   Something aimed at end-result intentions.

occupational categories   Groupings of job titles with similar levels of responsibility or skill requirements.

Occupational Safety and Health Administration (OSHA)   The federal agency within the Department of Labor that is responsible for safety in workplaces other than mines.

offshoring   The relocation of functions or work to another country.

oral employment contract   Verbal agreement involving promises of duration or conditions in the employment relationship.

oral warning   Verbal notice that a rule or policy has been violated and further discipline will result if the behavior is repeated.

organizational culture   The way an organization treats its employees, customers, and others.

organizational development   The process of structured analysis and planning for strategic organizational accomplishment.

organizational restructuring   Radical change to an organization's internal and external relationships.

organizing   Union efforts to convince employees to support a union as the designated bargaining agent for a workgroup.

orientation   A process or program introducing new employees to their jobs, organization, and facility.

outplacement   A program that assists employees in finding jobs when their job is eliminated.

outside sales exemption   Exemption from overtime payment based on several qualifying factors such as the primary duty being making sales or obtaining orders for products or services. Work must be customarily and regularly engaged away from the employer's place of business.

outsourcing   Contracting for services with a third party rather than having them performed in the organization.

P2P   Person-to-person.

paid holidays   Designated days each year that are awarded to employees as paid time off.

paid leaves   Paid time off for a specific designated reason.

paid sick leave   Accrued paid time off usually based on length of service.

paid time off (PTO)   A bank of hours in which an employer pools sick days, vacation days, and personal days that employees can use as the need arises.

paid vacation   Accrued paid time off, usually based on length of service.

parent-country nationals (PCN)   Employees sent from the home country to a remote country for a work assignment.

partially self-funded plans Health insurance programs where the employer purchases one or two types of stop-loss insurance coverage.

part-time Employees who work fewer than the number of hours required to be considered full-time.

pass rates The number of people shown as a percentage, who were successful in passing an exam.

pay differentials Additional compensation paid to an employee as an incentive to accept what would normally be considered adverse working conditions, usually based on time, location, or working conditions.

pay grades The way an organization organizes jobs of a similar value into job groups or pay grades as a result of the job evaluation process.

pay ranges Pay amounts constrained by the upper and lower boundaries of each pay grade.

pay survey Collections of data on prevailing market pay rates and information on starting wage rates, base pay, pay ranges, overtime pay, shift differentials, and incentive pay plans.

payroll The function of recordkeeping and computation of compensation for each employee that results in issuance of a check or electronic deposit and collection and deposit of payroll taxes and other withholdings.

payroll administration The act of managing the payroll function.

payroll systems Usually computerized software programs designed to accept work time data and generate paychecks or electronic deposits.

percentiles Distribution of data into percentage ranges, such as top 10 percent.

performance appraisal A process of evaluating how employees perform in their jobs.

performance grants Stock-based compensation that is linked to organizational performance.

performance improvement program (PIP) A written plan that a supervisor provides an underperforming employee that specifies performance results required by a specified date.

performance management The process used to identify, measure, communicate, develop, and reward employee performance.

performance standards Indicators of what a job is to accomplish and how it is to be performed.

performance-based merit pay system A system with pay determined based on individual job performance.

permissible bargaining issues Issues that may be discussed by employer and union during contract negotiations. They are neither required nor prohibited.

perquisites Special privileges for executives, including club memberships, company cars, reserved parking, use of the company airplane, and other such benefits.

personal protective equipment (PPE) Equipment worn by employees as protection against injury or illness hazards on the job.

person-based system Employee capabilities rather than how the job is performed determine the employee's pay.

personnel file One or more sets of documents held by an employer that contain information about the employee's employment status, performance evaluations, disability accommodations, and so forth, collectively considered one personnel file.

phantom stock plan Employee benefit program giving selected senior management employees pretend stock rather than actual stock, with the same financial benefits over time.

phased retirement Partial retirement while continuing to work a reduced schedule.

PHRca PHR credentials for experts in employment regulations and legal mandates specific to the state of California.

picketing Technique used by unions to announce to the public a problem with an employer over issues involving working conditions or benefits.

plateau curve A type of learning curve in which learning is fast at first but then flattens out.

point of service plan A type of managed-care plan that is a hybrid of HMO and PPO plans.

point-factor job evaluation An approach using specific compensable factors as reference points to measure relative job worth.

policies Statements describing how an organization is to be managed.

polycentric A condition that occurs when jobs at headquarters are filled with people from other countries and positions in remote countries are filled with people from the headquarters country.

preferred provider organization Healthcare program including an in-network and an out-of-network option for services.

premium pay Payment at rates greater than straight pay for working overtime, or other agreed condition.

premium-only plans   Authorized under the IRS Code, Section 125; allows employer-sponsored premium payments to be paid by the employee on a pretax basis instead of after-tax basis. Sometimes they are called *POP plans*.

prepaid legal insurance   Employer financial support for cost of routine legal services such as developing a will, real estate matters, divorces, and other services.

prescription drug plans   Medical insurance programs that cover some or all of the cost of prescription drugs for subscribers.

procedures   Methods to be used in fulfilling organizational responsibilities and policies.

process-flow analysis   A diagram of the steps involved in a process.

productivity-based system   When pay is determined by the employee's production output.

professional employer organization   Vendor that, as a co-employer, provides qualified workers to a client organization.

professional exemption   Exemption from overtime payment based on several qualifying factors, including minimum pay requirement, advanced knowledge, or education and use of professional discretion and judgment.

Professional in Human Resources (PHR)   Credential that demonstrates mastery of the technical and operational aspects of HR practices and U.S. laws and regulations.

profit & loss statement (P&L)   A financial statement that summarizes the revenues, costs, and expenses incurred during a specific period of time.

profit-sharing plans   Direct or indirect payments to employees that depend on the employer's profitability.

program evaluation and review technique (PERT)   A project management tool used to organize, coordinate, and schedule tasks and people.

progressive discipline   A system of penalties involving increasing sanctions that can be taken if unwanted behaviors recur.

prohibited bargaining issues   Issues that may not be discussed by employer and union during contract negotiations. These are illegal issues under the NLRA.

project hire   An employee who is hired for the duration of a project. Once the project is completed, the employee is dismissed or laid off. See *term employee*.

project management   Guiding the implementation of a program from beginning to end.

project management concepts   The study of project management styles and techniques.

project team   A group of people with specific talent or experience brought together to resolve a problem or accomplish some other organizational goal.

promotion   Usually considered to be an increase in responsibility or compensation or both.

proof of identity   Document such as a passport or driver's license that contains a photo of the individual that proves that person's identity.

proof of work authorization   Document such as a Social Security card or alien work registration authorization that proves the individual is authorized to work in the United States.

punitive damages   Translation of punishment into dollar amounts usually applied to employers who have done something egregious. The damages are intended to deter a defendant from engaging in conduct similar to that which was the basis of a lawsuit.

qualitative analysis   Research that explores the reasoning behind human behavior; often uses open-ended interviewing.

quantitative analysis   Research based on quantifiable data.

quartiles   Distribution of data into four quadrants: bottom quarter, lower-middle quarter, upper-middle quarter, and top quarter.

range spreads   Dispersion of pay from the lowest boundary to the highest boundary of a pay range.

ratio analysis   Comparison of current results or historic results at a specific point in time.

reasonable accommodation   Adjustment to a job condition or workplace that will allow an employee to perform the essential job duties.

reasonable cause   One possible determination from a state or federal enforcement agency concerning an investigation of a charge of illegal discrimination.

recency error   Occurs when an evaluator gives greater weight to recent events of performance.

recognition   Acknowledgment of accomplishments by individual employees.

recordkeeping   Documentation involving any aspect of employee management from discussions to personal employee information.

red circle rates   Pay at a rate higher than the maximum for the assigned pay range.

regiocentric   Orientation to culture in a specific region or collection of countries in regions such as Asia, South America, or Europe.

regression analysis   A statistical process of estimating the relationships among variables.

rehire   A former employee who is hired back onto the payroll.

repatriates Employees who return to their home country following a work assignment in a different country.

request for proposal (RFP) A written document asking for vendor input and suggestions along with cost estimates for any given work to be performed in the establishment.

responsibility A required part of a job or organizational obligation.

results measurement Methods for monitoring the amount of progress that has been accomplished toward a stated goal or objective.

retention Measurement of the quantity of employees remaining with the employer over a given period of time.

retiree An ex-employee who met the qualification requirements for retirement under the organization's definition or plan.

return on investment (ROI) The calculation showing the value of expenditures versus the investment.

return to work Clearance to return to active employment activities following an illness, injury, or other absence.

risk management Identifies and manages potential liabilities that come from operating an employer organization.

role-play Technique for simulating individual participation in real-life roles involving performance or action with regard to solving a problem.

safety audit The process of evaluating the workplace for safety hazards and determining any needed corrective action.

sales personnel incentive programs Bonuses or commissions based on predetermined formulas involving performance and time.

scaffolding Teacher modeling skills and thinking for students, allowing students to take over those expressions based on the initial structure provided by the teacher.

scatter diagram A graphical tool that depicts the relationship among variables.

seasonal employee A worker hired for a specific seasonal surge in work levels, common in retail industry and also agriculture and other food processing businesses.

Section 125 cafeteria plans Allows employees to pay certain qualified expenses on a pre-tax basis. See also *premium-only plans*.

self-directed team A group of people with a specific assignment permitted to select its own leadership and direction to take toward the problem or task.

self-funded plans Health insurance programs where the employer assumes all the risk as a self-insured entity.

Senior Professional in Human Resources (SPHR)   Credential for those who have mastered the strategic and policy-making aspects of HR management in the United States.

seniority pay increases   A pay increase based solely on length of service.

severance package   Voluntary payment by some employers to laid-off employees. This may include pay for designated number of workdays, job retraining, outplacement services, and/or paid benefits premium assistance.

short-term disability   Begins where sick leave ends. It covers some or all of employee's income for up to a specified period, usually six months.

simulations   Learning exercises designed to be as realistic as possible without the risk of a real-life circumstance.

single or flat-rate system   When each worker in the same job has the same rate of pay regardless of seniority or job performance.

Six Sigma   A data-driven approach and method for eliminating defects.

skill-based system   When pay is based on the number and depth of skills that an employee has applicable to their job.

SMART goal model   Model for creating goals that are specific, measurable, attainable/achievable, relevant/realistic, and timed.

Society of Human Resource Professionals (SHRM)   The world's largest HR membership organization devoted to human resource management. It represents more than 275,000 members in more than 160 countries.

solution analysis   Statistical comparison of various potential solutions.

specific stop-loss coverage   When the health plan is protected against the risk of a major illness for one participant, or one family unit, covered by the plan.

standard deviation   Scores in a set of data that spread out around an average.

standards   The yardstick by which amount and quality of output are measured.

state employment service   The agency responsible for assisting citizens with job placement and unemployment benefits in each state.

statistical forecasts   Use of mathematical formulas to identify patterns and trends.

step rate with performance considerations   A system allowing performance to influence the size or timing of a pay increase along the step system.

storytelling   Use of multimedia technology such as PowerPoint to present interactive opportunities involving any subject.

straight piece rate system   When the employee receives a base rate of pay and is awarded additional compensation for the amount of output produced.

strategic business management   That which formulates and produces HR objectives, programs, practices, and policies.

strategic planning   Identifying organizational objectives and determining what actions are required to reach those objectives.

strategies   Specific direction that outlines objectives to achieve long-term plans.

strike   Work stoppage resulting from a failed negotiation between employer and union.

subject matter expert   A person who is well versed in the content of a specific knowledge area.

subjective measurement   Assessment of a result using opinion or perception.

substance abuse   Personal use of alcohol or drugs in excess of amounts prescribed by a medical professional, or any use of illegal substances. Abuse generally results in an impairment of the individual's physical or mental capacities.

succession planning   Identification of future key job openings and individuals who will be ready to fill those jobs.

supplemental unemployment benefits   An unemployment benefit in addition to government benefits offered by some employers.

supply analysis   Strategic evaluation of job candidate sources, plant locations, and other factors.

suspension   Temporary hiatus of active employment, usually as a disciplinary step, that can be paid or unpaid.

SWOT analysis   A process in strategic planning that looks at an organization's strengths, weaknesses, opportunities, and threats.

talent management   The management and integration of all HR activities and processes that align with the organization's goals and needs.

talent retention   The retention of key talent, those employees who are the strongest performers, have high potential, or are in critical jobs.

task force   A group of people assembled to address major organizational issues.

teacher exemption   Exemption from overtime payment based on several qualifying factors, including the primary duty of teaching in an educational establishment.

teams   A group of people focused on specific organizational issues.

temp-to-lease   Conversion of a temporary agency–provided employee to regular employee status in the client organization.

term employee   An employee who is hired for the duration of a project. Once the project is completed, the employee is dismissed or laid off. See *project hire*.

termination   End of the employment relationship.

third party   Someone other than the two primary parties involved in an interaction.

third-country nationals (TCN)   Employees who are moved from one remote location to another remote location for a work assignment.

third-party administrator plan   Health insurance programs in which the employer assumes all of the risk but hires an independent claims department.

time-based differential pay   Shift pay, which is generally time-based rewards for employees who work what are considered undesirable shifts such as night shifts.

time-based step rate system   Determining pay rate based on the length of time in the job.

total quality management (TQM)   A management system for achieving customer satisfaction using quantitative methods to improve processes.

total rewards   Financial inducements and rewards as well as nonfinancial inducements and rewards, such as the value of good job content and good working environment.

trainability   The readiness and motivation to learn.

training   The process whereby people acquire skills, knowledge, or capabilities to perform jobs.

training effectiveness   Measurement of what students are expected to be able to do at the end of the training course or module.

training techniques   Approaches to training including virtual, classroom, on-the-job, and one-on-one tutoring.

transactional leadership   A leadership style that focuses on either rewards or threat of discipline in an effort to motivate employees.

transfer   Movement of current employee to a different job in a different part of the organization.

transformational leadership   A leadership style that motivates employees by inspiring them.

travel pay   Extra pay provided for travel time, either under legal requirement or by other agreement.

trend analysis   Comparison of historical results with current results to determine a trend.

tuition reimbursement   Employer financial support for employee continuing education efforts.

turnover analysis   Comparison of the reasons for employees leaving the workforce and the organizational problems that may be causing them.

Uniform Guidelines   Federal regulations that specify how job selection tools must be validated.

unpaid sick leave   Accrued unpaid time off, usually based on length of service.

validity   The extent to which a test measures what it says it measures.

values   The principles or standards of behavior that are most important to either an individual or an entity.

veteran   A former member of the U.S. military service in any branch.

veto   The action of canceling or postponing a decision or bill in the U.S. legislature.

vision care plans   Medical insurance programs that cover some or all of the cost of vision care (exams and corrective lenses) for subscribers.

vision statement   A statement that describes the desired future of an organization.

voluntary separations   Individuals leaving the payroll for voluntary reasons, including such things as retirement, obtaining a different job, returning to full-time education, or personal reasons.

weighted average   An average result taking into account the number of participants and each participant's pay.

workers' compensation   Program that provides medical care and compensates employees for part of lost earnings as a result of a work-related disability.

workforce analysis   Assessment of the workforce and things that are influencing it.

workforce planning and employment   The processes performed by an employer of recruiting, interviewing, staffing, ensuring equal employment opportunity, affirmative action orientating new employees, managing, retention, termination, and proper employee records.

workplace violence   Personal behavior that ranges from shouting to hitting or worse taking place on an employer's premises.

written employment contract   Written agreement involving promises of duration or conditions in the employment relationship.

written warning   Written notice that a rule or policy has been violated and further discipline will result if the behavior is repeated.

zero-based budgeting   A model of budgeting that is based on expenditures being justified for each budget year.

zero-sum   A system in which the sum of the gains equals the sum of the losses.

INDEX

Numbers

16-point program, 187–188
80 percent rule
  adverse impact calculations, 441
  beyond, 382
  defined, 571
  measuring adverse impact for reduction in force, 381–382
360-degree appraisals, 231, 275

A

AAPs (affirmative action plans), 188, 190
ACA. *See* Patient Protection and Affordable Care Act (PPACA) of 2010
acceptance, of union-organizing efforts, 528
accounting
  core knowledge requirements, 89
  leadership and strategy knowledge, SPHR, 416–418
  organizations affecting employee benefits, 312–316
  planning for financial security, 132–133
  terms used in, 417
accounts payable, 417
accounts receivable, 417
acquisitions, 205–206, 585
acronyms, list of common HR, 545–549
action plan
  in career development, 267
  for change strategy, 412
  for financial risk, 133
  for handling substance abuse incident, 133
  managing risk of workplace violence, 132
ad hoc, assigning international compensation, 505
ADA (Americans with Disabilities Act) of 1990
  ADA Amendments Act of 2008, 46–47, 107
  overview of, 46–49
ADDIE (Analysis, Design, Development, Implementation, Evaluation) model
  defined, 571
  needs assessment and analysis, 247–248
  training and development via, 246–247
ADEA. *See* Age Discrimination in Employment Act (ADEA) of 1967
administration, payroll, 309–310
administrative closure, EEOC investigation findings, 182
administrative exemption, 202, 571
administrative services-only (ASO) plan, 319, 571
adult learning processes
  core knowledge requirements, 91–92
  defined, 571

learning curves, 250–252
learning levels, 252–253
learning styles, 250
motivation concepts, 253–256
overview of, 249–250
adverse impact (or disparate impact)
  defined, 571
  illegal employment discrimination as, 53
  measurements and analysis of, 501
  measuring during reduction in force, 381–382
  overview of, 441
  statistical analysis beyond, 382
  Uniform Guidelines on Employee Selection Procedures, 184–185
adverse treatment
  defined, 571
  illegal employment discrimination as, 53
advertisements
  gender-neutral job, 198
  sourcing external recruits, 211–212
affirm relationship, conflict resolution, 370
affirmative action
  Civil Rights Act of 1964 and, 179
  defined, 571
  diversity and inclusion programs, 365–366
  EEOC and, 179–180
  EEOC complaint investigation procedures, 180–182
  EEOC guidelines, 182–186
  equal employment opportunity and, 178–179
  as Executive Order 11246 in 1965, 55
  federal contracting and, 186–188
  OFCCP and, 194–197
  OFCCP compliance evaluations, 189–190
  outreach and recruiting requirements, 196
  placement-rate goals and good faith efforts, 191–194
  reporting requirements, 190–191
  self-identifying in job applications, 218, 221–222
affirmative action plans (AAPs), 188, 190
Affordable Care Act (ACA). *See* Patient Protection and Affordable Care Act (PPACA) of 2010
Age Discrimination in Employment Act (ADEA) of 1967
  overview of, 54
  OWBPA amendment to, 445–446
  retention of payroll records, 310
agency shop, 349
aggregate stop-loss coverage, healthcare plan, 319, 571
aging
  analysis of survey data, 298
  making outdated data current, 571